Time Out

LONDON
FOR LONDONERS
timeout.com

Published by Time Out Guides Ltd, a wholly owned subsidiary of Time Out Group Ltd.
Time Out and the Time Out logo are trademarks of Time Out Group Ltd.

© **Time Out Group Ltd 2006**

10 9 8 7 6 5 4 3 2

This edition first published in Great Britain in 2006 by Ebury Publishing
Ebury Publishing is a division of The Random House Group Ltd, 20 Vauxhall Bridge Road,
London SW1V 2SA

Random House Australia Pty Limited 20 Alfred Street, Milsons Point, Sydney,
New South Wales 2061, Australia
Random House New Zealand Limited 18 Poland Road, Glenfield, Auckland 10, New Zealand
Random House South Africa (Pty) Limited Isle of Houghton, Corner Boundary Road &
Carse O'Gowrie, Houghton 2198, South Africa

Random House UK Limited Reg. No. 954009

Distributed in USA by Publishers Group West
1700 Fourth Street, Berkeley, California 94710

Distributed in Canada by Penguin Canada Ltd
10 Alcorn Avenue, Toronto, Ontario, Canada M4V 3B2

For further distribution details, see www.timeout.com

ISBN
To 31 December 2006: 1-904978-52-5
From 1 January 2007: 978-1-904978-52-7

A CIP catalogue record for this book is available from the British Library

Colour reprographics by Icon, Crowne House, 56-58 Southwark Street, London SE1 1UN

Printed and bound by Firmengruppe APPL, aprinta druck, Wemding, Germany
Papers used by Ebury Publishing are natural, recyclable products made from wood grown in
sustainable forests

Somerset House

Overlooking the Thames, by Waterloo Bridge, Somerset House is the inspirational setting for the world famous collection of the **Courtauld Institute of Art Gallery**, the decorative arts of the **Gilbert Collection** and the **Hermitage Rooms**, showcasing objects from the State Hermitage Museum in St Petersburg.
The spectacular Edmond J. Safra Fountain Court provides a unique venue for open-air performances and, in winter, becomes a glamorous ice paradise with London's most beautiful ice rink and the thrilling ice climbing wall.

For further information:
020 7845 4600
info@somerset-house.org.uk
www.somerset-house.org.uk

Somerset House Trust, Somerset House, Strand, London WC2
Registered charity no. 1063640

Time Out Guides Limited
Universal House
251 Tottenham Court Road
London W1T 7AB
Tel + 44 (0)20 7813 3000
Fax + 44 (0)20 7813 6001
Email guides@timeout.com
www.timeout.com

Editorial

Editor Tom Lamont
Copy Editors Phil Harriss, Lisa Ritchie
Researchers Helen Babbs, Lily Dunn, Roland
Lloyd-Parry, Patrick Welch
Listings Editors Cathy Limb, Jill Emeny
Proofreader Marion Moisy
Indexer Jackie Brind

Editorial/Managing Director Peter Fiennes
Series Editor Sarah Guy
Deputy Series Editor Cath Phillips
Business Manager Gareth Garner
Guides Co-ordinator Holly Pick
Accountant Kemi Olufuwa

Design

Art Director Scott Moore
Art Editor Pinelope Kourmouzoglou
Senior Designer Josephine Spencer
Graphic Designer Henry Elphick
Digital Imaging Dan Conway
Ad Make-up Jenny Prichard

Picture Desk

Picture Editor Jael Marschner
Deputy Picture Editor Tracey Kerrigan
Picture Researcher Helen McFarland

Advertising

Sales Director & Sponsorship Mark Phillips
Sales Manager Alison Wallen
Advertising Sales Michelle Clements, Jason Trotman
Advertising Assistant Kate Staddon
Copy Controller Amy Nelson

Marketing

Group Marketing Director John Luck
Marketing & Publicity Manager, US Rosella Albanese

Production

Production Director Mark Lamond
Production Controller Marie Howell

Time Out Group

Chairman Tony Elliott
Managing Director Mike Hardwick
Financial Director Richard Waterlow
General Manager Nichola Coulthard
Art Director John Oakey
Online Managing Director David Pepper
Production Director Steve Proctor
IT Director Simon Chappell

Contributors

Neighbourhoods, Restaurants & cafés, Bars & pubs and Shops written by Joseph Bindloss, James Bramble, Tim Cooper, Guy Dimond, Eli Dryden, Lily Dunn, Janice Fuscoe, Sarah Guy, Arwa Haider, Phil Harriss, Ronnie Haydon, Sophie Heawood, David Jenkins, Tom Lamont, Sam Le Quesne, Jenny Linford, Roland Lloyd-Parry, Alexia Loundras, Fiona McAuslan, Stuart McGurk, Felix Miln, Natalie Moore, Mark O'Flaherty, Cath Phillips, Kate Riordan, Lisa Ritchie, Andrew Shields, Andrew Staffell.
Additional writing, interviews and research by Helen Babbs, Jill Emeny, Neon Kelly, Cathy Limb, Justin Talbot, Patrick Welch, Sabrina Wolfe.
The Editor would like to thank all the estate agents, parents and Londoners who agreed to be interviewed.

Maps by JS Graphics (john@jsgraphics.co.uk).

Cover photography by Philip Ebeling, taken at Raoul's Café, 13 Clifton Road, W9 1SZ (7289 7313).
Photography by pages 3, 37, 127, 153, 160, 233, 239, 242, 249, 317, 322 Fiona Compton; pages 7, 34, 60, 69, 72, 99, 103, 112, 128, 141, 167, 182, 187, 197, 201, 202, 207, 227, 245, 257, 265, 273, 276, 285, 287, 306, 315 Heloise Bergman; pages 17, 21, 27, 44, 56, 79, 81, 104, 109, 117, 144, 217 Andrew Brackenbury; page 31 Gordon Rainsford; page 41 Ming Tang Evans; pages 49, 246, 262, 268 Alys Tomlinson; page 53 Piers Allardyce; pages 75, 171 Hadley Kincade; pages 83, 133, 174, 191, 253, 260 Matt Carr; pages 87, 91, 92, 282, 296 Aine Donovan; pages 95, 193, 211 Viktor Pesenti; pages 121, 122, 125, 137, 149 Jonathan Perugia; page 163 Kevin Nicholson; page 179 Michael Franke; page 218 Dominic Dibbs, page 223 Tricia de Courcy Ling; page 301 Janie Airey.

Contents

About the Guide

How the guide is arranged

Thanks to centuries of haphazard growth, a chaotic street plan and various changes in the division and administration of the capital's districts, London is a defiantly disordered city. To cope with contradictory postcode lines, electoral wards and borough boundaries, we've divided this guide into 24 chapters, each focusing on an inner-London borough.

In the case of the most central of these (City of Westminster, City of London, Tower Hamlets, Hackney, Islington, Camden, Kensington & Chelsea, Hammersmith & Fulham, Wandsworth, Lambeth, Southwark and Lewisham), each chapter covers the borough in its entirety; in other, slightly more outlying boroughs, such as Greenwich and Brent, the portions closest to central London are covered; in outer boroughs such as Waltham Forest and Redbridge only key areas are covered. Each chapter is then broken down by neighbourhood or cluster of neighbourhoods, followed by guides to restaurants and cafés, bars and pubs, shops and other essentials within the borough.

Neighbourhoods

Inevitably, neighbourhoods don't neatly follow borough boundaries. In cases where one district straddles two or more boroughs, we have included it in the most suitable chapter. Knightsbridge, for example, straddles both Kensington & Chelsea and Westminster, but is included in the former chapter. To make life a bit easier, we've included a map of each borough, plus an overview map (on page 14) of all the boroughs covered by this guide.

Amenities & essentials

No guide to the city's amenities can be completely comprehensive: we have tried to select the best of each borough's restaurants, cafés, bars, pubs, shops and other amenities. Addresses, telephone numbers and websites were all checked and correct as we went to press; in most cases, listings for large chains are omitted.

Open spaces covers all publicly accessible outdoor spaces of reasonable size or intrigue. Sport & fitness covers all publicly funded sports centres plus key private chains and facilities. Schools covers all state secondary schools plus any landmark private schools. Local estate agents are listed within each chapter; for London-wide chains, turn to Useful contacts on page 328.

While every effort has been made to ensure the accuracy of information in this guide, the publishers cannot accept any responsibility for any errors it may contain.

Statistics

Our statistics have been gathered from a variety of sources. Borough population and housing stock figures are taken from the DEFRA municipal waste management survey 2003-2004 (www.capitalwastefacts.com); ethnic origin, student and retiree figures from the 2001 Census (www.statistics.gov.uk); crime figures from the 'Recorded Crime for Key Offences 2004-2005' report by the Crime & Disorder Reduction Partnership (www.homeoffice.gov.uk/rds/); and CPA (Comprehensive Performance Assessment) ratings from the Audit Commission's new 'Harder Test', published in December 2005 (www.audit-commission.gov.uk/cpa/).

Let us know what you think

We hope you enjoy this book and we'd like to know what you think of it. We welcome tips for places you consider we should include in future editions and take note of your criticism of our choices. Email us at guides@timeout.com.

Realty check

Illustration by Daniel Mackie

Nobody seems to like estate agents. At best, they're seen as a necessary annoyance; at worst, servants of the devil. But what about the view from their side of the For Sale sign? Fibbing owners, phoney bidders, divorcing couples and the occasional undisclosed corpse... **Stuart Husband** learns what the people that everyone-loves-to-hate really hate about us.

Not long ago, an estate agent was trying to sell a house in a highly desirable quarter of south-west London. 'It was a beautiful property, and it should have been a cinch,' he recalls. 'But the vendor wasn't the most hygienic person, to put it mildly; he'd had cats and dogs and God knows what else running wild through the place. So we ripped out all the carpets, removed the soft furnishings, and scoured the sodden floorboards – we even had the place fumigated. But there was still this,

you know, bad smell hitting you as you entered. I could see would-be buyers flinching. So we got some guys to go right through the place. They sawed a hole through the stud wall in the kitchen and found decades of animal excrement in a pile behind the partition.' He sighs. 'It was a literal case of being landed in the shit.'

In the sliding scale of modern infamy, estate agents occupy an unenviable spot. Above Gary Glitter, sure, but nipping at the heels of, say, Dr Crippen. 'I see myself as a member of the service industry,' says a north London agent, 'but most people treat you like some kind of snake-oil salesman. They think we're all Gordon Gekko clones in shiny suits with fat ties and hair gel, braying into our camera-phones while driving our BMW Z-5s.' He pauses. 'Actually, I do know more than a few agents like that. But mostly, I think, it's grossly unfair. We have to act as a combined nanny-nursemaid-counsellor to people who are going through the biggest and most stressful transactions of their lives. And what does it teach you about human nature? You learn that when it comes down to people's own money, all notions of virtue, manners and decorum fly out the window. They'll do things and react in ways you wouldn't believe.'

And if this is a general truism, the situation is intensified in London. 'It's a hot-house atmosphere,' says a City agent. 'So many people are constantly looking to buy, and there are virtually no sellers. So people take liberties all the time.'

The prevailing rule of thumb, sighs an agent in the Finchley area (all spoke on condition of anonymity), is that no sticking-point is too petty. 'Sales have fallen through over a completion money difference of £100,' he says. 'In the end, we've stepped in to pay it simply to stop everything falling apart. I've paid for a courier to make a Manchester-London round-trip because someone has refused to send a contract by recorded delivery. But my best one was the Great Bookshelf Dispute. The seller had this swanky free-standing bookshelf on wheels that he insisted he was taking with him; the buyer assumed it was a fixture of the property. They haggled over this thing for weeks. Eventually we had to pay a grand for the bookshelf to keep it in the flat before they murdered each other over it. These things end up like leylandii boundary disputes. It's practically pistols at dawn.'

The flipside of this niggardliness is a cavalier attitude to pledges and agreements. 'You'd sometimes love to have a polygraph machine,' says a Hampstead agent. 'People agree a price and then switch buyers for thousands more without telling us. Or buyers will meet the owner directly and try to cut us out of the equation completely. I've been to court twice in those instances. People seem to forget that we're trying to

work on their behalf; I mean, if the sale doesn't go through, we don't get paid.'

This doesn't stop people disappearing on two-week skiing holidays as completion dates loom (without, needless to say, informing their agents), or sellers pulling out, in a case quoted with open-mouthed incredulity by a Clapham estate agent, because their spiritual advisor had informed them that the planetary alignment for a house-move was unpropitious. 'People often suggest that agents should be licensed,' says the City agent wearily, 'and my usual response is: so should vendors and buyers.'

'I was almost gagging'

It would be wrong to deduce from this litany of backstabbing and ransom-holding that the prevailing attitude of most agents to their more wayward charges is one of resigned cynicism. In fact, says an agent in London Bridge, it's more like a Spielbergian sense of wonder at the lengths to which people are – or aren't – prepared to go. Take viewings,' he says. 'If you or I were putting our place on the market, we'd want it to look at least acceptable, right? Desirable even? Once I was selling the flat of a high-flying City banker in Borough. What did I find when I got in there? Months of washing-up on every surface. Layers of grease and grime. McDonald's wrappers overflowing from the bins. I was almost gagging. It was only when I threatened to report her to Health & Safety that she got a cleaning company to scour the place.

'And there was another property,' he adds, sotto voce, 'another banker's place. I'm taking a client round it, and we come to the bedroom. I haven't had time to check it out beforehand, so I just swing the door open… and find *filthy* sheets strewn over the bed. You know, stained. And a rolled-up picture of David Beckham lying there in the middle.'

Other sellers take a Year Zero approach to fixtures and fittings. 'I've had instances where people have removed all the light bulbs and taken up all the carpets,' says the Hampstead agent. 'I've had people who've not only taken up the carpets, but actually taken the tacks away. Some make off with doors. The doors!'

Again, there's a flipside. 'I've had sellers leave a whole load of furniture for the buyer to come in and sort out,' says the Clapham agent. 'I call it stealth dumping. It costs the buyer a fortune to dispose of it all. And ▶

TOP FIVE
ESTATE AGENT GRIPES

1 Tyre-kickers

The 'nosey parkers' who serially turn out for viewings – and even put in phantom offers – with no intention of buying (named after their close cousins who haunt second-hand car showrooms, booting tyres to check vehicular veracity).

....

2 Specialist questions

'Some people expect you to be a walking encyclopaedia,' says an agent in Borough. 'I was showing a loft conversion to a designer and he asked, in all seriousness, "What's the solar gain for this place?" Not a bloody clue.'

....

3 Divorces

'It makes everything much harder,' says a Hampstead agent, 'because you have to negotiate with both parties. And they usually hate each other. I had one selling couple who'd had a last-minute offer – an extra £20,000. The husband told me to turn it down without his wife's knowledge, because he loathed her so much he'd rather forsake £10,000 than let her have hers. Horrible.'

....

4 Drive-by surveyors

Where a property is assessed from a car window. 'You can have something down-valued because it's above commercial premises,' says an agent in Finchley, 'whereas if the surveyor had gone in they'd have known that it's actually down a corridor to the back of the building and not above the shopfront at all. But they're too fat and lazy to go and look.'

....

5 Living too close

'I once had a flat in the Barbican while I was selling there,' says a City agent. 'Never again. I got accosted on the doorstep by people I'd sold to. "My windows don't fit properly!" "What's mine worth now, then?" I fled to Battersea as soon as I could.'

then people seem to have a vague idea of what completion time actually means. Just to be clear, it's when the money leaves the buyer's account and arrives in the account of the seller's solicitor. From that point on, the flat belongs to the buyer. But you get calls to say that people have got muddled up and there are two sets of removal vans facing off in the street. Let me tell you, those removal firms can be pretty hardcore. I tried to mediate in a dispute once and a guy threatened to break my legs.'

Given all this, you would infer that agents sign off on a deal with a sigh of relief and a Jameson's or two. And they do. But then, in some cases, they're called upon to administer after-care. 'People sometimes forget that we have lives too,' bemoans the City agent. 'I mean, if I'm in the middle of a big deal, I don't object to taking calls at 9pm. But someone phoned at that time the other night saying their kitchen door had fallen off. I've also had a call at 6.30am on a Saturday from someone complaining that their front door's a bit sticky.' He shakes his head. 'I try and explain that it's no longer my responsibility. I sometimes wonder how some people get from one end of the day to the other.'

All agents stress that – bad press, ram-raided life and the caprice of clients notwithstanding – 90 per cent of sales are reasonably problem-free. 'After a while you get hardened to it,' says the London Bridge agent. 'There are always going to be people who refuse to believe we're human beings. Once you, as an agent, realise that trying to keep everyone happy is a doomed endeavour, you can move forward.' He grins. 'And you certainly see all types of human life in the job.'

He illustrates this with an anecdote. A while ago, his company canvassed a Well-Known City Housing Development, looking to see if anyone was interested in selling their apartment. 'A guy wrote back to say we might be interested in his place,' he recalls, 'except that under his bath we'd find the mashed-up flesh of his murdered wife. So whoever bought the place would have to dispose of her remains.' He raises his eyebrows and smiles. 'So you can add confessor to the list of roles we perform. This job can be humiliating, infuriating and enervating, but I guess you can say that it's rarely ever dull.'

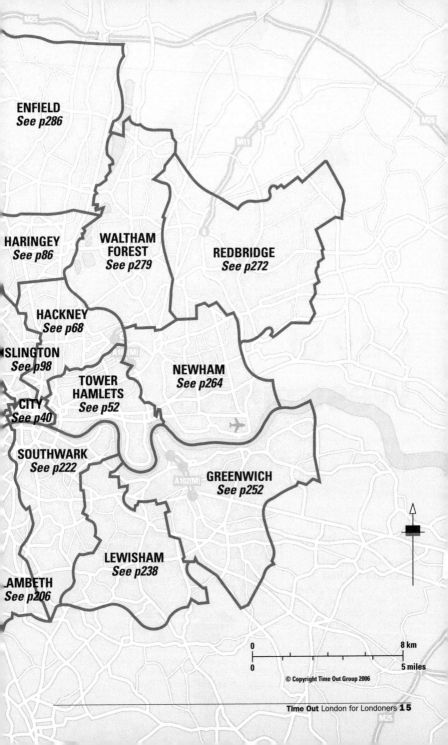

ENFIELD
See p286

HARINGEY
See p86

WALTHAM
FOREST
See p279

REDBRIDGE
See p272

HACKNEY
See p68

ISLINGTON
See p98

NEWHAM
See p264

TOWER
HAMLETS
See p52

CITY
See p40

SOUTHWARK
See p222

GREENWICH
See p252

LEWISHAM
See p238

LAMBETH
See p206

0   8 km
0   5 miles

© Copyright Time Out Group 2006

'This is a serious working and residential city. There are a lot of things that tourists are welcome to come and visit, but it is not a theme park.'

**Alan Bradley, City of Westminster councillor
and Pimlico resident for 30 years**

City of Westminster

Its sights are familiar throughout the world, its West End is among the planet's greatest entertainment centres, and in Belgravia and Mayfair, it has some of the priciest property on earth – but Westminster also contains nuggets of lesser-known urban life: villagey Marylebone, classy St John's Wood, lovely Little Venice and bedsitter Bayswater.

Neighbourhoods

Covent Garden and the Strand

There's more to this flamboyant enclave in the heart of the city than the tourist-thronged Piazza. If it were not for Covent Garden's dedicated residents, the WC2 honey pot would have turned into a decidedly sour network of through roads, conference centres and business hotels. Fortunately, the locals rose up against the planners after the original wholesale fruit

and vegetable market was moved to Nine Elms in 1973. The best place to witness Covent Garden's charms is at Neal's Yard, a picturesque little square full of co-operative and wholefood cafés, alternative therapy rooms and herbalists. It's just a stone's throw away from Seven Dials, once notorious for slums, now sleek with modish clothing boutiques and coffee shops. Away from the largely pedestrianised streets and community squares, towards Charing Cross Road, the lights of Theatreland meld into the neon of Leicester Square.

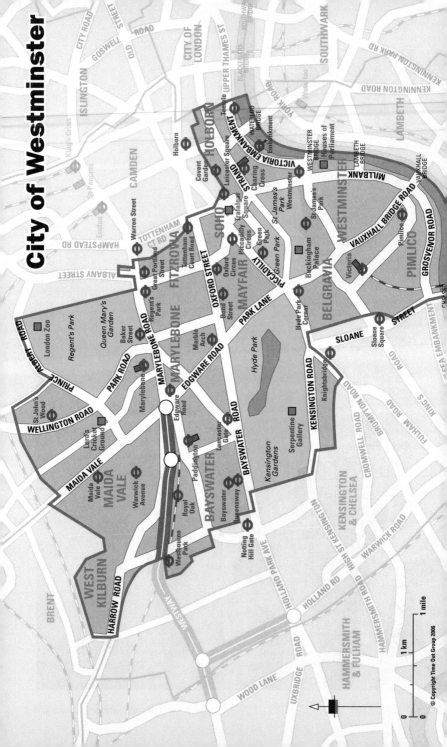

Turn away from the overcrowded horror of the Charing Cross Road end of Cranbourn Street and look towards the side streets around the Wyndham and Albany theatres: the gaslit Goodwin's Court with its 17th-century housing; or Brydges Place, surely the tiniest alley in central London. Desirable residential areas can be found at Ching Court, off Shelton Street, and the flats opposite Phoenix Garden (the wildlife garden built on an old car park on Stacey Street).

Connecting Westminster to the City, the Strand has widened its tourist appeal with the successful makeover of Somerset House, whose annual ice rink gets very crowded at peak times. The Savoy Theatre and Hotel and posh Simpson's-in-the-Strand have always attracted rich tourists and expense-accounters, but, come dusk, the homeless still bed down in various doorways along the stretch. Villiers Street, at the Charing Cross end of the Strand, takes you down to the Embankment, built in the 1860s.

Soho

Time was you couldn't escape the sex in Soho; now you have to go looking for it. The sleazy undercurrent still exists, but it flows alongside a cocktail of less obvious charms that give these streets their beguiling character.

Highs & Lows

▲ **Convenience** Discover the joys of walking to work – and save a fortune on late-night taxis
Residents' perks A free Westminster ResCard (www.rescard.com) gets you great discounts on arts and entertainment
Marylebone Village It's a five-minute walk from the hordes of Oxford Street, but has the feel of a (very chic) market town – and Regent's Park is but a jog away

Tourists Get your elbows out around Oxford Street and Covent Garden
Noise Unless you live in a mews (or have double glazing), the cacophony is relentless in most of the borough
Drunks West Enders suffer pee on the doorstep and tuneless
▼ 2am singalongs

Soho's outposts are marked in boisterous fashion by four Circuses: Oxford, St Giles, Cambridge and Piccadilly. The district within – and the southern subsection of Chinatown – is residential, touristy, intellectual, and historically complex. You'll need to mug up on it. Londoners are expected to know the order of the streets that run northwards from Old Compton Street to Oxford Street. So, notepads at the ready: from east to west, it goes Greek, Frith (both terminating at Soho Square, where Soho Street picks up the trail), Dean and Wardour.

Everyone adores Meard Street, between Dean and Wardour, for its picture-perfect Queen Anne houses. Wardour, Brewer and Berwick Streets used to form the seedy centre of Soho's sex industry. When, in 2004, Walker's Court lost its Raymond Revue Bar – the first ever licensed strip club – after 46 years of topless action, it looked like the end of a dirty raincoat era. Now, a revue bar is one element to the glitz of a different persuasion dished out by the Too 2 Much Club. Nearby, Old Compton Street has become a vibrant focal point for Soho's gay community in the past decade, featuring bars, cafés and gay-friendly businesses.

The streets around here still bear traces of the cheap perfume of sleaze, but Berwick Street market is an attraction for more wholesome reasons, fresh dates and wet fish among them. Westminster Council continues to make overtures to redevelop what seems an already lively, thriving area, but it is repeatedly rebuffed by businesses and residents. The council's latest attempt, in the summer of 2005, backfired and cost more than £500,000 in consultants' and architects' fees.

Near Piccadilly Circus, Great Windmill Street has a range of institutions that perfectly sums up Soho. The historic Windmill Theatre, which once attracted red-faced gentlemen from the shires with its erotica, is today 'probably the most exciting men's club in the world'. Wedged between this fallen theatre and the Soho Cabaret sits Soho Parish School, where local children gambol in the cramped playground.

South of Shaftesbury Avenue is Chinatown, centred on pedestrianised Gerrard Street. You can't miss its ridiculous ersatz oriental street trimmings. The Chinese community first opened restaurants and shops here in the 1950s; it's another part of Soho whose way of life was established in the halcyon days of cheap rents and slummy streets. Today, these streets represent valuable real estate; plans are already under way to redevelop the eastern edge of Chinatown, near Charing Cross Road. Many of the businesses here fear they'll be driven away by soaring rents.

Holborn

A buffer between the businesslike City of London and the ditsy West End, stolid Holborn – divided between three different boroughs – is the traditional home of the legal profession. It is hardly a glamorous locale, and is plagued by strident people in dark suits with mobiles clamped to their ears, but its history and architecture are intriguing, its ancient streets, alleys and courtyards full of mystery.

Most of Holborn's residential property tends to be on the Covent Garden side of Kingsway. Despite the district's stock of desirable-looking Georgian houses, people who live here usually have to make do with expensive flats, often in big Victorian buildings such as decommissioned primary schools. Minutes from Holborn tube, crossing the border into Camden borough, quiet Macklin Street and Newton Street have a number of such conversions. Queen Square, north of High Holborn, is also a favoured (expensive) residential area.

The Aldwych and Kingsway edge of the district has a more worldly air. Theatreland peters out at the Aldwych Crescent and gives way to equally self-regarding institutions: the BBC (whose World Service will continue to broadcast from Bush House until Marylebone's Broadcasting House takes over in 2008) and various constituents of the University of London. Houghton Street is home to the London School of Economics (LSE) Students' Union, and there's a large amount of student accommodation in the vicinity.

Just beyond St Clement Danes church on the Strand sit the Royal Courts of Justice, the splendid Gothic buildings that house 76 courts open to anyone who wants to go in and see British justice in action. Further south lie Inner Temple, Middle Temple (with its 16th-century hall) and Temple church (King's Bench Walk), oft visited by *Da Vinci Code* readers. Back on the

Strand, Temple Bar marks the boundary between the borough of Westminster and the City of London. It is guarded by a bronze griffin, mounted here in 1878 to replace Wren's archway.

Mayfair

Piccadilly, one of the capital's grandest roads (if you ignore the rather grubby bits around the Circus at the eastern end), separates swanky Mayfair from St James's. Blue blood has long coursed through this district's arteries (in 1926 the Queen was born on Bruton Street) and evidence of money is everywhere. In 2004, a parking space (six feet by nine feet since you ask) was sold in a Mayfair underground car park for £65,000.

Although few normal people can afford to live around here, Mayfair feels more eccentric than snotty; the bored shop assistants in the dottily exclusive Piccadilly Arcade are only too pleased to turn on the charm for a customer. There are some delightful pubs in the heart of Mayfair, too, where the local office crowd comes after work. Shepherd Market has a couple of decent boozers, a handful of interesting shops, good restaurants and an association with other fleshly pursuits (prostitutes still work in the area, although probably not so obviously as in Jeffrey Archer's heyday). Nearby Farm Street is largely residential and stunningly attractive. The pretty local library, on South Audley Street, speaks of a lucky, literate residential community.

Marylebone

Unless you're going to a wedding at photogenic Marylebone Town Hall, visiting the excellent library, or trying to hail a taxi, the horrendously busy Marylebone Road is no place for pedestrians. The Marylebone for strollers and weekenders is the rebranded 'Village', which takes in the High Street and surrounding squares. The area's fashionableness grows year on year and property prices are now astronomical.

Marylebone High Street, the best shopping street in London to our mind, is picturesque, useful and classy. Newcomers to the district marvel that a neighbourhood so close to Oxford Street can have such a refined buzz to it. To the east, in Langham Place, Broadcasting House is undergoing the final stages of an extensive renovation programme; from 2008 it will be the new

Chinatown, the inner-city focus for London's Chinese community. *See p19.*

home of BBC News. North of Marylebone Road, the district is less picturesque than Marylebone Village, but it does have London's most low-key railway terminus (Marylebone station) and the excellent Alfie's Antique Market.

Fitzrovia

Bloomsbury (part of the borough of Camden; *see p116*) barges into Fitzrovia at various points east along Cleveland Street, adding to the rakish charm of this area of north-central London. It's a district that raises a number of questions among Londoners – 'Where is it?' being a common one. Roughly speaking, it lies west of Great Portland Street, bordered by Euston Road to the north, Oxford Street to the south and Charlotte Street to the east. The name comes from Fitzroy Square (which falls into Camden), built by one Honourable Charles Fitzroy in the 18th century. Estate agents favour the utterly absurd term Noho (short for North Soho).

Unlike its neighbours, Marylebone and Bloomsbury, whose lofty terraces, crescents and squares were prescribed by the empire-building of wealthy landowners, Fitzrovia was developed on a smaller scale, by several minor landowners, so the streets are less schematic. The area, whatever the estate

agents and style gurus say, doesn't have a trendy feel to it, instead emitting a more low-key, arty, crafty and businesslike vibe.

Within this district you'll find a few fashion wholesale businesses, various former departments of the old Middlesex Hospital (now moved to University College Hospital on Euston Road), BT and other communications offices under the iconic Tower, and a whole load of restaurants, cafés and pubs.

The Fitzrovia Neighbourhood Association (Tottenham Street) was established in the 1970s with the battle cry 'The people live here', when the area's residents stood up against would-be developers. The association established the annual community festival and still works for the neighbourhood today – although building goes on regardless, if the new Qube housing development on Whitfield Street is anything to go by.

Westminster and St James's

The headquarters of the British monarchy and the government are separated by the serene acreage of Green Park and St James's Park. Tourists throng outside both powerhouses: Buckingham Palace to the west, the Houses of Parliament to the east. This is where iconic monuments can be

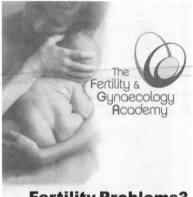

ticked off sightseeing lists, and Londoners must constantly remind themselves not to be rude, as the activities of these pavement-clogging visitors are grist to the city's mill.

In many ways, Westminster is like London's 'best room'. It is kept spick and span for our guests, its tube station is clean and impressively modern, and its made-over and traffic-calmed central square, Trafalgar Square, is a source of pride. Whitehall, on the other hand, is unfriendly to passing strollers; this is po-faced civil-servant country, and the big ministries that line the road are off-limits, as is the heavily guarded, security-gated Downing Street. Moving into the knot of streets around Victoria, through Peter Street, Old Pye Street (where Henry Purcell grew up) and Marsham Street (which has one of the oldest street signs in the country) returns you to community Westminster. There are residential streets around here, and Peabody estates for low-paid key workers – it can't be bad having Westminster Abbey as your local church.

Victoria bustles with backpackers, office workers and Catholics on pilgrimage (Westminster Cathedral is their goal and the view from its campanile is miraculous). It has the dubious honour of possessing London's busiest tube station and is the main shopping area in the district.

Pimlico

The people of Belgravia don't like to be associated with Pimlico, and Pimlico people aren't happy with the suggestion they live in Victoria. Theirs is a mysterious neighbourhood; residents say that the lack of community identity comes from the fact that so many politicians live here (it's handy for the office). Another mark of Pimlico's exclusivity is the baffling Dolphin Square, which is both a hotel and a self-contained village of pieds-à-terre for important people. The fortress-like, red-brick 1930s block has a health club, smart restaurant and a little art deco parade of shops. Such exclusivity is absent in the Westminster Boating Base, which has its headquarters just across Grosvenor Road, on the river. This excellent institution has been teaching urban youth the joys of water sports for 30 years.

Pimlico has its council blocks too, although they're far from ordinary. One, the Lillington (with a high-density, low-rise,

red-brick design, built in the 1970s), has grade II listed status. Belgrave Road, which starts smartly in Pimlico as Bessborough Gardens and turns into Eccleston Street when it crosses into Belgravia, is a boring stretch of hotels, some very down at heel.

Belgravia

Belgravia is the apotheosis of posh: road after road of gracious six-storey stucco houses, some reported to be worth in excess of £10m. Ordinary mortals can comfort themselves with the fact that many of the residences are occupied by embassies and offices. Belgravia has edges that blur with Knightsbridge, Chelsea and the less monied districts of Pimlico and Victoria. It describes more a state of extreme wealth than a geographical area. The centre of the district, should you wish to stand there, is Belgrave Square, laid out by the property contractor Thomas Cubitt for the second Earl Grosvenor in the 1820s. You can't stand in the gorgeous gardens, however, because they're private.

One advantage of Belgravia's refusal to join the real world is the fact that pubs originally built as modest affairs (for servants of the resident aristocracy) have not been allowed to be superseded by the big chain boozers. Hence you'll find many relatively understated watering holes like the Star Tavern and the Nag's Head.

Bayswater

For all its proximity to the refined, old-money Kensington Gardens, Bayswater manages to retain a vaguely unshaven, plebeian air. Some would say the only place worth visiting is Whiteleys, the largest shopping centre in central London. Apart from this grand, Edwardian relic, Queensway is a rough-and-ready high street with a mixture of chains, cafés and bakeries of many nationalities and, nearer Bayswater Road, tourist tat shops – though you'll also find some top-notch Chinese restaurants along its length. Behind Queensway, Queensborough Terrace is scruffy: cheap hotels, B&Bs, bedsits and studio flats have been crammed into what could, in another life, have been desirable residences. The result of Bayswater's profusion of tiny and temporary accommodation is a diverse population. You're likely to hear a whole world of accents as you stroll through the district, which has significant Brazilian,

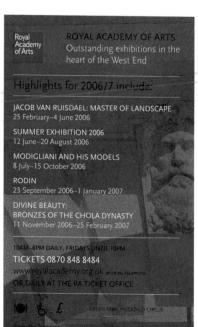

Arab and Greek populations (the Greek Orthodox Cathedral of St Sophia is on Moscow Road). The huge, 800-flat Hallfield Estate – designed by Sir Denys Lasdun in 1952, now a mixture of private and council tenants – swells the numbers further. A big Bayswater attraction is the Porchester Spa (attached to the Porchester Centre), an invigorating series of hot rooms and icy plunge pools with original art deco fittings and a slightly institutional aura.

North of Bayswater lies Westbourne Green, an area high on Westminster Council's 'to do' list for redevelopment as it has a distinctly deprived feel. The council is aiming to provide a new secondary school and health centre, as well as improved housing and a bit of green space to relieve the grey grimness all around the council estates near the unappealing Westway and Harrow Road confluence.

Paddington

The people of 'mournful' Paddington (as Peter Ackroyd would have it) are used to living in a building site. For decades this slice of central London's grand but slightly slummy houses have been the focus of property developers, small and large, but no regeneration project since Docklands has seen the transformation of such a vast area of inner city as the Paddington Waterside Project. The building work began in 2000 with the draining of the basin and went on over five years to transform an area the size of Soho into a very 21st-century ideal of waterside living, designed for young urban professionals who want to walk to work in the West End. The area around the cleaned-up basin, with its barges, pontoons, big-windowed flats and a futuristic Marks & Spencer's headquarters designed by Richard Rogers, is a far cry from down-at-heel Paddington, once deplored for its overcrowding and vice.

It's not all new and gleaming, however. A walk along Praed Street, Norfolk Place and Sussex Gardens reveals that many of the once grand stucco houses are still serving as rather seedy hotels or have been carved into bedsits. And the northern edge of the district has the Westway roaring through it (as well as Paddington Green high-security police station, where terrorist suspects are questioned). You'll also find a bit of a mess around the station, where the

ongoing Bishop's Bridge Project, which stopped the traffic for over two years, is due to be completed by mid 2006.

Westbourne Terrace, towards Bayswater, hailed as the finest street in London in its heyday, still boasts some fantastically handsome houses. Many residents here say they live in Hyde Park or Lancaster Gate or even Bayswater – so long as they can avoid the use of the word Paddington, which still sounds a bit working class.

Maida Vale

That piece of paradise where the Grand Union and Regent's Canals meet, Little Venice is the bit of Maida Vale that sticks in the memory. Perfect for a Sunday afternoon stroll, the area is pretty enough to confound out-of-town visitors about urban decay. Pelargonium-adorned narrowboats contain cafés, galleries and (during winter) a children's puppet theatre, and the atmosphere is generally friendly. Continuing west on the canal path leads the unwary to the rather less attractive Westbourne Green. Strolling east along the towpath seems a better option, as it takes you to Regent's Park.

Around Little Venice and Clifton Gardens the area is affluent. The houses are tall, white stucco, and the shops are geared to the luxury market. Stucco is exchanged for less classy red brick as you explore north-west towards Paddington Recreation Ground, at Maida Vale's northerly extreme, where the Kilburn craic starts to impinge on Maida Vale's sanity. Elgin Avenue bisects the district west to east, and the pretty, residential roads leading off it are lined with solid Victorian terraces with wrought-iron balconies and handsome blocks of well-proportioned mansion flats. It's a quiet, cosy part of the world with few shops and businesses. The handsome flats of Westside Court and pretty Delaware Road are much sought after.

St John's Wood

The comfortably off, north-western edge of Westminster borough would have the air and appeal of a wealthy market town if it weren't for the district's claims to pop music and sporting fame that keep the pilgrims beating a path to its tube station. The first is Abbey Road, whose recording studios were made legendary by... oh, you know already. The second is Lord's Cricket

Ground, whose pod-like NatWest Media Centre caused a bit of a stir among the largely conservative residents accustomed to the classical Victorian architecture that draws so many loaded business-folk to the area. The Fab Four association, in particular, gives St John's Wood year-round cred, so the Italian café by the tube, which does a brisk trade in Beatles memorabilia, is often full of young European students on their way back from taking photos of themselves striding over that zebra crossing. The Wood also has some very pretty residential streets with larger houses for well-to-do families. Parents in shiny Mercs ferry their blazered prep-school princes and princesses to independent educational establishments in the area.

West Kilburn

Westminster borough's westerly protuberance sprawls on to territories administered by the neighbouring boroughs of Brent (*see p303*) and Kensington & Chelsea (*see p143*), and arouses a great deal of interest among acquisitive young folk who aspire to Notting Hill but can't afford it. For those to whom modish postcodes are important, West Kilburn is a hop and a skip (albeit across the dismal Harrow Road) from Ladbroke Grove, and the houses, though modest, are pretty, with gabled porches and decorative brickwork.

These Victorian terraces form the extensive Queen's Park Estate conservation area, with its mundanely monikered avenues (First to Sixth), bordered by Harrow Road (and the comedic-sounding Droop Street) to the south and Brent's own Kilburn Lane to the north. Queen's Park, built by the Artisans' Labourers' and General Dwellings Company, is distinct from the large, family-friendly Corporation of London park of the same name on the other side of the railway tracks. Elsewhere in West Kilburn, there are tall blocks of council flats, which save the district from fancily gabled, IKEA-interiored ponciness.

Restaurants & cafés

Westminster has an astounding diversity of eating places. Here's a taste; for the whole menu, see the *Time Out London Eating & Drinking Guide*, and for the latest openings, check *Time Out* magazine's 'Food & Drink' section.

Covent Garden and the Strand contain two of London's oldest British restaurants: Rules (game a speciality) and Simpson's-in-the-Strand (famed for roasts). Streets around the Piazza are populated by tourist-luring eateries, but there's quality nearby, including the elegant Christopher's (North American). Closer to Trafalgar Square is sushi specialist Hazuki, and beneath St Martin's church the handy Café in the Crypt. Near Seven Dials you'll find vegetarian beaneries Food for Thought, Neal's Yard Salad Bar and World Food Café, and chippie Rock & Sole Plaice. West of St Martin's Lane on discreet

STATISTICS
BOROUGH MAKE-UP
Population 185,110 (during the day, number of people exceeds 1,000,000)
Average weekly pay £610.90
Ethnic origins
White 73.21%
Mixed 4.13%
Asian or Asian British 8.88%
Black or Black British 7.44%
Chinese or other 6.35%
Students 11.88%
Retirees 7.88%

HOUSING STOCK
Borough size 22km^2
No. of households 113,759
Detached 1%
Semi-detached 1.9%
Terraced 8%
Flats (purpose-built) 59.2%
Flats (converted) 27.9%
Flats (both) 87.1%

CRIME PER 1,000 OF POPULATION
(English average in brackets)
Burglary 8 (6.4)
Robbery 7 (1.4)
Theft of vehicle 5 (4.5)
Theft from vehicle 16 (10)
Violence against the person 47 (16.5)
Sexual offences 3 (0.9)

MPs & COUNCIL
MPs *Cities of London & Westminster* Mark Field (Conservative); *Holborn & St Pancras* Frank Dobson (Labour); *Regent's Park & Kensington North* Karen Buck (Labour)
CPA 4 stars; improving well

backstreets are two prime celeb hangouts: the Ivy (Mod Euro) and J Sheekey (fish). Towards the river the choice includes the handsome Admiralty (French), with a great location in Somerset House. Just along the Strand is cherished budget Indian the India Club. Swish Modern European enterprises can be found at Bank Aldwych and at One Aldwych hotel (Indigo and Axis).

Soho is the crucible of London's restaurant revolution. L'Escargot Marco Pierre White (classic French) and Andrew Edmunds (Modern European) are here, along with Irishman Richard Corrigan's Lindsay House. There are some great Italian restaurants too, from flash venues (Quo Vadis, Vasco & Piero's Pavilion) to first-rate pizza and pasta joints (Italian Graffiti, Spiga), and classic Italian caffs (New Piccadilly). Other communities have added to the thrilling variety: Afro-Caribbean (budget caff Mr Jerk), Korean (Nara), Hungarian (politicians' haunt Gay Hussar), Indian (Masala Zone for value; Red Fort for sheer class), and pan-oriental (Grocer on Warwick Café). Japanese caffs populate Brewer Street (including conveyor-belt sushi joint Kulu Kulu).

Most oriental choices, however, lie south of Shaftesbury Avenue in Chinatown: some specialising in dim sum (Hong Kong), some in regional cuisine (ECapital for Shanghainese, Fook Sing for Fujian) and several in authentic Cantonese (New Mayflower is our fave). Terrific dim sum is also found just outside the district at fashionable Yauatcha. Soho is also noted for cafés: from vegetarian haunts like Beatroot to famous landmark Maison Bertaux.

Unsurprisingly, Mayfair restaurants tend towards exclusivity. Some of Britain's most celebrated chefs operate here: Gordon Ramsay at Claridge's, Michel Roux at Le Gavroche. Our current haute cuisine favourites include the Greenhouse (playground of fusion-food meister Bjorn van der Horst), and Maze (exquisite tapas-sized dishes). Mayfair is also where to find classy dining Japanese-style (Chisou, Nobu), Indian-style (Tamarind) and Italian-style (Alloro). Chic North African Momo attracts the beau monde, while ladies-who-lunch frequent Nicole's (below the Nicole Farhi shop). It's possible to have a modestly priced meal – perhaps a pizza at Rocket – but that may be missing the Mayfair métier.

Paddington Waterside. *See p25.*

Marylebone is less showy – yet you can still find excellent eating. There's a popular branch of fishmonger's-cum-restaurant FishWorks, as well as Orrery (Terence Conran's grandiloquent Modern European venture). On Seymour Street is top Italian Locanda Locatelli. Cafés are a forte, with La Fromagerie's cheese-based eaterie, Quiet Revolution's organic stop-off and, in Regent's Park, the retro-chic Garden Café. A branch of Thai canteen Busaba Eathai and vegetarian diner Eat & Two Veg also provide quick bites. Other highlights include exquisite dim sum at Royal China; smashing fish and chips at the Golden Hind; two decent kosher restaurants (Reuben's and Six-13); and authentic Singaporean, Rasa Singapura. The frenetic Chapel is a decent gastropub.

Fitzrovia's dining district is centred on Charlotte Street, on Westminster's border with Camden (for restaurants here, *see p124*). Away from Charlotte Street, fish lovers should try Back to Basics; nearby is Özer (classy Turkish). Carluccio's Caffé and the smart Latium are two good Italians in the vicinity. Heading towards Marylebone, you'll find restaurant-bar-deli Villandry.

Westminster contains a few choice venues. Cinnamon Club, one of London's best Indians, is a favourite with scheming politicos; Quirinale (Italian) is another.

St James's has a rarefied vibe, as exemplified by the very grand Wiltons; Green's is in a similar upmarket piscine vein. Inn The Park is a sleek breakfast-to-dinner British restaurant in St James's Park. The Avenue is our current pick of the Modern European venues, though Italian Fiore also delivers exciting flavours. Noura Central (Lebanese) is good value, and great for vegetarians.

Pimlico is residential and its few restaurants can be divided into pit-stops near Victoria station (the Seafresh chippie; Thai-in-a-pub, Page) and highfalutin venues such as Tate Britain Restaurant (Mod Euro food and fine wine) and Allium (haute).

Belgravia restaurants are quietly select. On the southern boundary, little Hunan is a first-rate Chinese venue specialising in spicy western cuisine. Close by are three great French eateries – Roussillon, La Poule au Pot and Le Cercle – and gastropub the Ebury. Quietly select also describes Belgravia's two Italians, the elegant Il Convivio and Sardinian specialist Olivo.

Prices in Bayswater are more amenable. Two prime gastropubs on the outskirts of Notting Hill fall into Westminster borough: the popular Westbourne and the excellent Cow Dining Room. Queensway holds some superb Chinese restaurants, including seafood specialist Mandarin Kitchen. There are trendy Italians too (Sardinian-accented Assaggi), plus chic Modern Euro venue Island Restaurant & Bar. Otherwise, dining is suitably multinational: Russian at Erebuni, Thai at the delightful Nipa.

Paddington restaurants can be drab, but an exception is smart new Indian Jamuna. Satay House (Indonesian) is worthwhile too. For more choice, head for the Edgware Road, where Middle Eastern is the gastronomic forte: try pretty Iranian caff Kandoo; glitzy Lebanese Maroush Gardens; or late-night kebabery Ranoush Juice Bar. Also here is superb Mandalay, London's only Burmese venue.

Maida Vale's relaxed restaurants cater to affluent locals. Try Raoul's (daytime brunch, night-time Mediterranean) or Red Pepper (pizzas and pasta). Mesón Bilbao also appeals with genuine Basque cooking.

Eateries along St John's Wood High Street feed well-heeled shoppers, who ogle pastries at Maison Blanc or tuck into Jewish dishes at Harry Morgan's.

Admiralty *Somerset House, Strand, WC2R 1LA (7845 4646/www.somerset-house. org.uk).*
Allium *Dolphin Square, Chichester Street, SW1V 3LX (7798 6888/www.allium.co.uk).*
Alloro *19-20 Dover Street, W1X 4LU (7495 4768/www.atozrestaurants.com).*
Andrew Edmunds *46 Lexington Street, W1F 0LW (7437 5708).*
Assaggi *First floor, 39 Chepstow Place, W2 4TS (7792 5501).*
The Avenue *7-9 St James's Street, SW1A 1EE (7321 2111/www.egami.co.uk).*
Axis *One Aldwych, 1 Aldwych, WC2B 4RH (7300 0300/www.onealdwych.com).*
Back to Basics *21A Foley Street, W1W 6DS (7436 2181/www.backtobasics.uk.com).*
Bank Aldwych *1 Kingsway, WC2B 6XF (7379 9797/www.bankrestaurants.com).*
Beatroot *92 Berwick Street, W1F 0QD (7437 8591).*
Busaba Eathai *8-13 Bird Street, W1U 1BU (7518 8080).*
Café in the Crypt *Crypt of St Martin-in-the-Fields, Duncannon Street, WC2N 4JJ (7766 1158/www.stmartin-in-the-fields.org).*
Carluccio's Caffè *8 Market Place, W1W 8AG (7636 2228/www.carluccios.com).*
Le Cercle *1 Wilbraham Place, SW1X 9AE (7901 9999).*
Chapel *48 Chapel Street, NW1 5DP (7402 9220).*
Chisou *4 Princes Street, W1B 2LE (7629 3931).*
Christopher's *18 Wellington Street, WC2E 7DD (7240 4222/www.christophersgrill.com).*
Cinnamon Club *The Old Westminster Library, 30 Great Smith Street, SW1P 3BU (7222 2555/ www.cinnamonclub.com).*
Il Convivio *143 Ebury Street, SW1W 9QN (7730 4099/www.etruscagroup.co.uk).*
Cow Dining Room *89 Westbourne Park Road, W2 5QH (7221 0021).*
Eat & Two Veg *50 Marylebone High Street, W1U 5HN (7258 8595/www.eatandtwoveg.com).*
Ebury *11 Pimlico Road, SW1W 8NA (7730 6784).*
ECapital *8 Gerrard Street, W1D 5PJ (7434 3838).*

City of Westminster

Erebuni *London Guards Hotel, 36-37 Lancaster Gate, W2 3NA (7402 6067).*
L'Escargot Marco Pierre White *48 Greek Street, W1D 4EF (7437 2679).*
Fiore *33 St James's Street, SW1A 1HD (7930 7100/www.fiore-restaurant.co.uk).*
FishWorks *89 Marylebone High Street, W1U 4QW (7935 9796/www.fishworks.co.uk).*
Food for Thought *31 Neal Street, WC2H 9PR (7836 9072).*
Fook Sing *25-26 Newport Court, WC2H 7JS (7287 0188).*
La Fromagerie *2-4 Moxon Street, W1U 4EW (7935 0341/www.lafromagerie.co.uk).*
Garden Café *Inner Circle, Regent's Park, NW1 4NU (7935 5729/www.thegardencafe.co.uk).*
Le Gavroche *43 Upper Brook Street, W1K 7QR (7408 0881/www.le-gavroche.co.uk).*
Gay Hussar *2 Greek Street, W1D 4NB (7437 0973).*
Golden Hind *73 Marylebone Lane, W1U 2PN (7486 3644).*
Gordon Ramsay at Claridge's *Claridge's Hotel, 55 Brook Street, W1A 2JQ (7499 0099/www.gordonramsay.com).*
Greenhouse *27A Hay's Mews, W1J 5NY (7499 3331/www.greenhouserestaurant.co.uk).*
Green's *36 Duke Street, SW1Y 6DF (7930 4566/www.greens.org.uk).*
Grocer on Warwick Café *21 Warwick Street, W1B 5NE (7437 7776/www.thegrocer onwarwick.com).*
Harry Morgan's *31 St John's Wood High Street, NW8 7NH (7722 1869/www.harryms. co.uk).*
Hazuki *43 Chandos Place, WC2N 4HS (7240 2530).*
Hunan *51 Pimlico Road, SW1W 8NE (7730 5712).*
India Club *Second Floor, Strand Continental Hotel, 143 Strand, WC2R 1JA (7836 0650).*
Indigo *One Aldwych, 1 Aldwych, WC2B 4RH (7300 0400/www.onealdwych.com).*
Inn The Park *St James's Park, SW1A 2BJ (7451 9999/www.innthepark.co.uk).*
Island Restaurant & Bar *Royal Lancaster Hotel, Lancaster Terrace, W2 2TY (7551 6070).*
Italian Graffiti *163-165 Wardour Street, W1F 8WN (7439 4668/www.italiangraffiti.co.uk).*
The Ivy *1 West Street, WC2H 9NQ (7836 4751).*
Jamuna *38A Southwick Street, W2 1JQ (7723 5056/www.jamuna.co.uk).*
J Sheekey *28-32 St Martin's Court, WC2N 4AL (7240 2565/www.caprice-holdings.co.uk).*
Kandoo *458 Edgware Road, W2 1EJ (7724 2428).*
Kulu Kulu *76 Brewer Street, W1F 9TX (7734 7316).*
Latium *21 Berners Street, W1T 3LP (7323 9123/www.latiumrestaurant.com).*
Lindsay House *21 Romilly Street, W1D 5AF (7439 0450/www.lindsayhouse.co.uk).*
Locanda Locatelli *8 Seymour Street, W1H 7JZ (7935 9088/www.locandalocatelli.com).*
London Hong Kong *6-7 Lisle Street, WC2H 7BG (7287 0352).*

Maison Bertaux *28 Greek Street, W1D 5DQ (7437 6007).*
Maison Blanc *37 St John's Wood High Street, NW8 7NG (7586 1982).*
Mandalay *444 Edgware Road, W2 1EG (7258 3696).*
Mandarin Kitchen *14-16 Queensway, W2 3RX (7727 9012).*
Maroush Gardens *1-3 Connaught Street, W2 2DH (7262 0222/www.maroush.com).*
Masala Zone *9 Marshall Street, W1F 7ER (7287 9966/www.realindianfood.com).*
Maze *10-13 Grosvenor Square, W1K 6JP (7107 0000/www.gordonramsay.com).*
Mesón Bilbao *33 Malvern Road, NW6 5PS (7328 1744).*
Mr Jerk *189 Wardour Street, W1F 8ZD (7287 2878/www.mrjerk.co.uk).*
Momo *25 Heddon Street, W1B 4BH (7434 4040/www.momoresto.com).*
Nara *9 D'Arblay Street, W1F 8DR (7287 2224).*
Neal's Yard Salad Bar *1, 2, 8 & 10 Neal's Yard, WC2H 9DP (7836 3233/www.nealsyard saladbar.co.uk).*
New Mayflower *68-70 Shaftesbury Avenue, W1B 6LY (7734 9207).*
New Piccadilly *8 Denman Street, W1D 7HQ (7437 8530).*
Nicole's *158 New Bond Street, W1F 2UB (7499 8408).*
Nipa *Royal Lancaster Hotel, Lancaster Terrace, W2 2TY (7262 6737/www.royallancaster.com).*
Nobu *Metropolitan Hotel, 19 Old Park Lane, W1K 1LB (7447 4747/www.nobu restaurants.com).*
Noura Central *22 Lower Regent Street, SW1Y 4UJ (7839 2020/www.noura.co.uk).*
Olivo *21 Eccleston Street, SW1W 9LX (7730 2505).*
Orrery *55 Marylebone High Street, W1U 5RB (7616 8000/www.orrery.co.uk).*
Özer *4-5 Langham Place, W1B 3DG (7323 0505/www.sofra.co.uk).*
Page *11 Warwick Way, SW1V 4LT (7834 3313/www.frontpagepubs.com).*
La Poule au Pot *231 Ebury Street, SW1W 8UT (7730 7763).*
Quiet Revolution *28-29 Marylebone High Street, W1V 4PL (7487 5683).*
Quirinale *North Court, 1 Great Peter Street, SW1P 3LL (7222 7080/www.quirinale.co.uk).*
Quo Vadis *26-29 Dean Street, W1T 6LL (7437 9585/www.whitestarline.org.uk).*
Ranoush Juice Bar *43 Edgware Road, W2 2JR (7723 5929).*
Raoul's *13 Clifton Road, W9 1SZ (7289 7313).*
Rasa Singapura *Regent's Park Hotel, 154-156 Gloucester Place, NW1 6DT (7723 6740).*
Red Fort *77 Dean Street, W1D 3SH (7437 2115/www.redfort.co.uk).*
Red Pepper *8 Formosa Street, W9 1EE (7266 2708).*
Reuben's *79 Baker Street, W1U 6RG (7486 0035).*
Rock & Sole Plaice *47 Endell Street, WC2H 9AJ (7836 3785).*

Rocket *4-6 Lancashire Court, off New Bond Street, W1Y 9AD (7629 2889/www.rocket restaurants.co.uk).*
Roussillon *16 St Barnabas Street, SW1W 8PE (7730 5550/www.roussillon.co.uk).*
Royal China *24-26 Baker Street, W1U 7AB (7487 4688/www.royalchinagroup.co.uk).*
Rules *35 Maiden Lane, WC2E 7LB (7836 5314/www.rules.co.uk).*
Satay House *13 Sale Place, W2 1PX (7723 6763/www.satay-house.co.uk).*
Seafresh Fish Restaurant *80-81 Wilton Road, SW1V 1DL (7828 0747).*
Simpson's-in-the-Strand *100 Strand, WC2R 0EW (7836 9112/www.fairmont.com/svy/simpsons).*
Six-13 *19 Wigmore Street, W1U 1PH (7629 6133/www.six13.com).*
Spiga *84-86 Wardour Street, W1V 3LF (7734 3444).*
Tamarind *20 Queen Street, W1J 5PR (7629 3561/www.tamarindrestaurant.com).*
Tate Britain Restaurant *Tate Britain, Millbank, SW1P 4RG (7887 8825/www.tate.org.uk).*
Vasco & Piero's Pavilion *15 Poland Street, W1F 8QE (7437 8774/www.vascosfood.com).*
Villandry *170 Great Portland Street, W1W 5QB (7631 3131/www.villandry.com).*
Westbourne *101 Westbourne Park Villas, W2 5ED (7221 1332/www.thewestbourne.com).*
Wiltons *55 Jermyn Street, SW1Y 6LX (7629 9955).*
World Food Café *First Floor, 14 Neal's Yard, WC2H 9DP (7379 0298).*
Yauatcha *15 Broadwick Street, W1F 0DL (7494 8888).*

Bars & pubs

Westminster's watering holes attract drinkers from across London, the UK and beyond. Problem is, there's so much variety you can waste valuable licensing hours finding your niche. Here's a selection of the essential venues, but for the full draught, consult the *Time Out London Bars, Pubs & Clubs Guide.*

Covent Garden is a case in point. If you want a crush of out-of-towners downing nitrokegs, head towards the Piazza. If not, you'll find the surrounding side streets more promising, yielding traditional old boozers like the Lamb & Flag (packed to its bare beams after 5pm) and the ultra-cosy Cross Keys. Expat haunts the Maple Leaf (Canada), Lowlander (Benelux) and the Africa Bar are great for cultural tourism. The Octave Jazz Bar blends champagne cocktails with cool blues. Bünker purveys own-brewed lager, while beer-haven the Porterhouse serves

tremendous Irish stout. Style bars Detroit (retro sci-fi) and Freud (minimalist) remain eternally hip. Near Leicester Square, basement wine bar the Cork & Bottle is a gorgeous oasis, while over by the Strand, three very different constituencies are served by the Nell Gwynne (friendly little pub), Gordon's (ancient subterranean wine bar) and the Savoy's swanky American Bar.

Provincials, tourists, gay hedonists, after-work gluggers, early-hours groovers – Soho is diverse enough to accommodate the lot. The gay scene is focused on the west end of Old Compton Street, around the Admiral Duncan, Comptons of Soho and, over on Wardour Street, Village Soho; lesbians have the Candy Bar. If you're after famous old boozers, squeeze into the French House or the lovely little Dog & Duck. Equally historic is Kettner's champagne bar, though real ale fans should start at the Pillars of Hercules. Further into the night, hit the clubs. Lab, 22 Below and Polka supply terrific cocktails, then there's funky DJ bar Thirst, exclusive Milk & Honey and sumptuous oriental Opium (open until 3am) to consider – along with rockin' music venue Ain't Nothin' But? The Blues Bar.

Holborn is somewhat more restrained, but does have a few pubs to be proud of, most notably the gorgeous little Seven Stars (favoured by lawyers), while former journalists' pub the Edgar Wallace has the best choice of real ales. For slicker environs, there's the dramatic Lobby Bar (in One Aldwych hotel) and, nearby, the bar at Bank Aldwych (*see p27*).

Snug pubs and glitzy bars are Mayfair's forte. The Moroccan-styled Mô Tea Room (next to Momo restaurant) is trendy but welcoming. Style is also much in evidence (along with pricey cocktails) at Zeta Bar and Hush. And those snug pubs? Head for the Guinea Grill (a Young's house) or the delightful Red Lion.

Marylebone has a wealth of pubs, many with the feel of a local. Try two-bar real ale den the Barley Mow, or attractive corner pub the Golden Eagle (beer from Cornwall, plus a resident pianist). Bars are scarce, but Low Life – a fuzzy bill-postered basement DJ venue – is popular with students. In contrast, Fitzrovia has a burgeoning bar culture. Venues veer from the Sanderson

Old Compton Street, the buzzing main drag of gay Soho. *See p19.*

Hotel's sleek and expensive Long Bar via multifaceted Market Place and the Social (both with food and basement DJ bar), to Scandinavian-themed Nordic and good-value good-time venue Wax. Pub-goers have plenty to cheer too, with cosy little gem the Newman Arms, great-value Sam Smith's boozer the Cock Tavern and loungey Crown & Sceptre, which also serves good food.

In Westminster, politicians cram into the Red Lion, complete with division bell and BBC Parliament. St James's has more (albeit pricey) choices, with classic cocktails served at Rivoli at the Ritz and cool lounge Calma. For an old-school pub, head for one of the three Lions – two Red (on Crown Passage and Duke of York Street) and one Golden.

Pimlico pubs are quiet affairs frequented by affluent locals and office workers: typical is the Morpeth Arms. Chimes bar-restaurant has a laudable choice of ciders. In Belgravia, the Berkeley's stylish, discreet Blue Bar is a good place to meet and sip a cocktail before you head off to a first-rate boozer: the likes of former servant's inn the Star Tavern or the cheerful little Nag's Head.

There are plenty of run-down pubs in Bayswater and Paddington, but also some wheat among the chaff. The Victoria, a tiny

Fuller's pub, is a lovely place, and towards Notting Hill, the Prince Bonaparte scores highly for food, beer and wine. Close by is sweet, kooky Tom & Dick's.

In Little Venice, don't miss the fabulous Bridge House. Across the water, the beautiful Prince Alfred has great food and drink, while, near Warwick Avenue tube, the Warrington is a palace of Edwardian splendour. St John's Wood also houses a few prime drinking establishments on its stern residential streets. Bonhomie-laden local boozer the Star is among the most welcoming, though gastropub the Abbey Road Pub & Dining Room is a comfy spot too (with a beer garden).

Westminster's West Kilburn enclave is best served by Little Venice venues or the drinking dens of Kensal Green and Queen's Park in Brent (*see p307*).

Admiral Duncan *54 Old Compton Street, W1D 5PA (7437 5300).*
Ain't Nothin' But? The Blues Bar *20 Kingly Street, W1B 5PZ (7287 0514).*
Africa Bar *Africa Centre, 38 King Street, WC2E 8JT (7836 1976).*
American Bar *Savoy Hotel, Strand, WC2R 0EU (7836 4343).*
Bank Aldwych *1 Kingsway, WC2B 6XF (7379 9797/www.bankrestaurants.com).*

Barley Mow *8 Dorset Street, W1U 6QW* *(7935 7318).*
Blue Bar *The Berkeley, Wilton Place, SW1X 7RL (7235 6000/www.the-berkeley.co.uk).*
Bridge House *13 Westbourne Terrace Road, W2 6NG (7432 1361).*
Bünker *41 Earlham Street, WC2H 9LD (7240 0606/www.bunkerbar.com).*
Calma *23 St James's Street, SW1A 1HA (7747 9380/www.shumi-london.com).*
Candy Bar *4 Carlisle Street, W1D 3BJ (7494 4041/www.thecandybar.co.uk).*
Chimes *26 Churton Street, SW1V 2LP (7821 7456).*
Cock Tavern *27 Great Portland Street, W1W 8QE (7631 5002).*
Comptons of Soho *51-53 Old Compton Street, W1D 6HJ (7479 7961/www.comptons-of-soho.co.uk).*
Cork & Bottle *44-46 Cranbourn Street, WC2H 7AN (7734 7807).*
Cross Keys *31 Endell Street, WC2H 9EB (7836 5185).*
Crown & Sceptre *26-27 Foley Street, W1W 6DY (7307 9971).*
Detroit *35 Earlham Street, WC2H 9LD (7240 2662/www.detroit-bar.com).*
Dog & Duck *18 Bateman Street, W1D 3AJ (7494 0697).*
Edgar Wallace *40 Essex Street, WC2R 3JE (7353 3120).*
French House *49 Dean Street, W1D 5BG (7437 2799).*
Freud *198 Shaftesbury Avenue, WC2H 8JL (7240 9933/www.freudliving.com).*
Golden Eagle *59 Marylebone Lane, W1U 2NY (7935 3228).*
Golden Lion *25 King Street, SW1Y 6QY (7925 0007).*
Gordon's *47 Villiers Street, WC2N 6NE (7930 1408/www.gordonswinebar.com).*
Guinea Grill *30 Bruton Place, W1J 6NL (7499 1210/www.theguinea.co.uk).*

RECYCLING

No. of bring sites 114 (for nearest, visit www.recycleforlondon.com)
Household waste recycled 13.1%
Main recycling centre There are three small sites in Marylebone (the biggest is on Paddington Street), but residents in the rest of the borough are encouraged to use the council's kerbside collection scheme
Other recycling services green waste collection; home composting; collection of white goods and furniture; computer recycling scheme
Council contact Environment & Leisure Department (Environmental Services), City Hall, 64 Victoria Street, SW1E 6QP (7641 2000)

Hush *8 Lancashire Court, Brook Street, W1S 1EY (7659 1500/www.hush.co.uk).*
Kettner's *29 Romilly Street, W1D 5HP (7734 6112/www.kettners.com).*
Lab *12 Old Compton Street, W1D 4TQ (7437 7820/www.lab-townhouse.com).*
Lamb & Flag *33 Rose Street, WC2E 9EB (7497 9504).*
Lobby Bar *1 Aldwych, WC2B 4RH (7300 1070/www.onealdwych.com).*
Long Bar *Sanderson Hotel, 50 Berners Street, W1T 3NG (7300 1400).*
Lowlander *36 Drury Lane, WC2B 5RR (7379 7446/www.lowlander.com).*
Low Life *34A Paddington Street, W1U 4HG (7935 1272).*
Maple Leaf *41 Maiden Lane, WC2E 7LJ (7240 2843).*
Market Place *11 Market Place, W1W 8AH (7079 2020/www.marketplace-london.com).*
Milk & Honey *61 Poland Street, W1F 7NU (7292 9949/0700 655 469/www.mlkhny.com).*
Morpeth Arms *58 Millbank, SW1P 4RW (7834 6442).*
Mô Tea Room *23 Heddon Street, W1B 4BH (7434 4040).*
Nag's Head *53 Kinnerton Street, SW1X 8ED (7235 1135).*
Neil Gwynne *1-2 Bull Inn Court, WC2R 0NP (7240 5579).*
Newman Arms *23 Rathbone Street, W1T 1NG (7636 1127/www.newmanarms.co.uk).*
Nordic *25 Newman Street, W1T 1PN (7631 3174/www.nordicbar.com).*
Octave Jazz Bar *27-29 Endell Street, WC2H 9BA (7836 4616/www.octave8.com).*
Opium *1A Dean Street, W1D 3RB (7287 9608/ www.opium-bar-restaurant.com).*
Pillars of Hercules *7 Greek Street, W1D 4DF (7437 1179).*
Polka *58-59 Poland Street, W1F 7NB (7287 7500).*
Porterhouse *21-22 Maiden Lane, WC2E 7NA (7836 9931/www.porterhousebrewco.com).*
Prince Alfred & Formosa Dining Rooms *5A Formosa Street, W9 1EE (7286 3287).*
Prince Bonaparte *80 Chepstow Road, W2 5BE (7313 9491).*
Red Lion *1 Waverton Street, W1J 5QN (7499 1307).*
Red Lion *48 Parliament Street, SW1A 2NH (7930 5826).*
Red Lion *23 Crown Passage, off Pall Mall, SW1Y 6PP (7930 4141).*
Red Lion *2 Duke of York Street, SW1Y 6JP (7321 0782).*
Rivoli at the Ritz *Ritz Hotel, 150 Piccadilly, W1J 9BR (7493 8181).*
The Salthouse *63 Abbey Road, NW8 0AE (7328 6626).*
Seven Stars *53 Carey Street, WC2A 2JB (7242 8521).*
Social *5 Little Portland Street, W1W 7JD (7636 4992/www.thesocial.com).*
Star *38 St John's Wood Terrace, NW8 6LS (7722 1051).*

Star Tavern 6 Belgrave Mews West, SW1X 8HT (7235 3019).
Thirst 53 Greek Street, W1D 3DR (7437 1977/www.thirstbar.com).
Tom & Dick's 30 Alexander Street, W2 5NU (7229 7711/www.tomanddicks.com).
22 Below 22 Great Marlborough Street, W1F 7HU (7437 4106/www.22below.co.uk).
Victoria 10A Strathern Place, W2 2NH (7724 1191).
Village Soho 81 Wardour Street, W1D 6QD (7434 2124).
Wax 4 Winsley Street, W1W 8HF (7436 4650/www.wax-bar.co.uk).
Warrington Hotel 93 Warrington Crescent, W9 1EH (7286 2929).
Zeta Bar 35 Hertford Street, W1J 7TG (7208 4067)/www.zeta-bar.com).

Shops

Rivalled only by posh Kensington & Chelsea, Westminster wins out as London's all-embracing shopping centre. We've surveyed the highlights here; consult the *Time Out London Shopping Guide* for more ideas and further details of stock.

Jostling, maddening Oxford Street is the borough's main retail drag. The Centre Point end is horrid, dominated by cheap clothes shops and tacky gift emporia. Move swiftly west towards Oxford Circus and, though the crowds swell, the choice is better. The omnipresent Topshop squats on the north-eastern corner of the Circus, apparently about to swallow up NikeTown next door (no mean feat). Sharing premises is Topshop's elder, quieter sister, Miss Selfridge, and, next door to that, Urban Outfitters. The line-up of big fashion chains continues westwards towards Marble Arch. Pedestrianised St Christopher's Place, with its combination of upmarket chains and designer shops, is a welcome respite from the crush. On Wigmore Street, where it emerges, don't miss exquisite modern interiors shop Mint.

While most of the city's department stores congregate on Oxford Street, petite Fenwick, known for its accessories and lingerie, perches demurely on nearby Bond Street and Fortnum & Mason – its famous food hall staffed by courtly tailcoated gents – is out on Piccadilly. John Lewis is king for homewares, haberdashery and other basics, but Selfridges, despite its propensity to stage over-hyped theme weeks, wins hands-down for its all-encompassing selection of clothes, global food, home goods and

gadgets. An equally famous department store is down Regent Street; Liberty shouldn't be snubbed just because the tourists love its printed silk scarves. The beauty department and menswear are fab.

Nip out of Liberty's side door and you're on Carnaby Street. If you visited this iconic strip a few years back, hoping for a lingering whiff of 1960s swinging London, you'll have found nothing but tourist tat. Try it again. The shops are rather label-heavy, granted, but the street has come a long way from its tawdry appearance late in the last century. American Apparel is good for cheap 'n' chic tees, and G Room is a trendy men's 'lifestyle' shop. Duck into Kingly Court – the small, three-floor shopping centre houses numerous good boutiques. Twinkled is one of the newest, stocking retro collectibles for the home. There are more small shops on cobbled Newburgh Street, running parallel to Carnaby Street to the east.

In Soho, Antipodium's second store of Aussie fashion imports for both sexes is worth a browse, and Souvenir's two designer womenswear boutiques are handily close to each other; the newer, Brewer Street shop focuses on higher-end labels. On the same street is the World According To…, which is more affordable, and slightly more eccentric. Berwick Street boasts central London's jolliest street market and the shops that back it up include independent record stores and cut-price home and textile shops. The original Broadwick Street outpost of luxury lingerie chain Agent Provocateur is at home in its slightly louche locale.

Continuing east towards Covent Garden, even seasoned shoppers can get lost around the cobbled streets of Seven Dials; make a beeline for Monmouth Street, which boasts Kiehl's for skincare, Koh Samui for designer womenswear – and, for an educated, deluxe approach to spanking, Coco de Mer. Just around the corner, on Earlham Street, is a handy Space NK (though don't forget Pout and Screenface, also nearby, for additional unusual beauty goods) and a new fashion shop for women that is well within most budgets, Motel. Neal Street and its offshoots heave with streetwear and trainer emporia, while on quieter Floral Street, the Tintin Shop rubs shoulders with designer chains like Paul Smith and Agnès b. Locals tend

Lovely **Phoenix Garden**. *See p19.*

to avoid Covent Garden Market itself, as it offers little beyond mainstream names and tourist trinkets – unless, of course, you're looking for snuff or traditional toys.

While most Londoners associate Charing Cross Road with books, due to the famous Foyles and several dusty second-hand stores, not everyone is aware of Cecil Court, a pedestrian alley connecting Charing Cross with St Martin's Lane. Lined with specialist antiquarian bookshops, it's a pleasant place to pass an afternoon.

Over in Mayfair, the price tags are frightening but it's still fun to browse. Ignore the big Bond Street names like Burberry and Pringle and head for Browns on South Molton Street, which has been showcasing beautiful, unusual labels for more than 35 years (also check out its sale shop, Labels for Less, in the same street). Stella McCartney's elegant townhouse shop is not far away either, on Bruton Street. Make a detour down Bruton Lane to Belgian designer's shop Maison Martin Margiela.

The old arcades are always a treat. Burlington Arcade, off Piccadilly, has

N Peal and Pickett for classy cashmere and accessories, while the more secluded Royal Arcade, off Old Bond Street, boasts perfumer Ormonde Jayne and, for the finest hot chocolate, Charbonnel et Walker. While you're plundering Westminster's cache of venerable shops, nip over to St James's Street and call in at Swaine Adeney Brigg, which introduced London to the invaluable brolly. Before hitting Savile Row's updated trad tailors Gieves & Hawkes and Richard James, cast your eye over Dover Street Market, the pricey but directional new retail concept from Comme des Garçons' Rei Kawakubo.

To the west, a few notable shops have colonised Shepherd Market: innovative shoe designer Georgina Goodman, British skincare line REN and a second branch of the Chocolate Society. The latter's original shop/café lies south-west in Belgravia, where charming Elizabeth Street also offers avant-garde footwear (Mootich), beautiful breads (Poilâne), rare perfumes (Les Senteurs), designer hats (Philip Treacy) and a chic dog boutique (Mungo & Maud).

Long a retail wasteland bar the old Army & Navy (renamed House of Fraser), Victoria now has Cardinal Place shopping centre. Its shops, interspersed with lunching options, seem geared towards well-groomed local office workers: Zara, Molton Brown, Hawes & Curtis shirtmakers. Bayswater boasts Edwardian shopping centre Whiteleys, which retains beautiful original features, but its 70 retail units are mainly occupied by chains. North-west, near the border with Kensington & Chelsea, boutiques proliferate around Westbourne Grove (*see p147*).

To the north, overexposed in the style mags though it is, Marylebone High Street deserves praise for so comprehensively casting aside its rather dusty image. Gone is the customer base of wealthy old ladies with small dogs and Harley Street face-lifts. Today foodies will find Nigella's favourite cheese shop, La Fromagerie, rare-breed butcher's Ginger Pig and quality choc shop Rococo, plus a good Sunday-morning farmers' market in the car park behind Waitrose. There's a terrific old travel bookshop (Daunt's) and an interesting designer boutique, Sixty 6, among the middle-to-upmarket clothing chains. Stunning jewellery is sold at both Cox & Power and Kabiri, and Fresh, Aveda and

Calmia will satisfy your beauty and well-being needs. For homeware there's a big Conran Shop or Skandium.

Don't forget the lesser-known Marylebone Lane, where the ancient River Tyburn flows unobserved beneath your feet. Here you'll find pretty Saltwater womenswear, Tracey Neuls' iconoclastic footwear and century-old deli Paul Rothe & Son.North of Marylebone Road, at the eastern end of Church Street, Alfie's Antique Market has stalls selling, among other things, 20th-century Italian furniture and glam vintage fashions. Outside is a large general street market that's at its best on Saturdays.

In St John's Wood, the high street has a pleasant, villagey atmosphere and high-class traditional provisions stores, including quality butcher's Kent & Sons, branches of Carluccio's and Maison Blanc, as well as a number of smart children's and women's boutiques. Towards Maida Vale is aromatherapist Michelle Roques-O'Neil's small Pure Alchemy clinic, where you can book in for a rub-down or buy her gorgeous products. However, there is little in the way of interesting retail in the Vale beyond isolated shops such as Raoul's Deli.

Agent Provocateur *6 Broadwick Street, W1V 1FH (7439 0229/www.agent provocateur.com).*

Agnès b *35-36 Floral Street, WC1N 9DJ (7379 1992).*

Alfie's Antique Market *13-25 Church Street, NW8 8DT (7723 6066/www.alfiesantiques.com).*

American Apparel *2-4 Carnaby Street, W1F 9DW (7734 4477/www.americanapparel.net).*

Antipodium *5A Carlisle Street, W1D 3BH (7287 3841/www.antipodium.com).*

Aveda *28-29 Marylebone High Street, W1U 4PL (7224 3157/www.aveda.com).*

Berwick Street Market *Berwick Street, Rupert Street, W1.*

Browns *23-27 South Molton Street, W1K 5RD (7514 0000/www.brownsfashion.com).*

Browns Labels for Less *50 South Molton Street, W1K 5RD (7514 0052/www.browns fashion.com).*

Calmia *52-54 Marylebone High Street, W1U 5HR (7224 3585/www.calmia.com).*

Cardinal Place *Victoria Street, SW1 (www.cardinalplace.co.uk).*

Charbonnel et Walker *1 The Royal Arcade, 28 Old Bond Street, W1S 4BT (7491 0939/ www.charbonnel.co.uk).*

The Chocolate Society *32-34 Shepherd Market, W1J 7QN (7495 0302/www.chocolate. co.uk).*

Church Street Market *Church Street, NW8.*

Coco de Mer *23 Monmouth Street, WC2H 9DD (7836 8882/www.coco-de-mer.co.uk).*

Conran Shop *55 Marylebone High Street, W1U 5RB (7487 5591/www.conran.com).*

Cox & Power *35C Marylebone High Street, W1U 4QA (7935 3530/www.coxandpower.com).*

Daunt Books *83-84 Marylebone High Street, W1U 4QW (7224 2295/www.dauntbooks.co.uk).*

Dover Street Market *17-18 Dover Street, W1S 4LT (7518 0680).*

Fenwick *63 New Bond Street, W1A 3BS (7629 9161/www.fenwick.co.uk).*

Fortnum & Mason *181 Piccadilly, W1A 1ER (7734 8040/www.fortnumandmason.co.uk).*

Foyles *113-119 Charing Cross Road, WC2H 0EB (7437 5660/www.foyles.co.uk).*

Fresh *92 Marylebone High Street, W1U 4RD (7486 4100/www.fresh.com).*

La Fromagerie *2-4 Moxon Street, W1U 4EW (7935 0341/www.lafromagerie.co.uk).*

Georgina Goodman *12-14 Shepherd Street, W1J 7JF (7499 8599/www.georgina goodman.com).*

Gieves & Hawkes *1 Savile Row, W1S 3JR (7434 2001/www.gievesandhawkes.com).*

Ginger Pig *8-10 Moxon Street, W1U 4EW (7935 7788).*

G Room *46 Carnaby Street, W1F 9PS (7734 5994/www.theg-room.com).*

John Lewis *278-306 Oxford Street, W1A 1EX (7629 7711/www.johnlewis.co.uk).*

Kabiri *37 Marylebone High Street, W1U 4QE (7224 1808/www.kabiri.co.uk).*

Kent & Sons *59 St John's Wood High Street, NW8 7NL (7722 2258).*

Kiehl's *29 Monmouth Street, WC2H 9DD (7240 2411/www.kiehls.com).*

Kingly Court *Carnaby Street, W1B 5PW (www.carnaby.co.uk).*

Koh Samui *65-67 Monmouth Street, WC2H 9DG (7240 4280/www.kohsamui.co.uk).*

Liberty *210-220 Regent Street, W1B 5AH (7734 1234/www.liberty.co.uk).*

Maison Martin Margiela *1-9 Bruton Place, W1J 6NE (7629 2682).*

Marylebone Farmers' Market *Cramer Street car park, behind Marylebone High Street, W1U 4EA (7833 0338/www.lfm.org.uk).*

Mint *70 Wigmore Street, W1U 2SF (7224 4406).*

Mootich *34 Elizabeth Street, SW1W 9NZ (7824 8113/www.mootich.com).*

Motel *16 Earlham Street, WC2H 9LN (7240 7571/www.donotdisturb.co.uk).*

Mungo & Maud *79 Elizabeth Street, SW1W 9PJ (7952 4570/www.mungoand maud.com).*

Ormonde Jayne *12 The Royal Arcade, 28 Old Bond Street, W1S 4SL (7499 1100/ www.ormondejayne.co.uk).*

Paul Rothe & Son *35 Marylebone Lane, W1U 2NN (7935 6783).*

Paul Smith *40-44 Floral Street, WC2E 9DG (7379 7133/www.paulsmith.co.uk).*

N Peal *37 & 71 Burlington Arcade, W1J 0QD (7493 5378/www.npeal.com).*

Philip Treacy *69 Elizabeth Street, SW1W 9PJ (7730 3992/www.philiptreacy.co.uk).*

Pickett *32-33 & 41 Burlington Arcade, W1J 0PZ (7493 8939/www.pickett.co.uk).*
Poilâne *46 Elizabeth Street, SW1W 9PA (7808 4910/www.poilane.fr).*
Pout *32 Shelton Street, WC2H 9JE (7379 0379/www.pout.co.uk).*
Pure Alchemy *3 Violet Hill, NW8 9EB (7624 1022/www.purealchemy.co.uk).*
Raoul's Deli *8-10 Clifton Road, W9 1SS (7289 6649).*
REN *19 Shepherd Market, W1J 7PJ (7495 5960).*
Richard James *29 Savile Row, W1S 2EY (7434 0605/www.richardjames.co.uk).*
Rococo *45 Marylebone High Street, W1U 5HG (7935 7780).*
Saltwater *98 Marylebone Lane, W1U 2QB (7935 3336/www.saltwater.net).*
Screenface *48 Monmouth Street, WC2H 9EP (7836 3955/www.screenface.com).*
Selfridges *400 Oxford Street, W1A 1AB (0870 837 7377/www.selfridges.com).*
Les Senteurs *71 Elizabeth Street, SW1W 9PJ (7730 2322).*
Sixty 6 *66 Marylebone High Street, W1U 5JF (7224 6066).*
Skandium *86 Marylebone High Street, W1U 4QS (7935 2077/www.skandium.com).*
Souvenir *53 Brewer Street, W1F 9UY (7287 8708/www.souvenirboutique.co.uk).*
Space NK *37 Earlham Street, WC2H 9LD (7379 7030/www.spacenk.com).*
Stella McCartney *30 Bruton Street, W1J 6LG (7518 3100/www.stellamccartney.co.uk).*
Swaine Adeney Brigg *54 St James's Street, SW1A 1JT (7409 7277/www.swaineadeney.co.uk).*
Urban Outfitters *200 Oxford Street, W1D 1NU (7907 0800/www.urbanoutfitters.com).*
The World According To... *4 Brewer Street, W1F 0SB (7437 1259/www.theworldaccording to.co.uk).*
Tintin Shop, *34 Floral Street, WC2E 9DJ (7836 1131/www.thetintinshop.uk.com).*
Tracey Neuls *29 Marylebone Lane, W1U 2NQ (7935 0039/www.tn29.com).*
Whiteleys *151 Queensway, W2 4YN (7229 8844/www.whiteleys.com).*

Arts & attractions

Cinemas & theatres

There's an incredible number of cinemas and theatres in the City of Westminster, most clustered in the district around Shaftesbury Avenue. This is an overview; for more – plus the latest developments, reviews and practical information – consult the 'Film' and 'Theatre' sections of the weekly *Time Out* magazine.

Adelphi Theatre *Strand, WC2E 7NA (0870 403 0303/www.adelphitheatre.co.uk).*
Curzon *0870 756 4620/www.curzoncinemas. com; Mayfair 38 Curzon Street, W1J 7TY; Soho 93-107 Shaftesbury Avenue, W1D 5DY.*

Dominion Theatre *Tottenham Court Road, W1T 0AG (0870 169 0116/www.ticket master.co.uk).*
Empire *Leicester Square, WC2H 7NA (0871 224 4007/www.odeon.co.uk).*
Lyceum Theatre *Wellington Street, WC2E 7DA (0870 243 9000/www.lyceum-theatre.co.uk).*
Open Air Theatre *Regent's Park, NW1 4NR (7935 5765/box office 0870 060 1811/ www.openairtheatre.org).* Alfresco theatre, perfect for summery Shakespeare romps.
Piccadilly Theatre *Denman Street, W1D 7DY (0870 060 0123).*
Prince Charles Cinema *7 Leicester Place, WC2H 7BP (7437 7003/www.princecharles cinema.com).* The best value in town for releases ending their first run elsewhere.
Prince of Wales Theatre *Coventry Street, W1D 6AS (0870 850 0393/www.delfont mackintosh.co.uk).*
Queen's Theatre *Shaftesbury Avenue, W1D 6DA (0870 890 1110/www.delfont mackintosh.co.uk).*
Novello Theatre *Aldwych, WC2B 4LD (0870 950 0940/www.delfontmackintosh.co.uk).* The Royal Shakespeare Company's new London home – they've taken up a five-year residence at this renovated Cameron Mackintosh theatre.
St Martin's Theatre *West Street, WC2H 9NZ (0870 164 8787/www.stmartins-theatre.co.uk).*
Screen on Baker Street *Baker Street, W1U 6TJ (7935 2772/www.screencinemas.co.uk).*
Shaftesbury Theatre *210 Shaftesbury Avenue, WC2H 8DP (7379 5399/ www.shaftesbury-theatre.co.uk).*
Theatre Royal Drury Lane *Catherine Street, WC2B 5JF (0870 890 1109/www.theatre royaldrurylane.co.uk).*
Victoria Palace Theatre *Victoria Street, SW1E 5EA (0870 895 5577/www.victoria-palace-theatre.co.uk).*

Galleries & museums

This borough is the site of most of London's principal museums, galleries and tourist attractions. Below is a selection; for a more complete guide, see the *Time Out London Guide* or consult the 'Art' and 'Around Town' sections of *Time Out* magazine.

National Gallery *Trafalgar Square, WC2N 5DN (information line 7747 2885/ www.nationalgallery.org.uk).* A national treasure, founded in 1824, now with more than 2,000 pieces spanning virtually every school of art.
National Portrait Gallery *St Martin's Place, WC2H 0HE (7306 0055/www.npg.org.uk).* This attractive, manageable museum has a lovely restaurant and bar on the top floor.
Royal Academy of Arts *Burlington House, Piccadilly, W1J 0BD (7300 8000/www.royal academy.org.uk).* Britain's first art school, better known these days for its galleries.

Somerset House *Strand, WC2R 0RN (Courtauld 7848 2526/www.courtauld.ac.uk/ gallery/Gilbert 7420 9400/www.gilbert-collection. org.uk/Hermitage 7845 4630/www.hermitage rooms.co.uk).* Incorporates the Courtauld Institute of Art Gallery, the Gilbert Collection and the Hermitage Rooms; the courtyard is also used for open-air concerts in summer and ice-skating in winter.

Tate Britain *Millbank, SW1P 4RG (7887 8888/ www.tate.org.uk).* Though the sexier Modern gets all the attention, don't forget this old stalwart: it contains London's second great collection of art, after the National Gallery.

Wallace Collection *Hertford House, Manchester Square, W1U 3BN (7563 9500/ www.wallacecollection.org).* Fine private art collection, bequeathed to the nation by Lady Wallace, widow of Sir Richard Wallace, in 1897.

Music & comedy venues

See the weekly *Time Out* magazine for full music and comedy listings in the borough.

Astoria *157 Charing Cross Road, WC2H 0EN (7434 9592/www.meanfiddler.com).* This 2,000-capacity sweat box attracts big alt.rock names.

The Coliseum *St Martin's Lane, WC2N 4ES (7632 8300/www.eno.org).* Home of the English National Opera.

Ronnie Scott's *47 Frith Street, W1D 4HT (7439 0747/www.ronniescotts.co.uk).* Famous jazz venue; closed in March 2006, with a date for reopening not set at time of writing.

Royal Opera House *Bow Street, WC2E 9DA (7304 4000/www.royaloperahouse.org).* Refurbished in 2000; a new sound system allows passers-by outside to hear the music.

Wigmore Hall *36 Wigmore Street, W1U 3BN (7935 2141/www.wigmore-hall.org.uk).* Top concert venue for chamber music and song.

Other attractions

Buckingham Palace & Royal Mews *SW1A 1AA (7766 7300/www.royal.gov.uk).*

Houses of Parliament *Parliament Square, SW1A 0AA (Commons info 7219 4272/ Lords info 7219 3107/tours 0870 906 3773/ www.parliament.uk).*

Institute of Contemporary Arts (ICA) *The Mall, SW1 5AH (7930 3647/www.ica.org.uk).* Its cinema shows London's artiest films, its theatre stages performance art and quality gigs, and its art exhibitions are always talking points.

Royal Courts of Justice *Strand, WC2A 2LL (7947 6000).* Members of the public are allowed to attend certain trials.

St Martin-in-the-Fields *Trafalgar Square, WC2N 4JJ (7766 1100/www.smitf.org).* 18th-century church known for its classical concerts.

Westminster Abbey *20 Dean's Yard, SW1P 3PA (7222 5152/tours 7654 4900/ www.westminster-abbey.org).*

Westminster Cathedral *Victoria Street, SW1P 1QW (7798 9055/www.westminster cathedral.org.uk).*

MY VIEW

ALAN BRADLEY
City of Westminster councillor

The City of Westminster is a tremendously exciting pace to live – the whole activity of the capital on your doostep.
The growth of the night-time economy in the West End is very exciting, but it doesn't exactly produce a great atmosphere for residents. One of the things Westminster City Council has to do is try to create balance – which is why we've been fairly tough when implementing the new licensing laws. This isn't because we want to be killjoys, but because we're conscious of the fact that a rather surprising number of residents live in areas like Soho. We're determined that this should remain so, because we think it's healthy to have a city with people living in it – one that doesn't become barren of residents in the evening.
Another thing we're trying to rectify is that those living in the centre of London either have to be in social housing – a very high proportion of Westminster's population – or be reasonably well-off. We've tried to produce policies that will help middle-income people be able to afford to live in Westminster.
What else would I change? People in Westminster tend to think of where they live in terms of their 'village' – be it Pimlico or Bayswater or Maida Vale – but we want to make them feel part of the same, cohesive community.

City of Westminster

Open spaces

Green Park *The Mall, SW1.*

Hyde Park *Park Lane, W1.* The adjoining Kensington Gardens spill into Kensington & Chelsea (*see p150*).

Phoenix Garden *21 Stacey Street (entrance on St Giles Passage), WC2H 8DG.* Once a car park, now a delightful green surprise in Covent Garden.

Queen's Park *Ilbert Street, W10.*

Regent's Park *Prince Albert Road, NW1.* From formal flower beds to extensive playing fields, this green space is a London treasure.

St James's Park *The Mall, SW1.* Lovely views and exotic birdlife.

Sport & fitness

The prices in council-run centres in Westminster are high, matching those found in private clubs in most other boroughs, but the facilities tend to be well maintained and of high quality. The independents are correspondingly pricey, but if you want personal attention and celeb-spotting opportunities, this borough's exclusive clubs should deliver.

Gyms & leisure centres

agua at Sanderson *50 Berners Street, W1T 3NG (7300 1414).* Private.

Berkeley Health Club & Spa *The Berkeley Hotel, Wilton Place, SW1X 7RL (7201 1699/ www.savoy-group.co.uk).* Private.

Cannons *www.cannons.co.uk; Endell Street, WC2H 9SA (7240 2446); 27-28 Kingly Street, W1B 5QE (7734 5002); 2 Sheldon Square, W2 6EZ (7289 4686).* Private.

Dorchester Spa *Dorchester Hotel, 53 Park Lane, W1A 2HJ (7495 7335).* Private.

Fitness First *www.fitnessfirst.co.uk; 6 Bedford Street, WC2E 9HD (7240 8411); Berkeley Square House, Berkeley Square, W1J 6BR (7493 2311); 1 Concourse Level, Embankment Place, WC2N 6NM (7839 5411); 15 Great Marlborough Street, W1F 7HR (7287 8911); 59 Kingly Street, W1B 5QJ (7734 6226); Roebuck House, Stag Place, Palace Street, SW1E 5BA (7931 8011); 136-150 Victoria Street, SW1E 5LD (7828 8221).* Private.

Health Club at St James *Court Crowne Plaza Hotel, 51 Buckingham Gate, SW1E 6AF (7963 8307).* Private.

Holmes Place *www.holmesplace.co.uk; Clifton Ford Hotel, Bulstrode Place, Marylebone Lane, W1U 2HU (7299 9595); 120 Oxford Street, W1N 9DP (7436 0500); Shell Mex House, 80 The Strand, WC2R 0DT (7395 9595).* Private.

Jubilee Hall *30 The Piazza, WC2E 8BE (7836 4007/www.jubileehallclubs.co.uk).* Private.

Jubilee Sports Centre *Caird Street, W10 4RR (8960 9629).*

LA Fitness *www.lafitness.co.uk; 7 Balcombe Street, NW1 6NA (7723 5757); Bayswater House, 6 Moscow Place, W2 4AP (0870 429 6385); 49 Hallam Street, W1W 6JW (7436 2881); Portland House, Stag Place, SW1E 5BH (7233 8444); Rex House, 4-12 Lower Regent Street, SW1Y 4PE (7839 8448); Le Meridien Waldorf Hotel, Aldwych, WC2B 4DD (7379 5606).* Private.

LivingWell *www.livingwell.com; 4 Millbank, SW1P 3JA (7233 3579); London Hilton, 22 Park Lane, W1Y 4BE (7208 4080); Hilton London Metropole, Edgware Road, W2 1JU (7616 6486).* Private.

Porchester Centre *Queensway, W2 5HS (7792 2919).*

Queen Mother Sports Centre *223 Vauxhall Bridge Road, SW1V 1EL (7630 5522).*

Seymour Leisure Centre *Seymour Place, W1H 5TJ (7723 8019).*

Zest! Health & Fitness Spa *Dolphin Square Hotel, Dolphin Square, SW1V 3LX (7798 8686/ www.dolphinsquarehotel.co.uk).* Private.

Other facilities

Paddington Recreation Ground *Randolph Avenue, W9 1PD (7641 3642/ www.westminster.gov.uk).* Facilities for tennis, cricket, football and athletics, plus a gym.

Queens Ice Rink & Bowling *17 Queensway, W2 4QP (7229 0172).*

Westminster Boating Base *136 Grosvenor Road, SW1V 3JY (7821 7389/www.westminster boatingbase.co.uk).* Boats, canoes and kayaks.

Spectator sports

Lord's Cricket Ground *St John's Wood Road, NW8 8QN (Marylebone Cricket Club 7289 1611/ tickets 7432 1000/www.lords.org).*

Schools

WHAT THE PARENTS SAY:

❛Overall the options in Westminster are limited. The state schools generally have poor reputations, and they get poorer as middle-class parents choose to take their kids out of the system. There are some fantastic tiny primary schools, though. Children I've met from little schools in Aldwych and Bloomsbury have had a great time because so few kids go there and they get lots of attention. In general, however, there are a lot of refugees and non-English-speaking children, leaving schools with transient, unsettled populations.

The state secondary schools are not great; many middle-class parents go private. However, Westminster City Boys' School has an excellent reputation. Quintin Kynaston is a mammoth comprehensive that used to have a terrible image, but seems to be coming up a bit.❜

Mother of three, Westminster

Primary

There are 35 state primary schools in the City of Westminster, 14 of which are church schools. There are also 17 independent primaries in the borough, including one Jewish school and one theatre school. See www.westminster.gov.uk and www.ofsted.gov.uk for more information.

Secondary

Grey Coat Hospital Girls' School
St Andrew's Building, Grey Coat Place, SW1P 2DY (7969 1998). Girls only.
North Westminster Community School
Upper School, North Wharf Road, W2 1LF (7641 8400).
Pimlico School *Lupus Street, SW1V 3AT (7828 0881/www.pimlicoschool.org.uk).*
Quintin Kynaston School *Marlborough Hill, NW8 0NL (7722 8141/www.qkschool.org.uk).*
St Augustine's CE School *Oxford Road, NW6 5SN (7328 3434/www.staugustines high.org).*
St George's Catholic School *Lanark Road, W9 1RB (7328 0904/www.stgeorgesrc.org).*
St Marylebone CE School *64 Marylebone High Street, W1U 5BA (7935 4704/ www.stmaryleboneschool.com).* Girls only; mixed sixth form.
Westminster City Boys' School *55 Palace Street, SW1E 5HJ (7641 8760/www.wcsch.com).* Boys only.

Property

WHAT THE AGENTS SAY:

6People who like to feel the hustle and bustle under their feet move to this borough. They're attracted by Covent Garden and the fact they are a stone's throw from some of the city's major parks. Mayfair is very posh and there's a status that goes with living there. Soho's really buzzy – the properties in the area are mostly commercial with flats above. Lots of fashion boutiques and colleges too, which give the area a younger feel. City workers needing to be within walking distance of tubes tend to move to Marylebone, which is more residential than Soho. Fitzrovia has come on in leaps and bounds over the last few years and is very sought after. We were one of only a few agents in the area a few years back – now there are more than 16 agencies competing over property. 9
Darren, Robert Irving & Burns, Soho

Average property prices

Detached £1,608,392
Semi-detached £1,205,408
Terraced £881,009
Flat £382,343

Local estate agents

Clevelands *98 Cleveland Street, W1T 6NR (7554 5300/www.clevelands.co.uk).*
Foley Estates *22 Foley Street, W1W 6DS (7323 9003/www.foleyestates.co.uk).*
Fox Gregory *102-104 Allitsen Road, NW8 7AY (7586 1500/www.foxgregory.co.uk).*
Manors *1A Baker Street, W1U 8ED (7486 5982/www.londonapartment.co.uk).*
Richard James & Company *7 New Quebec Street, W1H 7RH (7723 7500/www.richard jamesandco.com).*
Robert Irving & Burns *23-24 Margaret Street, W1W 8LF (7637 0821/www.rib.co.uk).*
Wallsway *22 Devonshire Street, W1G 6PF (7224 0959/www.wallsway.co.uk).*
York Estates *81-82 Crawford Street, W1H 4AT (7724 0335/www.yorkestates.co.uk).*

Other information

Council

Westminster City Council *PO Box 240, Westminster City Hall, 64 Victoria Street, SW1E 6QP (7641 6000/www.westminster.gov.uk).*

Hospitals

The Heart Hospital *16-18 Westmoreland Street, W1G 8PH (7573 8888/www.uclh.nhs.uk).*
St Mary's Hospital *Praed Street, W2 1NY (7886 6666/www.uclh.nhs.uk).*

Legal services

Central London Law Centre *19 Whitcomb Street, WC2H 7HA (7839 2998).*
Westminster CAB *0870 126 4040/ www.adviceguide.org.uk.* Phone advice only.

Local newspapers

Westminster Independent *8961 3345/ www.londonlocals.co.uk.*
Westminster Reporter *7641 3041/ www.westminster.gov.uk.* Magazine distributed free by the council six times a year. Also available online.
Westminster Times/Wood & Vale *7433 0000/www.westminstertimes.co.uk.*

Allotments

There are no allotments in City of Westminster.

COUNCIL TAX		
A	up to £40,000	**£412.00**
B	£40,001-£52,000	**£480.67**
C	£52,001-£68,000	**£549.33**
D	£68,001-£88,000	**£618.00**
E	£88,001-£120,000	**£755.33**
F	£120,001-£160,000	**£892.66**
G	£160,001-£320,000	**£1,030.00**
H	over £320,000	**£1,236.00**
(differs in Montpelier Square only)		

> *'It's hard not to feel a little proprietorial if you live here. I find myself muttering "Thanks for coming, don't forget to take your litter away…"'*

Damian Wayling, writer and Barbican resident

City of London

For an outsider, it's easy to see the appeal of living bang in the centre of London – who could resist the idea of a pre-breakfast stroll along the Embankment or nipping round the corner for lunch by St Paul's? But residents of the Square Mile must also deal with weekend closing and a lack of schools and parks.

Neighbourhoods

The City

Over the course of an average day, the City suffers a Jekyll and Hyde-like transformation. By day, it's mobbed by nearly half a million office workers, plus a veritable army of tourists, white van drivers, cycle couriers and City of London police officers. By night (and at weekends), the streets are eerily quiet and after-office drinkers take sanctuary in the islands of noise and light near the stations at Liverpool Street, Fenchurch Street, Cannon Street, Moorgate and Blackfriars. In fact, fewer than one in 300 of the workers who clock in for duty on Monday morning are still here when the last train leaves Liverpool Street on Monday night.

The boundaries of the City are roughly delineated by the Roman city walls, but the 8,000 full-time residents of the district are squeezed into a much smaller area. Most of the elegant town houses built after the Great Fire of London were destroyed by German bombing in World War II, or transformed into offices by generations of town planners, leaving residents to make the best of small pockets of residential housing tucked away between the tower blocks, Wren churches and national monuments. With the massive focus on office space, amenities such as schools, parks and children's play areas are in short supply.

Most desirable are the handful of Georgian town houses that escaped the firestorm of the Blitz, found in clusters around Fleet Street, Fenchurch Street and Liverpool

City of London

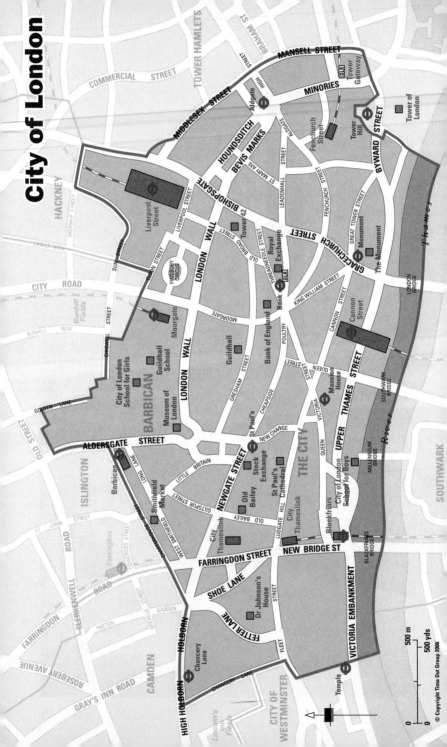

Street station. If one of these properties comes on the market, snap it up; the chance to live in a genuine piece of London history doesn't come along very often. Most of the town houses are broken up into luxury apartments, attracting the young and trendy who enjoy the proximity of the bars and restaurants in Islington and Tower Hamlets.

Inflated property prices tend to restrict the City to the wealthier sections of society – executives, stockbrokers, architects, advertising creatives and international high-fliers who like to keep a pied-à-terre in the centre. Gardens and parking spaces are almost unheard of, but most residents are happy to trade the luxury of space for the convenience of living five minutes from the office. The soaring congestion charge isn't really an issue; few bother with cars when the only available parking is in private car parks (besides, residents are eligible for a 90 per cent discount). With 1,200 police officers patrolling the streets, crime of the kind that affects home-owners is well below the London average. However, after-work binge drinking is one black mark on this otherwise enviable record – let's just say that the Saturday morning street cleaners around Bishopsgate have one of the more odious jobs in the City.

Another inconvenience is the tidal nature of the daytime population. Many shops, pubs and restaurants close over the weekend, and buying essentials after hours can involve an expedition to the nearest train station with a Tesco Express. On the other hand, this is one of the easiest places in London to flag down a black cab, and with train and tube stations every few hundred yards, workers who live and work in the City face one of the shortest commutes in the history of transport.

Smithfield and Barbican

In recent years, renovation of the area around Smithfield Market has provided new loft apartments in converted warehouses and office buildings. The atmosphere here most resembles next-door Clerkenwell (in the borough of Islington; see p104); there are still local shops and small businesses, as well as destination restaurants and bars. Aside from the handsome meat market, the main landmark is historic St Bartholomew's Hospital. The pretty streets between St

Barts and Aldersgate contain some very covetable houses – the area oozes character.

The Barbican is easily the City's most famous residential address. The Barbican Estate was built on space largely created by World War II bomb damage; the government wanted to repopulate the City (down to around 5,000 residents in the 1950s), even though far more money could have been made by using the land for commercial purposes. Designed by architects Chamberlain, Powell & Bon, the Barbican terraces and towers were built between 1964 and 1975 (though the complex was officially opened in 1969 and the Barbican arts centre not finished until 1982).

The Estate covers around 40 acres and has just over 2,000 apartments (of well over 100 different types, ranging from studio flats to penthouses). It also contains the City of London School for Girls, the Museum of London and the Guildhall School of Music & Drama. Opinion about the landmark concrete complex (now grade II listed) has always been divided – not everyone appreciates its stark charms, and the layout can initially be confusing – but residents

Highs & Lows

▲ **London on your doorstep** Fancy a Thames-side stroll every morning? Seeing Monument or St Paul's from your bedroom window? This is the place
No more commutes Remove the hell of journeying to and from the City every day by living there in the first place
Low crime Some 1,200 police officers roaming the small area of the City makes it safer than most other boroughs

Closing times With the majority of the City's population only there to work during the day, most pubs and almost all shops shut very early
Inflated property prices With so many wealthy City execs around, house (or rather flat) prices are bloated and prohibitive
Schools Few and far between. Almost no state provision, and only a few private ones ▼

Space to breathe in the middle of the City – the lake at the **Barbican**. *See p43*.

City of London

tend to fall in love with the place, and flats are highy sought after. As they become more and more expensive, the Golden Lane Estate (just north, on Fann Street) is becoming increasingly popular. Designed by the same architects as the Barbican (and also listed grade II), Golden Lane was completed in the mid 1960s and holds 557 flats.

Restaurants & cafés

The City proper is open Monday to Friday; residents have to look to the fringes for weekend dining options. Smithfield, bordering restaurant-rich Clerkenwell, is the most fruitful location: both hotel restaurant Brasserie de Malmaison and the four-storey Smiths of Smithfield (the complex holds two bars and two restaurants, which run from casual dining to high-end British – in Top Floor at Smiths) are open daily, for lunch and dinner. Other Smithfield restaurants tend to be open on Saturday nights at least: try the Bar & Grill (steak-based American dishes), Café du Marché (traditional French) and Club Gascon (deluxe French). In the Barbican complex itself is Searcy's, a low-key venue offering Modern British cuisine.

Inevitably, the City is not a cheap place to eat. Expense account dining at its most obvious is represented by the likes of Caravaggio, Chamberlain's, 1 Lombard Street, Bonds and Novelli in the City – all

serve top-notch food in impressive spaces. Gary Rhodes's place Rhodes Twenty Four has the added attraction of amazing views from the 24th floor of Tower 42. Slightly less imposing (and just a little cheaper) are the likes of 1 Blossom Street, Refettorio, the Chancery and Lanes.

Sir Terence Conran has a few stand-alone restaurants in the area: Paternoster Chop House (British) on handsome Paternoster Square, and Le Coq d'Argent (regional French) with its skyline views. Conran also runs the glam Grand Café & Bar, and French Sauterelle in the Royal Exchange. His big-hitter, however, is the Great Eastern Hotel, next to Liverpool Street station. It houses four very different restaurants: most casual is brasserie-style Terminus; Fishmarket specialises in fish and seafood; Miyabi offers Japanese dishes; Aurora is the poshest option.

An antidote to all this monied dining can be found at the Place Below, where breakfasts and vegetarian lunches are served in the Norman crypt of St Mary-le-Bow church. Ethnic restaurants tend to be more affordable too; near Aldgate there's Indian restaurant Kasturi (upmarket Indian is represented by the excellent Café Spice Namaste, just round the corner).

Other options are Noto and K-10 (both Japanese); Dolma and Haz (Turkish); Barcelona Tapas Bar y Restaurante, and Mesón Los Barriles (Spanish); and Nakhon Thai, Singapura and Silks & Spice (all oriental). The gastropub part of the White

Swan also qualifies as a budget option, though its lovely first-floor Dining Room does not. Brasserie fare can be had at Just The Bridge, located near the Millennium Bridge. In addition, the City has more than enough chains – there are Pizza Expresses and Wagamamas all over.

Interesting one-offs include: Vivat Bacchus, where a serious wine list is balanced by an easygoing attitude and South African-influenced food; Missouri Grill, for quality meat; Rosemary Lane, an intimate French place at the eastern edge of the City; and Bevis Marks Restaurant, a stylish kosher venue, next to the 18th-century synagogue of the same name. Sandeman's port, sherry and wine company was housed in what is now the appealing Don Bistro & Restaurant. And there's nowhere more characterful than our favourite City haunt – trad fish restaurant Sweetings. Only open at lunch, it's unpretentious and charming, and merits a special trip, even if you don't live here.

Aurora *Great Eastern Hotel, 40 Liverpool Street, EC2M 7QN (7618 7000/www.aurora-restaurant.co.uk).*
The Bar & Grill *2-3 West Smithfield, EC1A 9JX (0870 442 2541/www.barandgrill.co.uk).*
Barcelona Tapas Bar y Restaurante *15 St Botolph Street, entrance at 1 Middlesex Street, EC3A 7DT (7377 5222).*
Bevis Marks Restaurant *Bevis Marks, EC3A 5DQ (7283 2220/www.bevismarks therestaurant.com).*
Bonds *Threadneedle Hotel, 5 Threadneedle Street, EC2R 8AY (7657 8088/www.theeton collection.com).*
Brasserie de Malmaison *Malmaison, 18-21 Charterhouse Square, EC1M 6AH (7012 3700/www.malmaison.com).*
Café du Marché *22 Charterhouse Square, Charterhouse Mews, EC1M 6AH (7608 1609).*
Café Spice Namaste *16 Prescot Street, E1 8AZ (7488 9242/www.cafespice.co.uk).*
Caravaggio *107 Leadenhall Street, EC3A 4AA (7626 6206/www.etruscagroup.co.uk).*
Chamberlain's *23-25 Leadenhall Market, EC3V 1LR (7648 8690/www.chamberlains.org).*
The Chancery *9 Cursitor Street, EC4A 1LL (7831 4000/www.thechancery.co.uk).*
Club Gascon *57 West Smithfield, EC1A 9DS (7796 0600).*
Le Coq d'Argent *No.1 Poultry, EC2R 8EJ (7395 5000/www.conran.com).*
Dolma *157 Commercial Street, E1 6BJ (7456 1006/www.dolmalondon.com).*
Don Bistro & Restaurant *The Courtyard, 20 St Swithin's Lane, EC4N 8AD (7626 2606/www.thedonrestaurant.com).*
Fishmarket *Great Eastern Hotel, Bishopsgate, EC2M 7QN (7618 7200/www.fish-market.co.uk).*
Grand Café & Bar *The Royal Exchange, EC3V 3LR (7618 2480/www.conran.com).*
Haz *9 Cutler Street, E1 7DJ (7929 7923/www.hazrestaurant.com).*
Just the Bridge *1 Paul's Walk, Millennium Bridge North Side, EC4V 3QQ (7236 0000/ www.justthebridge.com).*
Kasturi *57 Aldgate High Street, EC3N 1AL (7480 7402/www.kasturi-restaurant.co.uk).*
K-10 *20 Copthall Avenue, EC2R 7DN (7562 8510/www.k10.net).*
Lanes *East India House, 109-117 Middlesex Street, E1 7JF (7247 5050/www.lanes restaurant.co.uk).*
Mesón Los Barriles *8A Lamb Street, E1 6EA (7375 3136).*
Missouri Grill *76 Aldgate High Street, EC3N 1BD (7481 4010).*
Miyabi *Great Eastern Hotel, Liverpool Street, EC2M 7QN (7618 7100/www.great-eastern-hotel.co.uk).*
Nakhon Thai *10 Copthall Avenue, EC2R 7DJ (7628 1555/www.nakhonthai.co.uk).*
Noto *2-3 Bassishaw Highwalk, off London Wall, EC2V 5DS (7256 9433/www.noto.co.uk).*
Novelli in the City *London Capital Club, 15 Abchurch Lane, EC4N 7BW (7717 0088/ www.londoncapitalclub.com).*

Glamour Grandeur
Sleaze Disease

Discover a great city in the making
FREE ENTRY

150 London Wall, EC2Y 5HN
 St Paul's, Barbican
www.museumoflondon.org.uk

BLOOD BLITZ
BANANAS

MUSEUM IN DOCKLANDS
How the world came to the East End
KIDS GO FREE

West India Quay, London E14 4AL

 Canary Wharf West India Quay   www.museumindocklands.org.uk

Registered charity number: 1060415

1 Blossom Street *1 Blossom Street, E1 6BX (7247 6530/www.1blossomstreet.com).*
1 Lombard Street *1 Lombard Street, EC3V 9AA (7929 6611/www.1lombardstreet.com).*
Paternoster Chop House *Warwick Court, Paternoster Square, EC4M 7DX (7029 9400/ www.conran.com).*
The Place Below *St Mary-le-Bow, Cheapside, EC2V 6AU (7329 0789/www.theplacebelow. co.uk).*
Refettorio *Crowne Plaza Hotel, 19 New Bridge Street, EC4V 6DB (7438 8052/ www.tableinthecity.com).*
Rhodes Twenty Four *24th floor, Tower 42, Old Broad Street, EC2N 1HQ (7877 7703/ www.rhodes24.co.uk).*
Rosemary Lane *61 Royal Mint Street, E1 8LG (7481 2602/www.rosemarylane.btinternet.co.uk).*
Sauterelle *The Royal Exchange, EC3V 3LR (7618 2483/www.conran.com).*
Searcy's *Level 2, Barbican, Silk Street, EC2Y 8DS (7588 3008/www.searcys.co.uk).*
Silks & Spice *Temple Court, 11 Queen Victoria Street, EC4N 4UJ (7248 7878/ www.silksandspice.com).*
Singapura *1-2 Limeburner Lane, EC4M 7HY (7329 1133/www.singapuras.co.uk).*
Smiths of Smithfield *67-77 Charterhouse Street, EC1M 6HJ (7251 7950/www.smithsof smithfield.co.uk).*
Sweetings *39 Queen Victoria Street, EC4N 4SA (7248 3062).*
Terminus *Great Eastern Hotel, 40 Liverpool Street, EC2M 7QN (7618 7400/www.terminus-restaurant.co.uk).*
Vivat Bacchus *47 Farringdon Street, EC4A 4LL (7353 2648/www.vivatbacchus.co.uk).*
White Swan Pub & Dining Room *108 Fetter Lane, EC4A 1ES (7242 9696).*

Bars & pubs

Two things will strike you about drinking in the City. First, with a population made up mostly of office workers, there's little night-time frolics before Thursday and Friday, and at weekends most venues don't open at all. Second, bar and pub chains have an incredibly strong presence.

Still, the City holds some wonderfully historic boozers, chain-affiliated or not. On and around Fleet Street, try the Viaduct Tavern (whose cellars are believed to be the last surviving cells of Newgate Prison), the Old Bell Tavern (which reputedly stands on the site of London's first print shop), the Black Friar (with its original 1905 interior), and labyrinth-like Ye Old Cheshire Cheese.

Impressive buildings include champagne specialist La Grande Marque and the Old Bank of England, now a Fuller's boozer. For great views, the Red Herring looks out

at the historic architecture around St Paul's, while the Samuel Pepys has a sweeping view of the Thames towards the South Bank. El Vino is a family-run wine bar that specialises in claret; fans of Guinness might like Tipperary, London's first Irish pub and the first to sell the black stuff.

On Chancery Lane (the border line between the Cities of London and Westminster), the prevailing sight is lawyers getting sloshed. Luckily the architecture around here saves the day: two ancient pubs – Ye Olde Mitre (dating back to 1546) and the Cittie of Yorke (1430) – are gorgeous.

Around Mansion House, Monument and Bank, wine and champagne top the menu at Bar Bourse, as it does at Bar Under the Clock (the sassiest branch of the Ball's Brothers chain). Bow Wine Vaults and Leadenhall Wine Bar are other decent venues in which to pop a cork; Leadenhall Market also has the fine Lamb Tavern. For more historic venues, try the rambling Williamson's Tavern, legend-heavy Ye Olde Watling, unpretentious Hatchet, and the atmospheric, half-timbered Bell – thought

---

TRANSPORT

Tube stations *Central* Chancery Lane, St Paul's, Bank, Liverpool Street; *Circle* Temple, Blackfriars, Mansion House, Cannon Street, Monument, Tower Hill, Aldgate, Liverpool Street, Moorgate, Barbican; *District* Temple, Blackfriars, Mansion House, Cannon Street, Monument, Tower Hill; *DLR* Bank, Tower Gateway; *Hammersmith & City* Liverpool Street, Moorgate, Barbican; *Metropolitan* Aldgate, Liverpool Street, Moorgate, Barbican; *Northern* Bank, Moorgate; *Waterloo & City* Bank

Rail stations *c2c* Fenchurch Street; *one* Liverpool Street; *Southeastern Trains* Cannon Street; *Thameslink* Blackfriars, City Thameslink, Barbican; *WAGN* Moorgate

Main bus routes dozens of buses run through the City of London – for a full list, visit www.tfl.gov.uk/buses; *night buses* N8, N11, N15, N21, N25, N26, N35, N47, N55, N63, N76, N133, N243; *24-hour buses* 23, 25, 43, 149, 214, 242, 271

River commuter and leisure boat services running east and west, with a pier at Blackfriars

to be the City's oldest pub (the Swan Tavern has a different claim to fame, as the City's smallest pub). Opposite Leadenhall Market, Prism is trying to break with tradition by investing itself with a more clubby, female-friendly atmosphere; Pacific Oriental on Bishopsgate is similarly dance-oriented.

The area around Liverpool Street has something of a dual personality. On Thursdays and Fridays, it heaves with City workers, all with annihilation on their minds. For the rest of the week, the pubs and bars are eerily empty. The vibe is smarter and dressier than in nearby Shoreditch or Old Street, but most establishments still don't open at weekends. The smart, understated George in Conran's Great Eastern Hotel is an exception, as is Hamilton Hall, a former ballroom restored to some kind of glory by JD Wetherspoon. Vertigo 42 – situated on the 42nd floor of the tallest edifice in the City – doesn't open at weekends, but with such spectacular views it would be churlish to complain.

West towards Tower Hill finds the Crutched Friar and Bar 38 Minories – both snug, if unexciting, City sanctuaries. Better to head in the other direction towards Islington for the trendy bars and clubs around Smithfield Market: thanks to Fabric (the achingly trendy destination club that draws enormous weekend queues), the bars on Charterhouse Street pull in a vibrant crowd – kookily designed Fluid and the multi-faceted Smiths of Smithfield (*see p44*) are both popular pre-club pit-stops.

RECYCLING

No. of bring sites 1 (Barbican Estate residents only)
Household waste recycled 19%
Main recycling centre The City of London does not have a site within the borough, so residents are directed to: Northumberland Wharf, Yabsley Street, Isle of Dogs, E14 9RG (7538 4526)
Other recycling services orange sack recycling service; Christmas tree recycling; collection of white goods and furniture; IT equipment
Council contact Caroline Telford, Recycling & Waste Strategy Officer, Walbrook Wharf, Upper Thames Street, EC4R 3TD (7606 3110 ext 2231/ www.cityoflondon.gov.uk/recycling)

Bar Bourse 67 Queen Street, EC4R 1EE (7248 2200/www.barbourse.co.uk).
Bar 38 Minories St Clare House, 30-33 The Minories, EC3N 1PD (7702 0470).
Bar Under the Clock 74 Queen Victoria Street (entrance on Bow Lane), EC4N 4SJ (7489 9895/www.ballsbrothers.co.uk).
Bell 29 Bush Lane, EC4R 0AN (7929 7772).
Black Friar 174 Queen Victoria Street, EC4V 4EG (7236 5474).
Bow Wine Vaults 10 Bow Churchyard, EC4M 9DQ (7248 1121/www.motcombs. co.uk).
Cittie of Yorke 22 High Holborn, WC1V 6BN (7242 7670).
Crutched Friar 39-41 Crutched Friars, EC3N 2AE (7264 0041).
El Vino 47 Fleet Street, EC4Y 1BJ (7353 6786).
Fabric 77A Charterhouse Street, EC1M 3HN (7336 8898/www.fabriclondon.com).
Fluid 40 Charterhouse Street, EC1M 6JN (7253 3444/www.fluidbar.com).
George Great Eastern Hotel, 40 Liverpool Street, EC2M 7QN (7618 7400/www.great-eastern-hotel.co.uk).
La Grande Marque 47 Ludgate Hill, EC4M 7JU (7329 6709/www.lagrandemarque.com).
Hamilton Hall Unit 32, The Concourse, Liverpool Street Station, EC2M 7PY (7247 3579/www.jdwetherspoon.co.uk).
Hatchet 28 Garlick Hill, EC4V 2BA (7236 0720).
Lamb Tavern 10-12 Leadenhall Market, EC3V 1LR (7626 2454).
Leadenhall Wine Bar 27 Leadenhall Market, EC3V 1LR (7623 1818).
Old Bank of England 194 Fleet Street, EC4A 2LT (7430 2255).
Old Bell Tavern 95 Fleet Street, EC4Y 1DH (7583 0216).
Pacific Oriental 1 Bishopsgate, EC2N 3AQ (7621 9988/www.pacificoriental.co.uk).
Prism 147 Leadenhall Street, EC3V 4QT (7256 3888/www.harveynichols.com).
Red Herring 49 Gresham Street, EC2V 7ET (7606 0399).
Samuel Pepys Stew Lane, High Timber Street, EC4V 3PT (7489 1871).
Swan Tavern Ship Tavern Passage, 77-80 Gracechurch Street, EC3V 1LY (7283 7712).
Tipperary 66 Fleet Street, EC4Y 1HT (7583 6470/www.tipperarypub.co.uk).
Vertigo 42 Tower 42, 25 Old Broad Street, EC2N 1HQ (7877 7842/www.vertigo42.co.uk).
Viaduct Tavern 126 Newgate Street, EC1A 7AA (7600 1863).
Williamson's Tavern 1 Groveland Court, off Bow Lane, EC4M 9EH (7248 5750).
Ye Olde Cheshire Cheese 145 Fleet Street, EC4A 2BU (7353 6170/www.yeoldecheshire cheese.com).
Ye Olde Mitre 1 Ely Court, Ely Place (beside 8 Hatton Gardens), EC1N 6SJ (7405 4751).
Ye Olde Watling 29 Watling Street, EC4M 9BR (7653 9971).

Black Friar, the most beautiful arts and crafts pub in London. *See p47.*

Shops

Unsurprisingly, most City shopping happens Monday to Friday. Equally predictably, chains predominate – the difference is, they tend to be pretty upmarket. Swankiest of the lot is the Royal Exchange complex. Here there's a raft of jewellers (Tiffany, Tateossian, De Beers, Royal Exchange Jewellers, Watches of Switzerland, Searle & Co, Wint & Kidd, Boodle & Dunthorne, Theo Fennell), perfumers (Penhaligon's, Jo Malone, L'Artisan Parfumeur), deluxe brands (Hermès, Gucci, Prada) and more quirky – though by no means budget – names such as Agent Provocateur, Lulu Guinness and Paul Smith.

Moving slightly downmarket, there's a useful mini version of the House of Fraser department store just north of London Bridge. Otherwise, high-street chains abound: on Moorgate you'll find Gap and a big (and uncrowded) Marks & Spencer; in and around Liverpool Street there are branches of Hobbs, Space NK and REN, plus a big Tesco; the adjacent Broadgate Centre has Reiss, Books etc and independent wine retailer Uncorked.

Cheapside has yet more chains (Tesco, Space NK and Gap), but also Austin Reed, and nearby, down Bow Lane, Jones the Bootmaker and a branch of Jigsaw with more accessories than most. Round the corner, on Queen Street, there's a Hugo Boss. Near St Paul's, Paternoster Square looks a treat, but the shops are run of the mill. Along Holborn Viaduct and Fleet Street, it's chainstores all the way, enlivened only by shops for the legal profession.

But it's not all identikit retailers. For more interesting shops, look to the fringes of the City; around Smithfield Market there are deli/cafés like Carluccio's (Italian), Comptoir Gascon (French) and Kipferl (Austrian), plus classy gift shop Ian Logan Design Company. Over to the east, Leadenhall Market is more historic building than market, but it is packed with high-class shops and there's a food market every Friday (10am-4pm).

Carluccio's *12 West Smithfield, EC1A 9JR (7329 5904/www.carluccios.com).*
Comptoir Gascon *61-63 Charterhouse Street, EC1M 6HJ (7608 0851).*
House of Fraser *68 King William Street, EC4N 7HR (0870 160 7274/www.houseof fraser.co.uk).*
Ian Logan Design Company *42 Charterhouse Square, EC1M 6EA (7600 9888/www.ian-logan. co.uk).*
Kipferl *70 Long Lane, EC1A 9EJ (7796 2229/ www.kipferl.co.uk).*
Leadenhall Market *Whittington Avenue, off Gracechurch Street, EC3.*
Royal Exchange *EC3V 3LR (www.theroyalexchange.com).*
Uncorked *Exchange Arcade, Broadgate Centre, EC2M 3WA (7638 5998/www.uncorked.co.uk).*

Arts & attractions

Cinemas & theatres

Barbican Centre *Silk Street, EC2Y 8DS (7638 8891/www.barbican.org.uk).* A major arts centre, with theatres, cinemas and an art gallery. Also the home of the London Symphony Orchestra.

Galleries & museums

Bank of England Museum *Entrance on Bartholomew Lane, EC2R 8AH (7601 5491/ www.bankofengland.co.uk/museum).*

Barbican Art Gallery *Level 3, Barbican Centre, Silk Street, EC2Y 8DS (7638 8891/ www.barbican.org.uk).* Contemporary art and photography exhibitions.

Clockmakers' Museum *Guildhall Library, Aldermanbury, EC2P 2EJ (7332 1868/ www.clockmakers.org).* Well-presented horological exhibition.

Dr Johnson's House *17 Gough Square, EC4A 3DE (7353 3745/www.drjohnsonshouse.org).* Wonderfully atmospheric museum celebrating the life and works of Samuel Johnson.

Guildhall Art Gallery *Guildhall Yard, off Gresham Street, EC2P 2EJ (7332 3700/ www.guildhall-art-gallery.org.uk).* Work by Constable, Reynolds and Rossetti.

Museum of London *London Wall, EC2Y 5HN (0870 444 3852/www.museumoflondon.org.uk).* The history of the capital.

Museum of Methodism & John Wesley's House *Wesley's Chapel, 49 City Road, EC1Y 1AU (7253 2262/www.wesleyschapel.org.uk).*

Tower Bridge Exhibition *Tower Bridge, SE1 2UP (7403 3761/www.towerbridge.org.uk).* The history of the bridge; offers stunning views from the high-level walkways.

Tower of London *Tower Hill, EC3N 4AB (0870 756 6060/www.hrp.org.uk).* The Crown Jewels, ravens, Beefeaters, tourists… and nearly 1,000 years of British royal history in this fortress on the Thames (actually within the borough boundary of Tower Hamlets).

Other attractions

Old Bailey *Central Criminal Court, Corner of Newgate Street & Old Bailey, EC4M 7EH (7248 3277/www.hmcourts-service.gov.uk).* The public galleries are open for viewing of trials in session.

College of Arms *Queen Victoria Street, EC4M 8AD (7248 2762/www.college-of-arms.gov.uk).* Heraldic and genealogical history.

Guildhall *Gresham Street, EC2P 2EJ (7606 3030/www.corpoflondon.gov.uk).* Home of the Corporation of London. The cathedral-like Great Hall is mainly used for ceremonial events.

The Monument *Monument Street, EC3R 8AH (7626 2717/www.towerbridge.org.uk).* Built in 1677 to commemorate the Great Fire of London. Spectacular views from the top.

St Bartholomew-the-Great *West Smithfield, EC1A 7JQ (7606 5171/www.greatstbarts.com).* The City's finest medieval church.

St Paul's Cathedral *Ludgate Hill, EC4M 8AD (7236 4128/www.stpauls.co.uk).* Wren's masterpiece. Renovation continues in preparation for its 300th anniversary in 2008.

Open spaces

Although without any full-sized parks, the City of London is home to over 150 small 'city gardens'.

Sport & fitness

The City is dominated by big-name private chains, although the exclusive Champneys and 24-hour Slim Jim's are slightly less identikit institutions. Changing areas often feel more like Savile Row fitting rooms, and atmospheres vary with the slightest fluctuation in the stock market. The one public centre is a charmer; the Golden Lane Leisure Centre offers an oasis of unpretentious calm amid high salaries and high towers, catering mostly to residents of the nearby estate and running a quality kids' sports camp during school holidays.

Gyms & leisure centres

Barbican YMCA *2 Fann Street, EC2Y 8BR (7628 0697/www.cityymca.org).* Private.

Cannons *Cousin Lane, EC4R 3XJ (7283 0101/ www.cannons.co.uk).* Private.

Champneys *Citypoint, 1 Ropemaker Street, EC2Y 9AW (7920 6200/www.champneys.com).* Private.

Fitness Exchange *www.fitness-exchange.net; Cutlers Gardens, 9 Devonshire Square, EC2M 4WY (7626 3161); 1 Broadgate, EC2M 7HA (7920 0192); 106 Fenchurch Street, EC3M 5JE (7369 0700); Lamb's Passage, Chiswell Street, EC1Y 8LE (7638 3811).* Private.

Fitness First *www.fitnessfirst.co.uk; Unit 12, Liverpool Street Station, EC2M 7PY (7247 5511); 55 Gracechurch Street, EC3V 6NN (7621 0911); 5-11 Fetter Lane, EC4A 1QX (7353 2311); 1 Thavie's Inn, EC4A 1AN (7822 0990); 1 America Square, EC3N 2LB (7488 9311).* Private.

Golden Lane Leisure Centre *Golden Lane Estate, Fann Street, EC1Y 0SH (7250 1464/ www.cityoflondon.gov.uk).*

Holmes Place *www.holmesplace.com; 97 Aldersgate, EC1A 4JP (7374 0091); 1 Exchange Place, Appold Street, EC2M 2QT (7422 6400); Ibex House, 1 Haydon Street, EC3N 7HP (7680 5000).* Private.

LA Fitness *www.lafitness.co.uk; 20 Little Britain, EC1A 7DH (7600 0900); 49 Leadenhall Street, EC3A 2BE (7488 2934); 48 London Wall, EC2M 5QB (7628 9876).* Private.

Slim Jim's Health Club *1 Finsbury Avenue, EC2M 2PF (7247 9982/www.slim-jims.co.uk).* Private.

City of London

Vie *122 Clerkenwell Road, EC1R 5DL (7278 8070/www.viehealthclubs.co.uk).* Private.

Other facilities

Broadgate Ice Rink *Broadgate Circle, EC2M 2QS (7505 4068/www.broadgateestates.co.uk).* Winter only.

Schools

WHAT THE PARENTS SAY:

'The choice of state education is very limited. We chose St Paul's Cathedral School above other independent primary schools because it had so much to offer. The school is co-ed and goes through to the end of year eight. The quality of the teaching staff is excellent, and the atmosphere is very friendly. For musical boys, the opportunity of being a chorister is second to none.

Where to go at secondary level is a problem that all parents in the borough face: there's no state school. The independent schools are prohibitively expensive, and scholarship places are hard to find. We might move to an area with better state secondary education.'
Georgina Hazlitt, mother of three,
City of London

Primary

There is only one state primary school within the City of London, the Sir John Cass Foundation Primary School. See www.cityoflondon.gov.uk for more information.

Secondary

City of London School for Girls *St Giles' Terrace, Barbican, EC2Y 8BB (7847 5500/ www.clsg.org.uk).* Girls only; private.
City of London School for Boys *Queen Victoria Street, EC4V 3AL (7489 0291/ www.clsb.org.uk).* Boys only; private.

Property

WHAT THE AGENTS SAY:

'The City is dead central and close to work, so you have no transport costs. Property prices are always going to be secure – buying a home would be a sound investment. Around Moorgate, we see a lot of second homes and pieds-à-terre. It can be a bit like a ghost town at weekends, but some people like that. There's lots to do nearby: you can walk to Shoreditch and Clerkenwell, or hop on the bus to Islington for buzzy bars and shops. The City isn't really a family area – there are some private schools, but pupils tend not to live locally.'
Sean McNaboe, Felicity J Lord, EC1

A	up to £40,000	**£537.66**
B	£40,001-£52,000	**£627.27**
C	£52,001-£68,000	**£716.88**
D	£68,001-£88,000	**£806.49**
E	£88,001-£120,000	**£985.71**
F	£120,001-£160,000	**£1,164.93**
G	£160,001-£320,000	**£1,344.15**
H	over £320,000	**£1,612.98**

'The Barbican is just very different to anything else – the location is fantastic for the City and the West End, and more people should go and see it to dispel the notion that it's a concrete jungle. There's greenery, landscaped gardening, and theatre and the arts in the Barbican Centre itself. The Barbican Estate has a choice of 2,000 apartments in 130 styles, ranging from studios to four-bedroom penthouse suites. Buyers are from across the board, from young first-timers to retired people.'
Nick Scott, Scott City, EC1

Average property prices

Detached, Semi-detached, Terraced n/a
Flat £273,424

Local estate agents

Bridge Estates *98A Curtain Road, EC2A 3AA (7749 1400/www.bridge.co.uk).*
Capital Dwellings *47 Fashion Street, E1 6PX (7375 1515/www.capitaldwellings.com).*
Frank Harris & Company *87 Long Lane, EC1A 9ET (7600 7000/www.frankharris.co.uk).*
Hamilton Brooks *73 Long Lane, EC1A 9ET (7606 8000/www.hamiltonbrooks.co.uk).*
Scott City *122 Newgate Street, EC1A 7AA (7600 0026/www.scottcity.co.uk).*
Square Mile Property Management *Global House, 5A Sandys Row, E1 7HW (7392 9111/ www.m2pm.com).*

Other information

Council

Corporation of London *PO Box 270, Guildhall, EC2P 2EJ (7606 3030/www.cityoflondon.gov.uk).*

Hospitals

St Bartholomew's Hospital *West Smithfield, EC1A 7BE (7377 7000/www.bartsandthe london.org.uk).*

Legal services

City of London CAB *32 Ludgate Hill, EC4M 7DR (7236 1156/www.adviceguide.org.uk).*

Local newspapers

City of London & Dockland Independent *8961 3345/www.londonlocals.co.uk.*

'Lush Victoria Park, elegant Victorian buildings… ugly post-war housing, industrial wastelands. There's a lot to delight and quite a bit to disgust – it's the paradox borough.'

Colin Grove, database manager and resident

Tower Hamlets

From east and west, rapacious financial districts are biting into the old East End, with the City encroaching on Spitalfields, and Docklands developments hogging the Limehouse waterfront. But alongside the extremes of wealth and deprivation, nuggets of gold remain: atmospheric Wapping, up-and-coming Victoria Park, and some of London's best street markets.

Neighbourhoods

Spitalfields and Brick Lane

For centuries, Spitalfields has been a first place of refuge for communities new to London. Over the years it has housed groups such as French Huguenots evading persecution by Catholics and Ashkenazi Jews escaping Russian pogroms. Today, its most prominent immigrant community is Bangladeshi, and numerous curry houses line both sides of Brick Lane. An influx of arty types, initially drawn to the area by cheap studio space, may mean that Spitalfields' role as a home for transient populations comes to an end, as property prices are pushed ever higher.

If you can get past the film crews shooting period dramas, peep through windows at the exquisitely ochred and panelled interiors of the houses on Hanbury, Princelet and Fournier Streets (in the shadow of Hawksmoor's recently restored Christ Church). Tracey Emin and writer Jeanette Winterson are among those who followed early pioneers Gilbert and George into restoring these formerly derelict Huguenot houses to Georgian splendour. Yet such preservation can make for oppression in the neighbourhood. Buyers who dare to install newfangled contraptions such as central heating have been known to find themselves shunned.

Evidence of the more gruesome elements of Spitalfields' history has disappeared.

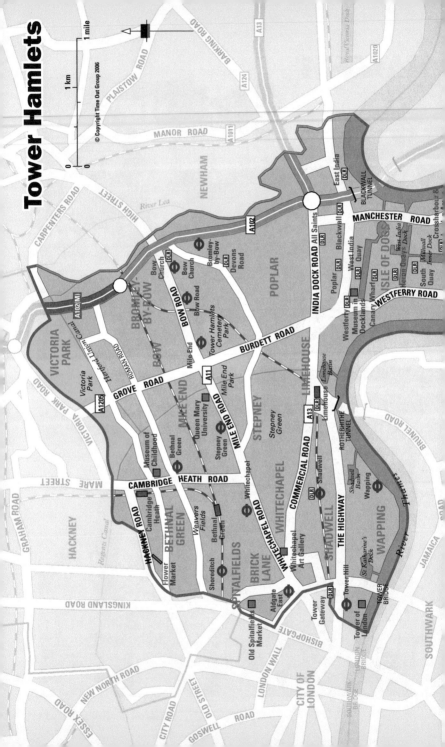

Even the Ten Bells pub, where Jack the Ripper used to source his prostitute victims, has stopped selling murder memorabilia and is now a light-flooded DJ bar. The only hassle you're likely to receive on a dark night comes from competing Brick Lane curry touts and illegal minicab drivers (though the ladies of the night are still here, offering their wares).

Trading, respectable or otherwise, is what Spitalfields has always been about, and Sundays are when the area's markets come to life. Brick Lane Market occupies the northern half of the street, extending east down Cheshire Street and west down Sclater Street. Cheap veg, household goods and general tat are still on offer, but it has also become a cult shopping haunt for lovers of vintage clothes and arty gifts. To the west, Dray Walk, by the Old Truman Brewery, has embraced café society; on a Sunday afternoon the street overflows with hipsters hiding their hangovers behind a latte and a lopsided fringe. Bars such as 93 Feet East, the Vibe Bar and the Spitz (on the edge of Spitalfields Market) have firmly established the area as a prime live music locale. Classical music comes to the fore during the Spitalfields Festival, which is held twice a year (June and December) in Christ Church and other venues in the neighbourhood.

In the background, the City looms large, with its traders encroaching ever further on to local turf. Half of Spitalfields Market has controversially been demolished to make way for further towers of Mammon (designed by Sir Norman Foster). According to the ominous warning of local chronicler Iain Sinclair, the neighbourhood is living through a stage it has to pass through before being 'totally colonised by the land greed of the City'.

Whitechapel and Stepney

The lower end of Brick Lane merges into the major thoroughfare of Whitechapel Road (aka the A11). The Whitechapel Art Gallery, East London Mosque and some Queen Anne architecture jolly it up somewhat, while an enormous branch of Sainsbury's helps appease consumers, as does Whitechapel Road street market. The brand-new, glass-walled Idea Store brings the concept of the public library into the 21st century (there are also two others in the borough, in Bow and Poplar).

But the relentless traffic is a downer; broad, sweeping boulevards may be Paris's greatest feature, but it's the most depressing aspect of east London, where juggernauts speed out of the capital to Essex and beyond. The nearest thing to café society you'll find here is teenage lads in bomber jackets congregating under the neon glare of fake KFCs. Commercial Road (A13), further south, is even worse.

Interesting pockets of housing are to be found behind the Royal London Hospital, especially the gigantic flat-fronted Victorian redbricks around Ashfield Street and Sidney Square. Things have improved since Dr Barnardo set up his first refuge in Stepney, and Albert Gardens and Arbour Square are well-hidden green spots. Stepney Green, where Richard II braved the peasants' revolt, now boasts weekend football and a swanky playground.

Bethnal Green

Like so much of east London, World War II bomb damage has left an architectural patchwork in Bethnal Green, with no single

The **East London Mosque**, on Whitechapel Road. *See p55.*

style or period monopolising. Yet the council estates never sprawl too high or wide here (unlike areas further east). The result is a neighbourhood that operates on a human scale, and each street seems to have its own character. Newcomers are often pleasantly surprised when they realise how central Bethnal Green is – much of the area is in Zone 1. The social attractions of Brick Lane and Shoreditch are within walking distance too, without being too close to transmit the nocturnal noise pollution.

On Sundays, Columbia Road Flower Market is a multicoloured frenzy, and the terraced cottages around neighbouring Jesus Green are the most highly prized in the area, selling for the best part of half a million pounds, despite being rather small.

Shopping is limited if you want any brand name more glamorous than Woolworths, but if it's Bengali wedding gear, bling gold jewellery or an enormous rotting jack fruit you're after, Bethnal Green Road will delight. You can also still sit down for a meal of pie, mash and jellied eels at a time-weathered local caff. Such bastions of the old East End might prompt thoughts of the district's more murky past. In the 1960s it was home to the Kray Twins. Don't joke out loud, though – thousands lined the streets for Ronnie Kray's funeral in 1995, and many locals still won't hear a bad word said against the brothers.

Mile End

Things have vastly improved since Mile End provided Pulp's Jarvis Cocker with his first London home ('We didn't have nowhere to live/We didn't have nowhere to go/'til someone said/I know this place off Burdett Road'). But like so much of east London, there are still vast, grim stretches. The legacy of wartime bomb damage and slum clearances means that Victorian terraces are interspersed with tower blocks.

The City may only be a mile away, but its glittering towers on the horizon seem to come from a different world. The completion of the Millennium Park project – an extraordinarily ambitious grass bridge (aka the Green Bridge) across Mile End Road – has perked things up considerably. Recent additions to the night-time lighting have made the area safer (muggings are down from 20 per month in the old park to almost zero). Kids love the park too, as it features wildlife-filled water pools beside the canal, the excellent Mile End Climbing Wall and an outdoor karting track.

Opposite the park, Queen Mary, University of London, gives a studenty feel to its stretch of Mile End Road, with majestic older buildings sitting alongside the award-winning modern architecture of the university's Student Village. Otherwise, the area is a little dull; one highlight, the Genesis cinema, is the only decent movie house for miles around, and shows all the latest blockbusters plus the odd foreign-language series.

Victoria Park

Despite being described by Dickens as 'one of the things which no student of London life should miss seeing', Victoria Park is still a remarkably well-kept secret. It is London's third largest cultivated green space, rivalled only by the parks Hyde and Regent's to the west, yet the East End location keeps it well off the tourist trail. Shaped like a wellington boot, the park was built in the mid 19th century in an attempt to bring health and vigour to the working classes – and to prevent illegal cockfighting and political meetings taking place in the area. Sadly, its

STATISTICS

BOROUGH MAKE-UP
Population 204,704
Average weekly pay £557.70
Ethnic origins
  White 51.40%
  Mixed 2.48%
  Asian or Asian British 36.62%
  Black or Black British 6.50%
  Chinese or other 3.00%
Students 12.31%
Retirees 7.68%

HOUSING STOCK
Borough size 16.8km²
No. of households 83,386 (over 80% are high-rise properties)
Detached 1%
Semi-detached 2.2%
Terraced 13%
Flats (purpose-built) 76.1%
Flats (converted) 6.5%
Flats (both) 82.6%

CRIME PER 1,000 OF POPULATION
(English average in brackets)
Burglary 8 (6.4)
Robbery 7 (1.4)
Theft of vehicle 9 (4.5)
Theft from vehicle 17 (10)
Violence against the person 38 (16.5)
Sexual offences 2 (0.9)

MPs & COUNCIL
MPs *Bethnal Green & Bow* George Galloway (Respect); *Poplar & Canning Town* Jim Fitzpatrick (Labour)
CPA 3 stars; subject to review

lido is no longer in use, but the lakes, deer enclosure and café nearly compensate, as do annual events such as music festivals, outdoor film screenings and fireworks.

Grove Road slices the park in two. If you follow it north as it turns into Lauriston Road, a wonderful hidden village appears (technically across the borough boundary in Hackney). There's a cluster of shops around the very pleasant junction with Victoria Park Road – not to mention a bevy of estate agents, cashing in on the area's family-friendly layout. The spacious Victorian houses and villagey feel have made this one of the most sought-after pockets of east London, despite the nearest tube stop (Bethnal Green) being a long walk down the Roman Road.

On the south side of the park runs the Hertford Union Canal, bordered by a variety of new-build flats and houses taking advantage of the waterside location. Follow the canal path along the park east to Cadogan Terrace and you'll find some fine four-storey houses with a fantastic view. Unfathomable council clearances in the 1960s robbed these houses of some of their neighbours, and those that remain have their backs to another unpleasant 1960s phenomenon – the A12 flyover, beyond which the canal connects to the River Lee Navigation.

Bow, Bromley-by-Bow and Poplar

Squint closely at the map on *EastEnders* and you'll see that the fictional borough of Walford is, in fact, Bow. Yet in reality, the similarities are few. If you want a tight-knit community based around a square where the local GP knows everybody's name, you'll have to look elsewhere.

The north part of Bow can be lovely, with Victorian family homes leading from the expensive Tredegar conservation area up and across the Roman Road to Zealand and Chisenhale Roads – home of artists' studios, a dance space and an art gallery in the Chisenhale building – and Victoria Park just beyond. Nearby, the canalside Bow Wharf development contains restaurants, bars, a gym and Jongleurs comedy club.

For a symbol of the East End's changing fortunes, look no further than the Bow Quarter development beside the A102,

Tower Hamlets

which is dominated by the massive Bryant & May match factory. Once the home of exploited factory girls, whose strike was pivotal to the 19th-century labour movement, this is now a luxury apartment complex, complete with swimming pools.

A few minutes down the road, the atmosphere changes starkly, with racial conflict still a huge local problem between white, black and Asian youths. Local estate agents may boast that Rachel Whiteread's *House* artwork was a cast of the last slum home to be cleared from Bow, but the mantle of deprivation has simply been transferred to the tower blocks. Located just south of Bow Church tube, the three towers of the Crossways Estate are notorious, not least with the local police. Ken Livingstone and Tony Blair's ideal of a multicultural London seems a myth here. 'We used to fight with kids from other estates. Now eight millimetres settle debates,' rapped local hero Dizzee Rascal about his childhood in Crossways.

The vibrant grime-rap scene Dizzee helped spawn is a great focus of energy for disaffected kids, centred on the Rhythm Division record shop on the shopping thoroughfare of Roman Road (which also hosts a large, thrice-weekly street market). The Bromley-by-Bow Centre has met with national acclaim too. Thanks to a very enthusiastic vicar at the helm, its mission to bring about social change through 'collective enterprise' has worked; its health centre, youth club and skills exchange employ more than 100 people.

The rest of Bromley-by-Bow is very ugly, excepting Three Mills, the site on the River Lee of former watermills and a grand, Byzantine-Gothic pumping station that are now listed buildings, complete with a visitors' centre. There's also an enormous television studio here – site of the first *Big Brother* TV show.

As for Poplar, its most notable landmark is Ernö Goldfinger's modernist Balfron Tower, a block of flats with a chimney-like lift shaft stuck on one side; the building mirrors Goldfinger's more famous Trellick Tower in west London. Chrisp Street is a popular thoroughfare containing Britain's first pedestrian shopping centre (built for the 1951 Festival of Britain), a local street market and another modern library-cum-community centre (aka Idea Store), but, other than that, Poplar seems lost, dwarfed by Docklands and flyovers.

What Bow excels at is public transport, with tubes, buses and the DLR all competing for your Oyster card. And with Crossrail and the nearby Olympic site yet to come, such facilities can only improve.

Wapping, Shadwell and Limehouse

The banks of the Thames may have been occupied for 12,000 years, but the glass-fronted luxury apartments of Wapping and Limehouse are resolutely modern developments and sit at odds with much of the world around them. Affluent incomers who buy flats off-plan might be shocked to see what exists outside the picture frame: endless estates and a brutal highway sucking traffic into the Rotherhithe Tunnel.

Nevertheless, at least one half of Wapping has managed to retain a villagey feel; the waterside area, with its old stevedores' pubs such as the Prospect of Whitby, is probably the loveliest example of restoration in the whole of east London. The other half of the district is another matter: the prison-like enclosure of 'Fortress Wapping', aka Rupert Murdoch's News International office complex and all-night-chugging printing press. This mighty edifice has been unable to shake off its association among locals with picket-line atrocities committed during the Thatcher years.

Westwards, on the edge of the City, lie the iconic pinnacles of Tower Bridge and the neighbouring turrets of the Tower of London (covered in the City of London; *see p50*), one of the capital's most historic – and most visited – monuments. History has been successfully glossed over in nearby St Katharine's Docks. Here, a glistening, yacht-filled marina is overlooked by upmarket sailing memorabilia shops and pricey, soulless restaurants.

Further east, Limehouse Basin marina has a similar feel, with some outstanding new (and old) architecture and a very good heritage trail. Nearby Shadwell mixes smart new housing with pockets of social deprivation; it has a lively canoeing and sailing centre on Shadwell Basin.

Docklands and the Isle of Dogs

Wonderfully evocative names such as Mudchute, Marsh Wall and Heron Quay summon images of a bird-watcher's paradise, but modern-day Docklands is a different story. Many of the names refer to the area's lost wildlife, or to former trading goods from a time when the docks were the funnel for London's lifeblood.

By the early 1980s, the docks had fallen into disuse, never having recovered from heavy bombing by the Luftwaffe and a decline in the shipping industry. The Isle of Dogs (actually a peninsula in the Thames) had become so cut off that, in the 1970s, a local group declared it a republic and named its own president. Those who had money moved to Essex; those who didn't remained. The latter are especially concentrated in the fiercely patriotic Millwall district, where union flags still hang outside pubs.

Margaret Thatcher decided to use the Isle of Dogs to create the most dramatic manifestation of her vision of Britain. The measure of her success remains a subject of fierce debate. The Canary Wharf development was an attempt to both rejuvenate the area and relocate London's growing financial centre. After a shaky start, it has finally paid off, with many major banks based in its gleaming towers, as well as the offices of the *Daily Telegraph* and the *Independent*. The extension of the Jubilee Line brought with it a space-age, Norman Foster-designed tube station. The Docklands Light Railway (DLR), with its driverless sky trains, adds yet another dimension to a landscape that already feels disorientingly like the set of *Blade Runner*. Cabot Place has a well-stocked shopping mall, while Canary Wharf has all the bars and restaurants you could need – which are now starting to fill up with families as well as suits. For movies, try the ten-screen multiplex at West India Quay.

Gastropubs are starting to flourish here, but there's a distinct lack of corner shops… probably because there's a distinct lack of corners. Where Wapping has made much of its older buildings, the 'Island' epitomises the modern, with angular waterside developments fringing West Ferry Road. Understandably, not all locals enjoy living alongside the money-making Wharfers, whose gated communities take advantage of fantastic views over the river to Greenwich and beyond by standing with their backs to the Isle of Dogs and its older communities, who occupy council flats or Victorian terraces (though many local families now live in Wimpey-style red-brick dwellings). On a day-to-day pedestrian level the Island feels distressingly impersonal. Attempts have been made to humanise the area, including the commissioning of a few token sculptures, but the juxtapositions of high-rise with low-rise, water with land, and industriousness with isolation can make the stroller feel small, even a little seasick.

Green space is not plentiful, but Mudchute Park is fantastic for children, with horse-riding, nature trails and the largest city farm in Europe. For an added adventure, walk through the pedestrian tunnel under the Thames to Greenwich.

TRANSPORT

Tube stations *Central* Bethnal Green, Mile End; *District/Hammersmith & City* Tower Hill, Aldgate East, Whitechapel, Stepney Green, Mile End, Bow Road, Bromley-by-Bow; *East London* Shoreditch, Whitechapel, Shadwell, Wapping; *DLR* Tower Hill, Tower Gateway, Shadwell, Limehouse, Westferry, Poplar; All Saints, Devons Road, Bow Church; Blackwall, East India; West India Quay, Canary Wharf, Heron Quays, South Quay, Crossharbour & London Arena, Mudchute, Island Gardens

Rail stations *c2c* Limehouse; *one* Bethnal Green, Cambridge Heath

Main bus routes *into central London* 8, 15, 25, 26, 48, 55, 100, 188, 205, 381, 388; *night buses* N8, N15, N26, N55, N106, N108, N277, N381; *24-hour buses* 8, 25, 108, 277

River commuter and leisure boat services to/from central London, with piers at St Katharine's Dock, Masthouse Terrace and Canary Wharf

Restaurants & cafés

Docklands and the borders of the City and Shoreditch are the areas where most restaurants are concentrated. The glossy office blocks and apartments of E14 provide the diners for an array of chain restaurants

All night, all day, 365 days a year. **Brick Lane Beigel Bake** is an institution.

that includes Carluccio's Caffè, Pizza Express, Moshi Moshi Sushi, Smollensky's, Tootsies Grill, Wagamama and Zizzi.

Many places have waterfront settings, including the laudable Royal China (Chinese), Curve (upmarket North American), the Gaucho Grill (Argentinian steaks) and Elephant Royale (Thai) – this last restaurant being at the tip of the Isle of Dogs, looking out over the Thames. The Gun – *Time Out*'s Best Gastropub in 2005 – also overlooks the Thames, though not from the dining room. Views are another USP: Ubon (the Docklands outpost of Nobu) has wonderful ones from its eyrie; Plateau (Conran-owned restaurant, grill and bar) has a slightly less impressive outlook, but the space age interior more than compensates.

Wapping offers more chains (Pizza Express, Pizza Paradiso and Smollensky's) but also Wapping Food, a fascinating arts space and Modern European eaterie in one huge building (formerly a hydraulic power station), and Il Bordello, an independent pizza and pasta joint. And almost in the City, St Katharine's Dock has Lightship

Ten (Modern European/Scandinavian food on a moored vessel), plus yet more chains.

As Spitalfields has been more and more developed, so the number of places to eat has grown; the brand-new market complex has branches of Pâtisserie Valerie and Giraffe, as well as Canteen (homely British food in a modish diner setting). Just opposite is sausage specialist S&M Café and the wood-panelled Market Coffee House. Inside Old Spitalfields Market is Arkansas Café, the most authentic barbecue joint in town, while opposite on Commercial Street is St John Bread & Wine, the best restaurant in the area – booking is advisable, and essential on Sundays. Also fabulous is OTT French outlet Les Trois Garçons, just off the northern end of the Lane.

The Indian restaurants that originally made Brick Lane's food name are now sad imitations of their former selves: there's no shortage of venues, but all serve just-adequate, identikit dishes; hesitate outside one, and touts descend, urging you inside. Much better casual budget eating can be had at the legendary Brick Lane Beigel Bake (a non-kosher Jewish bakery, like Rinkoff's further east), the Big Chill Bar (*see p62*) and Story Deli (excellent for pizza).

Along and around Columbia Road there's Jones Dairy Café, gastropub the Royal Oak, café/bar the Fleapit, tapas bar Laxeiro, brasserie Perennial and StringRay Globe Café, Bar & Pizzeria. Moving east, Bistrotheque provides a delightful cocktail of Anglo-French food, great attitude and groovy bar in a converted warehouse.

There are several pie and mash shops in the borough – G Kelly and S&R Kelly on Bethnal Green Road (also the home of ace greasy spoon E Pellicci), plus G Kelly in Bow. The Morgan Arms gastropub and Winkles fish restaurant are also in Bow, while two vegetarian restaurants, Gallery Café and Wild Cherry, are near neighbours in E2. After that, notable eateries are few and far between: even though it's a property hotspot, all Victoria Park can muster is Frocks bistro and Vietnamese outlet Namo.

Arkansas Café *Unit 12, Old Spitalfields Market, E1 6AA (7377 6999).*
Bistrotheque *23-27 Wadeson Street, E2 9DR (8983 7900/www.bistrotheque.com).*
Il Bordello *81 Wapping High Street, E1W 2YN (7481 9950).*
Brick Lane Beigel Bake *159 Brick Lane, E1 6SB (7729 0616).*
Canteen *Unit 2, Crispin Place, off Brushfield Street, E1 6DW (0845 686 1122/www. canteen.co.uk).*
Curve *London Marriott Hotel, West India Quay, 22 Hertsmere Road, E14 4ED (7093 1000 ext 2622).*
Elephant Royale *Locke's Wharf, Westferry Road, E14 3AN (7987 7999/www.elephant royale.com).*
E Pellicci *332 Bethnal Green Road, E2 0AG (7739 4873).*
Fleapit *49 Columbia Road, E2 7RG (7033 9986/www.thefleapit.com).*
Frocks *95 Lauriston Road, E9 7HJ (8986 3161).*
Gallery Café *21 Old Ford Road, E2 9PL (8983 3624).*
Gaucho Grill *29 Westferry Circus, Canary Riverside, E14 8RR (7987 9494/www.gaucho-grill.com).*
G Kelly *600 Roman Road, E3 2RW (8983 3552).*
G Kelly *414 Bethnal Green Road, E2 0DJ (7739 3603).*
Gun *27 Coldharbour, Isle of Dogs, E14 9NS (7515 5222).*
Jones Dairy Café *23 Ezra Street, E2 7RH (7739 5372/www.jonesdairy.co.uk).*
Laxeiro *93 Columbia Road, E2 7RG (7729 1147).*
Lightship Ten *5A St Katharine's Way, St Katharine's Dock, E1W 1LP (7481 3123/ www.lightshipten.com).*

Market Coffee House *50-52 Brushfield Street, E1 6AG (7247 4110).*
Morgan Arms *43 Morgan Street, E3 5AA (8980 6389/www.geronimo-inns.co.uk).*
Namo *178 Victoria Park Road, E9 7HD (8533 0639).*
Perennial *110-112 Columbia Road, E2 7RG (7739 4556/www.perennial-restaurant.co.uk).*
Plateau *Canada Place, Canada Square, E14 5ER (7715 7100/www.conran.com).*
Rinkoff's *79 Vallance Road, E1 5BS (7247 6228).*
Royal China *30 Westferry Circus, E14 8RR (7719 0888/www.royalchinagroup.co.uk).*
Royal Oak *73 Columbia Road, E2 7RG (7729 2220).*
S&M Café *48 Brushfield Street, E1 6AG (7247 2252/www.sandmcafe.co.uk).*
S&R Kelly *284 Bethnal Green Road, E2 0AG (7739 8676).*
St John Bread & Wine *94-96 Commercial Street, E1 6LZ (7247 8724/www.stjohnbread andwine.com).*
StringRay Globe Café, Bar & Pizzeria *109 Columbia Road, E2 7RL (7613 1141/ www.stringraycafe.co.uk).*
Story Deli *3 Dray Walk, The Old Truman Brewery, 91 Brick Lane, E1 6QL (7247 3137).*
Les Trois Garçons *1 Club Row, E1 6JX (7613 1924/www.lestroisgarcons.com).*
Ubon *34 Westferry Circus, Canary Wharf, E14 8RR (7719 7800/www.noburestaurants.com).*
Wapping Food *Wapping Hydraulic Power Station, Wapping Wall, E1W 3ST (7680 2080/ www.thewappingproject.com).*
Wild Cherry *241-245 Globe Road, E2 0JD (8980 6678).*
Winkles *238 Roman Road, E2 0RY (8880 7450/www.winklesseafood.com).*

Bars & pubs

If Brick Lane is known in restaurant terms for its curry houses, its two dominant bars – 93 Feet East and the Vibe Bar – are known for their fantastic outdoor spaces. Both have expansive courtyards: a huge attraction in the summer when barbecues lure punters from the beats inside (both are thriving music venues too). Nearby, the Big Chill Bar competes with its cool, car-park aesthetics, while the Spitz offers a bar, bistro, art gallery and cross-genre music events. Real ale fans, meanwhile, should head to the unpretentious Pride of Spitalfields.

Away from Brick Lane, in Whitechapel and Stepney, the pub scene ain't so savoury (although Kray Twins favourite the Blind Beggar does have two open fires – complete with two cats). Bar and club life is hidden, but more promising: Indo offers a laid-back vibe and all-day breakfasts, while the

Rhythm Factory once played host to early Libertines gigs and helped the revival of London's guitar scene (though now puts on latin, salsa and techno nights).

Bethnal Green also has its share of rough, no-frills hostelries – sprinkled with tastier bars. Trendies who can't be bothered to journey to Hoxton frequent the handsome, bare-bricked Napoleon Bar, attached to hip restaurant Bistrotheque (see p61). For cheaper booze, locals join the invariably enthusiastic crowd at music venue Pleasure Unit on Bethnal Green Road.

South to Limehouse and Wapping reveals a smattering of riverside pubs, many that have existed in some form or another for centuries: the Grapes in Limehouse (built 1720) and the Prospect of Whitby in Wapping (built 1520) are prime examples.

Though considered the netherland between the fashionable East End and the wilder expanses of east london, Mile End and Bow contain a number of boozers that are improving – or trying to. Take the curious Greenwich Pensioner, recent recipient of a wildly unlikely renovation from downtrodden pub to stripped-wood bar with hi-energy house on the jukebox, or, less hilariously, the Morgan Arms, now a stylish, spacious gastropub (see p61). Elsewhere, the area's population of students, locals and middle-class incomers tend to sup apart – in the New Globe, Bow Bells and Royal Inn on the Park, respectively; defying this, L'Oasis draws a mixed crowd with its accommodating hubbub. As for the Palm Tree: 1950s cash register, aged gold wallpaper, regulars of equally varied time-periods… with a drum kit and piano in the corner and would-be Sinatras showing their wives they've still got the magic, you really couldn't make this place up.

The Docklands nightscene isn't quite so magical; of an early evening, pubs and chain wine bars are rammed with suited ladies and gents (ties loosened), and the lack of imagination is depressing. Highlights are the waterside Cat & Canary (not as ancient as it looks, it was in fact built in 1992), the Ferry House (the only 'propah' locals pub on the Isle of Dogs?), and classy gastropub Gun (see p60), with its spectacular Thames views.

Big Chill Bar *Old Truman Brewery, off Brick Lane, E1 6QL (7392 9180/www.bigchill.net).*
Blind Beggar *337 Whitechapel Road, E1 1BU (7247 6195).*
Bow Bells *116 Bow Road, E3 3AA (8981 7317).*
Cat & Canary *1-24 Fisherman's Walk, E14 4DH (7512 9187).*
Ferry House *26 Ferry Street, E14 3DT (7537 9587).*
Grapes *76 Narrow Street, E14 8BP (7987 4396).*
Greenwich Pensioner *2 Bazely Street, E14 0ES (7987 4414).*
Indo *133 Whitechapel Road, E1 1DT (7247 4926).*
Napoleon Bar *Bistrotheque, 23-27 Wadeson Street, E2 9DR (8983 7900/ www.bistrotheque.com).*
New Globe *359 Mile End Road, E3 4QS (8980 6689).*
93 Feet East *150 Brick Lane, E1 6QN (7247 3293/www.93feeteast.co.uk).*
L'Oasis *237 Mile End Road, E1 4AA (7702 7051/www.loasisstepney.co.uk).*
Palm Tree *127 Grove Road, E3 5RP (8980 2918).*
Pleasure Unit *359 Bethnal Green Road, E2 6LG (7729 0167/www.pleasureunitbar.com).*
Pride of Spitalfields *3 Heneage Street, E1 5LJ (7247 8933).*
Prospect of Whitby *57 Wapping Wall, E1W 3SH (7481 1095).*
Rhythm Factory *16-18 Whitechapel Road, E1 1EW (7375 3774/www.rhythmfactory.co.uk).*
Royal Inn on the Park *111 Lauriston Road, E9 7HJ (8985 3321).*
Spitz *Old Spitalfields Market, 109 Commercial Street, E1 6BG (7392 9032/www.spitz.co.uk).*
Vibe Bar *The Old Truman Brewery, 91-95 Brick Lane, E1 6QL (7377 2899/www.vibe-bar.co.uk).*

Shops

With more markets and independent shops than you can shake a stick at, Tower Hamlets is one of London's most creative boroughs, with hosts of fashion and art college graduates striking out on their own each year. The three main shopping areas of Brick Lane, Columbia Road and Spitalfields are all within easy walking distance of one another. Given that many of the shops don't open during the week, the weekend is the sensible time for a spree and the occasion to capture the vibrant spirit of the area.

Silent during the week, Columbia Road blossoms into life on Sunday morning. Plants, cut flowers and gardening accessories are the stock in trade, but these days the hordes flock here for the one-off shops as much as

'Tower Hamlets takes its name from the hamlets, or villages, that provided the militiamen who manned the Tower of London. The term was in use by 1636 and probably much earlier. These days, the beauty is that people from all walks of life are living and working here. The diversity brings a richness of culture and food, and harmony to the borough.'

**Zoinul Abidin, Swanlea School governor
and lifelong Whitechapel resident**

the flora. It's testimony to the street's huge success that trading on Sunday mornings alone is enough to sustain the shopkeepers. Gems include retro and modern designs at Columbia Lights, well-priced Poole pottery and 20th-century homeware accessories at One Three Six, vintage silk tea dresses at Marcos & Trump, plus hat specialist Fred Bare and perfumier Angela Flanders.

Brick Lane and nearby Cheshire Street come up trumps for directional fashion: this is the breeding ground for many of London's streetstyle trends. Rummage for vintage denim, cowboy boots and baseball jackets in Rokit, and everything from 1950s to '80s wares at Beyond Retro. You'll find many-hued leather bags at Mimi, quirky homeware accessories at Shelf, and posh gardening and kitchen accessories at Labour & Wait. Comfort Station is a great place for fashion finds, while Mar Mar has a well thought-out collection of Scandinavian homeware.

The Old Truman Brewery on Brick Lane makes a handy shortcut to Spitalfields; hip but classy menswear boutique A Butcher of Distinction and imported trainer store Gloria's are worth seeking out, and the Sunday market is thriving. Spitalfields Market has shrunk, following the demolition of two-thirds of the original market building, but still offers an eclectic mix of stalls, including organic fruit and veg. The new shop units on the old market site are worth a look too – there are a few one-off shops, plus branches of small chains, such as make-up specialist Benefit. Nearby you'll find original jewellery designs at Ben

Day, and delis A Gold (British specialities) and Verde & Co (Italian-biased).

Brick Lane and Petticoat Lane Markets are a throwback to a different era, with geezers selling cheap pants and knock-off watches; visit for the East End atmosphere, not for the bargains.

Back where Brick Lane meets Bethnal Green Road (leaving behind the smell of leather from the jacket shops at this junction), either nip north to visit hip jewellers Tatty Devine and affordable, innovative furniture makers Unto This Last, or walk east along Bethnal Green Road. Here a string of nondescript discount stores and cheap supermarkets is brightened up by numerous Asian designer clothes shops, wedding shops and jewellers. Bethnal Green Road Market is a lively place to by the usual mix of odds 'n' ends and domestic wares, and there's also a large Tesco Metro.

The desolate commercial cabins in Bow Wharf house a gym and several restaurants. The nicest shopping enclave around here is actually north of Victoria Park, just over the borough line in Hackney. Here, along and off Lauriston Road, small, independent shops such as friendly boutique Sublime and sweet toyshop Play, plus a handful of gift and antique shops, provide succour to well-heeled locals.

Tatty shops tend to prevail when Bethnal Green Road gives way to Roman Road, but there are a few above-average clothes shops: Blush sells funky streetwear for women (labels include Miss Sixty and K Swiss), while its brother store Rockafella caters for

Tower Hamlets

men (Criminal and Komodo, plus Converse and Gola shoes). Further east there are some designer options: swish boutique Pure, which sells shoes and bags by the likes of D&G, plus men's and women's branches of mini chain Zee & Co. Roman Road is also home to a great one-off record shop: Rhythm Division, locally adored for its mean stock of vinyl. True to its name, Roman Road continues straight all the way to Bow, but there is little of interest east of Globe Road.

Stepney and Whitechapel offer more Asian clothes stores and grocers, plus the market stalls of Whitechapel Market on Whitechapel Road and a huge Sainsbury's. On Mile End Road in Stepney Green you'll find a very different shopping experience: a giant retail park, with branches of PC World, Halfords and Currys. Over in Wapping, meanwhile, a large Safeway has recently been joined by a new branch of Waitrose – much to the relief of shop-starved employees of the News International citadel.

East into the Isle of Dogs, the best shopping can be found in the complex of subterranean malls and streets around Canary Wharf, where a host of upmarket chainstores cater to the legions of suited drones that flood the place on their lunch breaks. With a ready-made, highly paid customer base, the shops in Cabot Place and Jubilee Place are by no means cheap or unique, but they're convenient nonetheless, with everything from Marks & Spencers and Boots to women's clothing and fashion options, such as Karen Millen, Monsoon, Oasis, Accessorize, Fiorelli, Phase Eight and Sweaty Betty. There are also several chic beauty salons, such as the Company Store (by invitation only); for men, fashion options are predictably business-oriented, with branches of Ted Baker, Reiss, Hackett, Thomas Pink and Church's English Shoes. Other highlights include classy body and beauty products at Molton Brown, bath products and confectionery at Crabtree & Evelyn and a branch of Waitrose.

Just north of Canary Wharf finds a shopping centre from a different age – the giant Billingsgate fish market (you'll see its great plastic sign from Trafalgar Way at the east end of the Canary Wharf complex). Catering mainly to wholesale customers, there are nevertheless great stalls here for the individual: seafood, snacks and all manner of accessories and cooking utensils.

After the sheen of Canary Wharf, the street market on Chrisp Street in Poplar is a desolate place: it offers the usual cheap clothes and fruit and veg. On nearby Markey Way, Polish grocery Polvital sells tinned food, Polish confectionery and excellent sourdough bread.

A Gold *42 Brushfield Street, E1 6AG (7247 2487/www.agold.co.uk).*
Angela Flanders *96 Columbia Road, E2 7QB (7739 7555).*
Ben Day *18 Hanbury Street, E1 6QR (7247 9977/www.benday.co.uk).*
Benefit *49 Brushfield Street, E1 6AA (7377 2684/www.benefitcosmetics.com).*
Beyond Retro *110-112 Cheshire Street, E2 6EJ (7613 3636/www.beyondretro.com).*
Blush *79 Roman Road, E2 0QN (8981 0011).*
Billingsgate Market *Trafalgar Way, E14 5ST (7987 1118).*
A Butcher of Distinction *11 Dray Walk, Old Truman Brewery, E1 6QL (7770 6111).*
Columbia Lights *142 Columbia Road, E2 7RG (7613 0517).*
Columbia Road Flower Market *Columbia Road, between Gosset Street & Royal Oak pub, E2.*
Comfort Station *22 Cheshire Street, E2 6EH (7033 9099/www.comfortstation.co.uk).*
Fred Bare *118 Columbia Road, E2 7RG (7729 6962/01904 624 579).*
Gloria's *6 Dray Walk, E1 6QL (7770 6024).*
Labour & Wait *18 Cheshire Street, E2 6EH (7729 6253/www.labourandwait.co.uk).*
Marcos & Trump *146 Columbia Road, E2 7RG (7739 9008).*
Mar Mar Co *16 Cheshire Street, E2 6EH (7729 1494/www.marmarco.com).*
Mimi *40 Cheshire Street, E2 6EH (7729 6699).*
One Three Six *136 Columbia Road, E2 7RG (7729 2740).*
Old Spitalfields Market *Commercial Street between Lamb Street & Brushfield Street, E1 (7247 8556/www.visitspitalfields.com).*
Play *89 Lauriston Road, E9 7HJ (8510 9960).*
Polvital *11 Market Way, E14 3TB (7093 4091).*

RECYCLING

No. of bring sites 55 (for nearest, visit www.recycleforlondon.com)
Household waste recycled 5.1%
Main recycling centre Northumberland Wharf, Yabsley Street, Isle of Dogs, E14 9RG (7538 4526)
Other recycling services furniture collection; home composting
Council contact London Borough of Tower Hamlets, Town Hall, Mulberry Place, Clove Crescent, E14 2BG (7364 6666)

Pure *430 Roman Road, E3 5LU (8983 2004/ www.puree3.com).*
Rhythm Division *391 Roman Road, E3 5QS (8981 2203/www.rhythmdivision.co.uk).*
Rockafella *81 Roman Road, E2 0QN (8981 5934).*
Rokit *101 & 107 Brick Lane, E1 6SE (7375 3864/www.rokit.co.uk).*
Shelf *40 Cheshire Street, E2 6EH (7739 9444).*
Sublime *99 Lauriston Road, E9 7HJ (8986 7243).*
Tatty Devine *236 Brick Lane, E2 7EB (7739 9009).*
Unto This Last *230 Brick Lane, E2 7EB (7613 0882/www.untothislast.co.uk).*
Verde & Co *40 Brushfield Street, E1 6AG (7247 1924).*
Whitechapel Market *Whitechapel Road, between Vallance Road & Cambridge Heath Road, E1.*
Zee & Co *www.zeeandco.co.uk;* women *416 Roman Road, E3 5LU (8980 2122);* men *454 Roman Road, E3 5LU (8983 3383).*

Arts & attractions

Cinemas & theatres
Chisenhale Dance Space *64-84 Chisenhale Road, E3 5QZ (8981 6617/www.chisenhale dancespace.co.uk).* Dance classes and workshops.
Mile End Genesis Cinema *93-95 Mile End Road, E1 4UJ (7780 2000/www.genesis-cinema.co.uk).*
UGC Cinema *West India Quay, 9 Hertsmere Road, E14 4AN (0870 907 0722/www.ugc cinemas.co.uk).*

Galleries & museums
Chisenhale Gallery *64-84 Chisenhale Road, E3 5QZ (8981 4518/www.chisenhale.org.uk).*
Denis Severs' House *18 Folgate Street, E1 6BX (7247 4013/www.dennissevershouse.co.uk).* Curious but fascinating period museum: a 'still-life drama' in a splendid Huguenot house.
Museum in Docklands *No.1 Warehouse, West India Quay, Hertsmere Road, E14 4AL (0870 444 3857/www.museumindocklands. org.uk).* Huge local museum covering everything from the Blitz to the area's controversial modern redevelopment.
Museum of Childhood *Cambridge Heath Road, E2 9PA (8983 5200/www.museumof childhood.org.uk).* The V&A's East End offshoot. Closed for redevelopment until autumn 2006.
Ragged School Museum *46-50 Copperfield Road, E3 4RR (8980 6405/www.raggedschool museum.org.uk).* Examining Dr Barnardo's Victorian education of the East End's urchins.
Royal London Hospital Archives & Museum *St Phillip's Church, Newark Street, E1 2AA (7377 7608/www.medicalmuseums.org).*
Whitechapel Art Gallery *80-82 Whitechapel High Street, E1 7QX (7522 7888/www. whitechapel.org).* One of the capital's leading contemporay galleries.

Music & comedy venues
Lee Hurst's Backyard Comedy Club *231 Cambridge Heath Road, E2 0EL (7739 3122/ www.leehurst.com).*
Jongleurs Bow *Bow Wharf, 221 Grove Road, E3 1AA (0870 787 0707/www.jongleurs.com).*

Open spaces
Bethnal Green Gardens *Cambridge Heath Road, E2.*
Island Gardens *Saunders Ness Road, E14.* Riverside park with splendid views over the water to Greenwich.
King Edward VII Memorial Park *The Highway, E1.*
Mile End Park *Rhodeswell Road, E14. (www.mileendpark.co.uk).*
Mudchute Park & Farm *Pier Street, E14 3HP (7515 5901/www.mudchute.org).*
Spitalfields City Farm *Weaver Street, E1 5HJ (7247 8762/www.spitalfieldscityfarm.org).*
Stepney Green & Stepping Stones Farm *Stepney Way, E1 3DG (7790 8204).*
Victoria Park *Old Ford Road, E3.* East London's most popular open space has a deer enclosure, lakes, tennis courts and playgrounds.
Weavers Fields *Bethnal Green Road, E1.*

Sport & fitness
The East End health club scene feels underdeveloped, and, in some cases, neglected. Many of the public venues are grim to look at and grubby inside, although the arrival of Greenwich Leisure in autumn 2005 should improve matters (the company successfully manages facilities in a number of other boroughs). York Hall – once a famous boxing venue – is currently undergoing a £4.2m facelift, including a makeover of its historic Turkish baths. Friendly, specialist clubs such as the body-buffing temple Muscle Works do much to improve the area's ultra-macho reputation, but for style and comfort the path leads unwaveringly to the private sector, especially in Docklands.

Otherwise, Mile End Climbing Wall draws climbers from across the capital, while the Docklands Sailing & Watersports Centre on Millwall Dock offers everything from dragon boat racing to Royal Yachting Association courses.

Gyms & leisure centres
Bodylines *461 Bethnal Green Road, E2 9QH (7613 1631/www.bodylinesfitness.co.uk).* Private.
Fitness Exchange *Spitalfields Health & Fitness Fruit Exchange Building, Brushfield*

Street, E1 6EP (7655 4316/www.fitness exchange.net); 15 Thomas More Square, E1 9YZ (7702 2777/www.fitnessexchange.net). Private.

Fitness First Bow Wharf, Grove Road, E3 5SN (8980 2442/www.fitnessfirst.com). Private.

Holmes Place West Ferry Circus, Canary Wharf, E14 8RR (7513 2999/www.holmes place.com). Private.

Island Sports Trust 100 Manchester Road, E14 3DW (7537 4762).

John Orwell Sports Centre Tench Street, E1 9QD (7488 9421/www.towerhamlets. gov.uk).

LA Fitness www.lafitness.co.uk; 90 Mansell Street, E1 8AL (7265 1544); West India Quay, 5 Hertsmere Road, E14 4AN (7531 0191). Private.

Muscle Works 2 Hague Street, E2 6HN (7256 0916/www.muscleworksgym.co.uk).

Reebok Sports Club Canada Square, E14 5ER (7970 0900/www.reeboksportsclub london.com). Private.

St George's Swimming Pool 221 The Highway, E1W 9BP (7709 9714/www.gll.org).

Tiller Centre Tiller Road, E14 8PX (7987 5211/www.gll.org).

Titan Fitness Centre 164-170 Mare Street, E8 3RD (8985 1287). Private.

Whitechapel Sports Centre Durwood Street, E1 5BA (7247 7538/www.gll.org).

York Hall Leisure Centre Old Ford Road, E2 9PJ (8980 2243/www.gll.org).

Other facilities

Docklands Sailing & Watersports Centre 235A Westferry Road, Millwall Dock, E14 3QS (7537 2626/www.dswc.org).

Mile End Climbing Wall Haverfield Road, E3 5BE (8980 0289/www.mileendwall.org.uk).

Mile End Karting Track 422-424 Burdett Road, Mile End park, E3 4AA (0120 679 9522/www.gokartinglondon.co.uk).

Schools

WHAT THE PARENTS SAY:

'We got lucky as we have a really good primary school across the road. Columbia Road Primary is splendid, and has an early years unit, so it takes kids from three years old. The school has changed a lot as the demographics of the area have changed, with the head teacher encouraging more white middle-class parents to choose the school. In general terms, Tower Hamlets has good primary schools, but on the fringes of the borough, where it borders Islington and Hackney, the schools aren't so great.

Secondary schools are more of a concern. Oaklands School, which is round the corner from us, is very, very good. It specialises in the

sciences and is also small, taking only 600 pupils. Haggerston Girls' School also has a fantastic reputation – but that's in Hackney. Bethnal Green Technology College has a bad reputation. It is under special measures and has seen a regular turnover of head teachers pass through its doors. Many of the kids are wild.

Most people we know in the area have stayed in the state sector, but an increasing number of people are moving out of London altogether when their kids get to secondary school age.'

Simon Rees, father of two, Bethnal Green

Primary

There are 73 state primary schools in Tower Hamlets, 18 of which are church schools. There are also five independent primary schools, including one faith school and two Montessori schools. See www.towerhamlets.gov.uk and www.ofsted.gov.uk for more information.

Secondary

Bethnal Green Technology College Gosset Street, E2 6NW (7920 7900/www.bgtc. org.uk).

Bishop Challoner Catholic Collegiate School Hardinge Street, E1 0EB (7790 3634/ www.bgtc.org.uk). Boys and girls taught separately; mixed sixth form.

Bow School Paton Close, Fairfield Road, E3 2QD (8980 0118). Boys only.

Central Foundation Girls' School College Terrace, E3 5AW (8983 1015). Girls only.

George Green's School 100 Manchester Road, E14 3DW (7987 6032).

Langdon Park School Byron Street, E14 0RZ (7987 4811).

Morpeth School Portman Place, E2 0PX (8981 0921).

Mulberry School for Girls Richard Street, Commercial Road, E1 2JP (7790 6327/ www.mulberry.towerhamlets.sch.uk/ learningeye). Girls only.

Oaklands School Old Bethnal Green Road, E2 6PR (7613 1014/www.oaklands.tower hamlets.sch.uk/welcome.php).

Raines Foundation School Approach Road, E2 9LY (8981 1231/www.rainesfoundation. org.uk).

St Paul's Way Community School Shelmerdine Close, E3 4AN (7987 1883/ www.st-paulsway.towerhamlets.sch.uk).

Sir John Cass Foundation & Redcoat School Stepney Way, E1 0RH (7790 6712/ www.sjcr.net).

Stepney Green Maths & Computing College Ben Jonson Road, E1 4SD (7790 6361). Boys only.

Swanlea School 31 Brady Street, E1 5DJ (7375 3267/www.swanlea.tower hamlets.sch.uk).

Property

WHAT THE AGENTS SAY:

❝There are a lot of City-based professionals in Docklands, predominantly working in Canary Wharf – about 80 per cent of our sales, I'd say. They are largely young people in their early and middle twenties, moving in from the suburbs to buy their first home. There aren't many families – there just aren't many big family homes to take over – and competition for the one or two secondary schools in the area is very high.❞
Paul Mitchell, Alex Neil Property Agents, Docklands

❝Bethnal Green is starting to get trendier – well, the Shoreditch end is. It's near central London, near Liverpool Street, so it's crowded, there's a hell of a lot of traffic, but it's certainly always alive. There's a real mixture of people, from upper-class City workers right down to the tramps in the streets. There is evidence of drugs on the streets, but crime is getting better. A lot of CCTV cameras have gone up; it's come a long way in the last few years. The pricey houses are on the Hackney side of Victoria Park, where three-storey houses go for £350K plus. On the Bow side, you're looking at £250K for a two-bed house. In Bethnal Green, you'd get an ex-council two-bed flat for around £150K.❞
Russell Parker, Hamilton Fox, Bethnal Green office

Average property prices
Detached £402,944
Semi-detached £299,501
Terraced £248,666
Flat £216,914

Local estate agents
Alex Neil Property Agents
www.alexneil.co.uk; 2 offices in the borough (Bow 8980 7431/Docklands 7537 9859).
APC London *14 Tiller Road, E14 8PX (7345 5171/www.apclondon.com).*
Atkinson Mcleod *www.atkinsonmcleod.com; 2 offices in the borough (Canary Wharf 7001 9670/Aldgate 7488 5536).*
Capital Dwellings *47 Fashion Street, E1 6PX (7375 1515/www.capitaldwellings.com).*
ea2 *Heritage Court, 8-10 Sampson Street, E1W 1NA (7702 3456/www.ea2.co.uk).*
Hamilton Fox *www.hamiltonfox.co.uk; 2 offices in the borough (Bethnal Green 7729 8777/Hackney 8985 5522).*
LND Residential *107 Burdett Road, E3 4JN (8983 9333/www.lndresidential.co.uk).*
Tarn & Tarn *4-10 Artillery Lane, E1 7LS (7377 8989/www.tarn-tarn.co.uk).*

COUNCIL TAX

A	up to £40,000	**£701.27**
B	£40,001-£52,000	**£818.15**
C	£52,001-£68,000	**£935.02**
D	£68,001-£88,000	**£1,051.90**
E	£88,001-£120,000	**£1,285.65**
F	£120,001-£160,000	**£1,519.41**
G	£160,001-£320,000	**£1,753.17**
H	over £320,000	**£2,103.80**

Other information

Council
Tower Hamlets Borough Council *The Town Hall, Mulberry Place, 5 Clove Crescent, E14 2BG (7364 5020/www.towerhamlets.gov.uk).*

Hospitals
London Chest Hospital *Bonner Road, E2 9JX (7377 7000/www.bartsandthelondon.org.uk).*
Mile End Hospital *Bancroft Road, E1 4DG (7377 7000).*
Royal London Hospital *Whitechapel Road, E1 1BB (7377 7000/www.bartsandthelondon.org.uk).*
St Andrews Hospital *Devas Street, E3 3NT (7476 4000).*
St Clements Hospital *Bow Road, E3 4LL (7377 7000).*

Legal services
Bow Road CAB *86 Bow Road, E3 4DL (0870 126 4014/www.adviceguide.org.uk).*
Tower Hamlets Advice Providers Directory *www.towerhamlets.gov.uk/data/ community/databases/regeneration/index.asp.*
Whitechapel CAB *Unit 32, Greatorex Street, E1 5NP (0870 126 4014/www.advice guide.org.uk).*

Local newspapers
East End Life *7364 3179/ www.towerhamlets.gov.uk.*
Free weekly newspaper distributed by the council and also available online. Includes 'Harmony', a section with stories in Bengali and Somali.
East London Advertiser *7790 8822/www.eastlondonadvertiser.co.uk.*
Tower Hamlets Recorder *8472 1421/www.threcorder.co.uk.*

Allotments
Cable Street Community Gardens *Corner of Cable Street & Hardinge Street, E1 (Jane Sill 7480 5456).*
Glamis Road Community Gardens *Glamis Road, E1 (Jane Sill 7480 5456).*
Reeves Road Allotment Society *1 Tibbetts Road, E3 (Mr T Fletcher 7515 7833).*
Stepping Stones Farm Allotments *Stepping Stones Farm, Stepney Way, E1 3DG (Lynne Bennett 7790 8204).*

'It's a tad grimy, but Hackney remains very real – I always want to tell other Londoners who've only discovered the "chocolate box" parts of the capital what they're missing'

Simon Carter, resident for 12 years

Hackney

Long plagued by deprivation, Hackney is now one of 21st-century London's most exciting boroughs. Persistent inner-city problems (crime, grime, unemployment) remain, but here too you'll find first-rate Turkish and Vietnamese food, a thriving arts scene, world-renowned clubs and bars – and the city's cutting-edge of cool.

Neighbourhoods

Shoreditch and Hoxton

Jutting down towards Liverpool Street from the south end of Hackney, Shoreditch is the classic East End slum made good. As recently as the 1960s, this was one of London's roughest neighbourhoods, living up to all the East End clichés of poverty, crime and neglect. All that changed in the 1990s, when artists and designers started moving into the fading warehouses around Old Street, attracted by low rents and a peer group that included Damien Hirst and Alexander McQueen.

That was then, this is now. Many of the artists moved out in the early Noughties, driven away by soaring rents and house prices. Since then, the irreverent bar scene that put Hoxton on the map has become as predictable as Saturday night at the Empire Leicester Square. City whiz-kids are more likely to live here now, in juxtaposition to residents of the sprawling council estates north of Hoxton Square.

Nevertheless, Shoreditch is still a desirable neighbourhood. It's about as close as you can get to living in the City without sleeping next to the office photocopier, and there are still a few Georgian terraces and Victorian loft apartments tucked away between the office blocks and car parks. The main residential area is north of Old Street; further south, every available inch has been given over to office space.

The perks of living in Shoreditch are obvious – Old Street and Hoxton Square are

Hackney

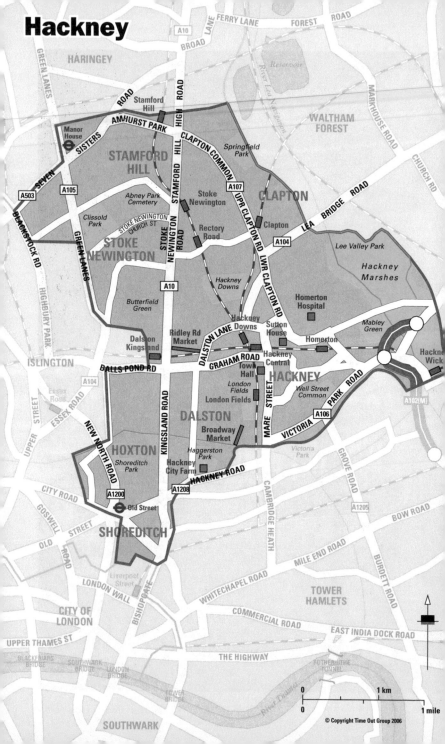

packed with bars and restaurants, and you can walk to the City in minutes. However, this is a young person's world and the attitude and novelty haircuts can get tiresome for the over-30s. Escape, though, is simple: Liverpool Street station gives easy access to Stansted and eastern England for when you need to see green fields.

North of Hoxton Square, council estates stretch as far as the eye can see. It's not the most salubrious place to live, but the location counts for something and Hoxton Street has a modest street market and one of London's last pie and mash shops. There are more greasy spoon cafés on Shoreditch High Street, along with a dwindling number of shoe and handbag wholesalers. If you tire of all-day breakfasts, head for the Vietnamese canteens on Kingsland Road near the Geffrye Museum (a gem of a place, showcasing changing domestic design down the centuries).

Some of the smartest housing is hidden in the north of Shoreditch, along the Regent's Canal. This is 'loft central', and most of the warehouses along the canal have been converted into luxury apartments. Perhaps

the most famous development is Gainsborough Studios, where Alfred Hitchcock shot *The Lady Vanishes*. Residents of the area generally work in the City and play in nearby Islington.

Despite the rapid spread of affluence, the district still has a seedy edge. Walls and shopfronts are plastered with graffiti and fly-posters; Shoreditch High Street is lined with grubby 'gentlemen's venues'. Of course, urban grit is part of the appeal for many. If you want genteel terraces and posh schools, move to Muswell Hill.

Hackney

The original working-class London suburb, Hackney was founded in Roman times near a ford across the River Lea. Once a rural idyll, it grew into a busy industrial centre in the Victorian era before sliding into rapid decline after World War II. Over the next few decades, Hackney became the heartland of social disintegration in the capital; stark housing estates mushroomed, unemployment soared and Hackney Council picked up the European record for most demolitions by a local authority. These days, gentrification is bringing new life to the borough, but Hackney is struggling to shake off a reputation for council mismanagement and for community projects that close within a few years of opening.

Most of the action takes place around Mare Street, which runs south past the 1920s Hackney Town Hall to Bethnal Green and Whitechapel. The area is known locally as Hackney Central, after the nearby train station. Following years of deprivation, the centre got a fresh start with the creation of the 'Hackney Cultural Quarter' around the Town Hall. First came Ocean, a flashy music venue, followed by the flashy public library complex and the glorious restoration of the Hackney Empire theatre. Sadly, Ocean went bankrupt after only two years (blamed variously on mismanagement, low visitor numbers and a boycott of homophobic reggae acts by British promoters). The Hackney Empire, in contrast, is still going strong, helped by a string of famous faces who got their breaks here in the 1980s; it's one of the best community theatres in London. The south end of Mare Street is home to Hackney's Vietnamese community, with restaurants and supermarkets that attract foodies from across the city.

Highs & Lows

▲ HIGHS & LOWS

Location A neighbour to both the City (for work) and Islington (for play)
World food The best Vietnamese, Turkish and Kurdish restaurants in London
Hackney Empire Restored to its turn-of-the-(previous)-century glory in 2004, this is one of the best community theatres in the city

No tube stations Weak transport links plague the borough, though tube stations Manor House and Old Street sit on the northern and southern borders
Seediness Urban grit is a lure for some, but swathes of Hackney are grim and intimidating – Clapton, in particular, has suffered a string of gun murders
Education Some of the worst-performing schools in Britain. Parents who can afford it look to private schools; higher-performing state students venture out of the borough ▼

A common sight: queuing outside **333** club. *See p80.*

Artistic endeavour in Hackney is focused on London Fields, just south of the centre. Driven from Old Street by soaring rents, painters and sculptors have colonised the warehouses and factories around the park. It's not yet the new Hoxton that supporters claim, but if the Flowers East art gallery and the Hothouse 'creative cluster' on Richmond Road are anything to go by, such fame won't be long in coming. Out of hours, artists hang out in the Pub on the Park on the edge of London Fields, or the pubs and cafés on trendy Broadway Market – a traditional market street that has seen a startling turnaround in its fortunes over the past decade. Further evidence of regeneration is to be found at the London Fields Lido, London's only 50-metre heated outdoor pool, which is due to reopen in the summer of 2006 after being closed for nearly two decades.

On the other (east) side of Mare Street, Hackney Wick has never quite recovered from the collapse of its Victorian industries. Along with nearby Homerton, the district was left to the criminal classes in Victorian times, and the neglect continues today. Both areas offer an unappealing mix of factories and council estates. The area abuts the new Olympic Park, however, so things will probably look very different come 2012.

The green expanse of Victoria Park is much used by Hackneyites (it's actually just over the borough border, in Tower Hamlets; *see p57*), as are the towpaths along the Regent's Canal and Hertford Union Canal. The residential roads around Well Street Common, just north of Victoria Park, are popular, with a cluster of shops and restaurants around Lauriston Road.

The overland train stations at Hackney Central, Hackney Downs and London Fields provide some compensation for the lack of a tube station, and buses run day and night to the City, Stoke Newington and Islington. However, Hackney loses marks for petty crime, high council taxes and some of the worst-performing schools in Britain.

Dalston

Dalston has picked up a bit of a reputation over the years, but the real Dalston isn't half as tough as residents like to pretend. Sure, it's overcrowded and the buildings on the main road could use a lick of paint, but the local population is invigoratingly diverse and the district is definitely on the way up.

For one thing, Dalston has a proper high street, with a Boots, an Argos and a Sainsbury's, plus a string of Turkish ocakbaşı restaurants and Afro-Caribbean supermarkets. Then there's the food market on Ridley Road, one of the best in north-east London and a great place to buy African and Caribbean ingredients. In recent years, these down-to-earth amenities have been joined by jazz bars, yoga centres and politically minded cafés. Another highlight is the Rio Cinema, a gorgeous art deco movie house screening everything from European arthouse to American schmaltz.

Before it was absorbed into the urban sprawl, the land beneath Dalston belonged to the gentry; neighbourhoods such as Kingsland and De Beauvoir still bear the names of their aristocratic former owners. The fields vanished under a maze of terraces in the 1840s and Dalston became very upmarket then very run-down in the space of a few generations. Of late, it has seen an influx of the upwardly mobile, and many estate agents now tip Dalston as the place to buy in the borough. Away from crowded Kingsland Road, the mood becomes more laid-back; things get quite posh on the approach to Islington's fringes. In De Beauvoir, the houses are tall and elegant – especially around De Beauvoir Square – and Hoxton and the City are on the doorstep.

On the other side of Kingsland Road, Haggerston doesn't have quite such des-res status; a handful of Victorian terraces sit in a sea of housing estates and warehouses, some undergoing the inevitable transition to loft apartments. The area isn't as cosy as De Beauvoir, but there are compensations – most notably the proximity of the City and the Regent's Canal, whose waterside path provides a scenic back route to Islington.

Dalston sits at the intersection of several transport lines. From Dalston Kingsland station, commuter trains run east to Stratford (and the new Olympic Park) and west to Hampstead and Camden, and then on to Richmond. Regular buses serve Clapton, Stoke Newington and the Square Mile, and the faithful No.38 runs day and night between Dalston, Islington and the West End.

Stoke Newington

Stoke Newington is a tale of two suburbs. The media classes congregate on bijou Stoke Newington Church Street, with its showy restaurants, estate agents and bric-a-brac shops, while the Gujarati and Anatolian communities live around busy Stoke Newington High Street (the A10). The change in atmosphere at the intersection of the two roads is striking.

Like many districts in north-east London, Stoke Newington was a peaceful village before it was engulfed by the city. As late as the 1860s, there were more trees than houses. Yet by the turn of the century, Stokey had evolved into a bustling suburb, with wide streets of terraced houses and hordes of commuters riding the trolley-buses down to Liverpool Street station.

STATISTICS

BOROUGH MAKE-UP
Population 208,769
Average weekly pay £461.60
Ethnic origins
  White 59.40%
  Mixed 4.19%
  Asian or Asian British 8.59%
  Black or Black British 24.66%
  Chinese or other 3.17%
Students 12.67%
Retirees 7.54%

HOUSING STOCK
Borough size 19.5km²
No. of households 91,043
Detached 1.5%
Semi-detached 3.9%
Terraced 18.8%
Flats (purpose-built) 51.7%
Flats (converted) 21.9%
Flats (both) 73.6%

CRIME PER 1,000 OF POPULATION
(English average in brackets)
Burglary 13 (6.4)
Robbery 9 (1.4)
Theft of vehicle 9 (4.5)
Theft from vehicle 17 (10)
Violence against the person 35 (16.5)
Sexual offences 2 (0.9)

MPs & COUNCIL
MPs *Hackney North & Stoke Newington* Diane Abbott (Labour); *Hackney South & Shoreditch* Meg Hillier (Labour)
CPA 1 star; improving adequately

Hackney

Today, residents define themselves by geographical location. The Church Street set is young, affluent, middle-class and predominantly employed in the media. You can identify such folk by their all-terrain baby buggies and next-generation mobile phones. In contrast, Stoke Newington High Street is edgier and rougher round the edges, but redeemed by a string of excellent Anatolian ocakbaşı restaurants and all-night Turkish grocers and delis. This split personality is partly a consequence of the location – Church Street leans towards Islington while the High Street looks to Dalston and Hackney Central.

Regardless of where they live, residents are united by their love of Clissold Park, a vast tree-dotted expanse with tennis courts, deer (in an enclosure), duck ponds, a kids' paddling pool and a pavilion café. On summer days, the park is carpeted by picnickers, and on match nights you can hear the distant roar of the crowd from the Arsenal stadium in Highbury. Clissold Leisure Centre, a £34m swimming and sports complex, was closed down almost as soon as it opened because of design problems; repairs are under way and it is set to reopen in summer 2006 – though angry locals aren't holding their breath.

Other highlights include Church Street's restaurants, the poshed-up pubs in the surrounding streets and the wonderfully overgrown Abney Park Cemetery, final resting place of the founder of the Salvation Army and the perfect setting for a George A Romero zombie movie. However, Stoke Newington loses points

Stoke Newington Bookshop. *See p81.*

for limited parking, car crime and anti-social teenagers. Begging is also a hassle at every ATM in the area.

Despite the drawbacks, residents are famously sentimental about this district. Businesses are named after bus routes. Restaurants have enough loyal customers for multiple branches on the same street. Even the lack of a tube station fails to faze the locals; shops sell nostalgic postcards of the bright red No.73 Routemasters that used to run along Church Street, now replaced by much-disliked bendy buses.

In fact, weak transport links are probably the biggest disadvantage to living in Stoke Newington. Reaching the City or the West End involves a 40-minute bus journey or a 20-minute overland train ride. The nearest tube stop, Manor House, is inconveniently located on Green Lanes, on the border with Haringey. On the other hand, buses pass through every few minutes, day and night, and you can cycle to Islington in ten minutes and the City in 20.

TRANSPORT

Tube stations *Northern* Old Street; *Piccadilly* Manor House
Rail stations *one* London Fields, Hackney Downs, Clapton, Rectory Road, Stoke Newington, Stamford Hill; *Silverlink* Dalston Kingsland, Hackney Central, Homerton, Hackney Wick
Main bus routes *into central London* 4, 8, 25, 26, 29, 30, 38, 43, 48, 55, 73, 76, 141, 149, 153, 205, 214, 242, 243, 253, 259, 271, 341, 476; *night buses* N8, N19, N26, N29, N35, N38, N41, N55, N73, N76, N106, N133, N236, N243, N253, N279; *24-hour buses* 23, 43, 149, 214, 236, 242, 243, 271, 277, 341

Stamford Hill

Few districts are as strongly associated with one community as Stamford Hill. This bustling neighbourhood of Victorian family residences and 1920s estates is home to most of London's 25,000-strong Hasidic Jewish community. Driven from continental Europe by pogroms and fascism, the Hasidim follow a strict form of Judaism. Yiddish is the lingua franca and Hasidic men dress identically in tasselled shirts, black suits and wide-brimmed hats. This is one of Hackney's most interesting districts, but there's a tangible divide between the Hasidic community and the rest of the local population. It's more a case of people not mixing than anything sinister, but it does make for a slightly disjointed atmosphere.

The main thoroughfare, Stamford Hill, is clogged with traffic and hemmed in by menacing-looking council blocks, but the surrounding terraces are bright and friendly. The prettiest area is north of Manor Road and Lordship Park; houses are positively palatial and the adjacent reservoir has the popular Castle Climbing Centre plus a water-sports venue.

Most of the shops and services are clustered around the intersection of Stamford Hill and Clapton Common; Seven Sisters tube stop is a short hop north, and Stamford Hill rail station is just west of the main junction. For a change of pace, it's less than a mile to the restaurants and middle-class sensibilities of Stoke Newington.

Clapton

Squeezed between Hackney Central and Walthamstow Marshes, Clapton is one of London's most neglected neighbourhoods, but it doesn't entirely deserve its gloomy reputation. There are plenty of genteel terraced streets between the faded council blocks, including the gorgeous Georgian terraces around Sutton House. Nevertheless, the area could clearly do with some love.

Clapton is divided in two by the massive Lea Bridge roundabout; Lower Clapton has the best of the shops and amenities, while Upper Clapton has the main train station. Commuter trains bound for Liverpool Street also pass through Hackney Downs in the south of the district. Parking is in short supply, and the tell-tale piles of glass next to empty parking bays provide a compelling reason to use public transport. Frequent day

and night buses connect Clapton with the City and surrounding districts.

Much of Clapton's reputation derives from its crime statistics. The main drag, Clapton Road – otherwise known as Murder Mile – has seen more than a dozen fatal shootings in the past five years. Clapton even featured in a movie, *Bullet Boy*, about gun crime in the capital. Although the risk to ordinary residents is pretty low, Clapton has seen less of a middle-class influx than other parts of Hackney. All that may change with the construction of the Olympic Village on the other side of the Lee Valley. Property investors are already eyeing up the Victorian townhouses around Upper Clapton Road; the area could easily be another Victoria Park (*see p57*) by 2012.

Perks of living in Clapton today include the child-friendly activities run by the National Trust at Sutton House, the proximity of the revitalised Hackney town centre, and the green open spaces of Springfield Park and Walthamstow Marshes. Although this latter is across the River Lee in Waltham Forest (*see p283*), 'Ackney kids can still take advantage of the ice-rink, riding school and rowing club, and walkers can stroll up to Springfield Marina to look at houseboats and feed the swans.

Restaurants & cafés

The Turkish/Kurdish and Vietnamese communities have stamped their mark on the borough. Between them, they provide most of the culinary interest – especially at

Hackney

an affordable level – in the area. From Dalston Kingsland rail station up the A10 to Stoke Newington Church Street, you are in the Turkish and Kurdish heart of Hackney. Intense competition means that restaurants and cafés come and go, and there's a constant race to provide different services and dishes. Try Bodrum Café, Dervish Bistro, Sölen, Tava, Testi and Turku (for meze with folk music). Café Z Bar mixes elements of café, bar, gallery and restaurant. Both 19 Numara Bos Cirrik II and the original branch down the road in Dalston do amazing belt-busting grills. Also, keep an eye open for ever-popular Best Turkish Kebab (superior versions of the English Turkish takeaway), and pâtisserie Özantepliler (perfect baklava). Old trooper Istanbul Iskembecisi stays open until 5am daily; the lengthy menu ranges from tripe soup (that gives the restaurant its name) through to a varied choice of meze. Mangal II is a step upmarket from the rather spartan (and now legendary) original Mangal Ocakbaşı round the corner and the Mangal Turkish Pizza sister across the way.

Away from the main drag, on Green Lanes, there's Beyti (which offers a slightly different northern Anatolian selection), and great fish specialist Sariyer Balik. A useful outpost on Mare Street is Anatolia Ocakbaşı, while smart newcomer Savarona can be found in Shoreditch.

The greatest concentration of Vietnamese restaurants is at the southern end of Kingsland Road. Au Lac, Hanoi Café, Loong Kee, Tay Do Café and pioneer Viet Hoa all provide excellent meals at low prices, but Sông Quê is still our favourite. Just around the corner on Old Street is Cây Tre, another contender for the top slot. Elsewhere, others worth checking out are Huong-Viet, Green Papaya and Tre Viet (the latter two also handy for the Hackney Empire).

In contrast, this is one London borough where Indian restaurants make a poor showing. Rasa in Stoke Newington is a vibrant, South Indian vegetarian exception to the rule; it also happens to be the best restaurant in Stokey, closely followed by its meat- and seafood-serving sibling, Rasa Travancore, across the road. Other choices are Mesclun (Mediterranean), Il Bacio (Italian), Itto (Oriental) and Blue Legume (all-day café) – all of them neighbourhood favourites, but not worth crossing town for.

Decent locals, dotted around the borough, include Faulkner's fish and chip shop and restaurant, quirky international joint LMNT, family-focused café Frizzante@City Farm, and Shanghai (a refurbished pie and mash shop serving Chinese food). Still serving pie and mash is F Cooke (branches on Hoxton Street and Broadway Market).

Gastropubs are just beginning to make an impact: the Fox Dining Room and, more recently, the Princess hold sway on Paul Street in Shoreditch; the Cat & Mutton on Broadway Market is a great local hangout. Also on this street are two very different Latin American restaurants, the pan-American Armadillo and Argentinian grill-house Santa Maria del Buen Ayre.

Inevitably, the most West End-like restaurants are in Shoreditch; the best-known is Jamie Oliver's Fifteen, but for culinary excellence there are other serious contenders. Eyre Brothers offers high-quality Iberian food in grown-up surroundings, the Great Eastern Dining Room (part of Will Ricker's stylish empire) serves a menu of pan-Asian dishes, while the Rivington Bar & Grill has a British slant. The Real Greek and its less formal branch Mezedopolio serve classy Greek dishes. At a less elevated (and less expensive) level, Cantaloupe is a landmark Shoreditch venue – an open-plan bar-cum-restaurant offering Spanish/North African food and good tunes; Cru is another lively bar-restaurant. On a different tip, Hoxton Apprentice trains student chefs in-house, the restaurant then provides them with an opportunity to exhibit their skills.

Anatolia Ocakbaşı *253 Mare Street, E8 3NS (8986 2223).*
Armadillo *41 Broadway Market, E8 4PH (7249 3633/www.armadillorestaurant.co.uk).*
Au Lac *104 Kingsland Road, E2 8DP (7033 0588/www.aulac.co.uk).*
Il Bacio *61 Stoke Newington Church Street, N16 0AR (7249 3833).*
Best Turkish Kebab *125 Stoke Newington Road, N16 8BT (7254 7642).*
Beyti *113 Green Lanes, N16 9DA (7704 3165).*
Blue Legume *101 Stoke Newington Church Street, N16 0UD (7923 1303).*
Bodrum Café *61 Stoke Newington High Street, N16 8EL (7254 6464).*
Café Z Bar *58 Stoke Newington High Street, N16 7PB (7275 7523).*
Cantaloupe *35-42 Charlotte Road, EC2A 3PD (7613 4411/www.cantaloupe.co.uk).*
Cat & Mutton *76 Broadway Market, E8 4QJ (7254 5599).*

Animals, green spaces and an award-winning café: **Hackney City Farm**. *See p82.*

Cây Tre *301 Old Street, EC1V 9LA (7729 8662).*
F Cooke *9 Broadway Market, E8 4PH (7254 6458).*
F Cooke *150 Hoxton Street, N1 6SH (7729 7718).*
Cru *2-4 Rufus Street, N1 6PE (7729 5252/ www.cru.uk.com).*
Dervish Bistro *15 Stoke Newington Church Street, N16 0NX (7923 9999).*
Eyre Brothers *70 Leonard Street, EC2A 4QX (7613 5346/www.eyrebrothers.co.uk).*
Faulkner's *424-426 Kingsland Road, E8 4AA (7254 6152).*
Fifteen *15 Westland Place, N1 7LP (0871 330 1515/www.fifteenrestaurant.com).*
Fox Dining Room *28 Paul Street, EC2A 4LB (7729 5708).*
Frizzante@City Farm *Hackney City Farm, 1A Goldsmith's Row, E2 8QA (7739 2266/ www.frizzanteltd.co.uk).*
Great Eastern Dining Room *54-56 Great Eastern Street, EC2A 3QR (7613 4545/ www.greateasterndining.co.uk).*
Green Papaya *191 Mare Street, E8 3QE (8985 5486/www.greenpapaya.co.uk).*
Hanoi Café *98 Kingsland Road, E2 8DP (7729 5610/www.hanoicafe.co.uk).*
Hoxton Apprentice *16 Hoxton Square, N1 6NT (7739 6022/www.hoxton apprentice.com).*
Huong-Viet *An Viet House, 12-14 Englefield Road, N1 4LS (7249 0877).*
Istanbul Iskembecisi *9 Stoke Newington Road, N16 8BH (7254 7291).*

Itto *226 Stoke Newington High Street, N16 7HU (7275 8827).*
LMNT *316 Queensbridge Road, E8 3NH (7249 6727/www.lmnt.co.uk).*
Loong Kee *134G Kingsland Road, E2 8DY (7729 8344).*
Mangal II *4 Stoke Newington Road, N16 8BH (7254 7888).*
Mangal Ocakbaşı *10 Arcola Street, E8 2DJ (7275 8981/www.mangal1.com).*
Mangal Turkish Pizza *27 Stoke Newington Road, N16 8BJ (7254 6999).*
Mesclun *24 Stoke Newington Church Street, N16 0LU (7249 5029/www.mesclun restaurant.com).*
Mezedopolio *14 Hoxton Market, N1 6HG (7739 8212/www.therealgreek.co.uk).*
19 Numara Bos Cirrik *34 Stoke Newington Road, N16 7XJ (7249 0400).*
19 Numara Bos Cirrik II *194 Stoke Newington High Street, N16 7JD (7249 9111).*
Özantepliler *30 Stoke Newington Road, N16 7XJ (7241 1514).*
Princess *76-78 Paul Street, EC2A 4NE (7729 9270).*
Rasa *55 Stoke Newington Church Street, N16 0AR (7249 0344/www.rasarestaurants.com).*
Rasa Travancore *56 Stoke Newington Church Street, N16 0NB (7249 1340/www.rasa restaurants.com).*
The Real Greek *15 Hoxton Market, N1 6HG (7739 8212/www.therealgreek.com).*
Rivington Bar & Grill *28-30 Rivington Street, EC2A 3DZ (7729 7053/www.rivington grill.co.uk).*

Santa María del Buen Ayre *50 Broadway Market, E8 4QJ (7275 9900/www.buenayre.co.uk).*
Sariyer Balik *56 Green Lanes, N16 9NH (7275 7681).*
Savarona *66 Great Eastern Street, EC2A 3JT (7739 2888/www.savarona.co.uk).*
Shanghai *41 Kingsland High Street, E8 2JS (7254 2878).*
Sölen *84 Stoke Newington High Street, N16 7PA (7923 3822).*
Sông Quê *134 Kingsland Road, E2 8DY (7613 3222).*
Tava *17 Stoke Newington Road, N16 8BH (7249 3666).*
Tay Do Café *65 Kingsland Road, E2 8AG (7729 7223).*
Testi *38 Stoke Newington High Street, N16 7XJ (7249 7151).*
Tre Viet *251 Mare Street, E8 3NS (8533 7390).*
Turku *79 Stoke Newington Road, N16 8AD (7254 0583).*
Viet Hoa *70-72 Kingsland Road, E2 8DP (7729 8293).*

Bars & pubs

Yes, the fins, mullets and bangs that once defined Hoxton and Shoreditch have long been cut, with many of the über-cool moving on entirely, but the Shoreditch Triangle – formed by Old Street, Great Eastern Street and Shoreditch High Street – still has plenty to offer as Hackney's focal nightspot. Soulless money-maker bars like Bluu and Zigrid around Hoxton Square draw the uninitiated; across the square, trendy mothership Mother Bar (attached to nightclub 333) has a more downbeat style and friendly vibe.

Round the corner, Shoreditch High Street brings the good stuff: near-perfect Bar Kick, with its authentic table football tables and unceasingly upbeat vibe; funky dim-sum-and-cocktail bar Drunken Monkey; and one-time railway warehouse Light Bar & Restaurant, with its large courtyard to take spill-over in the warm months. Aesthetes will love Loungelover, a glorious riot of camp and gaudy decor; the more subdued drinker might prefer to trip back towards Old Street for an endearing trio of boozers, the Bricklayer's Arms, Barley Mow and, north-east towards Islington, the Wenlock Arms. Turning from Old Street on to Kingsland Road reveals a run of popular bars: best are pulsating Caribbean venue Anda de Bridge (under a bridge, naturally) and understated, signless Catch (or Catch 22, depending on who you ask).

In Hackney proper, pickings are slimmer, but 291 – once a church – has to be one of the most visually impressive bars in London; the Marie Lloyd Bar is an interesting recent addition to the Hackney Empire, while the Dove Freehouse and Pembury Tavern are good choices for real ale lovers. In London Fields, the Pub on the Park attracts hordes in good weather, while the nearby Prince George is a great example of an unpretentious local pub.

Northwards to Stoke Newington, Church Street offers most of the action: friendly old boozer the Auld Shillelagh (order Guinness or go somewhere else); matey Rose & Crown; and French bistro-style Fox Reformed, with its range of liqueurs and eccentric crowd. Elsewhere, the Shakespeare is pure Stokey: raffish, lefty, vaguely bohemian… but friendly and fun. Clapton's a different story altogether. Most of the pubs are forbidding boozers that have seen better days – though the Eclipse on Elderfield Road is a reasonable sanctuary from the gruesome surrounds.

Anda de Bridge *42-44 Kingsland Road, E2 8DA (7739 3863/www.andadebridge.com).*
Auld Shillelagh *105 Stoke Newington Church Street, N16 0UD (7249 5951).*
Bar Kick *127 Shoreditch High Street, E1 6JE (7739 8700/www.cafekick.co.uk).*
Barley Mow *127 Curtain Road, EC2A 3BX (7729 3910).*
Bluu *1 Hoxton Square, N1 6NU (7613 2793/ www.bluu.co.uk).*
Bricklayer's Arms *63 Charlotte Road, EC2A 3PE (7739 5245).*
Catch *22 Kingsland Road, E2 8DA (7729 6097/www.thecatchbar.com).*
Dove Freehouse *24-28 Broadway Market, E8 4QJ (7275 7617/www.belgianbars.com).*
Drunken Monkey *222 Shoreditch High Street, E1 6PJ (7392 9606/www.thedrunken monkey.info).*
Eclipse *57 Elderfield Road, E5 0LF (8986 1591).*
Fox Reformed *176 Stoke Newington Church Street, N16 0JL (7254 5975/www.fox-reformed. co.uk).*
Light Bar & Restaurant *233 Shoreditch High Street, E1 6PJ (7247 8989/www.thelight e1.com).*
Loungelover *1 Whitby Street, E1 6JU (7012 1234/www.loungelover.co.uk).*
Marie Lloyd Bar *289 Mare Street, E8 1EJ (8510 4500/www.hackneyempire.co.uk).*
Mother Bar *333 Old Street, EC1V 9LE (7739 5949/www.333mother.com).*
Pembury Tavern *90 Amhurst Road, E8 1JH (8986 8597/www.individualpubs.co.uk/pembury).*
Prince George *40 Parkholme Road, E8 3AG (7254 6060).*

Pub on the Park *19 Martello Street, E8 3PE (7275 9586).*
Reliance *336 Old Street, EC1V 9DR (7729 6888).*
Rose & Crown *199 Stoke Newington Church Street, N16 9ES (7254 7497).*
Shakespeare *57 Allen Road, N16 8RY (7254 4190).*
333 *333 Old Street, EC1V 9LE (7739 5949/ www.333mother.com).*
291 *291 Hackney Road, E2 8NA (7613 5676/ www.291gallery.com).*
Wenlock Arms *26 Wenlock Road, N1 7TA (7608 3406/www.wenlock-arms.co.uk).*
Zigfrid *11 Hoxton Square, N1 6NU (7613 1988/www.zigfrid.com).*

Shops

While no one could accuse Hackney of being a glam destination, the borough does certain things very well and, in pockets, the retail choice gets more interesting all the time.

The Turkish/Kurdish shops and bakeries (dotted everywhere, but especially around Green Lanes, along Kingsland Road into Stoke Newington High Street, and notably at the Turkish Food Centre on Ridley Road) give a welcome blast of Mediterranean colour and flavour. In the Vietnamese enclave along Mare Street (Hackney is home to the largest Vietnamese community in London) are numerous small supermarkets, such as Huong-Nam, the Vietnam and Lê-Mi. For the ultimate Vietnamese experience, London Star Night Supermarket & Video is the place to go. Not only does it stock fresh seafood, but the shelves are also full of cooking utensils, miniature Buddhist altars and Vietnamese pop music. Dalston's crowded Ridley Road Market is immensely popular with the area's African and Caribbean community. Here you'll find everything from specialist hair products to bags of gari (a type of Nigerian grits) alongside fruit and veg.

The sudden growth and popularity of the Saturday food and crafts market on Broadway Market highlights the changing nature of parts of the borough – here, Hackney's wealthier residents stock up on artisan olive oils, own-made jams and real bread; stand-out shops on this patch are French deli L'Eau à la Bouche, shoe and accessory shop Black Truffle and funky florist Rebel Rebel. The other two established middle-class shopping enclaves are around Lauriston Road (covered in the

Basketball at **Space**. *See p84.*

Tower Hamlets chapter; *see p63*) and Stoke Newington Church Street.

In N16 the mix of shops includes Fresh & Wild (part of the organic and natural foods supermarket chain; this branch has a café), various child-and-parent-centred outlets (Born, Popcorn, Route 73 Kids), a farmers' market (10am-2.30pm Sat), vintage and second-hand shops, and the likes of Hub boutique. Just around the corner, on Stoke Newington High Street, is the independent Stoke Newington Bookshop.

However, the most dynamic retail action takes place down in Shoreditch. Start is the glossiest of a bunch of groovy boutiques, but staff are very welcoming and there are free makeovers available at their Becca cosmetics counter. Relax Garden, no-one and Hoxton Boutique are also worth checking out. Otherwise, the stand-out store is SCP, one of London's leading design stores for expertly sourced contemporary furniture, lighting, ceramics, glass, textiles and accessories, plus some excellent design books. Also worth a peek are Smallfish (electronica, experimental and mainstream dance on vinyl and CD, plus a great little café in the basement), and delis Leila's and the Food Hall.

Finally, randomly dotted about the borough, but useful in their different ways, are North One Garden Centre, the Burberry Factory Shop and London Fields Cycles.

Black Truffle *74 Broadway Market, E8 4QJ (7923 9450/www.blacktruffle.com).*
Born *168 Stoke Newington Church Street, N16 0JL (0845 130 2676/www.borndirect.com).*
Broadway Market *Broadway Market, E8 (www.broadwaymarket.co.uk).*
Burberry Factory Shop *29-53 Chatham Place, E9 6LP (8328 4287).*
L'Eau à la Bouche *49 Broadway Market, E8 4PH (7923 0600/www.labouche.co.uk).*
Food Hall *374-378 Old Street, EC1V 9LT (7729 6005).*
Fresh & Wild *32-40 Stoke Newington Church Street, N16 0LU (7254 2332/www.freshand wild.com).*
Hoxton Boutique *2 Hoxton Street, N1 6NG (7684 2083/www.hoxtonboutique.co.uk).*
Hub *49 & 88 Stoke Newington Church Street, N16 0AR (7254 4494).*
Huong-Nam Supermarket *185-187 Mare Street, E8 3RD (8985 8050).*
Leila's *17 Calvert Avenue, E2 7JP (7729 9789).*
Lê-Mi *257A Mare Street, E8 3NS (8533 1020).*
London Fields Cycles *281 Mare Street, E8 1PJ (8525 0077/www.londonfieldscycles.co.uk).*
London Star Night Supermarket & Video *213 Mare Street, E8 3QE (8985 2949).*
no-one *1 Kingsland Road, E2 8AA (7613 5314/www.no-one.co.uk).*
North One Garden Centre *The Old Button Factory, 25A Englefield Road, N1 4EU (7923 3553).*
Popcorn *121 Stoke Newington Church Street, N16 0UH (7241 1333).*
Rebel Rebel *5 Broadway Market, E8 4PH (7254 4487/www.rebelrebel.co.uk).*
Relax Garden *40 Kingsland Road, E2 8DA (7033 1881/www.relaxgarden.com).*
Ridley Road Market *Ridley Road, off Kingsland High Street, E8.*
Route 73 Kids *92 Stoke Newington Church Street, N16 0AP (7923 7873).*
SCP *135-139 Curtain Road, EC2A 3BX (7739 1869/www.scp.co.uk).*
Smallfish *329 Old Street, EC1V 9LE (7739 2252/www.smallfish.co.uk).*
Start *42-44 Rivington Street, EC2A 3BN (7729 3334/www.start-london.com).*
Stoke Newington Bookshop *159 Stoke Newington High Street, N16 0NY (7249 2808).*
Stoke Newington Farmers' Market *William Patten School, Stoke Newington Church Street, N16 0NX (7502 7588/www.growing communities.org).*
Turkish Food Centre *89 Ridley Road, E8 2NH (7254 6754).*
Vietnam Supermarket *193A Mare Street, E8 3QE (8525 1655).*

Arts & attractions

Cinemas & theatres
Arcola Theatre *27 Arcola Street, E8 2DJ (7503 1646/www.arcolatheatre.com).* Enterprising fringe theatre.
Hackney Empire *291 Mare Street, E8 1EJ (8985 2424/www.hackneyempire.co.uk).* Restored Edwardian music hall; shows run from stand-up comedy to Shakespeare.
Rio Cinema *107 Kingsland High Street, E8 2PB (7241 9410/www.riocinema.org.uk).*

Galleries & museums
Flowers East *82 Kingsland Road, E2 8DP (7920 7777/www.flowerseast.com).* Contemporary art gallery.
Geffrye Museum *136 Kingsland Road, E2 8EA (7739 9893/www.geffrye-museum.org.uk).* Domestic interiors from 1600s to the present, housed in Georgian almshouses. The annual Christmas exhibition is a must-see.
Hackney Museum *Technology & Learning Centre, 1 Reading Lane, off Mare Street, E8 1GQ (8356 3500/www.hackney.gov.uk).* Celebrates the cultural diversity of the area.
Sutton House *2 & 4 Homerton High Street, E9 6JQ (8986 2264/www.nationaltrust.org.uk).* This atmospheric red-brick Tudor mansion is the oldest home in east London.
Victoria Miro Gallery *16 Wharf Road, N1 7RW (7336 8109/www.victoria-miro.com).* Contemporary art gallery.
White Cube *48 Hoxton Square, N1 6PB (7930 5373/www.whitecube.com).* Contemporary art gallery.

Music & comedy venues
Comedy Café *66-68 Rivington Street, EC2A 3AY (7739 5706/www.comedycafe.co.uk).*
Dalston Jazz Bar *4 Bradbury Street, N16 8JN (7254 9728).*
Vortex Jazz Club *11 Gillett Street, N16 8JH (7254 4097/www.vortexjazz.co.uk).* One-time Stoke Newington staple, now moved to a new site in Dalston; no longer as characterful, but certainly smarter, with improved sightlines.

Open spaces
Abney Park Cemetery & Nature Reserve *Stoke Newington High Street, N16 (www.abney-park.org.uk).* Decaying monuments add romance to a nature reserve where the foliage is now in ascendance over the long-dead.
Clissold Park *Green Lanes, N4 & Stoke Newington Church Street, N16 (www.clissold park.com).* The much-loved green heart of Stokie.
Hackney City Farm *1A Goldsmiths Row, E2 8QA (7729 6381/www.hackneycityfarm.co.uk).*
Hackney Downs *Downs Park Road, E5.*
Hackney Marshes *Homerton Road, E9.* The largest concentration of football pitches in Europe.

Clissold Park

Haggerston Park *1 Queensbridge Road, E2.*
London Fields *Richmond Road, Lansdowne Drive, Westgate Street & London Fields West Side, E8.*
Mabley Green *Homerton Road, E9.*
Shoreditch Park *New North Road, N1.*
Springfield Park *Springfield Lane, Upper Clapton, E8.* Extensive park backing on to the River Lea, with tennis courts, cricket pitch, nature reserve and a very popular café.
Well Street Common *Victoria Park Road, E9.*

Sport & fitness

The management of most of Hackney's council-owned centres was taken over by Greenwich Leisure in autumn 2005. Alongside these, Hackney has a smattering of private clubs, from top-notch health and beauty salons to places such as Sunstone, a secluded haven for women, and the internationally renowned martial arts studio Bob Breen Academy. Canoeing and sailing take place at the West Reservoir Sports Centre, while in the old waterworks next door is the Castle, an impressive indoor climbing wall.

Gyms & leisure centres
Britannia Health & Fitness Centre *40 Hyde Road, N1 5JU (7729 4485/www.gll.org).*
Clissold Leisure Centre *63 Clissold Road, N16 9EX (www.gll.org).* Due to reopen in summer 2006.
Kings Hall Leisure Centre *39 Lower Clapton Road, E5 0NU (8985 2158/www.gll.org).*
Queensbridge Sports & Community Centre *30 Holly Street, E8 3XW (7923 7773/www.qscc.co.uk).*
Space Centre *Falkirk Street, N1 6HF (7613 9525).* Private.
Sunstone Health & Leisure Club for Women *16 Northwold Road, N16 7HR (7923 1991/www.sunstonewomen.com).* Private.

Other facilities
Bob Breen Academy *16 Hoxton Square, N1 6NT (7729 5789/www.bobbreen.co.uk).* Private martial arts studio.
Castle Climbing Centre *Green Lanes, N4 2HA (8211 7000/www.castle-climbing.co.uk).*
West Reservoir Sports Centre *Green Lanes, N4 2HA (8442 8116/www.gll.org).*

Schools

WHAT THE PARENTS SAY:

‘My daughter has ended up going to Gladesmore School in Tottenham. We are incredibly impressed, but it's in Haringey, not Hackney. A lot of parents send their children out of the borough, either to private schools or to the Latymer School in Enfield (*see p292*). Latymer is a mixed grammar school with an entrance exam and a high academic reputation, and kids from all over north London compete to get into it.

All the middle-class parents want their kids to go to the Stoke Newington School, an arts and media college. It has a great image but seems to be cruising on its reputation somewhat. The Mossbourne Community Academy opened two years ago, housed in a new Norman Foster building. It's early days, but I haven't heard wonderful things about it. There are some good girls' schools, particularly Clapton Girls'. There's not much for boys – Homerton College of Technology is expected to close soon because not enough people put it down as a first choice on their selection lists.

Hackney has a lot to do when it comes to secondary schools. There has been under-investment and although two or three new schools are due to open in the next few years, there just isn't enough secondary provision in the borough.’
Jim Heinemann, father of two, Stoke Newington

Primary
There are 55 state primary schools in Hackney, 11 of which are church schools and two of which are Jewish schools. There are also 21 independent primaries, including 18 faith schools. For more information, see www.learningtrust.co.uk and www.ofsted.gov.uk.

Secondary
Cardinal Pole RC School *Kenworthy Road, E9 5RB (8985 5150).*
Clapton Girls' Technology College *Laura Place, Lower Clapton Road, E5 0RB (8985 6641/www.clapton.hackney.sch.uk).* Girls only.
Hackney Free & Parochial *Paragon Road, E9 6NR (8985 2430/www.hackneyfree. hackney.sch.uk).*
Haggerston School *Weymouth Terrace, E2 8LS (7739 7324/www.haggerston. hackney.sch.uk).* Girls only.
Homerton College of Technology *Homerton Row, E9 6EB (8986 8144/www. homerton.hackney.sch.uk).* Boys only (expected to close summer 2006).
Mossbourne Community Academy *100 Downs Park Road, E5 8JY (8525 5200/ www.mossbourne.hackney.sch.uk).*
Our Lady's Convent High School *6-16 Amhurst Park, N16 5AF (8800 2158/ www.ourladys.hackney.sch.uk).* Girls only; mixed sixth form.

Petchey Academy *Shacklewell Lane, E8 2EY (7254 8722/www.petcheyacademy.org.uk).* New school, opens September 2006.
Skinners' Company's School for Girls *www.skinnerscompanys.hackney.sch.uk;* Lower School *Mount Pleasant Lane, E5 9JG (8806 3128);* Upper School *117 Stamford Hill, N16 5RS (8800 7411).* Girls only.
Stoke Newington School *Clissold Road, N16 9EU (7254 0548/www.sns.hackney.sch.uk).*
Yesodey Hatorah Senior for Girls *Egerton Road, N16 6UB (8826 5500).* Jewish; girls only.
Yesodey Hatorah Senior for Boys *224 Amhurst Park, N16 5AE (8800 8612).* Jewish; boys only.

Property

WHAT THE AGENTS SAY:

❝Hackney has a very diverse range of properties – from period to new-build – and a lively ethnic mix, largely Turkish, Vietnamese and African. It's close to the City, there are good bus connections, and it has good venues like the Rio Cinema and the Hackney Empire. You've also got Broadway Market and Ridley Road Market. We've recently had an influx of people moving from neighbouring boroughs due to the cheaper prices, so the area is becoming more gentrified. Hackney is shedding its old image of high crime, unemployment, lack of infrastructure and poor-performing schools. We still have some problems, obviously, but it is getting better. Dalston is set to be on the tube by 2010. The Olympics will have some impact – there will be more jobs and more housing (both shared-ownership and private). Overall, it's a good area to live in and a good place in which to invest.❞
Tim Gorgulu, Courtneys, Hackney

❝We have a very high rate of new families in Stoke Newington; Church Street has an incredible number of shops catering specifically for newborns. First-time buyers find it hard to get on the property ladder, though. A lot of people who do buy tend to work in the City. For the price of a house in Tottenham, you'd only get a one-bed flat in Stokey. Clissold Park is nice and Church Street is very popular – it has loads of bars and

restaurants. Stokey isn't far from becoming another Islington. There's no tube, but the No.73 bus is excellent – it goes through Islington and into central London.❞
Shakeel Bucktowar, Bairstow Eves, Stoke Newington

Average property prices
Detached £297,343
Semi-detached £332,510
Terraced £259,758
Flat £178,129

Local estate agents
Bunch & Duke *360 Mare Street, E8 1HT (8986 3521/www.bunchandduke.com).*
Courtneys *544 Kingsland Road, E8 4AH (7275 8000/www.courtneys-estates.com).*
Excel Properties *140 Albion Road, N16 9PA (7923 2211/www.xlproperties.com).*
Hamilton Fox Estate Agents *326 Mare Street, E8 1HA (8985 5522/www.hamiltonfox.co.uk).*
Homefinders *86 Amhurst Road, E8 1JH (8533 6461/www.home-finders-uk.com).*
Phillips Estates *7 Stoke Newington Church Street, N16 0NX (7241 0292/www.phillips estates.co.uk).*
Robert Alan Homes *170 Victoria Park Road, E9 7HD (8986 2222/www.robertalanhomes.com).*
Shaw & Co *29 Lower Clapton Road, E5 0NS (8986 7327/www.shawco.com).*

Other information

Council
London Borough of Hackney Council *Town Hall, Mare Street, E8 1EA (8356 5000/ www.hackney.gov.uk).*

Hospitals
Homerton University Hospital *Homerton Row, E9 6SR (8510 5555/www.homerton.nhs.uk).*

Legal services
Dalston CAB *491-493 Kingsland Road, E8 4AU (0870 126 4013/www.adviceguide.org.uk).*
Hackney Community Law Centre *8 Lower Clapton Road, E5 0PD (8985 8364).*
Mare Street CAB *236-238 Mare Street, E8 1HE (0870 126 4013/www.adviceguide.org.uk).*

Local newspapers
Hackney Gazette *7790 8822/www.hackney gazette.co.uk.*
Hackney Today *8356 3275/www.hackney.gov.uk.* Distributed free by the council; available online.
N16 The Mag *7249 9943/www.n16mag.com.*

Allotments
Hackney Allotment Society *Secretary, c/o 41 Dynevor Road, N16 0DL (www.hackney allotments.org.uk).*

COUNCIL TAX		
A	up to £40,000	**£835.38**
B	£40,001-£52,000	**£974.61**
C	£52,001-£68,000	**£1,113.84**
D	£68,001-£88,000	**£1,253.07**
E	£88,001-£120,000	**£1,531.53**
F	£120,001-£160,000	**£1,809.99**
G	£160,001-£320,000	**£2,088.45**
H	over £320,000	**£2,506.14**

Hackney

'Haringey gets into the news for all the wrong reasons, and not even the council seems to know how to spell its name properly. But you won't find a better kebab than on Green Lanes, and Alexandra Park has the best view in town.'

Daniel Trilling, student and resident

Haringey

Embracing inner-city enclaves and outer London 'burbs, Haringey is a borough of juxtapositions. Here you can find the middle-class bohemia of Crouch End, the multicultural variety of Green Lanes and Stroud Green Road, and some of the city's prime music sites at Finsbury Park and Ally Pally.

Neighbourhoods

Finsbury Park
and Stroud Green

Finsbury Park is a tricky area to classify; this part of town straddles the border with Islington borough (*see p98*), and while its main roads are more hectic than a conventional suburb, it feels like a route to somewhere else. As one local resident put it, 'one of the best things about Finsbury Park is the ease with which one can leave.'

Not that the area is without certain lures of its own. Dating back to 1869, the council-run park itself is a destination, thanks mainly to the numerous outdoor festivals it hosts – notably annual Irish roots celebration the Fleadh, but also

events such as Big Gay Out, and gigs from the likes of Oasis and Kiss. Curfews are strict, so don't expect late-night revelry. As this guide went to press, the park was in the final stages of a £5m restoration programme, bringing a new café, upgraded tennis courts and extensive re-landscaping. The open spaces are popular for softball games, and a Sunday market was launched here in late 2005.

Encompassing Finsbury Park's train, tube and bus terminus, Station Place is a fairly grotty hub of activity, currently undergoing a 21st-century makeover. Its Arsenal World of Sport 'megastore' reminds you that you're in Gooner territory. Across the road, Rowans Tenpin Bowl provides pleasingly old-fashioned entertainment. Finsbury Park Mosque, a modern building,

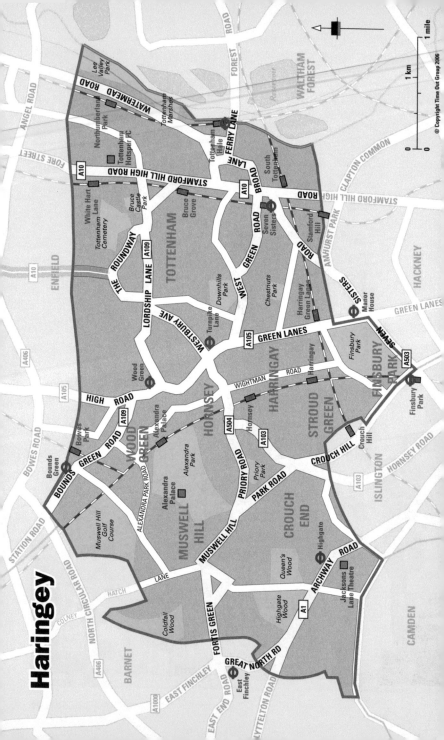

has gained unfortunate notoriety in the past few years through its links to controversial hook-handed cleric Sheikh Abu Hamza.

Local amenities are concentrated on Stroud Green Road (on the Islington border) – the heart of a popular residential area mixing Victorian and Edwardian buildings and council blocks, connecting Finsbury Park to Crouch End. You only need to look at the local shops to sense how international the district is, from the multicoloured displays of the wig stores at the Finsbury Park end, to traditional boozers flanking late-opening Turkish and Afro-Caribbean grocers, Italian delis, Latin American and Thai restaurants. By day, the choice of shopping is impressive; and these family-run businesses make for a distinctly homely buzz in the evenings.

Crouch End

In the horror spoof *Shaun of the Dead*, suburban Crouch End is terrorised by swarms of the undead. In reality, it's not zombies you'll run screaming to avoid, but mums at the helms of their titanium three-wheeler buggies; venture out during the daily school run, and the danger of being unceremoniously mown down is high.

Crouch End is a hotbed of middle-class bohemia, where media types, actors and musicians, drawn by the laid-back vibe and exclusively priced townhouses, build their family nests (even Bob Dylan looked for a house here in the mid 1990s). Things become increasingly less polished further up Tottenham Lane towards Turnpike Lane tube; Crouch End's residential smugness is kept in check by the scattering of looming estates on its fringes.

Radiating from the neighbourhood's historic Clock Tower – a locally prized red-brick monument that dates from 1895 – are streets lined with browsable shops and restaurants. Residents fought against the invasion of Starbucks, Costa and their ilk, only succumbing in 2004. Nevertheless, shopping here retains an independent feel. Food-wise the place is a bubbling stew-pot of multicultural culinary choice, and while buzzy nightlife is not a local priority, Crouch End is home to one of London's finest comedy clubs, Downstairs at the King's Head.

On the whole, though, the district is better geared towards healthy living than boozy nights out, offering a good selection of gyms, public pools and tennis courts. Green spaces are also within easy reach – which, if nothing else, legitimise the use of those ubiquitous off-road buggies. Alexandra Park backs on to the top end of Hornsey, while Priory Park (where a new skate park is to be built) lies north of the Clock Tower. The sylvan Highgate Wood and Queen's Wood are only a short walk away, easily reached via the equally lovely old railway line, the Parkland Walk.

In fact, Crouch End lacks only two things: a proper-sized supermarket (residents make do with the much-maligned Budgens, a small M&S food store and a Tesco Express) and a tube station. Some would suggest the neighbourhood's cosy atmosphere is a reasonable trade-off. Besides, with a range of handy bus routes serving rail stations at Finsbury Park, Hornsey and Crouch Hill, Northern Line stations at Highgate and Archway, and the Piccadilly and Victoria Lines at Finsbury Park all within a mile and a half, getting around is no real problem.

Highs & Lows

▲ **Great gigs** Alexandra Palace is a popular venue for live events, while Finsbury Park is famous as the site of outdoor festivals such as Fleadh
Indie shops Crouch End retains a butcher, baker and greengrocer, and you can't beat the riches of Green Lanes and Stroud Green Road for sheer international variety
Park life Ally Pally's manicured parkland and the ancient oaks of Highgate and Queen's Woods are great draws

Impoverished pockets Wood Green and Tottenham compete for the title of Haringey's grottiest neighbourhood – though there are plans to improve the latter
Green Lanes traffic Though Green Lanes is unrivalled for its excellent kebab shops, riding a bus (or driving) down this traffic-choked road is an exercise in human endurance
▼ **Spelling woes** Haringey or Harringay or Harringey or Haringay… a headache for letter-writers everywhere

Muswell Hill

Sitting atop a steep hill that leads up from Crouch End, Muswell Hill is its bigger, more mature sibling. While Crouch End is full of prams and trendy young parents, Muswell Hill is where such folk move when the kids have grown a little older. Immigration from boroughs like Islington with measurably poorer schools is very common.

Formerly part of the forest of Middlesex – which explains the ancient tree still standing in the grounds of Alexandra Palace – this hill-top site has been affording residents amazing views over the capital since it was first inhabited in the 12th century. Although Muswell Hill is tubeless, it is still well connected (situated just off the A1 and on the cusp of the North Circular; a train serves Alexandra Palace and buses run to nearby underground stations at Highgate, Finsbury Park and Hampstead). The bustling, villagey Broadway features a Tardis-like Sainsbury's and is dotted with homely independent shops and restaurants.

Aside from a beautiful, though somewhat undervalued, grade II listed art deco Odeon, Alexandra Palace is the area's foremost entertainment hub. The ornate building was opened in 1873, but had to be rebuilt after burning to the ground just 16 days after the grand opening. Reopened two years later, it went on to become the site of the first BBC television broadcast in 1936 (the BBC still uses the building for telecommunications). There's an ice rink at the building's north end, but the palace's main purpose is as an exhibition centre. And having hosted legendary gigs in its past – most notably by Pink Floyd in 1967 – Ally Pally is once again a top London concert venue.

Wood Green and Bounds Green

Wood Green isn't pretty, based as it is around a high road that is busy, dirty and habitually frequented by drunks, screaming schoolkids and assorted crazies. The district's prime attraction, its Shopping City, only adds to the clone-town feel of a high street that is otherwise overpopulated by pound shops. It is, of course, easy to be snotty about an area that is one of the poorest in the capital. Yet while other such neighbourhoods have an edgy vibrancy (look further down Green Lanes, to the 24-hour bustle between Turnpike Lane and Manor House), Wood Green really could do with a bit of a clean-up.

Bounds Green is the gateway between the grimness of 'Wooders' and the staid (if comparatively safe) suburbia of Palmers Green. Like PG, it's primarily residential and, apart from streets of fairly large terraced houses, there's very little going on. A smattering of takeaways and grocery shops mark the tube station as a tiny hub, but the neighbourhood's far from buzzing.

Harringay

Cut in two by railway tracks, Harringay is an area of sharp contrasts. The western half is just a short walk from the village-like amenities of Crouch End and is essentially an extension of that boho neighbourhood.

Haringey

STATISTICS

BOROUGH MAKE-UP
Population 218,246
Average weekly pay £499
Ethnic origins
  White 65.62%
  Mixed 4.55%
  Asian or Asian British 6.71%
  Black or Black British 20.03%
  Chinese or other 3.08%
Students 11.74%
Retirees 8.07%

HOUSING STOCK
Borough size 30.3km²
No. of households 96,000
Detached 3.1%
Semi-detached 9.5%
Terraced 31.8%
Flats (purpose-built) 27.4%
Flats (converted) 26.4%
Flats (both) 53.8%

CRIME PER 1,000 OF POPULATION
(English average in brackets)
Burglary 14 (6.4)
Robbery 6 (1.4)
Theft of vehicle 9 (4.5)
Theft from vehicle 13 (10)
Violence against the person 28 (16.5)
Sexual offences 2 (0.9)

MPs & COUNCIL
MPs *Hornsey & Wood Green* Lynne Featherstone (Liberal Democrat); *Islington North* Jeremy Corbyn (Labour); *Tottenham* David Lammy (Labour)
CPA 3 stars; improving well

Stroud Green Road. *See p89.*

The residential roads are lined with £500,000 family homes and dotted with trees and the odd Montessori nursery. There are great views of Alexandra Palace, too.

On the other side of the tracks, as cliché dictates, the picture is rather different. The Harringay Ladder (a glance at a street map reveals the name's inspiration: rows of Victorian terraces running perpendicular to Green Lanes) is home to a mixed community of Turks, Kurds, Albanians, Italians, South Americans, Indians and Greeks. Bordered by Green Lanes to the east and Finsbury Park to the south, the area is a bit rough round the edges. But shopping here is like wandering down an international street market full of sticky sweet shops, friendly independent stores and some of the best kebabs in London.

Harringay is a confused district (even the spelling, different from that of the borough of the same name, is a head-scratcher), but it has good bus links and a Zone 2 tube station in Manor House. And, hey, if you ever crave lamb doners or need Oxo cubes at 4am, this is the place to be.

Tottenham

Bordered by Harringay in the west, Tottenham Hale in the east, the North Circular in the north and Hackney to the south, Tottenham contains housing that is inexpensive for London… but for obvious reasons. This is one of the poorest districts in western Europe, and crime rates are high. Home buyers, however, may be tempted by the many Victorian terraces.

After decades of neglect, the obvious potential of the area, notably its excellent transport links to central London (Victoria Line and rail stations at Tottenham Hale and Seven Sisters, plus three more rail stations at Bruce Grove, South Tottenham and White Hart Lane), is at last being recognised, and millions of pounds of regeneration money have been promised.

In common with much of present-day north London, Tottenham existed as a relatively small parish until its rapid development in the 19th century. The area on the west side of the High Road, particularly in Church Road and Cemetery Road, contains Tottenham's best surviving terraces from that era. The nearby 16th-century Bruce Castle, occupying the site of a castle once owned by Robert the Bruce, is a source of some local pride and features a small museum. The oldest stretch of the High Road is to receive Heritage Lottery funding to install heritage lamp-posts and restore the shops to something of their former glory, but the rest of Tottenham

Haringey

is firmly stuck in the present, with the usual takeaways and uninviting pubs. Spurs fans, however, will relish the fact that every other shop seems to be an outlet for THFC merchandise.

Restaurants & cafés

When it comes to eating out in Haringey, there's a stark east-west divide. You'd be hard-pressed to find anything beyond standard takeaway fodder in down-at-heel Tottenham, while at the other end of the scale, affluent Crouch End's array of eating-out options, mainly clustered around Tottenham Lane and Park Road, seems almost excessive. Together with neighbouring Hornsey, it boasts a trio of good French restaurants – Les Associés, Bistro Aix and Le Bistro. The Pumphouse Dining Bar occupies a converted industrial building in Hornsey, while Crouch End brasserie Banners still draws crowds with its global menu. Further international options include stand-out Vietnamese Khoai Café and authentic Spanish food bar La Bota.

Muswell Hill is a bit more chain-dominated, with branches of child-friendly Giraffe, Fine Burger Company and ASK, but also has famed fish-and-chip shop Toff's, gastropub Victoria Stakes and a superior Turkish restaurant, Bakko. There's more Turkish fare in Harringay: amid the numerous cheap ocakbaşi joints on Green Lanes, we recommend Antepliler and Yayla. Over in Finsbury Park, Yildiz and excellent Ethiopian restaurant Senke are worth seeking out. To the north, Stroud Green Road offers a smorgasbord of ethnic cuisines, including cracking Colombian Los Guaduales, South Indian (and vegetarian) Jai Krishna, and a lively branch of pizza chain La Porchetta; the Triangle café is another highlight (steak and chips to more exotic North African-influenced fare). Wood Green is blessed with cosy Greek gem Vrisaki and Pumphouse sibling Mosaica @ the factory, but little else beyond cheap chain offerings. As you might expect, pickings are even slimmer in Tottenham.

Antepliler *46 Grand Parade, Green Lanes, N4 1AG (8802 5588).*
Les Associés *172 Park Road, N8 8JT (8348 8944).*
Bakko *172-174 Muswell Hill Broadway, N10 3SA (8883 1111/www.bakko.co.uk).*
Banners *21 Park Road, N8 8TE (8348 2930/ www.banners.co.uk).*
Le Bistro *36 High Street, N8 7NX (8340 2116).*
Bistro Aix *54 Topsfield Parade, Tottenham Lane, N8 8PT (8340 6346/www.bistroaix.co.uk).*

The Mall Shopping City. *See p94.*

La Bota *31 Broadway Parade, Tottenham Lane, N8 9DB (8340 3082).*
Fine Burger Company *256 Muswell Hill Broadway, N10 3SH (8815 9292/www.fine burger.co.uk).*
Los Guaduales *53 Stroud Green Road, N4 3EF (7561 1929).*
Jai Krishna *161 Stroud Green Road, N4 3PZ (7272 1680).*
Khoai Café *6 Topsfield Parade, Tottenham Lane, N8 8PR (8341 2120).*
Mosaica @ the factory *The Chocolate Factory, Clarendon Road, N22 6XJ (8889 2400/ www.mosaicarestaurants.com).*
La Porchetta *147 Stroud Green Road, N4 3PZ (7281 2892).*
Pumphouse Dining Bar *1 New River Avenue, N8 7QD (8340 0400/www.mosaica restaurants.com).*
Senke *1B-1C Rock Street, N4 2DN (7359 7687).*
Toff's *38 Muswell Hill Broadway, N10 3RT (8883 8656).*
The Triangle *1 Ferme Park Road, N4 4DS (8292 0516/www.thetrianglerestaurant.co.uk).*
Victoria Stakes *1 Muswell Hill, N10 3TH (8815 1793/www.victoriastakes.co.uk).*
Vrisaki *73 Myddleton Road, N22 8LZ (8889 8760).*
Yayla *429 Green Lanes, N4 1HA (8348 9515).*
Yildiz *163 Blackstock Road, N4 2JS (7354 3899).*

Bars & pubs

Blame it on the buggy contingent to the west or budget-conscious folk to the east, but there isn't a massive choice of good boozers in Haringey's enclaves. That's not to say there are none. A short skip from Finsbury Park tube, the stately Victorian Salisbury Hotel offers a strong list of real ales, live jazz and roasts by the fireside. Smaller and more intimate (and the other side of Finsbury Park, along Stroud Green Road), Chapter One has a long list of cocktails. The ever popular Harringay Arms is further towards Crouch End and attracts a blokey but friendly crowd. The King's Head is best known for stand-up (*see p95*), but has a relaxed bar upstairs.

In Crouch End itself, the Queen's Hotel has most things covered: a pool table, a TV for football, as well as quieter areas for intimacies. Up in Hornsey, community-oriented Viva Viva bar and restaurant aims to bring café culture to the area.

Then there are the steep slopes into Muswell Hill, offering beautiful views. The Phoenix, tucked into a corner of Alexandra Palace, has the best; on the other side of Muswell Hill, a friendly crowd rocks to the

TRANSPORT

Tube stations *Piccadilly* Finsbury Park, Manor House, Turnpike Lane, Wood Green, Bounds Green; *Northern* Highgate, East Finchley; *Victoria* Finsbury Park, Seven Sisters, Tottenham Hale
Rail stations *one* Stamford Hill, Seven Sisters, Bruce Grove, White Hart Lane, Totteham Hale, Northumberland Park; *Silverlink* Crouch Hill, Harringay Green Lines, South Tottenham; *WAGN* Finsbury Park, Harringay, Hornsey, Alexandra Palace, Bowes Park
Main bus routes *into central London* 4, 19, 29, 43, 73, 76, 91, 134, 141, 149, 243, 253, 259, 271, 341, 359, 476; *night buses* N19, N29, N41, N73, N76, N91, N243, N253, N279; *24-hour buses* 43, 134, 149, 214, 243, 271, 341

funky weekend beats at Over the Hill. Near the centre of Muswell Hill is good gastropub Victoria Stakes (*see p92*). Chain bars are kept to a minimum here, although there is an All Bar One in Crouch End and an O'Neills in a converted church in Muswell Hill. To the east in Tottenham, drinking options are confined to unremarkable or insalubrious pubs.

Chapter One *143 Stroud Green Road, N4 3PZ (7281 9630/www.chapteronebar.com).*
Harringay Arms *153 Crouch Hill, N8 9QH (8340 4243).*
King's Head *2 Crouch End Hill, N8 8AA (8340 1028).*
Over the Hill *96 Alexandra Park Road, N10 2AE (8444 2524).*
Phoenix *Alexandra Palace Way, N22 7AY (8365 4356).*
Queen's Hotel *26 Broadway Parade, N8 9DE (8340 2031).*
Salisbury Hotel *1 Grand Parade, Green Lanes, N4 1JX (8800 9617).*
Viva Viva *18 High Street, N8 7PB (8341 0999/www.viva-viva.co.uk).*

Shops

Unsurprisingly, the bulk of the borough's interesting shops are in well-heeled Muswell Hill and Crouch End. The former even has a branch of empire-building skincare emporium Space NK, plus the original outpost of expanding upmarket shoe chain Kate Kuba. Other shops cater to the family-oriented demographic: kids' clothes and toys, high-quality foodstuffs and homewares.

Haringey

Lovely deli/café Oliver's Deli on the Hill and the self-explanatory Cheeses rub shoulders with toyshops Hills and Fagin's and the Children's Bookshop on Fortis Green Road, while the Broadway boasts superior fishmonger Walter Purkis & Sons (there's a branch in Crouch End), old-fashioned grocer W Martyn, and the Scullery kitchen shop.

There's more kids' stuff in Crouch End: Soup Dragon, born out of a market stall, sells unusual clothes and toys for babies and children; Mini Kin has natural bath products and merino wool babygros as well as a children's hairdressing salon. Treehouse offers globally sourced treats for adults, such as embroidered cushions from India and Venetian glass jewellery. As well as fashionable boutiques and hairdressers, residents are well served by an organic butcher's, a friendly greengrocer's and the venerable Dunn's Bakery (established 1820).

The Mall Shopping City dominates Wood Green, but is a useful local resource with branches of Argos, TK Maxx and HMV alongside cheaper-end high street names (Topshop, New Look, Next), as well as numerous smaller shops. There's also a farmers' market on selected Sunday mornings at Alexandra Palace.

Stroud Green Road is lined with Middle Eastern and Mediterranean food stores and the excellent France Fresh Fish. To the north in Harringay, Green Lanes is known for its Turkish and Middle Eastern food shops – try Turkish Food Market and Yasar Halim. Nearby, Andreas Michli & Son stocks Greek, Cypriot and Turkish specialities such as figs flown in from Cyprus. Dandies without Gieves & Hawkes budgets can get outfitted by Savile Row-trained tailor George Christodoulou.

Given the low incomes of most of Tottenham's denizens, it's hardly surprising it isn't exactly a shoppers' paradise – although fans of its football team may be tempted by the abundance of replica kit, leisurewear and accessories at the Spurs Megastore. There's also an excellent reggae shop, Body Music, in South Tottenham. If you do decide to buy and renovate a bargain property, the B&Q and other home-related superstores of Tottenham Hale Retail Park will no doubt become a weekend fixture.

Alexandra Palace Farmers' Market *Hornsey Gate Entrance, Alexandra Palace Way, Wood Green, N22 7AY (8365 2121).*
Andreas Michli & Son *405-411 St Ann's Road, N15 3JL (8802 0188).*
Body Music *261 High Road, N15 4RR (8802 0146).*
Cheeses *13 Fortis Green Road, N10 3HP (8444 9141).*
Children's Bookshop *29 Fortis Green Road, N10 3HP (8444 5500).*
Dunn's Bakery *6 The Broadway, N8 9SN (8340 1614/www.dunns-bakery.co.uk).*
Fagin's Toys *84 Fortis Green Road, N10 3HN (8444 0282).*
France Fresh Fish *99 Stroud Green Road, N4 3PX (7263 9767).*
George's Tailors *50 Wightman Road, N4 1RU (8341 3614).*
Hills *58 Fortis Green Road, N10 3HN (8883 4644).*
Kate Kuba *71 Muswell Hill Broadway, N10 3HA (8444 1227/www.katekuba.co.uk).*
The Mall Shopping City *159 High Road, N22 6YQ (8888 6667).*
Mini Kin *22 Broadway Parade, N8 9DE (8341 6898).*
Oliver's Deli on the Hill *56 Fortis Green Road, N10 3HN (8883 0117).*
Scullery *123 Muswell Hill Broadway, N10 3RS (8444 5236).*
Soup Dragon *27 Topsfield Parade, Tottenham Lane, N8 8PT (8348 0224/ www.soup-dragon.co.uk).*
Space NK *238 Muswell Hill Broadway, N10 3SH (8883 8568).*
Spurs Megastore *1-3 Park Lane, N17 0HJ (8365 5042).*
Treehouse *7 Park Road, N8 8TE (8341 4326).*
Turkish Food Market *385-387 Green Lanes, N4 1EU (8340 4547).*
Walter Purkis & Sons *52 Muswell Hill Broadway, N10 3RT (8883 4355).*
W Martyn *135 Muswell Hill Broadway, N10 3RS (8883 5642).*
Yasar Halim *495 Green Lanes, N4 1AL (8340 8090).*

RECYCLING

No. of bring sites 75 (for nearest, visit www.recycleforlondon.com)
Household waste recycled 8.6%
Main recycling centre Park View Road Reuse & Recycling Centre, Park View Road, Tottenham, N17 9AY (8489 5659)
Other recycling services green waste collection; home composting; white goods and furniture collection; electrical equipment/IT recycling
Council contact Haringey Accord Customer Care Team, Contract House, Park View Road, Tottenham, N17 9AY (8885 7700)

Arts & attractions

Cinemas & theatres

Cineworld Wood Green *The Mall Shopping City, High Road, N22 6YA (0871 220 8000/ www.cineworld.co.uk).*

Jacksons Lane Theatre *269A Archway Road, N6 5AA (8341 4421/www.jacksons lane.org.uk).* Arts centre housed in a converted Edwardian church, offering a wide range of activities and workshops.

Odeon Muswell Hill *Fortis Green Road, N10 3HP (0871 224 4007/www.odeon.co.uk).*

Showcase Wood Green *Hollywood Green, High Road, N22 6EJ (0870 162 8960/ www.showcasecinemas.co.uk).* Cinema.

Galleries & museums

Bruce Castle Museum *Lordship Lane, N17 8NU (8808 8772/www.haringey.gov.uk).* Tottenham's local history museum.

Music & comedy venues

Alexandra Palace *Alexandra Palace Way, Wood Green, N22 7AY (8365 2121/ www.alexandrapalace.com).*

Downstairs at the King's Head *2 Crouch End Hill, N8 8AA (8340 1028/www.downstairs atthekingshead.com).*

Red Rose Comedy Club *129 Seven Sisters Road, N7 7QJ (0871 332 4436/www.redrose comedy.co.uk).* Steeped in socialist history, this venue and pub also stages debates.

Open spaces

Alexandra Park *Alexandra Palace Way, N22 (www.alexandrapalace.com).* The 196-acre grounds of Alexandra Palace include a boating lake, skate park, an animal enclosure and indoor ice-skating rink.

Finsbury Park *Endymion Road, N4.* The park has a boating lake, recently upgraded tennis courts and a Sunday market.

Highgate Wood/Queen's Wood *Muswell Hill Road, N10.* Ancient woodlands. Highgate Wood (managed by the Corporation of London) has a playground and playing fields; Queen's Wood is also a nature reserve, supporting diverse flora and bird life.

Lordship Recreational Ground *Lordship Lane, N17.*

Parkland Walk *Finsbury Park through Highgate to Alexandra Palace along a disused railway line, N4-N10.*

Priory Park *Priory Road, Middle Lane, N8.*

Sport & fitness

Haringey has four large and well-equipped leisure centres: Finsbury Park Track & Gym; Park Road Leisure Centre (formerly Park Road Swimming Pools); Tottenham

Haringey

Green Leisure Centre; and White Hart Lane Community Sports Centre. The council has been busy updating its facilities: both Park Road and Tottenham Green have been given swanky new gyms, plus chill-out features such as steam rooms and saunas. The borough also has some desirable private options, such as the luxurious (and pricey) Laboratory Spa & Health Club and down-to-earth yet aesthetically pleasing women's gym Paradise Walk, housed in a former dairy factory.

As for spectator sports, White Hart Lane draws Spurs fans from all over the capital.

Gyms & leisure centres

Bodyworks Gym *Unit 5, Fountayne House, Fountayne Road, N15 4QL (8808 6580/ www.bodyworksgym.co.uk).* Private.
Dragons Health Club *Hillfield Park, N10 3PJ (8444 8212/www.dragons.co.uk).* Private.
Finsbury Park Track & Gym *Hornsey Gate, Endymion Road, N4 0XX (8802 9139/ www.haringey.gov.uk/leisure).*
Fitness First *570-590 Tottenham High Road, N17 9TA (8808 7171/www.fitnessfirst.co.uk).* Private.
Flex Fitness *Unit A, Cypress House, 2 Coburg Road, N22 6UJ (8881 8222/ www.flexfitness.co.uk).* Private.
Holmes Place *(www.holmesplace.com) 98-100 High Street, N22 6YQ (8889 6161); 31 Topsfield Parade, Tottenham Lane, N8 8PT (8347 7763).* Private.
Hornsey YMCA Fitness Centre *184 Tottenham Lane, N8 8SG (8340 6088/ www.ymcahornsey.org.uk).* Private.
Laboratory Spa & Health Club *The Avenue, N10 2QJ (8482 3000/www.labspa. co.uk).* Private.
Paradise Walk *17 Crouch Hill, N4 4AP (7272 6857/www.paradisewalk.com).* Private.
Park Road Leisure Centre *Park Road, N8 8JN (8341 3567/www.haringey.gov.uk/leisure).*
Selby Centre *Selby Road, N17 8JL (8885 5499).* Private.
Tottenham Green Leisure Centre *1 Philip Lane, N15 4JA (8489 5322/www.haringey.gov. uk/leisure).*
White Hart Lane Community Sports Centre *White Hart Lane, N22 5QW (8881 2323/www.haringey.gov.uk/leisure).*

Other facilities

Muswell Hill Golf Club *Rhodes Avenue, N22 7UT (8888 1764/www.muswellhill golfclub.org.uk).* Private members' club.
Rowans Tenpin Bowl *10 Stroud Green Road, N4 2DF (8800 1950/www.rowans.co.uk).*

Spectator sports

Tottenham Hotspur FC *Bill Nicholson Way, 748 High Road, N17 0AP (8365 5000/ticket office 0870 420 5000/www.spurs.co.uk).*

Schools

WHAT THE PARENTS SAY:

‘We were lucky enough to get our kids into a well-regarded primary school in Highgate, St Michael's. The teaching staff are excellent and the parents very committed. The top criteria for admission is regular attendance at St Michael's Church, followed by another one in Highgate. On a Sunday, the church is packed with two-year-olds and their parents.

There are a number of other excellent primary schools in the area, including Muswell Hill Primary, Tetherdown, the Catholic Our Lady of Muswell and the Anglican, St James'.

Secondary schools are a daunting prospect for any parent. Fortismere is the top secondary school in the borough and there is fierce competition to get in. House prices close to the school reflect this. Most of the middle-class kids in the area tend to get extra tuition, which helps with the league tables.

When my daughter left St Michael's, we opted for Alexandra Park School. The headmistress was inspirational and we were sold after a parents' evening. My daughter spent a year there, but we weren't happy. The classes were too big and many of the children didn't want to work so there was a lot of disruption. The school had only been going for three years then and most of the parents in the area had opted for Fortismere. So after 12 months, we decided to send her to a private school.

From my experience the primary schools in Haringey have a good reputation, but the secondary schools are just too big and, unless your child is a keen scholar, they can get lost in the system.’
Nichola Coulthard, mother of two, Muswell Hill

Primary

There are 54 state primary schools in Haringey, 16 of which are church schools. There are also ten independent primaries, including one Montessori school and one Steiner school. See www.haringey.gov.uk and www.ofsted.gov.uk for more information.

Secondary

Alexandra Park School *Bidwell Gardens, N11 2AZ (8826 4880/www.alexandrapark. haringey.sch.uk).*
Fortismere School *South Wing, Tetherdown, N10 1NE; North Wing, Creighton Avenue, N10 1NS (South Wing 8365 4470/North Wing 8365 4400/www.fortismere.haringey.sch.uk).*
Gladesmore Community School *Crowland Road, N15 6EB (8800 0884/www.gladesmore. haringey.sch.uk).*

Greig City Academy *High Street, N8 7NU (8609 0100/www.greigcityacademy.co.uk).*
Highgate Wood School *Montenotte Road, N8 8RN (8342 7970/www.hws.uk.com).*
Hornsey School for Girls *Inderwick Road, N8 9JF (8348 6191/www.hornseyschool.com).* Girls only.
John Loughborough school *Holcombe Road, N17 9AD (8808 7837/www.john-loughborough.haringey.lgfl.net).*
Northumberland Park Community School *Trulock Road, N17 0PG (8801 0091/www.northumberlandpark.haringey.sch.uk).*
Park View Academy *Langham Road, N15 3RB (8888 1722/www.parkview.haringey.sch.uk).*
St Thomas More RC School *Glendale Avenue, N22 5HN (8888 7122/www.stthomasmoreschool.org.uk).*
White Hart Lane Secondary School *White Hart Lane, N22 5QJ (8889 6761).*

Property

WHAT THE AGENTS SAY:

'Excellent transport facilities keep Finsbury Park buoyant: it's in Zone 2, on two tube lines, plus it has the overground into Liverpool Street and loads of buses. There are a lot of postgrads, young professionals and media people living here – it's near Islington and relatively cheap for this part of north London. You wouldn't call Finsbury Park poncey – it feels more real than Crouch End. But there are no good secondary schools here; you'd have to go private, or up to Muswell Hill and Highgate. A lot of people who rented here as students end up buying in the area; Finsbury Park is maligned but loved by those who live here.'
Malcolm Levy, Davies & Davies, Finsbury Park

'Wood Green has the largest shopping centre north of the river, apart from Brent Cross, and Ally Pally is a great park. As for transport, there's the Piccadilly Line and good rail links. Housing is still relatively well priced; half a mile down the road in Muswell Hill, prices are huge – and it has none of our network links. Middlesex University campus in Bounds Green recently moved to Trent Park and the site is rumoured to be up for redevelopment. There's been a lot of investment here recently – we know of plans for at least five new housing developments within half a mile of the tube. Things are looking up.'
Andrew Cooney, WJ Meade, Wood Green

Average property prices

Detached £933,582
Semi-detached £412,321
Terraced £249,000
Flat £171,483

Local estate agents

Browne & Nathan *697 Seven Sisters Road, N15 5LA (8800 7677).*
Castles *5 Turnpike Lane, N8 0EP (8341 6262/www.castles.uk.com).*
Davies & Davies *85 Stroud Green Road, N4 3EG (7272 0986/www.daviesdavies.co.uk).*
Liberty *www.libertyproperty.co.uk; 2 offices (Crouch End 8348 6669/Finsbury Park 7281 3773).*
Tatlers *www.tatlers.co.uk; 2 offices (Muswell Hill 0871 271 7537/Crouch End 0871 271 7535).*
Thomas & Co *415 High Road, N17 6QN (8801 6068/www.thomasproperty.net).*
WJ Meade *1 Gladstone House, Gladstone Avenue, N22 6JS (8888 9595/www.wjmeade.co.uk).*

COUNCIL TAX

A	up to £40,000	£881.93
B	£40,001-£52,000	£1,028.91
C	£52,001-£68,000	£1,175.89
D	£68,001-£88,000	£1,322.88
E	£88,001-£120,000	£1,616.84
F	£120,001-£160,000	£1,910.83
G	£160,001-£320,000	£2,204.80
H	over £320,000	£2,645.76

Other information

Council

London Borough of Haringey *Civic Centre, High Road, N22 8LE (8489 0000/www.haringey.gov.uk).*

Hospitals

St Ann's Hospital *St Ann's Road, N15 3TH (8442 6000/www.haringey.nhs.uk).*
North Middlesex University Hospital *Sterling Way, N18 1QX (8887 2000/www.northmid.nhs.uk).*

Legal services

Hornsey CAB *7 Hatherley Gardens, N8 9JJ (0870 126 4030/www.adviceguide.org.uk).*
Tottenham CAB *Town Hall Approach, N15 4RY (0870 126 4030/www.adviceguide.org.uk).*
Turnpike Lane CAB *14A Willoughby Road, N8 0JJ (0870 126 4030/www.adviceguide.org.uk).*

Local newspapers

Haringey independent *www.haringeyindependent.co.uk.*
Muswell Hill & Crouch End Times *www.crouchendtimes.co.uk.*
Tottenham & Wood Green independent *www.shoppersworld.co.uk.*

Allotments

There are 25 sites in the borough and the majority have long waiting lists. For further information, contact the council's parks services on 8489 5670.

*'When I was young
my friends and I wanted
to move into one of the creepy
old factories by the canal.
Now they've actually been
turned into flats.'*

Eve Bennett, resident for 20 years

Islington

Over the past 30 years, Islington has come to symbolise upwardly mobile London, as evidenced by its wealth of modish shops and bars, and its renovated Georgian and Victorian property. Yet the area also holds spirited reminders of its working-class roots, including a top Premiership football team and a corking street market.

Neighbourhoods

Angel and Pentonville

Named after a famous Victorian pub that's now a Co-op bank, the Angel is a tremendously busy hub at the Pentonville Road end of Upper Street. This part of Islington caters for pretty much everything that folk from its many satellite neighbourhoods demand. Transport links come via Angel tube station (the deepest in London) and the congested interchange at the Pentonville Road traffic junction (one of London's three busiest, which buses must negotiate on their way to the City or the West End). Shopping options are provided by the many boutiques of Upper Street and Camden Passage, plus the more mainstream chains of the N1 Shopping Centre. Food is supplied by the numerous eateries along Upper Street; drink comes courtesy of the street's similarly voluminous pubs and bars scene.

This last – boozing – is probably what the Angel is best known for, evidenced by the hundreds of revellers who meet every Friday and Saturday outside the tube station before their night out. In recent years, rowdy chain pubs have lowered the high-end tone of the local night scene that trendy cocktail bars seek to preserve. This makes for a fluctuating atmosphere, depending on the clock. After work, the area buzzes; as the bars start to empty at midnight, a sober walk along the strip is about as pleasant as the kebab wrappers strewn across the pavement.

Islington

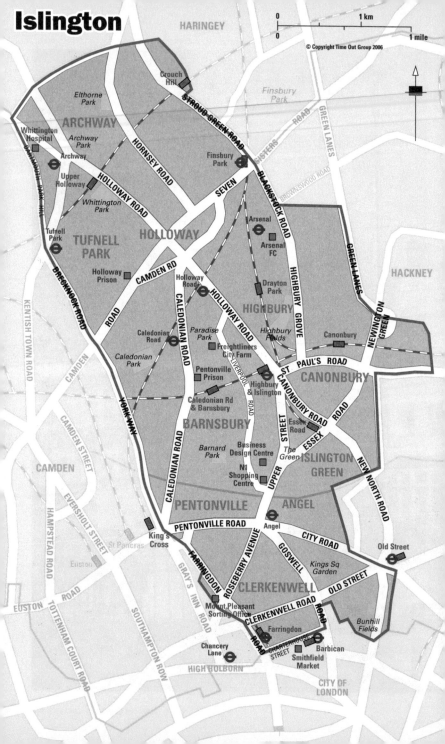

During the day, Angel is equally frenetic, though mostly with crowds rushing from tube to work, work to lunch, and so on. Chapel Market is a gloriously downmarket run of stalls hawking fruit and veg, linen, partywear, baked potatoes, DVDs – just about anything you can imagine. The street also contains some popular late-opening bars at its western end. This, combined with the early morning traders, makes Chapel Market and its surroundings a residential location best suited to heavy sleepers.

Running parallel to Chapel Market, Pentonville Road is a grim, grey main route, sloping down towards King's Cross. Along its length are offices and warehouses, brightened occasionally by small areas of green space (on Cumming Street), the Crafts Council gallery and lively Castle pub near Angel, and the twin towers of NatWest building Newton House (perhaps the most inoffensive of the offices around here).

Islington Green and Canonbury

Islington Green, the area, runs east of its eponymous square (a tiny, greenish spot, actually on Upper Street's Angel end, under the glow of the Screen on the Green cinema's iconic sign). This residential neighbourhood is the most obvious example of Islington's dual personality: the swanky and the hard-bitten, side by side. Young affluent families with all-terrain buggies (kids not yet old enough to necessitate the move to Muswell Hill for better schools) live in Georgian terraced flats behind wrought-iron gates. Next door, grim council blocks harbour miscreants who forever threaten to propel water balloons or egg cartons on to lingering pedestrians. Roving gangs of annoying teenagers make constant use of the wide streets around Packington Square to do wheelies on their bikes and shout obscenities. Spoiling their fun, the Metropolitan Police sometimes uses Islington Green to train horse-backed officers. This, and the constant crawl of learner drivers, tempers the quietness of the area's pretty, tree-lined roads.

Essex Road and New North Road have more than enough traffic for all the district. The former is a noisy, polluted, but not uncharming thoroughfare: one that retains many quaint and decade-weathered shops (a butcher, a fishmonger… a taxidermist). New North Road is a fairly bleak route south to the trendy flats and council blocks around Regent's Canal. Accommodation on and around both of these main roads – as well as offshoots Balls Pond Road and Southgate Road – is not peaceful. Living on principal bus arteries, residents must put up with chugging and stalling engines that run all through the night.

Yet the area is not without tranquil spots. Canonbury, running north from Essex Road station to Highbury Corner, is markedly posher and less ragged than its neighbours. This, together with a smattering of quiet squares and the exorbitant price of property, makes it a much-hawked area among estate agents (their signs, we predict, will soon outnumber residents). Of particular note is Canonbury Square, the Regency-era square at the northern tip of the neighbourhood, once home to George Orwell and Evelyn Waugh (in Nos.27 and 17A respectively).

Highs & Lows

▲ **Food shops** Spread throughout the borough, so you'll never go short of artisanal cheese and sun-dried tomatoes

Cyclists With plenty of cycle routes and keen pedallers, this is one of London's most bike-friendly neighbourhoods

Free wi-fi In June 2005, Islington council launched 'Technology Mile', a free wireless internet zone that stretches the length of Upper Street

Owning a car Parking's a bit of a nightmare, and the intersection at the Angel end of Upper Street is one of London's busiest

Secondary schools A poor lot, so most parents leave the borough or move to private schools if they can afford it

Troublesome teens Ubiquitous wherever you go in inner London, yet Islington seems to have more than its fair share of wall-kicking, BMX-patrolling, obscenity-shouting young 'uns. Essentially harmless but always ▼ a nuisance

Islington

Highbury

Roughly encompassing the postal district of N5, Highbury is best known for the football team housed in its midst. Without exception, pubs, shops and takeaway outlets make their allegiance clear with the red-and-white regalia of Arsenal FC's 'gooner' following. On match days, the streets around Highbury Stadium (Aubert Park, Highbury Hill, Gillespie and Avenell Roads) are choc-full, but the palpable excitement is likely to ensnare football fan and foe.

Yet things are to change. In 1999, Arsenal FC announced its intention to move north and west a bit, to a new home – the 60,000-seat Emirates Stadium – off Holloway Road. The club is due to move in summer 2006. What will happen to Highbury after its heart is removed? Probably very little. The old stadium is being redeveloped into 2,500 new homes (at least 40 per cent being 'affordable housing') and the new Ashburton Grove site is only a 20-minute walk away; parking will still be sorely limited on match-days and rowdy fans will still roam the streets.

But the neighbourhood has more to offer than the beautiful game. Highbury Fields is the local showpiece. With tennis courts, football pitches, children's play areas and a well-equipped pool, it is Islington's largest outdoor space. A stroll across here takes you from busy Upper Street past imposing period terraces to Highbury Barn, a trendy enclave boasting several excellent food shops, restaurants and cafés. Nearby, on the other side of Arsenal's current stadium, hides the lesser-known Gillespie Park, with its range of beautiful wildlife habitats and Ecology Centre (popular with children).

East towards the Hackney border, Newington Green marks the gateway to gentrified Stoke Newington. As a roundabout at the southern tip of Green Lanes, this is an important thoroughfare, but traffic is rarely intrusive. The green itself has a pleasant playground (accessed by many buggy-friendly zebra crossings) and the square is lined with a handful of decent cafés – both the French-inspired and trad-English variety.

Barnsbury

Liverpool Road begins behind the N1 Shopping Centre and Upper Street's modern, glass-fronted Business Design Centre. Overshadowed by Upper Street in almost every department except length (it runs further, to Holloway Road), the road offers none of the glitz, glamour or, indeed, sleaze of its sister thoroughfare. Instead, it serves as a residential refuge, with Edwardian terraces – mostly converted into flats – and a smattering of independent retailers. Despite having ample speed bumps, Liverpool Road draws much of Angel's spillover traffic; wailing police cars in a hurry to settle closing-time brawls on Upper Street are a particular local woe. Apart from the intimidating Sutton Estate, the roads between Liverpool Road and Upper Street contain many of Islington's choicest treats; Almeida Street is a joy, hosting two delightful 'Almeidas': one a theatre, the other a Conran restaurant.

STATISTICS

BOROUGH MAKE-UP
Population 178,028
Average weekly pay £573.60
Ethnic origins
White 75.35%
Mixed 4.11%
Asian or Asian British 5.39%
Black or Black British 11.86%
Chinese or other 3.28%
Students 11.08%
Retirees 7.84%

HOUSING STOCK
Borough size 14.9km²
No. of households 85,844
Detached 1%
Semi-detached 2.7%
Terraced 16%
Flats (purpose-built) 49.2%
Flats (converted) 29.8%
Flats (both) 79%

CRIME PER 1,000 OF POPULATION
(English average in brackets)
Burglary 14 (6.4)
Robbery 7 (1.4)
Theft of vehicle 7 (4.5)
Theft from vehicle 20 (10)
Violence against the person 42 (16.5)
Sexual offences 2 (0.9)

MPs & COUNCIL
MPs *Islington North* Jeremy Corbyn (Labour); *Islington South & Finsbury* Emily Thornberry (Labour)
CPA 3 stars; improving well

'Angel wings' at the **N1 Shopping Centre**. *See p98.*

Further to the west – though still running parallel – Caledonian Road is scruffier and, thanks to bars and pubs patronised by indie bands, trendier. Excellent travel links (a Piccadilly Line stop and a rail station) plus lower-end prices make the road popular with buyers and renters, though most of its offerings are grotty two-beds above takeaway outlets and betting shops, or ex-local authority conversions on estates. For the artfully dishevelled Pete Doherty-alikes (who abound), the urban grit is a lure. Other locals, like pitbull-walking Arsenal fans and hordes of bored teenagers in puffer jackets, probably have less choice in the matter. Talking of which, the 'Cally' Road's principal other residents are those serving at Her Majesty's pleasure, in Pentonville Prison.

Archway, Tufnell Park and Holloway

With their relatively affordable Victorian terraces within sniffing distance of Highgate and Hampstead, Archway, Tufnell Park and Holloway have long attracted London's media types. These are very different areas of Islington to the New Labour heartland of Angel to the south.

Holloway is the meat around Holloway Road, a main arterial route for London (the A1) that's kept fairly clear by its red route designation. As a result, passing trade rarely stops, yet local shops seem prosperous. The area also benefits from the University of North London and an Odeon cinema that can almost be described as grand. Built in the 1930s, this beauty was once the site of Lord Tufnell's manor house (which sat at the end of a long driveway, now Tufnell Park Road; halfway up the road, two posts mark the original entrance). Tufnell Park itself is pleasant, with fairly priced housing. It's also in Zone 2: half an hour's walk to Hampstead Heath, less to Kentish Town.

Archway is somewhat scruffier than its neighbours, largely the result of some unlovely 1960s developments such as the monolithic Archway Tower (disliked by 93 per cent of residents, according to a council survey). Discussions regarding a major redevelopment are ongoing, and considering the area's proximity to Highgate, its potential as a house-buying hotspot is high. For now, though, Archway serves principally as a transport hub for cars, tubes and buses, and as a kebab pit-stop for their drivers and passengers. Unsurprisingly, residents are keen on alterations to its transport system.

Clerkenwell and Farringdon

Stretching south from the Angel junction, St John Street and Rosebery Avenue lead into the mysterious province of Finsbury – a name that causes much confusion, due to the better-known Finsbury Park miles to the north (an entirely separate neighbourhood, on the border with Haringey). Though fallen to disuse as a geographical label, Finsbury still appears on maps and in the names of certain public buildings. Regardless of title, it is an attractive, lively area. City University on Northampton Square keeps the district young; Sadler's Wells theatre brings culture; and the pedestrianised Exmouth Market (opposite Royal Mail's Mount Pleasant Sorting Office) is fast turning into a foodie destination, with its mix of excellent restaurants, bars and delis.

South down St John Street lies Clerkenwell. Bordered by Farringdon Road to the west (a charmless thoroughfare that has little distinction other than being home to the

Guardian and nearby *Observer*) and Smithfield meat market to the south, the neighbourhood follows Clerkenwell Road east as it turns into Old Street. The area is primarily residential these days, but was once a home to jewellers, furniture makers, clock and watchmakers – plus an enormous printing trade. Some of the old trades live on in a few workshops run by the Clerkenwell Green Association (a charity providing affordable studios for small crafts businesses). Otherwise, as the area is so close to the City, almost every former office or warehouse building has been converted into flats.

Clerkenwell Green is a pretty local focal point; on the corner stands what was once the county courthouse and is now the London Masonic Centre (you can see men creeping in and out in dark suits in the evening). The area is now best known for its night scene; enormously popular Fabric, on Charterhouse Street, and the tag-along bars around it (covered in the City of London; *see p48*), attract youthful crowds from miles around. Close by, St John restaurant at the base of St John Street has won international plaudits for its British menu.

The district east along Old Street is sometimes known as St Luke's (the lovely Hawksmoor church of the same name is now used for rehearsals by the London

Mega-club **Turnmills** attracts the most international crowd in town. *See p109.*

Symphony Orchestra), but locals refer to it simply as Old Street; the busy roundabout above the station of the same name is a local landmark of sorts, with its modern, arched advertising hoarding. Running south from the roundabout towards Moorgate, City Road becomes rather picturesque (at least in great contrast to its concrete soullessness north-west of Old Street). Here you'll encounter the greenery of Finsbury Square, entrance to the Honourable Artillery Company barracks, and famous Bunhill Fields Nonconformists cemetery (one of the oldest in the capital and home to the bones of Daniel Defoe, John Bunyan and William Blake).

Restaurants & cafés

Where to start? Upper Street, of course: the central spine of Islington and home to its highest concentration of restaurants. Some see the strip as over-saturated, others as a source of plentiful choice. Either way, new restaurants are extremely vulnerable and the closure rate is high – except for bullet-proof chains such as Pizza Express, ASK, Strada and Est Est Est. A few eateries have been around for years, however: compact bistro Le Mercury, highly recommended Turkish eaterie Pasha, hidden-away Italian attic Casale Franco, the forever-packed outlets of meze-specialists Gallipoli. Other, more recent ventures are enjoying success too (sexy Thai Isarn, popular marine-chain FishWorks, Brazilian buffet-style Rodizio Rico), but many succumb to competition and retire to the Upper Street in the sky. No.127, in particular, seems to be a tough pitch; since infamous Tony Blair-haunt Granita closed a few years ago, four different businesses have occupied the site (current resident is a cheesy Tex-Mex bar).

The Angel end of Upper Street is the road's most popular and attractive stretch; look out for the atrium interior of bistro Lola's, upstairs in the old London Electricity building. But the grittier Highbury Corner end shouldn't be written off; Maghreb (Moroccan) and Gem (Kurdish) are often unjustly overlooked by passers-by, while cooked-to-order kebabery Flaming Nora is as fresh and fun as fast food gets. Off the main strip, Georgian restaurant Tiblisi on Holloway Road is worth the extra stroll.

Back towards the Angel, Terence Conran's classy Almeida (opposite the theatre of the same name) and Morgan Meunier's Morgan M (on Liverpool Road) are two of the capital's best French restaurants. Hidden off the junction with Essex Road (behind straightforward well-priced pit-stop, Afghan Kitchen), Camden Passage houses treats like the authentic Italian bistro Trattoria Aquilino and good-looking gastropub Elk in the Woods. Down Essex Road, sausage and mash at S&M Café makes for a quick, happy fix, while family-friendly Giraffe is a popular haunt.

If you're willing to venture further still from Upper Street, you'll be rewarded with three excellent gastropubs (the Duke of Cambridge near Regent's Canal, the Northgate on Southgate Road, and the House on Canonbury Lane). Continue to Highbury, and you'll discover superb Turkish restaurant İznik.

With so many bijou Islingtonians to fill with coffee, cafés are well-represented throughout the area. Pick of the bunch are Italian deli Saponara on Islington Green, La Belle Epoque on Newington Green, and two Upper Street shacks: Mem & Laz (known for their excellent Turkish breakfasts) and Tinderbox (a much-loved caffeine stop near Angel tube, cherished not least for its later-than-Starbucks opening hours). Slightly off the beaten track, the Candid Arts Trust (see p113) has an atmospheric, candle-lit café on its upper floor.

Moving away from Upper Street towards Clerkenwell, no less than four first-rate gastropubs can be found, each orbiting a key institution of the area: the Easton (behind Mount Pleasant Sorting Office), the Eagle and the Coach & Horses (near the offices of the Guardian) and the Peasant (near City University). Pedestrianised Exmouth Market, these days something of a foodie haven, houses louche and friendly restaurant Medcalf (British) and perennially popular Moro (Spanish). At the Market's northern mouth, pizzeria La Porchetta draws the party crowds; at the other end there's a branch of the pizza chain Strada.

On Farringdon Road, the Quality Chop House is popular for its old-school British fare; Little Bay offers a one-price Mediterranean menu. Running parallel, St John Street competes with cute café Pho (Vietnamese), the easy-going brasserie in

Islington

LETS FILL THIS TOWN WITH ARTISTS
BEST CHOICE TOP BRANDS LOW PRICES

EASELS

£49.95
DALER-ROWNEY
SALISBURY EASEL
RRP £200

75% OFF

70% OFF

70% OFF

£12.95
WINSOR & NEWTON
DART SKETCHING EASEL
RRP £39.99

£9.95
DALER-ROWNEY
EDINBURGH
TABLE BOX EASEL
RRP £29.50

PAINTS

DALER-ROWNEY
SYSTEM 3
250ML ACRYLIC
ALL HALF PRICE

HALF PRICE

WINSOR & NEWTON
14ML ARTISTS WATERCOLOUR
ALL HALF PRICE

HALF PRICE

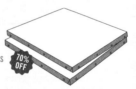

HALF PRICE

WINSOR & NEWTON
ARTIST OIL 37ML
ALL HALF PRICE

BRUSHES

WINSOR & NEWTON ARTIST
HOG BRUSH SET RRP £26
NOW £12.95 HALF PRICE

HALF PRICE

CANVAS

WINSOR & NEWTON
ARTIST QUALITY CANVAS
UP TO 70% OFF

70% OFF

SETS & GIFTS

PRESENTATION PORTFOLIOS
MANY HALF PRICE ITEMS

HALF PRICE

£9.47
WINSOR & NEWTON 8X14ML
DRAWING INKS SET RRP £18.95

HALF PRICE

LESS THAN HALF PRICE

A4 - £3.50, A5 - £2.75
DALER-ROWNEY EBONY HARDBACK SKETCH PAD
RRP (A4) £8.50, (A5) £6.25

£4.75
FABER-CASTELL 9000
12 ART PENCILS
8B-2H IN TIN RRP £9.50

HALF PRICE

HALF PRICE

REMBRANDT PASTELS
MANY HALF PRICE SETS

CASS PROMISE
CREATIVITY AT THE LOWEST PRICES. WE'RE
CONFIDENT OUR PRICES CAN'T BE BEATEN.

ISLINGTON OPENING JUNE 2006
66-67 COLEBROOKE ROW ISLINGTON N1

CASS ART LONDON

13 CHARING CROSS ROAD WC2
020 7930 9940
220 KENSINGTON HIGH STREET W8
020 7937 6506
24 BERWICK STREET W1
020 7287 8504
WWW.CASSART.CO.UK

the Zetter hotel (Italian), smart Clerkenwell Dining Rooms (Modern European) and lovely newcomer Vinoteca (foodie wine bar). Best of all here is Fergus Henderson's St John; whether you call it 'nose to tail eating' (like him) or offal (like most), the quirky British menu is outstanding. There's also a bevy of restaurants around the famous Smithfield meat market (which fall into the City of London; see p44).

To the north of the borough, Archway and Tufnell Park may not have a surplus of top restaurants, but there are a trio of worthy gastropubs: St John's, Dartmouth Arms and the Lord Palmerston.

Afghan Kitchen *35 Islington Green, N1 8DU (7359 8019).*
Almeida *30 Almeida Street, N1 1AD (7354 4777/www.conran.com).*
Belle Epoque Pâtisserie *37 Newington Green, N16 9PR (7249 2222/www.belleepoque.co.uk).*
Casale Franco *Rear of 134-137 Upper Street, N1 1QP (7226 8994).*
Clerkenwell Dining Room *69-73 St John Street, EC1M 4AN (7253 9000/www.theclerkenwell.com).*
Coach & Horses *26-28 Ray Street, EC1R 3DJ (7278 8990/www.thecoachandhorses.com).*
Dartmouth Arms *35 York Rise, NW5 1SP (7485 3267/www.dartmoutharms.co.uk).*
Duke of Cambridge *30 St Peter's Street, N1 8JT (7359 3066).*
Eagle *159 Farringdon Road, EC1R 3AH (7837 1353).*
Easton *22 Easton Street, WC1X 0DS (7278 7608/www.theeaston.co.uk).*
Elk in the Woods *39 Camden Passage, N1 8EA (7226 3535/www.the-elk-in-the-woods.co.uk).*
FishWorks *134 Upper Street, N1 1QP (7354 1279/www.fishworks.co.uk).*
Flaming Nora *177 Upper Street, N1 1RG (0845 835 6672/www.flamingnora.com).*
Gallipoli *102 Upper Street, N1 1QN (7359 0630/www.gallipolicafe.co.uk).*
Gallipoli Again *120 Upper Street, N1 1QP (7359 1578/www.gallipolicafe.co.uk).*
Gallipoli Bazaar *107 Upper Street, N1 1QN (7226 5333/www.gallipolicafe.co.uk).*
Gem *265 Upper Street, N1 2UQ (7359 0405).*
House *63-69 Canonbury Road, N1 2DG (7704 7410/www.inthehouse.biz).*
Isarn *119 Upper Street, N1 1QP (7424 5153).*
İznik *19 Highbury Park, N5 1QJ (7354 5697).*
Little Bay *171 Farringdon Road, EC1R 3AL (7278 1234/www.little-bay.co.uk).*
Lola's *The Mall Building, 359 Upper Street, N1 0PD (7359 1932/www.lolas.co.uk).*
Lord Palmerston *33 Dartmouth Park Hill, NW5 1HU (7485 1578).*
Maghreb *189 Upper Street, N1 1RQ (7226 2305).*
Mem & Laz *8 Theberton Street, N1 0QX (7704 9089).*
Medcalf *40 Exmouth Market, EC1R 4QE (7833 3533/www.medcalfbar.co.uk).*

Le Mercury *140A Upper Street, N1 1QY (7354 4088).*
Morgan M *489 Liverpool Road, N7 8NS (7609 3560/www.morganm.com).*
Moro *34-36 Exmouth Market, EC1R 4QE (7833 8336/www.moro.co.uk).*
Northgate *113 Southgate Road, N1 3JS (7359 7392).*
Pasha *301 Upper Street, N1 2TU (7226 1454).*
Peasant *240 St John Street, EC1V 4PH (7336 7726/www.thepeasant.co.uk).*
Pho *86 St John Street, EC1M 4EH (7253 7624).*
La Porchetta *84-86 Rosebery Avenue, EC1R 4QY (7837 6060).*
Quality Chop House *92-94 Farringdon Road, EC1R 3EA (7837 5093/www.qualitychophouse.co.uk).*
Rodizio Rico *77-78 Upper Street, N1 0NU (7354 1076).*
S&M Café *4-6 Essex Road, N1 8LN (7359 5361/www.sandmcafe.co.uk).*
St John *26 St John Street, EC1M 4AY (7251 0848/www.stjohnrestaurant.com).*
St John's *91 Junction Road, N19 5QU (7272 1587).*
Saponara *23 Prebend Street, N1 8PF (7226 2771).*
Tbilisi *91 Holloway Road, N7 8LT (7607 2536).*
Tinderbox *21 Upper Street, N1 0PQ (7354 8929).*
Trattoria Aquilino *31 Camden Passage, N1 8EA (7226 5454).*
Vinoteca *7 St John Street, EC1M 4AA (7253 8786).*
Zetter *86-88 Clerkenwell Road, EC1M 5RJ (7324 4455/www.thezetter.com).*

TRANSPORT

Tube stations *Bakerloo* King's Cross, Farringdon, Barbican; *Circle* King's Cross, Farringdon, Barbican; *Metropolitan* King's Cross, Farringdon, Barbican; *Piccadilly* King's Cross, Caledonian Road, Holloway Road, Arsenal, Finsbury Park; *Northern* King's Cross, Old Street, Angel, Tufnell Park, Archway; *Victoria* King's Cross, Highbury & Islington, Finsbury Park
Rail stations *Silverlink* Caledonian Road & Barnsbury, Highbury & Islington, Canonbury, Upper Holloway, Crouch Hill; *Thameslink* King's Cross Thameslink; *WAGN* Old Street, Essex Road, Highbury & Islington, Drayton Park, Finsbury Park, King's Cross
Main bus routes *into central London* 4, 19, 29, 30, 38, 43, 55, 56, 73, 76, 141, 153, 205, 214, 274, 341; *night buses* N19, N29, N38, N41, N55, N73, N253; *24-hour buses* 43, 214, 236, 243, 271, 274, 277, 341, 390

Islington

Bars & pubs

As with eating, Upper Street is the place in Islington to start when it comes to drinking. Hefty chains like O'Neill's and Walkabout take their share of the stretch near Angel station, bringing with them the inevitable Topshop-fitted lads and lasses, plus plenty of bus-stop trouble at closing time. Don't despair, there are several worthy independents too: upbeat Cuba Libre (with its raucous vibe and Cuban tapas menu); industrially styled Keston Lodge (a classy, if heaving, two-floored refuge for after-work suits); unpretentious Matt & Matt Bar (whose friendly staff and late opening hours keep the punters coming); and trendy Medicine Bar (tatty, noisy, full to capacity every weekend, and older brother to an outfit of the same name in Shoreditch).

There are also two equally worthy, though vastly different, boozers: the buzzy, well-fitted Bull; and long-standing theatre pub, the King's Head. As with restaurant choice, venturing up Upper Street towards Highbury Corner sees pickings slim, but there are some goodies, notably indie-kid pub Hope & Anchor (which hosts guitar music in its basement), a branch of well-stocked beer specialists Bierodrome, and intimate, cosy bars Lush and 25 Canonbury Lane.

As Upper Street's less-favoured sibling, Essex Road is often overlooked by those emerging from Angel station, but it holds just as many treats: throbbing Embassy Bar (for our money, a contender for the title of coolest bar in Islington), relaxed boozer the Old Queen's Head, and relative newcomers the Warwick (a small DJ bar) and Colebrooke's (an even smaller wine-and-cheeseboard venture).

Stretching in the opposite direction, away from the hub of the Angel, Chapel Market hosts a brace of stylish DJ bars (Anam and the recently renovated Salmon & Compass) plus a branch of popular pool hall chain Elbow Room. Round the corner is late-opening-but-free-to-enter Jay Cubed (once old-man boozer the Three Jays). Beyond to Pentonville, the Castle provides a warm welcome in the winter and an excellent roof-terrace in the summer; Filthy McNasty's is less conventional, with its no-frills decor, cheery scruffnik staff, and live music in the back room. In the other direction, on

RECYCLING

No. of bring sites 66 (for nearest, visit www.recycleforlondon.com)
Household waste recycled 7.6%
Main recycling centre Household Reuse & Recycling Centre, Hornsey Street, N7 8HR (8884 5645)
Other recycling services green and kitchen waste collection; home composting; white goods collection
Council contact Caroline Brimblecombe, Principal Waste Minimisation Officer, 36 North Road, N7 9TU (7527 4766)

Liverpool Road, the Angelic's stunning open-plan interior and exceptional service make it as popular as any of the above.

The Mucky Pup, a relatively recent addition to the Islington pubscape, is pleasing enough to wrench many Upper Street devotees from their comfort zone and out into Islington Green to the south. The canalside Narrow Boat and eccentric theatre pub Rosemary Branch might not be quite special enough to bring about similar upheaval, but the Island Queen certainly is: classy, friendly and just spectacular to look at, this is the sort of 'London, England' pub that Hollywood types would set a film in.

North in Holloway, the scene isn't quite as picturesque. Despite being distinctly rough and ready, this neighbourhood hasn't been spared the inexorable spread of the chain bar. Holloway's finest venues are to be found away from the main thoroughfare, such as well-kept secret the Swimmer at the Grafton Arms (hidden down an unassuming side-street), low-key watering hole the Landseer, and Liverpool Road's smartened-up Duchess of Kent. Though Tufnell Park and Archway boast gastropubs (*see p107*), the choice of decent boozers is slim: try the Settle Inn.

South towards Clerkenwell, Exmouth Market is home to the excellent Café Kick, a multi-hued, worn and weathered shack with table-football tables (the bar's signature, like sister outfit Bar Kick in Shoreditch). On the same stretch, Al's Café Bar is a bustling Euro-beer den with pavement tables; across the road, the Old China Hand serves real ale and, um, dim sum. Down in the mini-valley of Mount Pleasant (just across the border with City of Westminster), the pretty Apple Tree pub welcomes an after-work crowd

Islington

from nearby newspaper offices, as does the compact Betsey Trotwood, opposite the *Guardian* HQ on Farringdon Road.

On Clerkenwell Road, Match EC1 is the standard bearer, with its excellent cocktail list designed by mix-mogul Dale DeGroff; DJ bar Dust and club Turnmills make worthy sidekicks, while the Jerusalem Tavern, tucked away on Britton Street, is a must-see for its marvellous interior and brews from Suffolk's St Peter's Brewery. Other notable pubs include the jocular Three Kings of Clerkenwell, new-built Slaughtered Lamb and handsome corner pub the Green.

Al's Café Bar *11-13 Exmouth Market, EC1R 4QD (7837 4821).*
Anam *3 Chapel Market, N1 9EZ (7278 1001).*
Angelic *57 Liverpool Road, N1 0RJ (7278 8433/www.theangelic.co.uk).*
Apple Tree *45 Mount Pleasant, WC1X 0AE (7837 2365).*
Betsey Trotwood *56 Farringdon Road, EC1R 3BL (7253 4285).*
Bierodrome *173-174 Upper Street, N1 1XS (7226 5835/www.belgo-restaurants.com).*
Bull *98-100 Upper Street, N1 0NP (7354 9174).*
Café Kick *43 Exmouth Market, EC1R 4QL (7837 8077/www.cafekick.co.uk).*
Castle *54 Pentonville Road, N1 9LA (7713 1858).*
Colebrooke's *69 Colebrooke Row, N1 8AA (7226 7517/www.colebrookes.co.uk).*

Cuba Libra *72 Upper Street, N1 0NY (7354 9998).*
Duchess of Kent *441 Liverpool Road, N7 8PR (7609 7104/www.geronimo-inns.co.uk).*
Dust *27 Clerkenwell Road, EC1M 5RN (7490 5120/www.dustbar.co.uk).*
Embassy Bar *119 Essex Road, N1 2SN (7226 7901/www.embassybar.com).*
Filthy MacNasty's *68 Amwell Street, EC1R 1UU (7837 6067/www.filthymacnastys.com).*
Green *29 Clerkenwell Green, EC1R 0DU (7490 8010/www.thegreen.co.uk).*
Hope & Anchor *207 Upper Street, N1 1RL (7354 1312).*
Island Queen *87 Noel Road, N1 8HD (7704 7631).*
Jay Cubed *73 White Lion Street, N1 9PF (7837 1892).*
Jerusalem Tavern *55 Britton Street, EC1M 5UQ (7490 4281/www.stpetersbrewery.co.uk).*
Keston Lodge *131 Upper Street, N1 1QP (7354 5550/www.kestonlodge.com).*
King's Head *115 Upper Street, N1 1QN (7226 0364/www.kingsheadtheatre.org).*
Landseer *37 Landseer Road, N19 4JU (7263 4658/www.thelandseer.com).*
Lush *235 Upper Street, N1 1RU (7704 6977).*
Match EC1 *45-47 Clerkenwell Road, EC1M 5RS (7250 4002/www.matchbar.com).*
Matt & Matt Bar *112 Upper Street, N1 1QN (7226 6035/www.mattandmatt.co.uk).*
Medicine Bar *181 Upper Street, N1 1RQ (7704 9536/www.medicinebar.net).*
Mucky Pup *39 Queen's Head Street, N1 8NQ (7226 2572/www.muckypup-london.com).*

Islington

Estorick Collection. *See p113.*

Narrow Boat *119 St Peter Street, N1 8PZ (7288 0572).*
Old China Hand *8 Tysoe Street, EC1R 4RQ (7278 7678).*
Old Queen's Head *44 Essex Road, N1 8LN (no phone).*
Rosemary Branch *2 Shepperton Road, N1 3DT (7704 2730/www.rosemarybranch.co.uk).*
Salmon & Compass *58 Penton Street, N1 9PZ (7837 3891/www.salmonandcompass.com).*
Settle Inn *17-19 Archway Road, N19 3TX (7272 7872).*
Slaughtered Lamb *34-35 Great Sutton Street, EC1V 0DX (7253 1516).*
Swimmer at the Grafton Arms *13 Eburne Road, N7 6AR (7281 4632).*
Three Kings of Clerkenwell *7 Clerkenwell Close, EC1R 0DY (7253 0483).*
Turnmills *63B Clerkenwell Road, EC1M 5NT (7250 3409/www.turnmills.co.uk).*
25 Canonbury Lane *25 Canonbury Lane, N1 2AS (7226 0955).*
Warwick *45 Essex Road, N1 2SF (7688 2882).*

Shops

Though Islington – along with most other boroughs – has its shopping twilight zones (the pound shops of Archway, anyone?), it also has some retail hotspots. At the very south of the borough, Clerkenwell Green (home to ace jeweller's Lesley Craze Gallery) and Exmouth Market hold a great selection of independent retailers. Exmouth Market highlights include convivial CD store Clerkenwell Music, the equally welcoming Metropolitan Books, Space EC1 (cards and gifts), Family Tree (idiosyncratic gifts and clothes) and EC One (modern jewellery); foodwise, there's Brindisa (Spanish delicacies) and Sweet (baker and pâtisserie). Just north, on Arlington Way, there's an intriguing mix of fashion and accessories at Saloon, while on Amwell Street the Emma Hope shoe store, textiles outlet Wallace Sewell and second-hand book dealer Amwell Book Company are worth a detour.

Several hundred yards on, you hit shopping central – Upper Street. High-street chains are clustered in and around the N1 Centre. Nearby there are the food, clothing and household goods stalls of Chapel Market, while more individual outlets are dotted the length of Upper Street. Furniture and fashion are the main focus. Modern furniture is sold at Aria, Atelier Abigail Ahern, Living Space, Twentytwentyone and Fandango; more trad but still funky stuff can be found at After Noah, Chest of Drawers and Castle Gibson. Florists include Angel Flowers and Paula Pryke.

Must-visit boutiques are Clusaz, Comfort & Joy, Diverse, Labour of Love, Palette London and Sefton; there are also branches of Whistles and Space NK, wedding store Morgan Davies, Tallulah Lingerie and jewellery outlets Canal, Dinny Hall, Stephen Einhorn and gill wing. The sheer range of shops gives the place individuality: bric-a-brac and second-hand clothing devotees love Past Caring; fancy dress and party goods can be found at Preposterous Presents; Loop Knit Salon sells exquisite wool and associated tools. There are delis aplenty, but food shops worth noting are Euphorium Bakery and Steve Hatt fish shop; and no shop exemplifies the area's rise in status as well as smart diner/deli Ottolenghi. There's also a farmers' market behind the Town Hall (10am-2pm Sunday).

The area around Camden Passage holds antiques shops galore, but also quirkier one-offs such as design store Cho Cho San, vintage clothing outlet Annie's, boutique Kein Yuki, costume jeweller Eclectia, 20th-century design haunt Origin Modernism, and quaint delicatessen Mr Christian's.

Interesting places peter out as Highbury Corner approaches; the main artery of Holloway Road is best avoided unless you're after Waitrose and Marks & Spencer, or the odd gem such as Back in Time (retro furniture at decent prices) and D&A Binder (stylish reclaimed shop fittings). Liverpool Road has a few unusual outlets, such as rental venture the Film Shop.

In the other direction, there's a cluster of shops at Highbury Barn, though the only one worth making a journey for is the original branch of deluxe cheese shop La Fromagerie. Further north, Blackstock Road is lined with Middle Eastern and Mediterranean food stores, many of them open late.

After Noah *121 Upper Street, N1 1QP (7359 4281/www.afternoah.com).*
Amwell Book Company *53 Amwell Street, EC1R 1UR (7837 4891).*
Angel Flowers *60 Upper Street, N1 0NY (7704 6312/www.angel-flowers.co.uk).*
Annie's Vintage Clothes *12 Camden Passage, N1 8ED (7359 0796).*
Aria *133 Upper Street, N1 1QP (7226 1021) & 295-297 Upper Street, N1 2TU (7704 1999/ www.aria-shop.co.uk).*
Atelier Abigail Ahern *41 Cross Street, N1 2BB (7354 8181/www.atelierbypost.com).*

Back in Time 93 Holloway Road, N7 8LT (7700 0744/www.backintimeuk.com).
Brindisa 32 Exmouth Market, EC1R 4QE (7713 1666/www.brindisa.com).
Canal 42 Cross Street, N1 2BA (7704 0222).
Castle Gibson 106A Upper Street, N1 1QN (7704 0927/www.castlegibson.com).
Chapel Market off Liverpool Road, N1.
Chest of Drawers 281 Upper Street, N1 2TZ (7359 5909/www.chestofdrawers.co.uk).
Cho Cho San 9 Camden Passage, N1 8EA (7359 6000/www.chochosan.co.uk).
Clerkenwell Music 27 Exmouth Market, EC1R 4QL (7833 9757/www.clerkenwellmusic.co.uk).
Clusaz 56 Cross Street, N1 2BA (7359 5596/www.clusaz.co.uk).
Comfort & Joy 109 Essex Road, N1 2SL (7359 3898).
D&A Binder 101 Holloway Road, N7 8LT (7609 6300).
Dinny Hall 292 Upper Street, N1 2TU (7704 1543/www.dinnyhall.com).
Diverse www.diverseclothing.com; women 294 Upper Street, N1 2TU (7359 8877); men 286 Upper Street, N1 2TZ (7359 0081).
Eclectica 2 Charlton Place, N1 8AJ (7226 5625).
EC One 41 Exmouth Market, EC1R 4QL (7713 6185/www.econe.co.uk).
Emma Hope Shoes 33 Amwell Street, EC1R 1UR (7833 2367/www.emmahope.co.uk).
Euphorium Bakery 202 Upper Street, N1 1RQ (7704 6905); 6A Chapel Market, N1 9EN (7837 7010).
Family Tree 53 Exmouth Market, EC1R 4QL (7278 1084/www.familytreeshop.co.uk).
Fandango 50 Cross Street, N1 2BA (7226 1777/www.fandango.uk.com).
Film Shop 239 Liverpool Road, N1 1LX (7700 7170).
La Fromagerie 30 Highbury Park, N5 2AA (7359 7440/www.lafromagerie.co.uk).
gill wing 182 Upper Street, N1 1RQ (7359 4378).
Islington Farmers' Market William Tyndale School, Upper Street, N1 (7833 0338/www.lfm.org.uk).
Kein Yuki 32 Duncan Street, N1 8BW (7833 1032/www.keinyuki.com).
Labour of Love 193 Upper Street, N1 1RQ (7354 9333/www.labour-of-love.co.uk).
Lesley Craze Gallery 33-35A Clerkenwell Green, EC1R 0DU (7608 0393/www.lesleycrazegallery.co.uk).
Living Space 36 Cross Street, N1 2BG (7359 3950/www.livingspaceuk.com).
Loop Knit Salon 41 Cross Street, N1 2BB (7288 1160/www.loop.gb.com).
Metropolitan Books 49 Exmouth Market, EC1R 4QP (7278 6900/www.metropolitanbooks.co.uk).
Morgan Davies 62 Cross Street, N1 2BA (7354 3414/www.morgandavieslondon.co.uk).
Mr Christian's 20 Camden Passage, N1 8ED (7359 4103/www.mrchristians.co.uk).
N1 Centre 21 Parkfield Street, N1 0PS (7359 2674/www.n1islington.com).

Deli/café **Ottolenghi**. See p111.

Ottolenghi 287 Upper Street, N1 2TZ (7288 1454).
Origin Modernism 25 Camden Passage, N1 8EA (7704 1326/www.origin101.co.uk).
Palette London 21 Canonbury Lane, N1 2AS (7288 7428/www.palette-london.com).
Past Caring 76 Essex Road, N1 8LT (no phone).
Paula Pryke Flowers The Flower House, Cynthia Street, N1 9JF (7837 7336/www.paula-pryke-flowers.com).
Preposterous Presents 262 Upper Street, N1 2UQ (7226 4166).
Saloon 23 Arlington Way, EC1R 1UY (7278 4497/www.saloonshop.co.uk).
Sefton women 271 Upper Street, N1 2UQ (7226 9822); men 196 Upper Street, N1 1RQ (7226 7076).
Space EC1 25 Exmouth Market, EC1R 4QL (7837 1344).
Space NK 299 Upper Street, N1 2TU (7704 2822/www.spacenk.co.uk).
Stephen Einhorn 210 Upper Street, N1 1RL (7359 4977/www.stepheneinhorn.co.uk).
Steve Hatt 88-90 Essex Road, N1 8LU (7226 3963).
Sweet 64 Exmouth Market, EC1R 4QP (7713 6777/www.sweetdesserts.co.uk).
Tallulah Lingerie 65 Cross Street, N1 2BB (7704 0066/www.tallulah-lingerie.co.uk).
Twentytwentyone 274 Upper Street, N1 2UA (7288 1996/www.twentytwentyone.com).
Wallace Sewell 24 Lloyd Baker Street, WC1X 9AZ (7833 2995/www.wallacesewell.com).
Whistles 135-136 Upper Street, N1 1QP (7226 7551/www.whistles.co.uk).

'Pubs have either closed to make way for wine bars, or now sell cashew nuts instead of crisps.'

Brett Martin, estate agent

Arts & attractions

Cinemas & theatres

Almeida Theatre *Almeida Street, N1 1TA (7359 4404/www.almeida.co.uk).*
King's Head *115 Upper Street, N1 1QN (7226 0364/www.kingsheadtheatre.org).* A pioneer of the pub theatre scene.
Little Angel Theatre *14 Dagmar Passage, off Cross Street, N1 2DN (7226 1787/www.little angeltheatre.com).* London's only permanent puppet theatre.
Odeon Holloway Road *Holloway Road, N7 6LJ (0871 224 4007/www.odeon.co.uk).*
Rosemary Branch *2 Shepperton Road, N1 3DT (7704 2730/www.rosemarybranch. co.uk).*
Sadler's Wells *Rosebery Avenue, EC1R 4TN (0870 737 7737/www.sadlerswells.com).* One of the premier dance venues in the world.
Screen on the Green *Islington Green, Upper Street, N1 0NP (7226 3520/www.screen cinemas.co.uk).*
Vue Islington *Parkfield Street, N1 0PS (0871 224 0240/www.myvue.com).*

Galleries & museums

Crafts Council *44A Pentonville Road, N1 9BY (7278 7700/www.craftscouncil.org.uk).* Home to innovatively designed exhibitions of contemporary crafts, together with a shop and reference library.
Estorick Collection of Modern Italian Art *39A Canonbury Square, N1 2AN (7704 9522/ www.estorickcollection.com).* Work by Italian painters such as Balla, Boccioni and Carra; also a museum, bookshop and café.
Museum & Library of the Order of St John *St John's Gate, St John's Lane, EC1M 4DA (7324 4000/www.sja.org.uk/history).* Charts the evolution of the medieval Order of Hospitaller Knights to its modern incarnation as the world-reknowned ambulance service.

Music & comedy venues

Carling Academy Islington *N1 Centre, 16 Parkfield Street, N1 0PS (7288 4400/ www.islington-academy.co.uk).* Slightly soulless shopping mall venue; however, the capital's lack of midsize spaces means it's become a default haunt for international cult acts.
Garage *20-22 Highbury Corner, N5 1RD (7607 1818/Ticketmaster 0870 534 4444).* Low-ceilinged shoebox with an ever-changing line-up of indie, rock, punk and metal acts.

Hen & Chickens *109 St Paul's Road, N1 2NA (7704 2001/www.henandchickens.com).* Well-established comedy joint hosting a mixture of known names and newcomers.
LSO St Luke's *161 Old Street, EC1V 9NG (7490 3939/www.lso.co.uk/lsostlukes).* Restored Hawksmoor church now used for rehearsals by the London Symphony Orchestra. Free lunchtime and occasional evening concerts.

Other attractions

Business Design Centre *52 Upper Street, N1 0QH (7359 3535/www.businessdesign centre.co.uk).* Trade fairs and conferences, including some major art and design shows.
Candid Arts Trust *3 Torrens Street, EC1V 1NQ (7837 4237/www.candidarts.com).* Two Victorian warehouses behind Angel station, converted into exhibition space that includes two loft-style galleries, 20 art studios, rehearsal space, a screening room and an excellent café.

Open spaces

Barnard Park *Copenhagen Street, N1.*
Bunhill Fields *City Road, EC1 (www.cityof london.gov.uk/openspaces).* Ancient graveyard that's become something of a secret garden, with mossy, titled graves and memorials to the likes of William Blake and Daniel Defoe.
Caledonian Park *Market Road, N7.*
Elthorne Park *Hazelville Road, N19.*
Finsbury Square *Finsbury Square, EC2.*
Freightliners City Farm *Paradise Park, Sheringham Road, off Liverpool Road, N7 8PF (7609 0467/www.freightlinersfarm.org.uk).*
Gillespie Park *Drayton Park, N5.* Features the Islington Ecology Centre (7354 5162/www. islington.gov.uk), an imaginative development of former railway land with woodlands, meadows, wetlands and ponds.
Highbury Fields *Highbury Crescent, N5.* Islington's largest open space, and once a refuge to 200,000 people fleeing the Great Fire of London.
Paradise Park *Sheringham Road, N7.*
Rosemary Gardens *Southgate Road, N1.*
Whittington Park *Holloway Road, N19.*

Sport & fitness

Aquaterra Leisure, which runs seven of Islington's eight public centres, is a charity organisation that invests the money spent by the public back into the facilities.

Islington

Although the buildings themselves could use a revamp, the scope of facilities and activities offered is impressive. Kids have everything from fun pools and team games to ice hockey and martial arts to amuse them. Saddlers Sports Centre is affiliated to the nearby City University, but is open to all. For something more luxurious, you'll need, as ever, to turn to the private sector: there's a wide choice between well-designed independents and the big-name chains.

Gyms & leisure centres

Archway Leisure Centre *McDonald Road, N19 5DD (7281 4105/www.aquaterra.org).*
Cally Pool *229 Caledonian Road, N1 0NH (7278 1890/www.aquaterra.org).*
Dowe Dynamics Gym *1-2 Central Hall Buildings, Archway Close, N19 3UB (7281 2267).* Private.
Esporta *Islington Green, 27 Essex Road, N1 3PS (7288 8200/www.esporta.com).* Private.
The Factory (& Tango London) *407 Hornsey Road, N19 4DX (7272 1122/www.tango london.com).* Private.
Finsbury Leisure Centre *Norman Street, EC1V 3PU (7253 2346/www.aquaterra.org).*
Fitness First *60-63 Bunhill Row, EC1Y 8NQ (7490 3555/www.fitnessfirst.co.uk); 67-83 Seven Sisters Road, N7 6BU (7281 8585).* Private.
Highbury Pool *Highbury Crescent, N5 1RR (7704 2312/www.aquaterra.org).*
Holmes Place *Coinwood Business Centre, Mercers Road, N19 4PJ (7561 5200/www.holmes place.com); 33 Bunhill Row, EC1Y 8LP (7448 5454).* Private.
Inspirations *Holiday Inn Hotel, 1 King's Cross Road, WC1X 9HX (7837 0115).* Private.
Ironmonger Row Baths *1-11 Ironmonger Row, EC1V 3QF (7253 4011/www.aqua terra.org).*
Maximum Fitness *144 Fortess Road, NW5 2HP (7482 3941/www.maxfit.co.uk).* Private.
Saddlers Sports Centre *122 Goswell Road, EC1V 0HB (7040 5656/www.city.ac.uk/ sportscentre).*
Sequin Park *240 Upper Street, N1 1RU (7704 9844/www.sequinpark.co.uk).* Private.
Sobell Leisure Centre & Ice Rink *Hornsey Road, N7 7NY (7609 2166/www.aquaterra.org).*
Virgin Active *333 Goswell Road, EC1V 7DG (0845 130 9222/www.virginactive.co.uk).* Private.

Other facilities

Islington Tennis Centre *Market Road, N7 9PL (7700 1370/www.aquaterra.org).*

Spectator sports

Arsenal FC *until May 2006 Arsenal Stadium, Avenell Road, N5 1BU (7704 4000/box office 7704 4040/tours 7704 4504/www.arsenal.com); from summer 2006 Emirates Stadium, Ashburton Grove, N7.*

Schools

WHAT THE PARENTS SAY:

‘ At primary level, Islington has a good selection of schools; Gillespie Primary School, near Arsenal Stadium, is popular for its cultural diversity and attached nursery. Elsewhere, the similarly small and cosy St John Evangelist RC Primary School has a good reputation – you need to have a proven church-going record to get in here (the local vic carries a tick-list). Similarly, St Joan of Arc RC Primary School – where the Blair children schooled – has recently benefited from a classroom expansion, but can be hard for non-Catholics to get in to. Ambler Primary School near Finsbury Park isn't as popular; some parents blame recent poor league-table performances on the frequent changes in headteacher. William Tyndale Primary School on Upper Street is held in high regard, but has quite a long waiting list.

At secondary level, things are more bleak. Many parents move or send their kids to private school rather than risk the Islington options. Islington Green School is not a popular choice, with poor exam results and Ofsted failure in its past. Highbury Grove School, in its ugly concrete building, has a dreadful reputation – bad results, and a teacher was stabbed there a few years ago. Tables-wise, Holloway School has fared little better, with one of the lowest GCSE turnouts in the borough.

I joined a group of parents who were concerned about the state of schools in the area. Nearly all of us ended up moving out of the borough, and the only two sets of parents I know who didn't ended up sending their kids to private school.’
Carrie Lambe, mother of two

Primary

There are 48 state primary schools in Islington, 16 of which are church schools. There are also seven independent primaries, including one Montessori school and one Steiner school. See www.islington.gov.uk/education and www.ofsted.gov.uk for more information.

Secondary

Central Foundation Boys' School *City Road, EC2A 4SH (7253 3741/www.cfbs.islington. sch.uk).* Boys only.
Elizabeth Garrett Anderson Language College *Risinghill Street, off Penton Street, N1 9QG (7837 0739/www.egas.islington.sch.uk).* Girls only.
Highbury Fields School *Highbury Hill, N5 1AR (7288 1888/www.highburyfields. islington.sch.uk).* Girls only.

Highbury Grove School *Highbury New Park,*
N5 2EG (7288 8900/www.highburygrove.
islington.sch.uk).
Holloway School *Hilldrop Road, N7 0JG*
(7607 5885/www.holloway.islington.sch.uk).
Islington Arts & Media School *Turle Road,*
N4 3LS (7281 3302/www.iamschool.co.uk).
Islington Green School *Prebend Street, N1*
8PQ (7226 8611/www.igschool.com).
Mount Carmel Technology College for
Girls *Holland Walk, Duncombe Road, N19 3EU*
(7281 3536/www.mountcarmel.islington.sch.uk).
Girls only.
St Aloysius RC College *Hornsey Lane, N6*
5LY (7263 1391). Boys only.

Property

WHAT THE AGENTS SAY:

❝Everything is here on Upper Street. Every other
shop is a café, restaurant or bar, and there are
plenty of places to go and enjoy yourself – it's
very social. The new N1 shopping centre has
brought high-street shops such as Gap and Karen
Millen, and then there's the big Vue cinema –
both have made the area more commercial. A
very diverse and artistic group of people live
here, from actors to lawyers and solicitors who
are only a walk away from their jobs in the City.
From Angel you can easily walk into work, and
because of Upper Street there's less need to go
into the West End for shopping. Camden Passage
is evolving – already famous for its antiques,
there are now more boutiques and jewellery
shops moving in and drawing the crowds. There
are still a lot of council houses in the borough;
also Georgian and Victorian terraces with
original period features, which are mostly
split into flats.❞
Emma Evans, Evans Baker, Angel

❝Archway, Holloway and Tufnell Park are
affordable neighbourhoods compared to
surrounding areas and for those that can't meet
the prices in Highgate. It has improved tenfold
in the past five or six years – the increase in
young professionals moving here has encouraged
a higher quality of shops and bars. The area
is over-run with first-time buyers, but is also
popular with families and couples. Once people
buy here, they tend to stay and it is yet to fulfil
its full potential.❞
Brett Martin, JTM Homes, Archway

Average property prices
Detached £548,222
Semi-detached £514,808
Terraced £453,242
Flat £240,617

Local estate agents
APS Estates *210-212 Caledonian Road, N1*
0SQ (7837 0203/www.apsestates.com).
Currell Estate Agents *321 Upper Street, N1*
2XQ (7226 4200/www.currell.com).
Evans Baker *6 Camden Walk, Camden*
Passage, N1 8DY (7354 0066/www.evans
baker.co.uk).
Jeffrey Nicholas *293 Upper Street, N1 2TU*
(7354 0707/www.jeffreynicholas.co.uk).
JTM Homes *695 Holloway Road, N19 5SE*
(7272 1090/www.jtmhomes.co.uk).
Moving On Property Services *79 Pitfield*
Street, N1 6BT (7336 8882/www.moving
onlondon.com).
myspace *328 Caledonian Road, N1 1BB*
(7609 3598/www.myspaceuk.com).
Thomson Currie *313 Upper Street, N1 2XQ*
(7354 5224/www.thomsoncurrie.co.uk).
Urban Spaces *70 Clerkenwell Road, EC1M*
5QA (7251 4000/www.urbanspaces.co.uk).

COUNCIL TAX

A	up to £40,000	**£771.08**
B	£40,001-£52,000	**£899.59**
C	£52,001-£68,000	**£1,028.10**
D	£68,001-£88,000	**£1,156.61**
E	£88,001-£120,000	**£1,413.63**
F	£120,001-£160,000	**£1,670.65**
G	£160,001-£320,000	**£1,927.69**
H	over £320,000	**£2,313.22**

Other information

Council
Islington Council *222 Upper Street, N1 1XR*
(7527 2000/www.islington.gov.uk).

Hospitals
Whittington Hospital *Highgate Hill, N19 5NF*
(7272 3070/www.whittington.nhs.uk).

Legal services
Islington CAB *The Advice & Learning Centre,*
86 Durham Road, N7 7DU (0870 751 0925/
www.adviceguide.org.uk).

Local newspapers
Islington Tribune *7419 9000/www.camden*
newjournal.co.uk.
Islington Gazette *8342 5700/www.islington*
gazette.co.uk.

Allotments
The waiting list for those hoping to secure an
allotment in the borough is now at least ten
years. This list has therefore been closed to
new applicants until further notice. For
further information on the subject, contact
the Greenspace & Leisure Support Services
Team on 7527 4953.

'There's a story that psychiatrists the world over used to send their patients to Camden to convalesce. The area is very tolerant of eccentricity.'

**Mary Cane, former mayor of Camden
and daily swimmer in Hampstead
Heath Swimming Ponds**

Camden

Like an upper-crust sandwich with a spicy filling, Camden embraces the elegant Georgian squares of Bloomsbury, salubrious Highgate, bookish Hampstead and posh Primrose Hill. At its centre, though, are the soon-to-be-transformed King's Cross, and the assault on the senses that is Camden Town.

Neighbourhoods

Bloomsbury

Elegant and reserved, Bloomsbury is quintessential central London, without the manic bustle of the neighbouring West End. A long-time haunt of the literati, it has accommodated centuries of thinking and drinking. The district famously lent its name to Virginia Woolf's fashionably arty, early 20th-century cohorts, the Bloomsbury Group. About half a century earlier, Charles Dickens lived in Tavistock Square – the site of the bus bombing on 7 July 2005.

Amid numerous pretty squares and a glut of hotels and expensive B&Bs, you'll find many centres of study here, most notably

the sprawling campus of the University of London. Its union (www.ulu.co.uk), based on Malet Street, includes a music venue and sports facilities that are open to the public.

High-rise landmarks include the imposing Senate House, where the Ministry of Information was based during World War II (apparently, it was George Orwell's inspiration for the Ministry of Truth in *1984*). It's now the university's biggest library. There's also no mistaking the domed roof of the British Museum. If you don't have time to view the museum's crowded exhibitions, come to see the light-flooded spectacle of the Great Court, designed by Norman Foster; it's an uplifting experience, even on the greyest London day. Sidestep the tacky souvenir shops in the locality, and you'll find some classy

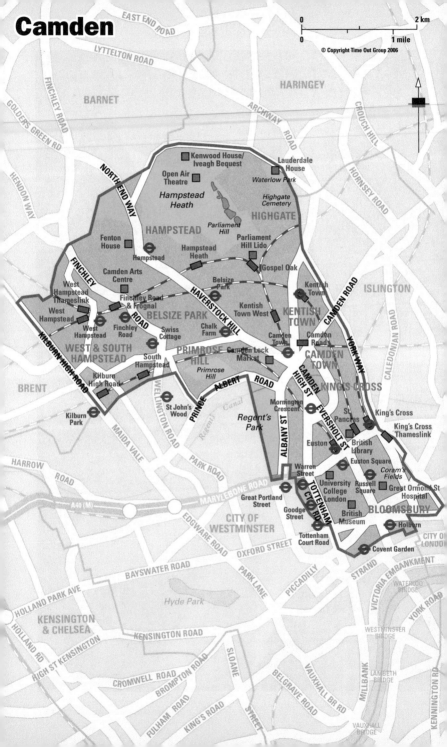

second-hand bookshops and art supplies. Some of the best occupy the ornate, pedestrianised Sicilian Avenue.

Of the neighbourhood's green spaces, Russell Square Gardens were tastefully landscaped in 2002, with a café and fountain at the centre; once an infamous gay cruising ground, they're now locked at night. Across the road from Russell Square tube station is the stark concrete architecture of Brunswick Square, which includes flats and a shopping centre (currently undergoing renovation to house incoming Starbucks, Nando's and the like; the closure of its delightful second-hand bookshop was a bitter local loss). The quirky Cartoon Museum, once the Cartoon Art Trust, moved from here in late 2005 (it reopened on Little Russell Street in February 2006) but the Renoir arthouse cinema remains. Coram's Fields is another striking open space nearby, which was once the site of the Foundlings Hospital established by Thomas Coram, the 18th-century philanthropist. The park signs state that adults are only admitted as the guest of a child. You might even find sheep grazing on its lawns.

To the south is the delightful Lincoln's Inn Fields, the largest garden square in London. It's beloved by four very distinct city tribes: the homeless, cabbies, local dog-walkers, and lawyers (although few barristers now live above the shop here). Tourists who've found their way to Sir John Soane's Museum also swell the lunching crowds in this serene corner of the city centre, but after business hours, the area's streets can appear quite empty.

Camden Town

More than any other part of London, Camden Town is a raucous clash of alternative culture and blatant commercialism. Since the 1970s, this neighbourhood has been inextricably linked with music; it has inspired countless songs, from the likes of Morrissey and Madness frontman Suggs, and was at the heart of the mid-1990s Britpop scene. Venues like the iconic Roundhouse (currently being redeveloped) once hosted Jimi Hendrix and the Doors, while the famous Barfly has been a sticky-floored launch pad for acts including the Strokes, Coldplay and Badly Drawn Boy.

The area around Camden Town tube is perpetually thronging – and sometimes intimidating, due to the population of drug-pushers touting their wares. Camden Market's far-reaching fame means that the area can become unbearably crowded at weekends (when tourists and excitable teens seem to dominate the masses); in response, the station is closed to exiting passengers on Sunday afternoons.

In fact, Camden Market comprises six different markets; Stables Market (weekends only) is the biggest, housed in a former Victorian horse hospital and specialising in vintage clothing and antiques. The distinctively colourful shop-fronts along Chalk Farm Road bear huge decorative sculptures of their wares (giant Doc Marten boots, leather jackets and the like) that haven't changed for years. In some respects, Camden Town can seem stuck in a time warp – but if you're after novelty DMs or cyberpunk hair extensions, look no further.

Local residents aged over 30 tend to avoid the market; unless your abode is on Chalk Farm Road, it's possible to live quite happily in the district without getting entangled in the weekend crowds. And you soon become oblivious to the mess created – after all, if you wanted middle-class seemliness, you wouldn't live here. Older, discerning Camdenites are more likely to hang out in Islington, Marylebone High Street or even Kentish Town (Bill Nighy is a regular spot, as is Jon Snow) – all of which are within easy reach. That's the joy of Camden: everything's on your doorstep. You could be in the mêlée of the market one minute, then walk a few hundred metres and find yourself in serene Primrose Hill. Or take a leisurely stroll along the Regent's Canal, which passes under the humpbacked bridges of Camden Lock.

Kentish Town

Walk up Kentish Town Road, away from the noisy sprawl of Camden Town, and the neighbourhood takes on an increasingly residential feel. There's no longer any sign of bucolic roots, or of the River Fleet, which once flowed through here from Hampstead. The nearest thing you'll find is Kentish Town City Farm (founded in 1972), offering animals, gardening space and horse-riding lessons. Should you crave more greenery, Hampstead Heath is only a short distance away.

On the whole, Kentish Town has a youthful feel to it (partly because of popular music venue, the Forum), but without the tourist clamour that Camden Town attracts. The cheapest house prices in the borough have traditionally been located in Kentish Town, up to Gospel Oak (although the area is going increasingly upmarket). The result is an engagingly diverse neighbourhood.

Transport links are very good (even though South Kentish Town tube station was closed in 1924 – you can still see its remains on Kentish Town Road), as is the range of local shops, including independent businesses. The street market at Queen's Crescent is very much a local affair, treasured by many in the vicinity who are fighting for its survival. There's also a decent selection of pubs; the Pineapple has a particularly convivial reputation.

The main roads of Kentish Town can seem dingy and rough around the edges, but there's big-scale beauty in its buildings, including the Grade II-listed St Pancras Public Baths and Victorian terraces. Off the beaten track, side streets reveal a surprisingly sedate side to this inner-city suburb.

King's Cross

King's Cross takes its name from a homage to King George IV, but its reputation has never been particularly regal. For many years, it was most notorious for drug deals, prostitution and homelessness, and the area around the stations still doesn't seem like somewhere you'd want to linger, with side streets dotted with massage parlours and unappealing takeaways. But King's Cross is undeniably in the throes of change. As we went to press, council applications were still being revised for the area's regeneration, with proposals including more public open space, community facilities and eco-friendly energy initiatives. Much of this radical redevelopment is linked to the forthcoming high-speed Channel Tunnel rail link, which is due to open in 2007. A new Thameslink station is currently under construction, while the tube station's expansion is scheduled to continue until 2009; for now, it's a messy interchange full of traffic cones and builders clad in fluorescent jackets.

West towards Euston, St Pancras Chambers has a wonderfully elaborate interior to match the building's Gothic façade; it's often used for film shoots, and a residential/hotel conversion has been mooted. Further along Euston Road sits the British Library – an absolute treasure, with a sweeping concrete courtyard (not as unappealing as it sounds) and a cavernous yet eminently peaceful interior. Books aside, King's Cross is also well served by a busy nightlife; key to this is the York Way Goods Depot, transformed into a clubby 'village' by night with three all-night venues (the Cross, EGG and Canvas, formerly Bagleys Studios). If you're looking for a different kind of wildlife, then visit Camley Street Natural Park, a surprising two-acre oasis of waters and woodland.

Belsize Park

A fancy pocket tucked between Camden Town and Hampstead, Belsize Park was at one time the scenic surrounds of a private mansion, Belsize House (demolished in the 1800s). In more recent years, it has gained a distinct identity, thanks mainly to a blend of exclusive residences (many of the Victorian and Edwardian townhouses have been converted into flats), chi-chi retailers and celebrity patronage. Don't expect many

Highs & Lows

▲ **Location** The greenery of Hampstead Heath or Regent's Park is nearby, yet the West End is only a quick bus journey away

Live music With iconic venues like the Barfly and the Forum, the intimate Jazz Café and a score of band-welcoming pubs and bars, Camden is a big player in the music scene

Camden Market A top London tourist attraction, this vibrant market is one of a kind...

Camden Market ...but residents who don't like crowds (or teenagers) give it a wide berth. The closure of the tube on Sunday is also a source of much vexation

Drug pushers Don't expect to get more than a few yards from Camden Town station without being asked 'Wan' weed?'

Hampstead prices It was once known as an enclave of artists and intellectuals, but how many ▼ can afford to live here now?

Kenwood House, a much-loved, much-used Hampstead landmark.

bargain price tags around here. What you will find, though, is plenty of green space, refurbished gastropubs and quaint, pedestrianised shopping areas. England's Lane, in the cosy heart of what is sometimes referred to as Belsize Village, is an enjoyable spot for pricey window shopping (although the usual chains are creeping in). Even the local cinema is comfortably tasteful; the Screen on the Hill is located opposite the tube station, and shows a mix of mainstream and independent films. The area also features a close-knit Jewish community, with two local synagogues.

Hampstead

Fashions come and go in London's property market, but NW3 is eternally desirable – and prohibitively expensive. To many envious eyes, Hampstead has it all: an expanse of semi-wild parkland; attractively steep streets; swathes of beautiful period housing; a view across the city; some great pubs; and delectable delis.

Hampstead has always pulled in the celebrities, from poets (Robert Louis Stevenson) to pop stars (Rachel Stevens). George Michael and Anthony Minghella are also here, along with a plethora of professional footballers. Other figures have come and gone: Dick Turpin was supposedly born at the whitewashed Spaniard Inn pub, which continues to

squeeze the traffic along the road of the same name; Keats House is where the poet penned his 'Ode to a Nightingale' in 1819; and the Freud Museum on Maresfield Gardens is the former residence of the famous psychoanalyst (Hampstead remains a popular home for therapists today).

The Heath is naturally one of the area's biggest assets; at its north end lies the elegant neo-classical Kenwood House. During the summer months, the north London intelligentsia turn up with picnics to enjoy the open-air classical music concerts. The Heath also contains three open-air swimming ponds – one for men, one for women and the third mixed. Local swimmers are fighting to keep them open.

House prices are predictably silly; large family homes go for over £1 million. So, although Hampstead has long had a reputation for attracting intellectuals and artists, in reality many have had to make way for wealthy financial types.

There's a surfeit of schools in the area, many of them private, so congestion is hellish during the school run. Controlled Parking Zones (CPZs) are another bone of local contention, as are the high rents charged to shops by Camden Council: a policy that might mean the loss of several treasured independents. Ominously, a Tesco Metro has started trading here in

College Lane, **Kentish Town**. *See p119.*

Thameslink and Silverlink trains both stop here, and there are vague plans for Chiltern Railways (to the Midlands) and the Metropolitan Line to stop off too. It is envisaged that there'll be one big station to house everything, including the existing Jubilee Line stop, but at present they're all separate, which is confusing for the uninitiated and tiresome for locals who have to walk between three stations.

Few Londoners know of the existence of South Hampstead as an area, unless they're familiar with yet another overland station (which takes you one stop to Euston in eight minutes on the Silverlink Metro) or have looked at the *A-Z*. What the place should be known for is Maryon Wilson Estate, which was built in the late 19th century and contains the area's priciest housing. Most property consists of stately red-brick mansion blocks or large detached villas such as those around Priory Road and Compayne Gardens. Several houses here remain gloriously spacious family homes, but many were converted into flats in the 1970s. Some of these are now quite scruffy and are one of the cheapest ways to buy into the area. Alternatively, plunder the large rental market. Further north, around Fortune Green, smaller Victorian terraces are proving increasingly popular with young families who could never afford Hampstead or Highgate.

Slightly shabby in parts, surprisingly grand in others, West Hampstead is still in its ascendancy. If you want to move to north-west London and live this side of Kilburn and Willesden, get in while you can.

the past year, and Marks & Spencer is due to open soon in South End Green.

And yet, especially in its beautiful backstreets, Hampstead still weaves a magical spell on the sensitive, artistic and merely aspirational – who come for a look and then fall so hard for its tree-lined roads, gorgeous vistas and discernible whiff of success that they don't even notice the four-wheel drives clogging the streets. What's more, as long as you stay off the Heath at night (and discount burglary), this is a remarkably safe place in which to live.

West and South Hampstead

Thanks to busy Finchley Road separating them, West Hampstead could never be classed as a mere dormitory of Hampstead proper. These days it's very much a district in its own right. West Hampstead is where you come for excellent transport links and a fairly priced bite to eat. Since West End Lane became a restaurant magnet, West Hampstead has emerged as a firm favourite with middle-class, pre-marriage-and-kids couples who aren't rich…yet.

Primrose Hill and Swiss Cottage

The quickest way to make enemies with Primrose Hill dwellers is to accuse them of living in Camden. This district is a genteel and well-heeled world away from its more raucous, easterly neighbour – and residents don't like you to forget it.

The eponymous mound provides lovely hilltop views of the city, within a smallish park. Regent's Park Road and Gloucester Avenue are the local focal points, containing a pretty sprinkling of boutiques, cafés and some constantly busy gastropubs. Most of the diminutive area that constitutes Primrose Hill, however, is residential and this remains the chief draw for the beautiful people who set up home here (as Jude Law and Sadie Frost once did). Rather like Hampstead, the neighbourhood has a reputation as a sanctuary for creative, bohemian types. In reality it's too pricey for most such folk, but they still just outnumber the banking whizzes who fancy a change from Kensington.

The big three-storey stuccoed houses close to the park – not only Primrose Hill but the much larger Regent's Park to the south-east – fetch £2 million if they haven't been converted into flats. Two-bed apartments in these same coveted streets such as Regent's Park Road and the Chaltons (Crescent, Road and Street), go for more than £500,000; one-beds leave you little change from the same amount. An alternative is to bag a flat in one of the area's few postwar blocks; it might not look as grand, but it's the cheapest way of getting your foot in a Primrose Hill door.

Up the hill from here is Swiss Cottage (named for a 19th-century inn fashioned after a chalet), a bit of a non-area that's wedged north of St John's Wood, south-east of West Hampstead and west of Belsize Park. Housing prices are pretty similar to West Hampstead; public transport is excellent (Swiss Cottage and Finchley Road tubes, plus several buses to the West End). The Cottage apart, the most notable building is the modernist landmark Swiss Cottage Library (designed by Sir Basil Spence and restored in 2003).

Highgate and Dartmouth Park

Spilling out from the borough of Camden into Haringey, Highgate is home to a wild and wonderful cemetery (wherein lies Karl Marx). It's far from dead, though, with a buoyant property market and one of the capital's most active community groups, the Highgate Society. The locality isn't quite as expensive to live in as Hampstead, but it's not far behind. Highgate shares many of Hampstead's advantages, such as its elevation and, of course, the Heath (lying to the south-west).

Dartmouth Park is due east of Highgate, just south of the cemetery – but it isn't a park at all. The land bought by and named after the 18th-century Earl of Dartmouth is a peaceful residential area on the slopes up

to Highgate, characterised by streets of late 19th-century terraced and semi-detached houses. Both Dartmouth Park and Highgate are close to the Parliament Hill end of the Heath, with its protected view over London. Once called Traitor's Hill, this elevation is now affectionately known as Kite's Hill, for obvious reasons. Families still make up a sizeable chunk of the local population.

Highgate Village is the prime place to reside in this neck of the woods – and talking of woods, Highgate Wood and Queen's Wood (both across borough boundaries in Haringey, but close) are very lovely. The Village's gated roads housing wealthy families are virtually free of the background hum of traffic. Such semi-rural serenity comes at a price, as does living anywhere very close to the Village, with

STATISTICS

BOROUGH MAKE-UP
Population 204,404
Average weekly pay £556.60
Ethnic origins
 White 73.17%
 Mixed 3.75%
 Asian or Asian British 10.38%
 Black or Black British 8.27%
 Chinese or other 4.43%
Students 14.16%
Retirees 6.98%

HOUSING STOCK
Borough size 21.6km²
No. of households 107,475
Detached 1.8%
Semi-detached 3.6%
Terraced 8.8%
Flats (purpose-built) 47.4%
Flats (converted) 35.7%
Flats (both) 83.1%

CRIME PER 1,000 OF POPULATION
(English average in brackets)
Burglary 11 (6.4)
Robbery 6 (1.4)
Theft of vehicle 6 (4.5)
Theft from vehicle 18 (10)
Violence against the person 36 (16.5)
Sexual offences 3 (0.9)

MPs & COUNCIL
MPs *Hampstead & Highgate* Glenda Jackson CBE (Labour); *Holborn & St Pancras* Rt Hon Frank Dobson (Labour)
CPA 4 stars; improving well

its pretty shops and famous pub, the Flask. Around Pond Square, most houses are Victorian or Georgian, while some even older properties, built around the time of Charles II, can be glimpsed on the Grove. Five-bedroomed, 18th-century piles command almost £3 million in this select enclave. High-end estates, such as the Holly Lodge Estate, are also popular, while Berthold Lubetkin's Highpoint flats, intended for workers in the 1930s, now house the chattering classes.

Public transport is a downside. The Northern Line station is a hike from the Village on congested Archway Road. Still, you can't argue with the locals: you're doing all right if you've made it to N6.

TRANSPORT

Tube stations *Central* Chancery Lane, Holborn, Tottenham Court Road; *Circle* King's Cross St Pancras, Euston Square, Great Portland Street; *Hammersmith & City* King's Cross St Pancras, Euston Square, Great Portland Street; *Jubilee* Swiss Cottage, Finchley Road, West Hampstead; *Metropolitan* King's Cross St Pancras, Euston Square, Great Portland Street, Finchley Road; *Northern* Tottenham Court Road, Goodge Street, Warren Street, Euston, King's Cross St Pancras, Mornington Crescent, Camden Town, Chalk Farm, Belsize Park, Hampstead, Kentish Town; *Piccadilly* Holborn, Russell Square, King's Cross St Pancras; *Victoria* Warren Street, Euston, King's Cross St Pancras
Rail stations *Silverlink* Camden Road, Kentish Town West, Gospel Oak, Hampstead Heath, Finchley Road & Frognal, West Hampstead, South Hampstead, Kilburn High Road; *Thameslink* King's Cross Thameslink, Kentish Town, West Hampstead
Main bus routes dozens of buses run through Camden and into central London – for a full list, visit www.tfl.gov.uk/buses; *night buses* N1, N7, N8, N10, N19, N28, N29, N31, N38, N41, N55, N63, N68, N73, N91, N98, N171, N253, N279; *24-hour buses* 14, 24, 25, 27, 88, 134, 139, 176, 189, 214, 242, 243, 274, 390
Development plans International railway station scheduled to open in 2007 with services direct to Paris and Brussels

Restaurants & cafés

Camden Town's eateries reflect the colourful, cosmopolitan nature of the area; try classic Lebanese cooking at Le Mignon, Vietnamese with a French twist at Bluu Grass, reliable tapas at El Parador (or the rowdier Bar Gansa), homely Greek at Andy's Taverna, superior Caribbean at Mango Room, or reliable Portuguese at Pescador. For something sweet afterwards, the puddings at newly opened vegetarian Green Note are sublime. This is also the home of Haché, *Time Out*'s best burger bar winner in 2005; if comfort food is your thing, also try Castle's on Royal College Street for traditional pie and mash. Café Corfu on Pratt Street is arguably London's finest purveyor of modern Greek cuisine; nearby Asakusa is a reasonably priced Japanese option. Also worth a nibble are Cambodian Lemongrass and an outpost of the Belgian chain restaurant, Belgo Noord. A short stroll up the hill finds Chalk Farm institution Marine Ices, known for its own-made ice-cream.

In Primrose Hill, restaurants get pricier and pubs take a swing towards gastro. Most of the dining options are to be found along the villagey Regent's Park Road. Lemonia and older sister Limani continue to serve a bustling crowd with their excellent mezze; Polish staple Trojka is close by, as is quietly romantic French-accented Odette's. Vegetarians, vegans and even meat-eaters should love the surprisingly tasty raw delights at Little Earth Café within the Triyoga centre; charming Manna is also a good herbivorous option. All this is before you get to Primrose Hill's trio of top-notch gastropubs: Queens, Landsdowne and Engineer.

Belsize Park's Hill is also a good gastropub; the rest of the area's culinary scene is dominated by chains (among them the ever-excellent Gourmet Burger Kitchen).

Things aren't great further up the hill in Hampstead: the feeble choice of eateries is always a surprise considering the money locals have to spend. Base meets its Mediterranean criteria well, though, while long-time favourites Jin Kichi (Japanese) and Safir (North African) please with their traditional cuisine. Pescador Two is a safe bet for fish dishes, while newcomer Room 68 hopes to make a splash with its well-worked Italian menu and classy decor. Off the Haverstock Hill to the east, you'll find reasonably priced Polish restaurant and vodka bar Zamoyski, unpretentious and efficient Turkish Zara, and family-friendly Fratelli la Bufala. Away from the busy streets and shoppers, enjoy tea and cake at the charming Brew House café in Kenwood House.

Westwards in the busy thoroughfare of Swiss Cottage, discreet Globe serves up tasty international fare when it's not being used as a cabaret joint (every Thursday), Eriki impresses with its Indian fare, and kids will love Japanese mini-chain Benihana, featuring performing chefs at each table. Further north up Finchley Road, Wakaba's Japanese food exceeds its slightly scruffy exterior. The O_2 Centre boasts a number of the usual chain names, plus Indian canteen Cumin and Cantonese China Red. Nearby, off Finchley Road, Tobia serves fine Ethiopian food on the first floor of the slightly drab community centre.

In West Hampstead, West End Lane keeps the resident middle classes well fed with Italian La Brocca, Modern European Walnut, and fine Cypriot taverna Mario's. Over in Highgate and its surrounds, gastropubs rule: the Bull in Highgate (in a stunning listed building), former *Time Out* award-winning gastropub Highgate to the south, spacious Junction Tavern in Dartmouth Park, and the recently opened Oxford on Kentish Town Road. Café culture is also important here; try Kalendar on Swains Lane and (over borough boundaries, in Haringey) the ever-popular Pavilion Café in Highgate Wood.

Back in King's Cross, dining options virtually disappear; things improve closer to Warren Street, with gastropub Queen's Head & Artichoke, Mexican newcomer Mestizo, and the intimate African Kitchen Gallery. Fish-and-chip shops Fish Bone and North Sea Fish Restaurant are two of the best. Directly south of Euston, Bloomsbury houses a concentration of restaurants between Guilford Street and Theobald's Road: try superior pizza at La Porchetta, great Spanish at Cigala, or Chinese at Sheng's Tea House; the Perseverance is a worthy gastropub, too. West of Tottenham Court Road and just within Camden borders is restaurant hotspot Charlotte Street; best are Tex-Mex shack La Perla, Southern

Vale of Health, **Hampstead**. *See p121.*

Indian Rasa Samudra, Italian Bertorelli, superior tapas joint Fino, classy Japanese Roka, and southern Italian Passione. Mini-chains Busaba Eathai (north on Store Street) and dim T café are also good. But if it's dim sum you're after, Hakkasan, nestled in the borough's south-west corner on Hanway Street, serves up arguably the best Chinese food in town.

African Kitchen Gallery *102 Drummond Street, NW1 2HN (7383 0918).*
Andy's Taverna *81-81A Bayham Street, NW1 0AG (7485 9718).*
Asakusa *265 Eversholt Street, NW1 1BA (7388 8533).*
Bar Gansa *2 Inverness Street, NW1 7HJ (7267 8909/www.gansa.co.uk).*
Base *71 Hampstead High Street, NW3 1QP (7431 2224/www.basefoods.com).*
Belgo Noord *72 Chalk Farm Road, NW1 8AN (7267 0718/www.belgo-restaurants.com).*
Benihana *100 Avenue Road, NW3 3HF (7586 9508/www.benihana.co.uk).*
Bertorelli *19-23 Charlotte Street, W1T 1RL (7636 4174/www.santeonline.co.uk).*
Bluu Grass *6 Plender Street, NW1 0JT (7380 1196).*
Brew House *Kenwood House, Hampstead Lane, NW3 7JR (8341 5384).*

La Brocca *273 West End Lane, NW6 1QS (7433 1989).*
Bull *13 North Hill, N6 4AB (0845 456 5033/www.inthebull.biz).*
Busaba Eathai *22 Store Street, WC1E 7DS (7299 7900).*
Café Corfu *7 Pratt Street, NW1 0AE (7267 8088/www.cafecorfu.com).*
Castle's *229 Royal College Street, NW1 9LT (7485 2196).*
China Red *O_2 Centre, 255 Finchley Road, NW3 6LU (7435 6888/www.chinared restaurant.com).*
Cigala *54 Lamb's Conduit Street, WC1N 3LW (7405 1717/www.cigala.co.uk).*
Cumin *O_2 Centre, 255 Finchley Road, NW3 6LU (7794 5616/www.cumin.co.uk).*
dim T café *32 Charlotte Street, W1T 2NQ (7637 1122/www.dimt.co.uk).*
Engineer *65 Gloucester Avenue, NW1 8JH (7722 0950/www.the-engineer.com).*
Eriki *4-6 Northways Parade, Finchley Road, NW3 5EN (7722 0606/www.eriki.co.uk).*
Fino *33 Charlotte Street, entrance on Rathbone Street, W1T 1RR (7813 8010/ www.finorestaurant.com).*
Fish Bone *82 Cleveland Street, W1T 6NF (7580 2672).*
Fratelli la Bufala *45A South End Road, NW3 2QB (7435 7814/www.fratellilabufala.com).*
Globe *100 Avenue Road, NW3 3HF (7722 7200/www.globerestaurant.co.uk).*
Gourmet Burger Kitchen *200 Haverstock Hill, NW3 2AG (7443 5335/www.gbkinfo.co.uk).*
Green Note *106 Parkway, NW1 7AN (7485 9899).*
Haché *24 Inverness Street, NW1 7HJ (7485 9100/www.hacheburgers.com).*
Hakkasan *8 Hanway Place, W1T 1HD (7907 1888).*
Highgate *53-79 Highgate Road, NW5 1TL (7485 8442).*
Hill *94 Haverstock Hill, NW3 2BD (7267 0033/ www.geronimo-inns.co.uk).*
Jin Kichi *73 Heath Street, NW3 6UG (7794 6158/www.jinkichi.com).*
Junction Tavern *101 Fortess Road, NW5 1AG (7485 9400/www.junctiontavern.co.uk).*
Kalendar *15A Swains Lane, N6 6QX (8348 8300).*
Lansdowne *90 Gloucester Avenue, NW1 8HX (7483 0409).*
Lemongrass *243 Royal College Street, NW1 9LT (7284 1116).*
Lemonia *89 Regent's Park Road, NW1 8UY (7586 7454).*
Limani *154 Regent's Park Road, NW1 8XN (7483 4492).*
Little Earth Café *6 Erskine Road, NW3 3AJ (7449 0700).*
Mango Room *10-12 Kentish Town Road, NW1 8NH (7482 5065/www.mangoroom.co.uk).*
Manna *4 Erskine Road, NW3 3AJ (7722 8028/ www.manna-veg.com).*
Marine Ices *8 Haverstock Hill, NW3 2BL (7482 9003).*

Mario's *153-155 Broadhurst Gardens, NW6 3AU (7625 5827).*
Mestizo *103 Hampstead Road, NW3 3EL (7387 4064).*
Le Mignon *98 Arlington Road, NW1 7HD (7387 0600).*
North Sea Fish Restaurant *7-8 Leigh Street, WC1H 9EW (7387 5892).*
Odette's *130 Regent's Park Road, NW1 8XL (7586 5486).*
Oxford *256 Kentish Town Road, NW5 2AA (7485 3521/www.realpubs.co.uk).*
El Parador *245 Eversholt Street, NW1 1BA (7387 2789).*
Passione *10 Charlotte Street, W1T 2LT (7636 2833/www.passione.co.uk).*
Pavilion Café *Highgate Woods, Muswell Hill Road, N10 3JN (8444 4777).*
La Perla *11 Charlotte Street, W1T 1RQ (7436 1744/www.cafepacifico-laperla.com).*
Perseverance *63 Lamb's Conduit Street, WC1N 3NB (7405 8278).*
Pescador *23 Pratt Street, NW1 0BG (7482 7008).*
Pescador Two *108 Heath Street, NW3 1DR (7443 9500).*
La Porchetta *33 Boswell Street, WC1N 3BP (7242 2434/www.laporchetta.co.uk).*
Queens *49 Regent's Park Road, NW1 8XD (7586 0408/www.geronimo-inns.co.uk).*
Queen's Head & Artichoke *30-32 Albany Street, NW1 4EA (7916 6206/www.the artichoke.net).*
Rasa Samudra *5 Charlotte Street, W1T 1RE (7637 0222/www.rararestaurants.com).*
Roka *37 Charlotte Street, W1T 1RR (7580 6464/www.rokarestaurant.com).*
Room 68 *68 Heath Street, NW3 1DN (7435 6140).*
Safir *116 Heath Street, NW3 1DR (7431 9888/www.safir-restaurant.co.uk).*
Sheng's Tea House *68 Millman Street, WC1N 3EF (7405 3697).*
Tobia *First Floor, Ethiopian Community Centre, 2A Lithos Road, NW3 6EF (7431 4213/www.tobiarestaurant.co.uk).*
Trojka *101 Regent's Park Road, NW1 8UR (7483 3765/www.troykarestaurant.co.uk).*
Wakaba *122A Finchley Road, NW3 5HT (7586 7960).*
Walnut *280 West End Lane, NW6 1LJ (7794 7772/www.walnutwalnut.com).*
Zamoyski Restaurant & Vodka Bar *85 Fleet Road, NW3 2QY (7794 4792).*
Zara *11 South End Road, NW3 2PT (7794 5498).*

Bars & pubs

Camden Town, like the nearby West End, has long been a popular place to drink, but also like the West End, it's threatened with transformation due to the change in licensing laws. Small venues like the Falcon and the Laurel Tree have already been ousted by the increase of chain pubs in the area, and there's concern that later opening hours will eventually stamp out independent ventures altogether. Luckily for residents, gems like the Lord Stanley are still hanging on and, nearby, the Camden Arms is settling in after many changes in management.

Further north, Hawley Arms has free nibbles and an awesome jukebox, while Monkey Chews, although nestled in a housing estate, has the authentic air of a Los Angeles drinking den; Enterprise, on Haverstock Hill, is a gem for those who like their speciality beers. A recent addition to the 'wrong' end of Kentish Town is the Abbey, with its atmosphere of airy chic and light jazz soundtrack. You can't go wrong with Pineapple, a true institution and thankfully untouched by modernisation, or the aesthetically pleasing Vine, which also serves decent food to rival local gastropubs the Oxford and the Highgate (see p125).

Back in Camden Town, what remains is a lively mix of DJ bars and studenty dives with a few genteel stops thrown in. Drink till 1am at Bar Solo on Inverness Street; soak up the intimate boudoir feel of Bartok on Chalk Farm Road; or hang out with a cocktail and enjoy the live music at Bullet on Kentish Town Road. Nearby, recently opened cocktail bar Peachy Keen hopes to get in on the action. Best of all is the much loved Lock Tavern: a tarted-up boozer with comfy chairs and chilled music. Tucked away off the main drag, the Crown & Goose (which also serves decent food), is worth a look. Finally, as a central meeting point, the huge World's End by Camden tube is unmissable – at least in the literal sense.

Despite their close proximity to raucous Camden Town, Belsize Park and Primrose Hill are places more suited to a quiet drink and a meal than DJs and shouting. Putting aside classy gastropubs the Landsdowne, Engineer and Queens (see p124), Pembroke Castle tops the bill in the relaxed and elegant boozer stakes. Other simple drinking dens include the unpretentious Albert and jazz-favouring Princess of Wales.

Carrying on up the hill to Hampstead, the smart public houses continue to beckon, most of them offering good food, decent draught bitter and wine by the glass; the Belsize is as good as any. On the area's southern fringe, the wonderful Washington

MY VIEW

MARY CANE
Former mayor of Camden (1985-1986)

I love Camden to bits and pieces. It welcomed me with open arms when I moved here as a single parent in my early 20s and needed to be in a community that accepted me and was kind to me. **That's the best thing about the borough: the tolerance of difference, the acceptance of eccentricity. It's diverse and that's a huge strength. Camden is many communities.** Of course, people roll their eyes when you mention Camden – without really understanding *why* it is so different. There's a very diverse population; there are also lots of people with mental health issues. But Camden welcomes them all – I'm proud to live here. **The market is Camden's heart. I've been in street markets in Brazil and elsewhere, and Camden's is one of the best. You're spoiled for choice.** I've been swimming in the Hampstead ponds every day, give or take a few, since 1984. Even through the winter. We have a regular race on Christmas Day. Obviously, most of the daily users live within a reasonable reach, but people come from all over the world to swim here. Katharine Hepburn used to swim regularly in the Hampstead ponds in the 1950s or '60s when she was in London. **It's a horrible shame that Camden Council's not going to refurbish the Kentish Town baths. They're beautiful and should be kept for the community. All my kids learned to swim there.**

Camden

Tapas taken to a higher level, at **Fino**. *See p125.*

Hotel & Bar accommodates dog-walkers, playwrights and dodderers alike. A short diversion to the west, meanwhile, brings you to Swiss Cottage, which boasts a notable Samuel Smith's pub in the form of Ye Olde Swiss Cottage (which gave its name to the surrounding area many moons ago). The O$_2$ Centre near Finchley Road tube has some chain names like Wetherspoons and Walkabout, but nothing worth making a trip for. North-west is the hilly village of West Hampstead and its main drag, West End Lane. Here you'll find the stylish Gallery and party destination No.77 Wine Bar (popular with rugger types).

Amid Hampstead's tangle of winding backstreets and leafy lanes are some intriguing old boozers, such as the Wells and the Spaniards Inn. Magdala on South Park Hill is where Ruth Ellis shot David Blakely in 1955, before becoming the last woman in Britain to be hanged; framed press cuttings and weathered bullet holes on the front wall mark the event. Further down the hill, back towards Belsize Park, the refined Freemasons Arms and Garden Gate have a less colourful history, but are worth a stop and a sip.

In Highgate, dozy old boozers filled with gossipy locals predominate; best are historic duo the Wrestlers and the Flask, or the pleasant Angel Inn. The Boogaloo on Archway Road (just outside the borough boundary) marks a total change of pace, with its upbeat vibe, impeccable jukebox, eclectic DJs (most Fridays and Saturdays) and occasional gigs.

Most people going for a night out in King's Cross tend to bypass the pubs and go straight to the popular trio of clubs at the top of eerie York Way (Canvas, the Key, and the Cross; EGG is also nearby). However, with regeneration in full swing, style bars are popping up: 06 St Chad's Place is the best indication of the gradual influx of trendy urbanites to the area; another is Smithy's in nearby Leeke Street. For a cosier atmosphere, the King Charles I boasts an open fire and rotating ales.

Teetering on the edge of the West End, Bloomsbury has a clutch of grand traditional pubs that draw tourists from the British Museum; the long-standing Museum Tavern was once a haunt of Orwell and Marx, while the Plough, the Lord John Russell and the Lamb just serve good beer. Catching the overspill from the West End, hip DJ bar AKA is popular; the recently revamped Point 101 is less impressive but always a worthy back-up option.

Snug Grape Street Wine Bar, courtyarded Truckles of Pied Bull Yard, and comfortable Angel are all in the near vicinity. Bar Oporto is the leading player in the bar-studded border area between Bloomsbury, St Giles, Holborn and the West End. There are also a number of hotel bars: myhotel's mybar and King's Bar at the Russell Hotel are decent (if expensive) stops if you're looking to avoid crowds.

West of Tottenham Court Road sees the beginning of Fitzrovia (half of which falls within Camden's borders). The area was once defined by the seminal Fitzroy Tavern, which still plays on its claim to London's literary past. Otherwise, the Bricklayers Arms or the more bohemian Bradley's Spanish Bar are smoky-but-cheery dens. Charlotte Street caters primarily for the well-moneyed media crowd: brave upmarket Crazy Bear, Shochu Lounge (below hipster Japanese eaterie Roka) or Oscar (smart drinks in a modish hotel setting) if you've got cash to flash. The Hope and the Newman Arms are more down-to-earth; for late night drinking and DJs, try Jerusalem.

06 St Chad's Place *6 St Chad's Place, WC1X 9HH (7278 3355/www.6stchads place.com).*
Abbey *124 Kentish Town Road, NW1 9QB (7267 9449/www.abbeypub.co.uk).*
AKA *18 West Central Street, WC1A 1JJ (7836 0110/www.akalondon.com).*
Albert *11 Princess Road, NW1 8JR (7722 1886).*
Angel *61 St Giles High Street, WC2H 8LE (7240 2876).*
Angel Inn *37 Highgate High Street, N6 5JT (8347 2921).*
Bar Oporto *168 High Holborn, corner of Endell Street, WC1V 7AA (7240 1548).*
Bar Solo *20 Inverness Street, NW1 7HJ (7482 4611/www.barsolo.co.uk).*
Bartok *78-79 Chalk Farm Road, NW1 8AR (7916 0595/www.meanfiddler.com).*
Belsize *29 Belsize Lane, NW3 5AS (7794 4910).*
Boogaloo *312 Archway Road, N6 5AT (8340 2928).*
Bradley's Spanish Bar *42-44 Hanway Street, W1T 1UT (7636 0359).*
Bricklayer's Arms *31 Gresse Street, W1T 1QY (7636 5593).*
Bullet Bar *147 Kentish Town Road, NW1 8PB (7485 6040/www.bulletbar.co.uk).*
Camden Arms *1 Randolph Street, NW1 0SS (7267 9829).*
Canvas *Bagley's Studios, King's Cross Goods Yard, N1 0UZ (7833 8301/www.canvas london.net).*

Crazy Bear *26-28 Whitfield Street, W1T 7DS (7631 0088/www.crazybeargroup.co.uk).*
Cross *Arches, 27-31 King's Cross Goods Yard, N1 0UZ (7837 0828/www.the-cross.co.uk).*
Crown & Goose *100 Arlington Road, NW1 7HP (7485 8008).*
EGG *200 York Way, N7 9AP (7609 8364/ www.egglondon.net).*
Enterprise *2 Haverstock Hill, NW3 2BL (7485 2659).*
Fitzroy Tavern *16 Charlotte Street, W1T 2LY (7580 3714).*
Flask *77 Highgate West Hill, N6 6BU (8348 7346).*
Freemasons Arms *32 Downshire Hill, NW3 1NT (7433 6811/www.freemasons arms.co.uk).*
Gallery *190 Broadhurst Gardens, NW6 3AY (7625 9184).*
Garden Gate *14 South End Road, NW3 2QE (7433 6891).*
Grape Street Wine Bar *222-224A Shaftesbury Avenue, WC2H 8EB (7240 0686).*
Hawley Arms *2 Castlehaven Road, NW1 8QU (7428 5979).*
Head of Steam *1 Eversholt Street, NW1 1DN (7383 3359).*
Hope *15 Tottenham Street, W1T 2AJ (7637 0896).*
Jerusalem *33-34 Rathbone Place, W1T 1JN (7255 1120/www.thebreakfastgroup.co.uk).*
Key *King's Cross Goods Yard, off York Way, N1 0UZ (7837 1027/www.thekeylondon.com).*
King Charles I *55-57 Northdown Street, N1 9BL (7837 7758).*
King's Bar *Russell Hotel, Russell Square, WC1B 5BE (7837 6470).*
Lamb *94 Lamb's Conduit Street, WC1N 3LZ (7405 0713).*
Lansdowne *90 Gloucester Avenue, NW1 8HX (7483 0409).*
Lock Tavern *35 Chalk Farm Road, NW1 8AJ (7482 7163).*
Lord John Russell *91 Marchmont Street, WC1N 1AL (7388 0500).*
Lord Stanley *51 Camden Park Road, NW1 9BH (7428 9488).*
Magdala *2A South Hill Park, NW3 2SB (7435 2503).*
Monkey Chews *2 Queen's Crescent, NW5 4EP (7267 6406/www.monkeychews.com).*
Museum Tavern *49 Great Russell Street, WC1B 3BA (7242 8987).*
mybar *11-13 Bayley Street, WC1B 3HD (7667 6000/www.myhotels.com).*
Newman Arms *23 Rathbone Street, W1T 1NG (7636 1127/www.newmanarms.co.uk).*
No.77 Wine Bar *77 Mill Lane, NW6 1NB (7435 7787).*
Oscar *Charlotte Street Hotel, 15 Charlotte Street, W1T 1RJ (7806 2000/www.charlotte streethotel.com)*
Oxford *256 Kentish Town Road, NW5 2AA (7485 3521/www.realpubs.co.uk).*
Peachy Keen *112 Kentish Town Road, NW1 9PX (7482 2300/www.peachy-keen.com).*

Pembroke Castle *150 Gloucester Avenue, NW1 8JA (7483 2927).*
Pineapple *51 Leverton Street, NW5 2NX (7284 4631/www.thepineapplelondon.com).*
Plough *27 Museum Street, WC1A 1LH (7636 7964).*
Point 101 *101 New Oxford Street, WC1A 1DB (7379 3112/www.101bar.com).*
Princess of Wales *22 Chalcot Road, NW1 8LL (7722 0354).*
Shochu Lounge *37 Charlotte Street, W1T 1RR (7580 9666/www.rokarestaurant.com).*
Smithy's *15-17 Leeke Street, WC1X 9HZ (7278 5949/www.smithyskingscross.com).*
Spaniards Inn *Spaniards Road, NW3 7JJ (8731 6571).*
Truckles of Pied Bull Yard *off Bury Place, WC1A 2JR (7404 5338/www.davy. co.uk).*
Vine *86 Highgate Road, NW5 1PB (7209 0038/www.thevinelondon.co.uk).*
Washington Hotel & Bar *50 England's Lane, NW3 4UE (7722 8842).*
Wells *30 Well Walk, NW3 1BX (7794 3785/www.thewellshampstead.co.uk).*
World's End *174 Camden High Street, NW1 0NE (7482 1932/www.theunderworldcamden. co.uk).*
Wrestlers *98 North Road, N6 4AA (8340 4297).*
Ye Olde Swiss Cottage *98 Finchley Road, NW3 5EL (7722 3487).*

Shops

Retail hotspots in the borough are limited to Hampstead, Primrose Hill and the fringes of the West End. And, of course, Camden Town, with its market, Lock and alternative stores. But shopping here is hard work and you should be prepared for a scrum at weekends, as tourists flood the streets and wade through the litter. The Lock, with its artisan shops and stalls, is the most palatable part, and has been smartened up lately. Head to the Stables Market for a hotchpotch of stalls selling retro furniture, vintage clothing and old-fashioned toys. More clothes and accessories can be rifled through at the newer Episode. Rokit is another reliable outlet for choice yet reasonably priced vintage goods.

The sedate streets of Primrose Hill offer a more select shopping experience. Newcomer Shikasuki stocks a modest-sized but well-presented vintage collection that's a pleasure to peruse. Boutiques include Miss Lala's Boudoir, a lingerie outlet crammed with everything from diaphanous whispers of silk to stout burlesque corsets. Anna, sister to the King's Road shop, appeals to women with a girlish streak; celebrities

persist in coming but prices have stayed sane. As well as posh clobber, it carries a range of ultra-glamorous denim labels like Rogan, and C&C California T-shirts to match. Press is also worth a visit if you fancy adopting the apparently effortless boho chic of the Primrose Hill native. Elias & Grace has cornered the burgeoning market – in this borough at least – for designer pregnancy ranges (such as See by Chloé and Sonia Rykiel). For shoes, there's Beatrix Ong (an ex-Jimmy Choo designer) and Spice; for books there's the small but perfectly formed Primrose Hill Books; gifts and girly stuff is provided by Graham & Green.

On Haverstock Hill, which links Belsize Park to Hampstead, is a branch of Daunt Books; there's also one in the charming enclave of South End Green, which holds the Delicatessen Shop too, recommended for its pesto and its chocolate. Other delis include the Belsize Village Deli, while in Hampstead itself, aside from popular branches of Paul and Maison Blanc, there's the stalwart Rosslyn Delicatessen. New kid Beetroot, a Polish food shop, makes for a welcome change – and it's not just about borscht. Also of eastern European extraction (but this time of over 40 years' standing), Louis' Pâtisserie provides Hungarian-style cakes. Hampstead has plenty of (mostly MOR) fashion too – the boutique YDUK is worth a visit, as are branches of Oxfam, Nicole Farhi, Jigsaw, Formes and Agnès b. The Well Walk Pottery Shop is also a prime attraction, and Happy Returns, on Rosslyn Hill, is a lovely toy shop.

Further east in (otherwise barren) Gospel Oak is Kristin Baybars' shop, full of exquisite miniaturist scenes and dolls' house kits; east again in Kentish Town there's not much apart from a busy but workaday high street (Kentish Town Road), on which the Owl Bookshop is the only gem. Highgate has Sound 323 (indie tunes) and Ripping Yarns (second-hand children's and illustrated books).

In the west of the borough, on and around the main artery of Finchley Road, are big names such as Habitat and Waitrose, upmarket modern furniture showrooms such as Charles Page and Interni, plus small East European deli the Birch. Isolated on nearby Abbey Road is party specialist Oscar's Den.

Camden

Towards the centre of town, retailing turns serious. Tottenham Court Road has too many electrical goods shops to mention, plus a clutch of homeware shops, including Heal's, Habitat, BoConcept and, most design-tastic of all, Purves & Purves. Further south-east lie the joys of Bloomsbury: here are James Smith & Son, venerable vendors of umbrellas, and in the streets around the British Museum, small shops (though not as many as there once were) selling everything from books to antiquarian maps and music scores. It's also home to the brutalist Brunswick Centre. For many years neglected, this residential and shopping complex is now being revamped: major high street names are scheduled to move in during 2006.

Further east, on the far side of Gray's Inn Road (home to a branch of ace baker's Konditor & Cook) is old-style Leather Lane Market (Monday to Friday only) and Hatton Garden, centre of London's jewellery-making activity.

Agnès b *58 Heath Street, NW3 1EN (7431 1995/www.agnesb.fr).*
Anna *126 Regent's Park Road, NW1 8XL (7483 0411/www.shopatanna.co.uk).*
Beatrix Ong *117 Regent's Park Road, NW1 8UR (7499 0480/www.beatrixong.com).*
Beetroot *92 Fleet Road, NW3 2QX (7424 8544/www.beetrootdeli.co.uk).*
Belsize Village Deli *39 Belsize Lane, NW3 5AS (7794 4258).*
Birch *297 Finchley Road, NW3 6DT (7794 0777).*
BoConcept *158 Tottenham Court Road, W1T 7NH (7388 2447/www.boconcept.co.uk).*
Charles Page *61 Fairfax Road, NW6 4EE (7328 9851).*

RECYCLING

No. of bring sites 101 (for nearest, visit www.recycleforlondon.com)
Household waste recycled 16.3%
Main recycling centre Regis Road Recycling Centre, Regis Road, NW5 3EW (7974 6914)
Other recycling services home composting bins; collection of furniture (8493 0900/www.restore communityprojects.org); recycling of IT equipment
Council contact Street Environment Services, 2nd Floor, Cockpit Yard, WC1N 2NP (7974 6914/www.camden. gov.uk/recycling)

Daunt Books *193 Haverstock Hill, NW3 4QL (7794 4006); 51 South End Road, NW3 2QB (7794 8206).*
The Delicatessen Shop *23 South End Road, NW3 2PT (7435 7315).*
Elias & Grace *158 Regent's Park Road, NW1 8XN (7449 0574/www.eliasandgrace.com).*
Episode *26 Chalk Farm Road, NW1 8AG (7485 9927).*
Formes *66 Rosslyn Hill, NW3 1ND (7431 7770/www.formes.com).*
Graham & Green *164 Regent's Park Road, NW1 8XN (7586 2960).*
Happy Returns *36 Rosslyn Hill, NW3 1NH (7435 2431).*
Heal's *196 Tottenham Court Road, W1T 7LQ (7636 1666/www.heals.co.uk).*
Interni *51-53 Fairfax Road, NW6 4EL (7624 4040).*
James Smith & Son *53 New Oxford Street, WC1A 1BL (7836 4731/www.james-smith. co.uk).*
Konditor & Cook *46 Gray's Inn Road, WC1X 8LR (7404 6300/www.konditorandcook.com).*
Kristin Baybars *7 Mansfield Road, NW3 2JD (7267 0934).*
Leather Lane Market *Leather Lane, EC1.*
Louis' Pâtisserie *32 Heath Street, NW3 6DU (7435 9908).*
Maison Blanc *62 Hampstead High Street, NW3 1QH (7431 8338/www.maisonblanc.co.uk).*
Miss Lala's Boudoir *144 Gloucester Avenue, NW1 8JA (7483 1888).*
Nicole Farhi *27 Hampstead High Street, NW3 1QA (7435 0866/www.nicolefarhi.com).*
Oscar's Den *127 Abbey Road, NW6 4SL (7328 6683/www.oscarsden.com).*
Owl Bookshop *207-209 Kentish Town Road, NW5 2JU (7485 7793).*
Oxfam *61 Gayton Road, NW3 1TU (7794 4474/www.oxfam.org.uk).*
Paul *43 Hampstead High Street, NW3 1QG (7794 8657/www.paul.fr).*
Press *3 Erskine Road, NW3 3AJ (7449 0081).*
Primrose Hill Books *134 Regent's Park Road, NW1 8XL (7586 2022).*
Purves & Purves *220-224 Tottenham Court Road, W1T 7PZ (7580 8223/www.purves.co.uk).*
Ripping Yarns *355 Archway Road, N6 4EJ (8341 6111).*
Rokit *225 Camden High Street, NW1 7BU (7267 3046/www.rokit.co.uk).*
Rosslyn Delicatessen *56 Rosslyn Hill, NW3 1ND (7794 9210/www.delirosslyn.co.uk).*
Shikasuki *67 Gloucester Avenue, NW1 8LD (7722 4442/www.shikasuki.com).*
Sound 323 *323 Archway Road, N6 5AA (8348 9595/www.sound323.com).*
Spice Shoes *162 Regent's Park Road, NW1 8XN (7722 2478).*
Stables Market *off Chalk Farm Road, opposite junction with Hartland Road, NW1 8AH (7485 5511/www.camdenlock.net).*
Well Walk Pottery Shop *49 Willow Road, NW3 1BT (7435 1046).*
YDUK *82 Heath Street, NW3 1DN (7431 9242).*

Camden

Arts & attractions

Cinemas & theatres

Camden People's Theatre 58-60 Hampstead Road, NW1 2PY (bookings 0870 060 0100/ www.cptheatre.co.uk).

Diorama Arts Centres Diorama 1, 34 Osnaburgh Street, NW1 3ND; Diorama 2, 3-7 Euston Centre, NW1 3JG (7916 5467/ www.diorama-arts.org.uk). Community arts centre with two galleries, a theatre and rehearsal space.

Etcetera Theatre 265 Camden High Street, NW1 7BU (7482 4857/www.etceteratheatre. com). Miniature theatre above the Oxford Arms pub.

Everyman Cinema 5 Holly Bush Vale, NW3 6TX (0870 066 4777/www.everyman cinema.com).

Hampstead Theatre Eton Avenue, NW3 3EU (7722 9301/www.hampsteadtheatre.com).

The Horse Hospital Colonnade, WC1N 1HX (7713 7370/www.thehorsehospital.com). Offbeat arts venue that describes itself as 'the true home of the avant-garde'.

Odeon Camden Town 14 Parkway, NW1 7AA (0871 224 4007/www.odeon.co.uk).

Odeon Swiss Cottage 96 Finchley Road, NW3 5EL (0871 224 4007).

Renoir Cinema Brunswick Square, WC1N 1AW (7837 8402/www.artificial-eye.com).

Screen on the Hill 203 Haverstock Hill, NW3 4QG (7435 3366/www.screencinemas.co.uk). Cinema.

Upstairs at the Gatehouse Corner of Hampstead Lane & North Road, Highgate Village, N6 4BD (8340 3488/www.upstairs atthegatehouse.com). Theatre pub.

Vue Finchley Road O_2 Centre, 255 Finchley Road, NW3 6LU (0871 224 0240/www.myvue. com).

Galleries & museums

British Museum Great Russell Street, WC1B 3DG (7323 8000/www.thebritishmuseum.ac.uk). Officially London's most popular tourist attraction; check out the glass-roofed Great Court, the largest covered space in Europe.

Camden Arts Centre Arkwright Road, NW3 6DG (7472 5500/www.camdenarts centre.org). Galleries, studios, a café and landscaped gardens.

Cartoon Museum Old Dairy, 35 Little Russell Street, WC1A 2HH (7631 0793/www.cartoon centre.com). Formerly the Cartoon Arts Trust, this museum recently relocated from the Brunswick Centre.

Fenton House Windmill Hill, NW3 6RT (7435 3471/information 01494 755563/ www.nationaltrust.org.uk). Collection of antique musical instruments and porcelain; the sunken gardens and orchard are a delight.

Freud Museum 20 Maresfield Gardens, NW3 5SX (7435 2002/www.freud.org.uk). Former home of Sigmund and his daughter Anna.

Jewish Museum 129-131 Albert Street, NW1 7NB (7284 1997/www.jewishmuseum.org.uk). Fascinating insight into one of Britain's oldest immigrant communities; sister museum in Finchley (see p299).

Keats House Keats Grove, NW3 2RR (7435 2062/www.cityoflondon.gov.uk/keats). Home of the Romantic poet from 1818 to 1820.

Kenwood House Hampstead Lane, NW3 7JR (8348 1286/www.english-heritage.org.uk). Impressive neo-classical house within Hampstead Heath; houses the Iveagh Bequest art collection.

Sir John Soane's Museum 13 Lincoln's Inn Fields, WC2A 3BP (7405 2107/www.soane.org). Atmospheric home of 18th-century architect showcases his collection of art and artefacts.

Music & comedy venues

Amused Moose Camden Enterprise, 2 Haverstock Hill, NW3 2BL (8341 1341/ www.amusedmoose.com). Comedy club.

Barfly 49 Chalk Farm Road, NW1 8AN (7691 4243/www.barflyclub.com). Music venue and bar.

Dublin Castle 94 Parkway, NW1 7AN (7485 1773/www.bugbearbookings.com). Music venue and pub.

Electric Ballroom 184 Camden High Street, NW1 8QP (7485 9006/www.electricballroom. co.uk). Music venue and club.

Forum 9-17 Highgate Road, NW5 1JY (7284 1001/www.meanfiddler.com). Music venue.

Jazz Café 5 Parkway, NW1 7PG (7916 6060/www.meanfiddler.com). Jazz venue.

Jongleurs Camden Middle Yard, Chalk Farm Road, Camden Lock, NW1 8AB (0870 787 0707/www.jongleurs.com). Comedy club.

KOKO 1A Camden High Street, NW1 7JE (0870 432 5527/www.koko.uk.com). Music venue and club; formerly the Camden Palace.

Monkey Business Camden Lush Bar, 31 Jamestown Road, NW1 7DB (07932 338203/ www.monkeybusinesscomedyclub.co.uk). Comedy club.

Roundhouse Chalk Farm Road, NW1 8EH (7424 9991/www.roundhouse.org.uk). Music venue, due to reopen after extensive redevelopment in spring 2006.

Scala 275 Pentonville Road, N1 9NL (7833 2022/www.scala-london.co.uk). Music venue and club.

Water Rats 328 Gray's Inn Road, WC1X 8BZ (7837 7269). Indie music venue.

Other attractions

British Library 96 Euston Road, NW1 2DB (0870 444 1500/www.bl.uk). Unjustly criticised by architecture critics when it opened in 1997, this enormous library is one of the greatest in the world. Access to the reading rooms requires a reader's pass (free, but subject to a rigorous interrogation by library staff).

Pirate's Castle Oval Road, NW1 7EA (7267 6605/www.thepiratecastle.org). A canalside activity centre for young people.

Woburn Walk, one of the prettiest shopping streets in Bloomsbury.

Open spaces

Camley Street Natural Park *12 Camley Street, NW1 0PW (7833 2311/www.wild london.org.uk).* Two acres of wild green space in urban King's Cross. Closed Fri.
Coram's Fields *93 Guilford Street, WC1.* Children's playground.
Gray's Inn Gardens *Theobald's Road, WC1.* Tranquil gardens open to the public on weekdays.
Hampstead Heath *Highgate Road, NW5.* Just over a mile in each direction, but the Heath's charming contours and woodlands conspire to make it seem larger than it is.
Highgate Cemetery *Swains Lane, N6 6PJ (8340 1834/www.highgate-cemetery.org).* Famous residents include Faraday, Karl Marx, George Eliot and Sir Ralph Richardson.
Kentish Town City Farm *1 Cressfield Close, NW5 4BN (7916 5421/www.aapi.co.uk/cityfarm).*
Lincoln's Inn Fields *Lincoln's Inn, WC2.* The largest public square in London, flanked by historic buildings.
Parliament Hill *Highgate Road, N6 & NW5.* The views from the top are stunning and on hot days the murky bathing ponds are a godsend.
Primrose Hill *Prince Albert Road, NW8.* The grassy hill that gave its name to the area, with fantastic views across the city.
Regent's Park *Inner Circle, NW1 (www.royal parks.org.uk).* Spills into Camden from the City of Westminster.

Russell Square Gardens *Russell Square, WC1.* Tastefully landscaped in 2002, with a café and public park in the centre.
Waterlow Park *Dartmouth Park Hill, N19.* Several lakes, Lauderdale House and grassy slopes that are great for picnicking.

Sport & fitness

Camden has done much to throw off the air of shabbiness that once pervaded its public sport and leisure centres. November 2002 saw the launch of the £6 million Talacre Community Sports Centre, complete with its unique (for Camden) gymnastics hall, which is run directly by Camden Council; the Swiss Cottage Leisure Centre has been transformed into a gleaming new facility, due to open shortly after this guide went to press. The Corporation of London-managed Hampstead Heath Swimming Ponds and the Parliament Hill Lido offer year-round open-air dips (mornings only in winter at the latter). In the private sector, the borough is blessed with the Central YMCA, one of the top sports centres in London, and the Kieser Training Centre, devoted to combating chronic back pain.

Gyms & leisure centres

Armoury *25 Pond Street, NW3 2PN (7431 2263/www.jubileehallclubs.co.uk).* Private.

Central YMCA *112 Great Russell Street, WC1B 3NQ (7343 1700/www.centralymca. org.uk/club).* Private.

Esporta *Unit 2, Level 1, O₂ Centre, 255 Finchley Road, NW3 6LU (7644 2400/ www.esporta.com).* Private.

Fitness First *www.fitnessfirst.co.uk; 128 Albert Street, NW1 7NE (7284 2244); 81-84 Chalk Farm Road, NW1 8AR (7284 0004); Coram Street, WC1N 1HB (7833 1887).* Private.

Gymbox *100 High Holborn, WC1V 6RD (7400 1919/www.gymbox.co.uk).* Private.

Holmes Place *50 Triton Square, NW1 3XB (7388 5511/www.holmesplace.co.uk).* Private.

Kentish Town Sports Centre *Prince of Wales Road, NW5 3LE (7267 9341/www. camden.gov.uk/sport).*

Kieser Training *Greater London House, Hampstead Road, NW1 7DF (0800 037 0370/www.kieser-training.com).* Back specialists; private.

LA Fitness *www.lafitness.co.uk; 53-79 Highgate Road, NW5 1TL (0870 607 2142); Lacon House, 84 Theobald's Road, WC1X 8RW (0870 607 2143).* Private.

Maitland Park Gym *Maitland Park Villas, NW3 2ET (7485 7004).*

Mallinson Sports Centre *Bishopswood Road, N6 4NY (8342 7272/www.highgate school.org.uk).* Private.

Mornington Sports & Fitness Centre *142-150 Arlington Road, NW1 7HP (7267 3600/www.hp-mornington.freeservers.com).*

Oasis Sports Centre *32 Endell Street, WC2H 9AG (7831 1804).*

Soho Gym *www.sohogyms.com; 193 Camden High Street, NW1 7JY (7482 4524); 12 Macklin Street, WC2B 5NF (7242 1290).* Private.

Spring Health Leisure Club *81 Belsize Park Gardens, NW3 4NJ (7483 6800/www.springhealth.net).* Private.

Swiss Cottage Leisure Centre *Adelaide Road, NW3 (7974 2012/ www.camden.gov.uk/sport).*

Talacre Community Sports Centre *Dalby Street, off Prince of Wales Road, NW5 3AF (7974 8765/www.camden.gov.uk/ sport).*

Other facilities

Hampstead Heath Swimming Ponds *Hampstead Heath, NW5 1QR (7485 4491).*

Parliament Hill Lido *Parliament Hill Fields, Gordon House Road, NW5 2LT (7485 5757).*

Triyoga *6 Erskine Road, NW3 3AJ (7483 3344/www.triyoga.co.uk).*

Schools

WHAT THE PARENTS SAY:

'Fitzjohn Avenue is notorious at 9am and 3pm, because it gets so congested with parents taking their children to local primary schools. They're mainly private (St Anthony's and Devonshire House are among the best), but state school Fitzjohn Primary has a fantastic reputation.

There's a wide choice at secondary level, but so much depends on where you live. Camden School for Girls is hugely popular, but you have to live virtually on the doorstep to get in – estate agents sell property off the back of proximity to the school. Another girls' school, Parliament Hill, doesn't have such a great image; for boys, William Ellis used to be considered on a par with Camden, but is no longer so desirable. Some of the pupils at Acland Burghley can be quite rough from what I hear. I have friends with kids at Hampstead School and they've all been very happy there. La Sainte Union is a good, sound Catholic girls' school – very straight and serious. Haverstock School has just added a great-looking new building.' Mother of two, Hampstead

Primary

There are 42 state primary schools in Camden, 19 of which are church schools. There are also 25 independent primary schools, including one French school, one international school and two Montessori schools. See www.camden.gov.uk and www.ofsted.gov.uk.

Secondary

Acland Burghley School *Burghley Road, NW5 1UJ (7485 8515/www.aclandburghley. camden.sch.uk).*

Camden School for Girls *Sandall Road, NW5 2DB (7485 3414/www.csfg.org.uk).* Girls only.

Hampstead School *Westbere Road, NW2 3RT (7794 8133/www.hampstead school.org.uk).*

Haverstock School *24 Haverstock Hill, NW3 2BQ (7267 0975/www.haverstock. camden.sch.uk).*

La Sainte Union Catholic Secondary School *Highgate Road, NW5 1RP (7428 4600/www.lsu.camden.sch.uk).* Girls only.

Maria Fidelis Convent School *34 Phoenix Road, NW1 1TA (7387 3856/ www.mariafidelis.camden.sch.uk).* Girls only.

Parliament Hill School *Highgate Road, NW5 1RL (7485 7077/www.parliamenthill. camden.sch.uk).* Girls only.

South Camden Community School *Charrington Street, NW1 1RG (7387 0126/www.sccs.camden.sch.uk).*

William Ellis School *Highgate Road, NW5 1RN (7267 9346/www.williamellis.camden. sch.uk).* Boys only.

Property

WHAT THE AGENTS SAY:

'Everyone wants to live in Camden; it's vibrant, cosmopolitan, full of young people, yet also has a well-established older population. You name it, it's got it – clubs, eateries, comedy clubs, music venues like the Jazz Café… plus it's brilliantly located, right on the edge of green spaces *and* just 15 minutes to the West End. It's got a similar buzzy vibe to Notting Hill, but it's more raw round the edges. Within a five-minute walk, you'll find dope-dealers by the canalside and then, just up the road, wonderful little enclaves like Gloucester Crescent, where Alan Bennett lives. The areas close to King's Cross and Euston have a lot of local authority buildings mixed in with nice Victorian villas – those are slowly being gentrified because of the Eurostar developments. That's going to be a property hotspot in the next five years or so.'
Jonathan Westray, Stickley & Kent, Camden

'Highgate's got it all – but the council tax is high and you probably don't get what you pay for in services. Families move here from Islington for the schools and quiet village charm. Once you've lived in Highgate, you tend to scale up or down within the area and not move away. If you can't afford Highgate, you live in Crouch End – prices have gone through the roof there.'
Stephen Day, Day Morris Associates, Highgate

Average property prices
Detached £1,309,593
Semi-detached £825,490
Terraced £602,487
Flat £302,726

Local estate agents
Alexanders *337 West End Lane, NW6 1RS (7431 0666/www.alexanders-uk.com).*
Christo & Co *148 Kentish Town Road, NW1 9QB (7424 9474/www.christo.co.uk).*
Day Morris Associates *www.daymorris. co.uk; 2 offices in the borough (Hampstead 7482 4282/Highgate 8348 8131).*
Jeremy Bass *50 Chalcot Road, NW1 8LS (7722 8686/www.jeremybass.co.uk).*
London Residential *172 Royal College Street, NW1 0SP (7267 0909/www.ldn-res.com).*
MBM Ringley *Ringley House, 349 Royal College Street, NW1 9QS (7267 2900/ www.ringley.co.uk).*

COUNCIL TAX

A	up to £40,000	£821.66
B	£40,001-£52,000	£958.60
C	£52,001-£68,000	£1,095.54
D	£68,001-£88,000	£1,232.48
E	£88,001-£120,000	£1,506.36
F	£120,001-£160,000	£1,780.24
G	£160,001-£320,000	£2,054.14
H	over £320,000	£2,464.96

Olivers *189 Kentish Town Road, NW5 2JU (7284 1222/www.olivers-estateagents.co.uk).*
Stickley & Kent *www.stickleykent.co.uk; 4 offices in the borough (Belsize Park 7722 8899/Covent Garden 7836 2888/Camden 7267 2053/Kentish Town 7267 1010).*

Other information

Council
Camden Council *Camden Town Hall, Judd Street, WC1H 9JE (7278 4444/www.camden. gov.uk).*
Camden Direct Information Service *7974 5974.*

Hospitals
Elizabeth Garrett Anderson & Obstetric Hospital *Huntley Street, WC1E 6DH (0845 155 5000/www.uclh.nhs.uk).*
Great Ormond Street Hospital *Great Ormond Street, WC1N 3JH (7405 9200).*
The National Hospital for Neurology & Neurosurgery *Queen Square, WC1N 3BG (7837 3611/www.uclh.nhs.uk).*
Royal Free Hospital *Pond Street, NW3 2QG (7794 0500).*
University College Hospital *235 Euston Road, NW1 2BU (0845 155 5000).*

Legal services
Camden Community Law Centre *2 Prince of Wales Road, NW5 3LQ (7284 6510/www.law centres.org.uk).*
Holborn CAB *3rd Floor, Holborn Library, 32-38 Theobalds Road, WC1X 8PA (0845 120 2965/www.adviceguide.org.uk).*

Local newspapers
Camden Gazette *8342 5777/ www.camdengazette.co.uk.*
Camden New Journal, Islington Tribune & West End Extra *7419 9000/ www.camdennewjournal.co.uk.*
Central London Independent *8961 3345/www.londonlocals.co.uk.*

Allotments
Council Allotments *Allotments Officer, c/o Parks and Open Spaces Section, Crowndale Centre, 218 Eversholt Street, NW1 1BD (7974 8819).*

Camden

'These days one would truly have to be born with a silver spoon in one's mouth to be able to afford such luxurious surroundings.'

Charmian Griffiths, Blue Badge guide

Kensington & Chelsea

It's the UK's wealthiest borough, so you won't be short of luxury shopping, classy restaurants and fabulous residences. Yet there are also student enclaves, world-renowned museums and run-down bedsits within these boundaries – not forgetting Europe's biggest street party.

Neighbourhoods

Kensington and Holland Park

Although Kensington High Street has lost any claim to cool (the famously offbeat indoor Kensington Market and edgy '80s designer emporium Hyper-Hyper are long gone), the upmarket chains and amenities are still popular; it sometimes feels like you're queuing just to move along the pavement. Kensington Church Street houses pricier boutiques and antiques parlours. The narrow surrounding roads contain a mix of handsome private residences and various foreign embassies.

As a rule, this area is much busier by day, although Kensington Roof Gardens (entrance at 99 Kensington High Street, above what was originally Derry & Toms department store, then Biba) is a ritzy private party venue and home to some of the borough's live peacocks (there are more in Holland Park).

Outdoor types, especially in-line skaters and cyclists, gravitate towards Kensington Gardens (which merges with Hyde Park). Here it's easy to forget the dense traffic of Kensington Road. At Kensington Palace, heartfelt tributes to its late resident, Princess Diana, are still regularly pinned to the golden gates.

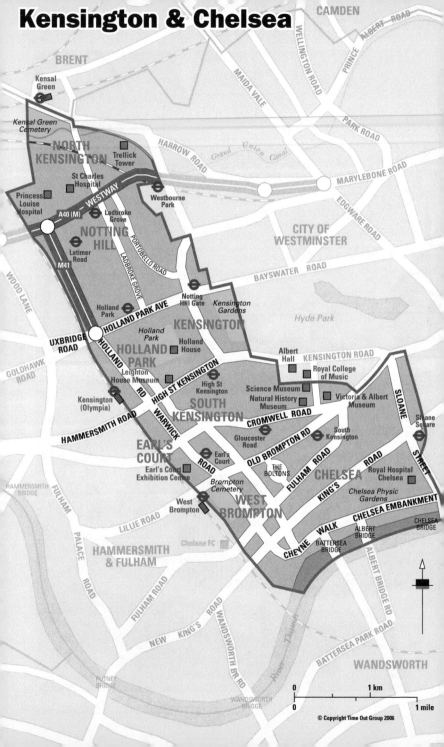

Kensington also incorporates Holland Park, which, tellingly, is where Edina and Patsy lived the high life in the TV sitcom *Absolutely Fabulous*. In real life, this area's extravagant Georgian and Victorian terraces are relatively tranquil, although myriad posh delis, beauty salons and vintage clothing boutiques (most of them on Holland Park Avenue or Portland Road) are signs of an undeniably ab-fab locale. Holland Park itself is an impressively planned, surprisingly untouristy public garden, including a Japanese garden, an art gallery and open-air theatre. Located a short stroll away, Leighton House Museum was once the residence of the Victorian artist Frederic, Lord Leighton. Visit for the lavish marble interiors and collection of paintings.

South Kensington, Earl's Court and West Brompton

Between Kensington High Street and Cromwell Road rests South Kensington, a distinctly elegant part of the capital. South Kensington tube station could do with modernisation, but the surrounding cluster of shops, cafés and restaurants lends this area a pleasingly homely identity, despite the crowds that pass by on their way to the nearby triumvirate of world-famous museums: the V&A, the Natural History Museum and the Science Museum.

There's architectural splendour at nearly every turn in this neighbourhood, from the florid Italianate style of Brompton Oratory Catholic church on Thurloe Place, to the iconic Royal Albert Hall on Kensington Gore (technically, just outside the borough – but this whole neighbourhood is sometimes referred to as 'Albertopolis' due to its Victorian heritage). Exhibition Road, named after the 1851 Great Exhibition, is a direct route to Hyde Park, lined with grand 19th- and 20th-century buildings. During the summer, don't miss the chance to eat or drink on the Goethe-Institut's bijou terrace, which opens on to a lovely private garden. Besides tourists and wealthy residents, South Kensington is home to a sizeable student population (the Royal College of Art, Royal College of Music, Imperial College and numerous language schools are all here) and lots of embassies.

It's a safe bet that almost every Londoner has passed through Earl's Court on a journey through the capital, with its busy District and Piccadilly line interchange. Above ground, Earl's Court connects with South Kensington via the very busy Cromwell Road (A4). Further local amenities can be found dotted around Gloucester Road. Otherwise, the area remains a sprawl of side streets, hotels, private garden squares, youth hostels and bedsits; the latter often have sadly crumbling interiors behind their imposing stuccoed façades. There's a transient spirit to the district, but this does make for an appealing cultural mix. Earl's Court has long been a base for Antipodean communities, while Hogarth Road has some interesting Filipino groceries and cafés. The Earl's Court Exhibition Centre – which has hosted concerts by the likes of Madonna, Kylie and Oasis, as well as annual events such as the *Daily Mail* Ideal Home Show – is very centrally located for a venue that covers 12 acres.

In contrast to Earl's Court, neighbouring West Brompton is a classy residential area, incorporating plenty of high-value property, including the facing crescents of the Boltons (which swarmed with paparazzi when Hugh Grant and Liz Hurley lived here). The district's most memorable landmark is Brompton Cemetery on Fulham Road, worth a visit for its 19th-century design; the many famous graves include that of the suffragette pioneer Emmeline Pankhurst. The cemetery also includes a chapel based on the Vatican's San Pietro. From here, it's

Highs & Lows

▲ **Retail** From Notting Hill to Knightsbridge, there are endless ways to spend, spend, spend
Culture Family-friendly museums, concerts and indie cinemas keep weekends packed
Notting Hill Carnival Residents get a ringside view when the circus comes to town, or rent their pad at a premium...

Notting Hill Carnival ...but it can be a headache for home-owners. Local businesses board up their storefronts against the mob
Property prices It's the UK's wealthiest borough – need we say more?
▼ **Weekend crowds** Battle tourists and day-trippers when you pop out for milk

a short walk to Stamford Bridge, home of Chelsea Football Club, actually just across the borough border in Hammersmith & Fulham (*see p157*).

Chelsea

This fancy neighbourhood is bisected by the King's Road, originally Charles II's private route from St James's Palace. For generations, the place has accommodated a unique blend of toffs and bohemians. Today, though more conventional shops have replaced the wayward boutiques of the King's Road's swinging 1960s and '70s heyday, you'll still find some intriguing contrasts.

High-end designers and private galleries are concentrated towards the Sloane Square end of the King's Road and on luxurious Sloane Street, which connects Chelsea to Knightsbridge (*see p141*). Sloane Square, named after its 18th-century owner Sir Hans Sloane, features a central fountain depicting Venus; on the whole, though, this paved space is rather dowdy. Nearby Duke of York Square is a pricey but pretty place to meet and pose. It's a focal point for the twice-yearly London Fashion Week Sale, and in winter it has a dinky ice rink. The Royal Court Theatre next to Sloane Square tube station is always worth a visit for its new plays. Otherwise, the area remains largely the preserve of ladies who lunch, and a sub-species of toff long known as the Sloane Ranger. At the other end of the King's Road is the once-notorious World's End estate, a large council development of tower blocks and a shopping complex built in the 1970s. The estate is slowly shaking off its reputation for drug-related crime – and estate agents are certainly keen to tout the area – but it's still very evidently the poorest pocket of Chelsea.

There's a wealth of English Heritage blue plaques in the area. The composer Thomas Arne is believed to have conceived *Rule Britannia* at his home, 215 King's Road. For truly famous neighbours, check out the quaint riverside Cheyne Walk, which dates back to the 18th century; residents have ranged from George Eliot, JMW Turner and Dante Gabriel Rossetti to the Rolling Stones' Keith Richards and Mick Jagger (at Nos.3 and 48 respectively). If you're not spotting names, look out for the Chelsea Pensioners in their dapper scarlet uniforms and tricorne hats. These retired servicemen live at Royal Hospital Chelsea, which was designed by Christopher Wren and Sir John Soane, among others, and whose grounds host the lavish Chelsea Flower Show every May.

For a great secret haven, visit Chelsea Physic Garden, founded in 1673, with acres of plants dedicated to the science of healing.

In recent years, newspapers including the *Daily Telegraph* have reported a 'mini crimewave' in Chelsea. You'd guess that there are rich pickings around here, and it's true that Cheyne Walk residents have lobbied the council for CCTV security; but that said, there's no discernible fear on the streets in this elegant part of town. In fact, a council report claims that crime in the borough decreased by 6.4 per cent between 2003 and 2004.

Not your average terraced housing – the streets of **Notting Hill**.

Knightsbridge

While much of Knightsbridge falls under Westminster's aegis, it seamlessly continues on from Sloane Street as a ritzy, label-saturated enclave. The main drag is dominated by two temples to conspicuous consumption: Harrods, whose traditional opulence has become comically OTT under Al Fayed's reign (case in point is the £20 million Egyptian Escalator), and the more restrained, slickly fashionable Harvey Nicks.

Residentially, Knightsbridge is almost entirely the preserve of the fabulously wealthy, although some students and key workers can rent tiddly bedsits in tucked-away streets not far from the tube.

Notting Hill

The 1999 Hugh Grant rom-com *Notting Hill* proved how pretty this part of town could look on the big screen – while somehow glossing over its economic disparities. The district is otherwise best known for hosting Europe's largest street party, the Notting Hill Carnival, a raucous celebration of the neighbourhood's Afro-Caribbean heritage. The Carnival emerged as a positive stand against the race riots of the 1960s. Forty years later, it draws around a million revellers to these streets and neighbouring North Kensington every August Bank Holiday weekend (many of the area's residents move out during the festivities).

There are enough fashionable shops and hangouts to keep the crowds flocking here throughout the year. Film buffs head to Notting Hill's atmospheric arty cinemas, the Gate, the Coronet and the Electric; at the latter you can book two-seater leather sofas for a special date.

Traffic-clogged Notting Hill Gate isn't a particularly attractive high street, lined as it is with unexceptional chain stores and eateries. But there are highlights: the wooden doors of No.21 open into Notting Hill Arts Club's intimate basement, where you'll find lively programming, art shows and international clubbers.

Hilly Ladbroke Grove, named after its affluent 19th-century landowners, branches into curved parades of Victorian townhouses. Some of the borough's hippest streets are to its east: Westbourne Grove, Portobello Road with its famous street market, and the self-consciously upmarket All Saints Road. Powis Square was the setting for the cult 1960s film *Performance* starring Mick Jagger.

Portobello Road Market is still a good place to find antiques and emerging designers, although there's a fair amount of tat. Most of the antiques stalls are at the Notting Hill Gate end; the most interesting clothing stalls are crammed beneath the Westway, an oddly romantic flyover that opened in 1970 and carries travellers in and out of central London on the A40(M). The Westway now has its own development trust (www.westway.org), which owns a sports centre and a nightclub (the Neighbourhood, *see p146*).

North Kensington

On the northern side of the Westway, North Kensington has the most suburban feel of any neighbourhood in the borough. The district was built around the local St Charles and Princess Louise hospitals. Buildings in the area certainly contrast with each other, from the snug-looking terraced houses around Barlby Road to the imposing 1911 Pall Mall Depository (also on Barlby Road), which now contains office units and a café.

North Kensington bursts into life during the Notting Hill Carnival, with many local kids involved in the parade. At its northernmost boundary, you'll find the green oasis of Kensal Green Cemetery, the first of London's grand Victorian burial grounds, and the striking canalside studios of Kensal Town. Here too is the borough-run Canalside Activity Centre, which focuses on youth recreation.

Finally, mention should be made of what is surely North Kensington's most famous building: Ernö Goldfinger's 31-storey Trellick Tower, originally designed as cheap social housing in 1972. It has shrugged off a troubled reputation in recent years to become one of the most sought-after addresses in the capital.

Restaurants & cafés

There's no shortage of restaurants in this borough – cuisine preferences and extent of budget are all that will hold you back (for the complete run-down, see the *Time Out London Eating & Drinking Guide*). The most sparsely populated area is just north of the Westway, but even here you'll find a cluster of Moroccan (Moroccan Tagine), Portuguese (Lisboa Pâtisserie, Oporto Pâtisserie) and Spanish (Galicia) places.

South of the Westway there are cafés galore, but this is where the glamour starts: E&O (hip oriental) is probably most popular with the beautiful people, but the Electric Brasserie (adjoining the Electric cinema), and Tom Conran's well-established deli/café Tom's Delicatessen have their fans too. A recent arrival is the Ledbury (strangely the immediate area's only 'serious' eaterie); at the other end of the scale is Books for Cooks (the tiny, much loved café attached to the bookshop of the same name). Makan and Nyona (both Malaysian and Indonesian) and the Gourmet Burger Kitchen are good affordable places too. Spilling over into the City of Westminster are Angie's (African and Caribbean), Mosob (Eritrean) and Rodizio Rico (Brazilian).

Also worth knowing about are the two fish-and-chip restaurants Costas and (more upmarket) Geales, just the other side of Notting Hill Gate; here you'll also find Modern European pioneers Kensington Place and Clarke's, as well as the venerable British restaurant Maggie Jones. Also of note are Wódka (stylish Polish) and Zaika (classy Indian), plus two upmarket Italians, Brunello and Timo. Kensington High Street is lined with chain eateries, but towering above it, overlooking the Roof Gardens, is Modern European restaurant Babylon. In Earl's Court, one-offs Nikita's (Russian), As Greek As It Gets and Lou Pescadou (fish) stand out from the chain gang.

Swanky South Kensington retains Polish stalwarts Daquise and Ognisko Polskie alongside such big guns as Bibendum and Tom Aikens; other options include Lebanese restaurant Al Bustan, and Spanish outlet Cambio de Tercio and its tapas-bar offshoot Tendido Cero. Chelsea is home to even more heavyweights: the Bluebird complex holds both the Bluebird Dining Rooms (high-end British) and the Bluebird (Modern European) as well as a café; people cross town to eat haute cuisine at Aubergine and Gordon Ramsay; ladies who lunch still flock to Daphne's (Italian).

Knightsbridge has a handful of excellent, but expensive, eating options, including Fifth Floor (Modern Euro) at Harvey Nicks, the Mandarin Oriental's Foliage (spellbinding food), and the Millennium's Mju (haute with an oriental accent). Glamour is also in evidence at Mr Chow along with surprisingly good Chinese food,

Once monstrous carbuncle, now architectural gem – **Trellick Tower**. *See p143.*

and at Knightsbridge's two top French restaurants: Racine and Brasserie St Quentin.

For a modestly priced Knightsbridge meal (ha!), you're limited to the chains; Harvey Nicks has a branch of Wagamama, and there's a Pâtisserie Valerie on the Brompton Road.

Chutney Mary is the best known of Chelsea's classy Indians; there's also Painted Heron, Rasoi Vineet Bhatia and Vama. Tugga, an upmarket Portuguese, is an interesting new arrival. Gastropubs include the Lots Road Pub & Dining Room and excellent newcomer Pig's Ear, while a welcome raucous note is supplied by the Big Easy (motto 'put a li'l South in yo' mouth'). Lots of noise can also be made in child-oriented brasserie Blue Kangeroo. But pockets of the past remain – try Foxtrot Oscar (very British old-school wine bar). Finally, wharfwards, you'll find Chinese outpost Yi-Ban.

Al Bustan *68 Old Brompton Road, SW7 3LQ (7584 5805).*
Angie's *381 Harrow Road, W9 3NA (8962 8761).*
As Greek As It Gets *233 Earl's Court Road, SW5 9AH (7244 7777/www.asgreek asitgets.com).*
Aubergine *11 Park Walk, SW10 0AJ (7352 3449).*
Babylon *7th Floor, 99 Kensington High Street, W8 5SA (7368 3993/www.roofgardens.com).*

Bibendum *Michelin House, 81 Fulham Road, SW3 6RD (7581 5817/www.bibendum.co.uk).*
Bibendum Oyster Bar *Michelin House, 81 Fulham Road, SW3 6RD (7589 1480).*
Big Easy *332-334 King's Road, SW3 5UR (7352 4071/www.bigeasy.uk.com).*
Bluebird *350 King's Road, SW3 5UU (7559 1000/www.conran.com).*
Bluebird Dining Rooms *350 King's Road, entrance in Beaufort Street, SW3 5UU (7559 1129/www.conran.com).*
Blue Kangaroo *555 King's Road, SW6 2EB (7371 7622/www.thebluekangaroo.co.uk).*
Books for Cooks *4 Blenheim Crescent, W11 1NN (7221 1992/www.booksforcooks.com).*
Brasserie St Quentin *243 Brompton Road, SW3 2EP (7589 8005/www.brasseriest quentin.co.uk).*
Brunello *Baglioni Hotel, corner of Palace Gate & Kensington Road, SW7 5BB (7368 5700/ www.baglionihotellondon.com).*
Cambio de Tercio *163 Old Brompton Road, SW5 0LJ (7244 8970/www.cambiodetercio.co.uk).*
Chutney Mary *535 King's Road, SW10 0SZ (7351 3113/www.realindianfood.com).*
Clarke's *124 Kensington Church Street, W8 4BH (7221 9225/www.sallyclarke.com).*
Costas Fish Restaurant *18 Hillgate Street, W8 7SR (7727 4310).*
Daphne's *112 Draycott Avenue, SW3 3AE (7589 4257/www.daphnes-restaurant.co.uk).*
Daquise *20 Thurloe Street, SW7 2LP (7589 6117).*
E&O *14 Blenheim Crescent, W11 1NN (7229 5454/www.eando.nu).*
Electric Brasserie *191 Portobello Road, W11 2ED (7908 9696/www.the-electric.co.uk).*

Fifth Floor *Harvey Nichols, Knightsbridge, SW1X 7RJ (7235 5250/www.harveynichols.com).*
Foliage *Mandarin Oriental Hyde Park Hotel, 66 Knightsbridge, SW1X 7LA (7201 3723/ www.mandarinoriental.com).*
Foxtrot Oscar *79 Royal Hospital Road, SW3 4HN (7352 7179).*
Galicia *323 Portobello Road, W10 5SY (8969 3539).*
Geales *2 Farmer Street, W8 7SN (7727 7528).*
Gordon Ramsay *68-69 Royal Hospital Road, SW3 4HP (7352 4441/www.gordonramsay.com).*
Gourmet Burger Kitchen *50 Westbourne Grove, W2 5SH (7243 4344/www.gbkinfo.co.uk).*
Kensington Place *201-209 Kensington Church Street, W8 7LX (7727 3184/www.egami.co.uk).*
The Ledbury *127 Ledbury Road, W11 2AQ (7792 9090/www.theledbury.com).*
Lisboa Pâtisserie *57 Golborne Road, W10 5NR (8968 5242).*
Lots Road Pub & Dining Room *114 Lots Road, SW10 0RJ (7352 6645/www.thespirit group.com).*
Lou Pescadou *241 Old Brompton Road, SW5 9HP (7370 1057).*
Maggie Jones *6 Old Court Place, Kensington Church Street, W8 4PL (7937 6462).*
Makan *270 Portobello Road, W10 5TY (8960 5169).*
Mju *The Millennium Knightsbridge, 16-17 Sloane Street, SW1X 9NU (7201 6330/ www.millenniumhotels.com).*
Moroccan Tagine *95 Golborne Road, W10 5NL (8968 8055).*
Mosob *339 Harrow Road, W9 3RB (7266 2012).*
Mr Chow *151 Knightsbridge, SW1X 7PA (7589 7347/www.mrchow.com).*
Nikita's *65 Ifield Road, SW10 9AU (7352 6326/www.nikitasrestaurant.com).*
Nyonya *2A Kensington Park Road, W11 3BU (7243 1800/www.nyonya.co.uk).*
Ognisko Polskie *55 Exhibition Road, Prince's Gate, SW7 2PN (7589 4635/www.ognisko.com).*
Oporto Pâtisserie *62A Golborne Road, W10 5PS (8968 8839).*
Painted Heron *112 Cheyne Walk, SW10 0DJ (7351 5232/www.thepaintedheron.com).*
Pâtisserie Valerie *215 Brompton Road, SW3 2EJ (7823 9971).*
Pig's Ear *35 Old Church Street, SW3 5BS (7352 2908/www.thepigsear.co.uk).*
Racine *239 Brompton Road, SW3 2EP (7584 4477).*
Rasoi Vineet Bhatia *10 Lincoln Street, SW3 2TS (7225 1881/www.vineetbhatia.com).*
Rodizio Rico *111 Westbourne Grove, W2 4UW (7792 4035).*
Tendido Cero *174 Old Brompton Road, SW5 0BA (7370 3685/www.cambiodetercio.co.uk).*
Timo *343 Kensington High Street, W8 6NW (7603 3888).*
Tom Aikens *43 Elystan Street, SW3 3NT (7584 2003/www.tomaikens.co.uk).*
Tom's Delicatessen *226 Westbourne Grove, W11 2RH (7221 8818).*

Tugga *312 King's Road, SW3 5UH (7351 0101/www.tugga.com).*
Vama *438 King's Road, SW10 0LJ (7351 4118).*
Wôdka *12 St Alban's Grove, W8 5PN (7937 6513/www.wodka.co.uk).*
Yi-Ban *5 The Boulevard, Imperial Wharf, Imperial Road, SW6 2UB (7731 6606).*
Zaika *1 Kensington High Street, W8 5NP (7795 6533/www.zaika-restaurant.co.uk).*

Bars & pubs

The King's Road might be the first Chelsea stretch that springs to mind when pondering a night out in the area, but it's far from the discerning boozer's best option. Yes, it houses flash Apartment 195 (one for the gents, thanks to its all-female, all-sexy staff), gorgeous cocktail lounge Nectar, and the Chelsea Potter pub (popular with Topshop misses and, on match days, Chelsea fans) – but rule number one of Chelsea drinking is this: get off the King's Road. Do so, and you'll find an engaging mix of top-notch gastropubs (*see p144*) plus some great locals tucked away in the backstreets, like Chelsea Ram (refined yet down-to-earth), raffish Cooper's Arms, quirky Cross Keys, and aptly named Surprise in Chelsea (an unadorned old boozer popular with toffs and toughs). North-east on Old Brompton Road, the bohemian Troubadour fills many roles admirably (delicatessen, café), not least as a wine bar and singer-songwriter venue in the evening.

Finding a decent watering hole in over-priced Knightsbridge isn't easy, but it's worth seeking out wine-bar-cum-pub Swag & Tails. The cocktail bar of sushi restaurant Zuma is the deluxe option.

In South Kensington, look past the curious mingle of Sloanes, rootless cosmopolitans and crims to find some of London's most pristine pubs and cocktail bars. Typical of the genre is the Collection: clever, expensive and a little soulless unless you're part of a moneyed clique. Better are the Anglesea Arms (hearty, friendly and allegedly where the Great Train Robbery was planned) and 190 Queensgate (an annexe of the Gore Hotel, it's a miracle of swankiness on an otherwise desolate stretch between the Albert Hall and the Bulgarian Embassy). Nearby, well-stocked beer room Drayton Arms and American-themed cocktail bar Cactus Blue are both worthy alternatives.

Considering its moneyed locals, Kensington itself is strangely lacking in quality drinking venues, though the Tenth Bar (on the tenth floor of the Royal Garden Hotel) offers fabulous views across Hyde Park; there's also a clutch of corking pubs, like the countrified Scarsdale Tavern, antique and unspoiled Windsor Castle and, star of the Kensington pub trail, the Churchill Arms – a tinker's yard of quirky paraphernalia with a frenetic, buzzy vibe. Venues around Holland Park add little to the scene, though the Prince of Wales can work up a good head of steam at the weekends; the serene Ladbroke Arms suits for a gentle pint.

No wonder the denizens of W11 often come across as smug: Notting Hill, particularly the area between Westbourne Park and Westbourne Grove, has nurtured a spate of quality new bars over the past few years that are easily the best in the borough. Cocktail bar Lonsdale pitches its crazy 1970s vision of space-age decor with enough chutzpah to make it work, while nearby Trailer Happiness has won just as many fans for its kitsch decor. Elsewhere on Portobello Road, there's the charmingly boho boozer Sun in Splendour, idiosyncratic Portobello Gold and low-key Visible. Moving towards the Westway reveals likeable and intimate drinks lounge Eclipse, lavish Elgin (W11's most handsome pub), plus newcomer Ten West, whose sweeping, high-ceilinged interior (once, apparently, a public toilet) makes it the perfect setting for classy cocktails. Under the Westway, club Neighbourhood (founded by Portobello local Ben Watt of Everything But The Girl) impresses a smartish crowd with its house-tilted music and excellent upstairs balcony.

There's also a clutch of venues east of Chepstow Road that fall under the borough of Westminster (see p28).

Anglesea Arms 15 Selwood Terrace, SW7 3QG (7373 7960/www.capitalpub company.com).
Apartment 195 195 King's Road, SW3 5ED (7351 5195/www.apartment195.co.uk).
Cactus Blue 86 Fulham Road, SW3 6HR (7823 7858).
Chelsea Potter 116 King's Road, SW3 4PL (7352 9479).
Chelsea Ram 32 Burnaby Street, SW10 0PL (7351 4008).
Churchill Arms 119 Kensington Church Street, W8 7LN (7727 4242).
Collection 264 Brompton Road, SW3 2AS (7225 1212/www.the-collection.co.uk).
Cooper's Arms 87 Flood Street, SW3 5TB (7376 3120).
Cross Keys 1 Lawrence Street, SW3 5NB (7349 9111/www.thexkeys.co.uk)
Drayton Arms 153 Old Brompton Road, SW5 0LJ (7835 2301).
Eclipse 186 Kensington Park Road, W11 2ES (7792 2063/www.eclipse-venues.com).
Elgin 96 Ladbroke Grove, W11 1PY (7229 5663).
Ladbroke Arms 54 Ladbroke Road, W11 3NW (7727 6648).
Lonsdale 48 Lonsdale Road, W11 2DE (7727 4080/www.thelonsdale.co.uk).
Nectar 562 King's Road, SW6 2DZ (7326 7450).
Neighbourhood 12 Acklam Road, W10 5QZ (7524 7979/www.neighbourhoodclub.net).
190 Queensgate 190 Queensgate, SW7 5EU (7584 6601).
Portobello Gold 95-97 Portobello Road, W11 2QB (7460 4900/www.portobellogold.com).
Prince of Wales 14 Princedale Road, W11 4NJ (7313 9321).
Scarsdale Tavern 23A Edwardes Square, W8 6HE (7937 1811).
Sun in Splendour 7 Portobello Road, W11 3DA (7313 9331).
Surprise in Chelsea 6 Christchurch Terrace, off Tite Street, SW3 4AJ (7349 1821).

TRANSPORT

Tube stations Bakerloo Kensal Green; Central Notting Hill Gate, Holland Park; Circle Sloane Square, South Kensington, Gloucester Road, High Street Kensington, Notting Hill Gate; District Sloane Square, South Kensington, Gloucester Road, High Street Kensington, Notting Hill Gate, Earl's Court, Kensington (Olympia), West Brompton; Hammersmith & City Westbourne Park, Ladbroke Grove, Latimer Road; Piccadilly Knightsbridge, South Kensington, Gloucester Road, Earl's Court

Rail stations Silverlink Kensal Green, West Brompton, Kensington (Olympia); Southern West Brompton, Kensington (Olympia)

Main bus routes into central London 7, 9, 10, 11, 12, 14, 18, 19, 22, 23, 27, 74, 94, 148, 414; night buses N3, N7, N9, N10, N11, N18, N19, N22, N28, N31, N52, N74, N207; 24-hour buses 14, 23, 27, 94, 148, 345

River commuter and leisure boat services running to/from central London, with stops at Cadogan Pier (under Albert Bridge) and Chelsea Harbour Pier

'Notting Hill is a vibrant, exciting place to live. The movie is actually a pretty good depiction. During the Carnival, the residents evacuate.'

James Bailey, estate agent

Swag & Tails *10-11 Fairholt Street, SW7 1EG (7584 6926/www.swagandtails.com).*
Tenth Bar *Royal Garden Hotel, 20-24 Kensington High Street, W8 4PT (7361 1910).*
Ten West *161-165 Ladbroke Grove, W10 6HJ (8960 1702).*
Trailer Happiness *177 Portobello Road, W11 2DY (7727 2700/www.trailerhappiness.com).*
Troubadour *265 Old Brompton Road, SW5 9JA (7370 1434/www.troubadour.co.uk).*
Visible *299 Portobello Road, W10 5TD (8969 0333).*
Windsor Castle *114 Campden Hill Road, W8 7AR (7243 9551/www.windsor-castle-pub.co.uk).*
Zuma *5 Raphael Street, SW7 1DL (7584 1010/ www.zumarestaurant.com).*

Shops

From the excess of Knightsbridge to the indie record stores and vintage stalls of Notting Hill, Kensington & Chelsea offers an embarrassment of retail riches. Knightsbridge may be a tourist-clogged nightmare on a Saturday afternoon, but on a weekday morning it's quiet enough to appreciate Harrods' sumptuous tiled Edwardian food halls and the beauty theme park that is the fifth floor Urban Retreat. For the latest designer fashion, though, head for coolly sophisticated Harvey Nichols. For more super-luxe labels, stroll down Sloane Street to take in the likes of Marni, Fendi and, closer to Sloane Square, boudoir-fabulous boutique Coco Ribbon and the Jimmy Choo flagship.

After its 1960s and '70s heyday, the King's Road had become a bland, chain-dominated strip, but it was given a boost a couple of years ago when the old Duke of York barracks was reborn as an attractive shopping square. More interesting retailers within its confines include Kate Kuba for shoes, Myla lingerie and a stunning branch of Jigsaw in the former chapel. Further along the King's Road, the new Shop at Bluebird, which took over Sainsbury's Market, is further proof of its revival, selling a combination of designer clothes, furnishings, books and gadgets. Austique

has a lovely collection of clothes, lingerie and accessories for women, much of it by Australian designers. Famed vintage emporium Steinberg & Tolkein is a tad overrated, but still worth a rummage, and Antiquarius has an interesting array of stalls selling everything from old Louis Vuitton trunks to rare glassware. You have to walk further (it may really feel like World's End by the time you get there) for Vivienne Westwood's eponymous store. On the way, take a detour down unassuming Old Church Street for master shoemaker Manolo Blahnik's long-standing salon.

South Kensington has a cache of designer shops at Brompton Cross, as well as the Conran flagship in the spectacular art nouveau Michelin building; the boutique trail continues on pretty Walton Street, where you'll find the Farmacia Santa Maria Novella for wonderful herbal products.

Chain-choked Kensington High Street is another former fashion star that lost its sparkle. Its 135-year-old department store, Barkers, has been taken over by American company Whole Foods to be reborn as an organic superstore. From Kensington High Street, Kensington Church Street – lined with rarefied antiques shops perhaps more suited to the serious collector than the casual browser – leads up to Notting Hill. The area around the intersection of Westbourne Grove and Ledbury Road (on the border with City of Westminster) has become Boutique Central: Aimé, Feathers, JW Beeton, Matches…the list goes on (make a detour west for the Cross). Also worth a look are J&M Davidson for beautifully crafted bags, Alice & Astrid's adorable lingerie, and British perfumer Miller Harris. Boys get a look in at Ilk, with a fine collection of hip menswear labels like Margaret Howell, Rag & Bone and Nudie. Chaps should also look to the handsome-but-pricey knitwear in kaleidoscopic colours at Ballantyne, plus perennial favourite Paul Smith's suits, casualwear and luxe knits. And

Kensington & Chelsea

there are not one, but two fab boutiques for year-round swimwear shopping: Heidi Klein and Pistol Panties (technically in Westminster but it feels like part of the Hill).

There's plenty of scope to kit out your home, with Themes & Variations' post-war and contemporary furniture and decorative art, and Brissi for dainty bibelots. Excellent independent music stalls and shops ensure vinyl junkies are well served – Intoxica! and Stand Out Collectors Records are two of the best. Blenheim Books sells a thoughtful assembly of design, gardening and art titles. Food-wise, delis R Garcia & Sons (Spanish), Lisboa (Portugese) and Le Maroc (Moroccan) are all in the area, plus picturesque butcher Kingsland and fishmonger Golborne Fisheries.

As for Saturday's Portobello Road Market, the antique stalls and arcades start at the Notting Hill end; further up are the food stalls, with everything from traditional fruit and veg to organic biscuits, bratwurst and crêpes. Up-and-coming designers and vintage clothes sellers set up shop next to the Portobello Green arcade (which also contains an interesting selection of units) under the Westway Flyover on Fridays and Saturdays. Those who keep walking are rewarded by Olivia Morris's shoes and even further, on Golborne Road, celebrated vintage emporium Rellik.

Aimé *32 Ledbury Road, W11 2AB (7221 7070/ www.aimelondon.com).*
Alice & Astrid *30 Artesian Road, W2 5DD (7985 0888/www.aliceandastrid.com).*
Antiquarius *131-141 King's Road, SW3 5EB (7351 5353/www.antiquarius.co.uk).*

RECYCLING

No. of bring sites 25 (for nearest, visit www.recycleforlondon.com)
Household waste recycled 16.1%
Main recycling centre Kensington & Chelsea's main recycling centre has closed; residents are directed to: Western Riverside Civic Amenity Site, Smugglers Way, SW18 1JS (8871 2788/www.wrwa.gov.uk)
Other recycling services orange bag recycling service; green waste collection; collection of furniture and white goods; home composting
Council contact Waste Management, The Council Offices, 37 Pembroke Road, W8 6PW (recycling hotline 7341 5148)

Austique *330 King's Road, SW3 5UR (7376 4555/www.austique.co.uk).*
Ballantyne *303 Westbourne Grove, W11 2QA (7792 2563).*
Blenheim Books *11 Blenheim Crescent, W11 2EE (7792 0777).*
Brissi *196 Westbourne Grove, W11 2RH (7727 2159/www.brissi.co.uk).*
Coco Ribbon *133 Sloane Street, SW1X 9AX (7730 8555/www.cocoribbon.com).*
The Conran Shop *Michelin House, 81 Fulham Road, SW3 6RD (7589 7401/www.conran.com).*
The Cross *141 Portland Road, W11 4LR (7727 6760).*
Farmacia Santa Maria Novella *117 Walton Street, SW3 2HP (7460 6600).*
Feathers *176 Westbourne Grove, W11 2RW (7243 8800).*
Fendi *20-22 Sloane Street, SW1X 9NE (7838 6280/www.fendi.com).*
Golborne Fisheries *75-77 Golborne Road, W10 5NP (8960 3100).*
Harrods *87-135 Brompton Road, SW1X 7XL (7730 1234/www.harrods.com).*
Harvey Nichols *109-125 Knightsbridge, SW1X 7RJ (7235 5000/www.harveynichols.com).*
Heidi Klein *174 Westbourne Grove, W11 2RW (7243 5665/www.heidiklein.com).*
Ilk *24 All Saints Road, W11 1HG (7221 5033).*
Intoxica! *231 Portobello Road, W11 1LT (7229 8010/www.intoxica.co.uk).*
J&M Davidson *42 Ledbury Road, W11 2AB (7313 9532/www.jandmdavidson.com).*
Jimmy Choo *32 Sloane Street, SW1X 9NR (7823 1051/www.jimmychoo.com).*
JW Beeton *48-50 Ledbury Road, W11 2AJ (7229 8874).*
Kate Kuba *24-25 Duke of York Square, King's Road, SW3 4LY (7259 0011/www.katekuba.co.uk).*
Kingsland, the Edwardian Butcher *140 Portobello Road, W11 2DZ (7727 6067).*
Lisboa *54 Golborne Road, W10 5NR (8969 1052).*
Manolo Blahnik *49-51 Old Church Street, SW3 5BS (7352 3863).*
Marni *26 Sloane Street, SW1X 9NH (7245 9520/www.marni.com).*
Le Maroc *94 Golborne Road, W10 5PS (8968 9783).*
Matches *60-64 & 85 Ledbury Road, W11 2AJ (7221 0255/www.matches.co.uk).*
Miller Harris *14 Needham Road, W11 2RP (7221 1545/www.millerharris.com).*
Myla *74 Duke of York Square, King's Road, SW3 3LY (7730 0700/www.myla.com).*
Olivia Morris *355 Portobello Road, W10 5SA (8962 0353/www.oliviamorrisshoes.com).*
Paul Smith *Westbourne House, 120 & 122 Kensington Park Road, W11 2EP (7727 3553/ www.paulsmith.co.uk).*
Pistol Panties *75 Westbourne Park Road, W2 5QH (7229 5286/www.pistolpanties.com).*
Portobello Road Market *Portobello Road, W10, W11; Goldborne Road, W10.*
Rellik *8 Golborne Road, W10 5NW (8962 0089/www.relliklondon.co.uk).*

Kensington & Chelsea

Holland Park: beautiful woods, formal gardens and a great playground. *See p150.*

R Garcia & Sons *248-250 Portobello Road, W11 1LL (7221 6119).*
The Shop at Bluebird *350 King's Road, SW3 5UU (7351 3873).*
Stand Out Collectors Records *2 Blenheim Crescent, W11 1NN (7727 8406).*
Steinberg & Tolkien *193 King's Road, SW3 5EB (7376 3660).*
Themes & Variations *231 Westbourne Grove, W11 2SE (7727 5531/www.themes andvariations.com).*
Vivienne Westwood *430 King's Road, SW10 0LJ (7352 6551/www.viviennewestwood.com).*

Arts & attractions

Cinemas & theatres

Chelsea Cinema *206 King's Road, SW3 5XP (7351 3742/www.artificial-eye.com).*
Ciné Lumière *Institut Français, 17 Queensway Place, SW7 2DT (7073 1350/www.institut-francais.org.uk).* Films in French, with English subtitles.
Cineworld *0871 200 2000/www.cineworld. co.uk:* Chelsea *279 King's Road, SW3 5EW;* Fulham Road *142 Fulham Road, SW10 6SD.*
Coronet Cinema *103 Notting Hill Gate, W11 2LB (7727 6705/www.coronet.org).*
Electric Cinema *191 Portobello Road, W11 2ED (7908 9696/www.electriccinema.co.uk).*
Gate Cinema *87 Notting Hill Gate, W11 3JZ (0871 223 6497/www.picturehouses.co.uk).*
Gate Theatre *11 Pembridge Road, W11 3HQ (7229 5387/www.gatetheatre.co.uk).* Small, ambitious theatre that produces international work.
Odeon Kensington *263 Kensington High Street, W8 6NA (0871 224 4007/www.odeon. co.uk).*
Royal Court Theatre *Sloane Square, SW1 8AS (7565 5000/www.royalcourttheatre.com).* One of London's best theatres, committed to producing new plays by up-and-coming writers.

Science Museum IMAX *Science Museum, Exhibition Road, SW7 2DD (0870 870 4771/ www.sciencemuseum.org.uk).*

Galleries & museums

Carlyle's House *24 Cheyne Row, SW3 5HL (7352 7087/www.nationaltrust.org.uk).* The home of writer Thomas Carlyle offers an intriguing snapshot of Victorian life.
Leighton House Museum & Art Gallery *12 Holland Park Road, W14 8LZ (7602 3316/ www.rbkc.gov.uk/leightonhousemuseum).* Sumptuous former studio and home of Victorian artist Frederic, Lord Leighton.
National Army Museum *Royal Hospital Road, SW3 4HT (7730 0717/www.national-army-museum.ac.uk).* Exhibitions ranging from 15th-century Agincourt to present-day peace-keeping.
Natural History Museum *Cromwell Road, SW7 5BD (information 7942 5725/switchboard 7942 5000/www.nhm.ac.uk).* Ever-popular museum of dinosaurs and stuffed animals.
Science Museum *Exhibition Road, SW7 2DD (7942 4454/booking & information line 0870 870 4868/www.sciencemuseum.org.uk).* Interactive, child-friendly exhibitions on science, industry, technology and medicine.
Victoria & Albert Museum *Cromwell Road, SW7 2RL (7942 2000/www.vam.ac.uk).* This renowned art and design museum holds 3,000 years' worth of global artefacts.

Music & comedy venues

Cadogan Hall *5 Sloane Terrace, SW1X 9DQ (7730 4500/www.cadoganhall.com).* The Royal Philharmonic are residents of this classical concert hall.
Earl's Court Exhibition Centre *Warwick Road, SW5 9TA (7385 1200/www.eco.co.uk).* Huge exhibition, conference and concert venue.
Notting Hill Arts Club *21 Notting Hill Gate, W11 3JQ (7460 4459/www.nottinghillarts club.com).* Specialist music and arts venue hosting club nights and gigs.

Royal Albert Hall *Kensington Gore, SW7 2AP (7589 8212/www.royalalberthall.com).* World-famous concert hall known for classical performances, including the Proms; also hosts pop and rock concerts.

Royal College of Music *Prince Consort Road, SW7 2BS (7589 3643/www.rcm.ac.uk).* Many concerts at this famous academy are free.

Other attractions

Brompton Oratory *Thurloe Place, Brompton Road, SW7 2RP (7808 0900).* Also known as the Oratory Catholic Church, this is the second largest cathedral in London (after Westminster).

Goethe-Institut *50 Princes Gate, Exhibition Road, SW7 2PH (7596 4000/www.goethe.de/ london).* German cultural institution.

Institut Français *17 Queensberry Place, SW7 2DT (7073 1350/www.institut-francais.org.uk).* French cultural institution, including Ciné Lumière (*see p149*).

Kensington Palace *W8 4PX (7937 9561/ bookings 0870 751 5180/www.hrp.org.uk).* Though still a royal residence, some rooms and apartments are open to the public.

Royal Hospital Chelsea *Royal Hospital Road, SW3 4FR (7881 5200/www.chelsea-pensioners. co.uk).* Home to about 350 dapper, red-coated Chelsea Pensioners. The grounds host the annual Chelsea Flower Show.

Open spaces

Brompton Cemetery *South Lodge, Fulham Road, SW10 (7351 9936/www.royalparks.gov.uk).* Famous graves and a picturesque chapel.

Chelsea Physic Garden *66 Royal Hospital Road, SW3 4HS (7376 3910/www.chelsea physicgarden.co.uk).* A secret garden in the city, but public opening hours are restricted.

Holland Park *Abbotsbury Road, Holland Park, Holland Walk & Kensington High Street, W14.* Romantic park whose formal gardens surround the remains of Holland House (bombed during World War II) plus Leighton House, an ecology centre and a smart Italian park café.

Kensal Green Cemetery *Harrow Road, W10 4RA (8969 0152).* More graves of the famous, including writers Trollope and Thackeray, and engineer Isambard Kingdom Brunel.

Kensington Gardens *Kensington Road, W8 (www.royalparks.gov.uk).* Covering 260 acres, these gardens are home to various Diana memorials (a walk, a fountain, a playground), another to Prince Albert (an overblown statue) and, of course, Kensington Palace.

Sport & fitness

Leisure centres here tend towards private, highly polished and pricey. Exceptions include the no-nonsense Club Kensington, while Portobello Green Fitness Club defies expectations (and its somewhat seedy

location) with a good range of community-driven, family-friendly activities at affordable prices. The borough also encompasses two of the capital's premier public facilities: Kensington Leisure Centre (excellent design and a wide scope of activities), while the Westway Sports Centre is a first-rate, floodlit haven, with everything from all-weather football pitches to a large indoor climbing wall.

Gyms & leisure centres

Aquilla Health Club *11 Thurloe Place, SW7 2RS (7225 0225/www.aquillahealthclub.com).* Private.

Chelsea Club *Chelsea Village, Fulham Road, SW6 1HS (7915 2200/www.thechelseaclub.com).* Private.

Chelsea Sports Centre *Chelsea Manor Street, SW3 5PL (7352 6985/www.cannons. co.uk).* Private.

Club Kensington *201-207 Kensington High Street, W8 6BA (7937 5386/www.club kensington.com).* Private.

David Lloyd *116 Cromwell Road, SW7 4XR (7341 6401/www.davidlloydleisure.co.uk).* Private.

Earl's Court Gym *254 Earl's Court Road, SW5 9AD (7370 1402/www.sohogyms.com).* Private.

Fitness First *Petersham House, 29-37 Harrington Road, SW7 3HD (7590 5000/ www.fitnessfirst.co.uk).* Private.

The Harbour Club *Watermeadow Lane, SW6 2RR (7371 7700/www.harbourclub.co.uk).* Private.

Holmes Place *3rd Floor, 17A Old Court Place, W8 4HP (7761 0000/www.holmesplace.co.uk); 119-131 Lancaster Road, W11 1QT (7243 4141).* Private.

Kensington Leisure Centre *Walmer Road, W11 4PQ (7727 9747).*

LA Fitness *63-81 Pelham Street, SW7 2NJ (7838 0500/www.lafitness.co.uk).* Private.

Lambton Place Health Club *Lambton Place, W11 2SH (7229 2291/www.lambton.co.uk).* Private.

Portobello Green Fitness Club *3-5 Thorpe Close, W10 5XL (8960 2221/www.westway. org.uk).* Private.

Other facilities

Canalside Activity Centre *Canal Close, W10 5AY (8968 4500).*

Westway Sports Centre & Climbing Wall *1 Crowthorne Road, W10 5XL (8969 0992/ www.westway.org).*

Schools

WHAT THE PARENTS SAY:

'Many parents in this area aspire to get their children into independent secondary schools in Hammersmith, such as Godolphin & Latymer or St Paul's (*see p165*), as there is no space for

playing fields in Kensington & Chelsea. Of the state schools, I've heard that Cardinal Vaughan is very good, but I should think entry is highly competitive. As for state primary schools, Avondale Park in Notting Hill is large with a big multi-ethnic following and Fox Primary in Kensington is a charming little number.'
Mother of one, Kensington

Primary
There are 27 state primary schools in Kensington & Chelsea, 15 of which are church schools. There are also 26 independent primaries, including one Spanish school and four French schools. See www.rbkc.gov.uk and www.ofsted.gov.uk for more information.

Secondary
Cardinal Vaughan Memorial School *89 Addison Road, W14 8BZ (7603 8478/ www.cvms.co.uk).* Boys only.
Holland Park Community School *Airlie Gardens, Campden Hill Road, W8 7AF (7727 5631).*
Sion Manning RC School for Girls *St Charles Square, W10 6EL (8969 7111/ www.sion-manning.com).* Girls only.
St Thomas More School *Cadogan Street, SW3 2QS (7589 9734/www.stm.rbkc.sch.uk).*

Property
WHAT THE AGENTS SAY:
'With the river, fantastic shops and restaurants, theatres, parks, culture and history, Chelsea has the lot. The most expensive street is the Boltons, a lovely garden crescent with huge Victorian houses – they can go up to £20 million. The only real downside is that there are not enough tube stations within the area, so you often have a bit of a walk or have to get a bus.'
Dominic Pasqua, Hamptons International, Chelsea

Average property prices
Detached £2,921,524
Semi-detached £2,009,467
Terraced £1,292,345
Flat £468,369

Local estate agents
Berkeley International
www.berkeleyinternational.com; 2 offices in the borough (Kensington 7792 1881/South Kensington 7581 8888).
Bruten & Co *4A Wellington Terrace, W2 4LW (7229 9262/www.brutens.com).*
Cavanagh Smith & Co *8 Addison Avenue, W11 4QR (7371 1111/www.cavanagh smith.com).*

Chelsea International *15 Radnor Walk, SW3 4BP (7349 9495/www.chelseainternational.co.uk).*
Coutts de Lisle *66 Pembroke Road, W8 6NX (7603 4444/www.cdlestates.co.uk).*
Executive Lettings *329 Chelsea Cloisters, Sloane Avenue, SW3 3EE (8870 2670/ www.executivelettings.com).*
Marsh & Parsons *www.marshandparsons.co.uk; 5 offices (Bayswater 7243 5390/Holland Park 7605 6890/Kensington 7368 4450/North Kensington 7313 8350/Notting Hill 7313 2890).*
Westways *20 Great Western Road, W9 3NN (7286 5757/www.westwaysuk.com).*

Other information
Council
The Royal borough of Kensington & Chelsea *The Town Hall, Hornton Street, W8 7NX (7361 3000/www.rbkc.gov.uk).*

Hospitals
Chelsea & Westminster Hospital *369 Fulham Road, SW10 9NH (8746 8000/ www.chelwest.nhs.uk).*
Princess Louise Hospital *St Quintin Avenue, W10 6DL (8969 0133/www.nhs.uk).*
Royal Brompton Hospital *Sydney Street, SW3 6NP (7352 8121/www.rbht.nhs.uk).*
Royal Marsden Hospital *203 Fulham Road, SW3 6JJ (7352 8171/www.royalmarsden.nhs.uk).*
St Charles Hospital *Exmoor Street, W10 6DZ (8969 2488/www.st-marys.nhs.uk).*

Legal services
Chelsea CAB *Old Town Hall, King's Road, SW3 5EE (0870 122 2313/www.adviceguide.org.uk).*
Kensington CAB *140 Ladbroke Grove, W10 5ND (0870 122 2313/www.adviceguide.org.uk).*
North Kensington Law Centre *74 Golborne Road, W10 5PS (8969 7473).* Free legal advice and representation for individuals and small community groups.
Nucleus Legal Advice Centre *298 Old Brompton Road, SW5 9JF (7373 6262/4005).*

Local newspapers
Kensington & Chelsea Independent *8961 3345/www.londonlocals.co.uk.*

Allotments
There are no allotments in Kensington & Chelsea.

COUNCIL TAX		
A	up to £40,000	**£654.60**
B	£40,001-£52,000	**£763.69**
C	£52,001-£68,000	**£872.79**
D	£68,001-£88,000	**£981.89**
E	£88,001-£120,000	**£1,200.09**
F	£120,001-£160,000	**£1,418.28**
G	£160,001-£320,000	**£1,636.49**
H	over £320,000	**£1,963.78**

'I love the borough, but parts of it are jolly dirty. It's odd that Hammersmith isn't more up-and-coming, considering its neighbours.'

Virginia Ironside, writer and chair of the Save Shepherd's Bush Streets campaign

Hammersmith & Fulham

Sharp contrasts abound in this borough. You'll find beauty (riverside hostelries) and the beast (traffic in Hammersmith), socialites and the socially excluded, and the representatives of a league of nations. The range of housing, dining and sporting opportunities – from Queen's Club tennis to Queen's Park Rangers FC – is correspondingly diverse.

Neighbourhoods

Shepherd's Bush

Situated between rarefied Notting Hill to the east and gritty Harlesden to the north, Shepherd's Bush can feel like the part of west London that gentrification forgot. It has long been home to a variety of immigrant communities. While travelling Antipodeans remain a strong presence in the area, many have now moved out to Acton. It is the large Muslim community (mostly Arabs, but also Egyptians, Lebanese and Syrians) to the west of Shepherd's Bush Green – the area's focal point – that now define it.

Surrounding compact Shepherd's Bush Common, the Green itself is not a lovely spot. At its best, it is a transport hub to almost anywhere in London: take your pick from the endless conga line of buses that encircle it or the two tube stations at either end, both called Shepherd's Bush but confusingly separate (one's on the Central Line, the other the Hammersmith & City Line). Served by a variety of newsagents, takeaway chicken outlets, and large, noisy

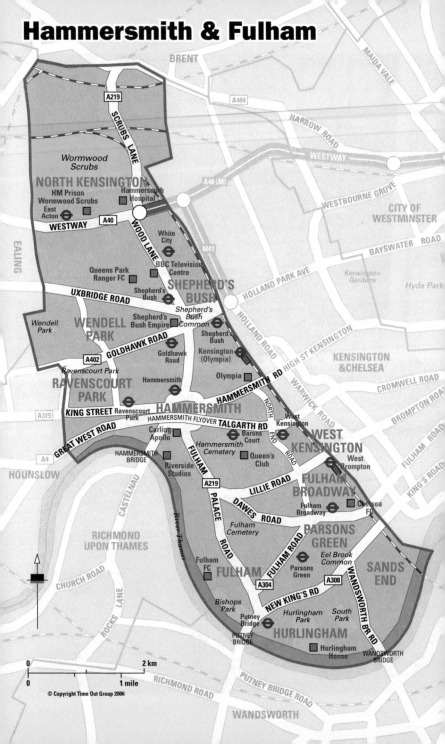

pubs – not to mention the ugly American-style West 12 shopping centre on the north side – it is not a place for picnics.

The surrounding streets offer all-purpose pound shops, late-night grocers and Muslim-friendly juice bars, while Shepherd's Bush Market (on the east side of the railway viaduct) is a lively and exotic experience, selling bargain-priced fruit and veg, fabrics, clothing and household goods. The spread of more upmarket restaurants and bars from Goldhawk Road has seen house prices rise, though the area remains affordable compared to its more affluent neighbours.

Within walking distance of the 'concrete doughnut' that is the BBC headquarters in White City, Shepherd's Bush has other links with the entertainment world, having spawned members of the Who, the Sex Pistols and current tabloid bête noire Pete Doherty. It's also famous for the Shepherd's Bush Empire, a venue that's just as likely to host top bands as a live session from Radio One; musos also frequent the more intimate Bush Hall. Other defining features include football ground Loftus Road, home to the 'Super Hoops' (Queen's Park Rangers), and the Daytona Raceway to the east. North of the Westway is Wormwood Scrubs common land, the largest open space in the borough, and adjoining it the infamous prison of the same name.

Hammersmith

The heart of Hammersmith has been torn in two by the thundering A4 and Hammersmith flyover. The adjacent roundabout, encircling Hammersmith tube (Piccadilly and District Lines) and bus station, and the Broadway Shopping Centre, is thus one of the busiest traffic intersections in London – often gridlocked. What remains of the centre is now noisy, built-up, polluted and less than aesthetically appealing.

Shopping is centred on the main street, King Street (which leads west to Chiswick). It's a grubby thoroughfare, providing the usual raft of Dixons, Boots and charity shops that you'd expect, plus another small shopping centre, Kings Mall. Noisy chain pubs dominate the area around the tube station; far better are the lovely riverside pubs west of green-and-gold Hammersmith Bridge, one of the prettiest bridges in London. Cultural offerings include the Carling Apollo (once the Hammersmith

Odeon), which hosts rock bands, pantos and even comedy stage shows; and the slightly shabby Hammersmith Palais (run by the Po Na Na group), which brings hordes of twentysomethings dressed as school kids for the regular School Disco nights on Saturdays. More upmarket are the Lyric Hammersmith – one of London's best and most diverse local theatres – and the Riverside Studios, specialising in performance arts and repertory cinema.

Socially diverse, Hammersmith includes large Irish, Afro-Caribbean, Asian and Polish communities – with Antipodean backpackers spilling over from nearby Earl's Court – but it's commerce, not community, that defines the area. King Street is lined with ethnic eateries, some good, many indifferent. Property is dominated by conversion flats – this is one of the largest private rented sectors in London – and you'll need to venture to leafy Brook Green to the north for converted family homes, along with medium-sized Victorian houses and modern luxury apartment blocks. St Paul's Girls, one of the best independent girls' schools in the country, is also here. Nearby, Olympia Exhibition Centre on the Kensington & Chelsea border hosts a variety of trade

Hammersmith & Fulham

Highs & Lows

▲ **The river** A Thames-side location is a boon to the southern section of the borough
Live music Shepherd's Bush spawned the likes of the Sex Pistols and the Who, and venues like the Empire and Bush Hall continue to host great acts today
Footie heaven The presence of three Premiership football teams means fans are never short of some sporting action

Hammersmith Flyover It leaves the surrounding area noisy, polluted and often gridlocked with traffic
West 12 Centre An ugly building that does little to improve Shepherd's Bush Green's already neglected appearance
▼ **Parking in Fulham** With an abundance of family cars, residents' parking permits are like gold dust

shows; locals tend to resent it for the traffic it creates. The area's transport is generally a plus, though, especially the fast links (by road and tube) to Heathrow airport – hence the presence of such multinational companies as Coca-Cola, EMI and Disney.

Brackenbury Village and Ravenscourt Park

Bounded by Goldhawk Road to the west and north, King Street to the south and Hammersmith Grove to the east, this is a very neighbourly, peaceful and gentrified area – quite distinct from surrounding Hammersmith and Shepherd's Bush. Huge Ravenscourt Park, a much-needed green lung in a very built-up part of the capital, adds to the community feel with its duck pond, lido, all-weather football pitch, several tennis courts, teahouse and – in summer – playday events and pony rides. Come Guy Fawkes Night, it offers the best fireworks display (and funfair) in west London.

Minimal traffic and one of London's best state primary schools (John Betts) make the area enormously popular with families. Such assets, combined with clever estate agent marketing (the 'Village' is a relatively recent addition to Brackenbury), also draw BBC staff eager for a quick commute to White City. Other middle-class attractions include a cluster of shops and restaurants on Brackenbury Road and a slew of excellent gastropubs. Ravenscourt Park tube is on the District Line, while Goldhawk Road and Hammersmith tubes are not far.

Cathnor Park and Wendell Park

This wedge-shaped area west of Shepherd's Bush is hemmed in by two major arteries – Goldhawk Road to the south and Uxbridge Road to the north. It leans towards the ethnic diversity of Shepherd's Bush, with a thriving Muslim community, though some deride the neighbourhood for a distinct lack of defining features.

Supposedly offering the greatest variety of any London street, Uxbridge Road boasts everything from 24-hour grocers with produce spilling out on to the street to ethnic restaurants, internet cafés and pound shops. Goldhawk Road, meanwhile, is torn between two worlds, simultaneously housing smart bar-restaurants like BBC fave the Bush Bar & Grill and old-style greasy caffs and Subway franchises. During the day, smallish Wendell Park can make an adequate setting for a sit or a stroll, but it is beset by its reputation as a hangout for the area's troublemaker teens. Buses stream regularly down both Uxbridge and Goldhawk Roads, but the closest tube stations are back near Shepherd's Bush Green.

West Kensington and Barons Court

West Kensington sits somewhat awkwardly between the sprawling concrete mass of Hammersmith to the west and well-heeled Kensington & Chelsea to the east, with the thundering Talgarth Road (aka the A4) slicing through its centre. It's the part of Kensington that fashionistas ignore; the name may sound posh to outsiders, but most residents of West Ken know this is the wrong side of the tracks. The long spine of the North End Road – pebble-dashed with kebab shops, mini-marts and a lively street market – cuts through the area from Olympia Exhibition Centre in the north to Fulham Broadway in the south.

The district is primarily residential, consisting mainly of Victorian terraces, plus newer apartment blocks. Properties become larger and smarter the nearer you get to Barons Court, which is also home to the Queen's Club, one of the capital's most exclusive tennis clubs. Transport is a strong point, with easy access to the A4 and three tube stations: Barons Court to the west, West Kensington in the centre, and Kensington (Olympia) to the north.

Fulham

Leafy Fulham has changed radically since the 1960s. The former Labour stronghold's tightly packed terraces, once home to working-class families employed in the heavy industry that dominated the riverside, are now full of young, monied professionals. The population is much less diverse than in neighbouring Hammersmith: there's truth to the clichéd image of private school-educated, Porsche-driving young men who work in the City and their blonde-bobbed spouses. Yet the area is just as popular with families, thanks to relatively crime-free streets combined with an abundance of private nurseries and prep schools.

'There are a lot of hospitals in Hammersmith, and a huge number of medical and nursing staff live in the area. The nurses rent, the doctors buy – that says it all.'

Rollo Miles, estate agent, Brook Green

Originally a market garden area, the architecture is largely Victorian, offering row upon row of neat terraced houses and converted flats. Gardens tend to be tiny (a drawback for families), except for the 'alphabet' streets between Fulham Palace Road and the river. Council blocks exist too, but many are set to undergo a revamp (and with this, their prices). Middle-class needs are met by a range of exclusive boutiques, antiques shops, upmarket bars and restaurants – many clustered along Fulham Road, the main retail street. Gyms servicing the hyper-achieving locals appear on almost every corner. Two major bugbears are a lack of parking spaces (mainly controlled by residents' parking permits) and traffic congestion. Public transport can be a problem. There is no overground rail service and the nearest tubes (Putney Bridge, Parsons Green and Fulham Broadway) are all a bit of a hike.

The only green area of any size is hugely popular Bishops Park. Bordering the river, it includes tennis courts, an ornamental park and grade I listed Fulham Palace (once the summer home of Bishops of London, now a museum) – and adjoins the loveliest allotments in London. It's also a great place to spot the many resident celebs. Next door is Craven Cottage, home of Fulham Football Club.

Parsons Green and Fulham Broadway

Avenues lined with stately plane trees give Parsons Green a village-like air. Complete with its own (eponymous) green, a church and the perennially popular White Horse pub, affectionately known as the 'Sloaney Pony', it's also slightly more affordable than neighbouring Chelsea. Eel Brook Common – offering children's play areas, tennis courts, football-cum-netball pitches and dog-free grass sections – is a big draw for families.

The twin thoroughfares of Fulham Road and the New Kings Road mean the shopping and dining opportunities are also excellent, if you can afford it. As in Fulham, a number of fitness clubs dot the streets, some more exclusive than others. Parsons Green tube station (District Line) is a distinct bonus.

The streets north-east of Parsons Green are noticeably busier but also highly desirable. Fulham Broadway itself is a thriving shopping area, with the standard high-street names, supermarkets, pubs, restaurants and the shiny new Fulham Broadway Centre atop the (revamped) tube station. An upper-class version of Shepherd's Bush's ugly West 12 centre, this US-style mall boasts assorted chain shops and eateries, plus a nine-screen cinema complex and a David Lloyd fitness club. Next door is Stamford Bridge, Chelsea FC's ground: congestion on match days is a major downer.

Peterborough Estate and Hurlingham

Lying south of the New Kings Road, this area is a tale of two estates. One is the exclusive Peterborough Estate, built in the 19th century for local workers. Conversions, extensions and the increasing gentrification from Chelsea's overspill have combined to make these elaborately detailed red-brick houses highly sought after. The original 500 'Lion' houses – so-named because of the miniature rooftop stone lions – now regularly go for over £1m (though few appear on the market). Nearby, meanwhile, sits the Sullivan Estate – an area known for 'hoodie' street gang kids and petty crime. The clash can be an uncomfortable one.

Catering to the richest residents is the exclusive Hurlingham Club, located at 18th-century Hurlingham House. Best described as a country mansion (site of many a glittering party), it sits in 42 acres

Hammersmith & Fulham

of grounds, which cater for tennis, croquet, cricket, bowls, golf, squash and swimming. Arrivistes beware – there is currently a ten-year waiting list for membership. Nearby is a smaller green space, South Park (open to all), while the proximity of both the New Kings Road and more affordable Wandsworth Bridge Road cover the retail side of life. As for transport, Putney Bridge tube and slow buses service the area.

Sand's End

Previously seen as Fulham's poor relation, Sand's End in the south-east corner of the borough is in a state of flux. The newly built Imperial Wharf – a dramatic residential complex featuring soaring glass towers, a ten-acre park and stunning riverside views – has given the area an aura of glamour that has local estate agents drooling. As part of the development, a new overground station is set to be completed by September 2006 (no promises, though), improving poor transport links. Moving inland from the river sees a mix of more affordable public and private housing, with facilities for those on lower incomes, such as the Sand's End Community Centre. Wandsworth Bridge Road is the main shopping street, containing pine and antiques shops, cosy cafés and one of the best butcher's in town (Randalls).

Restaurants & cafés

Shepherd's Bush has a fine spread of restaurants, helped by the area's racially mixed population and the increasing number of upwardly mobile residents. The latter have yet to make much visible impact on the district's main streets, though notable exceptions include long-standing Mod Euro bar-restaurant Bush Bar & Grill on grimy Goldhawk Road. Also on Goldhawk Road, boho haven Blah Blah Blah serves first-rate vegetarian food; classic caff Harris' Café Rest draws admirers for its 1950s decor and huge portions. Down the road, modish Bush Garden Café is popular with local yummy-mummies.

Otherwise, Shepherd's Bush is great for sampling world cuisines, ranging from Syrian (low-budget, high-quality Abu Zaad) to South-east Asian (unassuming Thai Esarn Kheaw), via East European (Polish old-timer Patio). Askew Road typifies the

district's forte in modest ethnic eateries: Adam's Café (Tunisian) is worth a look.

Travelling south on the Shepherd's Bush Road towards Hammersmith, Snows on the Green is a smart Mediterranean restaurant with Italian leanings. In Hammersmith itself, only the River Café makes good use of a curvaceous stretch of the Thames; close behind in the fame stakes is the excellent vegetarian Gate. At a less exalted level, King Street has long been known for its Polish and Indian restaurants. You'll get the whole East European experience within the concrete block of the Lowiczanka Polish Cultural Centre, while homely Polish cooking at low prices is the remit of deli-restaurant Polanka. As for the South Asian contenders, best are low-priced Sagar (South

Hammersmith & Fulham

Brackenbury Village. *See p156.*

Indian) and Agni (pan-Indian). King Street also houses Azou (North African/Middle Eastern), Saigon Saigon (Vietnamese) and Tosa (Japanese).

Away from the major thoroughfares, the pocket of gentility that is Brackenbury Village and Ravenscourt Park has the Brackenbury, a cherished Mod Euro venue; you'll find similarly moneyed clientele at gastropub the Anglesea Arms. Nearby, Ravenscourt Park has its own daytime café. But our current top choice for a meal in this neighbourhood is Chez Kristof, with its marvellous regional French cuisine.

West Kensington is a good place to look for a cheap eat, the market street North End Road being well served with takeaways (best is Turkish Best Mangal). Further down the same street is 222 Veggie Vegan, with its (you guessed it) vegan menu. At West Ken's northern boundary is Olympia, boasting some great Middle Eastern restaurants and cafés like Chez Marcelle (Lebanese) and Yas (Iranian), plus Popeseye Steak House. As for gastropubs, the genial Cumberland Arms has a good-value Mediterranean and North African menu, while the Atlas, at the back of Earl's Court Exhibition Centre, is also worth a look.

Like its neighbour Chelsea, Fulham's restaurants mainly cater to the area's young professionals. Some, like the Blue Kangaroo brasserie, also tend to the offspring of these folk. Off towards Fulham Broadway, the Farm (Mod Euro) is more grown-up. Around Fulham Broadway, Zimzun (oriental), Blue Elephant (Thai), Olé (Spanish), and pizzeria Napulé are all recommended. Nearby you'll find the buzzing cocktail bar and Latin American eaterie 1492. Fulham's fish lovers head for the river, where Deep serves a fascinating, Scandinavian-influenced menu. Equally new and enticing is Wizzy ('modern Korean') at the Parsons Green end of Fulham Road.

Two more options worth considering in this neck of the woods are Darwesh (Middle Eastern) and Fulham's own River Café – unlike its illustrious Hammersmith namesake, this one is a 1950s Italian caff serving omelette and chips.

Abu Zaad *29 Uxbridge Road, W12 8LH (8749 5107).*
Adam's Café *77 Askew Road, W12 9AH (8743 0572).*
Agni *160 King Street, W6 0QU (8846 9191/ www.agnirestaurant.com).*
Anglesea Arms *35 Wingate Road, W6 0UR (8749 1291).*
Atlas *16 Seagrave Road, SW6 1RX (7385 9129/www.theatlaspub.co.uk).*
Azou *375 King Street, W6 9NJ (8563 7266).*
Best Mangal *104 North End Road, W14 9EX (7610 1050).*
Blue Elephant *4-6 Fulham Broadway, SW6 1AA (7385 6595/www.blueelephant.com).*
Blue Kangaroo *555 King's Road, SW6 2EB (7371 7622/www.thebluekangaroo.co.uk).*
Blah Blah Blah *78 Goldhawk Road, W12 8HA (8746 1337).*
Brackenbury *129-131 Brackenbury Road, W6 0BQ (8748 0107).*
Bush Bar & Grill *45A Goldhawk Road, W12 8QP (8746 2111/www.bushbar.co.uk).*
Bush Garden Café *59 Goldhawk Road, W12 8EG (8743 6372).*
Chez Kristof *111 Hammersmith Grove, W6 0NQ (8741 1177/www.chezkristof.co.uk).*
Chez Marcelle *34 Blythe Road, W14 0HA (7603 3241).*
Cumberland Arms *29 North End Road, W14 8SZ (7371 6806/www.thecumberland armspub.co.uk).*
Darwesh *6 Fulham High Street, SW6 3LQ (7736 8777).*
Deep *The Boulevard, Imperial Wharf, SW6 2UB (7736 3337/www.deeplondon.co.uk).*
Esarn Kheaw *314 Uxbridge Road, W12 7LJ (8743 8930).*
The Farm *18 Farm Lane, SW6 1PP (7381 3331/www.thefarmfulham.co.uk).*

1492 *404 North End Road, SW6 1LU (7381 3810/www.1492restaurant.com).*
The Gate *51 Queen Caroline Street, W6 9QL (8748 6932).*
Harris' Café Rest *39 Goldhawk Road, W12 8QQ (8743 1753).*
Lowiczanka Polish Cultural Centre *1st Floor, 238-246 King Street, W6 0RF (8741 3225).*
Napulé *585 Fulham Road, SW6 5UA (7381 1122).*
Olé *Broadway Chambers, Fulham Broadway, SW6 1EP (7610 2010/www.olerestaurants.com).*
Patio *5 Goldhawk Road, W12 8QQ (8743 5194).*
Polanka *258 King Street, W6 0SP (8741 8268).*
Popeseye Steak House *108 Blythe Road, W14 0HD (7610 4578).*
Ravenscourt Park Café *Ravenscourt Tea House, Ravenscourt Park, W6 0UL (8748 1945).*
River Café *1 Station Approach, SW6 3UH (7736 6296).*
The River Café *Thames Wharf, Rainville Road, W6 9HA (7386 4200/www.rivercafe.co.uk).*
Sagar *157 King Street, W6 9JT (8741 8563).*
Saigon Saigon *313-317 King Street, W6 9NH (0870 220 1398).*
Snows on the Green *166 Shepherd's Bush Road, W6 7PB (7603 2142/www.snowsonthe green.co.uk).*
Tosa *332 King Street, W6 0RR (8748 0002).*
222 Veggie Vegan *222 North End Road, W14 9NU (7381 2322/www.222veggie vegan.com).*
Wizzy *616 Fulham Road, SW6 5PR (7736 9171/www.wizzyrestaurant.co.uk).*
Yas *7 Hammersmith Road, W14 8XJ (7603 9148).*
Zimzun *Fulham Broadway Retail Centre, Fulham Road, SW6 1BW (7385 4555/ www.zimzun.co.uk).*

Bars & pubs

Once notable for very little other than a half-decent music venue, Shepherd's Bush is slowly liberating itself from the chain pubs and grotty boozers that once held sway here. There's still some way to go, but at least the local drinker need not venture into Notting Hill to find some class-act bars; with luck, newcomers such as the Defector's Weld, with its smart pub, 'snug' cocktail bar and unobtrusive DJ sounds, are a sign of things to come. Similarly promising, the gorgeous and unaffected Albertine is great for a quiet chat. Ale lovers will be in their element in the Crown & Spectre on Melinda Road; on the other side of Goldhawk Road is another

fine boozer, the Anglesea Arms gastropub (*see p160*). The Seven Stars Bar & Dining Room further west down Goldhawk Road serves good cocktails in elegant surroundings. Heading towards Kensington, nestled on a quiet residential road, is the Havelock Tavern, one of London's original gastropubs; it was recently closed due to fire damage but plans to reopen by spring 2006. Close to Shepherd's Bush tube, the string of chain pubs is unlikely to set your interest aflame.

South towards Hammersmith is traditional pub land – you won't find many places for a cocktail, but you will find some fine views of the Thames. The cluster of pubs on the western side of Hammersmith Bridge, on Upper Mall, include the Old Ship, with its happy marriage of river views, outside space and a lively crowd, and the tiny, snug, wood-panelled Dove. Both serve Fuller's beers, and are prime spots for watching the Boat Race in spring (or rowers in general, thoughout the year). Just north from the river is the beautifully ornate Salutation; further north still you can enjoy Young's beers and live jazz, blues or comedy at the Victorian Brook Green Hotel. Bringing a less genial vibe to the area is the Hammersmith Palais, with its popular School Disco theme nights.

Even though Fulham covers such a large area, from the riverside to the busy lower

TRANSPORT
Tube stations *Central* Shepherd's Bush, White City, East Acton; *District* Kensington (Olympia), West Kensington, Baron's Court, Hammersmith, Ravenscourt Park, West Brompton, Fulham Broadway, Parsons Green, Putney Bridge; *Hammersmith & City* Shepherd's Bush, Goldhawk Road, Hammersmith; *Piccadilly* Barons Court, Hammersmith
Rail stations *Silverlink* Willesden Junction, Kensington (Olympia), West Brompton; *Southern* Kensington (Olympia), West Brompton
Main bus routes *into central London* 7, 9, 10, 11, 14, 22, 27, 74, 94, 148, 211, 414; *night buses* N7, N9, N10, N11, N22, N28, N74, N97, N207; *24-hour buses* 14, 27, 72, 85, 93, 94, 148, 220, 266

stretches of the King's and Fulham Roads, there's not a great deal to shout about before you reach the pastoral pleasures of Parsons Green, where posh locals hang out at the White Horse, one of London's finest pubs.

Also in this area is a newish outcrop of the La Perla chain, with its overabundance of Tex-Mex kitsch and a wide-reaching drinks menu; Aragon House on New Kings Road is a fine neo-Georgian boozer with an ivy-clad exterior and a lovely garden. Just out of the borough to the east, on the other side of Fulham Broadway tube and in close proximity to Chelsea's football ground, is the grand Finch's and the charming, unpretentious Fox & Pheasant.

Albertine 1 *Wood Lane, W12 7DP* *(8743 9593).*
Anglesea Arms 35 *Wingate Road, W6 0UR* *(8749 1291).*
Aragon House 247 *New Kings Road, SW6 4XG (7731 7313/www.aragonhouse.net).*
Brook Green Hotel 170 *Shepherd's Bush Road, W6 7PB (7603 2516).*
Crown & Sceptre 57 *Melina Road, W12 9HY* *(8746 0060).*
Defector's Weld 170 *Uxbridge Road, W12 8AA (8749 0008).*
Dove 19 *Upper Mall, W6 9TA (8748 5405).*
Finch's 190 *Fulham Road, SW10 9PN* *(7351 5043).*
Fox & Pheasant 1 *Billing Road, SW10 9UJ* *(7352 2943).*
Havelock Tavern 57 *Masbro Road, W14 0LS* *(7603 5374/www.thehavelocktavern.co.uk).*
La Perla 803 *Fulham Road, SW6 5HE* *(7471 4895/www.cafepacifico-laperla.com).*
Old Ship 25 *Upper Mall, W6 9TD (8748 2593/ www.oldshipw6.co.uk).*
Salutation 154 *King Street, W6 0QU* *(8748 3668).*

RECYCLING

No. of bring sites 45 (for nearest, visit www.recycleforlondon.com)
Household waste recycled 14.4%
Main recycling centre Western Riverside Civic Amenity Site, Smugglers Way, Wandsworth, SW18 1JS (8871 2788/www.wrwa.gov.uk).
Other recycling services green waste collection; home composting; fridge and freezer collection; collection of furniture, by either the council, Furnish (8969 3332) or the Notting Hill Housing Group Furniture Store (8960 3005)
Council contact Direct Services Department, DS03, 25 Bagleys Lane, SW6 2QA (8753 1100)

Seven Stars Bar & Dining Room 243 *Goldhawk Road., W12 8EU (8748 0229/ www.sevenstarsdining.co.uk).*
White Horse 1-3 *Parsons Green, SW6 4UL* *(7736 2115).*

Shops

In retail terms, the borough is best known for the colourful, cut-price bazaar that is Shepherd's Bush Market and the refined interiors and antiques shops of Fulham. Running between Uxbridge and Goldhawk Roads, the former offers an intriguing mix of just about everything you can think of, from produce and fabrics to reggae music and wedding gowns. There is also an impressive array of food shops on Uxbridge Road, including global supermarket Al-Abbas. Otherwise, the area's retail draws are limited; the West 12 mall contains basic chains such as Boots and Books Etc.

Hammersmith is a lure for keen bargain-hunters, as two cheap-as-chips clothes emporia – TK Maxx and Primark – face each other on the main shopping drag, King Street. The small Kings Mall shopping centre houses a branch of Habitat, and there are more chains at the Broadway mall in the centre of the tube/bus station complex. Soil Association-registered Bushwacker Wholefoods is popular, while Hepsibah Hats (by appointment only) is worth a detour to Brackenbury Road for Jayne Hepsibah Sullivan's made-to-order creations.

Residents of Hammersmith, West Kensington and Fulham converge to stock up on comestibles at the North End Road street market; it's also worth seeking out the delightful Prima deli a few streets north. Unsurprisingly, affluent Fulham has the lion's share of browse-worthy shops, beyond the Sainsbury's and workaday chains of the Fulham Broadway Centre.

The stretch of the Fulham Road near Parsons Green has enough upmarket chains (Cologne & Cotton, Cath Kidston, Emma Bridgewater) and interesting one-offs (Cine Art Gallery, Judy Greenwood Antiques) to occupy the locals on a Saturday afternoon. Men can get outfitted in handmade Italian shirts and unstructured tailoring at Palmer. Towards the river on Fulham High Street are glam vintage clothes boutiques Circa and Old Hat, where cash-strapped dandies can pick up a (previously worn) Savile Row suit.

The **Atlas** gastropub, near Earl's Court Exhibition Centre. *See p160.*

On the food front, there's a trio of upmarket delis in the locale – Elizabeth King, Megan's and Moroccan/Middle Eastern Del'Aziz (next to Aziz restaurant) – plus excellent butcher Randalls.

This end of the King's Road and Wandsworth Bridge Road are known for smart furniture and interiors shops. You'll find traditional pieces at Sasha Waddell, bed specialist Simon Horn and upholsterer George Smith. Modern options include Pop UK and Harmer. If you're looking for affordable artworks to decorate your Fulham pad, try Will's Art Warehouse.

Lillie Road's line-up of antiques shops yields some unusual items. Graham Kirkland Religious Art & Antiques is the place to stock up on chapel chairs or life-size plaster Virgin Marys; Curious Science (open by appointment only) sells such conversation-starters as a Victorian dildo or an Edwardian glass eye. Among several businesses in the area catering to growing families is a branch of toy shop Cheeky Monkeys. For big boys' toys, Warr's stocks lots of new and used Harley-Davidsons.

Al-Abbas *258-262 Uxbridge Road, W12 7JA (8740 1932).*
Broadway Shopping Centre *The Broadway, W6 (www.hammersmithbroadway.co.uk).*
Bushwacker Wholefoods *132 King Street, W6 0QU (8748 2061).*
Cheeky Monkeys *94 New Kings Road, SW6 4UL (7731 3031).*
Cine Art Gallery *759 Fulham Road, SW6 5UU (7384 0728/www.cineartgallery.com).*
Circa Vintage Clothes *8 Fulham High Street, SW6 3LQ (7736 5038/www.circavintage.com).*

Curious Science *307 Lillie Road, SW6 7LL (7610 1175/07956 834 094/www.curious science.com).*
Del'Aziz *24-32 Vanston Place, SW6 1AX (7386 0086).*
Elizabeth King *34 New Kings Road, SW6 4ST (7736 2826/www.elizabethking.com).*
Fulham Broadway Centre *Fulham Road, SW6 (www.fulhambroadway.com).*
George Smith *587-589 King's Road, SW6 2EH (7384 1004/www.georgesmith.co.uk).*
Graham Kirkland Religious Art & Antiques *271 Lillie Road, SW6 7LL (7381 3195/www.grahamkirkland.co.uk).*
Harmer *253 New Kings Road, SW6 4RB (7736 5111/www.harmer.uk.com).*
Judy Greenwood Antiques *657-659 Fulham Road, SW6 5PY (7736 6037/ www.judygreenwoodantiques.co.uk).*
Hepsibah Hats *112 Brackenbury Road, W6 0BD (8741 0025).*
Megan's Delicatessen *571 King's Road, SW6 2EB (7371 7837/www.megansdeli.com).*
North End Road Market *North End Road, between Walham Grove & Lillie Road, SW6.*
Old Hat *66 Fulham High Street, SW6 3LQ (7610 6558).*
Palmer *771 Fulham Road, SW6 5HA (7384 2044).*
Pop UK *88 Wandsworth Bridge Road, SW6 2TF (7731 5544/www.popuk.com).*
Prima Delicatessen *192 North End Road, W14 9NX (7385 2070).*
Randalls Butchers *113 Wandsworth Bridge Road, SW6 2TE (7736 3426).*
Sasha Waddell *269 Wandsworth Bridge Road, SW6 2TX (7736 0766/www.sasha waddell.com).*
Shepherd's Bush Market *East side of the railway viaduct, off Goldhawk Road, W12.*
Simon Horn *117-121 Wandsworth Bridge Road, SW6 2TP (7731 1279/www.simonhorn.com).*

Hammersmith & Fulham

Warr's *611 King's Road, SW6 2EL (7736 2934/www.warrs.com).*
West 12 Centre *The Broadway, W12 (www.west12online.com).*
Will's Art Warehouse *Unit 3, Heathmans Road, SW6 4TJ (7371 8787/www.wills-art.com).*

Arts & attractions

Cinemas & theatres
Bush Theatre *Shepherd's Bush Green, W12 8QD (7610 4224/www.bushtheatre.co.uk).*
Cineworld Hammersmith *207 King Street, W6 9JT (0871 220 8000/www.ugccinemas.co.uk).*
Lyric Hammersmith *Lyric Square, King Street, W6 0QL (0870 050 0511/www.lyric.co.uk).*
Riverside Studios *Crisp Road, W6 9RL (8237 1111/www.riversidestudios.co.uk).*
Vue *0871 224 0240/www.myvue.com;* Fulham Broadway *Fulham Broadway Centre, Fulham Road, SW6 1BW;* Shepherd's Bush *West 12 Centre, Shepherd's Bush Green, W12 8PP.*

Music & comedy venues
Bush Hall *310 Uxbridge Road, W12 7LJ (8222 6955/www.bushhallmusic.co.uk).* Stages chamber concerts and low-key rock shows.
Carling Apollo Hammersmith *Queen Caroline Street, W6 9QH (0870 606 3400).* Powerhouse music venue with a 5,000 capacity.
Shepherd's Bush Empire *Shepherd's Bush Green, W12 8TT (8354 3300/www.shepherds-bush-empire.co.uk).* Great mid-sized music venue.

Open spaces

Bishops Park *Stevenage Road, SW6.*
Eel Brook Common *New Kings Road, SW6.*
Normand Park *Lillie Road, SW6.*
Ravenscourt Park *Ravenscourt Road, W6.*
South Park *Peterborough Road, SW6.*
Wendell Park *Wendell Road, W12.*
Wormholt Park *Sawley Road, W12.*
Wormwood Scrubs *Scrubs Lane, W12.*

Sport & fitness

Things are changing in Hammersmith & Fulham. Although there is only one public swimming complex in the borough (managed by Holmes Place, which also has private facilities in the same building), work is under way on a new £4m pool in White City, which will be linked to the recently opened Phoenix Fitness Centre.

The borough is also home to three football clubs – Chelsea, Fulham and QPR – as well as the prestigious Queen's tennis club, which hosts the Stella Artois Championship (an annual, men-only precursor to Wimbledon).

Gyms & leisure centres
Charing Cross Sports Club *Aspenlea Road, W6 8LH (8741 3654/www.ccsclub.co.uk).* Private.
David Lloyd *Unit 24, Fulham Broadway Retail Centre, Fulham Road, SW6 1BW (7386 2200/ www.davidlloydleisure.co.uk).* Private.
Fitness First *West 12 Centre, W12 8PP (8743 4444/www.fitnessfirst.co.uk).* Private.
Fulham Pools *Normand Park, Lillie Road, SW6 7ST (7471 0450/www.holmesplace.com).*
Hammersmith Fitness & Squash Centre *Chalk Hill Road, W6 8DW (8741 4640).*
Holmes Place *www.holmesplace.com; 181 Hammersmith Road, W6 8BS (8741 0487); 188A Fulham Road, SW10 9PN (7352 9452).* Private.
Lillie Road Fitness Centre *Lillie Road, SW6 7PH (7381 2183/www.gll.org).*
Phoenix Fitness Centre & Janet Adegoke Swimming Pool *Bloemfontein Road, W12 0RQ (8735 4900/www.gll.org).*

Other facilities
Linford Christie Outdoor Sports Centre *Artillery Way, W12 0DF (8749 6758).*
Queen's Club *Palliser Road, W14 9EQ (7385 3421/www.queensclub.co.uk).* Private.

Spectator sports
Chelsea FC *Stamford Bridge, Fulham Road, SW6 1HS (0870 300 2322/www.chelseafc.com).*
Fulham FC *Craven Cottage, Stevenage Road, SW6 6HH (0870 442 1222/www.fulhamfc.com).*
Queen's Park Rangers FC *Loftus Road Stadium, South Africa Road, W12 7PA (8743 0262/www.qpr.co.uk).*

Schools

WHAT THE PARENTS SAY:
‘Hammersmith & Fulham is pretty bad for state schools. There are too many private schools and they have a really negative impact on the state sector. The primaries, particularly, tend to have really bad reputations, and many are failing. However, my youngest goes to All Saints, a church primary that I rate highly. As far as secondary schools go, I wouldn't touch any except for Lady Margaret School, which every girl in the borough wants to go to. It gets good results. The intake is 40 per cent from churches, but they accept all denominations. For boys, the London Oratory School also gets good results and is famous for being the school Tony Blair's kids went to. There's absolutely no point in applying unless you are a Catholic, though.’
Mother of four, Fulham

Primary
There are 37 state primary schools in Hammersmith & Fulham, including 12 church schools. There are also 13 independent primaries,

including one faith school, three French schools and one theatre school. See www.lbhf.gov.uk and www.ofsted.gov.uk for more information.

Secondary

Burlington Danes CE School *Wood Lane, W12 0HR (8735 4950).*
Fulham Cross *Munster Road, SW6 6BP (7381 0861/www.fulhamcross.lbhf.sch.uk).* Girls only.
The Godolphin & Latymer School *Iffley Road, W6 0PG (8741 1936/www.godolphin andlatymer.com).* Private; girls only.
Henry Compton School *Kingwood Road, SW6 6SN (7381 3606/www.henrycompton school.ik.org).* Boys only.
Hurlingham & Chelsea School *Peterborough Road, SW6 3ED (7731 2581).*
Lady Margaret School *Parson's Green, SW6 4UN (7736 7138/www.ladymargaret. lbhf.sch.uk).* Girls only.
The London Oratory School *Seagrave Road, SW6 1RX (7385 0102/www.london-oratory.org).* Boys only; mixed sixth form.
Phoenix High School *The Curve, W12 0RQ (8749 1141).*
Sacred Heart High School *212 Hammersmith Road, W6 7DG (8748 7600/ www.sacredhearthighschool.org.uk).* Girls only.
St Paul's Girls' School *Brook Green, W6 7BS (7603 2288/www.spgs.org).* Private; girls only.

Property

WHAT THE AGENTS SAY:

❛Fulham's proximity to central London and areas like Chelsea and Kensington makes it perpetually desirable. It's also pretty good for transport links and has always maintained reasonable house prices. It's very residential with good schools – there are lots of families here. Many residents have moved here from areas further out, such as Clapham and Battersea.

Arguably, Fulham isn't as well served for large open spaces as some areas in south London – the big commons in Clapham and Wimbledon, for example – but there are a couple of small parks.❜
Alex Bignell, John Hollingsworth, Fulham

Average property prices

Detached £681,188
Semi-detached £671,566
Terraced £496,422
Flat £260,238

Local estate agents

Aspire *www.aspire.co.uk: 1 office in the borough (Fulham 7736 6110).*
Chard *www.chard.co.uk; 2 offices in the borough (Brook Green 7603 0603/Fulham 7731 5115).*

Faron Sutaria *www.faronsutaria.co.uk; 3 offices in the borough (Brook Green 7348 0016/Fulham 7610 2080/Shepherd's Bush 8740 7766).*
John Hollingsworth *www.johnhollingsworth. co.uk; 2 offices in the borough (Fulham 7731 3888/West Kensington 7602 8511).*
Lawsons & Daughters *68 Fulham Palace Road, W6 9PL (8563 0202/www.lawsonsand daughters.com).*
Ravenscourt Residential *3 Seven Stars Corner, Paddenswick Road, W12 8ET (8740 5678/www.ravenscourtresidential.co.uk).*
Sebastian Estates *www.sebastianestates. co.uk; 2 offices in the borough (Fulham 7610 6716/Hammersmith 7381 4998).*
Tauntons *95 Uxbridge Road, W12 8NR (8740 6666/www.tauntons.co.uk).*

Other information

Council

London Borough of Hammersmith & Fulham Council *Hammersmith Town Hall, King Street, W6 9JU; Fulham Town Hall, Fulham Broadway, SW6 1ET (8748 3020/ www.lbhf.gov.uk).*

Hospitals

Charing Cross Hospital *Fulham Palace Road, W6 8RF (8846 1234/www.hhnt.org).*
Hammersmith Hospital/Queen Charlotte & Chelsea Hospital *Du Cane Road, W12 0HS (8383 1000/www.hhnt.org).*
Ravenscourt Park Hospital *Ravenscourt Park, W6 0TN (8846 7777/www.hhnt.org).*

Legal services

Hammersmith & Fulham CAB *The Pavilion, 1 Mund Street, W14 9LY (0845 458 2515/ www.fulhamcab.org.uk).*
Shepherd's Bush Advice Centre *338 Uxbridge Road, W12 7LL (8753 5913).*

Local newspapers

Hammersmith & Fulham Independent *8961 3345/www.londonlocals.co.uk.*

Allotments

Fulham Palace Meadow Allotments Association *c/o Fulham Palace Museum, Bishops Avenue, SW6 6EA (7731 6055).*

COUNCIL TAX		
A	up to £40,000	**£772.03**
B	£40,001-£52,000	**£900.70**
C	£52,001-£68,000	**£1,029.37**
D	£68,001-£88,000	**£1,158.04**
E	£88,001-£120,000	**£1,415.38**
F	£120,001-£160,000	**£1,672.72**
G	£160,001-£320,000	**£1,930.07**
H	over £320,000	**£2,316.08**

'There's nothing better in winter than having a pint in a pub along the river, beside an open fire, then walking home along the foggy lanes.'

Omer Ali, resident

Richmond upon Thames

There's good reason why the wealthy are wowed by Richmond: villagey enclaves, wide-open spaces, alluring boutiques, quaint cottages and, wending its way across the borough, a gorgeous stretch of the Thames. Yes, Richmond is swanky, but here you can combine the best in country and city living – or at least dream that dream.

Neighbourhoods

Barnes

At the far east of Richmond borough, the Thames describes a sharp meander referred to as the Tideway; the Oxford and Cambridge boat crews race this stretch each year, finishing at Mortlake. The knuckle of land which the curve encircles is Barnes. Practically half of this district is open land: the London Wetland Centre (a bird reserve converted from defunct reservoirs) sits to the east of Castelnau, the long spine that leads up from Hammersmith Bridge to

Barnes proper; and wild and wooded Barnes Common creates a buffer zone to the south.

At the centre of Barnes is a large duck pond and adjoining green (site of a popular annual midsummer fair). From here a mix of shops, restaurants and pubs radiates out along Barnes High Street, Church Street and Station Road. The cosy, semi-rural atmosphere is more typical of a Surrey village than a capital city. Such attractions, combined with regular train connections to Waterloo from Barnes and Barnes Bridge stations, plus good (private) schools, draw affluent families and retirees to the area.

Richmond upon Thames

Richmond upon Thames

© Copyright Time Out Group 2006

Typical properties are Edwardian, Victorian or earlier – including some very large mansions around the pond, one once the home of writer Henry Fielding. Seven-figure house prices are common. The cost reflects the twin benefits of the seclusion afforded by Barnes' geography, and the proximity to Hammersmith just over the bridge. Barnes Bridge also allows easy access to the meadows and allotments of Chiswick (in the borough of Hounslow).

Barnes has an oddly musical heritage: Gustav Holst lived in a bow-fronted river-facing property; the Rolling Stones, Led Zeppelin, Jimi Hendrix and others made recordings at the Olympic studios; and the Bull's Head riverside pub has been a famous jazz venue since the 1950s.

Sheen and Mortlake

Most of what's considered to be Sheen sits between the Upper Richmond Road and the northern fringe of Richmond Park. This area is entirely residential, and the houses, in many cases newer than Richmond's but still classed as 'period' properties, sell for equally astronomical prices. Housing ranges from large Victorian and Edwardian villas near the park (the Parkside and Palewell Park areas are particularly sought after) to clusters of cute labourers' cottages around the railway tracks.

Residents say that the introduction of a Red Route a few years ago has turned Sheen into a thoroughfare rather than a village. Certainly the Upper Richmond Road (aka the South Circular/A205), the area's commercial artery, is unpleasantly busy. It is lined with shops (including a surprising number of charity outlets), restaurants, cafés and a branch of Waitrose.

To the north lies Mortlake, sandwiched between the Upper Richmond Road and the Thames. This is something of a no-man's land, any village atmosphere long since vanished with the widening of Mortlake High Street. Still, property prices are significantly lower than in neighbouring Barnes. The looming Budweiser brewery – the air is often thick with beery odours – occupies a large site next to the river. Just south of Kew is North Sheen, a relatively small pocket hemmed in by two major thoroughfares: the Lower Richmond Road (A316) and Mortlake Road (A205).

There's no tube in Sheen, which explains why the area is a little more secluded and a little less cosmopolitan than Richmond, but the overground from North Sheen and Mortlake stations still gets commuters to work in a jiffy – though the numerous level crossings are a constant source of annoyance to local drivers.

Richmond

After Henry VIII built his palace here in the late 15th century he took it upon himself to rename the area, then called Shene, after one of his favourite rural retreats: Richmond, Yorkshire. It was a prescient gesture. Today, Richmond is just what it says in the name: a very, very rich mound (on a hill rising up from the Thames). After Kensington & Chelsea, this is the most affluent borough in England. The pretty riverside setting, huge green spaces and stunning period houses have proved an irresistible lure for monied professionals, especially since the City is scarcely half an hour away by train. Yet Richmond avoids the haughtiness of K&C, retaining a buzzing villagey air and a harmonious sense of community. It is clean, safe, peaceful (except for the relentless Heathrow air traffic) and has excellent schools.

Richmond Park is London's largest: 2,500 acres of rolling woodland, where the Queen's deer graze. The park was first enclosed for hunting by Charles I and not much has changed since (though fewer bloodsports take place nowadays). Within, the Isabella Plantation – a carefully tended enclosure of azaleas and rhododendrons – is at its most splendid and colourful in May.

West of the Park is Richmond Hill, where Mick Jagger and Pete Townshend's palatial mansions enjoy an unrivalled, idyllic view over the Thames and the pastures of Surrey. Gracing the hill, on the steeper side, are the Terrace Gardens, another pristine enclosure of parterres and winding stone pathways. Near the top of the hill sits a dainty cluster (shops, restaurants, a pub) known as Richmond Village.

The road down the hill takes you into the confusingly planned town centre, a hive of shopping, eating and drinking establishments. Tucked away behind George Street (essentially the high street) is Richmond Green, one of the borough's

Richmond upon Thames

proudest assets. Remnants of Henry VIII's palace still stand in one corner, now converted into lodgings. When the sun's out, the Green is invariably strewn with lounging locals – except when cricket is being played on it, in authentically casual, village-green fashion. The Green has a diminutive adjunct, the Little Green; opposite this is Richmond's most famous cultural venue, its Victorian theatre.

Kew

Like Barnes, Kew is a little peninsula carved out by the Thames' wayward path. And also like Barnes, half of Kew is given over to unpopulated land. But unpopulated here doesn't mean undeveloped. The Royal Botanic Gardens, Kew (Kew Gardens to you and me) is an exquisitely planned extravaganza of biodiversity attracting a million visitors a year. But it's not the only expanse of green: adjoining the Gardens to the south is the Old Deer Park and the exclusive Royal Mid-Surrey Golf Course, while Kew Green (scene of many a summer cricket match) abuts the northern end.

Kew's other asset is its little village, a short stroll from the Victoria Gate of Kew Gardens. Considering there's a tube and rail station here, it's surprising that it has kept its serenity, but the local shops, cafés and restaurants dotted around the station retain a characterful, independent air.

Property in Kew is as highly sought after as in the rest of the borough, and relatively varied: Queen Anne to Victorian houses, converted flats and modern purpose-built apartments. Good primary schools and easy access to the A4 and M4 just over Kew Bridge are added attractions for prosperous middle-class families.

Twickenham

The world knows Twickenham for its Rugby Stadium. Locals know it for its pleasant riverside location (with eyots or islands to boot) and more palatable property prices (compared with Richmond, at least). Well-kept late Victorian and Edwardian terraces dominate its residential districts. Admittedly, the High Street is a noisier, busier thoroughfare than Richmond's intimate George Street (and nowhere near as attractive), but proud Twickenham residents would assert that they have Church Street instead – a cobbled lane off the main road flanked by restaurants, pubs, boutiques and gift shops. In summer, Church Street's restaurants mobilise, bringing their tables out into the street for an alfresco display that other parts of London can only envy.

Twickenham is served by overland rail, but no tube, though the M3 is easily accessible. Riverside walks and green spaces are a bonus.

Restaurants & cafés

The borough's demographic – white, wealthy, plenty of families but few immigrants – is mirrored in its eating options. There's no shortage of kid-friendly chain restaurants (Giraffe, Nando's, Pizza Express, ASK, Strada, Wagamama) or classy, white-tableclothed restaurants for the grown-ups, but bargain-priced ethnic cafés are conspicuous by their absence. Longevity matters more than fashion, so expect smart neighbourhood restaurants that have built up their reputation and clientele over decades, rather than the latest culinary trends.

Richmond's restaurants tend to be reliable rather than outstanding, with good options including Spanish veteran Don Fernando's, regional French specialist Chez Lindsay,

Highs & Lows

↑ **Greenery** Richmond has more green space than any other borough and Richmond Park is London's largest park
Not-so-secret gardens The Royal Botanic Gardens in Kew are exquisite
Good schools Some of the best in London are in Richmond and Barnes; most of these, though, are private

Air traffic The noise over Richmond caused by flights to and from Heathrow is relentless, a persistent local complaint
Property prices Seven-figure sales tags are not uncommon in Richmond, Kew and Barnes. In Twickenham, prices are more palatable
↓ **Cultural diversity** Or lack of it. Richmond has the most limited ethnic spread of any borough in London

Horticultural delights at the **Royal Botanic Gardens** in Kew.

and Japanese newcomer Matsuba. Canyon is worth a visit for its beautiful riverside setting, less so for its variable American food; a short walk along the river you'll find Bavarian sausages at Stein's kiosk (Easter to Christmas only). Upmarket Petersham Nurseries Café – winner of *Time Out*'s Best Alfresco Dining award in 2005 and definitely not your average garden centre caff – is ideal for summer lunches.

East Sheen offers excellent pan-Indian Sarkhel's, Modern European neighbourhood fave Redmond's, and smart gastropub-cum-hotel the Victoria. In Barnes, much-praised Sonny's (Modern European) and Riva (Italian) are perennially popular. Riverside brasserie the Depot is less formal, while MVH, over the road, is one of London's most enjoyably eccentric restaurants, for both cooking and decor.

Twickenham has its share of chains (Pizza Express, Zizzi, Loch Fyne), as well as two casual French brasseries, Brula and Ma Cuisine (also with a branch in Kew), and two first-rate one-offs: A Cena (Italian) and McClements (Modern European). Also Mod Euro in style, and equally polished, is the Glasshouse, next to Kew Gardens station.

A Cena *418 Richmond Road, Twickenham, Middx TW 1 2EB (8288 0108).*
Brula *43 Crown Road, St Margarets, Middx TW1 3EJ (8892 0602).*
Chez Lindsay *11 Hill Rise, Richmond, Surrey TW10 6UQ (8948 7473).*
The Depot *Tideway Yard, 125 Mortlake High Street, SW14 8SN (8878 9462/www. depotbrasserie.co.uk).*
Don Fernando's *27F The Quadrant, Richmond, Surrey TW9 1DN (8948 6447/ www.donfernando.co.uk).*
The Glasshouse *14 Station Parade, Kew, Surrey TW9 3PZ (8940 6777/www.glasshouse restaurant.co.uk).*
Ma Cuisine *6 Whitton Road, Twickenham, Middx TW1 1BJ (8607 9849); 9 Station Approach, Kew, Surrey TW9 3QB (8332 1923).*
Matsuba *10 Red Lion Street, Richmond, Surrey TW9 1RW (8605 3513).*
McClements *2 Whitton Road, Twickenham, Middx TW1 1BJ (8744 9610).*
MVH *5 White Hart Lane, SW13 0PX (8392 1111).*
Petersham Nurseries Café *Church Lane, off Petersham Road, Petersham, nr Richmond, Surrey TW10 7AG (8605 3627).*
Redmond's *170 Upper Richmond Road West, SW14 8AW (8878 1922/www.redmonds.org.uk).*
Riva *169 Church Road, SW13 9HR (8748 0434).*
Sarkhel's *199 Upper Richmond Road West, East Sheen, SW14 8QT (8876 6220/www. sarkhels.com).*

wagamama

**fast and fresh noodles and rice dishes
from london's favourite noodle restaurant**

for locations around london visit
www.wagamama.com

Sonny's *94 Church Road, SW13 0DQ (8748 0393/www.sonnys.co.uk).*
Stein's *Richmond Towpath, west of Richmond Bridge, Richmond, Surrey TW10 6UX (8948 8189/www.stein-s.com).*
Victoria *10 West Temple Sheen, SW14 7RT (8876 4238/www.thevictoria.net).*

Bars & pubs

The *rus in urbe* allure of its vast park and Thameside wetlands makes Richmond something of a beacon for active, wholesome Londoners who like their pubs to be equipped with such things as real ale and picturesque views. Both of these can be found at the Cricketers overlooking Richmond Green (get your Old Speckled Hen in a plastic glass in summer and stretch out by the boundary for a few wickets) and the riverside London Apprentice, where Henry VIII used to work on his beer belly. Also on the Green, the Prince's Head is looking spruce (with its original oak panelling still intact) after a 2004 refurb. The White Cross draws summer crowds to the riverbank, while real ale enthusiasts prefer to sup at the low-key Red Lion.

Down Twickenham way, the White Swan (located in a maze of impossibly idyllic little streets) and the Eel Pie both overlook the countercultural bastion of Eel Pie Island.

Barnes and Mortlake also have good riverside pubs: the former's Ye White Hart offers a perfect view of the Varsity boat race once a year; the latter's Ship is a sedate, perfectly pleasant tap at which to while away an afternoon. The Sun Inn on Barnes village green has to be one of the most idyllically positioned boozers in the borough, while jazz lovers should head to legendary venue the Bull's Head. Over in Kew, the Coach is an airy and congenial pub that'll make a visit to nearby Kew Gardens seem like an even better idea. Their full English is famous around these parts.

Bull's Head *373 Lonsdale Road, SW13 9PY (8876 5241/www.thebullshead.com).*
Coach & Horses *8 Kew Green, Richmond, Surrey TW9 3BH (8940 1208).*
Cricketers *The Green, Richmond, Surrey TW9 1LX (8940 4372).*
Eel Pie *9-11 Church Street, Twickenham, Middx TW1 3NJ (8891 1717).*
London Apprentice *62 Church Street, Isleworth, Middx TW7 6BG (8560 1915).*
Prince's Head *28 The Green, Richmond, Surrey TW9 1LX (8940 1572).*

Red Lion *92-94 Linkfield Road, Isleworth, Middx TW7 6QJ (8560 1457).*
The Ship *10 Thames Bank, SW14 7QR (8876 1439).*
Sun Inn *7 Church Road, SW13 9HE (8876 5256).*
White Cross *Water Lane, Richmond, Surrey TW9 1TH (8940 6844).*
White Swan *Riverside, Twickenham, Surrey TW1 3DN (8892 2166).*
Ye White Hart *The Terrace, SW13 0NR (8876 5177).*

Shops

Richmond is by far the biggest shopping centre in the borough, with enough options to rival the West End. High-street chains dominate, but there's also a serious number of high-end fashion shops catering to local ladies-who-lunch. The main thoroughfare,

Richmond upon Thames

Montpellier Row, **Twickenham**.
See p170.

the Quadrant/George Street, leading left from the station into a confusing tangle of one-way streets, is lined with familiar names (Boots, French Connection, Gap, HMV, Jigsaw, Monsoon, Reiss et al, even a branch of Topshop), plus large branches of Habitat, M&S and Waterstone's. Anchoring it all is a small outlet of Dickens & Jones.

As with property in these parts, the higher you climb the higher the aspirations – and prices. Head up Hill Street and its extension Hill Rise for top-end fashion from Caroline Charles, Joseph, Kate Kuba, Matches, MaxMara, Ronit Zilkha and Whistles. More posh frocks can be found at Fenn Wright Mason (back in the town centre) and Margaret Howell (on pretty Richmond Green). Specialist food shops include smart wholefood emporium Source, a branch of French pâtisserie/café Maison Blanc and chocolatier William Curley. Weary offspring can be placated at toy shops Tridias and the Farmyard. Further along the Thames is Petersham Nurseries, one of London's largest and swankiest outlets for all things horticultural.

East Sheen offers a less attractive retail experience, with shoppers having to negotiate the constant traffic on the busy Upper Richmond Road. But there's plenty of choice, from Woolworths, Boots, Superdrug, WH Smith and a Waitrose to charity shops,

smarter outlets (Kew for womenswear, Oliver Bonas for gifts) and some one-offs.

For a quieter and quainter time, head to Barnes. Locals are very proud of its old-fashioned villagey atmosphere, complemented by the duck pond and traditional butcher, baker, fishmonger and greengrocer – all found on Barnes High Street/Church Street. Other independents include the Real Cheese Shop, a branch of the Farmyard toy shop, and a smattering of upmarket fashion boutiques, including Jesus Lopez and Question Air. Tasteful, Swedish-style furniture is available at Blue Door Yard, while White Hart Lane in adjoining Mortlake offers posh deli goods at Gusto & Relish and antique and modern home accessories at Tobias & the Angel.

In Kew, there's a cluster of independent outlets around Kew Gardens station. For high-street brands, visit user-friendly Kew Retail Park, off the A205, which has a huge M&S, the Gap, Boots, Mothercare, Next and lots of parking.

Middle-class incomes and tastes mean there are no less than three farmers' markets in the borough, in Barnes, Richmond and Twickenham (all held on Saturdays). Mega-supermarkets include Waitrose next to Richmond station, and Sainsbury's off the A316 (Lower Richmond Road) at Manor Circus roundabout.

Blue Door Yard *74 Church Road, SW13 0DQ (8748 9785/www.bluedoorbarnes.co.uk).*
Caroline Charles *18 Hill Rise, Richmond, Surrey TW10 6UA (8948 7777).*
The Farmyard *54 Friars Stile Road, Richmond, Surrey TW10 6NQ (8332 0038/www.the farmyard.co.uk); 63 Barnes High Street, SW13 9LF (8878 7338).*
Fenn Wright Manson *4 The Square, Richmond, Surrey TW9 1DZ (8940 6852/ www.fennwrightmanson.com).*

TRANSPORT

Tube stations *District* Kew Gardens, Richmond
Rail stations *South West Trains* Barnes, Barnes Bridge, Mortlake, North Sheen, Richmond, St Margarets, Twickenham, Whitton, Strawberry Hill, Hampton Wick, Teddington, Fulwell, Hampton; *Silverlink* Kew Gardens, Richmond
Bus routes *night buses* N22, N74; *24-hour buses* 65, 72, 285

Jesus Lopez *20 Barnes High Street, SW13 9LW (8878 5388).*
Joseph *28 Hill Street, Richmond, Surrey TW9 1TW (8940 7045).*
Kate Kuba *22 Hill Street, Richmond, Surrey TW9 1TW (8940 1004/www.katekuba.co.uk).*
Margaret Howell *1 The Green, Richmond, Surrey TW9 1HP (8948 5005/www.margaret howell.co.uk).*
Matches *13 Hill Street, Richmond, Surrey TW9 1FX (8332 9733/www.matches.co.uk).*
MaxMara *32 Hill Street, Richmond, Surrey TW9 1TW (8332 2811).*
Petersham Nurseries *Church Lane, off Petersham Road, Petersham, Richmond, Surrey TW10 7AG (8940 5230/www. petershamnurseries.com).*
Question Air *129 Church Road, SW13 9HR (8741 0816/www.question-air.co.uk).* Sale shop at No.86.
Real Cheese Shop *62 Barnes High Street, SW13 9LF (8878 6676).*
Ronit Zilkha *54 Hill Street, Richmond, Surrey TW9 1TW (8948 8333/www.ronitzilkha.co.uk).*
Source *27D The Quadrant, Richmond, Surrey TW9 1DN (8439 9866/www.sourcefood.co.uk).*
Tobias & the Angel *68 White Hart Lane, SW13 0PZ (8878 8902/www.tobiasandthe angel.com).*
Tridias *6 Lichfield Terrace, Sheen Road, Richmond, Surrey TW9 1AS (0870 420 8632/ www.tridias.co.uk).*
Twickenham Farmers' Market *Holly Road car park, Twickenham, Middx TW1 4EA (7833 0338/www.lfm.org.uk).*
Whistles *19 Hill Street, Richmond, Surrey TW9 1SX (8332 1646/www.whistles.co.uk).*
William Curley *10 Paved Court, Richmond, Surrey TW9 1LZ (8332 3002/www.william curley.co.uk).*

Arts & attractions

Cinemas & theatres

Odeon Richmond *72 Hill Street, Richmond, Surrey TW9 1TW (0871 224 4007/www.odeon. co.uk).*
Orange Tree Theatre *1 Clarence Street, Richmond, Surrey TW9 2SA (8940 3633/ www.orangetreetheatre.co.uk).*
Richmond Theatre *The Green, Richmond, Surrey TW9 1QJ (0870 060 6651/www.the ambassadors.com/richmond).*
Richmond Film House *3 Water Lane, Richmond, Surrey TW9 1TJ (8332 0030/ www.richmondfilmhouse.co.uk).*
Vue Staines *Two Rivers, Mustard Mill Road, Staines, Middx TW18 4BL (0871 224 0240/ www.myvue.com).*

Galleries & museums

Museum of Richmond *Old Town Hall, Whittaker Avenue, Richmond, Surrey TW9 1TP (8332 1141/www.museumofrichmond.com).* A loyal parade of Richmond's regal history.

Orleans House Gallery *Riverside, Twickenham, Middx TW1 3DJ (8831 6000/ www.richmond.gov.uk/arts).* The borough's principal art gallery.

Music & comedy venues

Bull's Head *373 Lonsdale Road, SW13 9PY (8876 5241/www.thebullshead.com).*

Other attractions

Ham House *Ham Street, Ham, Richmond, Surrey TW10 7RS (8940 1950/www.national trust.org.uk).* Lavish riverside mansion built in 1610, with an Orangery and a terrace café.
Hampton Court Palace *East Molesey, Surrey KT8 9AU (0870 751 5175/information 0870 752 7777/www.hrp.org.uk).* Dazzling palace with an famous maze, changing interior exhibitions, and an ice rink in the winter.
Marble Hill House *Richmond Road, Twickenham, Middx TW1 2NL (8892 5115/ www.english-heritage.org.uk).* Strikingly elegant Palladian house built in 1724 by George II for his mistress, Henrietta Howard.
National Archives *Ruskin Avenue, Kew, Richmond, Surrey TW9 4DU (8876 3444/ www.nationalarchives.gov.uk).* Accessible archives office, housing 1,000 years of official government and law records.

Open spaces

Barnes Common *Church Road, SW13.*
Bushy Park *Hampton Court Road, Hampton, Middx TW12 (www.royalparks.gov.uk).*
East Sheen Common *Fife Road, SW14 7EW.*
Ham Common *Richmond, Surrey TW10.*
Marble Hill Park *Richmond Road, Twickenham, Middx TW1.*
Old Deer Park *Twickenham Road, Richmond, Surrey TW9.*

Richmond upon Thames

Richmond Park *Holly Lodge, Richmond, Surrey TW10 5HS (www.royalparks.gov.uk).*
Royal Botanic Gardens (Kew Gardens) *Kew, Richmond, Surrey TW9 3AB (8332 5655/www.rbgkew.org.uk).*
London Wetland Centre *Queen Elizabeth Walk, SW13 9SA (8409 4400/www.wwt.org.uk).*

NEC Harlequins *Twickenham Stoop Stadium, Langhorn Drive, Twickenham, Middx TW2 7SX (8410 6000).*
Twickenham Stadium *Rugby Road, Twickenham, Middx TW1 1DZ (0870 405 2001/www.rfu.com).* Home to both the England rugby team and the Museum of Rugby; on non-match days there are stadium tours.

Sport & fitness

Surprisingly, Richmond is not the best equipped borough for leisure facilities. The council-run centres are decent, but not state-of-the-art. However, as you'd expect, no one gets short-changed on quality at Richmond's private health clubs.

Gyms & leisure centres

Cannons *www.cannons.co.uk; Stoop Memorial Ground, Langhorn Drive, Twickenham, Middx TW2 7SX (8892 2251); Richmond Athletic Ground, Kew Foot Road, Richmond, Surrey TW9 2SS (8948 3743).* Private.
Cedars Health & Leisure Club *144-150 Richmond Hill, Richmond, Surrey TW10 6RW (8332 1010/www.soliohotels.co.uk/cedars).* Private.
Fitness First *First floor, 20-28 Broad Street, Teddington, Middx TW11 8QZ (8614 6650/www.fitnessfirst.com).* Private.
Hampton Sport, Arts & Fitness Centre *Hanworth Road, Hampton, Middx TW12 3HB (8941 4334/www.richmond.gov.uk).*
Pools on the Park/Springheath Leisure Club *Old Deer Park, Twickenham Road, Richmond, Surrey TW9 2SF (8940 0561/www.springhealth.net).*
Richmond Hill Health Club *Lewis Road, Richmond, Surrey TW10 6SA (8948 5523/www.fit4ever.co.uk).* Private.
Shene Sports & Fitness Centre *Sheen International School, Park Avenue, SW14 8RG (8878 7578/www.richmond.gov.uk).*
Teddington Pools & Fitness Centre *Vicarage Road, Teddington, Middx TW11 8EZ (8977 9911/www.richmond.gov.uk).*
Teddington Sports Centre *Teddington School, Broom Road, Teddington, Middx TW11 9PJ (8977 0598/www.richmond.gov.uk).*
Whitton Sports & Fitness Centre *Percy Road, Whitton, Middx TW2 6JW (8898 7795/www.richmond.gov.uk).*

Other facilities

Ham Polo Club *The Polo Office, Petersham Road, Richmond, Surrey TW10 7AH (8334 0000/www.hampoloclub.org.uk).*
Hampton Heated Open Air Pool *High Street, Hampton, Middx TW12 2ST (8255 1116/www.hamptonpool.co.uk).*

Spectator sports

London Welsh Rugby Club *Old Deer Park, Kew Road, Richmond, Surrey TW9 2AZ (8940 2368/www.london-welsh.co.uk).*

Schools

WHAT THE PARENTS SAY:

'There are some very good schools in Richmond, but if you restrict yourself to state schools then the standard definitely goes down a little. There are quite a lot of private schools, which reflects the social make-up of Richmond. People seem to think they should pay for a good education, which makes the state schools worse.

Government league tables will tell you that Richmond is good for primary schools. East Sheen Primary has a great reputation: the school population is mixed and multicultural, and it is more arty and creative than most state primaries.

There are far fewer options at secondary level, and there is a marked difference between the private and the state schools. The two sectors don't mix. I am considering two private schools for my son: St Paul's, and the Harrodian School. I know kids who have gone to the latter and changed for the better as a result. Plus they teach all the way through from age six to 18, so parents and children can avoid the difficult jump from primary to secondary.'
Derek Pearce, East Sheen Primary PTA chairman

Primary

There are 41 state primary schools in Richmond, including 15 church schools, plus seven independents. See www.route2learn.co.uk and www.ofsted.gov.uk for more information.

Secondary

Christ's School *Queen's Road, Twickenham, Middx TW10 6HW (8940 6982/www.christs.richmond.sch.uk).*
Grey Court School *Ham Street, Ham, Richmond, Surrey TW10 7HN (8948 1173/www.greycourt.richmond.sch.uk).*
Hampton Community College *Hanworth Road, Hampton, Middx TW12 3HB (8979 3399/www.hcc.richmond.sch.uk).*
Hampton School *Hanworth Road, Hampton, Middx TW12 3HD (8979 5526/www.hampton school.org.uk).* Boys only; private.
The Harrodian School *Lonsdale Road, SW13 9QN (8748 6117/www.harrodian.com).* Private.
Lady Eleanor Holles School *Hanworth Road, Hampton, Middx TW12 3HF (8979 1601/www.lehs.org.uk).* Girls only; private.

Richmond upon Thames

Orleans Park School *Richmond Road, Twickenham, Middx TW1 3BB (8891 0187/www.orleanspark.richmond.sch.uk).*
St Paul's *Lonsdale Road, SW13 9JT (8748 9162/www.stpaulsschool.org.uk).* Boys only; private.
Shene School *Park Avenue, SW14 8RG (8876 8891/www.shene.richmond.sch.uk).*
Teddington School *Broom Road, Teddington, Middx TW11 9PJ (8943 0033/www.teddington. richmond.sch.uk).*
Waldegrave School *Fifth Cross Road, Twickenham, Middx TW2 5LH (8894 3244/ www.waldegrave.richmond.sch.uk).* Girls only.
Whitton School *Percy Road, Twickenham, Middx TW2 6JW (8894 4503/www.whitton. richmond.sch.uk).*

Property

WHAT THE AGENTS SAY:

‘Barnes has the feel of a small country village – complete with pond and pub – but is just 20 minutes from central London. There's a natural progression of young couples from Fulham and Kensington who move to Barnes to have families, stay here for 25 or 30 years, then move out to Sussex to retire. Regeneration? No! Most people want to keep Barnes as quiet and quaint as it is.’
Jeremy Boileau Wright, Boileaus, Barnes

‘To keep on the ladder in Richmond you'd have to really be a professional from another affluent area, such as Notting Hill. Richmond Hill is probably the most expensive area around here – about £550 per sq ft. It's all big Victorian houses, very traditional. Richmond's transport links are very attractive indeed: you've got the M3 and M4 in and out of London, the tube and the overland. Obviously, the parks, open spaces and river are a big draw for families. There isn't much land for new-builds – a lot of it is owned by the Crown around here.’
Damien Hodgson, Chancellors, Richmond

Average property prices
Detached £1,309,593
Semi-detached £825,490
Terraced £602,487
Flat £302,726

Local estate agents
Antony Roberts *www.antonyroberts.co.uk; 2 offices in the borough (Kew 8940 9401/ Richmond 8940 9403).*
Boileaus *135 Church Road, SW13 9HR (8741 7400/www.boileaus.com).*
Major Son & Phipps *5A The Square, Richmond, Surrey TW9 1DX (8940 2233/ www.major-estateagents.com).*

Marquis & Co *Marquis House, 54 Richmond Road, Twickenham, Middx TW1 3BE (8891 0222/www.marquisandco.co.uk).*
Pemberstone Residential *212B Upper Richmond Road West, SW14 8AH (8876 4445/www.pemberstone.co.uk).*
Philip Hodges *www.philip-hodges.co.uk; 4 offices in the borough (Hampton Hill 8783 1007/Richmond Bridge 8891 2121/St Margarets 8891 6391/Teddington 8977 6633).*
W Hallet & Co *6 Royal Parade, Station Approach, Kew Gardens, Surrey TW9 3QD (8940 1034).*

Other information

Council
London Borough of Richmond upon Thames Council *Civic Centre, 44 York Street, Twickenham, Middx TW1 3BZ (8891 1411/ customer services 8891 7841/out of office hours 8831 6482/www.richmond.gov.uk).*

Hospitals
Barnes Hospital *South Worpole Way, SW14 8SU (8878 4981/www.swlstg-tr.nhs.uk)*
Richmond Royal Hospital *Kew Foot Road, Richmond, Surrey TW9 2TE (8940 3331/ www.swlstg-tr.nhs.uk).*
Teddington Memorial Hospital *Hampton Road, Teddington, Middx TW11 0JL (8408 8210/www.richmondandtwickenham.nhs.uk).*

Legal services
Civic Centre *44 York Street, Twickenham, Middx TW1 3BZ (8487 5005/www.richmond. gov.uk).*
Richmond upon Thames CAB *61 Heath Road, Twickenham, Middx TW1 4AW (8940 2501).*

Local newspapers
Richmond & Twickenham Times *8940 6030/www.rttimes.co.uk.*

Allotments
Council allotments *The Allotments Officer, Civic Centre, 44 York Street, Twickenham, Middx TW1 3BZ (mornings only 8831 6110).*
Royal Paddocks Allotments *Park Road, Hampton Wick (www.paddocks-allotments.org.uk).*

COUNCIL TAX		
A	up to £40,000	**£923.95**
B	£40,001-£52,000	**£1,077.94**
C	£52,001-£68,000	**£1,231.93**
D	£68,001-£88,000	**£1,385.92**
E	£88,001-£120,000	**£1,693.90**
F	£120,001-£160,000	**£2,001.88**
G	£160,001-£320,000	**£2,309.87**
H	over £320,000	**£2,771.84**

> *'Away from the Commons,
> council tax is lower than in
> any other borough.'*
>
> **Sheelagh Wells, resident**

Wandsworth

Putney, Clapham, Battersea and Wandsworth have long been desirable, middle-class areas, with a wealth of Victorian property and good facilities. Fast-tracking professionals love the transport links and the thriving restaurant and bar scene; young families dig the green spaces and the child-friendly amenities.

Neighbourhoods

Battersea

Battersea started life as an island in the Thames, known as Batrices Ege ('Badric's Isle') in the early medieval period. After the marshes to its south were drained, the area became known for market gardening. It also provided a home to gentry seeking refuge from the filth of London. The opening of the London & Southampton Railway in 1838, which had its terminus at Nine Elms, brought a huge influx of people to the area; large factories were established in the late 19th century. After World War II the industry waned, and Battersea went into decline. It wasn't until the 1980s boom that the well-heeled settled here again.

Battersea's excellent park, power station and dog refuge have all made it famous. Battersea Park, the largest in Wandsworth, hosts an incredible number of activities. Its attractions include a boating lake, a gallery, an athletics track, a children's zoo and the riverside peace pagoda. Such a backdrop has made the park attractive to film-makers – it is London's second most popular movie location. Disused Battersea Power Station, with its iconic four white towers, is still the most distinctive piece of architecture around. Several attempts to redevelop the hulking ruin have failed. The latest plan, proposed by Hong Kong company Parkview, is set to involve the destruction and reconstruction of the station's corroding towers; residents oppose this, fearing the rebuild will never happen. If the company's

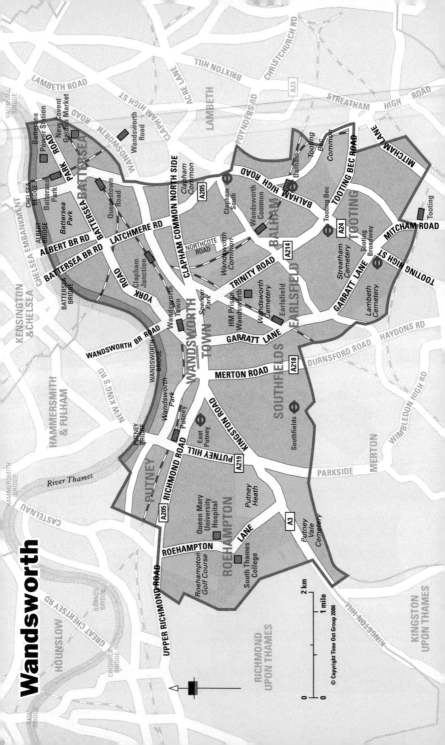

promises are delivered, the project could create 9,000 jobs for the area and a world-class complex of apartments, attractions and amenities.

The Queenstown Road district is popular because of its proximity to Battersea Park and Queenstown Road train stations. The Parktown Estate conservation area – nicknamed 'the Diamond' – is liked for its Victorian cottages. The streets on the south side of the park boast imposing Victorian mansions; those to the west contain some attractive houses but no train links. At the heart of this area is pedestrianised Battersea Square (dubbed Battersea Village after a recent redevelopment), with its cobblestones and cafés. Dotted between these districts are some fairly unappealing high-rise flats, especially to the north of the Diamond over the train tracks.

To the east of Battersea, Nine Elms is now chiefly known as the venue for New Covent Garden Market, which straddles the border with Lambeth. Britain's biggest horticultural wholesale market, it moved here in 1974.

Clapham Junction and Clapham Common

The Hive Honey Shop on Northcote Road houses an amazing glass-fronted beehive some five feet high: it's home to 20,000 live bees, connected to the outside world by tubes. The shop's location is apt, as this district is one of south London's most buzzy neighbourhoods. With Clapham Junction at its centre, the area is extremely popular with young professionals and families, who are attracted by the smart houses, the proximity to two commons (Clapham and Wandsworth), the good transport links and the terrific amenities, including many independent shops and restaurants.

Transport hub Clapham Junction station proudly proclaims itself to be the busiest in Europe, but Wandsworth Council has rightly identified flaws and put together a ten-point plan listing its aspirations for the station and connected transport links. For now, the subway remains congested and leaky, and the queues get ever longer (tip: for Travelcards or Oyster card top-ups, go to the nearby newsagents).

North of the station, around Falcon Road, the neighbourhood still has a somewhat scruffy demeanour (the Winstanley Estate

Highs & Lows

▲ **Council tax** In most of the borough, council tax is lower than any other in central London; in areas around the Commons only the City of Westminster's council tax is cheaper
Green fields With Clapham, Wandsworth and Tooting Bec Commons, Battersea Park and Putney Heath, you're never short of a picnic spot
Battersea Power Station An iconic feature of the London skyline, long may it last...

Property prices Always on the rise. Even Tooting and Balham are becoming too expensive for first-time buyers
Secondary schools There just aren't enough good options, so many residents look outside the borough
Too many 4WDs The gas-guzzling, road-hogging SUV rules in Wandsworth. Too many la-di-da sports cars too. Haven't these ▼ people heard of buses?

is a particularly grim example). Yet just to the south-east is the Shaftesbury Park Estate, a selection of unusual cottages with Gothic Revival flourishes, built by the Artisans', Labourers' & General Dwellings Company in the late 19th century.

South of Clapham Junction – around Northcote Road, St John's Road and Lavender Hill (home to the *Lavender Hill Mob* of Ealing Studios fame) – is where the area's greatest appeal lies. By day, this is an attractive shopping area. You'll find the usual chains along St John's Road and Lavender Hill – along with Battersea Arts Centre – but Northcote Road is especially alluring, with independent shops and cafés and a lovely street market. In summer, outside seating makes this street the place to be seen. By night, the area takes on a different character. The many bars and restaurants are often full, especially with out-of-towners at the weekends, and things can get pretty chaotic.

The area around Northcote Road is renowned for attracting young middle-class families; estate agents prefer to describe it as 'between the Commons', though the cliché 'Nappy Valley' is more often used. It contains some very smart rows of Victorian terraces notable for their light grey or white bricks, which make a welcome change from the usual red brick of Wandsworth. Clapham Common West, which overlooks the park, is especially grand.

The flat green expanse of Clapham Common itself, with its busy events schedule, is favoured by a younger crowd (and at night by gay men). The borough boundary with Lambeth cuts through its centre. Wandsworth Common – and the collection of posh shops and restaurants along Bellevue Road – is more family-oriented, and a fine place for a summer picnic or Sunday afternoon stroll.

Wandsworth Town

From the late 1500s, the village of Wandsworth gave refuge to Protestant craftsmen fleeing religious persecution in Europe. Dutch metalworkers were followed by French Huguenots in the late 1600s. The many skills of these newcomers – particularly in hat-making, iron and copperware – greatly benefited the area. You can still see the Huguenots' cemetery on Huguenots Place.

Today the best-known local industry is the Young's Ram Brewery, which has a long history of beer making. Shire horse-carts still deliver barrels from the brewery to local pubs. Wandsworth's historic legacy is harder to appreciate these days, however, as the district is sliced up by some hectically busy roads and intersections. The worst congestion occurs where the A3 into south London hits the notorious 'Wandsworth bottleneck' one-way system.

The Victorian cottages in the streets between Wandsworth Town rail station and the A3 form a neat little enclave, dubbed 'the Tonsleys' – home to many upwardly mobile young couples and their sports cars. Some pleasant shops on the Old York Road add a villagey feel. The area is also popular with rugby fans, who find their skills come in handy in the morning scrum at the station. If you can squeeze on to a train, the journey to Waterloo takes only ten minutes.

Some light industry is still based along the river, meaning that the only expansive view of the Thames is from the excellent Ship Inn on Jew's Row, or from one of the riverside apartment blocks. There are also two sites of major residential development on this stretch: the construction of riverside housing block Battersea Reach at the sound end of Wandsworth Bridge, and the conversion of York Road's old candle factory into loft apartments.

There is decent housing south of the A3, an area that also has the advantage of being near the newly developed Southside Shopping Centre on Garratt Lane, and also Wandsworth Common with its tennis courts, bowling green and cricket pitch. Midway between Wandsworth Town and Clapham Junction stations, the St John's Hill Grove estate features some fairly grand late-Victorian and Edwardian properties that aren't too far from Northcote Road's delights.

Putney

To many of its residents, Putney is a suburban Eden. It offers them all the benefits of the riverside, country living (well, plenty of greenery), some beautiful houses, good schools and amenities – and

Tooting Bec station

'Wandsworth can feel like somewhere you pass through, but I have a lot of love for the place. It's like a tight pair of loose-fit jeans – comfortable. It's pretty chilled.'

Shubs Golder, musician and resident

yet is only 12 minutes by train from Waterloo. Not surprisingly, the disadvantages include astronomical house prices and nightmare traffic congestion. Putney is also directly under a Heathrow flight path.

Swathes of greensward are plentiful, with Wandsworth Park on the river, densely wooded Putney Heath to the south and (over in the borough of Richmond upon Thames), Richmond Park to the west. Putney Wharf is the centre of much rowing and sailing action, with numerous rowing clubs along the water. Every spring, the Boat Race attracts a huge rowing crowd and various hangers-on, though events like the Great River Race (held in autumn) are much more fun to watch. Stride out along the riverside path to Barnes for one of the area's most delightful walks.

Putney contains some fine examples of Victorian and Edwardian housing – around 50 per cent of it is a designated conservation area. Streets south of the Upper Richmond Road (aka the South Circular/A205) contain the most spacious and well-to-do abodes: houses in the roads west of Putney Hill and between Chartfield Avenue and Upper Richmond Road, for instance, are so large and desirable that prices of £1m have become ordinary. Coalecroft Road and Parkfields, with their terraced Victorian cottages, original lamp-posts and herringbone brick roads, rank among the most attractive. More interesting, however, is the area between the South Circular and the river. This includes the delightfully idiosyncratic Lower Common South on the edge of Putney Lower Common, and the quaint, cosy streets around Cardinal Place. The bevy of estate agents at the junction of Putney High Street and the Upper Richmond Road shows how lively the property market is around these parts.

Given all this wealth and beauty, Putney High Street is a disappointment with its amusement arcades dotted among high-street chains. It gets more interesting down towards the river, where a clutch of trendy bars and restaurants liven things up at night. The smart Exchange Shopping Centre is worth a look, as is the smattering of quirky shops down Lacy Road.

Putney has an air of permanence about it – more so than elsewhere in Wandsworth. Residents tend to buy their houses and settle down, and neighbours make the effort to get to know each other.

Roehampton

Roehampton is a tale of two towns. Its name will forever be linked with the infamous Alton Estate in the south-east corner of Richmond Park. This vast swathe of concrete, built in the Le Corbusier-inspired 1950s and '60s, became a byword for modernist monstrosity, but is now grade II listed (though many still consider the architecture ugly). Still, the location is fantastic and there are great views across the park from some of the flats.

To the north, either side of the district's main thoroughfare (busy Roehampton Lane/A306) sit Roehampton University, South Thames College and Queen Mary's Hospital, the main structure of which was built in 1712 and enlarged by Sir Edwin Lutyens a couple of centuries later.

The second 'town' is to the east of Roehampton Lane. The Dover House and Westmead Estates, near Putney Heath, resemble something you might find in a suburban Surrey town, with simple, unpretentious, ex-council housing. At the north-west corner of Putney Heath, Roehampton Village is a charming little area featuring picturesque terraced buildings, a High Street of local shops, a pub and a parish church. In contrast, the Putney Heath district, with its huge elaborate Edwardian houses, seems to belong more in the stockbroker belt than this corner of south-west London.

Wandsworth

Southfields and Earlsfield

Southfields and Earlsfield are both predominantly residential areas. The quiet and well-ordered streets of Southfields have been a middle-class retreat for many years. Earlsfield's rise in property values and subsequent influx of young professionals is a more recent phenomenon.

The large gardens of many Southfields homes, together with the peaceful, sober atmosphere, mean that the area is popular with families. The neat rows of terraced Victorian housing in the district known as 'the Grid' (south-east of Southfields station) are the most sought after. Similar properties around Wimbledon Park Road are also popular. The pleasant cafés and shops on low-key Replingham Road give the place the air of a Home Counties town.

West of the tube line you'll find tree-dotted hills overlooking lush Wimbledon Park, a golf course and the famous All England Lawn Tennis Club, site of the annual tennis championships (all across the borough boundary in Merton). The architecture is an odd mix of 1960s estates and grand mock-Tudor residences.

East of the overland train line, Earlsfield is dominated by the spacious Magdalen Park estate with its 1920s and '30s ex-council cottages. To the north of Earlsfield station are mainly Victorian and Edwardian terraces. The select choice of shops and restaurants around the station lend the district a cosy, small-town atmosphere. Earlsfield, however, is not quite as posh as Southfields, Putney or Wimbledon.

Balham

'Hasn't Balham come up in the world?' is a remark frequently heard at south London dinner parties. The neighbourhood has certainly changed markedly since World War II, when Balham High Road took a massive direct hit, and has even come a fair way since the days when Jimmy White, who was born here in a prefab, used to skip school to visit the Tooting snooker clubs. But considering the high price of property in Balham nowadays, the district hasn't come as far as you might hope. Though there are a few decent bars and restaurants, Balham High Road continues to be dominated by chainstores and pound shops. And as you head south towards Tooting, the street becomes increasingly humdrum.

So what's all the fuss about? Crucially, Balham is on the Northern Line. It is in the middle of three Commons: Tooting Bec, Wandsworth and Clapham. It is full of increasingly well-presented Victorian terraces, as well as flats in huge 1930s blocks, such as Du Cane Court. Balham Man likes living close to town in an unpretentious area, away from the graduate City types of Clapham. He is doing alright, but doesn't like to shout about it. Here you can spend a seven-figure sum on a pukka house south of Wandsworth Common and chi-chi Bellevue Road and tell people you live in Tooting – the nearest tube station.

Mention must be given to the Heaver Estate conservation area, which backs on to Tooting Bec Common. Its 11 avenues boast magnificent, red-brick, two- and three-storey Victorian houses with large gardens and plenty of ornate tile, window and stucco work. Wide, tree-lined Streathbourne Road is the finest example.

In the north of the district, the most desirable address is Nightingale Square. Cut off from the traffic, it has two schools on one side and plumes of wisteria spouting from elegant façades overlooking a peaceful green. Come to think of it, Balham improves the more you get to know it.

Tooting

Tooting used to have two main attractions: good Indian restaurants, and cheap housing. The Indian restaurants are still here, along

---

RECYCLING

No. of bring sites 35 (for nearest, visit www.recycleforlondon.com)
Household waste recycled 17.3%
Main recycling centre Western Riverside Civic Amenity Site, Smugglers Way, Wandsworth, SW18 1JS (8871 2788/www.wrwa.gov.uk); Cringle Dock Civic Amenity Site, Cringle Street, Battersea, SW8 5BX (7622 6233/www.wrwa.gov.uk)
Other recycling services printer cartridge recycling banks; home composting; collection of white goods
Council contact Deborah Gill, Waste Management, Room 57A, Town Hall, Wandsworth High Street, SW18 2PU (8871 6233/www.wandsworth.gov.uk/wastemanagement)

---

the curry corridor on the High Street and Upper Tooting Road, and still cheap and still excellent. But house prices have more than doubled in some parts of Tooting within the past decade. As house-hunters have been pushed even further south from neighbouring Clapham and Balham, they've discovered the Heaver Estate (on the border with Balham) and Furzedown (near Tooting Bec), and the more affordable Edwardian terraced housing of Tooting Broadway. The Northern Line takes you to the West End or City in half an hour, and – unlike at Balham and Clapham – you can get a seat on the tube in the mornings.

Some people, of course, actually work in Tooting – St George's Hospital is one of the biggest employers in Wandsworth, and dominates the ebb and flow of people around Tooting Broadway. After hours, the hinterland of Tooting Broadway tube attracts its regular drunks, as busy tube stations everywhere seem to. That apart, Tooting is a pretty quiet place in which to live. There are no appealing pubs, bars or clubs of any note. Beyond a good selection of budget Pakistani, South Indian and Gujarati restaurants, there's nowhere special to eat either, and no cinema – just a bingo hall.

For shopping, Broadway Market and Tooting Market provide an alternative to Sainsbury's, but apart from the Afro-Caribbean food stalls, the traders sell the usual fruit and veg and tacky goods you can find anywhere. Several of the Asian greengrocer's are excellent, though. As for the great outdoors, Tooting Lido is fun in summer, and Tooting Bec Common is popular with joggers, though a trip to Wimbledon Common is more rewarding for the discerning dog-walker or stroller.

Restaurants & cafés

Northcote Road is the focal point of the varied restaurant scene around Battersea and Clapham Junction. For high-quality fast food, try Gourmet Burger Kitchen; for child-friendly cafés there's Boiled Egg & Soldiers, and Crumpet. Young couples yet to procreate flock to well-loved Italian Osteria Antica Bologna, or more pricey Modern Euro bar-restaurant Niksons. Heading towards Battersea Rise, you'll come across budget oriental diner Banana Leaf Canteen, and shabby-chic sushi den Tokiya. Nearby are

good-time pizza and pasta joint Pizza Metro, South American steak house La Pampa Grill and top-notch French brasserie, Le Bouchon Bordelais. Francophiles should also make the trip to Queenstown Road to sample Eric Guignard's enticing modern French menu at the Food Room.

Off towards Clapham, on Lavender Hill, there's Donna Margherita, a local favourite for pizza, and global fusion specialist Cinnamon Cay. Bellevue Road has well-regarded veteran Chez Bruce, with its superb regional and classic French cuisine, plus kiddie-friendly American joint Dexter's Grill & Bar. First-rate seafood options include budget bistro Fish in a Tie, and chippy Fish Club. Until recently, Battersea was lacking in decent gastropubs; now the Greyhound has more than redressed the balance. Ransome's Dock near Battersea Bridge is a established favourite for its classy Mod Euro food and excellent wine list.

Wandsworth is blessed with one of London's best fish and chip restaurants in Brady's, but also has a trio of good gastropubs: the Ship, the Alma (sister to the Ship) and the Freemasons.

Putney's eateries tend to reflect the district's affluent suburban location. There are two main roads where restaurants cluster: Upper Richmond Road and Putney High Street. The former contains well-loved Indian Ma Goa, family-run French bistro L'Auberge, South African newcomer Chakalaka and one of London's most authentic Japanese restaurants, Chosan. Putney High Street has family-geared café

TRANSPORT

Tube stations *District* East Putney, Southfields; *Northern* Clapham South, Balham, Tooting Bec, Tooting Broadway
Rail stations *Silverlink* Clapham Junction; *Southern* Battersea Park, Wandsworth Road, Clapham Junction, Wandsworth Common, Balham, Tooting; *South West Trains* Queenstown Road, Clapham Junction, Wandsworth Town, Putney, Earlsfield
Main bus routes *into central London* 14, 19, 22, 35, 74, 77, 77A, 137, 239, 344, 414; *night buses* N19, N22, N35, N44, N74, N77, N133, N137, N155; *24-hour buses* 14, 37, 72, 85, 220, 264, 345

Upper Tooting Road.

WWW.TIMEOUT.COM
London for Londoners
every day

**NOW WITH FULLY
SEARCHABLE LISTINGS**
New for 2006

Eddie Catz, classy Italian Enoteca Turi, popular tapas bar La Mancha and the area's best pizza joint, Il Peperone, plus branches of Maison Blanc and Wagamama.

However, two of Putney's top restaurants are elsewhere: the Phoenix Bar & Grill, near the river, offers Mod Euro cooking and an outstanding wine list, while Royal China, just off the High Street, has some of south London's best dim sum.

Despite being fairly well-off areas, Roehampton and Earlsfield can barely come up with a decent restaurant between them. Southfields fares little better, but can muster a branch of upmarket pan-Indian Sarkhel's, gastropub the Earl Spencer and, best of all, Turkish restaurant Kazans.

In contrast, Balham is buzzing, with new restaurants opening apace. Bedford Hill is where it's all happening, with a branch of the Fine Burger Company joining bustling brasserie Balham Kitchen & Bar, budget south Indian venue Sadya, modish Persian restaurant Dish-Dash and low-priced oriental eaterie the Paddyfield. Possibly Balham's best restaurant is Lamberts, a rising Modern European star near the station, while two new ventures, Tagine (North African) and Ciullo (pizza and pasta) further broaden the local choice.

Tooting has long been famed for Indian cuisine, with many different regions of the subcontinent represented. Two favourites are Kastoori (East African Gujarati vegetarian) and Radha Krishna Bhavan (south Indian with wacky decor). Good, cheap (and often fierily hot) food is also the speciality of two local Sri Lankan cafés, Apollo Banana Leaf and Jaffna House. European alternatives to the Tooting south Asian norm are provided by Rick's Café (casual Mod Euro with a Spanish edge), and Harrington's (traditional pie and mash).

Alma 499 Old York Road, SW18 1TF (8870 2537).
Apollo Banana Leaf 190 Tooting High Street, SW17 0SF (8696 1423).
L'Auberge 22 Upper Richmond Road, SW15 2RX (8874 3593/www.ardillys.com).
Balham Kitchen & Bar 15-19 Bedford Hill, SW12 9EX (8675 6900/www.balhamkitchen.com).
Banana Leaf Canteen 75-79 Battersea Rise, SW11 1HN (7228 2828).
Boiled Egg & Soldiers 63 Northcote Road, SW11 1NP (7223 4894).
Le Bouchon Bordelais 5-9 Battersea Rise, SW11 1HG (7738 0307/www.lebouchon.co.uk).
Brady's 515 Old York Road, SW18 1TF (8877 9599).

Chakalaka 136 Upper Richmond Road, SW15 2SP (8789 5696/www.chakalakarestaurant.co.uk).
Chez Bruce 2 Bellevue Road, SW17 7EG (8672 0114/www.chezbruce.co.uk).
Chosan 292 Upper Richmond Road, SW15 6TH (8788 9626).
Cinnamon Cay 87 Lavender Hill, SW11 5QL (7801 0932/www.cinnamoncay.co.uk).
Ciullo 31 Balham High Road, SW12 9AL (8675 3072).
Crumpet 66 Northcote Road, SW11 6QL (7924 1117).
Dexter's Grill & Bar 20 Bellevue Road, SW17 7EB (8767 1858).
Dish-Dash 11-13 Bedford Hill, SW12 9ET (8673 5555/www.dish-dash.com).
Donna Margherita 183 Lavender Hill, SW11 1EQ (7228 2660/www.donna-margherita.com).
Earl Spencer 260-262 Merton Road, SW18 5LY (8870 9244/www.theearlspencer.co.uk).
Eddie Catz First floor, 68-70 Putney High Street, SW15 1SF (0845 201 1268/www.eddiecatz.com).
Enoteca Turi 28 Putney High Street, SW15 1SQ (8785 4449/www.enotecaturi.com).
Fine Burger Company 37 Bedford Hill, SW12 9EY (8772 0266/www.fineburger.co.uk).
Fish Club 189 St John's Hill, SW11 1TH (7978 7115/www.thefishclub.com).
Fish in a Tie 105 Falcon Road, SW11 2PF (7924 1913).
The Food Room 123 Queenstown Road, SW8 3RH (7622 0555/www.thefrenchtable.co.uk).
Freemasons 2 Wandsworth Common Northside, SW18 2SS (7326 8580/www.freemasonspub.com).
Gourmet Burger Kitchen 44 Northcote Road, SW11 1NZ (7228 3309/www.gbkinfo.co.uk).
Greyhound 136 Battersea High Street, SW11 3JR (7978 7021/www.thegreyhoundatbattersea.co.uk).
Harrington's 3 Selkirk Road, SW17 0ER (8672 1877).
Jaffna House 90 Tooting High Street, SW17 0RN (8672 7786/www.jaffnahouse.co.uk).
Kastoori 188 Upper Tooting Road, SW17 7EJ (8767 7027).
Kazans 607-609 Garratt Lane, SW18 4SU (8739 0055/www.kazans.com).
Lamberts 2 Station Parade, Balham High Road, SW12 9AZ (8675 2233).
Ma Goa 242-244 Upper Richmond Road, SW15 6TG (8780 1767/www.ma-goa.com).
Maison Blanc 125 Putney High Street, SW15 1SU (8789 6064/www.maisonblanc.co.uk).
La Mancha 32 Putney High Street, SW15 1SQ (8780 1022/www.lamancha.co.uk).
Niksons 172-174 Northcote Road, SW11 6RE (7228 2285).
Osteria Antica Bologna 23 Northcote Road, SW11 1NG (7978 4771/www.osteria.co.uk).
The Paddyfield 4 Bedford Hill, SW12 9RG (8772 1145).
La Pampa Grill 60 Battersea Rise, SW11 1EG (7924 4774).
Il Peperone 26 Putney High Street, SW15 1SL (8788 3303).
Phoenix Bar & Grill 162-164 Lower Richmond Road, SW15 1LY (8780 3131/www.sonnys.co.uk).

Pizza Metro *64 Battersea Rise, SW11 1EQ (7228 3812).*
Radha Krishna Bhavan *86 Tooting High Street, SW17 0RN (8682 0969).*
Ransome's Dock *35-37 Parkgate Road, SW11 4NP (7223 1611).*
Rick's Café *122 Mitcham Road, SW17 9NH (8767 5219).*
Royal China *3 Chelverton Road, SW15 1RN (8788 0907).*
Sadya *90 Bedford Hill, SW12 9HR (8673 5393/www.sadya.co.uk).*
Sarkhel's *199 Replingham Road, SW18 5LY (8870 1483).*
Ship *41 Jew's Row, SW18 1TB (8870 9667/ www.theship.co.uk).*
Tagine *1-3 Fernlea Road, SW12 9RT (8675 7604).*
Tokiya *74 Battersea Rise, SW11 1EH (7223 5989/www.tokiya.co.uk).*

Bars & pubs

Few boroughs can rival Wandsworth's versatility when it comes to drinking options. Take Battersea's Northcote Road, where young, loud professionals pack into style bars like the Holy Drinker to compare haircuts and show off their new clothes (and that's just the blokes), while, nearer to the park, S Bar and Dovedale House are splendidly intimate haunts. Or there's the beer lover's paradise of Microbar, the theatrical Latchmere and cocktail- and DJ-fuelled Dusk.

Putney's riverside options include Bar M, popular with the local after-work crowd, and the more sedate Duke's Head; nearby is the Half Moon, one of London's best live music pubs, and friendly Fuller's outlet the Whistle & Flute.

In Wandsworth Town, gastropubs the Alma and the Ship (for both, *see p186*) are the top boozers, but ditto is a nice, polite place in which to get a glass of wine, while laid-back East Hill boasts a library and stacks of board games. By the Common, fairy-lit gem the Hope and stylish gastropub Freemasons (*see p186*) are popular too.

Down in Balham, many of the pubs lead a double life, catering for both sides of the gentrification divide: the Duke of Devonshire, for example, with its older local customers at the front and its hipster cocktail crowd in the back room. The Bedford hosts top-notch comedy nights and low-key acoustic performances in its back rooms, while maintaining a noisy bar

up front. Elsewhere, two bars offset their grim locations with swankiness within: the Lounge (under a railway bridge) and Exhibit (adjoined to a supermarket car park).

The pick of the bunch in Tooting is undoubtedly the Trafalgar Arms, a glorious pub drawing both a gay and a straight crowd with its combination of transvestite bingo, camp karaoke, and more mainstream lures such as burgers, beers and board games. The King's Head and Spirit Bar Café are chiefly haunted by football fans.

Finally, Earlsfield is awash with the kinds of hostelries that affluent residential areas need to keep their affluent residents happy. The first kind is of the Friday night, time-to-forget-the-pinstripes variety, of which the Garage is a prime example. The

STATISTICS

BOROUGH MAKE-UP
Population 264,671
Average weekly pay £575.80
Ethnic origins
White 77.95%
Mixed 3.35%
Asian or Asian British 6.93%
Black or Black British 9.63%
Chinese or other 2.14%
Students 8.62%
Retirees 7.40%

HOUSING STOCK
Borough size 34.3km²
No. of households 124,719
Detached 2.3%
Semi-detached 7.1%
Terraced 26.3%
Flats (purpose-built) 40.2%
Flats (converted) 23.1%
Flats (both) 63.3%

CRIME PER 1,000 OF POPULATION
(English average in brackets)
Burglary 10 (6.4)
Robbery 5 (1.4)
Theft of vehicle 5 (4.5)
Theft from vehicle 10 (10)
Violence against the person 22 (16.5)
Sexual offences 1 (0.9)

MPs & COUNCIL
MPs *Battersea* Martin Linton (Labour);
Putney Justine Greening (Conservative);
Tooting Sadiq Khan (Labour)
CPA 4 stars; improving strongly

Lie back and think of the property prices, on **Wandsworth Common**. *See p193.*

second kind is that genre of pub where a glowing hearth, well-behaved kids, sleepy dogs and decent draught beers are all likely to be found: of these, gastropub the Earl Spencer (*see p189*) and the Leather Bottle are the best. Wine bar Willie Gunn is worth noting too.

Bar M *The Star & Garter, 4 Lower Richmond Road, SW15 1JN (8788 0345/www.barm.co.uk).*
Bedford *77 Bedford Hill, SW12 9HD (8682 8940).*
ditto *55-57 East Hill, SW18 2QE (8877 0110/ www.doditto.co.uk).*
Dovedale House *441 Battersea Park Road, SW11 4LR (7223 7721).*
Duke's Head *8 Lower Richmond Road, SW15 1JN (8788 2552).*
Duke of Devonshire *39 Balham High Road, SW12 9AN (8673 1363).*
Dusk *339 Battersea Park Road, SW11 4LF (7622 2112/www.duskbar.co.uk).*
East Hill *21 Alma Road, SW18 1AA (8874 1833).*
Exhibit *12 Balham Station Road, SW12 9SG (8772 6556/www.exhibitbars.com).*
Garage *20 Replingham Road, SW18 5LS (8874 9370).*
Holy Drinker *59 Northcote Road, SW11 1NP (7801 0544/www.holydrinker.co.uk).*
Hope *1 Bellevue Road, SW17 7EG (8672 8717).*
King's Head *84 Upper Tooting Road, SW17 7PB (0871 332 5739).*
Latchmere *503 Battersea Park Road, SW11 3BW (7223 3549).*
Leather Bottle *538 Garratt Lane, SW17 0NY (8946 2309).*
Lounge *76 Bedford Hill, SW12 9HR (8673 8787/www.thebalhamlounge.co.uk).*
Microbar *14 Lavender Hill, SW11 5RW (7228 5300/www.microbar.org).*
S Bar *37 Battersea Bridge Road, SW11 3BA (7223 3322).*

Spirit Bar Café *94 Tooting High Street, SW17 0RR (8767 3311).*
Trafalgar Arms *148 Tooting High Street, SW17 0RT (8767 6059).*
Whistle & Flute *46-48 Putney High Street, SW15 1SQ (8780 5437).*
Willie Gunn *422 Garratt Lane, SW18 4HW (8946 7773).*

Shops

Wandsworth encompasses wide variations in atmosphere and demographic, from the Sloaney affluence of Battersea to the multi-ethnic edginess of Tooting. Shopping highlights in Battersea include former stylist Jacquie Allmond's globally sourced vintage clothing at Gadjo Dilo, Minh Mang's luxurious eastern-vibe accessories, and milliner Edwina Ibbotson's Ascot creations.

Northcote Road is undoubtedly the retail hub of the borough. A foodies' fantasy, it boasts a busy market as well as excellent individual shops. Young professionals with no time to cook rely on the fresh pasta and antipasti at Italian deli I Sapori di Stefano Cavallini. The beekeeper-owned Hive sells a huge array of honeys; the Lighthouse Bakery produces small-batch speciality loaves; Hamish Johnston offers around 150 cheeses; and traditional butcher A Dove & Sons supplies the best of British meat. Reflecting, perhaps, local habits, the stretch is awash with upmarket wine merchants, including the Grape Shop, Philglas & Swiggot and Vingt.

But it's not all about food and drink. The small Antiques Market is worth a nose for collectable china and restored furniture.

As you'd expect from this child-centric neighbourhood, there are several kids' clothes shops across the age spectrum, including Jojo Maman Bébé, Quackers and Tomboy Kids. There's scope for browsing in upmarket gift shops Huttons and Oliver Bonas and bookshop Bolingbroke's. An ex-Neal's Yarder is behind the high-quality botanical toiletries at Verde, while Opus has a tempting array of footwear and accessories.

Apart from concrete retail parks at either end of Wandsworth Bridge, Wandsworth Town's local shopping resources have been given a boost with the development of the Southside Shopping Centre, housing Waitrose, Virgin Active health club, a 14-screen Cineworld and 65 high-street stores, from H&M to HMV. In Putney, the Exchange Shopping Centre offers a less extensive and slightly more upmarket mall mix. Designer cast-offs from the likes of Voyage and Prada abound at Frock Market, and furniture by Le Corbusier, Ron Arad and Philippe Starck is on offer at Pop UK. The chilled Ark Health & Beauty can keep stress levels down with reiki and hot stone massage.

Roehampton doesn't offer much beyond domestic necessities, but Sikelia, which sells artisanal produce from Sicily and freshly made Italian dishes, is a new draw in Southfields. Tooting's ethnic diversity is reflected in the availability of Afro-Caribbean produce in the covered 1930s arcades of Broadway Market and Tooting Market, and the line-up of Indian food shops on Upper Tooting Road. Deepak Cash & Carry on Garratt Lane is the place to go for Asian staples and every spice imaginable.

Elsewhere in the borough, contemporary interiors company Ocean (formerly mail order only) has an outpost in Lavender Hill, while Dwell in Balham offers affordable modern furniture. And early risers can buy bargain blooms in bulk at New Covent Garden Market.

A Dove & Sons *71 Northcote Road, SW11 6PJ (7223 5191).*
Ark Health & Beauty *339 Putney Bridge Road, SW15 2PG (8788 8888/www.arkhealth andbeauty.com).*
Bolingbroke Bookshop *147 Northcote Road, SW11 6QB (7223 9344).*
Broadway Market & Tooting Market *Upper Tooting Road, SW17.*
Deepak Cash & Carry *953-959 Garratt Lane, SW17 0LW (8767 7819).*
Dwell *264 Balham High Road, SW17 7AN (0870 600 182/www.dwell.co.uk).*

Edwina Ibbotson *45 Queenstown Road, SW8 3RG (7498 5390).*
Exchange Shopping Centre *High Street, SW15 1TW (8780 1056/www.theexchange sw15.com).*
Frock Market *50 Lower Richmond Road, SW15 1JT (8788 7748).*
Gadjo Dilo *531 Battersea Park Road, SW11 3LB (7585 1770).*
Grape Shop *135 Northcote Road, SW11 6PX (7924 3638).*
Hamish Johnston *48 Northcote Road, SW11 1PA (7738 0741).*
Hive Honey Shop *93 Northcote Road, SW11 6PL (7924 6233/www.thehivehoney shop.co.uk).*
Huttons *29 Northcote Road, SW11 1NJ (7223 5523).*
I Sapori di Stefano Cavallini *146 Northcote Road, SW11 6RD (7228 2017).*
JoJo Maman Bébé *68 Northcote Road, SW11 6QL (7228 0322/www.jojomamanbebe.co.uk).*
Lighthouse Bakery *64 Northcote Road, SW11 6QL (7228 4537/www.lighthousebakery.co.uk).*
Minh Mang *182 Battersea Park Road, SW11 4ND (7223 6030/www.minhmang.co.uk).*
New Covent Garden Market *Covent Garden Market Authority, Covent House, SW8 5NX (7720 2211/www.cgma.gov.uk).*
Northcote Road Antiques Market *155A Northcote Road, SW11 6QB (7228 6850).*
Northcote Road Market *Northcote Road, SW11.*
Ocean *201-207 Lavender Hill, SW11 5TB (7228 3671/www.oceanuk.com).*
Oliver Bonas *137 Northcote Road, SW11 6PX (7223 5223/www.oliverbonas.com).*
Opus *57 Northcote Road, SW11 1NP (7978 4240/www.opusshoes.co.uk).*
Philglas & Swiggot *21 Northcote Road, SW11 1NG (7924 4494/www.philglas-swiggot.co.uk).*
Pop UK *278 Upper Richmond Road, SW15 6TQ (8788 8811/www.popuk.com).*
Quackers *155D Northcote Road, SW11 6QB (7978 4235).*
Sikelia *3 Replingham Road, SW18 5LT (8877 3257).*
Southside Shopping Centre *SW18 4TF (8870 2141/www.southsidewandsworth.com).*
Tomboy Kids *176 Northcote Road, SW11 1RE (7223 8030/www.tomboykids.com).*
Verde *75 Northcote Road, SW11 6PJ (7223 2095/www.verde.co.uk).*
Vingt *20 Northcote Road, SW11 1NX (7924 6924/www.vingt.co.uk).*

Arts & attractions

Cinemas & theatres
Battersea Arts Centre (BAC) *Lavender Hill, SW11 5TN (7223 6557/www.bac.org.uk).* Forward-thinking theatre specialising in new writers and companies.
Cineworld Wandsworth *Southside Shopping Centre, Wandsworth High Street, SW18 4TF (0871 220 8000/www.cineworld.co.uk).*

Odeon Putney *26 Putney High Street, SW15
1SN (0871 224 4007/www.odeon.co.uk).*
Putney Arts Theatre *Ravenna Road, SW15
6AW (8788 6943/www.putneyartstheatre.org.uk).*

Galleries & museums

Albion *8 Hester Road, SW11 4AX (7801 2480/
www.albion-gallery.com).* Stunning riverside art
gallery near Battersea Park.
London Sewing Machine Museum *312
Balham High Road, SW17 7AA (8682 7916/
www.sewantique.com).*
Pump House Gallery *Battersea Park, SW11
4NJ (7350 0523).* Tiny art gallery in a 19th-
century building.
Wandsworth Museum *The Courthouse,
11 Garratt Lane, SW18 4AQ (8871 7074).*
Small space offering temporary exhibitions
about the borough throughout the year.

Music & comedy venues

Half Moon *93 Lower Richmond Road, SW15
1EU (8780 9383/www.halfmoon.co.uk).* One of
London's longest-running music venues, this
jovial Young's pub has hosted almost everyone
(the Stones, Elvis Costello, the Who, U2…).

Other attractions

Battersea Dogs & Cats Home *4 Battersea
Park Road, SW8 4AA (7622 3626/www.dogs
home.org).* Casual visitors welcome at this
famous sanctuary.

Open spaces

Battersea Park *Prince of Wales Drive, SW11.*
Over 200 acres of riverside parkland with a
boating lake, a sports centre and the Pump
House Gallery.
Clapham Common *Clapham Common
Northside, SW4.* This green and pleasant
expanse, surrounded by the roar of traffic,
straddles the borough boundary with Lambeth.
King George's Park *Merton Road, SW18.*
Leaders Garden *Ashlone Road, SW15.*
Dainty little riverside park, with two play
areas and tennis courts.
Putney Heath *Putney Heath Lane, SW15
(8788 7655/www.wpcc.org.uk).* The eastern
edge of the huge piece of common land that
eventually becomes Richmond Park and
Wimbledon Common.
Putney Vale Cemetery *Kingston Road/
Stag Lane, SW15.* Famous names in this burial
ground on the edge of Putney Heath include
Howard Carter, discoverer of Tutankhamen's
tomb, writer Enid Blyton, footballer Bobby
Moore and racing driver James Hunt.
Tooting Bec Common *Tooting Bec Road,
SW17.* Includes Tooting Bec Lido, an athletics
track and horse riding facilities.
Wandsworth Common *Bolingbroke Grove,
SW11.* Breezy expanse with ornamental areas,
sports pitches, tennis courts and a lake.
Wandsworth Park *Putney Bridge Road, SW15.*

MY VIEW

ROB DOVE
Butcher, A Dove & Sons,
Northcote Road, SW11

My grandfather opened this butcher's
shop in 1889, so our family has been
here for over 100 years. In the 1960s
there were 14 butchers, five bakers,
and no restaurants or estate agents
on this street. Today there's only one
other butcher. So we have very little
competition, and are now considered
quaint!
**Supermarkets and parking controls
have destroyed high-street shopping,
but there's definitely a renewed
interest in small independent shops.**
Wandsworth used to be a very working-
class area, but the make-up has
changed. We now see lots of high-
earning professionals in the shop.
Lawyers, media types, newsreaders,
political journalists… Jack Dee! Our
customers are more remote from us
than in years past.
**So-called working-class people are out
of the loop around here. My employees
certainly can't afford to live in the
area, and it can be difficult to get hold
of good staff. My old man bought his
house for £15,000. It's now worth
£1.5 million – silly money.**
We don't have kids hanging around on
street corners here – they spend their
time at the pony club or deciding where
to ski. I couldn't retire here. I'd look like
an old git with no money.

Sport & fitness

The council's public leisure centres were taken over by DC Leisure in 2000, under the name of Wandsworth Community Leisure Association, with the result that all its public centres have achieved superior standards.

The private sector is dominated by the big-name chains. The smaller clubs tend to be long-established bodybuilding centres which see no need to embrace a more modern, holistic approach to fitness.

Gyms & leisure centres

Balham Leisure Centre *Elmfield Road, SW17 8AN (8772 9577/www.balhamleisurecentre.co.uk).*
Cannons *www.cannons.co.uk; King George's Park, Burr Road, SW18 4SQ (8874 1155); Sheepcote Lane, Burns Road, SW11 5BT (7228 4400).* Private.
Esporta *Smugglers Way, SW18 1DG (8875 2222/www.esporta.com).* Private.
Fitness Exchange *St John's Hill, SW11 1SA (7738 0067/www.fitness-exchange.net).* Private.
Fitness First *www.fitnessfirst.co.uk; 279-291 Balham High Road, SW17 7BA (8672 2904); 276-288 Lavender Hill, SW11 1LJ (7924 5252).* Private.
Holmes Place *154-160 Upper Richmond Road, SW15 2SW (8246 6676/www.holmesplace.com).* Private.
Latchmere Leisure Centre *Burns Road, SW11 2DY (7207 8004).*
Physical Culture Studios *21-22 The Arches, Winthorpe Road, SW15 2LW (8780 2172).* Private.
Profiles for Women *56-70 Putney High Street, SW15 1SF (8788 5700).* Private.
Putney Leisure Centre *Dryburgh Road, SW15 1BL (8785 0388/www.putneyleisurecentre.co.uk).*
Roehampton Recreation Centre *Laverstoke Gardens, SW15 4JB (8785 0535).*
Wandle Recreation Centre *Mapleton Road, SW18 4DN (8871 1149/www.wandlerecreation centre.co.uk).*
Yorky's *24-28 York Road, SW11 3QA (7228 6266).* Private.

Other facilities

Tooting Bec Lido *Tooting Bec Road, SW16 1RU (8871 7198).* Largest open-air pool in Europe, within Tooting Bec Common.

Schools

WHAT THE PARENTS SAY:

'St Anselm's in Tooting Bec and St Boniface in Tooting are both excellent Catholic primary schools, with caring atmospheres. St Boniface has improved steadily in recent years, while St Anselm's has always been near the very top of the league tables. Honeywell Junior School in Battersea is also a popular choice. Generally, the primary sector is strong in Wandsworth and there's no need to go private.

However, Wandsworth is not blessed with an abundance of top secondary schools, and many parents look outside the borough – to Merton, Lambeth and Hammersmith. Some families move south towards Kingston or Wallington for the grammar schools. One of the very best local secondary schools is Graveney School in Tooting. A modern, forward-thinking set-up has made this the most sought-after school in the borough; the campus layout is an added attraction. However, unless you live within a stone's throw of the school gates, your child will need to score extremely highly in the school's logic-based assessment tests to stand a chance of admission.

While Graveney has improved dramatically over the years, Putney High School has always been a consistent performer, and Emanuel School in Battersea is doing well. One school not to rush to is Ernest Bevin College in Tooting, which doesn't enjoy the best of reputations.'
Mark Wareham, father of two, Tooting

Primary

There are 59 state primary schools in Wandsworth, 18 of which are church schools. There are also 25 independent primaries, including one Montessori school and one Steiner school. See www.wandsworth.gov.uk and www.ofsted.gov.uk for more information.

Secondary

ADT College *100 West Hill, SW18 2UT (8877 0357/www.adtcollege.org.uk)*
Battersea Technology College *401 Battersea Park Road, SW11 5AP (7622 0026/www.battersea-tech.wandsworth.sch.uk).*
Burntwood School *Burntwood Lane, SW17 0AQ (8946 6201/www.burntwoodschool.com).* Girls only; mixed sixth form.
Chestnut Grove School *45 Chestnut Grove, SW12 8JZ (8673 8737/www.chestnutgrove.wandsworth.sch.uk).*
Elliot School *Pullman Gardens, SW15 3DG (8788 3421).*
Emanuel School *Battersea Rise, SW11 1HS (8870 4171/www.emanuel.org.uk).* Private.
Ernest Bevin College *Beechcroft Road, SW17 7DF (8672 8582/www.ernestbevin.org.uk).* Boys only; mixed sixth form.
Graveney School *Welham Road, SW17 9BU (8682 7000/www.graveney.org).*
John Paul II RC School *Princes Way, SW19 6QE (8788 8142).*
Putney High School *35 Putney Hill, SW15 6BH (8788 4886/www.gdst.net/putneyhigh).* Private; girls only.
Salesian College *Surrey Lane, SW11 3PB (7228 2857/www.salesiancollege.co.uk).* Boys only.

Southfields Community College *333 Merton Road, SW18 5JU (8875 2600/ www.southfields.wandsworth.sch.uk).*
St Cecilia's, Wandsworth School *Sutherland Grove, SW18 5JR (8780 1244/ www.saintcecilias.wandsworth.sch.uk).*

Property

WHAT THE AGENTS SAY:

❛The fact that we are surrounded by so many Commons appeals to young families – they are the core market. Young professionals and first-time buyers are attracted to the good-value housing, transport links and great bars and restaurants.

People tend to start off buying a property at the cheaper end of the market, such as in Tooting, then gradually move on to areas such as Battersea or Wandsworth Common; both are extremely expensive and desirable places to live. Buying a property in Tooting Bec would be a great investment: it's affordable and, despite what people say, not so far from the action.

Nearby Balham is an emerging market despite being ignored for many years: good-quality properties without having to spend too much, plus good transport links and trendy bars and restaurants. Since 1996 there has been a massive rejuvenation and prices have rocketed.❜
Glen Penman, Penmans, Wandsworth

Average property prices

Detached £1,027,846
Semi-detached £514,801
Terraced £362,042
Flat £219,307

Local estate agents

Andrews *233 Lavender Hill, SW11 1JR (7326 8171/www.andrewsonline.co.uk).*
Craigie & Co *309 Garratt Lane, SW18 4DX (8874 7475/www.craigie-co.co.uk).*
Desouza Residential *173 Garratt Lane, SW18 4DP (8870 4161/www.desouzaresidential.co.uk).*
First Union *www.first-union.co.uk; 2 offices (Battersea 7771 7100/Wandsworth 8480 4444).*

John Thorogood *140 Northcote Road, SW11 6QZ (7228 7474/http://john-thorogood.co.uk).*
Penmans *260 Balham High Road, SW17 7AN (8672 4422/www.penmansestateagents. co.uk).*
Rolfe East *168 & 178 Putney High Street, SW15 1RS (8780 3355/www.rolfe-east.com).*
Time2move *28 London Road, SW17 9HW (8640 0146/www.time2move.com).*

Other information

Council

Wandsworth Borough Council *The Town Hall, Wandsworth High Street, SW18 2PU (8871 6000/www.wandsworth.gov.uk).*

Hospitals

Queen Mary's Hospital *Roehampton Lane, SW15 5PN (8789 6611/www.wandsworth-pct.nhs.uk).*
Springfield University Hospital *SW London & St George's Mental Health NHS Trust, 61 Glenburnie Road, SW17 7DJ (8682 6000).*
St George's Hospital *Blackshaw Road, SW17 0QT (8672 1255/www.st-georges. org.uk).*

Legal services

Battersea CAB *14 York Road, SW11 3QA (8333 6960).*
Battersea Law Centre *14 York Road, SW11 3QA (7585 0716).*
Roehampton CAB *1 Portswood Place, off Danebury Avenue, SW15 4ED (8333 6960).*
Tooting & Balham CAB *4th floor, Bedford House, 215 Balham High Road, SW17 7BQ (8333 6960).*

Local newspapers

South London Press *8769 4444/ http://icsouthlondon.icnetwork.co.uk.*
Wandsworth Borough News & Wandsworth Guardian *8646 6336/www.wb-news.co.uk/www.wandsworthguardian.co.uk.*

Allotments

Council allotments *8871 6441/ www.wandsworth.gov.uk.*
Roehampton Garden Society *Paula Alderson 8789 5836.*

COUNCIL TAX

		Main borough area	Commons area
A	up to £40,000	£406.32	£420.91
B	£40,001-£52,000	£474.04	£491.06
C	£52,001-£68,000	£541.75	£561.21
D	£68,001-£88,000	£609.47	£631.36
E	£88,001-£120,000	£744.91	£771.66
F	£120,001-£160,000	£880.34	£911.96
G	£160,001-£320,000	£1,015.79	£1,052.27
H	over £320,000	£1,218.94	£1,262.72

Wandsworth

'Lady Hamilton said she'd like to row Admiral Nelson down the Nile – but Merton's River Wandle was the next best thing'

Trudy Finch, resident for 11 years

Merton

As a borough, Merton is a relatively youthful addition to London – it was born in 1965 after the fusion of suburbs such as Wimbledon and Mitcham. In contrast, the place feels rather grown-up in spirit: it has considerable history (dating back to the tenth century) and great green spaces, and is growing livelier at a steady pace.

Neighbourhoods

Wimbledon, Wimbledon Village and Wimbledon Park

Anyone for tennis? Wimbledon inevitably evokes thoughts of racket sports, and the area is noticeably spruced up during the championship fortnight starting in late June. At any given time, though, central Wimbledon forms the accessible hub of Merton – a thronging high street (the Broadway) serviced by tubes, trains, trams and buses, and surrounded by residential roads. Chain retailers are concentrated in the Centre Court shopping centre, which used to be Wimbledon's town hall. The busy cinema, restaurants and bars are also identikit chains, but there are some interesting exceptions: Bar Sia's tiled basement was once a Turkish bath used by actors from Wimbledon Theatre; and you'll also find a few specialist shops catering for the burgeoning South African and Polish communities. In addition, the acclaimed Polka Theatre entertains kids from around the borough and far beyond.

Central Wimbledon can get rowdy on weekend nights, but a trip up Wimbledon Hill Road leads to the upmarket 'alternative centre' of Wimbledon Village. Here you'll discover charmingly old-fashioned pubs, stylised bars, boutiques, riding stables, and multi-million pound residences on private roads. The atmosphere is particularly buzzy during Wimbledon fortnight (although the All England Lawn Tennis Museum is open throughout the year),

Merton

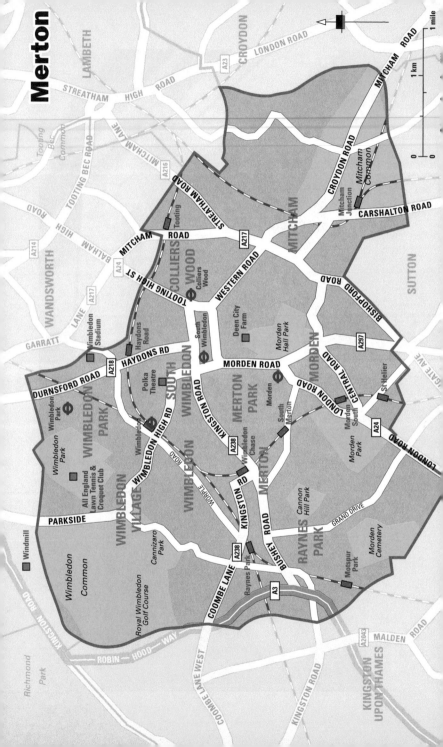

when entrepreneurial Villagers rent out their driveways and set up unofficial stalls.

Wimbledon Common (the birthplace of Elisabeth Beresford's classic eco-characters *The Wombles*) offers vast areas of woodland to explore, as well as a windmill and golf club. The romantic landscaped gardens of Cannizaro House hotel (West Side Common) are equally unmissable; Cannizaro Park features an aviary and numerous sculptures – including a bust of Emperor Haile Selassie, who sought refuge in Merton in the 1930s.

One tube stop along the District Line, the compact satellite of Wimbledon Park provides another local green haven; tennis courts, bowling greens, football pitches and a boating lake ensure it is frequented by all ages. The tube station is located on Arthur Road, which has lost many distinctive local businesses over the years (there's an infestation of estate agents around the station), but the industrial estates off busy Durnsford Road conceal some retail treats – a favourite is the Sardinian cuisine specialist, Vallebona. Wimbledon Park also hosts a small but popular farmers' market every Saturday morning. Local foodies are better catered for than football fans. Plough Lane, the one-time ground of Wimbledon FC, has long been reduced to rubble (and currently looks set to accommodate flats), while the team has been banished to Milton Keynes. A renegade team, AFC Wimbledon, is based in Ham, Surrey. Nevertheless, tennis isn't the only spectator sport left here. Wimbledon Stadium hosts regular greyhound and speedway racing: a 'propah saaf Landan' night out.

South Wimbledon, Colliers Wood and Merton Park

Wimbledon Broadway used to look noticeably shabbier towards South Wimbledon, but more recently shiny new apartments and offices have sprung up at a frantic rate. At the end of the Broadway, Merton High Street leads towards Colliers Wood, where an up-and-coming feel pervades due to the many twenty- and thirtysomethings who've flocked to cheaper property here. In response, there's a growing cluster of late-night bars and soulless but convenient retail parks. ITV's police drama *The Bill* has been filmed around these parts and in neighbouring Mitcham for years.

The area has always reflected a cultural mix, from Asian grocers to Irish pubs, but its history is poorly preserved overall. In 1963, the Beatles played at the Wimbledon Palais on Merton High Street – a site now home to bland residences. The 12th-century Merton Abbey once educated the likes of Thomas A'Becket; its ruins can be seen behind the Savacentre supermarket car park.

The former Liberty silk works at Abbey Mills hosts a weekend craft and book market that's popular with families, as is the Colour House Theatre on the site. In summer this is a pleasant spot for a drink and to listen to musicians, alongside the River Wandle.

Nearby, Merton Park was planned by John Innes in the early 20th century; it's a kind of experiment in suburbia. Naval hero Admiral Horatio Nelson lived with his lover Emma Hamilton in this area around 1801 – a fact echoed in the names of various local pubs (the couple's home in Merton Place has long since been demolished). When Nelson departed for the Battle of Trafalgar, he wrote in his diary: 'I drove from dear, dear Merton where I left all that I hold dear in this world to go and serve my king and country.' There's a recommendation for you.

Highs & Lows

▲ **Wimbledon Common** Nature trails, horse tracks, cycle paths, sports grounds – and Wombles
Tennis For two weeks a year, the nation's attention turns to SW19 for the Wimbledon tournament; more enterprising residents set up stalls on their driveways
Wimbledon Stadium One of only two greyhound tracks left in London – a real south London treat

Grim patches There's a reason Colliers Wood is so often used as the location for episodes of *The Bill*...
Football exile With the move of the official Wimbledon team to Milton Keynes – and the unofficial, 'rebel' team to Ham in Richmond – football fans need to look outside the borough to show their support
Morden and Mitcham Morden Hall Park is nice, but the streets of these two districts are not over-welcoming at night

Raynes Park, Morden and Mitcham

Today they might all be described as commuter suburbs, but what Raynes Park, Morden and Mitcham have in common is rural roots – though only a few traces of these remain. Raynes Park is clearly the most affluent of the three, boasting the biggest family residences this side of Wimbledon Village (particularly on Grand Drive), and the lowest crime rates. It's sometimes referred to as West Wimbledon (an estate agent phrase). 'The Apostles area' – the name apparently coined by local boy scouts in the 1960s – refers to the 12 side streets off Kingston Road, from Bronson Road to Gore Road. You'll find the borough's best indoor and outdoor sports facilities here, at the David Lloyd Centre.

STATISTICS

BOROUGH MAKE-UP
Population 190,231
Average weekly pay £519.90
Ethnic origins
  White 74.97%
  Mixed 3.12%
  Asian or Asian British 11.07%
  Black or Black British 7.78%
  Chinese or other 3.05%
Students 7.76%
Retirees 9.94%

HOUSING STOCK
Borough size 38km^2
No. of households 77,090
Detached 5.9%
Semi-detached 18.1%
Terraced 40.6%
Flats (purpose-built) 23%
Flats (converted) 11.8%
Flats (both) 34.8%

CRIME PER 1,000 OF POPULATION
(English average in brackets)
Burglary 5 (6.4)
Robbery 2 (1.4)
Theft of vehicle 5 (4.5)
Theft from vehicle 6 (10)
Violence against the person 20 (16.5)
Sexual offences 1 (0.9)

MPs & COUNCIL
MPs *Mitcham & Morden* Siobhain McDonagh (Labour); *Wimbledon* Stephen Hammond (Conservative)
CPA 2 stars; improving well

Right at the end of the Northern Line, Morden is where Merton Council is based, in the grim Crown House tower block on traffic-heavy London Road. There's no specific town centre and scant nightlife. Morden Hall Park is a welcome retreat, including meadows, wetlands, waterways and the Old Snuff Mill environmental education centre. Head to the park's northern side for Deen City Farm, home to sheep, rabbits and many other animals. The farm incorporates a riding school and tends to be a big hit with kids.

Like Morden, Mitcham's streets don't seem particularly welcoming after dark, but its local shops and greens also feature a few gems. You might find it hard to believe, but this sprawling neighbourhood was once full of lavender fields; and remains of a Roman settlement were found near the gasworks. Mitcham can also lay claim to having the world's oldest cricket green (dating from 1730); these days, players have to cross busy Cricket Green Road to reach the pavilion.

Restaurants & cafés

Chain restaurants beset many parts of this borough; Wimbledon accommodates outlets of Strada, Tootsies Grill, Giraffe and, over on Wimbledon Hill Road, Wagamama. Less ubiquitous mini-chains in the vicinity include chic modern American diner Jo Shmo's, the busy Korean-owned Japanese restaurant Makiyaki (offering 45 weird and wonderful types of maki sushi) and, just south of Wimbledon Park, Dalchini – under the same ownership as East Sheen's Sarkhel's, but serving an enticing choice of rarely found Indo-Chinese dishes.

Yet one-offs do exist. In South Wimbledon, Service-Heart-Joy is unique: a peaceful, sunny vegetarian/vegan café with a choice of Asian- and European-inspired dishes. The borough's most upmarket suburban corner, Raynes Park, also has two of its most attractive eating options. Cah Chi – an outpost of New Malden's thriving Korean community – is one of the capital's best Korean restaurants, with helpful staff and unbeatable food (bring your own wine). Nearby, on a barren shopping parade, Cocum rises above its unpromising location by offering a fantastic South Indian menu. The centres of Mitcham

Wimbledon Village, near the Common, has the borough's smartest shopping...

and Morden are not as promising, though each contains a handful of Indian restaurants, along with the odd local Chinese and Thai.

Cah Chi *34 Durham Road, SW20 0TW (8947 1081).*
Cocum *9 Approach Road, SW20 8BA (8540 3250).*
Dalchini *147 Arthur Road, SW19 8AB (8947 5966/www.dalchini.co.uk).*
Jo Shmo's *33 High Street, SW19 5BY (8879 3845/www.joshmos.com).*
Makiyaki *149 Merton Road, SW19 1ED (8540 3113).*
Service-Heart-Joy *191 Hartfield Road, SW19 3TH (8542 9912).*

Bars & pubs

Wimbledon Village is the mainstay of Merton's otherwise unexceptional drinking scene. Here you'll find solid middle-class hostelries like the Rose & Crown (a cosy old spot with Young's beers; it was once a favourite of the poet Swinburne), the 19th-century Alexandra and the adjoining, buzzy Smart Alex wine bar. Similarly well-heeled customers also frequent the stylish Fire Stables (good for food and great for wine) and the Eclipse (a popular evening venue, where smartly attired punters splash out on deli-style snacks and cocktails). Close to the Common is the Fox & Grapes, a former riding stables that once served as changing rooms for Wimbledon FC; now, walkers come to refuel on ale and pub grub. Also

nearby is ancient pub the Hand in Hand, which dates back to the 17th century and is rumoured to have a ghost.

But it's not all snoozing gents and crackling fires, as several Wimbledon venues are capable of turning up the heat for a night out: Bar Sia (where DJs play on Thursday and Friday) and the Common Room (a comfortable cocktail bar).

South Wimbledon's large Irish community is served by the area's traditional boozers, one such being the Grove Tavern, which hosts regular rock sessions. A short walk north up Haydons Road is the Marquis of Lorne, a gay pub where the local lesbian and gay branch of CAMRA meets.

Towards Colliers Wood, the Sultan may have a modest backstreet location but is a magnet for real ale lovers seeking the delights of Salisbury's Hopback Brewery. A short stagger south (off Meratun Way, near the Merton Abbey Mills crafts enclave), the William Morris features a beer garden by the River Wandle and is a popular place for a pint after the weekend market. There's little reward in venturing further south towards Morden and Mitcham, or south-west towards Raynes Park, as decent pubs are few and far between.

Alexandra & Smart Alex *33 Wimbledon Hill Road, SW19 7NE (8947 7691).*
Bar Sia *105-109 The Broadway, SW19 1QG (8540 8339/www.barsia.com).*

Common Room *18 High Street, SW19 5DX
(8944 1909/www.jamiesbars.co.uk).*
Eclipse *57 High Street, SW19 5EE
(8944 7722/www.eclipse-ventures.com).*
Fire Stables *27-29 Church Road, SW19 5DQ
(8946 3197).*
Fox & Grapes *9 Camp Road, SW19 4UN
(8946 5599).*
Grove Tavern *2 Morden Road, SW19 3BH
(8543 2023).*
Marquis of Lorne *117 Haydons Road,
SW19 1HH (8542 3306).*
Rose & Crown *55 High Street, SW19 5BA
(8947 4713).*
Sultan *78 Norman Road, SW19 1BT
(8542 4532).*
William Morris *20 Watermill Way, SW19 2RD
(8540 0216).*

Shops

Most of Merton's choicest amenities are to
be found in Wimbledon, but a handful of
unique shops and markets are scattered
across the surrounding neighbourhoods.
The Broadway is the borough's main
shopping strip, where you'll find high-street
chain stores, and a few independents, at
the Centre Court shopping mall (housed
in the old town hall). There are more large-
scale chains in the Priory retail park on
Merton High Street.

As with the bars and pubs, the shopping
turns upmarket as you head north-west

from the Broadway towards Wimbledon
Village. One of the highlights here is the
stunning Mark J West shop on the High
Street, packed with dazzling antique glasses
and decanters, some of them costing
thousands of pounds. Matches boutique is
dripping with luxe designer labels.

The Wedding Dress Shop in Wimbledon
Park has a high-quality range of ready-to-
wear and custom-made dresses. Across
the main Durnsford Road from here, set in
the industrial retail space east of the Park,
is Vallebona Sardinian Gourmet. Stock
includes highly enticing imports of both
food and wine from the Mediterranean
island, and regular tastings are held.

On the High Street in Colliers Wood,
Burge & Gunson is a bathroom centre with
strikingly designed furniture and fittings,
as well as high-tech toys for those who want
to take bathing to a new level with a TV
screen and ultrasound whirlpool. Nearby,
the Boat Harbour is a well-stocked nautical
shop – and the only place you can get your
jet skis fixed in this neck of the Wood.

For fresh market goods, Merton's main
attractions are the Saturday farmers'
market in Wimbledon Park First School
and (for groceries and clothing, street-
market style) the Wimbledon Stadium
Market, held in the greyhound stadium
on Sunday morning.

...eating and drinking options.

Merton

For gifts and collectibles, stroll around the Merton Abbey Mills market at the weekend; it's a hotchpotch of antiques and crafts stalls, plus vans selling exotic hot dishes and English breakfasts. Further south, in otherwise unremarkable Morden, DJs and record collectors should check out Marks Classics, a surprising haven for rare and deleted dance vinyl.

The Boat Harbour 40 High Street, SW19 2AB (8542 5857).
Burge & Gunson 13-27 High Street, SW19 2JE (8543 5166).
Centre Court 4 Queens Road, SW19 8YA (8944 8323).
Mark J West 39B High Street, SW19 5BY (8946 2811).
Marks Classics 25 Abbotsbury Road, SM4 5LJ (8646 4605).
Matches 34 High Street, SW19 5BY (8947 8707).
Merton Abbey Mills Watermill Way, SW19 2RD (8543 9608/www.mertonabbeymills.com).
Priory Retail Park Colliers Wood, SW19.
Vallebona Sardinian Gourmet Unit 14, 55-59 Weir Road, SW19 8UG (8944 5665/www.vallebona.co.uk).
The Wedding Dress Shop 174 Arthur Road, SW19 8AQ (8605 9008).
Wimbledon Farmers' Market Wimbledon Park First School, Havana Road, SW19 8EJ (7833 0338/www.lfm.org.uk).
Wimbledon Stadium Market Wimbledon Stadium Car Park, Plough Lane, SW17 0BL (8946 8000).

Arts & attractions

Cinemas & theatres
Colour House Theatre Merton Abbey Mills, Watermill Way, SW19 2RD (8640 5111/www.wheelhouse.org.uk).
New Wimbledon Theatre & Studio Theatre The Broadway, SW19 1QG (0870 060 6646/www.theambassadors.com/newwimbledon).
Odeon Wimbledon 39 The Broadway, SW19 1QB (0871 224 4007/www.odeon.co.uk).
Polka Theatre for Children 240 The Broadway, SW19 1SB (8543 4888/www.polka theatre.com).

Galleries & museums
Wimbledon Lawn Tennis Museum Centre Court, All England Lawn Tennis & Croquet Club, Church Road, SW19 5AE (8946 6131/www.wimbledon.org/museum). Scheduled to reopen as this guide is published, with new interactive displays enhancing its collection of costumes, memorabilia and film footage.
Wimbledon Society Museum of Local History 22 Ridgway, SW19 4QN (8296 9914/www.wimbledonmuseum.org.uk). Charting the 3,000 year history of the area.

TRANSPORT
Tube stations District Wimbledon Park, Wimbledon; Northern Colliers Wood, South Wimbledon, Morden
Rail stations South West Trains Wimbledon, Raynes Park, Motspur Park; Thameslink Tooting, Haydons Road, Wimbledon, Wimbledon Chase, South Merton, Morden South, St Helier, Mitcham Junction
Tram stops Croydon Tramlink Wimbledon, Dundonald Road, Merton Park, Morden Road
Main bus routes into central London no direct service; night buses N44, N77, N155; 24-hour buses 93, 264

Wimbledon Windmill Museum Windmill Road, Wimbledon Common, SW19 5NR (8947 2825/www.wimbledonwindmillmuseum.org.uk). This old dear, built in 1817, is still working, but only on high days and holidays.

Other attractions
Buddhapadipa Temple 14 Calonne Road, Wimbledon Parkside, SW19 5HJ (8946 1357/www.buddhapadipa.org). London's first Buddhist temple.
Cannizaro House West Side, SW19 4UD. Huge mansion, now a hotel; the fabulous gardens are open to the public.
Merton Priory off Merantun Way, Merton Abbey, SW19 2RD (8543 9608/www.merton priory.org). 12th-century Augustine priory.
Southside House 3-4 Woodhayes Road, Wimbledon Common, SW19 4RJ (8946 7643/www.southsidehouse.com). Regal house, open to visitors and the site of concerts and lectures.

Open spaces

Cannizaro Park West Side, SW19.
Cannon Hill Common Cannon Hill Lane, SW20.
Colliers Wood South Gardens, SW19.
Deen City Farm 39 Windsor Avenue, SW19 2RR (8543 5300/www.deencityfarm.co.uk). Tidy-sized community farm within the grounds of the beautiful Morden Hall Park Estate.
Mitcham Common Commonside West, CR4.
Morden Hall Park Morden Hall Road, SM4. Uncommonly beautiful former deer park on the River Wandle.
Mostyn Gardens Mostyn Road, SW19.
Raynes Park Taunton Avenue, SW20.
Wandle Park Wandle Bank, SW19.
Wimbledon Common Windmill Road, SW19 (www.wpcc.org.uk). Huge, wild, partly wooded park, criss-crossed by paths, horse tracks and nature trails.
Wimbledon Park Home Park Road, SW19. Site of a boating lake.

Merton

RECYCLING

No. of bring sites 28 (for nearest, visit www.recycleforlondon.com)
Household waste recycled 13%
Main recycling centres Weir Road Reuse & Recycling Centre, 36 Weir Road, SW19 8UG (8274 4902); Merton Reuse & Recycling Centre, 63-69 Amenity Way, Garth Road, SM4 4NJ (8274 4902)
Other recycling services green waste collection; home composting; collection of white goods and furniture; Squirrels Community Scrap Scheme (8640 9510) take unwanted materials for use by local groups in educational and creative arts play
Council contact Waste Services, Environment & Regeneration, 63-69 Amenity Way, Morden, Surrey SM4 4NJ (8274 4902)

Sport & fitness

Since entering into a non-profit partnership with Greenwich Leisure, Merton Council has dramatically improved its leisure provision. Most notable is the installation of high-tech Wellness Fitness Centres at the Canons and Wimbledon centres. Merton's private health clubs have to battle for business with the popular chains, but there's probably enough elitism among the racket-loving Wimbledon Village locals for a continued reign by the independent clubs.

Gyms & leisure centres

Browns *127-129 High Street, SW19 2HR (8542 7884/www.browns-gym.co.uk).* Private.
Cannons *The Broadway, SW19 1QB (8947 9627/www.cannons.co.uk).* Private.
Canons Leisure Centre *Madeira Road, CR4 4HD (8640 8543/www.gll.org.uk).*
Christopher's Squash & Fitness Club *Wimbledon Stadium, Plough Lane, SW17 0BL (8946 4636/www.christopherssportsclub.co.uk).* Private.
David Lloyd *Bushey Road, SW20 8TE (8543 8020/www.davidlloydleisure.co.uk).* Private.
Esporta *21-33 Worple Road, SW19 4JS (8545 1700/www.esporta.com).* Private.
Fitness First *1-3 Upper Green East, CR4 2PE (8640 9944/www.fitnessfirst.co.uk).* Private.
Holmes Place *Battle Close, North Road, SW19 1AQ (8544 9111/www.holmesplace.co.uk).* Private.
King's Club *Woodhayes Road, SW19 4TT (8255 5401/www.kcs.org.uk).* Private.
Morden Park Pool *Morden Park, London Road, SM4 5HE (8640 6727/www.gll.org.uk).*

Wimbledon Club *Church Road, SW19 5AG (8971 8090).* Private.
Wimbledon Leisure Centre *Latimer Road, SW19 1EW (8542 1330/www.gll.org.uk).*
Wimbledon Racquets & Fitness Club *Cranbrook Road, SW19 4HD (8947 5806/ www.wsbc.co.uk).* Private.
YMCA *200 The Broadway, SW19 1RY (8542 9055/www.kwymca.org.uk).* Private.

Spectator sports

All England Lawn Tennis Club *Church Road, SW19 5AE (8946 2244/www.wimbledon.org).* Site of annual Wimbledon tournament.
Wimbledon Stadium *Plough Lane, SW17 0BL (0870 840 8905/www.wimbledonstadium. co.uk).* Greyhound and speedway racing.

Schools

WHAT THE PARENTS SAY:

'Many parents in Merton look at private education for their kids if they can. At primary level, the Rowans School has an excellent reputation, as do boys' schools like Squirrels, Willington School and Rokeby. Girls can start at Wimbledon High School as young as four. There are a number of excellent primary schools that now take children up to the age of 11, including Bishop Gilpin, which is highly competitive to get in to. Other primary schools with a good reputation are Pelham and Dundonald.

Secondary schools in the borough are not as popular as primaries – many parents go private or look outside the borough. Coombe Girls' School (in Kingston) is very highly regarded, but places are usually snapped up by those living close by. In contrast, Ricards Lodge has a rather poor reputation. King's College School provides education for boys from seven to 18 and is extremely popular – the catchment area is large, with boys coming in from Surrey and elsewhere. Wimbledon College has a good reputation among schools in the maintained sector.'
Mother of two, Merton

Primary

There are 43 state primary schools in Merton, 11 of which are church schools. There are also eight independent primaries, including one Norwegian school. See www.merton.gov.uk/learning and www.ofsted.gov.uk for more information.

Secondary

Bishopsford Community School *Lilleshall Road, SM4 6DU (8687 1157/ www.bishopsford.org).*
King's College School *Southside, Wimbledon Common, SW19 4TT (8255 5300/www.kcs. org.uk).* Private; boys only.

Mitcham Vale School *Acacia Road, CR4 1SF (8648 6627/www.mitchamvale.merton.sch.uk).*
Raynes Park High School *Bushey Road, SW20 0JL (8946 4112/www.raynespark.merton.sch.uk).*
Ricards Lodge High School *Lake Road, SW19 7HB (8946 2208/www.richardslodge. merton.sch.uk).* Girls only.
Rutlish School *Watery Lane, SW20 9AD (8542 1212/www.rutlish.merton.sch.uk).* Boys only.
Tamworth Manor High *Wide Way, CR4 1BP (8623 1000/www.tamworthmanor.co.uk).*
Ursuline High School *Crescent Road, SW20 8HA (8255 2688/www.ursulinehigh.merton. sch.uk).* Girls only (mixed sixth form with Wimbledon College).
Wimbledon College *Edge Hill, SW19 4NS (8946 2533/www.wimbledoncollege.org.uk).* Boys only (mixed sixth form with Ursuline High School).

Property

WHAT THE AGENTS SAY:

‘Wimbledon has lots of City-based professionals and young families who have moved out from places like Knightsbridge for the greenery. There's a nice mix of town and countryside, we've no planes (unlike Richmond and Barnes) and, of course, there's the Common. Plus there are very good rail connections – just 12 minutes to Waterloo. And, despite all the bars, it doesn't get rowdy at the weekends. We also get a lot of the top players renting properties here during Wimbledon. It's all very low-profile, obviously – we're an understated bunch here.’
Malcolm Gee, Hawes & Co, Wimbledon

Average property prices
Detached £863,355
Semi-detached £329,612
Terraced £228,006
Flat £169,394

Local estate agents
Christopher St James *61 High Street, SW19 2JF (8296 1270/www.christopher-st-james.plc.uk).*

Cross & Prior *85 The Broadway, SW19 1QE (8540 2299/www.crossprior.co.uk).*
Dicksons *194 Merton High Street, SW19 1AX (8542 8595/www.dicksons-estate.com).*
Eddison White *34 Christchurch Road, SW19 2NX (8540 9828/www.eddisonwhite.co.uk).*
Ellisons *www.ellisons.uk.com; 3 offices in the borough (Wimbledon 8944 9494/Raynes Park 8944 9595/Morden 8543 1166).*
Hawes & Co *www.hawesandco.co.uk; 4 offices in the borough (Wimbledon Village 8946 1000/ Wimbledon Broadway 8542 6600/Wimbledon Park 8947 1000/Raynes Park 8946 3000).*
Reynolds *44 Coombe Lane, SW20 0LD (8946 6511/www.reynolds-estates.co.uk).*

Other information

Council
London Borough of Merton Council
Civic Centre, London Road, Morden, Surrey SM4 5DX (8274 4901/www.merton.gov.uk).
Out-of-hours emergency service
8543 5974.
Out-of-hours Social Services standby service *Sutton Civic Offices 8770 5000.*

Hospitals
Nelson Hospital *Kingston Road, SW20 8DB (8296 2000/www.suttonandmerton.nhs.uk).*
St George's Hospital *Blackshaw Road, SW17 0QT (8672 1255/www.st-georges.org.uk).*
St Helier Hospital *Wrythe Lane, SM5 1AA (8296 2000/www.epsom-sthelier.nhs.uk).*

Legal services
Wandsworth & Merton Law Centre
14th Floor, The Tower, 125 High Street, SW19 2JR (8333 6960/www.lawcentres.org.uk).

Local newspapers
My Merton *www.merton.gov.uk/mymerton.*
Council magazine distributed across the borough every two months; also available online.
Wimbledon Guardian
www.wimbledonguardian.co.uk.
Wimbledon News *www.wimbledonnews.co.uk.*

Allotments
For council allotments, visit www.merton. gov.uk/allotments or call 8545 3665.

COUNCIL TAX		Main borough	Wimbledon Common area
A	up to £40,000	£829.28	£843.87
B	£40,001-£52,000	£967.49	£984.51
C	£52,001-£68,000	£1,105.70	£1,125.16
D	£68,001-£88,000	£1,243.91	£1,265.80
E	£88,001-£120,000	£1,520.33	£1,547.09
F	£120,001-£160,000	£1,796.75	£1,828.37
G	£160,001-£320,000	£2,073.19	£2,109.67
H	over £320,000	£2,487.82	£2,531.60

'Lambeth is London, pre-gentrification. Maybe we should appreciate the discarded syringes while we can – in ten years, we'll be recalling the area as unspoilt.'

Laura Fergusson, student and resident for 20 years

Lambeth

London's main cultural complex, a buzzing market, Portuguese enclaves, a Test Match cricket ground, a thriving club culture, great bars aplenty, premium Victorian housing, ungainly estates and one of London's best commons – you'll find them all, during a Lambeth walk (oi!).

Neighbourhoods

South Bank, Waterloo and Lambeth North

Lambeth's northerly tip, known to council folk as Bishop's Ward, has the borough's lowest population, but its tourist-friendliness brings in the money. The South Bank is the sweet spot. Visitors spend their dosh along the river promenade between Westminster Bridge and Blackfriars Bridge. Tourist-drawing highlights, from west to east, include the London Aquarium, the London Eye, the Royal Festival Hall, the Hayward Gallery, an IMAX cinema, the National Film Theatre and the National Theatre. The Saatchi Gallery (www.saatchi-gallery.co.uk), however, is moving, and will reopen at a new site in Chelsea in late 2006.

Although the South Bank isn't solely the preserve of visitors, setting up home here is prohibitively expensive. Penthouse flats in the Perspective apartment complex near Lambeth North tube (100 Westminster Bridge Road – the old MI6 headquarters) cost from £500,000 up to a whopping £4.5m, which goes to show what sustained regeneration can do for a rather mouldy, if central area. Round the corner, in Baylis Road, modest local authority housing still exists, but the South Bank effect is clearly filtering down Lambeth way. It probably won't be long before 'doing the Lambeth Walk' describes well-heeled locals looking for a decent gastropub. That's still some way off; although the market and shops of the legendary Lambeth Walk have died a death, and the shopping precinct put up in the 1970s is being demolished to make way

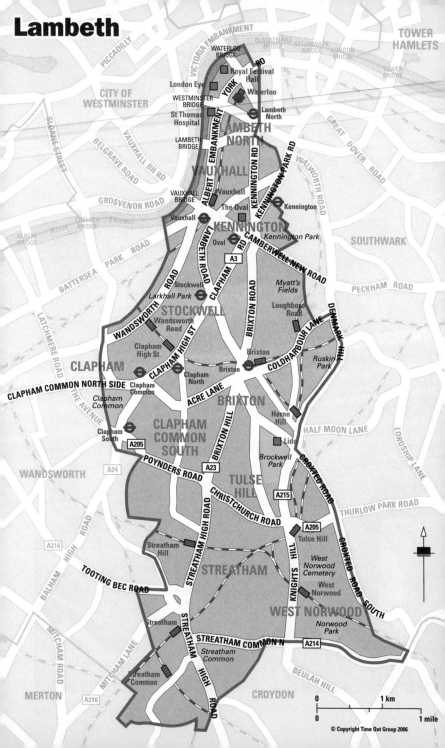

for modern flats, the area still has an unreconstructed, seedy look.

Between gritty Lambeth and the swanky South Bank lies Waterloo, a quarter that's always had a bit of an identity crisis, Kinks tune notwithstanding. Most people only know Waterloo for its station (the UK's largest), where the International Terminal faces the ignominy of bowing out to King's Cross in 2007, once the new Channel Tunnel Rail Link is completed. Waterloo also suffers from terminal ugliness at the Westminster Bridge Road end, where hideous scenes of dereliction greet the visitor at the confluence of the busy streets that lead to better things. Dive into Lower Marsh for the street market and restaurants, and continue east towards the Cut for a better view of Waterloo, at sunset or any other time.

Vauxhall

Vauxhall is an odd place: smack on the river in Zone 1, sitting across from Tate Britain and Millbank Tower… yet with the feel of a forgotten backwater. Hugely busy A-roads criss-cross the area's heart at Vauxhall Cross, and dripping railway arches run like a seam across a great section of the neighbourhood. It can feel like a route to somewhere else rather than a place in itself.

It wasn't always like this. What are now known as Vauxhall Spring Gardens were once the famed Vauxhall Pleasure Gardens, a vast expanse of ground dedicated to leisure for Londoners from the late 17th to the early 19th century. The area changed once Vauxhall Bridge was completed in 1816, bringing industry with it. A few famous names (Royal Doulton, Marmite and the Vauxhall Iron Works, which became the car manufacturer) were all based here.

Although the area's workers now toil in offices (including, of course, the spies and suits of MI6, whose idiosyncratic building sits at the base of Vauxhall Bridge), the industrial heritage has left behind some characterful streets. The new bus station, with its sleek, soaring architecture, could be the hint of things to come, with regeneration plans perhaps finally coming to fruition.

As with Stockwell, though, the best aspects of Vauxhall are its hidden spaces: lovely pubs such as the Royal Oak and the Lavender; intriguing cafés like the Madeira and Luis Deli (*see p216*) under the railway arches on Albert Embankment. Further

softening the area's hard edges are a wonderful city farm and, nearby, bounded by Glasshouse Walk and Oswald's Place, some well-tended allotments.

Kennington

Kennington sits at the junction of several Roman roads, with Kennington Road (A23) and Kennington Lane (A3204) forming Kennington Cross (a lively parade of shops, pubs and restaurants) at the very heart of the neighbourhood. Spanning out from here, the streets are lined with genteel Georgian and Victorian terraces that manage to rise serenely above the petrol fumes. The area is popular with politicians – indeed, photos of Jack Straw, Gordon Brown and chums feature prominently in the window of one of the local curry houses – and has the feel of a village about it, despite its perch on the outskirts of the Congestion Charge zone.

Kennington's greatest claim to fame is the Oval: once a cabbage patch, now the home of Surrey County Cricket Club and one of the most prestigious leather-on-willow grounds in the world. Otherwise it's mostly residential in feel, with a surprising variety of property – from pristine Georgian squares such as Cleaver Square (nestled behind Kennington Park Road) and the

<table>
<tr><td colspan="2">

Highs & Lows

</td></tr>
<tr><td>▲</td><td>**Culture on the South Bank** How about having the NFT as your local cinema? Or the Riverside Book Market as your bookshop?
A taste of Portugal Custard tart lovers take note: Vauxhall and Stockwell have some fantastic Portuguese delis
The vibe in Brixton The heartland of London's Afro-Caribbean culture, and one of the most vibrant neighbourhoods in the capital</td></tr>
<tr><td>▼</td><td>**The crime in Brixton** Muggings and bag-snatchings are, sadly, another feature of Brixton life
Boozy excess The non-stop party in parts of Clapham and Brixton can be exhausting
Ugly intersections Vauxhall Cross and the Westminster Road end of Waterloo are prime examples of urban unpleasantness</td></tr>
</table>

Lambeth

Duchy of Cornwall cottages (to the west of Kennington Cross), to the large LCC estates of various vintages surrounding the park.

Stockwell and South Lambeth

High crime rates and an over-abundance of concrete give Stockwell a reputation as an area of urban blight. This notoriety isn't helped by the glum, uninspiring parade of shops and estates around the tube station. Look harder, though: Stockwell may be scruffy on the surface, but there are gems to be found if you're willing to dig.

The area just above Clapham Road contains Larkhall Park, tree-lined Victorian crescents, great local pubs and one of London's real-life Albert Squares. This area is also home to the magnificent Stockwell Bus Garage, built in 1952 by Adie, Button & Partners – surely the only listed bus garage in London. Vincent Van Gogh even saw fit to make Stockwell his home, as the little blue plaque on Hackford Road, to the east of Clapham Road, attests.

Property is a mix of Victorian terraces and council (or ex-council) estates; the large Latin American and African communities ensure there's an abundance of interesting neighbourhood eateries. Stockwell's rather nebulous boundaries also encompass the area slightly to the north known as South Lambeth, a wonderful Portuguese enclave with bars, restaurants, shops and bakeries. Wandering along South Lambeth Road in the early evening, you'll find the atmosphere is as much Lisbon as London – especially when there's a Porto versus Sporting football match on satellite TV.

Brixton

Synonymous over the years with social unrest, poverty and crime, Brixton has become an increasingly popular place to live without quite reaching the tipping point of gentrification that has threatened since the late 1990s.

The neighbourhood's largely Caribbean population is its life and soul, from the market (a glorious collection of indoor arcades and outdoor stalls) to the barber shops, food joints and record stores peppered along Coldharbour Lane and Atlantic Road. The network of streets hemmed in by the railway line running to the north and east is a maze of colourful awnings and eclectic wares – tattoos, wigs, cows' feet: anything is up for grabs if you know where to look. The grubby main drag along Brixton Road is less interesting, although well appointed with the usual high-street stores. Hectic doesn't even begin to describe it: touts hamper the crowds by the tube station, hawking tickets to whatever act is appearing that night at the Brixton Academy, while preachers belt out their convictions outside KFC.

The bustle doesn't simmer down much in the evening, with Brixton's bar and club scene drawing enthusiasts from all over London. Locals also have one of the capital's best independent cinemas on their doorstep, the Ritzy. There's an urban, modern vibe to the area, yet splashes of local history are found everywhere, from the slightly forlorn Windrush Square (commemorating the large Caribbean influx of the post-war years) to Electric Avenue, Britain's first electrically lit shopping street. The neighbourhood even retains its very own windmill, a relic of the early 19th century, which stands in the residential district to the west of Brixton Hill, a stone's throw from Brixton Prison.

The only thing the area lacks is a decent-sized green space, although Max Roach Park does offer swings, slides and a nature trail for kids; ten minutes' walk away, Brockwell Park, with its outdoor pool and sports facilities, is a refuge from the chaos.

In bricks-and-mortar terms, Brixton is about as mixed as can be found in London, encompassing the early 19th-century cottages of Brixton Water Lane, the petite Victorian terraces in the 'Effra' neighbourhood (around Effra Road and the Effra pub), and the sprawling estates that stretch off towards Loughborough Junction. Ultimately, Brixton's best feature is its strong sense of community. Many places lay claim to the badge of multiculturalism, but Brixton truly owns it.

Clapham and Clapham North

SW4 is the home of colonic irrigation, posh butchers and designer boutiques. Nevertheless, there are still some old-school retail dinosaurs in the locality (including a Sainsbury's on the High Street).

At the north of the district, Wandsworth Road remains a stretch of industrial wasteland on the border of Battersea.

The neighbouring Old Town, just north of Clapham Common tube, is far more pleasing: a genteel quadrangle of boutiques, tarted-up pubs, premium-value Victorian property, and even three Queen Anne-style houses (at Nos.39, 41 and 43). Despite the fact that it doubles as a bus depot, the quadrangle is ideal for meandering in fine weather, when it is populated by newly settled, straight-laced, twenty- and thirtysomething professionals, spilling out of pubs, Staropramen or Mojito in hand. Although markedly more middle class than neighbouring Brixton, Clapham is very much the contemporary urban village, with council blocks sitting next to cool £1 million-plus dream homes.

The northern stretch of the High Street has a high turnover of bars and restaurants, with frequent franchised newcomers. There remains, however, a superb selection of unique-to-Clapham businesses in all flavours – the quirky, the bohemian and the Michelin-worthy.

Clapham Common South and Clapham Park

Not quite Balham, not quite Clapham proper, Clapham Common South has managed to develop its own identity over the last decade. The area is split between two boroughs, Lambeth and Wandsworth (*see p178*), with the dividing line running through the Common (though Lambeth manages the whole area). It now has far more than this vast expanse of green to justify its existence and no longer feels like an elongated roundabout (around Clapham South tube) for motorists turning off for Streatham or en route to Brighton.

Boutiquey bars and cafés have sprouted in recent years, manifestations of Clapham Park's move upmarket. Abbeville Road 'up and came' long before the glossy Chablis and Sancerre franchises appeared on the High Street to the north. Its smart Victorian terraces now boast a varied batch of shops and eateries.

The lovely Common itself is reason enough to want to live here. In high summer, when not playing host to one of numerous festivals, the entirely flat expanse behind the Windmill Pub becomes a jumbo picnic blanket. Yes, there are plenty of well-heeled rugby boys treating the Common as one vast beer garden with their future yummy-

Lambeth

mummy girlfriends, but this is a very democratic green space; you're as likely to encounter pre-sundown gay cruisers who have strayed from the bijou wooded stretch to the west as you are kite-flying kids, sunbathing chavsters, Jamaican barbecuers and bell-ringing dope sellers.

Streatham

Streatham has provided a first rung on the accommodation ladder for newcomers to London for decades. Estate agents tend to describe the area as Brixton Hill, to suggest the Victoria Line is in close proximity. It isn't (there's no tube at all south of Brixton), but this neighbourhood is just central enough to make the commute relatively painless and just inconvenient enough to make rents reasonable.

For many, Streatham still conjures up visions of Cynthia Payne and luncheon vouchers. Today, prostitutes still inhabit several streets in the St Leonard's area (this has been the centre of the trade since a move from Tooting in the 1980s). On top of this, Streatham High Road, with its endless traffic jams and flanks of ugly shops, has to be one of the most unprepossessing thoroughfares in London. Yet there are also some wonderful green spaces and imposing homes in the locality that hint at its origins as a wealthy agricultural community. Local amenities are abundant too: there's a good multiplex cinema, competitive supermarkets, and an ice rink. (Admittedly, the local nightlife might resemble that of a satellite town, and the boys tend to sport button-down shirts *sans* jackets even in February.)

Tulse Hill and West Norwood

Hugging the South Circular, West Norwood and Tulse Hill could be described as south London's gateway to suburbia. Though the area borders some of the rougher parts of London, much of it looks far edgier than it really is – even when you venture away from the rows of net-curtained terraced houses into less lovely-looking estates.

Norwood High Street has come up in the world of late, and CCTV has covered all of the scarier urban bases in the district. Campaigns are in full swing to regenerate the neighbourhood and to plant more greenery. As a result, a new generation of families has taken up residence. There's no tube station, but there are few parts of

London that have better bus and rail links. You won't have to travel far for abundant parkland and commercial centres either (towards the West End as well as further out of town).

The Victorian grandeur of West Norwood Cemetery gives a flavour of a more genteel era. In contrast, if you walk through the area of an afternoon, you're likely to run the gauntlet of raucous secondary-school children en route to the nearest chippy. With its own kind of charm, this part of Lambeth is definitely more 'sarf' than 'south'.

Restaurants & cafés

Many of the restaurants around Waterloo and the South Bank rely on a transitory population: either tourists, theatre- and concert-goers, or those taking a quick bite before a train journey. The Archduke wine bar, near the Royal Festival Hall, caters for all these folk with its bar menu and pricier restaurant. Ozu, specialising in traditional Japanese cuisine, is probably the best of the venues occupying the old County Hall on the riverfront, though an oriental alternative popular with lunchtime workers is Inshoku (Japanese and Thai food), on Lower Marsh.

There's a Pizza Express on Belvedere Road and, nearby, a branch of Chez Gérard, but our choice for seasonally based French cuisine would be RSJ behind Gabriel's Wharf. Pizza Paradiso has a branch on the Lambeth side of the Cut; the Anchor & Hope (also on the Cut) is one of London's best gastropubs. To the south, Lambeth North is sufficiently far from the tourist attractions to have cherished local caffs like Perdoni's (fry-ups and Italian standards a speciality).

Vauxhall has a paucity of eating venues, although it does boast a stray Portuguese, Madeira Pâtisserie (*see p216*). On Vauxhall Grove, the Bonnington Centre Café, an eccentric vegetarian caff, has a strong local following, though the food is very variable. Kennington has intimate fish restaurant the Lobster Pot, pizza-specialising brasserie the Lavender and upmarket modern Indian the Painted Heron. For a budget meal, try classic chippy the Windmill Fish Bar.

Stockwell is at the heart of the capital's Portuguese community, with several restaurants and bars on the South Lambeth Road. Bar Estrela is a perennially popular spot, though the tapas and hearty meals at

Grelha D'Ouro also have their fans. Nearby, tapas bar/restaurant Rebato's provides a Spanish take on the Iberian theme, while the Hot Stuff caff serves a budget menu of Indian and West African food. On Stockwell Road there are more Portuguese enterprises, the best of which is bar-restaurant O Cantinho de Portugal.

While you would expect to find good African and Caribbean fare in Brixton (try Asmara for Eritrean specials, or the great-value Bamboula for Caribbean cooking), the local restaurant scene is diversifying. The selection now includes the likes of oriental canteen New Fujiyama, budget Thai pit-stop Baan Thai, Colombian caff Coma y Punto, a branch of trendy pizza joint Eco, and Modern European newcomer Upstairs Bar & Restaurant.

Clapham is a restaurant hotspot, with a varied choice of cuisines in both high and low price brackets. Close to Clapham North tube, Tsunami is one of the city's best Japanese restaurants. Nearby are first-rate chippy Sea Cow and budget Tex-Mex joint Café Sol. Francophiles are provided for by ever-so-French bistro Gastro on Venn Street; just down the same road, on opposite sides, are siblings the Rapscallion and the Sequel which both serve adventurous international cuisine (and great weekend brunch).

Jostling for space among the chain bars of Clapham High Street, Café Wanda is a versatile all-day spot for hearty Polish cooking as well as pâtisserie and English breakfasts. The High Street is blessed with pizzerias too, including the original branch of Eco, plus there's a neighbourhood pizza and pasta joint, Verso, down Clapham Park Road. Despite its position off the main drag, pan-Hispanic tapas bar El Rincón Latino is a regular haunt of the district's youthful hordes. Over in Clapham Old Town, the Polygon Bar & Grill serves a modish international menu, but is especially busy for weekend brunch. Top-end dining is provided by Modern European outfit Morel, while even closer to Clapham Common tube is local Thai, Pepper Tree. Away from the mêlée in Clapham Common South, Newtons brasserie has long been catering to the upwardly mobile of Abbeville Road.

The Streatham dining scene has yet to get off the ground; one of the more promising outfits, Caribbean Trini's, recently closed down; alternatives include a branch of Pizza Express and La Pergola, where you can eat Italian accompanied by the yelping of an Elvis impersonator. Tulse Hill and West Norwood fare even worse, though the restaurants of Herne Hill and Dulwich (over the border in Southwark; see p229) aren't far away.

Anchor & Hope 36 The Cut, SE1 8LP (7928 9898).
Archduke Concert Hall Approach, SE1 8XU (7928 9370).
Asmara 386 Coldharbour Lane, SW9 8LF (7737 4144).
Baan Thai 401 Coldharbour Lane, SW9 8LQ (7737 5888).
Bamboula 12 Acre Lane, SW2 5SG (7737 6633).
Bar Estrela 111-115 South Lambeth Road, SW8 1UZ (7793 1051).
Bonnington Centre Café 11 Vauxhall Grove, SW8 1TD (7820 7466/www.bonningtoncafe.co.uk).

Lambeth

Café Sol *56 Clapham High Street, SW4 7UL (7498 9319/www.cafesol.net).*
Café Wanda *153 Clapham High Street, SW4 7SS (7738 8760).*
O Cantinho de Portugal *137 Stockwell Road, SW9 9TN (7924 0218).*
Chez Gérard *9 Belvedere Road, South Bank, SE1 8YS (7202 8470/www.santeonline.co.uk).*
Coma y Punto *94-95 Granville Arcade, Coldharbour Lane, SW9 8PS (7326 0276).*
Eco *www.ecorestaurants.com; 162 Clapham High Street, SW4 7UG (7978 1108); 4 Market Row, Brixton Market, Electric Lane, SW9 8LD (7738 3021).*
Gastro *67 Venn Street, SW4 0BD (7627 0222).*
Grelha D'Ouro *151 South Lambeth Road, SW8 1XN (7735 9764).*
Hot Stuff *19 Wilcox Road, SW8 2XA (7720 1480).*
Inshoku *23-24 Lower Marsh, SE1 7RJ (7928 2311).*
Lavender *112 Vauxhall Walk, SE11 5ER (7735 4440).*
Lobster Pot *3 Kennington Lane, SE11 4RG (7582 5556/www.lobsterpotrestaurant.co.uk).*
Morel *14 Clapham Park Road, SW4 7BB (7627 2468/www.morelrestaurant.co.uk).*
New Fujiyama *5-7 Vining Street, SW9 8QA (7737 2369/www.newfujiyama.com).*
Newtons *33-35 Abbeville Road, SW4 9LA (8673 0977/www.newtonsathome.co.uk).*
Ozu *County Hall, Westminster Bridge Road, SE1 7BH (7928 7766/www.ozulondon.com).*
Painted Heron *205-209 Kennington Lane, SE11 5QS (7793 8313).*
Pepper Tree *19 Clapham Common Southside, SW4 7AB (7622 1758).*
Perdoni's *18-20 Kennington Road, SE1 7BL (7928 6846).*
La Pergola *66 Streatham High Road, SW16 1DA (8769 2646).*
Pizza Paradiso *61 The Cut, SE1 8LL (7261 1221/www.pizzaparadiso.co.uk).*
Polygon Bar & Grill *4 The Polygon, SW4 0JG (7622 1199/www.thepolygon.co.uk).*
Rapscallion *75 Venn Street, SW4 0BD (7787 6555/www.therapscalliononline.com).*
Rebato's *169 South Lambeth Road, SW8 1XW (7735 6388/www.rebatos.com).*
El Rincón Latino *148 Clapham Manor Street, SW4 6BX (7622 0599).*
RSJ *33A Coin Street, SE1 9NR (7928 4554/www.rsj.uk.com).*
Sea Cow *57 Clapham High Street, SW4 7TG (7622 1537).*
Sequel *75 Venn Street, SW4 0BD (7622 4222/www.thesequelonline.com).*
Tsunami *5-7 Voltaire Road, SW4 6DQ (7978 1610/www.tsunamijapaneserestaurant.co.uk).*
Upstairs Bar & Restaurant *89B Acre Lane, SW2 5TN (7733 8855).*
Verso *84 Clapham Park Road, SW4 7BX (7720 1515).*
Windmill Fish Bar *211 Kennington Lane, SE11 5QS (7582 5754).*

Bars & pubs

Containing well-to-do party village Clapham and clubby Brixton, Lambeth throbs with drinkers and dancers after dark. Brixton has, in the last decade, become London's epicentre of gritty urban cool, proved by its surplus of stylish (occasionally pretentious) pubs and DJ bars, plus London's hard dance mecca, Fridge Bar. Other lively ones are the raucous Dogstar, the art students' favourite Sun & Doves and the more sophisticated but no less feisty Tongue & Groove. Then, for the morning after – or, indeed, a weekend lunch or quiet post-commute pint – pubs like the Effra, the Trinity Arms and the Far Side are all suitably warm and fuzzy. Towards Streatham Hill there's trendy bar White Horse, and the Windmill – an indie rock joint with bands playing most nights.

Kennington also has a few fashion-conscious bars, chief among them the trendy Dog House and, up toward Lambeth North, the more stylish Three Stags (now unrecognisable as the blue-collar pub in which Chaplin's father drank himself to death). The area's more homely locals include the Greyhound and the Prince of Wales. Stockwell, though not the best area for bar-hopping, also has one or two spots worth seeking out. The north of the South Lambeth Road has a cluster of convivial Portuguese establishments, of which Bar Estrela is the star. There's also warm neighbourhood local the Canton Arms, quality alehouse the Priory Arms, and the Antipodean-friendly Swan.

Then there's Clapham. The area east of the Common belongs to Lambeth, and this is where the greatest concentration of pubs, bars and restaurants is to be found. The seductive after-hours den of Sand, tiny Bar Local, lounge-bar-cum-restaurant Grafton House, the leftist Bread & Roses and rugger-bugger central, the Coach & Horses, pretty much sum up the length and breadth of what's on offer here. In a word: everything.

Bar Estrela *111-115 South Lambeth Road, SW8 1UZ (7793 1051).*
Bar Local *4 Clapham Common Southside, SW4 7AA (7622 9406/www.barlocal.co.uk).*
Bread & Roses *68 Clapham Manor Street, SW4 6DZ (7498 1779/www.breadandroses pub.com).*

Lambeth

Canton Arms *177 South Lambeth Road, SW8 1XP (7587 3819).*
Coach & Horses *173-175 Clapham Park Road, SW4 7EX (7622 3815/www.barbeerianinns.com).*
Dog House *293 Kennington Road, SE11 6BY (7820 9310).*
Dogstar *389 Coldharbour Lane, SW9 8LQ (7733 7515/www.thedogstar.com).*
Effra *38A Kellet Road, SW2 1EB (7274 4180).*
Far Side *144 Stockwell Road, SW9 9TQ (7095 1401).*
Fridge Bar *1 Town Hall Parade, Brixton Hill, SW2 1RJ (7326 5100).*
Grafton House *13 Old Town, SW4 0JT (7498 5559).*
Greyhound *336 Kennington Park Road, SE11 4PP (7735 2594).*
Priory Arms *83 Lansdowne Way, SW8 2PB (7622 1884).*
Prince of Wales *48 Cleaver Square, SE11 4EA (7735 9916/www.shepherdneame.co.uk).*
Sand *156 Clapham Park Road, SW4 7DE (7622 3022).*
Sun & Doves *61-63 Coldharbour Lane, SE5 9NS (7733 1525/www.sunanddoves.co.uk).*
Swan *215 Clapham Road, SW9 9BE (7978 9778/www.theswanstockwell.co.uk).*
Three Stags *67-69 Kennington Road, SE1 7PZ (7928 5974).*
Tongue & Groove *50 Atlantic Road, SW9 8JN (7274 8600).*
Trinity Arms *45 Trinity Gardens, SW9 8DR (7274 4544).*
White Horse *94 Brixton Hill, SW2 1QN (8678 6666/www.whitehorsebrixton.com).*
Windmill *22 Blenheim Gardens, SW2 5BZ (8671 0700/www.windmillbrixton.co.uk).*

Shops

Although served by a wealth of betting shops, dry-cleaners, uninviting greasy spoons and corner shops, the borough of Lambeth – ignoring Clapham – lacks destination shops and chic boutiques. Where it does excel, however, is in its food shops: with such a mixed ethnicity, the borough has an absolute surplus of interesting international delis.

In Vauxhall, under the railway arches of Albert Embankment, the Madeira Pâtisserie is a fantastic source of Portuguese baked goods: it supplies most of the cafés in the area, and the shop on site doesn't disappoint (buy a custard tart). Next door the Luis Deli (Portuguese again). Stockwell, too, is tinged with a flavour of Portugal: Funchal Bakery sell pastries, soups and ready-prepared meals; tiny Sintra, attached to a popular café next door, overflows with confectionery, breads and condiments.

For other international foodstuffs, Wandsworth Road has the Ryad Halal Way Butchers & Deli (for halal meat, sausages, spice mixes and other intriguing sundries), while, for Italian fare, South Lambeth has Di Lieto Bakery & Deli and Brixton Road has Delicatessen Alberobello. Down in Streatham, Korona is a one-stop shop for French, Italian, eastern European and South African deli goods. The Old Post Office Bakery (the oldest in south London) in Clapham North stocks a huge selection of breads. South-west in Clapham Common, M Moen & Sons is a well-respected organic butcher's; North Street Deli offers top-quality charcuterie, breads and cakes. Less well ordered but far more fun is Brixton Market. The stalls along Electric Avenue are piled high with yams, plantains, mangoes, papayas and more exotic items. Opposite, stalls and stores sell halal meats and an incredible variety of fish.

To focus solely on food, though, would do Brixton Market a disservice: move on to Atlantic Road for clothes, towels and wallets, then to Brixton Station Road for second-hand wear (Saturdays only). In Brixton Village (once Granville Arcade) there are African and Caribbean food stores, household goods and crafts. One of the market's strongest suits, though, is music, with three of the best specialist record shops in the capital: stock up on reggae, gospel and soca at Supertone, jazz

---

TRANSPORT

Tube stations *Bakerloo* Waterloo, Lambeth North; *Northern* Waterloo, Kennington, Oval, Stockwell, Clapham North, Clapham Common, Clapham South; *Victoria* Vauxhall, Stockwell, Brixton

Rail stations *South Eastern Trains* Brixton, Herne Hill; *Southern* Waterloo East; Wandsworth Road, Clapham High Street; Streatham, Tulse Hill, West Norwood, Streatham Common; *South West Trains* Waterloo, Vauxhall; *Thameslink* Loughborough Junction, Herne Hill

Main bus routes *into central London* 2, 3, 35, 36, 42, 45, 59, 68, 77, 77A, 88, 133, 137, 159, 344, 436, X68; *night buses* N2, N3, N35, N44, N68, N77, N133, N137, N155, N159; *24-hour buses* 12, 88, 250, 345

National Film Theatre. *See p218.*

Lambeth

and hip hop at Reds, and soul and roots at Selectors Music Emporium. Coldharbour Lane has some African and West Indian record stores, plus ace furniture store Bleu. Further Brixton worthies are sneaker shop My Trainers and new-age bookstore Book Mongers.

For literature elsewhere, Soma Books in Kennington imports a wide range of texts from India. And, of course, there's the fantastic Riverside Walk Book Market under Waterloo Bridge, in front of the NFT.

In Clapham, tiny Places & Spaces has one of the most interesting selections of furniture, lighting and accessories in London; south on Abbeville Road, Josephine Ryan Antiques & Interiors is an essential stop for chic furniture and trinkets. Nearby, Tessa Fantoni's photo albums, desk accessories and toiletries make excellent gifts, while the branch of high-end toyshop Cheeky Monkeys will delight kids. The Common Sense clinic next to Clapham Common (smell the pun) stocks a host of alternative remedies.

South in Streatham, the High Road has all the usual amenities (and a great many charity shops). More interesting is Cenci,

over in West Norwood: once based in Covent Garden, this vintage clothes store has a fantastic collection from the 1960s.

Bleu *403 Coldharbour Lane, SW9 3QR (7733 4999).*
Book Mongers *439 Coldharbour Lane, SW9 8LN (7738 4225).*
Brixton Market *Electric Avenue, Pope's Road, Brixton Station Road, Atlantic Road, SW9.*
Cenci *4 Nettlefold Place, SE27 0JW (8766 8564/www.cenci.co.uk).*
Cheeky Monkeys *24 Abbeville Road, SW4 9NH (8673 5215/www.cheeky monkeys.com).*
Common Sense *7-7A Clapham Common Southside, SW4 7AA (7720 8817/www.south londonnaturalhealthcentre.com).*
Delicatessen Alberobello *2 Brixton Road, SW9 6BU (7735 2121).*
Di Lieto Bakery & Deli *175 South Lambeth Road, SW8 1XW (7735 1997).*
Funchal Bakery *141 Stockwell Road, SW9 9TB (7733 3134).*
Josephine Ryan Antiques & Interiors *63 Abbeville Road, SW4 9JW (8675 3900/ www.josephineryanantiques.co.uk).*
Korona *30 Streatham High Road, SW16 1DB (8769 6647).*
Madeira Pâtisserie/Luis Deli *46A-46C Albert Embankment, SE1 7TL (7820 1117).*
M Moen & Sons *24 The Pavement, SW4 0JA (7622 1624/www.moen.co.uk).*

Brockwell Park, one of Lambeth's lungs.

My Trainers *3 Brixton Station Road, SW9 8TA (7274 0022/www.mytrainers.com).*
North Street Deli *26 North Street, SW4 0HB (7978 1555).*
Old Post Office Bakery *76 Landor Road, SW9 9PH (7326 4408/www.oldpostoffice bakery.co.uk).*
Places & Spaces *30 Old Town, SW4 0LB (7498 0998/www.placesandspaces.com).*
Reds *500 Brixton Road, SW9 8EQ (7274 4476).*
Riverside Walk Book Market *Outside the National Film Theatre, under Waterloo Bridge, SE1 9PX.*
Ryad Halal Way Butchers & Deli *248 Wandsworth Road, SW8 2JS (7738 8811).*
Selectors Music Emporium *100B Brixton Hill, SW2 1AH (7771 2011).*
Sintra *146-148 Stockwell Road, SW9 9TG (7733 9402).*
Soma Books *38 Kennington Lane, SE11 4LS (7735 2101/www.childrens-books.uk.com).*
Supertone Records, Videos & CDs *110 Acre Lane, SW2 5RA (7737 7761).*
Tessa Fantoni *73 Abbeville Road, SW4 9JN (8673 1253/www.tessafantoni.com).*

Arts & attractions

Cinemas & theatres

BFI London IMAX
1 Charlie Chaplin Walk, SE1 8XR (0870 787 2525/www.bfi.org.uk/incinemas/imax). 3-D spectaculars at the UK's biggest cinema screen.
Clapham Picture House *76 Venn Street, SW4 0AT (7498 3323/www.picturehouses.co.uk).* Arthouse and quality mainstream films.
National Film Theatre *Belvedere Road, South Bank, SE1 8XT (7928 3232/www.bfi.org.uk/ incinemas/nft).* London's best cinema, with an unrivalled programme of retrospective seasons and previews.
Odeon Streatham *44-47 Streatham High Road, SW16 1PW (08712 244 007/www. odeon.co.uk).*
Ritzy *Brixton Oval, Coldharbour Lane, SW2 1JG (7733 2229/www.picturehouses.co.uk).* Much-loved local cinema, with café, jazz bar and Saturday art fairs.
Royal National Theatre *South Bank, SE1 9PX (info 7452 3400/box office 7452 3000/ www.nationaltheatre.org.uk).* Under artistic

director Nicholas Hynter, the National gets better and better. Three theatres (Olivier, Lyttleton, Cottesloe) present an eclectic mix of new plays and classics.

Galleries & museums

Dalí Universe *County Hall Riverside Building, Queen's Walk, SE1 7PB (7620 2720/www. daliuniverse.com).* More than 500 works by surrealist artist Salvador Dali, displayed in suitably labyrinthine galleries.

Florence Nightingale Museum *St Thomas's Hospital, 2 Lambeth Palace Road SE1 7EW (7620 0374/www.florence-nightingale. co.uk).* Honours the remarkable life and Crimean war work of 'the lady with the lamp'.

Hayward Gallery *South Bank Centre, SE1 8XX (0870 380 0400/www.hayward.org.uk).* One of London's major contemporary art galleries.

Museum of Garden History *Lambeth Palace Road, SE1 7LB (7401 8865/ www.cix.co.uk/~museumgh).* The world's first horticultural museum, complete with replica 17th-century knot garden.

The Type Museum *100 Hackford Road, SW9 0QU (7735 0055/www.typemuseum.org).* Printing and typographical exhibitions.

Music & comedy venues

Brixton Academy *211 Stockwell Road, SW9 9SL (7771 3000/www.brixton-academy.co.uk).* Major concert venue staging anyone from US death metal bands to crooners such as James Blunt.

South Bank Centre *Belvedere Road, SE1 8XX (0870 380 0400/www.rfh.org.uk).* Three concert halls – the Royal Festival Hall, the smaller Queen Elizabeth Hall, and the tiny Purcell Room – covering classical and contemporary music and dance. The RFH is closed until June 2007 for major redevelopment.

Other attractions

British Airways London Eye *Riverside Building, next to County Hall, Westminster Bridge Road, SE1 7PB (0870 500 0600/www. ba-londoneye.com).* Superb views over London and beyond from the capital's favourite new icon.

London Aquarium *County Hall, Riverside Building, Westminster Bridge Road, SE1 7PB (7967 8000/www.londonaquarium.co.uk).* One of Europe's largest exhibitions of global aquatic life, displayed in giant tanks and touch pools.

Open spaces

Agnes Riley Gardens *Atkins Road, Clapham Park, SW12.*

Brockwell Park *Dulwich Road, SE24.* Large hilly park, with café, children's play area, sports facilities and Brockwell Lido (*see p220*).

Clapham Common *Windmill Drive, SW4.* Clapham's major asset has ponds, cafés, a paddling pool and acres of grass for lounging.

Hillside Gardens *Hillside Road, SW2.*
Jubilee Gardens *Belvedere Road, SE1.* Next to the London Eye.
Kennington Park *Kennington Park Road, SE11.* Historic meeting place now hosts festivals; facilities for tennis, football, cricket and netball.
Larkhall Park *Courland Grove, SW8.*
Max Roach Park *Brixton Road, SW9.*
Myatt's Fields Park *Cormont Road, SE5.*
Norwood Park *Salters Hill, SE19.* Walk to the top of the hill for great views of London.
Ruskin Park *Denmark Hill, SE5.*
Spring Gardens *Tyers Street, SE11.*
Streatham Common *Streatham High Road, SW16.* Woods, grassland, wild flower meadows, two paddling pools and fab views.
Vauxhall City Farm *165 Tyers Street, SE11.*
Vauxhall Park *Lawn Lane, SW8.* Victorian-style park with play area and model village.
Waterloo Millennium Green *Waterloo Road, SE1.*

Sport & fitness

Lambeth is home to over a quarter of a million Londoners, almost 60 per cent under 35, yet it has only five council-owned sports centres (admittedly, one of these is the enormous six-storey Brixton Recreation Centre). Private clubs range from small operations squeezed between big buildings and main roads to large facilities in quieter, more remote areas. Unique to the borough is London's only exclusively gay, all-male club, the Paris Gym in Vauxhall.

Gyms & leisure centres

Brixton Recreation Centre *27 Brixton Station Road, SW9 8QQ (7926 9780/ www.lambeth.gov.uk).*
Clapham Leisure Centre *141 Clapham Manor Street, SW4 2AU (7926 0700/ www.lambeth.gov.uk).*

Ferndale Community Sports Centre
*Nursery Road, SW9 8PB (7733 4282/
www.lambeth.gov.uk).*
Fitness First (*www.fitnessfirst.co.uk*) *Basement,
London Bridge Hotel, 80-81 London Bridge
Street, SE1 9SG (7378 7811); Blue Star House,
234-244 Stockwell Road, SW9 9FP (7733 5522).*
Private.
Flaxman Sports Centre *Carew Street, SE5
9DF (7926 1054/www.lambeth.gov.uk).*
Holmes Place (*www.holmesplace.co.uk*)
*4-20 North Street, SW4 0HB (7819 2555);
20 Ockley Road, SW16 1UB (8769 8686).*
Private.
Oval Health & Fitness Club *The Oval,
SE11 5SS (7820 5755/www.surreycricket.com).*
Private.
Paris Gym *73 Goding Street, SE11 5AW
(7735 8989/www.parisgym.com).* Men only;
private.
Soho Gym *95-97 Clapham High Street,
SW4 7TB (7720 0321/www.sohogyms.com).*
Private.
South Bank Club *124-130 Wandsworth
Road, SW8 2LD (7622 6866/www.southbank
club.co.uk).* Private.
Streatham Leisure Centre *384 High
Road, SW16 6HX (7926 6744/www.lambeth.
gov.uk).*
21st Century Gym *33 Westow Hill, SE19
1TQ (8655 7367).* Private.

Other facilities
Brockwell Lido *Lido Park Gardens,
Brockwell Park, Dulwich Road, SE24 0PA
(7274 3088/www.thelido.co.uk).* This lovely
1930s lido reopened in summer 2005 after
an impressive revamp.
Streatham Ice Arena *386 Streatham High
Road, SW16 6HT (8769 7771/www.streatham
icearena.co.uk).*

Spectator sports
The Oval *Surrey County Cricket Club,
Kennington, SE11 5SS (7582 6660/
www.surreycricket.com).*

Schools

WHAT THE PARENTS SAY:
❛Lambeth's primary schools are decent and
reasonably plentiful. Some are very good, though
to get into these you have to be careful choosing
where you live. You also have to be lucky; every
year, admissions policies are different.

At secondary level, Dunraven School in
Streatham is popular (and over-subscribed)
and Lilian Baylis Technology School in Oval is
doing well in a brand-new building, with a very
talented head teacher leading from the front.

On the whole, though, the borough is a
nightmare at secondary level. There are far
too few year seven places, and the majority of

families have to move. That said, parents have
been vigorously campaigning for years to get
Lambeth to invest in new secondary schools
and we've had some success. Lambeth Academy
in Clapham opened in September 2004 and is
hugely over-subscribed (about 1,000 applicants
for 180 places each year). The school is off to a
brilliant start; it accepts all local children without
making them sit an exam. Another school like
this will open in Norwood in September 2007,
and yet another in East Brixton in September
2008. Parents are also campaigning for the
Nelson Mandela School to open on Brixton
Hill, in the centre of the borough.

Most of the secondary school places in Lambeth
are at faith schools and girls' schools (60 per cent
each); coupled with the general shortage of year
seven places, this means that 70 per cent of
children aged 11-18 are being educated outside
the borough. The council is not moving as
quickly on this as local people would like.❜
Devon Allison, mother of two and chair of the
Secondary Schools Campaign in Lambeth

Primary
There are 59 state primary schools in Lambeth,
22 of which are church schools. There are also
ten independent primary schools, including one
French school. See www.lambeth.gov.uk
www.ofsted.gov.uk for more information.

Secondary
Elmcourt School – set up by a group of parents
with the support of Lambeth council – will open
in West Norwood in September 2007. See
www.elmcourt.co.uk.

Archbishop Tenison's CE School *55
Kennington Oval, SE11 5SR (7735 3771).*
Boys only.
Bishop Thomas Grant RC School *Belltrees
Grove, SW16 2HY (8769 3294/www.btg-
secondary.lambeth.sch.uk).*
Charles Edward Brooke CE School
Langton Road, SW9 6UL (7274 6311).
Girls only.
Dunraven School *94-98 Leigham Court
Road, SW16 2QB (8677 2431/www.dunraven-
school.org.uk).*
Lambeth Academy *Elms Road, SW4 9ET
(7498 5004/www.lambeth-academy.org).*
Lilian Baylis Technology School
*323 Kennington Lane, SE11 5QY (7091
9500).*
London Nautical School *61 Stamford
Street, SE1 9NA(7928 6801/www.lns.org.uk).*
Boys only.
Norwood School *Crown Dale, SE19 3NY
(8670 9382/www.norwood-secondary.
lambeth.sch.uk).* Girls only.
La Retraite RC School *Atkins Road, SW12
0AB (8673 5644/www.laretraiteclapham
school.co.uk).* Girls only.

St Martin-in-the-Fields CE School *155 Tulse Hill, SW2 3UP (8674 5594/www.st martins.lambeth.sch.uk).* Girls only.
Stockwell Park High School *Clapham Road, SW9 0AL (7733 6156/www.stockpark. lambeth.sch.uk).*

Property

WHAT THE AGENTS SAY:

❛Kennington is a forgotten area, but it's cracking in terms of architecture – we have some perfect Georgian terraces and grade II listed properties dating back to 1750. Half of Kennington is in the Congestion Charge zone, although it doesn't seem to make any difference to people moving here. It's not really a young, trendy area, but there are good restaurants and pubs that are fairly laid-back. It's also very popular with the gay community and thirtysomething couples. Transport is a main attraction, with the Victoria and Northern lines, and lots of buses and cycle routes. It's easy to get to Canary Wharf, the City and the West End.

Vauxhall is doing well at the moment. Generally, expectations have lowered and people are willing to pay a lot more for property in this area as they see it as an investment. Geographically, it's central London yet still feels quite suburban. Because Stockwell was bombed during World War II, architecture is a real mix: council estates (some of which are quite ugly), beautiful garden squares and old houses.❜
Justin Bhoday, Kinleigh, Folkard & Hayward, Kennington office

Average property prices
Detached £464,336
Semi-detached £349,184
Terraced £293,298
Flat £194,991

Local estate agents
Aspire *www.aspire.co.uk; 2 offices in the borough (Clapham South 8675 1222/North Clapham 7840 3700).*
Harmens *www.harmens.co.uk; 2 offices in the borough (Brixton 7737 6000/Streatham 8769 4777).*
Hooper & Jackson *76 Streatham High Road, SW16 1BS (8769 8000/www.hooper jackson.com).*
Keating Estates *25 Clapham Common South Side, W4 7AB (7720 2113/www.keating estates.com).*
Martin Barry *www.findaproperty.co.uk/ martinbarry; 2 offices in the borough (Brixton 7738 5866/Clapham 7720 7237).*

Murray Estates *92-96 Stockwell Road, SW9 9HR (7733 4203/www.murrayestates.com).*
Opendoors Estates *91 Acre Lane, SW2 5TU (7733 4000/www.opendoorsestates.com).*
Time2move *www.time2move.com; 2 offices in the borough (Streatham 8769 9999/West Norwood 8670 2000).*

Other information

Council
Lambeth Council *Town Hall, Brixton Hill, SW2 1RW(7926 1000/Lambeth advice line 7926 9000/www.lambeth.gov.uk).*

Hospitals
Kings College Hospital *Denmark Hill, SE5 9RS (7737 4000/www.kingsch.nhs.uk).*
Lambeth Hospital *108 Landor Road, SW9 9NT (7411 6190/www.slam.nhs.uk).*
St Thomas' Hospital *Lambeth Palace Road, SE1 7EH (7188 7188/www.guysandstthomas. nhs.uk).*

Legal services
Lambeth Law Centre *7737 9780/www.lambeth.gov.uk.*
Streatham Hill CAB *Ilex House, 1 Barrhill Road, SW2 4RJ (8715 0707/www.adviceguide.org.uk).*

Local newspapers
Lambeth Life *7926 2485/www.lambeth.gov.uk.* Distributed free by the council and also available online.
South London Press & The Streatham Post *8769 4444/http://icsouthlondon.ic network.co.uk.*
Streatham Guardian *8646 6336/ www.streathamguardian.co.uk.*

Allotments
Lorn Road Allotments *Lorn Road, SW9 (Lambeth Parks 7926 9000, option 7).*
Rosendale Allotments Association *227 Rosendale Road, SE21 8LR (www.rosendale-allotments.org.uk).*
Streatham Vale Allotments, *SW16, c/o Streatham Vale Property Occupiers Association (www.svpoa.org.uk).*
Vauxhall Allotments *Tyers Street, SE11, c/o Vauxhall City Farm, 24 St Oswald's Place, SE11 5JE (7582 4204).*

Lambeth

*'Every building and
street has a history – it's a
lifetime's work getting
to know it all.'*

Marion Marples, pastoral care worker, Southwark Cathedral

Southwark

Old London is becoming rejuvenated, and nowhere is this more apparent
than in Southwark. Here a new tube extension, a reinvention of an old
market, an art gallery made from a disused power station and – across
the borough – widespread refurbishment of Victorian properties have
worked wonders.

Neighbourhoods

Borough and Bankside

Southwark, more than any other borough,
represents London regeneration, and
Borough and Bankside are arguably its
brightest examples to date. Bankside's
south-eastern stretch of riverfront runs
from the Oxo Tower's stylised restaurant
and retail units to the cobbled backstreets
and high-end eateries of Butler's Wharf,
taking in numerous intrigues along the way.
Its incredible revival has been accelerated
by the opening of the thatched Shakespeare's
Globe theatre in 1997, and Tate Modern
art gallery in 2000, the latter famously
converted from a tall-chimneyed power
station. In their wake, restaurants and bars
have mushroomed in the once-downbeat
surrounding area. Another modern icon in
these parts is the architect Norman Foster's
pedestrian-only Millennium Bridge (still
referred to as 'the wobbly bridge' as it
had to be closed for this reason soon after
opening), which affords a romantic vista of
the Thames and St Paul's Cathedral opposite.

Next to Tower Bridge, the glass-and-steel
City Hall, also designed by Foster, is where
the Mayor of London's office is based; there
is public access to its foyer and occasionally
the top-floor panorama, known as 'London's
Living Room'. Alongside the building,
there's a concrete amphitheatre ('the Scoop'),
which hosts excellent free entertainment
(open-air film screenings and performance)
in summer. You'll often find interesting art
installations around here too. This enclave,

Southwark

Southwark

COMMERCIAL ROAD
TOWER HAMLETS
INDIA DOCK RD
THE HIGHWAY
River Thames
WESTFERRY ROAD

BLACKFRIARS BRIDGE
SOUTHWARK BRIDGE
LONDON BRIDGE
Tate Modern
Southwark
Borough Market
TOWER BRIDGE
ROTHERHITHE TUNNEL
A200
City Hall
Rotherhithe
Ecological Park
BRUNEL ROAD

YORK ROAD
Waterloo
BOROUGH
London Bridge
JAMAICA ROAD
Bermondsey
Canada Water
ROTHERHITHE

Lambeth North
Borough
Guy's Hospital
A24
BERMONDSEY
Surrey Quays
LOWER
ROAD

Imperial War Museum
NEWINGTON
NEW KENT ROAD
SOUTHWARK PARK ROAD
Southwark Park
ROTHERHITHE NEW ROAD
South Bermondsey
A200
EVELYN ROAD

KENNINGTON PARK RD
Elephant & Castle
GREAT DOVER ROAD
WALWORTH
OLD KENT ROAD
ROTHERHITHE NEW ROAD

KENNINGTON ROAD
Kennington
WALWORTH ROAD
Burgess Park
LEWISHAM WAY

CAMBERWELL NEW ROAD
CAMBERWELL
A215
PECKHAM ROAD
A202 QUEENS ROAD
Queens Road Peckham

BRIXTON ROAD
LAMBETH
St Giles Church
The Maudsley Hospital
Peckham Rye
Nunhead

COLDHARBOUR LANE
DENMARK HILL
Denmark Hill
EVALINA ROAD
Nunhead Cemetery

East Dulwich
NUNHEAD
Peckham Rye Common

HERNE HILL
HERNE HILL
EAST DULWICH
Peckham Rye Park
Aquarius Golf Course

Herne Hill
North Dulwich
Camberwell New Cemetery

LORDSHIP LANE
Camberwell Old Cemetery
LEWISHAM

CROXTED ROAD
DULWICH
Dulwich College
Dulwich Park
STANSTEAD ROAD

Belair Park
THURLOW PARK ROAD
West Dulwich
Dulwich & Sydenham Golf Course
A205 LONDON RD

KNIGHTS HILL
SYDENHAM HILL
Dulwich Wood
SYDENHAM ROAD

CROXTED ROAD SOUTH
Sydenham Hill
CRYSTAL PALACE PARK ROAD
BROMLEY

0   1 km
0   1 mile

© Copyright Time Out Group 2006

the oddly named, ultra-slick More London, links the riverfront to Tooley Street. Nearby, Hay's Galleria has an impressive atrium dating back to the mid 19th century, when it formed part of a wharf. Quirky shops and crafts stalls now fill the interior.

Borough High Street combines offices, convenience stores and an international student population (Guy's/St Thomas's Medical School is nearby) – but the obvious focal point is Borough Market, with its gourmet food stalls and rich history (records date from 1276 when the market caused traffic jams on London Bridge). Open on Fridays and Saturdays, it's massively popular with visitors. The market and its surrounding area are also extremely atmospheric, and have provided a backdrop for numerous films, including *Bridget Jones's Diary* and *Lock, Stock and Two Smoking Barrels*. The district offers great choices for eating out – the Cut, near Southwark tube station (on the border with Lambeth, *see p206*), is worth a look too.

History and entertainment are often entwined around here – from a replica of Sir Francis Drake's ship, the *Golden Hinde*, to the London Dungeon, Clink Prison Museum and Old Operating Theatre Museum. Even stately Southwark Cathedral, dating back to the 13th century, is occasionally a venue for avant-garde music events. The local pubs once attracted the likes of Shakespeare and Chaucer; their modern (and not so modern) equivalents are still doing a roaring trade.

The City is mere minutes away, via three bridges – Southwark, London and Tower – lining up in quick succession; or there's the major transport interchange of London Bridge station, plus tube stops at Southwark and Borough.

Newington, Elephant & Castle and Walworth

Sandwiched between Borough and Bermondsey, Newington is not to be confused with Stoke Newington in Hackney (*see p73*). In fact, this whole district is generally referred to as Elephant & Castle, distinctive for its two horrendously busy roundabouts, its shopping centre (which, until the late 1990s, was painted a gaudy pink; it is due to be demolished in 2010 in a local regeneration programme), the imposing Metropolitan Tabernacle Church, and dingy subways. Though the area is

visually unappealing, you'll find a few interesting shops and continental delis.

Elephant & Castle has also forged a strong reputation for nightlife, including Britain's original superclub, the Ministry of Sound, which celebrated its 14th birthday in 2005, and more recently the Coronet, converted from an old cinema. On the cultural side, the impressive Imperial War Museum operates various temporary exhibitions throughout the year, as well as displaying its stock collection of guns, war toys and frontline poetry.

The network of A-roads in the locality includes the Old Kent Road (the cheapest square on the Monopoly board) and New Kent Road (which forms part of the Congestion Zone boundary). Heading towards Camberwell, Walworth Road contains a variety of takeaways, including a handy 24-hour bagel bakery. It's also notable for the cheap and cheerful East Street Market, with stalls selling fruit 'n' veg, clothes and household goods. Head towards the border with Lambeth borough, and the backstreets blossom into Surrey Gardens and relatively sedate residential squares: a jumble of spruced-up terraces and sprawling council estates.

Bermondsey

From its original rough reputation and industrial roots (evoked in addresses such as Leathermarket Street), this part of town has steadily emerged as a fashionable place in which to live. Bermondsey is another neighbourhood that has been made more accessible by 1999's extension to the Jubilee Line tube, which boasts some of the smartest stations in the capital. Bermondsey Street bears the most obvious signs of the new prosperity, featuring arty cafés, studios and boutiques, and most prominently, the zany multi-hued façade of the Fashion & Textiles Museum, founded by the designer and local resident Zandra Rhodes.

The RV1 bus service is a pleasant, deliberately meandering route through the area, ending up across the river in Covent Garden; it's aimed at holidaymakers, but used by everybody. You can pick it up on Tooley Street, by London Bridge station.

Bermondsey was once known as 'London's Larder' because of its concentration of food-processing plants, including national institutions Crosse & Blackwell and Jacobs.

Although none of these businesses remains in the neighbourhood, various manufacturing works and warehouses have been converted into exclusive gated communities; one prime example is the former Hartley's Jam factory off Tower Bridge Road, which now comprises expensive apartments – and still seems at odds with the surrounding estates.

A long-time local draw is Bermondsey Antiques Market, also known as the New Caledonian Market. This has shaken off its reputation for stolen goods, and opens on Fridays from before dawn until midday. It draws more than 500 traders every week, with a focus on British vintage.

Rotherhithe

Rotherhithe's historic docks had all closed down by the 1980s. The central Surrey Docks was renamed Surrey Quays and is now given over to a utilitarian shopping and entertainment complex alongside Canada Water, including a multiplex cinema and bowling alley. There's still a rather desolate feel to the district – sprawling roads and car parks – but flocks of swans lend an elegant air to the waterside development, which includes high-rise Docklands residences.

Independent shops are concentrated around Lower Road, while South Dock Marina (the capital's largest working marina, with over 200 berths) provides a swanky contrast. For a sense of this neighbourhood's heritage, stroll or cycle along the scenic Thames Path. Here you'll find such landmarks as Brunel Engine House, where the world's first underwater path was opened in 1843. Originally a foot tunnel, it now forms part of the East London tube line.

Rotherhithe once accommodated a Scandinavian seafaring community, and Swedish, Norwegian and Finnish churches remain in the area; you'll come across addresses such as Helsinki Square and Queen of Denmark Court too. This is also where the Pilgrim Fathers set sail for the New World in 1620; their ship lends its name to the Mayflower – one of several highly popular boozers with riverside views.

Camberwell

Built around the old village green, Camberwell has a church that predates the Domesday Book. Today's church of St Giles, the patron saint of cripples, features stained-glass windows by one-time resident John Ruskin. Camberwell rapidly expanded in Victorian times, bequeathing attractive terraced architecture, though the jewel in its crown, Camberwell Grove, also features listed Georgian properties.

Stray World War II bombs aimed at the City destroyed much north of the green, which today consists of uninspiring estates and occasional pockets of Victoriana. The green itself has a certain jaded charm and provides a community hub. The best roads for property lie south of Camberwell Church Street, running east from the Grove and offering relatively good value considering their proximity to central London.

There are two major hospitals on Denmark Hill: King's College and the Maudsley, treating body and mind respectively. Immediately south of King's College Hospital (just inside Lambeth's borders) is Ruskin Park, with impressive views of the Houses of Parliament.

The arts flourish here too, with the Camberwell College of Arts and South London Gallery testament to Ruskin's memory. This vibrant mix of hospital staff and art students (many of whom stay on in the area), plus a strong post-war Caribbean and Greek-Cypriot influence, give the

Highs & Lows

Borough Market Endorsed by many a celebrity chef, and a *Time Out* favourite, this is foodie heaven. Prices are high, but quality matches

Literary past *The Canterbury Tales* began here, Dickens set many a scene here, and some chap called Shakespeare put on a few plays here

Allotments Southwark has more than any other central borough

Elephant & Castle roundabout Surely one of the most visually unappealing spots in London; bring on the regeneration

Secondary education Top-notch private schools, but lousy state ones – so poorer parents suffer

No tube Once you get past Elephant & Castle, you're relying on trains and buses, so it can feel very cut off. Locals tend to see this as a plus

The old **Hartley's Jam factory**, now a landmark apartment development.

neighbourhood a creative buzz. The influx of young professionals, once held back because of the lack of the tube, continues apace as more and more Londoners realise the benefits of the bus and Camberwell's central position on the network. Denmark Hill station offers a rail alternative.

Peckham and Nunhead

Unfairly pigeon-holed by fools, horses and the tragic death of Damilola Taylor, Peckham is a neighbourhood of two halves. The area north of Peckham Road was completely flattened in the war and comprises the uninspiring Burgess Park and the estates that give Peckham its hackneyed image. However, over £300m has been invested here since the mid 1990s. South of Peckham Road you'll find a charming architectural mix of Regency, Georgian and Victorian properties, mainly situated west of Rye Lane, and getting ever more desirable stretching south towards East Dulwich.

The Regency villas of Holly Grove and nearby detached houses are as highly sought-after now as they were when suburban Peckham was renowned for market gardening in the 1800s. Bellenden Road, home to design shops, excellent restaurants and funky street architecture, forms a community hub to the largely Victorian housing of the locale; and Will Alsop's striking, award-winning library is a recent improvement. Nevertheless, the heart

and soul of Peckham proper is Rye Lane and its markets, supporting a cosmopolitan and colourful community. East of here remains fairly desolate. The same cannot be said of Peckham Rye Park and Common (shared with East Dulwich and Nunhead), one of south London's greatest green spaces where the boy William Blake had his vision of angels in the oak trees.

Nunhead, the forgotten man of SE15, lies east of the park and is split in two by the old cemetery, now an important and highly valued nature reserve. Property here remains quietly popular, and there is the boon of the Aquarius Golf Course.

East Dulwich and Herne Hill

The march upmarket of East Dulwich began in the mid 1990s and has continued with a speed to rival that of the late 19th century, when nearly all the uniformly attractive Victorian properties were built. Not many neighbourhoods have such charmingly homogeneous architecture, with red-brick, gables and decorative finials in abundance. The area's spine is busy Lordship Lane, where almost every shop is now a designer bar, restaurant, organic specialist or estate agent. The icing on the cake is the recent arrival of award-winning organic butcher's, William Rose (decamped from Kennington because of the congestion charge).

North Cross Road juts east with some arty shops and a weekend market specialising in organic and speciality foods,

Southwark

but the rest of the branches off Lordship Lane are quiet residential streets ideally suited to couples and young families. Goose Green, at the bottom of Lordship Lane, is the old village centre backed by some lovely tall townhouses not far from the main train station and a Sainsbury's. Heading south means heading uphill, where some properties have sublime views of the Houses of Parliament and the City. The heights of East Dulwich are sandwiched between the lungs of Dulwich and Peckham Rye Parks. They are the first major hills to the south of London. The district was badly bombed in the Blitz – but here damaged property was sympathetically restored.

To the west lies Herne Hill, a largely residential area bordered by Brixton, Brockwell Park and East Dulwich Grove. Housing stock is mainly Victorian and Edwardian, on tree-lined streets off Half Moon Lane. There's a peppering of shops and restaurants, and a small but lively centre around Herne Hill train station. The park (inside Lambeth's borders) is a major attraction – particularly its 1930s Lido in the summer – hosting major events and commanding one of London's finest views. Sadly, the surrounding traffic is often gridlocked.

Dulwich and Sydenham Hill

The fact that Dulwich retains its village charm, now coupled with a highly exclusive feel, owes much to an Elizabethan actor by the name of Edward Alleyn, who set up Dulwich College to help educate the poor. On his death, the freehold of the land passed to the College which, ever since, has blocked the overdevelopment of the area (the toll on College Road, instituted in 1789, is still in force and currently stands at £1). The College is now one of the best private schools in London.

Good schools and green spaces equate to high property prices in London; Dulwich doesn't disappoint. Dulwich Village is name to both village and road and is the epicentre of the area. It has a countrified, refined feel. The architecture is largely grand Georgian in style, with many of the newer properties well-built replicas bordered by a smattering of Edwardian terraces. The Dulwich Picture Gallery is one of the finest art galleries in London; there's a strong literary heritage too, with writers like PG Wodehouse and

Raymond Chandler former College pupils. Byron also schooled here.

Dulwich Park is extremely well kept, with excellent children's facilities, boating lake and sporting areas. South of the traffic-choked A205 lies yet more playing fields, a golf course and the Dulwich/Sydenham Hill Woods: once renowned for highwaymen, now reserved for nature. Sydenham Hill is a varied mix of large detached houses, terraced flats and a tired high street that seems to be slowly on the turn.

Restaurants & cafés

The stretch along and just behind the riverfront has the giant's share of good eateries in this borough. Once you leave Waterloo behind, there's Oxo Tower (two Modern European restaurants with great views, and a bar) and Baltic (stylish Polish) before you get to Bankside. The opening of Tate Modern and the blossoming of Borough Market has led to a huge amount of restaurant activity in the area (some of it within the Tate itself, as with the café on the second floor). There are quite a few big chains – Pizza Express, inevitably – but also some smaller, more interesting ones: Turkish mini-chain Tas has several outlets (Tas, Tas Café and Tas Pide); plus there's a branch of the Real Greek Souvlaki & Bar, and one of ace baker's Konditor & Cook. Must-visit one-offs include bustling no-bookings-taken Tapas Brindisa, intimate Swedish joint Glas and new, big-noise British restaurant Roast. A Julyan Wickam-designed steel and glass edifice holds fish!, while Vinopolis is home to Cantina Vinopolis (and Wine Wharf wine bar, see p231). Closer to Borough tube is South American snack bar El Vergel.

Around London Bridge station are Fina Estampa and Tito's (both Peruvian), Champor-Champor and Georgetown (both Malaysian), Kwan Thai (Thai), and, at the station, a branch of French baker's Paul. Slightly south east of here there's charming Mod Brit restaurant/gallery Delfina, then Bermondsey Kitchen (more Modern British cooking, in a wine bar setting) and a couple of gastropubs, Garrison and the Hartley, plus pie and mash stalwart M Manze's.

Between Tower Bridge and the Design Museum (home to the excellent Modern European Blueprint Café) are a clutch of

Conran places: Butlers Wharf Chop House, Cantina del Ponte and Le Pont de la Tour, all with views over the river. Otherwise the area holds chains such as Ask and Pizza Express, plus upmarket Italian Tentazioni. Further south into Bermondsey is another Italian, budget-concious Arancia.

The unlovely Elephant & Castle complex boasts a branch of Nando's; otherwise nearby there's Pizzeria Castello; further into Walworth is WJ Arment's pie and mash shop. Camberwell is similiarly bereft of decent places to eat – there's another Nando's on Denmark Hill, Chumleigh Gardens Café in Burgess Park and pizza joint Mozzarella e Pomodoro at Camberwell Green. And it's the same story in Peckham, where there are a couple of pie and mash places (M Manze's and Bert's), an appealing café, Petitou, and low key South Indian Ganapati. East Dulwich does rather better, with the Green (family-friendly brasserie), Franklins (small British restaurant and bar), Sea Cow (excellent fish and chips), Upstairs at the EDT (decent pizza place above a pub), the Palmerston (gastropub) and – most interesting of the lot – Green & Blue (wine bar-cum-shop).

Dulwich is the biggest puzzle, however; there's lots of money sloshing about, and very few places in which to spend it. There are a few chain restaurants, and a couple of cafés – posh Au Ciel and Pavilion Café in the park. But Beauberry House, serving Japanese-French food in an elegant setting, is the only smart option.

Arancia *52 Southwark Park Road, SE16 3RS (7394 1751/www.arancia-uk.co.uk).*
WJ Arment *7 & 9 Westmoreland Road, SE17 2AX (7703 4974).*
Au Ciel *1A Carlton Avenue, SE21 7DE (8488 1111).*
Baltic *74 Blackfriars Road, SE1 8HA (7928 1111).*
Bermondsey Kitchen *194 Bermondsey Street, SE1 3TQ (7407 5719).*
Bert's *3 Peckham Park Road, SE15 6TR (7639 4598).*
Beauberry House *Belair Park, Gallery Road, SE21 7AB (8299 9788).*
Blueprint Café *Design Museum, 28 Shad Thames, SE1 2YD (7378 7031/www.conran.com).*
Butlers Wharf Chop House *Butlers Wharf Building, 36E Shad Thames, SE1 2YE (7403 3403/www.conran.com).*
Cantina del Ponte *Butlers Wharf Building, 36C Shad Thames, SE1 2YE (7403 5403/www.conran.com).*
Cantina Vinopolis *1 Bank End, SE1 9BU (7940 8333/www.cantinavinopolis.com).*

Champor-Champor *62-64 Weston Street, SE1 3QJ (7403 4600/www.champor-champor.com).*
Chumleigh Gardens Café *Chumleigh Gardens, Burgess Park, SE5 0RJ (7525 1070).*
Delfina *50 Bermondsey Street, SE1 3UD (7357 0244/www.delfina.org.uk).*
Fina Estampa *150 Tooley Street, SE1 2TU (7403 1342).*
fish! *Cathedral Street, Borough Market, SE1 9AL (7407 3803/www.fishdiner.co.uk).*
Franklins *157 Lordship Lane, SE22 8HX (8299 9598/www.franklinsrestaurant.com).*
Ganapati *38 Holly Grove, SE15 5DF (7277 2928).*
Garrison *99-101 Bermondsey Street, SE1 3XB (7089 9355/www.thegarrison.co.uk).*
Georgetown *10 London Bridge Street, SE1 9SG (7357 7359).*
Glas *3 Park Street, SE1 9AB (7357 6060).*

STATISTICS
BOROUGH MAKE-UP
Population 251,657
Average weekly pay £496.60
Ethnic origins
 White 63.02%
 Mixed 3.74%
 Asian or Asian British 4.06%
 Black or Black British 25.90%
 Chinese or other 3.28%
Students 13.29%
Retirees 7.96%

HOUSING STOCK
Borough size 28.9km²
No. of households 116,817
Detached 2%
Semi-detached 6%
Terraced 17.6%
Flats (purpose-built) 60.3%
Flats (converted) 13.1%
Flats (both) 73.4%

CRIME PER 1,000 OF POPULATION
(English average in brackets)
Burglary 11 (6.4)
Robbery 9 (1.4)
Theft of vehicle 9 (4.5)
Theft from vehicle 14 (10)
Violence against the person 37 (16.5)
Sexual offences 2 (0.9)

MPs & COUNCIL
MPs *Camberwell & Peckham* Harriet Harman QC (Labour); *Dulwich & West Norwood* Tessa Jowell (Labour); *North Southwark & Bermondsey* Simon Hughes (Liberal Democrat)
CPA 3 stars; improving well

The Green *58-60 East Dulwich Road, SE22 9AX (7732 7575/www.greenbar.co.uk).*
Green & Blue *38 Lordship Lane, SE22 8HJ (8693 9250/www.greenandbluewines.com).*
Hartley *64 Tower Bridge Road, SE1 4TR (7394 7023/www.thehartley.com).*
Konditor & Cook *10 Stoney Street, SE1 9AD (7407 5100/www.konditorandcook.com).*
Kwan Thai *The Riverfront, Hay's Galleria, Tooley Street, SE1 2HD (7403 7373).*
M Manze's *87 Tower Bridge Road, SE1 4TW (7407 2985/www.manze.co.uk).*
M Manze's *105 Peckham High Street, SE15 5RS (7277 6181).*
Mozzarella e Pomodoro *21-22 Camberwell Green, SE5 7AA (7277 2020).*
Oxo Tower Restaurant, Bar & Brasserie *Eighth floor, Oxo Tower Wharf, Barge House Street, SE1 9PH (7803 3888).*
Palmerston *91 Lordship Lane, SE22 8EP (8693 1629).*
Paul *The Vaults, London Bridge Station, Railway Approach, SE1 9SP (7403 7457).*
Pavilion Café *Dulwich Park, SE21 7BQ (8299 1383).*
Petitou *63 Choumert Road, SE15 4AR (7639 2613).*
Pizzeria Castello *20 Walworth Road, SE1 6SP (7703 2556).*
Le Pont de la Tour *36D Shad Thames, SE1 2YE (7403 8403/www.conran.com).*
The Real Greek Souvlaki & Bar *Units 1&2, Riverside House, 2A Southwark Bridge Road, SE1 9HA (7620 0162).*
Roast *The Floral Hall, Borough Market, Stoney Street, SE1 (7940 1300).*
Sea Cow *37 Lordship Lane, SE22 8EW (8693 3111).*
Tapas Brindisa *18-20 Southwark Street, SE1 1TJ (7357 8880/www.brindisa.com).*
Tas *72 Borough High Street, SE1 1XF (7403 7200).*
Tas Café *76 Borough High Street, SE1 1QF (7403 8557).*
Tas Pide *20-22 New Globe Walk, SE1 9DR (7633 9777).*
Tate Modern Café: Level 2 *Second floor, Tate Modern, Sumner Street, SE1 9TG (7401 5014).*
Tentazioni *2 Mill Street, SE1 2BD (7237 1100)*
Tito's *4-6 London Bridge Street, SE1 9SG (7404 7787).*
Upstairs at the EDT *First floor, East Dulwich Tavern, 1 Lordship Lane, SE22 8EW (8693 1817).*
El Vergel *8 Lant Street, SE1 1QR (7357 0057/www.elvergel.co.uk).*

Bars & pubs

Snooty Dulwich, multicultural Elephant and the geezerish 'sarf' all rub shoulders within the Southwark boundaries, resulting in a wide array of drinking options. In areas like

Bermondsey and Rotherhithe you'll find boozers that have sent the Pilgrim Fathers on their way to the New World (the Mayflower), those that serve good food and fine wines to the area's loft-dwelling yuppies (the Garrison, *see p229*), and those that still shelter the Arthur Daleys of this world from the ubiquitous 'Er Indoors (too numerous to mention). Camberwell, Peckham, East Dulwich and Herne Hill are home to a trendier crowd who prefer to do their socialising in the slick surroundings of bars such as Liquorish, the EDT (East Dulwich Tavern), the Sun & Doves, the Old Dispensary, the Commercial or the Castle, before staggering on for some killer cocktails and a dance at Funky Munky.

In Dulwich Village, meanwhile, the pace is more stately, as wonderful old pubs like the Crown & Greyhound offer up their fireside sofas to rosy-cheeked dog walkers and City types in GAP mufti with three-wheel pushchairs in tow. Similarly cosy (although not as grand), Peckham Rye's Clock House and the Palmerston (*see p230*) on bar-saturated Lordship Lane are both good bets. However, despite Elephant's cast-iron nightlife rep (thanks to the world-famous Ministry of Sound, plus the recently converted Coronet), good pubs are very thin on the ground.

The best of the borough's drinking, though, can be found in Borough and neighbouring Southwark itself. Places such as the George Inn, the city's last remaining galleried coaching inn, the deservedly popular Market Porter and the real ale paradise of the Royal Oak are among the finest pubs in London. Also excellent is Wine Wharf, the oenological bar attached to Vinopolis. But the jewel in Southwark's crown must surely be the anachronistic Dulwich Wood House, whose wood-panelled interior (designed by Sir Joseph Paxton of Crystal Palace fame) is straight out of Somerset Maugham.

Castle *65 Camberwell Church Street, SE5 8TR (7277 2601).*
Clock House *196A Peckham Rye, SE22 9QA (8693 2901).*
Commercial *210-212 Railton Road, SE24 0JT (7501 9051).*
Coronet *28 New Kent Road, SE1 6TJ (7701 1500).*
Crown & Greyhound *73 Dulwich Village, SE21 7BJ (8299 4976).*
Dulwich Wood House *39 Sydenham Hill, SE26 6RS (8693 5666).*

East Dulwich Tavern *1 Lordship Lane, SE22 8EW (8693 1316/1817).*
Funky Munky *25 Camberwell Church Street, SE5 8TR (7277 1806).*
George Inn *77 Borough High Street, SE1 1NH (7407 2056).*
Liquorish *123 Lordship Lane, SE22 8HU (8693 7744/www.liquorish.com).*
Market Porter *9 Stoney Street, SE1 9AA (7407 2495).*
Mayflower *117 Rotherhithe Street, SE16 4NF (7237 4088).*
Ministry of Sound *103 Gaunt Street, SE1 6DP (0870 060 0010/www.ministryof sound.com).*
Old Dispensary *325 Camberwell New Road, SE5 0TF (7708 8831).*
Royal Oak *44 Tabard Street, SE1 4JU (7357 7173).*
Sun & Doves *61-63 Coldharbour Lane, SE5 9NS (7733 1525/www.sunanddoves. co.uk).*
Wine Wharf *Stoney Street, SE1 9AD (7940 8335/www.winewharf.co.uk).*

Shops

Borough Market is the best food market in London, with everything from Iberian acorn-fed ham to organic cakes and breads on offer. Its reputation stretches far and wide and Saturday mornings are rightly very busy. Not foodie-oriented but with a charm all its own, Bermondsey Antiques Market (sometimes called New Caledonian Market) specialises in ramshackle

TRANSPORT

Tube stations *Bakerloo* Elephant & Castle; *East London* Rotherhithe, Canada Water, Surrey Quays; *Jubilee* Southwark, London Bridge, Bermondsey, Canada Water; *Northern* Kennington, Elephant & Castle, Borough, London Bridge
Rail stations *South Eastern Trains* London Bridge; Elephant & Castle, Denmark Hill, Peckham Rye, Nunhead; West Dulwich, Sydenham Hill; *Southern* London Bridge, South Bermondsey, Queens Road Peckham, Peckham Rye, East Dulwich, North Dulwich
Main bus routes *into central London* 1, 12, 36, 40, 42, 45, 47, 63, 68, 133, 148, 171, 172, 176, 185, 188, 343, 381, 436, 453; *night buses* N1, N21, N35, N36, N47, N63, N68, N133, N155, N171, N343, N381; *24-hour buses* 12, 37, 53, 148, 176, 345, 453

Victoriana, including delicate plates, silver-plated cutlery and jewellery.

Elephant & Castle is probably best known for its hideous central shopping centre (demolition and redevelopment is planned for 2010), but the neighbourhood's East Street Market is a fun, bustling place to pick up food and essentials. Heading north-east, options get swisher: on the banks of the river in the very corner of the borough, is the Oxo Tower, with its numerous small design shops and studios. Among those that shine out are Bodo Sperlein's delicate porcelain, work by designer-enamelists at Studio Fusion and stained-glass designs from Kate Maestri. Further east along the river, Hay's Galleria is a draw, with its historic atrium sheltering the likes of stylish gift shop Obsessions and the Christmas Shop, which sells baubles, tinsel and seasonal regalia all year round. Further along, fitness freaks should check out the massive branch of the French sports superstore Decathlon (the only outlet in the capital) in Surrey Quay's large shopping complex. Sited in two neighbouring annexes, it caters for any active pursuit you can imagine.

In Camberwell and Peckham, pickings are slimmer. Peckham's Rye Lane and its surrounding markets, purveying fruit, veg and all the usuals, keep the neighbourhood ticking; there's also a farmers' market on Sunday mornings in Peckham Square. Elsewhere, shopping is cheap and plentiful, though the High Street is tired. In Camberwell, seek out Mixed Blessings, a Caribbean bakery. Old-school purveyor Men's Traditional Shoes, in business since 1861, is also an interesting stop; labels include Trickers, Church's and Loakes.

In the south of the borough, dinky gift shops suit Dulwich's genteel air. Dulwich Trader on Croxted Road (the border with Lambeth) has a well-edited collection of furniture, clothing, ceramics and textiles, including Cath Kidston, Lulu Guinness and jewellery from Lola Rose. Stock comes from 200 suppliers at Grace & Favour, many of them independent; look for hand-dyed shirts, antique birdcages and cushions. Dulwich Garden Centre is an excellent place to stock up with all things horticultural. There's also the excellent Dulwich Music Shop, with its range of wind, brass and stringed instruments. In food terms, there's

Southwark

rich – and smelly – pickings at the Cheese Block (over 250 types of cheese), Italian and Spanish artisan products at East Dulwich Deli, pan-Asian supplies at Fusebox, and a thorough selection of wine at Green & Blue. The area's biggest coup came with the arrival of butcher William Rose.

Herne Hill's Half Moon Lane is packed with interesting one-off shops. You'll find excellent applied arts and masses of unique jewellery designs at the Artemidorus gallery; deli goods at Mimosa; and dance shoes galore at Duo Dance. Family specialists include Merry Go Round (baby and maternity wear), Tales on Moon Lane (children's books) and Just Williams (toys). Near the station, Stardust is a good choice for trendy and unusual gifts.

Artemidorus *27B Half Moon Lane, SE24 9JU (7737 7747).*
Bermondsey Antiques Market *Corner of Bermondsey Street & Long Lane, SE1 4QB (7525 6000/www.southwark.gov.uk).*
Bodo Sperlein *Unit 105, Oxo Tower Wharf, Bargehouse Street, SE1 9PH (7633 9413/ www.bodosperlein.com).*
Borough Market *8 Southwark Street, SE1 1TL (7407 1002/www.boroughmarket.org.uk).*
Cheese Block *69 Lordship Lane, SE22 8EP (8299 3636).*
Christmas Shop *Hay's Galleria, 55A Tooley Street, SE1 2QN (7378 1998/www.thechristmas shop.co.uk).*
Decathalon *Canada Water Retail Park, Surrey Quays Road, SE16 2XU (7394 2000/ www.decathlon.co.uk).*
Dulwich Garden Centre *20-22 Grove Vale, SE22 8EF (8299 1089/www.dulwichgarden centre.co.uk).*
Dulwich Music Shop *2 Croxted Road, SE21 8SW (8766 0202).*
Dulwich Trader *9-11 Croxted Road, SE21 8SZ (8761 3457).*
Duo Dance *11 Half Moon Lane, SE24 9JU (7274 4517/www.duodance.co.uk).*
East Dulwich Deli *15-17 Lordship Lane, SE22 8EW (8693 2525).*
East Street Market *East Street, SE17.*
Fusebox *12 Stoney Street, SE1 9AD (7407 9888/www.fuseboxfoods.com).*
Grace & Favour *35 North Cross Road, SE22 9ET (8693 4400).*
Green & Blue *38 Lordship Lane, SE22 8HJ (8693 9250/www.greenandbluewines.com).*
Just Williams *18 Half Moon Lane, SE24 9HU (7733 9995).*
Kate Maestri *Unit 2.11, Oxo Tower Wharf, Bargehouse Street, SE1 9PH (7620 0330/ www.katemaestri.com).*
Men's Traditional Shoes *171 Camberwell Road, SE5 0HB (7703 4179).*
Merry Go Round *21 Half Moon Lane, SE24 9JU (7737 6452).*

MY VIEW

MARION MARPLES
Pastoral care worker,
Southwark Cathedral

Regeneration has brought a lot of money and expertise into Southwark, but I'm still very aware of the huge gulf between the wealthy riverside area and poorer areas like the Old Kent Road and Peckham. **The constant change and pressure from redevelopment is difficult. As residents, we suffer from 'consultation fatigue' – we give our best response to new plans, only to find that the suggestions are ignored and the plans completely changed.** At the moment I'm most concerned about the proliferation of plans for tall buildings. When you cross Blackfriars Bridge to the south the buildings are on a reasonably human scale, but towers and big developments will destroy the intimate character that just about lingers from our Victorian industrial past. **Developers think that the riverside is up for grabs, ignoring the fact there are communities of people enjoying life as it is, and that even people who come into the area for work want shops and open spaces to enjoy.**

Mimosa *16 Half Moon Lane, SE24 9HU (7733 8838).*

Mixed Blessings *12-14 Camberwell Road, SE5 0EN (7703 9433).*

Obsessions *Hay's Galleria, 55A Tooley Street, SE1 2HD (7403 2374/www.obsessions.co.uk).*

Peckham Farmers' Market *Peckham Square, Peckham High Street, SE15 5QN (7833 0338/ www.lfm.org.uk).*

Rye Lane Market *Rye Lane & around, SE15.*

Stardust *294 Milkwood Road, SE24 0EZ (7737 0199/www.stardustkids.co.uk).*

Studio Fusion *Unit 106, Oxo Tower Wharf, Bargehouse Street, SE1 9PH (7928 3600/www.studiofusiongallery.co.uk).*

Tales on Moon Lane *25 Half Moon Lane, SE24 9JU (7274 5759/www.talesonmoonlane.co.uk).*

William Rose *26 Lordship Lane, SE22 8HD (8693 9191).*

Arts & attractions

Cinemas & theatres

Menier Chocolate Factory *51-53 Southwark Street, SE1 1RU (7907 7060/www.menier chocolatefactory.com).* Arts complex including a gallery, restaurant, theatre and rehearsal space.

Odeon Surrey Quays *Surrey Quays Leisure Park, Redriff Road, SE16 7LL (0871 224 4007).*

Peckham Multiplex *95A Rye Lane, SE15 4ST (0870 0429 399/www.peckhamplex.com)*

The Scoop *South Bank, between London Bridge & Tower Bridge, SE1 (www.morelondon.com).* Open-air sunken amphitheatre featuring drama, street shows, visual arts and music – all for free.

Shakespeare's Globe *21 New Globe Walk, Bankside, SE1 9DT (7401 9919/tours 7902 1500/www.shakespeares-globe.org).* Recreation of the original Elizabethan theatre, complete with thatched roof and standing room for the peasants.

Shunt Vaults *Joiner Street, London Bridge Station, SE1 9SP (7452 3000/www.national theatre.org.uk).* Offbeat theatre in an odd, under-station location.

Galleries & museums

Bramah Museum of Tea & Coffee *40 Southwark Street, SE1 1UN (7403 5650/ www.bramahmuseum.co.uk).* First museum dedicated to the nation's favourite warm drinks.

Brunel Museum *Railway Avenue, SE16 4LF (7231 3840/www.brunelenginehouse.org.uk).* Honours the world's first underwater tunnel.

Clink Prison Museum *1 Clink Street, SE1 9DG (7403 0900/www.clink.co.uk).* Prison exhibition with recreation of original cells.

Design Museum *28 Shad Thames, SE1 2YD (7403 6933/www.designmuseum.org).* Museum of modern and contemporary design.

Dulwich Picture Gallery *Gallery Road, SE21 7AD (8693 5254/www.dulwichpicturegallery. org.uk).* An exquisite collection of old masters, housed in England's first purpose-built art gallery, designed by Sir John Soane in 1811.

Fashion & Textiles Museum *83 Bermondsey Street, SE1 3XF (7407 8664/www.ftmlondon.org).* Pink-and-orange shrine to the fashion industry.

Imperial War Museum *Lambeth Road, SE1 6HZ (7416 5000/www.iwm.org.uk).* Extensive collection of military weapons, war paintings and associated exhibitions, plus a reconstructed Somme trench.

London Dungeon *28-34 Tooley Street, SE1 2SZ (7403 7221/www.thedungeons.com).* Ever-popular recreation of the unpleasant aspects of London's history.

Old Operating Theatre Museum & Herb Garret *9A St Thomas's Street, SE1 9RY (7188 2679/www.thegarret.org.uk).* A 16th-century herb loft and 17th-century operating theatre.

South London Gallery *65 Peckham Road, SE5 8UH (7703 6120/www.southlondon gallery.org).* Contemporary art.

Tate Modern *Bankside, SE1 9TG (7887 8000/ www.tate.org.uk).* Iconic leader of London's modern art scene.

Winston Churchill's Britain at War Experience *64-66 Tooley Street, SE1 2TF (7403 3171/www.britainatwar.co.uk).* Recreation of an Anderson shelter during an air raid.

Other attractions

City Hall *The Queen's Walk, SE1 2AA (7983 4100/www.london.gov.uk).*

Dulwich Festival *8299 1011/www.dulwich festival.co.uk.* Annual shindig of music, theatre, poetry and art, held in May.

Golden Hinde *St Mary Overie Dock, Cathedral Street, SE1 9DG (0870 011 8700/www.golden hinde.co.uk).* Replica of Sir Francis Drake's 16th-century flagship.

HMS Belfast *Morgan's Lane, Tooley Street, SE1 2JH (7940 6300/www.iwm.org.uk).* Retired World War II battlecruiser, open to view.

St Giles Camberwell *81 Camberwell Church Street, SE5 8RB (7703 4504).* Church with stained-glass windows by John Ruskin.

Southwark Cathedral *London Bridge, SE1 9DA (7367 6700/tours 7367 6734/www.dswark. org/cathedral).* Small, handsome cathedral, the oldest of its kind in London.

The changing face of Peckham, at the local **farmers' market**. *See p232.*

Open spaces

Belair Park *Gallery Road, SE21.*
Brenchley Gardens *Brenchley Gardens, SE22.* Small but beautiful flower garden.
Burgess Park *Albany Road, SE5.*
Dulwich Park *College Road, SE21.*
Geraldine Mary Harmsworth Park *Lambeth Road, SE1.* Site of the Imperial War Museum.
Nunhead Cemetery *Limesford Road or Linden Grove, SE15.* An uncultivated but tranquil Victorian resting place.
Nunhead Nature Reserve *Linden Grove & Limesford Road, SE15.*
One Tree Hill *Brenchley Gardens, SE23.*
Peckham Rye Park/Peckham Rye Common *Peckham Rye, SE22.*
Russia Dock Woodlands *Redriff Road, SE16.*
Southwark Park *Southwark Park Road, SE16.* London's oldest municipal park.
Stave Hill Ecological Park *Salter Road, SE16.* Superb views over Docklands.
Sydenham Hill Wood *Sydenham Hill, SE26.* Woodland nature reserve managed by the London Wildlife Trust.

Sport & fitness

Southwark benefits from a well-organised, grant-funded operation called Fusion, which maintains the borough's public leisure facilities. And while the Fusion venture is expanding – its trademark, wipe-clean cardiovascular machines replacing more antiquated sweat boxes – the diversity of Southwark's various community sports centres remains virtually unaltered, each with a personality all its own. Dulwich Leisure Centre and the Colombo Centre are especially worth tracking down, as is the the Surrey Docks Watersports Centre for the more adventurous.

The area also has a some unique private clubs: the recently refurbished Miami Health Club is a well-disguised gem, while the Physical Arts centre is a beacon for wannabe Karate Kids and kick-boxing champions.

Gyms & leisure centres

Camberwell Leisure Centre *Artichoke Place, off Camberwell Church Street, London SE5 8TS (7703 3024/www.fusion-lifestyle.com).*
The Club at County Hall *County Hall, SE1 7BP (7928 4900).* Private.
Colombo Centre *34-68 Colombo Street, SE1 8DP (7261 1658/www.colombo-centre.org).*
Dojo Physical Arts *10-11 Milroy Walk, Upper Ground, SE1 9LW (7928 3000/ www.physical-arts.com).* Private.
Dulwich Leisure Centre *45 East Dulwich Road, SE22 9AN (8693 1833/www.fusion-lifestyle.com).*
Elephant & Castle Leisure Centre *22 Elephant & Castle, SE1 6SQ (7582 5505/ www.fusion-lifestyle.com).*
Fitness Exchange *(www.fitness-exchange.net) Cottons, Tooley Street, SE1 2QN (7403 1171); London Bridge Health & Fitness, Swan Lane, EC4R 3TR (7623 6895).* Private.
Fitness First *First floor, 332-344 Walworth Road, SE17 2NA (7252 4555/www.fitness first.co.uk).* Private.
Hamlets Health Club *Edgar Kail Way, Dog Kennel Hill, SE22 8BD (7274 8707).* Private.
K4 Fitness *127 Stamford Street, SE1 9NQ (7401 9357/www.kclsu.org/k4).* Private.

LivingWell *265 Rotherhithe Street, SE16 5HW (7064 4421/www.livingwell.com)*. Private.
Miami Health Club *208-210 Old Kent Road, SE1 5TY (7703 9811/www.miamihealth club.co.uk)*. Private.
Peckham Pulse Healthy Living Centre *10 Melon Road, SE15 5QN (7525 4999/www. fusion-lifestyle.com)*. Pools currently undergoing structural repairs; scheduled to reopen late 2006.
Seven Islands Leisure Centre *Lower Road, SE16 2TU (7237 3296/www.fusion-lifestyle.com)*.
Surrey Docks Watersports Centre *Rope Street, off Plough Way, Greenland Dock, SE16 7SX (7237 4009/www.fusion-lifestyle.com)*.
Tokei Martial Arts & Fitness Club *Lion Court, 28 Magdalen Street, SE1 2EN (7403 5979/www.tokeicentre.org)*. Private.
Waverley School Sports Centre *Homestall Road, SE22 0NR (7732 2276)*.

Other facilities
Aquarius Golf Club *Marmora Road, SE22 0RY (8693 1626)*
Dulwich Croquet Club *Burbage Road, SE12 7JA (7274 1242/www.dulwichsportsclub.com)*.
Dulwich & Sydenham Hill Golf Club *Grange Lane, College Road, SE21 7LH (8693 3961)*.
Hollywood Surrey Quays *The Mast Leisure Park, Teredo Street, SE16 7LW (7237 3773/ www.hollywoodbowl.co.uk)*. Bowling alley.
London Palace Superbowl *First floor, Elephant & Castle Shopping Centre, SE1 6TE (7277 0001/www.palacebowl.com)*. Bowling alley.

Schools

WHAT THE PARENTS SAY:

❝Primary schools in Southwark don't look very good on paper, but they are improving. A few years ago the three primary schools that everyone was competing to get into were Goodrich, Dog Kennel Hill and Dulwich Village CE, which is quite posh and gets good results. Our daughter couldn't get into any of these; we were 67th on the waiting list for Goodrich. She got into Heber Primary School, which previously had a terrible reputation, poor facilities, and had been put on emergency measures.

A new headmaster joined the year we started looking, and we heard good things through the parent grapevine. Three years on, and Heber is getting better results than Goodrich. There are only 24 kids in my daughter's class, although the school is really broke because they get funding based on numbers. However, the Heber parents' association is really active, and has raised lots of money for new facilities. The school even has a phonics programme sponsored by the *Financial Times*. As the Southwark demographic has changed, a new set of savvy, pushy parents have helped primary schools to improve.

Friends are looking at secondary schools in Southwark, but the state ones have a very bad reputation, plus there aren't enough. The Charter School is four years old and is the only one that anybody wants to get into, although its catchment area gets ever smaller. It has a liberal approach, and the parents are heavily involved. The Waverley School has new sports facilities, but doesn't do well academically. There's a lot of movement to the independent sector after primary. Southwark plays host to three very expensive private schools – Dulwich College, James Allen's Girls' School and Alleyn's – and we are already starting to save just in case we have no other option.❞
Jessica Cargill Thompson, mother of two, East Dulwich

Primary
There are 65 state primary schools in Southwark, 18 of which are church schools. There are also seven independent primary schools, including two faith schools. See www.southwark.gov.uk and www.ofsted.gov.uk for more information.

Secondary
The Academy at Peckham *112 Peckham Road, SE15 5DZ (7703 4417/www.peckham academy.southwark.sch.uk)*.
Alleyn's *Townley Road, SE22 8SU (8557 1500/www.alleyns.org.uk)*. Private.
Archbishop Michael Ramsey Technology College *Farmers Road, Camberwell, SE5 0UB (7701 4166)*.
Aylwin Girls' School *55 Southwark Park Road, SE16 3TZ (7237 9316/www.southwark.tv/ aylwin/agshome.asp)*. Girls only.
Bacon's College *Timber Pond Road, SE16 6AT (7237 1928/www.baconsctc.co.uk)*.
Charter School *Red Post Hill, SE24 9JH (7346 6600/www.charter.southwark.sch.uk)*.
Dulwich College *SE21 7LD (8693 3601/www.dulwich.org.uk)*. Boys only; private.
Geoffrey Chaucer Technology College *Harper Road, SE1 6AG (7407 6877)*.
James Allen's Girls' School *144 East Dulwich Grove, SE22 8TE (8693 1181/ www.jags.org.uk)*. Girls only; private.
Kingsdale School *Alleyn Park, Dulwich, SE21 8SQ (8670 7575)*.
Notre Dame RC Girls' School *118 St George's Road, SE1 6EX (7261 1121)*. Girls only.
Sacred Heart RC School *Camberwell New Road, SE5 0RP (7274 6844)*.
St Michael's RC School *John Felton Road, SE16 4UN (7237 6432)*.
St Saviour's & St Olave's CE School *New Kent Road, SE1 4AN (7407 1843/ www.ssso.southwark.sch.uk)*. Girls only.
Walworth School *Shorncliffe Road, SE1 5UJ (7450 9570)*.
Waverley School *Homestall Road, SE22 0NR (7732 2276)*. Girls only.

Property

WHAT THE AGENTS SAY:

'The north of Southwark doesn't tend to attract many family-oriented buyers. It's more suited to City workers and students who are studying at nearby Guy's Hospital. People move for the central location (within walking distance of the City) plus the exceptional local amenities, the Conran restaurants, Borough Market, museums and theatres. And after all that, it's only a £15 cab fare to Soho and the West End.'
Simon Roy, Hastings International, Rotherhithe

'People who would have once bought in Clapham or Battersea are moving to East Dulwich and Peckham instead, because it's better value. There's no tube, but both rail stations take you into central London. The area around Lordship Lane has changed massively with lots of boutiques and interesting shops appearing. Honor Oak and Forest Hill make for good investments – they have similar transport to Dulwich and it looks there'll be a lot of money being poured into the area soon.'
Alex Patton, Winkworth, Dulwich

'Surrey Quays has been compared to Milton Keynes in the past – not its biggest selling point, agreed – but it's very new, very purpose-built, and it's still growing as an area. There's been a lot of investment and development around the docks and once some bars and restaurants are introduced, it will become less of a soulless housing development and more of a lively area to live.'
Paul Mitchell, Alex Neil, Docklands

Average property prices

Detached £623,621
Semi-detached £316,077
Terraced £245,990
Flat £197,142

Local estate agents

Alex Neil www.alexneil.co.uk; 1 office in the borough (Surrey Quays 7394 9988).

COUNCIL TAX

A	up to £40,000	**£732.51**
B	£40,001-£52,000	**£854.59**
C	£52,001-£68,000	**£976.68**
D	£68,001-£88,000	**£1,098.76**
E	£88,001-£120,000	**£1,342.93**
F	£120,001-£160,000	**£1,587.09**
G	£160,001-£320,000	**£1,831.27**
H	over £320,000	**£2,197.52**

Burnet Ware & Graves www.b-w-g.co.uk; 3 offices in the borough (East Dulwich 8693 4201/Herne Hill 7733 1293/Surrey Quays 7232 0333).
Dulwich & Village Residential www.dulwichhomes.com; 2 offices in the borough (Dulwich 8693 7999/East Dulwich 8693 7999).
Field & Sons 54 Borough High Street, SE1 1XL (7407 1375/www.fieldandsons.co.uk).
Hastings International www.hastings international.com; 3 offices in the borough (Borough 7378 9000/Rotherhithe 7231 4973/ Shad Thames 7407 1066).
Oliver Burn 5 Half Moon Lane, Herne Hill, SE24 9JU (7274 3333/www.oliver burn.com).
Osbourne Stewert 106 Grove Vale, SE11 8DR (8299 1444/www.osbourne-stewart.com).
Roy Brooks 2 Barry Parade, Barry Road, SE22 0JA (8299 3021/www.roybrooks.co.uk).

Other information

Council
Southwark Council Town Hall, 31 Peckham Road, SE5 8UB (7525 5000/www.southwark. gov.uk).

Hospitals
Guy's Hospital St Thomas Street, SE1 9RT (7188 7188/www.guysandstthomas.nhs.uk).
King's College Hospital Dulwich East Dulwich Grove, SE22 3PT (7737 4000/ www.kingsch.nhs.uk).
London Bridge Hospital 27 Tooley Street, SE1 2PR (7407 3100/www.londonbridgehospital.com).
The Maudsley Hospital Denmark Hill, SE5 8AZ (7703 6333/www.slam.nhs.uk).
St Giles Hospital St Giles Road, SE5 7RN (7771 3300).

Legal services
Bermondsey CAB 8 Market Place, Southwark Park Road, SE16 3UQ (0870 121 2016/ www.adviceguide.org.uk).
Cambridge House Law Centre 137 Camberwell Road, SE5 0HF (7703 3051).
Peckham CAB 97 Peckham High Street, SE15 5RS (0870 121 2016/ www.advice guide.org.uk).

Local newspapers
Southwark News/Southwark Weekender 7231 5258/ www.southwarknews.co.uk.
South London Press 8769 4444/http://icsouthlondon.icnetwork.co.uk.

Allotments
For a full list of allotments in the borough, including contact details, visit Southwark Council's website (www.southwark.gov.uk).

'This is a borough of contrasts – often edgy, but always interesting and with areas of incredible architectural and environmental beauty.'

Louise Palmer, schools education manager, Horniman Museum

Lewisham

Stretching from Deptford by the river south to Bromley, Lewisham is a borough undergoing regeneration. Improvements continue apace, sweeping away the architectural assaults suffered after World War II. Locals have always cherished beautiful Blackheath, but there are now excellent reasons to celebrate all of this mercurial, multicultural area.

Neighbourhoods

New Cross and Telegraph Hill

Away from the jarring traffic of the A2, all seems calm in New Cross, the only district in the borough with a tube station. This, and the presence of one of London's best state secondary schools (Haberdashers' Aske's Hatcham College, whose entrance requirements make grown men cry), have made for a most desirable area.

While queuing in traffic you can admire the various sites of Goldsmiths College (University of London), the other fine educational establishment to dominate the district. The Ben Pimlott Building, a dramatic glass and steel construction, is the new landmark on the New Cross

skyline. The huge metal sculpture that sits astride the fifth-floor terrace causes many a double take among bored drivers. Goldsmiths has also moved into the fabulously ornate old Deptford Town Hall building, down the road from its main site on Lewisham Way.

Up the steeply climbing wide roads from all the hullabaloo of the main drag, Telegraph Hill is a largely unspoilt residential area with some impressive Edwardian bay-fronted houses. The park here affords inspiring views over the city and has recently undergone a facelift.

Deptford and St John's

Deptford may not have all the World Heritage Site kudos – and tourist and traffic gridlock – of Greenwich (*see p252*), but it

Lewisham

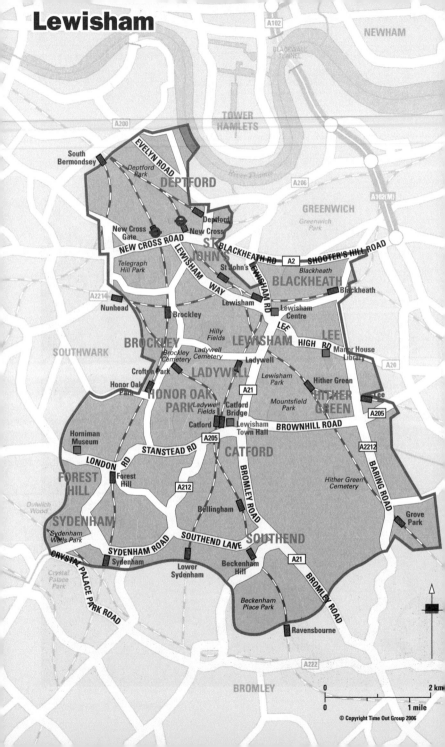

does possess a wealth of inner-city earthiness, history and character. The waterfront area once known as Deptford Strand, selected by Henry VIII as a worthy place for a dockyard, is now prime real estate territory. As the old wharves give way to yet more new blocks of riverside flats, local residents worry about Deptford's character being sacrificed. Safely preserved sites further inland include St Nicholas's Church (where Christopher Marlowe is rumoured to have been buried following his violent end in a Deptford pub), the vast baroque St Paul's church, and Albury Street, a narrow little residential terrace off the High Street, first laid out in 1706-17.

Modern-day Deptford is hugely entertaining. Its High Street, complete with a brilliant market, was rated the best in London according to a formula devised by the Yellow Pages business directory – scoring highly for its diversity and vibrancy. Creekside, following the course of Deptford Creek before it joins the Thames, is Deptford's artists' quarter, full of studios and workshops. Nearby, Laban, Europe's leading contemporary dance centre, is housed in a fascinating, iridescent, coloured-perspex building – a fantastic sight when passed on the DLR. The Creekside Renewal project, completed in 2002, created green spaces like Twinkle Park, the Ahoy Centre for Deptford's modern sailors, and the Ha'penny Hatch Bridge spanning the Creek from Deptford to Greenwich.

St John's is the name given to the district away from the river, called New Deptford when it was developed in the mid 19th century. Now a conservation area, it contains some beautiful Victorian and Edwardian houses around its own station and the loftily spired church of St John.

Blackheath

The pride of the borough, well-to-do Blackheath Village burgeoned in Victorian times with the coming of the railway. Today, the preponderance of specialist shops along the main street continues to mark out the Village as a classy area. It's highly popular too, and the streets are traffic-choked at weekends, when the restaurants and bars at the heath end of the Village play host to Blackheath's gilded youth and merchant bankers.

Blackheath, the flat common land against whose southern edge the Village nestles, has a remarkable history. Watling Street, the Roman road to Canterbury (now the A2), ran through it, Wat Tyler assembled his revolting peasants here in 1381, and Henry VIII marshalled the full force of pomp and circumstance when he arranged to meet Anne of Cleves here in 1540 (which he must have regretted). These days, the heath's airy acres are used by circuses, kite fliers, dog-walkers and sporting clubs.

Traffic is a major problem. Try crossing the A2 to Greenwich Park and you can lose the will to live. All the houses overlooking the heath are grand, but the smartest address of all is surely the Paragon (the barriered entrance is just beyond the pond by South Row). This graceful semi-circle of seven colonnaded houses was designed around 1800 by Michael Searles. The southern end of the Village, on the road to Lee, is home to the Blackheath Conservatoire (an old-established music school) and Blackheath Halls (now part of Greenwich's Trinity College of Music).

Lewisham

Arriving in central Lewisham by train or DLR, you're confronted by the A20 and a perpetually busy, irredeemably ugly roundabout that must be negotiated before you reach the shops. It's not an impressive introduction to south-east London's most populous town centre. The charmless shopping centre was built in 1975; just opposite, the new, enormous police station frowns out at the crowds.

The old rivers Ravensbourne and Quaggy, which meet at Lewisham, have figured strongly in the proposed Urban Renaissance programme. A more natural environment is planned to replace the ugly concrete channels through which the waters currently flow. The programme will also provide a central green space and park, and a paved walkway to run from the stations to the High Street. All this will not happen for some years, but the prospect of a facelift, and the presence since 2000 of a DLR connection into the City, have improved Lewisham's status. Incomers attracted by the good transport (there's a bus station too) are encouraged by estate agents to explore areas around Lewisham Park, Belmont Hill and the roads

Blackheath – where the only problem is the traffic. *See p241*.

connecting the High Street to Ladywell.
They're seduced by the size and relative
cheapness of the houses, easily accessible
from town via wide, tree-lined roads.

A short walk from such pleasures,
Lewisham town centre throbs with life.
Highlights include a rowdy street market
outside the shopping centre, and the wide
choice of cuisines in local restaurants and
cafés: from pie and mash to Turkish grills.
And for a spot of romance after a meal,
stroll along the Lewisham Promenade
– where the trees glow with blue lights
at night – in the direction of Catford.

Ladywell, Brockley and Honor Oak

Ladywell's cheerful little knot of
independent businesses (bakery, hardware
store, trendy cafés and arty shops) gives
the impression of being surrounded by
countryside. To the south-east there's
Ladywell Fields, home to a somewhat
underused running track, tennis and
basketball courts, a new ranger station and
café. Here too is the River Ravensbourne,
separating the fields from the newly
expanded Lewisham University Hospital.

To the west, connecting Ladywell to
Brockley, is Brockley Cemetery, as much
a nature reserve as a final resting place.
Across wide and traffic-calmed Adelaide
Avenue rises Hilly Fields: a lovely, airy
park with Prendergast Girls' School at its
centre and grassy slopes that look out over
Lewisham town centre. Houses in roads
surrounding the park command huge prices.
Hilly Fields has a mini stonehenge: a stone
circle of 12 granite boulders with two tall
shadow-casting stones, erected to mark the
new millennium. The astronomically-correct
circle has become a place for poetic
Lewisham souls to mark the solstice.

Artistic types tend to settle here and in
Brockley, where local artists have done
much to improve the look of the area.

Brockley's famous site is the Brockley Jack, a lively pub-theatre rebuilt in Victorian times. The original Jack was reputed to be a haunt of highwaymen. The grand old Rivoli Ballroom, with its magnificent dancefloor, is used for tea dances and classes.

Brockley's station is Crofton Park. The housing here is dominated by modest Victorian terraces built for local workers. The Lewisham edge of Brockley and Ladywell, near the wide and once-prosperous Wickham Way, contains some fabulously lofty detached houses. Brockley Rise takes you to Honor Oak, a hilly residential area just over the borough boundary in Southwark. The main road through the area is called Honor Oak Park, as is the local overground station. For great views and springtime woodpeckers, climb One Tree Hill, where there's a beacon (last lit for the millennium).

Highs & Lows

Low crime rate Especially in the borough's outer neighbourhoods (New Cross lets the team down)
The arts scene Thanks largely to the excellent Broadway and Albany theatres, Lewisham draws a high proportion of artists, musicians, comedians and writers (some of them are celebrities!). To some people, of course, this might constitute a low
Country neighbours Easy access to comfortable suburbs like Beckenham and Bromley, plus the countryside of Kent, makes for excellent green getaways; while the proximity of Bluewater shopping centre negates the need to travel to urban inner London at all

Architectural manoeuvres in the dark Bombed heavily during World War II, the borough suffers from some hideous architectural decisions made in the 1960s
No cinema A near-criminal absence, though the Broadway theatre occasionally screens arthouse films
Lewisham Hospital Has performed consistently badly in hospital league tables (and is surrounded by a number of funeral directors)

Lee and Hither Green

The burghers of Lee enjoy the genteel pleasures of neighbouring Blackheath without the prohibitive property prices. Their main shopping and eating centre is at Lee Green, but it's the housing and ease of access into both the city and Kent that attract most people.

The Lee Conservation Area, bounded by Burnt Ash Road, Manor Lane and Southbrook Road, contains some graceful Victorian and Edwardian semis. Manor House, a 1775 mansion built for Sir Francis Baring, the banker, has survived the test of time to become the local library. In the garden, an old ice house is opened to the public on high days and holidays. The rest of Baring's land now forms a well-maintained park with a lake and café.

From Manor House Gardens, a walk west brings you to Hither Green, where the terraced housing looks more mundane. Hither Green was once a hamlet in the Great North Wood. Today it has an unfounded reputation of being a bit of a backwater. This densely populated residential area has a major railway junction (London Bridge is 11 minutes away) and is a short walk from Lewisham town centre. Its population is growing, courtesy of a massive residential development of the old hospital and grounds. Travelling south from Hither Green, down Baring Road past the cemetery, eventually brings you to Grove Park and Chinbrook Meadows, at the borough's most south-easterly edge.

Catford

A giant black and white cat leaps out from the entrance of the almost comically ugly shopping centre at Catford. Built by a ford in a river where there were once wild cats, this town centre has been the victim of some criminal town-planning decisions. Its once-beautiful Broadway market area now cowers behind a 1971 carbuncle containing Lewisham Town Hall and Civic Suite; another culprit, Laurence House (across the dreadful A205 gyratory), houses the local library. Brutal tower blocks – Eros House, Rosenthal House and the horrible council flats known as Milford Towers (crouching murderously above the shopping centre) – have given Catford's centre, which suffered greatly from bomb damage in World War II, a run-down look.

Until 2004, the greyhound track endeared the world to Catford, but its sudden closure, followed by the suspicious 'arson attack' on the historic tote board building standing in the way of the developers, has taken that bright spot away. Now the main attraction is the 1932 Broadway Theatre, an elegant art deco building with a diverse programme of ballets, comedy and family shows. A small independent cinema was opened in the building following a furore about the borough's cinema-less status.

Further along the A205, St Dunstan's public school, in a handsome red-brick building, is a pricey alternative to Lewisham's education options.

Away from the Catford gyratory, green spaces and huge, reasonably priced,

Edwardian family houses are reasons enough for settling here. Towards Hither Green the well-built houses of the Corbett Estate (built by Archibald Cameron Corbett MP around 1900) are coveted for their generous proportions. There are no pubs near Corbett houses, though: the developer was a strict Presbyterian. Mountsfield Park, between Rushey Green and Hither Green, is the scene of Lewisham's People's Day every summer.

Forest Hill and Sydenham

The centrepiece of the hilly, wooded, bottom-left corner of the borough is the Horniman Museum, one of London's treasures. The area's views over the city and the North Downs are best experienced from the museum's gardens, or on the steep residential roads to the north.

Forest Hill's Great North Wood origins lend it a wholesome air, although the station's entrance on to the traffic-clogged A205/South Circular might dispel all ideas of breezy heights if you come by train. Dartmouth Road, the main shopping street leading from the station to Sydenham, offers some interesting independent shops and restaurants, however, and Kirkdale, further on, has various quirky outlets for books, antiques and period furniture.

Wide residential roads with spacious detached houses branch off to the left and right as you travel south down Kirkdale to Sydenham, which borders Bromley. One of the most attractive roads takes you to Sydenham Wells Park, which was created on the site of medicinal springs. Crowds of the wealthy, including George III, used to flock here to take the waters.

Upper Sydenham was considered the smart area. Its undulating countryside and gracious residences got it noticed by a bohemian set; Byron was a frequent visitor. The arrival of the Crystal Palace, which moved from Hyde Park after the Great Exhibition of 1851 to Crystal Palace Park (just over the borough border, in Bromley), added to its fashionable cachet. To this day, musicians, actors and artists favour the area. Lower Sydenham – around where the gas containers and Savacentre now look out over highways of Bromley-bound traffic – has always been poorer and meaner.

The transport future's bright for Forest Hill and Sydenham. Both areas will benefit

The pride of Catford, the **Broadway Theatre**.

from the development of the East London Line Project, poised to provide a metro-style (National Rail) train service north to Highbury & Islington, south to West Croydon and west to Clapham Junction. Phase one of the project, from New Cross Gate south to Crystal Palace and West Croydon, should be completed by June 2010.

Restaurants & cafés

Eating in Lewisham town takes you into the glycaemic stratosphere, thanks to the doughnut, noodle and sausage vans, plus hefty fish and chip lunches at Something Fishy. Eating is more exciting up Lee High Road, where Arru Suval, a Sri Lankan caff, doles out decent high-street curries for indecently low prices (spend more than seven quid and you might explode). The cheap and spicy theme continues in the other direction, on Loampit Hill, where Everest Curry King, another Sri Lankan, has cramped surroundings and raging hot curries and snacks.

In New Cross, Goldsmiths students fuel up on fiery dishes from Esarn and Laos at tiny Thailand, or Turkish barbecued meats, meze and pide at Meze Mangal. North of New Cross Road, Deptford's budget eating places include AJ Goddard's and Manze's eel, pie and mash shops, and the welcoming Vietnamese West Lake. There's a dearth of upmarket restaurants in the borough, but Chapters café (inside Laban dance centre) offers refined risottos, pastas and soups, while its sister, Blackheath's posh Chapter Two, has a Modern European menu replete with veloutés and remoulades. Blackheath is also home to Laicram, a cosy neighbourhood Thai, and various organically inspired deli-cafés. El Pirata is a family-friendly Spanish tapas restaurant overlooking the heath.

Few people would consider eating out in Catford unless they knew about the uncannily good Japanese restaurant Sapporo Ichiban, and its not-half-bad Rushey Green rival, Hello Tokyo. Catfordites also fill up on noodles at Tai Won Mein and handmade pizzas at La Pizzeria Italiana, which attracts incongruous numbers of middle-class diners to its premises under a block of flats.

The biggest noise in Brockley is the newly refurbished Babur Brasserie, where fab tandoori dishes are served with great aplomb and modest bills. In Forest Hill, Fu Lee is Thai/Chinese and friendly, filling and cheap. As if to prove it's on the up, Forest Hill also has Organic Republic, a wholesome deli-café, and Lewisham's only gastropub: the excellent alehouse Dartmouth Arms has gone all leek tart and raspberry coulis. It's actually rather good.

AJ Goddard *203 Deptford High Street, SE8 3NT (8692 3601).*
Arru Suval *19 Lee High Road, SE13 5LD (8297 6452).*
Babur Brasserie *119 Brockley Rise, SE23 IJP (8291 4881/2400).*
Chapters *Laban, Creekside, SE8 3DZ (8469 9514/www.laban.org).*
Chapter Two *43-45 Montpelier Vale, SE3 OTJ (8333 2666/www.chaptersrestaurants.co.uk).*
Dartmouth Arms *7 Dartmouth Road, SE23 2NH (8488 3117/www.thedartmoutharms.com).*
Everest Curry King *24 Loampit Hill, SE13 7SW (8691 2233).*
Fu Lee *25 Dartmouth Road, SE23 3HN (8699 4000).*
Hello Tokyo *81 Rushey Green, SE6 4AF (8285 1988) .*
Laicram *1 Blackheath Grove, SE3 ODD (8852 4710).*
El Pirata *15-16 Royal Parade, SE3 OTL (8297 1880).*
La Pizzeria Italiana *Eros House, Brownhill Road, SE6 2EF (8461 4606).*
Manze's *204 Deptford High Street, SE8 3PR (8692 2375).*
Meze Mangal *245 Lewisham Way, SE4 1XF (8694 8099).*
Organic Republic *49 London Road, SE23 3TY (8699 8400).*

Lewisham

TRANSPORT

Tube stations *East London* New Cross Gate, New Cross
Rail stations *South Eastern Trains* South Bermondsey, Deptford, Nunhead, Lewisham, Blackheath, Crofton Park, Catford, Catford Bridge, Bellingham, Beckenham Hill, Ravensbourne, New Cross, St Johns, Ladywell, Lower Sydenham, Hither Green, Grove Park, Lee; *Southern* New Cross Gate, Brockley, Honor Oak Park, Forest Hill, Sydenham
Main bus routes *into central London* 21, 47, 53, 171, 172, 176, 185, 188, 343, 436, 453; *night buses* N21, N47, N89, N171, N343; *24-hour buses* 53, 75, 108, 176, 453

Sapporo Ichiban *13 Catford Broadway, SE6 4SP (8690 8487).*
Something Fishy *117-119 Lewisham High Street, SE13 6AT (8852 7075).*
Tai Won Mein *90-92 Rushey Green, SE6 4HW (8690 8238).*
Thailand *15 Lewisham Way, SE14 6PP (8691 4040).*
West Lake *207 Deptford High Street, SE8 3NT (8465 9408).*

Bars & pubs

They may both be in the same borough, but Blackheath, one of the capital's loveliest, leafiest villages, and neighbouring Lewisham, which looks as if a malevolent child made it from Lego, have little else in common. The only pubs worth visiting in Lewisham (unless you enjoy WKD and fighting) are those at a decent remove from the centre, such as the homely Dacre Arms (be prepared for a walk). In Blackheath, it's a different story. Of the many fine boozers, the centuries-old Hare & Billet and the Georgian Princess of Wales are the grandest. Livelier options include Zero Degrees, with its microbrewed beers and inventive bar food, the upbeat Railway, and Cave Austin, a slick wine bar with basement club and chill-out room.

Elsewhere in the borough, down-to-earth Deptford has the real ales, good Sunday lunches and unpretentious charm of the Dog & Bell, and the late-night revelry of the Live Bar to recommend it. In New Cross, former grunge emporium Goldsmiths Tavern has been transformed into an oasis of squishy sofas, fine wine and sea bass; in contrast, the Hobgoblin remains resolutely studenty. For live music, indie-leaning Amersham Arms and kitsch Montague Arms are popular; a third Arm, the Forresters Arms, south in Forest Hill, hosts popular jazz nights.

Amersham Arms *388 New Cross Road, SE14 6TY (8692 2047).*
Cave Austin *7-9 Montpelier Vale, SE3 OTA (8852 0492/www.caveaustin.co.uk).*
Dacre Arms *11 Kingswood Place, SE13 5BU (8852 6779).*
Dog & Bell *116 Prince Street, SE8 3JD (8692 5664).*
Forresters Arms *53 Perry Vale, SE23 2NE (8699 3311).*
Goldsmiths Tavern *316 New Cross Road, SE14 6AF (8691 8875).*
Hare & Billet *1A Elliot Cottages, Hare & Billet Road, SE3 OQJ (8852 2352).*
Hobgoblin *272 New Cross Road, SE14 6AA (8692 3193).*

Bridge Leisure Centre, Lewisham's premier public fitness facility. *See p250.*

Live Bar *41-42 Deptford Broadway, SE8 4PH (8469 2121).*
Montague Arms *289 Queens Road, SE14 2PA (7639 4923).*
Princess of Wales *1A Montpelier Row, SE3 0RL (8297 5911).*
Railway *16 Blackheath Village, SE3 9LE (8852 2390).*
Zero Degrees *29-31 Montpelier Vale, SE3 0TJ (8852 5619/www.zerodegrees.co.uk).*

Shops

Since losing its depressing playground and banning smoking, the retail heart of the area, the Lewisham Centre, has improved a touch. Many high-street chains are within, but WH Smith is your only hope for books, apart from discount store the Works.

Outside, more individuality prospers at the daily market, where there's a wide range of household goods, fruit and veg, wet fish, haberdashery and plants (Deptford's buzzing, colourful market is, however, better – and was rated the best in London by the Yellow Pages). Opposite here, Rolls & Rems textiles shop is fab for one-off bolts of unusual fabrics, and the coffee- and cheese-scented Genarro Deli serves the borough's large Italian community.

Ladywell makes like a village centre, with its florists, bakers, barber and hardware shops. Creare should satisfy your paper-craft needs, and there's even a tatooist.

Lee High Road reveals a few surprises. Harlequin is a fancy-dress hire and sales shop with good budget accessories. A few doors away, Snapdragon contains an attractive jumble of pots, planters and vases for the garden, as well as candles, cards, pottery and sundry gifts. Keep going to find Allodi Accordions, which has several rooms of accordions and a repair workshop.

Outside Hither Green train station lies the Staplehurst Road shops, overseen by FUSS (Friends & Users of Staplehurst Road Shops). These doughty shopkeepers keep the community close. You Don't Bring Me Flowers – a florist that also encompasses a café, knitting group and writers' club – is central to this arty scene. Over the road, the Education Interactive maths initiative has a shop full of number puzzles and the sort of toys bought by conscientious parents.

Blackheath Village provides the genteel antidote to Lewisham. Independent traders are the norm (discreet chains include Neal's Yard Remedies, Phase Eight, Fat Face and Ryman). Upmarket gourmet shops such as Hand Made Food and the Village Deli help shunt up the grocery bill. Madame Chocolat and Jade Boulangerie provide the sweet course and breakfast croissants. Proper sweets, such as rosy apples and cola cubes, are the forte of the gift shop in Blackheath's atmospheric Age Exchange centre (see p249). There are far too many gift shops, but 2nd Impressions is a joy to explore, as it has many floors and an extensive toy department. Near the heath, Cookery Nook is a large kitchen equipment shop, while at the Lee end, Hortus is a pricey garden accessories store. Blackheath's association with hockey and cricket is evident in the specialist sports shop, Furley & Baker.

In Forest Hill – with its recently poshed-up Sainsbury's – there's Organic Republic deli-café (see p246) for healthy grub and Silkroute for oriental furniture, homeware and rugs. On Dartmouth Road, sassy boutique Bunka has been joined by the slick Mayo Maker for men's designer wear. Next door, the Antoinette Costume Hire's frontage looks fusty by comparison. A large ski, snowboarding and mountain-biking store, Finches Ski Emporium, hides behind the South Circular on Perry Vale. Sydenham and Kirkdale also have fine shopping areas, strong on arts and antiques. The Kirkdale bookshop and

gallery provides art and literature, Oola Boola Antiques is brilliant for furniture and collectibles, and Behind the Boxes Art Deco has furniture, ceramics, jewellery and glass.

Allodi Accordions *143-145 Lee High Road, SE13 5PF (8244 3771/www.accordions. co.uk).*
Antoinette Costume Hire *10A Dartmouth Road, SE23 3XU (8699 1913).*
Behind the Boxes Art Deco *98 Kirkdale, SE26 4BG (8291 6116/www.behindtheboxes-artdeco.co.uk).*
Bunka *4 Dartmouth Road, SE23 3XU (8291 4499/www.bunka.co.uk).*
Cookery Nook *32 Montpelier Vale, SE3 0TA (8297 2422).*
Creare *89 Ladywell Road, SE13 7JA (8690 9514).*
Deptford Market *Douglas Way & Deptford High Street, SE8.*
Education Interactive *10 Staplehurst Road, SE13 5NB (8318 6380/www.education-interactive.co.uk).*
Finches Ski Emporium *25-29 Perry Vale, SE23 2NE (8699 6768/www.finches-ski.com).*
Furley & Baker *34 Montpelier Vale, SE3 0TA (8463 0752/www.furleyand baker.com).*
Gennaro Delicatessen *23 Lewis Grove, SE13 6BG (8852 1370).*
Hand Made Food *40 Tranquil Vale, SE3 0BD (8297 9966/www.handmade food.com).*
Harlequin *254 Lee High Road, SE13 5PR (8852 0193).*
Jade Boulangerie *44 Tranquil Vale, SE3 0BD (8318 1916).*
Kirkdale Bookshop & Gallery *272 Kirkdale, SE26 4RS (8778 4701).*
Lewisham Centre *33A Molesworth Street, SE13 7HB (8852 0094/www.lewisham centre.co.uk).*
Lewisham Market *Lewisham High Street, SE14.*
Madame Chocolat *21 Tranquil Vale, SE3 0BU (8852 9817/www.madame chocolat.co.uk).*
Mayo Maker *8 Dartmouth Road, SE23 3XU (8314 4050).*
Oola Boola Antiques *139-147 Kirkdale, SE26 4QJ (8291 9999).*
Rolls & Rems *111 High Street, SE13 6AT (8852 8686).*
2nd Impressions *10 Montpelier Vale, SE3 0TA (8852 6192).*
Silkroute *56 London Road, SE23 3HF (8699 9888/www.silkroute-rugs.co.uk).*
Snapdragon *266 Lee High Road, SE13 5PL (8463 0503).*
Village Deli *1-3 Tranquil Vale, SE3 0BU (8852 2015).*
You Don't Bring Me Flowers *15 Staplehurst Road, SE13 5ND (8297 2333/www.youdont bringmeflowers.co.uk).*

RECYCLING

No. of bring sites 48 (for nearest, visit www.recycleforlondon.com)
Household waste recycled 8.2%
Main recycling centre Landmann Way Reuse & Recycling Centre, Landmann Way, off Surrey Canal Road, SE14 5RS (8314 7171)
Other recycling services green garden rubbish collection; home composting; white goods and furniture collection; paint reuse (www.communityrepaint. org.uk)
Council contact Beth Sowden, Waste Education Officer, Wearside Service Centre, Wearside Road, SE13 7EZ (8314 2053/www.lewisham.gov.uk/ recycling)

Arts & attractions

Cinemas & theatres

Albany *Douglas Way, SE8 4AG (8692 4446/www.thealbany.org.uk).* Deptford's busy community arts centre; 'Family Sundays' involve brunch and music.

Blackheath Halls *23 Lee Road, SE3 9RQ (8463 0100/www.blackheathhalls.com).* Concerts (classical and contemporary), community events and more.

Broadway Theatre *Rushey Green, SE6 4RU (8690 0002/www.broadwaytheatre.org.uk).* Handsome art deco theatre that is scruffy Catford's pride and joy.

Brockley Jack Theatre *410 Brockley Road, SE4 2DH (8291 6354/www.brockleyjack.co.uk).* Popular theatre (and pub) that hosts drama productions, plus music, comedy and live events.

Laban *Creekside, SE8 3DZ (8691 8600/ www.laban.org).* Independent conservatoire for contemporary dance training, housed in stunning, award-winning premises designed by Herzog & de Meuron, architects of Tate Modern.

Galleries & museums

Horniman Museum *100 London Road, SE23 (8699 1872/www.horniman.ac.uk).* Eccentric art noveau museum, with natural history and anthropological displays, a spacious café, lovely gardens and an animal enclosure.

Lewisham Arthouse *140 Lewisham Way, SE14 6PD (8244 3168/www.lewishamarthouse.co.uk).* Gallery in an impressive Edwardian hall.

Other attractions

Age Exchange Reminiscence Centre *11 Blackheath Village, SE3 9LA (8318 9105/ www.age-exchange.org.uk).* Nostalgic museum experience that aims to improve quality of life for elderly people by emphasising the value of memories.

Goldsmiths College *University of London, SE14 6NW (7919 7171/www.goldsmiths.ac.uk).* Famous art college with various sites around New Cross and Deptford; the fabulously ornate building on Lewisham Way (once Deptford Town Hall) is particularly attractive.

Manor House Library & Gardens *Old Road, SE13 5SY (8852 0357/www.lewisham.gov.uk).* One of the grandest local libraries in London, built in 1772.

Rivoli Ballroom *346-350 Brockley Road, SE4 2BY (8692 5130).* Grand old ballroom used for tea dances and classes.

Open spaces

Blackheath *Tranquil Vale, Montpelier Row, Shooter's Hill Road, SE3.* The huge flat grassy common that lends its name to the neighbourhood.

Brockley Cemetery *Brockley Road, SE4.* Also a nature reserve; adjoins Ladywell Cemetery.

MY VIEW

LOUISE PALMER
Schools education manager,
Horniman Museum

You probably couldn't get much more of a social mix: there's the lively arts scene, with theatres such as the Broadway and the Albany, plus the smaller Brockley Jack and Laban. **Goldsmiths College brings a big student population; the DLR brings professionals who work in Docklands and the City; and on top of this there are large West African, Afro-Caribbean and Turkish communities.** It also seems friendlier than other areas of London. People are very down to earth and it is not uncommon to actually have conversations with people on public transport – unheard of elsewhere. **Yes, intense traffic means a lot of noise and a frantic pace to life, but there's always a sizeable green space to retire to – such as the 16 acres of parkland at the Horniman Museum, where I go for my lunchtime stroll.** What can you do here that you can't do anywhere else? Visit a museum with an overstuffed walrus (at the Horniman Museum) and dance in an original ballroom (at the Rivoli).

Lewisham

Deptford Park *Evelyn Street, Grinstead Road, Scawen Road, SE8.*
Hilly Fields *Adelaide Avenue, Hilly Fields Crescent, Montague Avenue, SE4 & SE13.* Airy public park and site of Prendergast Girls' School.
Ladywell Fields *Albacore Crescent, Doggett Road, Malyons Road, SE6 & SE13.*
Mountsfield Park *Brownhill Road, George Lane, Station Road, SE6.* Hosts Lewisham People's Day every summer.
Sydenham Wells Park *Longton Avenue, Taylors Lane, Wells Park Lane, SE26.*
Telegraph Hill Park *Drakefell Road, Kitto Road, Pepys Road, SE14.*
Twinkle Park *Watergate Street, SE8.*

Sport & fitness

Lewisham is on the up. The Downham Lifestyle Centre, due to open in 2007, will include a pool, fitness centre and community health facilities, along with music and drama studios and a café. Some of the borough's existing centres are more basic, however, though others have already benefited from a spruce-up. Wavelengths Leisure Centre, famous for its large 'fun pool', has been updated, while Lewisham's flagship – the Bridge Leisure Centre – almost makes up for the others' failings with a setting and facilities that exceed those at many private venues. Ladywell Leisure Centre is under threat from a controversial scheme to replace it with a secondary school. Overall, if you're looking for a regular workout haunt or an unusual fitness class, you'll be more than adequately served by the borough's collection.

Gyms & leisure centres

Bridge Leisure Centre *Kangley Bridge Road, SE26 5AQ (8778 7158/www.leisure-centre.com).*
Coliseum *15 Davids Road, SE23 3EP (8699 3342).* Private.
Colfe's Leisure Centre *Horne Park Lane, SE12 8AW (8297 9110).* Private.
Fitness First *61-71A High Street, SE13 5JX (8852 4444/www.fitnessfirst.co.uk).* Private.
Forest Hill Leisure Centre *Dartmouth Road, SE23 3HZ (8699 3096).*
Ladywell Leisure Centre *261 Lewisham High Street, SE13 6NJ (8690 2123/www.leisure-centre.com).*
LA Fitness *291 Kirkdale, SE26 4QE (8778 9818/www.lafitness.co.uk).* Private.
One to One Fitness *19B Marischal Road, SE13 5LE (8318 5630).* Private.
Skyline Gym *96-102 Rushey Green, SE6 4HW (8314 1167).* Private.
TakeShape *17A Brandram Road, SE13 5RT (8852 2009).* Private.

Wavelengths Leisure Centre *Giffin Street, SE8 4RJ (8694 1134/www.leisure-centre.com).*

Other facilities
AMF Bowling *11-29 Belmont Hill, SE13 5AU (www.amfbowling.co.uk).*

Spectator sports
Millwall FC *The New Den, Zampa Road, SE16 3LN (7231 9999/www.millwallfc.co.uk).*

Schools

WHAT THE PARENTS SAY:

'Schools in Lewisham are a bit rough. I'm really lucky that there's a primary school, Perrymount, practically opposite my house. I'm pleased with it to a point – it's very mixed, made up of kids from all different cultures and backgrounds, and is considered to be one of Lewisham's good primaries.

I'm worried about secondary schools, though, and am hoping to be able to put my son into a private school. The state schools just aren't good enough; none stands out as having a good academic reputation or good facilities. Forest Hill is a relatively poor, working-class area and the schools seem to reflect this. There's been no influx of middle-class parents to help bring about changes… I don't think many people move to Lewisham for its schools.'
Claire Clifford, mother of one, Forest Hill

Primary
There are 69 state primary schools in Lewisham, 21 of which are church schools. There are also six independents, including two faith schools. See www.lewisham.gov.uk/educationand learning and www.ofsted.gov.uk for more information.

Secondary
Addey & Stanhope School *472 New Cross Road, SE14 6TJ (8305 6100/www.as.lewisham.sch.uk).*
Bonus Pastor RC School *Winlaton Road, Downham, BR1 5PZ (8695 2100/www.bp.lewisham.sch.uk).*
Catford Business & Enterprise College *Bellingham Road, SE6 2PS (8697 8911/www.catford-girls.lewisham.sch.uk).* Formerly girls only; accepting boys from September 2006.
Crofton School *Manwood Road, SE4 1SA (8690 1114/www.crofton.lewisham.sch.uk).*
Deptford Green School *Amersham Vale, SE14 6LQ (8691 3236/www.deptfordgreen.lewisham.sch.uk).*
Forest Hill Boys' School *Dacres Road, SE23 2XN (8699 9343/www.foresthill.lewisham.sch.uk).* Boys only.

Haberdashers' Aske's Hatcham College
Pepys Road, E14 5SF (7652 9500/www.hahc. org.uk).
Haberdashers' Aske's Knights Academy
Launcelot Road, BR1 5EB (8698 1025/ www.hahc.org.uk). New school, with initial enrolment of 150 pupils in 2006.
Northbrook CE School *Taunton Road, SE12 8PD (8852 3191/www.northbrook. lewisham.sch.uk).*
Prendergast School *Hilly Fields, Adelaide Avenue, SE4 1LE (8690 3710).* Girls only.
St Dunstan's College *Stanstead Road, SE6 4TY (8516 7200/www.stdunstans.org.uk).* Private.
St Joseph's Academy *Lee Terrace, SE3 9TY (8852 7433/www.sja.lewisham.sch.uk).* Boys only.
Sedgehill School *Sedgehill Road, SE6 3QW (8698 8911/www.sedgehill.lewisham. sch.uk).*
Sydenham School *Dartmouth Road, SE26 4RD (8699 6731/www.sydenham. lewisham.sch.uk).* Girls only.

Property

WHAT THE AGENTS SAY:

❝People are attracted to Lewisham by the good reputation of the borough's council, improvements in transport, and generally the good value for money. The primary schools have a good reputation although the secondary schools don't; you tend to get a lot of young families moving here. Younger buyers who work in Canary Wharf move here too – it's only 13-15 minutes on the DLR and you can buy a three-bedroom house with a garden for the same price as a smaller property in Canary Wharf. There's quite a lot of green space compared to areas further in such as Brixton and Peckham, which are also both more densely populated. The quality of life in Lewisham is better.

Forest Hill, Brockley and Honor Oak Park are very popular; there are no big tower blocks and fewer people. Many people are choosing to swap their one-bedroom in Clapham for a three-bedroom in Forest Hill. The price is similar, but it's the difference between sharing a house or having it to yourself.❞
Robert Whimparley-Dixon, Sebastian Roche, Lewisham

Average property prices
Detached £385,941
Semi-detached £223,276
Terraced £178,866
Flat £161,257

COUNCIL TAX

A	up to £40,000	**£799.15**
B	£40,001-£52,000	**£932.34**
C	£52,001-£68,000	**£1,065.53**
D	£68,001-£88,000	**£1,198.72**
E	£88,001-£120,000	**£1,465.10**
F	£120,001-£160,000	**£1,731.48**
G	£160,001-£320,000	**£1,997.87**
H	over £320,000	**£2,397.44**

Local estate agents
Beaumont Residential *111B Rushey Green, SE6 4AF (8695 0123/www.beaumont-residential.com).*
1st Avenue *343 Lee High Road, SE12 8RU (8852 9444/www.1stavenue.co.uk).*
James Johnston *8 Montpelier Vale, SE3 0TA (8852 8383/www.jamesjohnston.com).*
Oak Estates *www.oakestates.co.uk; 3 offices in the borough (Brockley 8692 9533/Forest Hill 8699 1600/Lewisham 8333 5252).*
Property World *1 & 4 Sydenham Road, SE26 5QW (8488 0011/www.propertyworlduk.net).*
Reeds Estate Agents *195 Deptford High Street, SE8 3NT (8691 9009).*
RJG Properties *118 Springbank Road, SE13 6SX (8695 1243).*
Sebastian Roche *www.sebastianroche.com; 2 offices in the borough (Forest Hill 8291 9441/ Lewisham 8690 8888).*

Other information

Council
Lewisham Council *Lewisham Town Hall, Catford Road, SE6 4RU (8314 6000/www. lewisham.gov.uk).*

Hospitals
BMI Blackheath Hospital *40-42 Lee Terrace, SE3 9UD (8318 7722/www.bmihealthcare.co.uk).* Private.
Lewisham Hospital *Lewisham High Street, SE13 6LH (8333 3000/www.lewisham.nhs.uk).*

Legal services
Catford CAB *120 Rushey Green, SE6 4HQ (0870 1264037/www.adviceguide.org.uk).*
Sydenham CAB *299 Kirkdale, SE26 4QD (0870 1264037/www.adviceguide.org.uk).*

Local newspapers
Lewisham & Greenwich Mercury *8769 4444/http://icsouthlondon.icnetwork.co.uk.*

Allotments
Council Allotments *c/o Greenscene, Main Building, Wearside Service Centre, Wearside Road, SE13 7EZ (8314 2047/www.lewisham.gov.uk).*
Network Rail Allotments *c/o Citex, Portsoken House, 155-157 Minories, EC3N 1LJ (7265 2550).*

> *'A seaside town
> in the depths of
> south-east London.'*

James Brazier, soldier and resident

Greenwich

The maritime sights of Greenwich are known to millions of visitors and Londoners, but alongside the tourist attractions is a thriving local community and a borough containing astonishing variations in housing and wealth – not to mention a Premiership football club, a deer enclosure and, ahem, the Millennium Dome.

Neighbourhoods

Greenwich

Residents of Greenwich take the district's status as a UNESCO World Heritage Site – famed for its horological and maritime history – well within their stride. The teeming tourist trail incorporates the National Maritime Museum, the Old Royal Naval College, the Queen's House, the *Cutty Sark*, the Royal Observatory and more, but beyond these spectacular sights, Greenwich is home to a lively community encompassing diverse backgrounds.

The main shopping area around Greenwich Church Street comprises many discount bookshops, independent boutiques selling contemporary and retro clothing,

and a couple of token high-street names. The covered market houses two galleries, a health-food store, designer jewellery shops, and a different selection of stall traders every day of the week. At the weekend (and especially on Sundays) the covered market gets mobbed by visitors, and dozens of crafts, retro fashion and antiques traders set up at various sites as Greenwich Market takes centre stage.

To discover the 'real' Greenwich, you'll need to sidestep the beaten track. The centre of town groans with below-average eateries and (invariably maritime-themed) pubs, but there are some great restaurants hidden away. Culture-wise, Greenwich is constantly developing: the Greenwich Theatre, Greenwich Playhouse and Up the Creek provide comedy, mainstream theatre, fringe

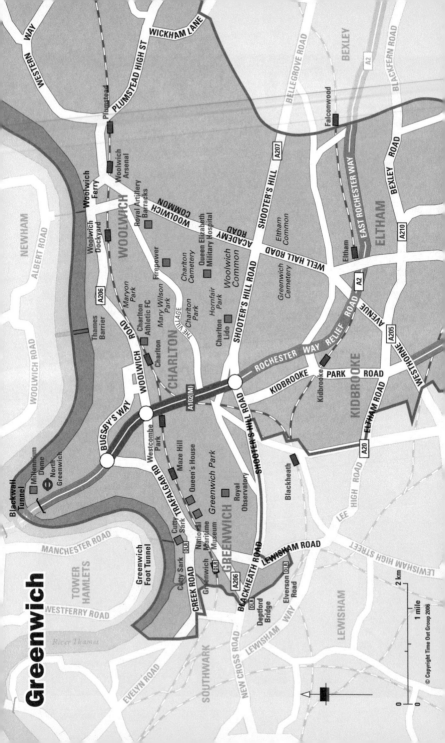

and children's events, and there's a programme of outdoor performances every summer. A new addition to the scene, Greenwich Picture House, shows popular movies and arthouse flicks; and lunchtime recitals are held in beautiful St Alfege's Church. Built by Nicholas Hawksmoor in 1714, it houses the remains of various local celebs of yesteryear, including General James Wolfe and composer Thomas Tallis.

Cherished by all is beautiful Greenwich Park, one of London's royal parks. The tranquil, undulating space includes a boating lake, a fabulous children's play area, flower gardens, a deer enclosure, and possibly the friendliest squirrels in London. The views from the top of One Tree Hill are magnificent, with the towers of Canary Wharf in the foreground, and Tower Bridge, the tip of the London Eye and the dome of St Paul's within sight on a clear day. A few minutes' walk north of the park you can view the Thames flowing past on its way towards the more industrial landscape of North Greenwich, which is dominated by the infamous Millennium Dome (currently still surrounded by a ghost town) and the entrance and exit ways to the Blackwall Tunnel. The Thames Path is well-used by walkers and cyclists. Less strenuous transport links are excellent, with a rail station (15 minutes to central London), various DLR stops, North Greenwich tube (on the Jubilee line, and a fifteen-minute bus ride from the centre of Greenwich), commuter river services and the old Greenwich Foot Tunnel to the Isle of Dogs.

The Georgian splendour of much of the housing in Greenwich belies the fact that 19 neighbourhoods within the wider borough are among the most deprived in Britain. However, the council is committed to its regeneration agenda, and has recently been awarded Beacon status for its affordable housing initiatives. Future developments are bound to cause an even greater influx of tourists: 2006 sees the opening of the first phase of the Time and Space project (the £15m regeneration of the Royal Observatory), and in 2012 the borough will host nine of the 21 Olympic events.

Kidbrooke

The lofty and elegant houses found at the north-western end of Kidbrooke, by the border with Blackheath, quickly make way for a bleak landscape of 1960s brutalist architecture and run-down tower blocks south of Kidbrooke rail station. A £550m redevelopment programme is currently under way, which will include the demolition of 2,000 dwellings on the infamous Ferrier Estate, and increasing access to the sports facilities and open spaces that are among Kidbrooke's plus points. At present, the David Lloyd leisure complex runs a range of classes and initiatives for children. Kidbrooke shot to fame recently as the focal point for Channel 4's series *Jamie's School Dinners*; Greenwich Council now proudly boasts that processed food is banned in all the borough's schools.

Charlton and Woolwich

Charlton encompasses an area of stark contrasts. Here you can find tree-lined, quiet residential streets (in the vicinity of Charlton Park), but also gain intimate knowledge of hoodie culture. The area's pride and joy is the Premiership football

Highs & Lows

▲ **Greenwich Park** Cherished by all, it's a huge, tranquil, undulating space – with possibly the friendliest squirrels in London

School food Thanks to Jamie Oliver (and his TV campaign), processed food is now banned across the borough's 80 schools

Thames development In Woolwich, where the Woolwich Ferry currently operates, the Thames Gateway Bridge is waiting for a project greenlight, and the DLR is planned to extend across the water by 2009

Tourists The *Cutty Sark* et al draw a never-ending crowd. Residents must grin, put up with it – and expect more in the build-up to 2012

The Dome An expensive, expensive tribute to misjudgement, the Millennium Dome stands without purpose, unoccupied (for now), surrounded by an ugly ghost town

Poverty Splendid Georgian property in parts of Greenwich belies the fact that almost 20 neighbourhoods in ▼ the borough are among the most deprived in the country

club Charlton Athletic, whose family-friendly approach and fairly priced tickets guarantee it a top spot in local affections. Match days are inevitably busy, but generally good-natured. Move east towards Woolwich Dockyard and the less affluent part of town and you'll discover shops, caffs and, on Beresford Square, a pretty good street market. In general, though, this is a fairly soulless district.

The area's attractions are overshadowed by those of neighbouring Greenwich, but Charlton House (a Jacobean mansion set in beautiful grounds) is magnificent, and vestiges of Charlton's village roots (such as the parish church, St Luke's) can be seen along the Village. Firepower (the Royal Artillery Museum) and the Thames Barrier Learning Centre also provide local diversions, and they are due to be joined in time for the 2012 Olympics by the London Aquatic Centre. There are many open spaces in the area, including Charlton Park and Woolwich Common (the latter located opposite the Queen Elizabeth Hospital). In summer, the art deco Charlton Lido is popular too.

The Woolwich Ferry is the only means of crossing the Thames at this point, though things will change dramatically for the district if and when the planned Thames Gateway Bridge is given the go-ahead, and when the DLR extends over the river (due for completion in 2009).

STATISTICS

BOROUGH MAKE-UP
Population 218,856
Average weekly pay £514.10
Ethnic origins
 White 77.11%
 Mixed 2.73%
 Asian or Asian British 6.78%
 Black or Black British 11.08%
 Chinese or other 2.29%
Students 9.47%
Retirees 10.34%

HOUSING STOCK
Borough size 50.9km²
No. of households 97,522
Detached 3.8%
Semi-detached 17.9%
Terraced 35.7%
Flats (purpose-built) 32.7%
Flats (converted) 9.2%
Flats (both) 41.9%

CRIME PER 1,000 OF POPULATION
(English average in brackets)
Burglary 8 (6.4)
Robbery 5 (1.4)
Theft of vehicle 8 (4.5)
Theft from vehicle 10 (10)
Violence against the person 35 (16.5)
Sexual offences 2 (0.9)

MPs & COUNCIL
MPs *Eltham* Clive Efford (Labour); *Greenwich & Woolwich* Nick Raynsford (Labour)
CPA 3 stars; improving well

Restaurants & cafés

Considering how much spare money there is sloshing about SE10 (not only many wealthy residents, but also a constant trail of tourists), Greenwich is a disappointment foodwise. You won't starve – there are quite a number of chain restaurants (Nando's, Pizza Express) – but there are very few notable stand-alones. The borough's best restaurant is Inside, a mellow Modern European place that's rightly treasured by locals. Another winner is Pavilion Tea House in Greenwich Park: real care goes into the food and the location is lovely (a fantastic garden and fabulous views over London). Buenos Aires Café & Deli is also a bit of a find, redolent with classy smells: wonderful arabica coffee, Italian deli sandwiches, croissants and pastries. Inc Bar & Restaurant (decor courtesy of Laurence Llewelyn-Bowen, inspired by the 'slum and splendour' of Georgian Greenwich) is worth a visit, while Bar du Musée, with its diverse dining and drinking spaces, is another address worth remembering.

New development towards the Dome in North Greenwich has brought in Peninsula, a Chinese restaurant that occupies the ground floor of a budget commuter hotel. It serves dim sum all afternoon, every afternoon, as well as evening meals. Also away from the main drag is classic café Gambardella – check out the unique moulded plywood revolving chairs while enjoying egg and chips.

Bar du Musée *17 Nelson Road, SE10 9JB (8858 4710/www.bardumusee.com).*
Buenos Aires Café & Deli *86 Royal Hill, SE10 8RT (8488 6764/www.buenos airesltd.com).*

Sir Christopher Wren's **Old Royal Naval College**. *See p260.*

Gambardella *47-48 Vanbrugh Park, SE3 7JQ (8858 0327).*
Inc Bar & Restaurant *7 College Approach, SE10 9HY (8858 6721).*
Inside *19 Greenwich South Street, SE10 8NW (8265 5060/www.insiderestaurant.co.uk).*
Pavilion Tea House *Greenwich Park, Blackheath Gate, SE10 8QY (8858 9695).*
Peninsula *Holiday Inn Express, Bugsby's Way, SE10 0GD (8858 2028/www.mychinesefood.co.uk).*

Bars & pubs

Even disregarding the tourists drawn by Greenwich's maritime sights, this is still one of the most bustling places in south-east London – particularly at night. Party zones like Polar Bar and Oliver's get things lively: the former is a late-opening DJ bar, the latter a cosy jazz cellar, ideal for fans of mellow music plus those wanting an intimate drink *à deux*. Although surpassed by these two, one-time premier venue North Pole on Greenwich High Road still gets some action: it's a stylish three-floor club-bar-restaurant with DJs downstairs at weekends. Davy's Wine Vaults, part of the London-wide Davy's wine bar chain, is handy for thirsty commuters (it's next to Greenwich train station). Popular eating and drinking spots Inc Bar & Restaurant and Bar du Musée (for both, *see p256*) also do their bit to contribute to the mêlée.

For a less hectic sip, head to the Ashburnham Arms, a great local pub with intimate bar, friendly folk, tasty food and excellent Shepherd Neame ales – outside, garden and patio complete the accomplished picture. Talk of real ale pricked your taste buds? Then try the Greenwich Union, flagship outlet of Alistair Hook's lauded Meantime Brewing Company: friendly and knowledgeable staff will serve you signature Union, Chocolate, Golden, Raspberry and Stout beers in miniature before you order.

Next door, exemplary Young's pub Richard I is a comfortable alternative; north to the river, the stately Trafalgar Tavern is another option, with its superb location by the lapping Thames. Finally, with its outside tables jutting on to the trestled morass of Greenwich Market, the Coach is a prime Greenwich boozer; at once a bar, pub and market meeting place, it offers hearty ales and fine wines by the fireplace and daily papers in the lower lounge (stake your claim early at weekends).

Charlton lays claim to some of the least salubrious pubs in south-east London; boozers around the station and football ground are either suspiciously dark from

London for Londoners
every week

Time Out London — Out every Tuesday

the outside, or plastered with England flags. Try your luck at neither. Kidbrooke, too, is similarly starved, though benefits from the many fine boozers and lively nightspots of neighbouring Blackheath, across borough borders in Lewisham (*see p246*).

Ashburnham Arms *25 Ashburnham Grove, SE10 8UH (8692 2007).*
Coach *13 Greenwich Market, SE10 9HZ (8293 0880).*
Davy's Wine Vaults *161 Greenwich High Road, SE10 8JA (8853 0585/www.davy.co.uk).*
Greenwich Union *56 Royal Hill, SE10 8RT (8692 6258/www.greenwichunion.co.uk).*
North Pole *131 Greenwich High Road, SE10 8JA (8853 3020/www.northpolegreenwich.com).*
Oliver's *9 Nevada Street, SE10 9JL (8858 5855).*
Polar Bar *13 Blackheath Road, SE10 8PE (8691 1555/www.polarbar.co.uk).*
Richard I *52-54 Royal Hill, SE10 8RT (8692 2996).*
Trafalgar Tavern *Park Row, SE10 9NW (8858 2909/www.trafalgartavern.co.uk).*

Shops

A trip to Greenwich, if you don't live there, has the feel of a visit to the seaside: you'll find a scenic stretch of river with obligatory pubs, some choice museums and plenty of shops and markets to potter over.

Greenwich Market – open on Saturday and Sunday – actually consists of three separate markets. The smallest, the Weekend Market, is mostly bric-a-bac and junk. For second-hand clothes head to the Village Market, where you'll find Chinese silk dresses plus home furnishings and ethnic ornaments. The covered Crafts Market is the most rewarding as it is jam-packed with stalls selling handicrafts, jewellery, home furnishing and clothes.

The shops on the fringes of the covered market are also worth investigating. Hide All has an excellent selection of bags including Orla Kiely, Amano, Hidesign and Tula; Greenwich Printmakers offers original artworks that are also affordable; Essential Music deals in CDs in all genres; and Compendia specialises in games from around the world like Mexican train dominoes and the Japanese board game Go.

Nearby, the Emporium has a fine stock of vintage clothes, at much better prices than in central London. Worth crossing town for, Pickwick Papers & Fabrics has a huge selection of wallpapers and fabric, including David Oliver's glam glitter

designs. Max out on kitsch at Flying Duck Enterprises, which has a huge collection of original pieces from the '50, '60s and '70s. Board games, chopper bikes and neon palm-trees bar signs as standard. Next door, Pets & the City has a witty selection of toys, clothes and accessories for cats and dogs.

Greenwich is also known for its antiquarian and second-hand bookshops; Halcyon Books is one of the best all-rounder second-hand bookshops in the capital; Marcet Books concentrates on maritime texts with an interesting sideline on Nelson and Drake; and Maritime Books covers naval and mercantile history up to the end of World War II, with contemporary and historical naval magazines to boot.

For more Nelson memorabilia, elegant brass porthole mirrors and even vintage china from an 1822 shipwreck, visit jaunty little marine shop Nauticalia.

The heart of Greenwich aside, the rest of the borough offers little shopping excitement. Bugsby's Way, which links North Greenwich to Charlton, is lined with huge supermarkets (Asda, Sainsbury's) and shopping centres containing fashion stores (including Matalan), B&Q, Comet and so on. The heart of Charlton provides an old-style high street experience, while Woolwich has a bigger shopping precinct with M&S, Mothercare and others. There's an air of faded glory about the place, though also hope that the extension of the DLR will revitalise things.

Compendia *10 Greenwich Market, SE10 9HZ (8293 6616/www.compendia.co.uk).*
The Emporium *330-332 Creek Road, SE10 9SW (8305 1670).*

TRANSPORT

Tube stations *DLR* Cutty Sark, Greenwich, Deptford Bridge, Elverson Road; *Jubilee* North Greenwich
Rail stations *South Eastern Trains* Greenwich, Maze Hill, Westcombe Park, Charlton, Woolwich Dockyard, Woolwich Arsenal, Plumstead; Blackheath, Kidbrooke, Eltham, Falconwood
Main bus routes *into central London* 53, 188; *night buses* N1, N21, N108; *24-hour buses* 53, 108
River Woolwich Ferry; commuter and leisure boat services to/from central London, with piers at Greenwich and Woolwich Arsenal

Glorious **Greenwich Park** – just one of the area's many assets.

Essential Music *16 Greenwich Market, SE10 9HZ (8305 1876).*

Flying Duck Enterprises *320-322 Creek Road, SE10 9SW (8858 1964/www.flying-duck.com).*

Greenwich Market *Greenwich Market, SE10 (enquiries 8293 3110/www.greenwichmarket.net).*

Greenwich Printmakers *1A Greenwich Market, SE10 9HZ (8858 1569/www.greenwich-printmakers.org.uk).*

Halcyon Books *1 Greenwich South Street, SE10 8NW (8305 2675/www.halcyonbooks.co.uk).*

Hide All *9 Greenwich Market, SE10 9HZ (8858 6104/www.hideall.co.uk).*

Marcet Books *4A Nelson Road, SE10 9JB (8853 5408/www.marcetbooks.co.uk).*

Maritime Books *66 Royal Hill, SE10 8RT (8305 1310).*

Nauticalia *25 Nelson Road, SE10 9JB (8858 1066/www.nauticalia.com).*

Pets & the City *334 Creek Road, SE10 9SW (8858 3527).*

Pickwick Papers & Fabrics *6 Nelson Road, SE10 9JB (8858 1205/www.pickwick papers.co.uk).*

Arts & attractions

Cinemas & theatres

Greenwich Playhouse *189 Greenwich High Road, SE10 8JA (8858 9256/www.galleontheatre.co.uk).*

Greenwich Picture House *180 Greenwich High Road, SE10 8NN (0870 755 0065/www.picturehouses.co.uk).*

Greenwich Theatre *Crooms Hill, SE10 8ES (8858 4447/www.greenwichtheatre.org.uk).* Musical theatre productions.

Odeon Greenwich *Bugsby's Way, SE10 0QJ (0871 224 4007/www.odeon.co.uk).*

Galleries & museums

Cutty Sark *King William Walk, SE10 9HT (8858 3445/www.cuttysark.org.uk).* Launched in 1869, and now the last surviving tea clipper in the world.

Fan Museum *12 Crooms Hill, SE10 8ER (8305 1441/www.fan-museum.org).* More than 3,000 fans from around the world.

Firepower *Royal Artillery Museum, Royal Arsenal, SE18 6ST (8855 7755/www.firepower.org.uk).* Artillery through the ages, from catapults to nuclear warheads.

National Maritime Museum *Romney Road, SE10 9NF (8858 4422/information 8312 6565/tours 8312 6608/www.nmm.ac.uk).* Charts the nation's seafaring history.

Old Royal Naval College *King William Walk, SE10 9LW (8269 4747/tours 8269 4791/www.greenwichfoundation.org.uk).* Built by Sir Christopher Wren at the turn of the 18th-century; originally a hospital, then a naval college and now part of the University of Greenwich.

Royal Observatory & Planetarium *Greenwich Park, SE10 9NF (8312 6565/www.rog.nmm.ac.uk).* Also by Wren, built for Charles II in 1675, and the home of Greenwich Mean Time and the Prime Meridian Line. The first phase of the new Time and Space project opens in 2006, and will eventually include a brand-new planetarium.

Thames Barrier Information & Learning Centre *1 Unity Way, SE18 5NJ (8305 4188/www.environment-agency.gov.uk).* Learn about London's flood defence system: the world's largest adjustable damn, built in 1982 at the cost of £535m. This small learning centre would be submerged if it stopped working.

Music & comedy venues

St Alfege's Church *Church Street, SE10 9RB (www.st-alfege.org).*

Up the Creek *302 Creek Road, SE10 9SW (8858 4581/www.up-the-creek.com).*

Other attractions

Age Exchange Reminiscence Centre *11 Blackheath Village, SE3 9LA (8318 9105/ www.age-exchange.org.uk).* A charity that emphasises the value of memories through exhibitions, theatre, books and educational programmes.

Charlton House *Charlton Road, SE7 8RE (8856 3951/www.greenwich.gov.uk).* Grand Jacobean manor house, now used as a community centre and library.

Eltham Palace *Court Yard SE9 5QE 8294 2548/www.elthampalace.org.uk).* Two sights in one: a medieval royal palace and an art deco home. Run by English Heritage.

Greenwich & Docklands Festivals *www.festival.org* A festivals and event producing organisation working across east London in the boroughs of Greenwich, Tower Hamlets and Newham.

Greenwich Tourist Information Centre *Pepys House, 2 Cutty Sark Gardens, SE10 9LW (0870 608 2000).* Includes an exhibition on the history of Greenwich.

Millennium Dome *Drawdock Road, SE10 OAX.* The blighted Dome remains a major landmark of the Docklands area. It will host gymnastics, trampolining and basketball events at the 2012 Olympics; before that, plans are still uncertain.

Queen's House *Romney Road, SE10 9NF (8312 6565/www.nmm.ac.uk).* Palladian house designed by Inigo Jones in 1616 for James I's wife. It's now home to the National Maritime Museum's art collection (including paintings by Hogarth and Gainsborough) – and a ghost.

Ranger's House (Wernher Collection) *Chesterfield Walk, SE10 8QX (8853 0035/ www.english-heritage.org.uk).* Medieval and Renaissance art, housed in an 18th-century villa next to Greenwich Park. Run by English Heritage.

RECYCLING

No. of bring sites 80 (for nearest, visit www.recycleforlondon.com)

Household waste recycled 9.7%

Main recycling centre Nathan Way Waste Transfer Station, Nathan Way, SE28 0AN (8311 5229)

Other recycling services garden waste collection; home composting; furniture and white goods collection

Council contact Peter Dalley, Greenwich Council, Waste Services, Birchmere Business Park, Thamesmead, SE28 8BF (8921 4641)

Open spaces

Abbey Wood *Abbey Wood Road, SE2.*

Avery Hill *Bexley Road, SE9.*

Charlton Park *Charlton Park Road, SE7.*

Eltham Common *Well Hall Road, SE18.*

Greenwich Park *Blackheath Gate, Charlton Way, SE10 (visitors centre 8858 2608/ www.royalparks.org.uk).* One of London's great parks, offering fantastic city views, plenty of history and the Royal Observatory.

Greenwich Peninsula Ecology Park *Thames Path, John Harrison Way, SE10 (8293 1904/www.urbanecology.org.uk).* Once derelict land, now a pond-dipping, bird-watching riverside haven.

Maryon Park *Maryon Road, SE18.*

Maryon Wilson Park *Thorntree Road, SE7.* More pleasant than the nearby Charlton Park; has a small farm that offers organised tours.

Oxleas Wood *Shooter's Hill, SE9.*

Sutcliffe Park *Meadowside, SE9.*

Woolwich Common *Shooter's Hill Road, SE9.*

Sport & fitness

National Lottery money, and the investment of Greenwich Leisure (which manages sports facilities in a number of London boroughs), have meant an upturn in fortunes for the public leisure centres in Greenwich – they can certainly give the private clubs a run for their money. The Waterfront Leisure Centre, in particular, is outstanding, with excellent swimming facilities and ample provision for other sports. The private sector can offer PhysioActive, a gym that specialises in sports injuries; Gordon's is the place if you're into body-building.

Charlton Lido – one of just three lidos in south-east London still in operation – is a local gem.

Gyms & leisure centres

Arches Leisure Centre *80 Trafalgar Road, SE10 9UX (8317 5020/www.gll.org.uk).*

Charlton Health & Fitness Centre *Charlton Athletic Football Club, The Valley, West Stand, Floyd Road, SE7 8BL (8853 5454/www.gll.org.uk).*

Coldharbour Leisure Centre *Chapel Farm Road, SE9 3LX (8851 8692/www.gll.org.uk).*

David Lloyd Kidbrooke *Kidbrooke Park Road, at Weigall Road, SE12 8HG (8331 3901/ www.davidlloydleisure.co.uk).* Private.

Eltham Health & Fitness Centre *Messeter Place, SE9 5DW (8850 1234/www.gll.org.uk).*

Eltham Pools *Eltham Hill, SE9 5SU (8859 0898/www.gll.org.uk).*

Fitness First *Unit 1, Macbean Street, SE1 6LW (8312 7190).* Private.

Gordon's Gym *29A Herbert Road, SE18 3SZ (8854 6273).* Private.

Meadowside Leisure Centre *Tudway Road, SE3 9XT (8856 0101/www.gll.org).*

PhysioActive *Old Bank House, Mottingham Road, SE9 4QZ (8857 6000/ www.physioactive.com).* Private.

Plumstead Leisure Centre *Speranza Street, SE18 1JL (8855 8289).*

Royal Herbert Leisure Club *Royal Herbert Pavilions, Shooter's Hill Road, SE18 4PE (8319 0720).* Private.

Thamesmere Leisure Centre *Thamesmere Drive, SE28 8RE (8311 1119/www.gll.org.uk).*

Waterfront Leisure Centre *High Street, SE18 6DL (8317 5000/www.gll.org.uk).*

Other facilities

Charlton Lido *Hornfair Park, Shooter's Hill Road, at Charlton Park Lane, SE18 4LX (8856 7180/www.gll.org.uk).*

David Beckham Academy *East Parkside, SE10 0JF (no phone/www.thedavidbeckham academy.com).* Open during school holidays, this football coaching centre aims to teach eight- to 15-year-olds how to bend it like the man himself.

Royal Blackheath Golf Club *Court Road, SE9 5AF (8850 1795/www.rbgc.com).* Reputedly the oldest golf club in England, established in 1608.

Shooters Hill Golf Club *Lowood, Eaglesfield Road, SE18 3DA (8854 1216).*

Spectator sports

Charlton Athletic FC *The Valley, Floyd Road, SE7 8BL (8333 4000/4010/www.cafc.co.uk).*

Schools

WHAT THE PARENTS SAY:

‘Overall, Greenwich is somewhere in the middle when it comes to the quality of its schools. Where the borough has done really well is with the under-fives. The Robert Owen Centre is a beacon of good practice and the council has invested a huge amount of money in it. The primary schools are generally good. Two of my children go to Halstow, a very good state primary; parents try hard to get their kids into it. There's also the much talked-about new Millennium primary school on the peninsula, which looks modern and interesting – from the outside at least.

Secondary schools are a real issue, and there's a lot of dissatisfaction. Thomas Tallis is incredibly popular, but impossible to get into. Middle-class parents move to get their children into it, but it also takes kids from the more deprived Kidbrooke estate, so the school's population is genuinely mixed. However,

Charlton Health & Fitness. *See p261.*

even though we live only a mile away, we were told not to even bother trying for our children.

There aren't any notoriously bad secondary schools. Crown Woods isn't considered to be great as it's too big; the John Roan School used to have a poor reputation, but a new head was appointed two years ago and it's now thought to be improving. Kidbrooke School has become famous because of the attention of Jamie Oliver [during Channel 4's school dinner makeover show, *Jamie's School Dinners*, shown in summer 2005].

At least a quarter of the children at Halstow primary will go on to a private school – Colfe's is in Greenwich – although a lot of children will leave the borough. The middle classes are very much playing the system and getting their kids into state schools outside Greenwich too, in places like Bexley and North Kent. My eldest daughter goes to a grammar school in Dartford. There's a sense that the council is trying, but that it's tackling education from the bottom up and hasn't cracked secondary schools.’

Mother of three, Greenwich

Primary

Greenwich has 65 state primary schools, 18 of which are church schools. There are also seven independents, including a Steiner school and a theatre academy. See www.greenwich.gov.uk and www.ofsted.gov.uk for more information.

Secondary

Abbey Wood School *Eynsham Drive, SE2 9AJ (8310 9175).*
Blackheath Bluecoat CE School *Old Dover Road, SE3 8SY (8269 4300).*
Colfe's School *Horn Park Lane, SE12 8AW (8852 2283/www.colfes.com).* Private.
Crown Woods School *Riefield Road, SE9 2QN (8850 7678).*
Eltham Green *Middle Park Avenue, SE9 5EQ (8859 0133/www.elthamgreen.co.uk).*
Eltham Hill Technology College for Girls *Eltham Hill, SE9 5EE (8859 2843/ www.elthamhill.greenwich.sch.uk).* Girls only.
The John Roan School *Maze Hill, SE3 7UD (8516 7555/www.thejohnroanschool.co.uk).*
Kidbrooke School *Corelli Road, SE3 8EP (8516 7977/www.kidbrooke.greenwich.sch.uk).*
Plumstead Manor School *Old Mill Road, SE18 1QF (8855 5011/www.plumstead manor.com).* Girls only.
St Paul's Academy *Wickham Lane, SE2 0XX (8311 3868).*
St Thomas More RC Comprehensive School *Footscray Road, SE9 2SU (8850 6700).*
St Ursula's Convent School *Crooms Hill, SE10 8HN (8858 4613).* Girls only.
Thomas Tallis School *Kidbrooke Park Road, SE3 9PX (8856 0115).*
Woolwich Polytechnic School *Hutchins Road, SE28 8AT (8310 7000).* Boys only.

Property

WHAT THE AGENTS SAY:

❛It's called 'Historic Greenwich', you know, like 'Historic Bath'. There are a lot of Tudor and Queen Mary houses, plus a lot of beautiful Georgian properties. It's on the river, there's the *Cutty Sark*, and Greenwich Park is just a magical, lovely place. As for the Dome – there's not a lot in there right now, but it's due to become a large entertainment centre: cinemas, theatres, eating places, a basketball stadium… Love it or hate it, the Dome really put Greenwich on the map for a lot of people. It's comparable to villagey areas in west London like Barnes and Putney, but is a bit more isolated in that the areas surrounding Greenwich are less, er, nice.❜
Mark Epps, Winkworth, Blackheath Village

COUNCIL TAX
A	up to £40,000	**£786.49**
B	£40,001-£52,000	**£917.57**
C	£52,001-£68,000	**£1,048.65**
D	£68,001-£88,000	**£1,179.73**
E	£88,001-£120,000	**£1,441.89**
F	£120,001-£160,000	**£1,704.05**
G	£160,001-£320,000	**£1,966.22**
H	over £320,000	**£2,359.46**

Average property prices
Detached £357,070
Semi-detached £203,983
Terraced £169,394
Flat £160,928

Local estate agents
Alan Ives Estates *118 Plumstead High Street, SE18 1SJ (8854 0101/www.alanives. co.uk).*
Cockburn *352 Footscray Road, SE9 2EB (8859 8590/www.cockburn-online.co.uk).*
Greenwich Estates *115A Trafalgar Road, SE10 9TS (8858 8833/www.greenwich-estates.co.uk).*
Harrison Ingram *www.harrisoningram.co.uk; 4 offices in the borough (Charlton 8858 3434/ Eltham 8859 4419/Plumstead 8316 6616/ Thamesmead 8312 4111).*
James Johnston *22 College Approach, SE10 9HY (Greenwich 8858 9986/www. jamesjohnston.com).*
Oliver Bond *38 King William Walk, SE10 9HU (8858 9595/www.oliverbond.co.uk).*
Redwood Estates *13 Cumberland House, Erebus Drive, SE28 0GE (8316 8990/ www.redwoodestates.co.uk).*
Urtopia *26 Corbidge Court, Glaisher Street, Millennium Quay, SE8 3ES (8692 7000/ www.urtopia.com).*

Other information

Council
London Borough of Greenwich *Town Hall, Wellington Street, SE18 6PW (8854 8888/ www.greenwich.gov.uk).*

Hospitals
Queen Elizabeth Hospital *Stadium Road, SE18 4QH (8836 6000/www.queenelizabeth. nhs.uk).*

Legal services
Greenwich CAB *Old Town Hall, Polytechnic Street, SE18 6PN (08451 202931/www. adviceguide.org.uk).*
Greenwich Community Law Centre *187 Trafalgar Road, SE10 9EQ (8305 3350).*

Local newspapers
The Lewisham & Greenwich Mercury *8769 4444/http://icsouthlondon.icnetwork.co.uk.*

Allotments
Council Allotments *8856 2232/ www.greenwich.gov.uk.*
Gavestone Allotments *off Alwick Road, SE12 (Mr C Tomlin 8851 9407).*
Kidbrooke Allotments *Kidbrooke Park Road, SE3 (John Morgan 8853 5803).*
Prior Street Allotments *Prior Street, SE10 (Jon Yorke 8858 3104).*

Newham

The steamships that plied the Royal Docks in the Victorian East End may have disappeared, but working-class Newham is again set to become part of the global village. It's a host borough of the 2012 Olympic Games, and the derelict plot separating Stratford from Hackney is to be home to the Olympic Park.

Neighbourhoods

Stratford and Forest Gate

Stratford has great claim to be the most pleasant and convenient corner of Newham. Local amenities include the Broadway shopping mall east of the rail/tube station and charming West Ham Park, which borders Stratford and West Ham. There's also a four-screen cinema behind the Broadway shops, and the legendary Theatre Royal Stratford East (showing a mix of stand-up comedy, live music and serious drama). These venues mark out the district from much of the rest of the borough where such entertainment options are scarce.

Residents are attracted to Stratford and its surrounding neighbourhoods by the relatively low cost of buying and renting. Pick of the local property is the pocket of Victorian terraced houses between West Ham Lane and the park. The area also has excellent transport links; Stratford is the hub of one of London's best-served boroughs, linking the Central and Jubilee tube lines, DLR, Silverlink and mainline routes to north London. You can be in the City in ten minutes and Oxford Street in 20. If this and the flurry of property buying that followed the Olympic announcement weren't enough, a Channel Tunnel rail link due for completion in 2007 will hook Stratford up to the Continent.

Students mill around the red-brick Stratford campus of East London University on Romford Road (the A118), the main route linking Stratford with Forest Gate. The neighbourhood gets scruffier north and east from Stratford towards Forest Gate and Manor Park, where the quiet terraced streets are markedly less cheerful and the shopping

sparser, prompting hopes that Olympic investments will radiate out beyond the immediate environs of the Games site.

Newham boasts of being the most ethnically diverse borough in London. The large African, Caribbean and Asian populations that have developed since the post-war reconstruction years have been joined recently by an influx of immigrants from eastern Europe, but no one group predominates. There is still a (subdued) Albert Square in Forest Gate – complete with the remains of a Queen Vic pub currently being redeveloped into something more modern – but in Stratford, with its ethnic mix, and most of its houses bought-to-let, the Cockney community of *EastEnders* feels far away.

Highs & Lows

▲ **The Olympics, of course** Ask anyone about Newham's prospects for the future, and the Games will be the first thing mentioned. It will mean a new Olympic Park, better sports facilities, and more money for one of London's poorest boroughs
Abundant public transport Stratford has the tube, trains, the DLR, and buses – the full quota. By 2007, there'll also be a Channel Tunnel link

Crime Rife in big swathes of Newham; much of it goes unrecorded according to a 2005 survey
Beckton With a vast sewage works on one side, and the rather soulless world of Custom House and the Excel Centre on the other, Beckton's not one of London's most desirable neighbourhoods ▼

Downtown **Stratford**, transport hub for the surrounding area.

Upton Park and West Ham

People come from all over to visit Green
Street, the heart of Upton Park – some for
its sari shops and jewellers, some to see
a match at the Boleyn football stadium
towering over the south end of the street.
The neighbourhood's pride in West Ham
United finds expression in a statue of
England's 1966 World Cup hero Bobby
Moore being hoisted aloft by his Hammers
team mates.

Vibrant Queen's Market next to Upton
Park tube station, housed in something
resembling a concrete bunker, deals in
multicultural food and clothes; it's under
threat from redevelopment, but locals are
fighting for its survival. East Newham's
highly visible Indian, Bangladeshi,
Pakistani and Sri Lankan communities
are also well represented on Green Street
itself, which bustles in the day and empties
at night, its takeaway restaurants and
handful of pubs calm except on match-day
afternoons. The Victorian terraces around
Plashet Road and Plashet Park are quiet
and anonymous.

Beyond Green Street, the ornate three-
screen Boleyn Cinema, a beacon of charm
among the fast-food shops on Barking Road,
screens a strict diet of Indian Bollywood
films, but such diversions are scarce, as are
decent places to eat and drink. The arterial
Barking Road that cuts Newham in half –
actually the A124, leading to Essex via East
Ham – has some colourful stretches of shops
and takeaways, but nothing extraordinary.

Upton Park's more genteel better half,
West Ham is a mix of old and new terraces
and estates interrupted by the vast, iron-
gated East London Cemetery at its heart.
The nicest houses are around West Ham
Park, a wonderful recreation ground for
local school children and families, with
sports grounds and ornamental flower beds.

Clichés of the rough, tough East End
aside, residents in Upton Park, Plaistow
and the Hams do complain of sometimes
feeling unsafe after dark, reflecting
Newham's unenviable record – in 2005
it was one of the top ten London boroughs
for recorded crime.

East Ham and Plaistow

Lined with Asian shops and businesses,
East Ham's High Street North rivals
Upton Park's Green Street and Stratford's
Broadway in the daytime for the title of
liveliest strip in Newham. This bustling

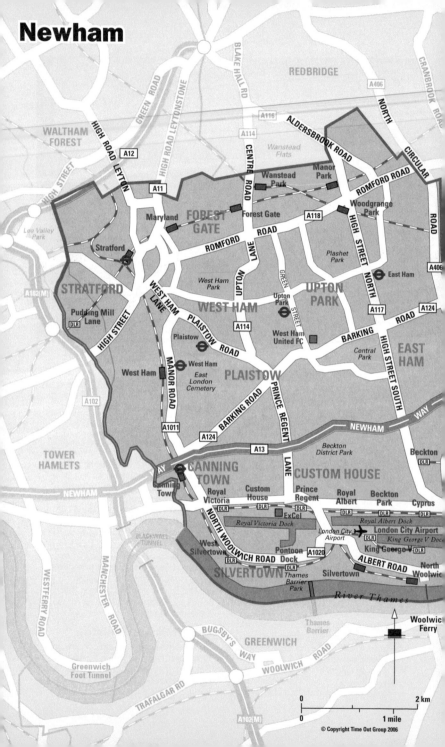

thoroughfare stretches south from Romford Road by Manor Park to the clock tower of Newham Council in East Ham. The council offices are in an attractive Victorian building at the junction of Barking Road and the High Street, adjoining East Ham Leisure Centre. Newham College of Further Education, just down the road, adds to the sense of community.

New residents are attracted to the Victorian terraced streets joining the High Street north of Plashet Park and in the grid known as the Burges Estate (in the area ranging east towards the Barking Relief Road). Central Park, an oasis of greenery that ties together many of the quieter Victorian residential streets in the heart of East Ham, is another popular area.

Stuck between East and West Ham, Plaistow is a nugget of ugliness lacking a centre. The area south of the tube station as far as Barking Road is made up of cheerless houses and high-rise estates, though the main artery, Prince Regent Lane, broadens and lightens in atmosphere around Newham Sixth Form College and Newham General Hospital, a modern building on a rise overlooking Plaistow. The streets teem with school kids on weekdays, reminding you that the borough of Newham has one of London's youngest populations. Nearby is the large, council-run Newham Leisure Centre, with track and field facilities as well as indoor pools. Traversing Plaistow is the Greenway, a pleasant four-mile tree-lined foot-and-cycle path linking Hackney with Beckton via the River Lea in Stratford and the East London Cemetery in West Ham.

Canning Town, Custom House and Silvertown

Stretching south to the old Royal Docks from the noisy A13, which severs it from the rest of Newham, Canning Town is a maze of residential streets and estates made convenient by a tube and rail station. The area was badly bombed, so much of the housing is post-World War II. The Royal Victoria Dock, now almost empty of boats, exists mainly for its aesthetic contribution to the giant Excel Exhibition Centre and the airport hotels that flank it, right under the path of jets landing at London City Airport.

The residential sprawl of Custom House continues into the modern estate housing of Beckton, an unpopular choice of home because of the vast sewage works nearby. There's green space at Beckton District Park and pigs and chickens at Newham City Farm, though the animals look rather forlorn in this part of the world.

South of the dock, the Victorian workers' township of Silvertown (named after the boss of a 19th-century rubber firm) is afflicted by the sickly rotten smell from the Tate & Lyle sugar refinery, and the roar of aeroplanes. A welcome green space comes in the form of the Thames Barrier Park, a modern, well-designed riverside park with great views of the space-age Thames Barrier (the visitor centre is on the other side of the river). Further east are more desolate estates in North Woolwich, while

The **Boleyn**, a vast Victorian pub next to West Ham United's ground.

the industrial space stretches west to Canning Town. Estate agents advertise flashy new apartments around Silvertown, Beckton and North Woolwich, but this neighbourhood still belongs to the factories.

Transport connections are good, though, with the DLR extension to London City Airport opening in December 2005, and the Woolwich Ferry providing a link to the south side of the Thames.

Restaurants & cafés

Brick Lane is dead – long live Green Street. The curry haven of Brick Lane may be better known, but it doesn't have the same authentic atmosphere (and variety of ingredients for sale) as the stretch of greengrocers, butchers, fishmongers and restaurants that is Green Street in Upton Park. Here, ethnic communities from all over the subcontinent rub shoulders, and the mix is reflected in the restaurants: best are Mobeen (a bright, clean, self-service Pakistani café) and Vijay's Chawalla (a Gujarati vegetarian sit-down-and-snack shop), plus Lazzat Kahari on nearby Plashet Grove (Punjabi food served buffet-style). This wouldn't be the East End without pie and mash, though, and East Ham is home to a classic server of the cheery treat: Robins.

Nowhere in the rest of Newham quite measures up to its eastern districts: apart from a handful of passable Indian and pizza restaurants, even Stratford and Forest Gate hardly pull their weight when it comes to eating opportunities. Barking Road from Canning Town to Plaistow has a thin smattering of fast-food shops, while people in the residential sprawl from Canning Town to Beckton tend to find themselves hailing the next bus in search of an interesting meal.

Lazzat Kahari *18 Plashet Grove, E6 1AE (8552 3413).*
Mobeen *222 Green Street, E7 8LE (8470 2419).*
Robins Pie & Mash *105 High Street, E6 1HZ (8472 1956).*
Vijay's Chawalla *268-270 Green Street, E7 8LF (8470 3535).*

Bars & pubs

Fingers are crossed that the planned transformation of Newham into an Olympic-worthy region will include the introduction of some medal-worthy drinking dens; as it stands, decent boozers are scarce. Take Stratford: though Olympic visitors will marvel at the many travel options (tube, rail, DLR, numerous bus routes), they'll wonder what its inhabitants do in the evening – other than use the transport facilities to go elsewhere. Only two boozers catch the eye: the King Edward VII (known locally as the King Eddie, with an upstairs restaurant and comfortable downstairs bar) and the Golden Grove. The latter is part of the JD Wetherspoon chain, which has introduced guest ales, cheerful food and a much-improved, family-luring cleanliness.

Down in bleak Plaistow, the friendly Black Lion is worth a mention, if only for its unusual puntership: the pub is home to both the West Ham Boys' Boxing Club, and the Phoenix Games Club, a role-playing games society (luckily, the former don't give the latter any trouble). For something totally different, try the palatial but friendly Boleyn, next to West Ham's football ground. During the week it's full of cheeky-chappy types; on match days it's a bit of a riot.

Black Lion *59-61 High Street, E13 0AD (8472 2351).*
Boleyn *1 Barking Road, E6 1PW (8472 2182).*
Golden Grove *146-148 The Grove, E15 1NS (8519 0750).*
King Edward VII *47 Broadway, E15 4BQ (8534 2313/www.kingeddie.co.uk).*

Shops

For Newham residents with a car, the biggest shopping draw actually lies outside the borough in Essex; indeed, Lakeside Shopping Centre, off the A13 that cuts across the borough as the Newham Way, has done quite some damage to the neighbourhood trade with its numerous chainstores and cafés. In Newham proper, the best retail action is in Stratford. The shopping centre on Broadway and the stretch of high street around it – including a small street market – caters for basic needs but offers few surprises.

In the centre of the borough, the main commercial activity is on Green Street in West Ham and the vast High Street running south from Plashet to East Ham. On Green Street, the discount stores and fast-food joints are interspersed with shops selling posh saris and jewellery, while Queen's Market is a well-stocked bustle of typical stalls selling cheap clothes and fresh foods. East Ham High Street has much of the same kind of pound shops and some high-street chains. For a touch more character, try the Myrtle Road Shopping Hall, an old covered arcade at the foot of the north stretch of the High Street in East Ham.

Arts & attractions

Cinemas & theatres

Boleyn Cinema *7-11 Barking Road, E6 1PN (8471 4884).*
Brick Lane Music Hall *443 North Woolwich Road, E16 2DA (7511 6655/www.bricklane musichall.co.uk).*
Stratford Picture House *Theatre Square, E15 1BN (8555 3366/bookings 0870 755 0064/www.picturehouses.co.uk).*
Theatre Royal Stratford East *Gerry Raffles Square, E15 1BN (0800 183 1188/8534 7374/www.stratfordeast.com).*

Other attractions

Discover *1 Bridge Terrace, E15 4BG (8536 5555/www.discover.org.uk).* Popular interactive play centre.
Excel Exhibition Centre *1 Western Gateway, Royal Victoria Dock, E16 1XL (7069 5000/ www.excel-london.co.uk).* Trade fairs, conferences, sporting events and concerts.

Newham

Open spaces

Beckton District Park *Strait Road, E6.*
Central Park *High Street South, E6.*
East Ham Nature Reserve *Norman Road,
E6 4HN (8470 4525). A small museum, as
well as nature trails through an overgrown
churchyard.*
East London Cemetery *Grange Road, E13
(www.eastlondoncemetery.co.uk).*
Newham City Farm *Stansfeld Road, E16
(7474 4960).*
Plashet Park *Plashet Grove, E6.*
Thames Barrier Park *Barrier Point Road,
off North Woolwich Road, E16 (www.thames
barrierpark.org.uk).*
West Ham Park *Upton Lane, E7.*

Sport & fitness

The private sector has hardly registered a
presence here. However, there's more than
adequate compensation in the very varied
shapes of its four public centres. East
Ham Leisure Centre opened in 2001 and
is justly Newham's flagship facility, but
a redevelopment programme at the other
venues, in conjunction with management
company Greenwich Leisure, has seen
usage grow in general. The private
Peacock Gymnasium in Canning Town is
an atmospheric and motivating place. Also
popular are the various watersports centres
in the old docks and the purpose-built cycle
circuit on the edge of Lee Valley Park.

Gyms & leisure centres

Atherton Leisure Centre *189 Romford
Road, E15 4JF (8536 5500/www.gll.org).*
Balaam Leisure Centre *Balaam Street,
E13 8AQ (7476 5274/www.gll.org).*
East Ham Leisure Centre *324 Barking
Road, E6 2RT (8548 5850/www.gll.org).*

RECYCLING

No. of bring sites 151 (for nearest,
visit www.recycleforlondon.com)
Household waste recycled 5.5%
Nearest recycling centre Jenkins Lane
Reuse & Recycling Centre, Jenkins
Lane, Barking, Essex IG11 0AD
(8504 5808)
Other recycling services home
composting; collection of white goods,
electrical goods, furniture and other
household items
Council contact The Recycling Team,
Central Depot, Folkestone Road,
E6 6BX (8430 3960)

Fit for Life *Second floor, Hawley House,
5-7 High Street, E13 0AD (8552 1776). Private.*
Newham Leisure Centre *281 Prince Regent
Lane, E13 8SD (7511 4477/www.gll.org).*
Peacock Gymnasium *Peacock House, Caxton
Street North, E16 1JL (7476 8427). Private.*

Other facilities

Docklands Equestrian Centre *2 Claps Gate
Lane, E6 6JF (7511 3917). Riding lessons
available for all ages.*
Docklands Watersports Club *Gate 14, King
George V Dock, Woolwich Manor Way, E16 2NJ
(7511 5000). Members of this jet-ski club need to
provide their own equipment and personal water
craft. Membership £350/yr.*
Lee Valley Cycle Circuit *Quartermile
Lane, E10 5PD (8534 6085/www.leevalleypark.
org.uk). Commonly known as Eastway, with
a road racing circuit, off-road trails and a
BMX track.*
London Regatta Centre *Dockside Road,
E16 2QT (7511 2211/www.london-regatta-
centre.org.uk). Located in the heart of the
Docklands, the centre provides training
facilities for rowing clubs, a fully equipped
gym and boat hire.*
Royal Victoria Dock Watersports Centre
*Gate 5, Tidal Basin Road, off Silvertown Way,
E16 1AF (7511 2326). The centre offers bell
boating, canoeing, raft building and sailing
lessons for both individuals and groups.*

Spectator sports

West Ham United FC *Boleyn Ground, Green
Street E13 9AZ (8548 2748/www.whufc.com).*

Schools

WHAT THE PARENTS SAY:

'Newham primary schools probably don't have
a great reputation as far as the league tables go,
but they all work really hard and schools in the
borough are very inclusive. I'm 100% satisfied
with the schooling my children have had. They
all went to New City Primary School in Plaistow.
It is a very big school, which I was anxious about,
but I needn't have worried – there's a real sense
of community there.

At secondary level, there are two single-sex
Catholic schools that people in Newham compete
to get into as they have very good academic
reputations. My eldest son went to the Royal
Docks Community School and did very well
in his GCSEs. My daughter is going to start at
Brampton Manor next year – it has improved
under a very strong head teacher, and when we
visited it seemed full of relaxed-looking teachers
and pupils who were excited about the future.
They also run a Saturday school.'
Mother of three, East Ham

Newham

Primary

There are 66 state primary schools in Newham, including ten church schools. There are also six independent primaries – all faith schools. See www.newham.gov.uk and www.ofsted.gov.uk for more information.

Secondary

Brampton Manor School *Roman Road, E6 3SQ (7540 0500).*
Cumberland School *Oban Close, E13 8SJ (7474 0231).*
Eastlea Community School *Exning Road, E16 4ND (7540 0400).*
Forest Gate Community School *Forest Street, E7 0HR (8534 8666).*
Kingsford Community School *Kingsford Way, E6 5JG (7476 4700).*
Langdon School *Sussex Road, E6 2PS (8471 2411/www.langdon.newham.sch.uk).*
Lister Community School *St Mary's Road, E13 9AE (8471 3311).*
Little Ilford School *Browning Road, E12 6ET (8478 8024/www.littleilford.newham.sch.uk).*
Newham College of Further Education *High Street South, E6 6ER (8257 4000/ www.newham.ac.uk).*
Newham Sixth Form College *Prince Regent Lane, E13 8SG (7473 4110/www.newvic.ac.uk).*
Plashet School *Plashet Grove, E6 1DG (8471 2418).* Girls only.
Rokeby School *Pitchford Street, E15 4RZ (8534 8946).* Boys only.
Royal Docks Community School *Prince Regents Lane, E16 3HS (7540 2700).*
St Angela's Ursuline Convent School *St George's Road, E7 8HU (8472 6022/www.anglia campus.com).* Girls only; mixed sixth form.
St Bonaventure's RC School *Boleyn Road, E7 9QD (8472 3844/www.lgfl.net/lgfl/leas/ newham/schools/st-bonaventures).* Boys only; mixed sixth form.
Sarah Bonnell School *Deanery Road, E15 4LP (8534 6791/www.sarahbonnell.newham. sch.uk).* Girls only.
Stratford School *Upton Lane, E7 9PR (8471 2415).*

Property

WHAT THE AGENTS SAY:

❝Stratford has become the centre of east London. There are lots of big firms here. It's like a second-rate copy of what's going on in the City – it's not the same right now, but it'll get there. Residents are mostly tenants – there's no real community feel, no real gelling of people, because it's broken up by tenanted property.

The ratio of people buying-to-let to those buying-to-live is about 70 per cent to 30 per cent – it's because of the Olympics making properties in the area attractive to investors. After London won the bid, we sold all our properties in about

four weeks. The scramble has since died down, but closer to the Olympics it'll probably snowball again. We're going to see massive development in the area; lots of jobs will be created.❞
Russell Hawkes, Charles Living & Son, Stratford

Average property prices

Detached £214,248
Semi-detached £171,411
Terraced £148,631
Flat £136,214

Local estate agents

Charles Living & Son *14-16 Romford Road, E15 4BZ (8534 1163/www.charlesliving.com).*
Marvel Estates *367 Katherine Road, E7 8LT (8471 0845/www.marvelestates.com).*
McDowalls *54-56 Barking Road, E6 3BP (8472 4422/www.mcdowalls.com).*
Samuel King *110A Barking Road, E16 1EN (7474 6000/www.samuelkingestateagents.co.uk).*
Spencer's Property Services *70 Woodgrange Road, E7 0EN (8555 5666/www.spencers property.co.uk).*

Other information

Council

London Borough of Newham Council
Newham Town Hall, Barking Road, E6 2RP (8430 2000/www.newham.gov.uk).

Hospitals

Newham General Hospital *Glen Road, E13 8SL (7476 4000/www.newham-healthcare.org).*
Plaistow Hospital *Samson Street, E13 9EH (8586 6251/8586 6240/www.newhampct.nhs.uk).*

Legal services

Newham CAB *Stratford Advice Arcade, 107-109 The Grove, E15 1HP (0870 126 4097/ www.adviceguide.org.uk).*

Local newspapers

Newham Recorder *8472 1421/ www.newhamrecorder.co.uk.*

Allotments

Council allotments *The Allotment Officer, 292 Barking Road, E6 3BA (8430 2455/3606).*

Redbridge

Ditch any preconceptions you might have about east London. Redbridge – sitting pretty astride the Essex border – exudes an air of well-to-do suburbia. It boasts first-rate schools and a choice selection of sports clubs, and is within easy reach of both central London and the East Anglian countryside.

Neighbourhoods

Wanstead

With its golf, cricket, tennis and bowls clubs, plus countless local societies, Wanstead is where suburbia begins. As you head east, it's the first place that has a life independent of the capital and is markedly different in character from grittier Leytonstone, one stop back down the Central Line. Though the county boundary is a couple of miles further out, this stretch of E11 is where Essex intrudes into London.

There's plenty of money round here, and an 'East End made good' mentality. For those who made their pile in Bow, but don't fancy moving to the so-called 'golden triangle' of Chigwell, Buckhurst Hill and Loughton, there are the lairy mansions near the golf course (cash only, please), private schools, and a David Lloyd centre just up the road.

The presence of the Central Line – there are stations at both ends of the High Street – means Wanstead is not entirely cut off from London (or, more specifically, from the City). The attractive 18th-century villas near Snaresbrook Crown Court and what locals call 'Swan Lake' were originally built for City merchants; easy tube access means this area continues to be popular with workers in the Square Mile. The general air of prosperity is reflected in property prices.

Central Wanstead and the Aldersbrook Estate (which is surrounded by the historic Wanstead Park and the vast playing fields of Wanstead Flats) consist of large, classic late-Victorian terraced houses. Most are occupied by families keen to maintain Wanstead's strong community feel; there are active churches, residents' associations and a High Street where people chat over coffee and choose to shop rather than

drive to Tesco. However, even powerful campaigns have been unable to prevent a number of pubs and bars gaining late licences, increasing residents' concerns about after-hours noise and aggravation. Christchurch Green is lovely by day, but can be rather forbidding at night.

When the M11-A12 link road was tunnelled through the area in the early 1990s, with protesters gaining national attention by creating the 'independent republic of Wanstonia', many feared that Wanstead's leafy character would be destroyed. That hasn't happened – it retains the feel of a small town within reach of, but at arm's length from, London.

South Woodford

South Woodford may help you change your mind about E numbers. With Epping Forest running continuously along one flank, and

Highs & Lows

▲ **Suburban contentment** Strongly residential, the area attracts families looking to settle; local amenities and activities meet this demand
Excellent schools At both primary and secondary levels, Redbridge has a range of well-performing schools. Parents move from miles away to take advantage

Garishness East End-made-good mentality means a lot of flash houses, fast cars and bling.
North Circular The noise from this six-lane beast, cutting through the otherwise pleasant streets of E18, is inescapable

Christchurch Green

many pockets of wealth, it has been a smart, middle-class residential area since the 19th century. A measure of its status – and pretensions – is a large branch of Waitrose.

At one end of E18 is the Drive: the local millionaires' row of 1930s mansions. At the other extreme, London shades into Essex at Woodford Green, with its postage-stamp cricket ground, bronze statue of former MP Sir Winston Churchill, and celebrity residents like Tamzin Outhwaite and Patsy Palmer (pop into Pizzeria Bel-Sit to look at the signed photos). In between are countless Victorian and Edwardian properties radiating from the shopping centre in George Lane. The area is popular with families because of the good local schools. The Odeon, the only mainstream cinema for miles around, keeps the local teenagers happy when they're not getting kicked out of the George next door.

City-rich singletons and couples snap up the luxury flats along the High Road, attracted by the decent cafés and bars and the fact that South Woodford is close to plenty more happening places.

There is, however, a scar running through the heart of E18. Six lanes of the North Circular lie in a deep cutting, with the High Road crossing over on a bridge. The noise is inescapable, spoiling the otherwise pleasant Victorian streets close by. Unlike in neighbouring Wanstead, where the A12 was tunnelled through the central town area to cause minimal blight, the planners of an earlier generation paid less heed to the physical and psychological damage caused by heavy traffic.

The thundering lorries on the A406 don't seem to harm South Woodford's appeal, though. It's prosperous but friendly, with only a hint of the Essex flash that's to come a mile or two further out.

Restaurants & cafés

The Wanstead restaurant scene has recently been shaken up by Applebee's, the offshoot of an upmarket fish stall in Borough Market. The impeccable provenance of their modern British menu has set a challenge to Hadley House, whose hefty meat dishes attract a regular, well-heeled clientele. Nam An is an oasis of oriental opulence serving high-quality Vietnamese food just yards from the A12 interchange , while Gastrodome is part of a small chain of diners specialising in grills and spit-roasted chicken. Of the cafés that dot the High Street, Nice Croissant is the best option for coffee, cake and a natter.

The South Woodford equivalent is the 1950s-styled Soul Stop Café, while good-value fish restaurant Ark and the noisy but good-natured Yellow Book Californian Café offer more substantial fare. You'll need to travel further afield to find the best ethnic options: Curry Special (North Indian) in Newbury Park and Mandarin Palace (Chinese), hard by the Gants Hill roundabout. If you've got kids to entertain, don't miss Pizzeria Bel-Sit in Woodford Green. Every inch of wall and ceiling is crammed with signed football shirts, balls and photos.

Redbridge

Redbridge

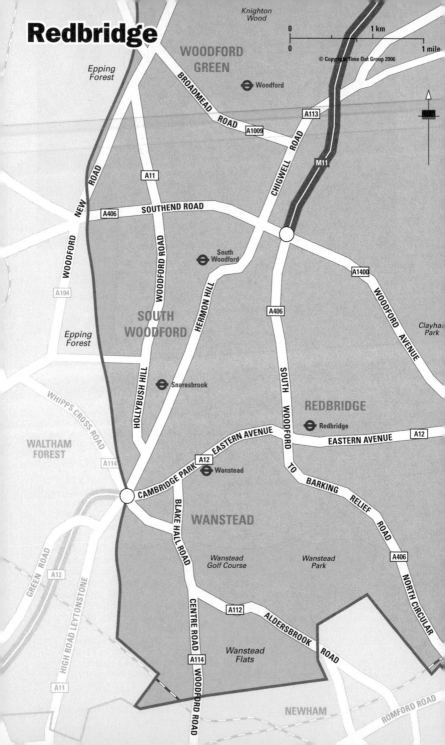

Knighton
Wood

WOODFORD
GREEN

0   1 km
0   1 mile
© Copyright Time Out Group 2006

Epping
Forest

BROADMEAD ROAD

Woodford

A113

A1009

CHIGWELL ROAD

M11

A11

NEW ROAD

A406   SOUTHEND ROAD

WOODFORD ROAD

HERMON HILL

South
Woodford

A104

A1400

WOODFORD AVENUE

Clayha
Park

A406

Epping
Forest

SOUTH
WOODFORD

HOLLYBUSH HILL

Snaresbrook

WHIPPS CROSS ROAD

WALTHAM
FOREST

SOUTH WOODFORD

REDBRIDGE

Redbridge

EASTERN AVENUE   A12

A114

CAMBRIDGE PARK   EASTERN AVENUE

A12

Wanstead

BLAKE HALL ROAD

WANSTEAD

TO   BARKING   RELIEF   ROAD

A406

GREEN ROAD

A12

HIGH ROAD LEYTONSTONE

Wanstead
Golf Course

Wanstead
Park

NORTH CIRCULAR

CENTRE ROAD

A112

ALDERSBROOK ROAD

Wanstead
Flats

A114

WOODFORD ROAD

A11

NEWHAM

ROMFORD ROAD

STATISTICS

BOROUGH MAKE-UP
Population 241,900
Average weekly pay £497.90
Ethnic origins
White 63.52%
Mixed 2.44%
Asian or Asian British 24.99%
Black or Black British 7.59%
Chinese or other 1.46%
Students 9.24%
Retirees 11.32%

HOUSING STOCK
Borough size 56.3km²
No. of households 94,174
Detached 5.6%
Semi-detached 26.8%
Terraced 40.3%
Flats (purpose-built) 19%
Flats (converted) 7.9%
Flats (both) 26.9%

CRIME PER 1,000 OF POPULATION
(English average in brackets)
Burglary 7 (6.4)
Robbery 5 (1.4)
Theft of vehicle 7 (4.5)
Theft from vehicle 12 (10)
Violence against the person 19 (16.5)
Sexual offences 1 (0.9)

MPs & COUNCIL
MPs *Chingford & Woodford Green* Iain
Duncan Smith (Conservative); *Leyton
& Wanstead* Harry Cohen (Labour)
CPA 2 stars; improving well

Applebee's *17 Cambridge Park, E11 2PU
(8989 1977).*
Ark *142 Hermon Hill, E18 1QH
(8989 5345).*
Curry Special *2 Greengate Parade, Horns
Lane, IG2 6BE (8518 3005).*
Gastrodome *17 High Street, E11 2AA
(8989 8943).*
Hadley House *27 High Street, E11 2AA
(8989 8855).*
Mandarin Palace *559-561 Cranbrook
Road, IG2 6JZ (8550 7661).*
Nam An *157 High Street, E11 2RL
(8532 2845).*
Nice Croissant *119A High Street, E11 2RL
(8530 1129).*
Pizzeria Bel-Sit *439 High Road, IG8 0XE
(8504 1164).*
Soul Stop Cafe *154 George Lane, E18 1AY
(8989 1849).*
Yellow Book Californian Café *190 George
Lane, E18 1AY (8989 3999).*

Bars & pubs

The watering holes along Wanstead's High
Street and South Woodford's George Lane
attract a young and often lairy clientele, so
don't turn up at the Cuckfield, Bar Room
Bar and Russells in E11, or the Hogshead
and Jets in E18, if you're after a quiet glass
of merlot. In each you'll find a fair selection
of perma-tanned Essex girls getting stoked
up for a night ogling the footballers and
Z-list soap stars at Faces, and far too
many Chelsea shirts quaffing badge lagers
(this is east London, lads).

Better drinking options are found
away from the main drag. Fine locals
with well-kept beer and a welcome are the
Nightingale in Wanstead and the Cricketers
and Travellers Friend in Woodford Green.
The last has never served keg beer and is
a TV- and fruit machine-free zone.

Bar Room Bar *33-34 High Street, E11
2AA (8989 0552/www.barroombar.com).*
The Cricketers *299-301 High Road, IG8
9HQ (8504 2734).*
The Cuckfield *31 High Street, E11 2AA
(8532 2431).*
Faces *458 Cranbrook Road, IG2 6LE
(8554 8899).*
Jets Wine Bar *77-79 George Lane, E18
1JJ (8989 2334).*
The Nightingale *51 Nightingale Lane,
E11 2EY (8530 4540).*
Russells *44 High Street, E11 2RJ (8518 8477).*
Travellers Friend *496-498 High Road,
Woodford Green, IG8 0PN (8504 2435).*

Shops

Ilford is the main destination for Redbridge
residents, with the Exchange Mall offering
most major names and a medium-sized
branch of Marks & Spencer. There's
also a farmers' market on the first and
third Saturday of each month on the
pedestrianised High Road.

Wanstead doesn't go without, though.
Its villagey ambience is enhanced by
an excellent butcher, AG Dennis, and a
quality greengrocer, JD Harvey & Sons
(which recently won a prize from residents'
association the Wanstead Society for
its friendly service). Up the road, South
Woodford offers branches of Sainsbury's
and Waitrose, while sausage lovers
should head for Joshua Hill's.

You'll find quality men's clothes at Santa
Fe and Men's Club in Wanstead, though

Redbridge

The suburban good life, at the **Nice Croissant**. *See p273.*

anyone getting ready for a night out at Faces may prefer the clobber at Jun-Qi in Woodford Green. Azzurra and Rio stock pricey women's shoes. To complete the look, Zoology is an award-winning hair salon. There's a home furnishings branch of Laura Ashley in South Woodford, though Devon House Interiors is the place to go if you've got serious money to spend. And if lugging that wardrobe home leaves more than your wallet screaming for mercy, the Back Pain Centre is run by Terry Chimes – the Clash's original drummer who's been a registered chiropractor since 1994.

AG Dennis *3 Clock House Parade, High Street, E11 2AG (8989 2691).*
Azzurra *119B High Street, E11 2RL (8532 9405).*
Back Pain Centre *50 Chigwell Road, E18 1LS (8989 3330).*

TRANSPORT

Tube stations *Central* Wanstead, Redbridge, Gants Hill, Newbury Park, Barkingside, Hainault, Grange Hill, Roding Valley, Woodford, South Woodford
Rail stations *one* Ilford, Seven Kings, Goodmayes, Chadwell Heath; *Silverlink* Wanstead Park
Main bus routes *into central London* 25; *night buses* N8, N55, N86; *24-hour buses* 25, 369

Devon House Interiors *3-5 Hermon Hill, E11 2AW (8518 8112/www.devonhouse interiors.co.uk).*
Exchange Mall *High Road, IG1 1RS (8553 3000).*
Ilford Farmers' Market *High Road, near Town Hall, IG1.*
JD Harvey & Sons *6 Clock House Parade, High Street, E11 2AG (8989 6369).*
Joshua Hill's Famous Sausages *126 George Lane, E18 1AD (8989 3083).*
Jun-Qi *172 High Road, IG8 9EF (8559 2122).*
Laura Ashley *12-14 Electric Parade, George Lane, E18 2LY (0871 223 1468).*
Men's Club *54A High Street, E11 2RJ (8530 4946).*
Rio Shoes *54 High Street, E11 2RJ (8530 3533).*
Santa Fe *119 High Street, E11 2RL (8518 8922).*
Zoology *145 High Street, E11 2RL (8530 3005).*

Arts & attractions

Cinemas & theatres
Cineworld Ilford *Clements Road, IG1 1EA (0871 220 8000/www.cineworld.co.uk).*
Kenneth More Theatre *Oakfield Road, IG1 1BT (8553 4464/box office 8553 4466/www.kenneth-more-theatre.co.uk).*
Odeon South Woodford *60-64 High Street, E18 2QL (0871 224 4007/www.odeon.co.uk).*

Galleries & museums
Redbridge Museum *Central Library, Clements Road, IG1 1EA (8708 2432/ www.redbridge.gov.uk/leisure/museum.cfm).* Local history museum.

Other attractions

Valentines Mansion *Emerson Road, IG1 4XA (no phone).* The traditional garden of this 17th-century mansion in Valentines Park is open to visitors.

Open spaces

Clayhall Park *Longwood Gardens, IG5.*
Hainault Forest Country Park *Romford Road, IG7.*
Loxford Park *Loxford Lane, IG1.*
Ray Park *Snakes Lane East, IG8.*
Valentines Park *Cranbrook Road, IG1.*
Wanstead Flats *Centre Road, E7 & E11.* Vast playing fields.
Wanstead Park *Northumberland Avenue, Warren Road, E11.* Heavily wooded, the park has several beautiful water features and a ruined temple.

Sport & fitness

This middle-class segment of east London suburbia plays host to countless sports clubs amid its green acres. The trust-run Redbridge Sports & Leisure Centre is superb – undoubtedly among the very best health centres in the capital. Physicals is the pick of the other private clubs, although the chains are establishing an ever-stronger presence. In contrast, public-sector provision is dreadful: just one sports centre (Wanstead) and two pools (Fullwell Cross and Ilford).

Gyms & leisure centres

David Lloyd *Roding Lane, IG9 6BJ (8559 8466/www.davidlloydleisure.co.uk).* Private.
Fitness First *261-275 High Road, IG1 1NJ (8514 7666/www.fitnessfirst.co.uk).* Private.
Fullwell Cross Leisure Centre *133 High Street, IG6 2FA (8550 2366/www.leisure-centre.com).*
Ilford Pools Leisure Centre *468 High Road, IG1 1UE (8553 0639/www.leisure-centre.com).*
Physicals *327 High Road, IG8 9HQ (8505 4914/www.physicalsfitness.co.uk).* Private.
Redbridge Sports & Leisure Centre *Forest Road, IG6 3HD (8498 1000/ www.rslonline.co.uk).* Private.
Wanstead Leisure Centre *Redbridge Lane West, E11 2JZ (8989 1172).*

Other facilities

Wanstead Golf Course *Overton Drive, E11 2LW (8989 3938/0604/www.wanstead golf.org.uk).*

RECYCLING

No. of bring sites 70 (for nearest, visit www.recycleforlondon.com)
Household waste recycled 9.6%
Main recycling centre Chigwell Road Reuse & Recycling Centre, Chigwell Road (opposite Maybank Road), South Woodford, IG8 8PP (8504 5808)
Other recycling services green waste collection; home composting; white goods collection
Council contact Cleansing Services, London Borough of Redbridge, Ley Street House, 497-499 Ley Street, Ilford, Essex IG2 7QY (customer contact centre 8554 5000)

Schools

WHAT THE PARENTS SAY:

'Lots of people move to Redbridge for its schools. At primary level, state schools are in the top ten nationally. Our children go to the Wanstead Church Primary School; Our Lady of Lourdes is another denominational school that does well. Church Fields in South Woodfood and Snaresbrook Primary are both popular too.

Secondary schools are even better, with excellent-quality teaching. There's fierce competition to get into Woodford County and Ilford County. Apart from Hainault Forest School, which is in special measures, all the other secondary schools are good. Redbridge parents also look out of borough to the Coopers' & Coborn school in Upminster, which is the most successful state school in the country. The idea that east London is at the bottom of the education pile is grossly untrue – if education is a factor in choosing where to live, then Redbridge should be the number one choice in London.'
Andrew Shields, father of three, Leytonstone

Primary

There are 51 state primary schools in Redbridge, including seven church schools and two Jewish schools. There are also 16 independent schools, including three faith schools. See www.redbridge.gov.uk/learning and www.ofsted.gov.uk for more information.

Secondary

Beal High School *Woodford Bridge Road, IG4 5LP (8551 4954/www.bealhighschool. org.uk).*
Canon Palmer Catholic School *Aldborough Road South, IG3 8EU (8590 3808/www.canonpalmer.redbridge.sch.uk).*

Caterham High School *Caterham Avenue, IG5 0QW (8551 4321/www.caterham. redbridge.sch.uk).*
The Chadwell Heath Foundation School *Christie Gardens, RM6 4RS (8252 5151/ www.chadwellheath.redbridge.sch.uk).*
Hainault Forest High School *Harbourer Road, IG6 3TN (8500 4266/www.hainault forest.redbridge.sch.uk).*
Ilford County High School for Boys *Fremantle Road, IG6 2JB (8551 6496/ www.ichs.org.uk).* Boys only.
Ilford Ursuline High School *Morland Road, IG1 4JU (8554 1995/www.ilford ursuline-high.org.uk).* Girls only.
King Solomon High School *Forest Road, IG6 3HB (8501 2083/www.kshsonline.com).*
Loxford School of Science & Technology *Loxford Lane, IG1 2UT (8514 4666).*
Mayfield School *Pedley Road, RM8 1XE (8590 5211).*
Oaks Park High School *45-65 Oaks Lane, IG2 7PQ (8590 2245).* Opened in 2003.
Seven Kings High School *Ley Street, IG2 7BT (8554 8935/www.skhs.net).*
Trinity Catholic High School *Mornington Road, IG8 0TP (8504 3419/www.trinity. redbridge.sch.uk).*
Valentines High School *Cranbrook Road, IG2 6HX (8554 3608/www.valentines-sch.org.uk).*
Wanstead High School *Redbridge Lane West, E11 2JZ (8989 2791/www.wanstead high.co.uk).*
Woodbridge High School *St Barnabas Road, IG8 7DQ (8504 9618).*
Woodford County High School for Girls *High Road, IG8 9LA (8504 0611/www. woodford.redbridge.sch.uk).* Girls only.

Property

WHAT THE AGENTS SAY:

‘Wanstead has two Central Line stations, plus access to the M11, or the A406 and A12 into Docklands, so it's convenient for work. We've also got good schools – state, church and private. The properties are largely turn of the century, with the odd bit of new-build thrown in, so it still looks good and retains a villagey atmosphere. The tree-lined High Street has a park and a nice mix of shops and places to eat. A cross-section of people live here: all races, all ages. There are some TV celebs in the pricier houses. We tend to leave them in peace – they live here too, just like us.’
Gary Clarke, Churchill Estates, Wanstead

Average property prices

Detached £286,899
Semi-detached £217,115
Terraced £170,104
Flat £114,908

COUNCIL TAX

A	up to £40,000	**£798.21**
B	£40,001-£52,000	**£931.24**
C	£52,001-£68,000	**£1,064.28**
D	£68,001-£88,000	**£1,197.31**
E	£88,001-£120,000	**£1,463.38**
F	£120,001-£160,000	**£1,729.44**
G	£160,001-£320,000	**£1,995.52**
H	over £320,000	**£2,394.62**

Local estate agents

Churchill Estates *32 High Street, E11 2RJ (8989 0011/www.churchill-estates.co.uk).*
Homes & Co *131 High Road, E18 2PA (8504 8844/www.homesandco.com).*
Ideal Residentials *88 Ley Street, IG1 4BX (8478 2999/www.idealresidentials.co.uk).*
Richard John Clarke *397 High Road, IG8 0XG (8559 1555/www.richardjohnclarke.com).*
Sandra Davidson *www.sandradavidson.com; 2 offices in the borough (Redbridge 8551 0211/ Seven Kings 8597 7372).*
Spencer's Property Services *www.spencers property.co.uk; 2 offices in the borough (Woodford Green 8559 2110/Ilford 8518 5411).*

Other information

Council

Redbridge Council *Town Hall, PO Box 2, Ilford, Essex IG1 1DD (8554 5000/ www.redbridge.gov.uk).*

Hospitals

Barking Hospital *Upney Lane, IG11 9LX (8983 8000/www.bhrhospitals.nhs.uk).*
Goodmayes Hospital *Barley Lane, IG3 8XJ (8983 8000/www.bhrhospitals.nhs.uk).*
King George Hospital *Barley Lane, IG3 8YB (8983 8000/www.bhrhospitals.nhs.uk).*
Mellmead House Day Hospital *4 Orchard Close, E11 2DH (8491 2181).*
Oldchurch Hospital *Waterloo Road, RM7 0BE (01708 345 533/www.bhrhospitals.nhs.uk).*

Legal services

Loughton CAB *St Mary's Parish Centre, High Road, IG10 1BB (8502 0031/ www.adviceguide.org.uk).*
Redbridge CAB *2nd Floor, Broadway Chambers, 1 Cranbrook Road, IG1 4DU (0870 126 4140/www.adviceguide.org.uk).*

Local newspapers

Wanstead & Woodford Guardian *www.guardian-series.co.uk.*

Allotments

Council Allotments *8th Floor, Lynton House, 255-259 High Road, IG1 1NY (8708 3091/ www.redbridge.gov.uk).*

Waltham Forest

Waltham Forest is holding its breath, hoping to realise its own Olympic dreams following the granting of the 2012 Games to nearby Stratford. Pluses include affordable housing, a community-minded football club, a top greyhound track and Europe's longest street market, but this remains a neglected borough.

Neighbourhoods

Walthamstow

When house prices in Hackney started to soar, first-time buyers bolted across the River Lea to the borough of Waltham Forest. Sadly, the days when you could buy a three-bedroom house in Walthamstow for the price of a one-bedroom flat in Stoke Newington have long gone. The influx of newcomers was already in process when Stratford was chosen as the location for the 2012 Olympics. Prices across the borough are set to rocket as the regeneration phase of the Olympic development gets under way.

Until the arrival of the railway in 1840, Walthamstow was a peaceful village, and at its heart you'll still find a self-sufficient atmosphere, despite some runaway industrial development. The most attractive neighbourhood – featuring interesting architecture from a variety of eras – is the area around the overgrown churchyard of St Mary's, one of the few parts of London deserving a 'village' tag. Highlights include a couple of good restaurants, pubs and the excellent Vestry House Museum.

Otherwise, the district contains a blend of dark-brick terraces and large-scale housing estates, home to a mix of young professionals and families from South Asia, Africa, Turkey and the Caribbean. Notable accommodation for first-time buyers or renters includes the 19th-century Warner Flats, purpose-built one- and two-bedroom abodes. At the north end of the district is Walthamstow Stadium – the only greyhound track still operating in the East End – and nearby is pretty Lloyd Park, childhood home to the late-Victorian craftsman, designer and socialist William Morris. All aspects of Morris's life are explored in the enjoyable museum housed on the premises, which is a popular summer destination for young mums.

Walthamstow is rightly proud of its street market, which is claimed to be the longest in Europe, sprawling along the mainly pedestrianised High Street. It's a lively, frenetic place, run by old East Enders and full of stalls selling mops and bags of fruit and veg for a pound.

Transport connections are good: Walthamstow is linked to central London by the Victoria Line and at least four rail stations, plus a plethora of buses. Nevertheless, the commute to and from town is invariably a crowded affair.

Leyton

Perched on the edge of the new Olympic Park, Leyton lacks the homely feel of Walthamstow Village but does have

Highs & Lows

▲ **Affordable housing** Many people buy their first flats in Leyton or Leytonstone before moving on, as tradition dictates, to Redbridge when they earn more money
Walthamstow street market The longest in Europe, apparently

Scruffiness Despite the efforts of Waltham Forest Council in recent years, large chunks of the borough remain distinctly down at heel
No cinema Since the controversial closure of the EMD cinema in Walthamstow, locals have to
▼ head to Stratford to catch a movie

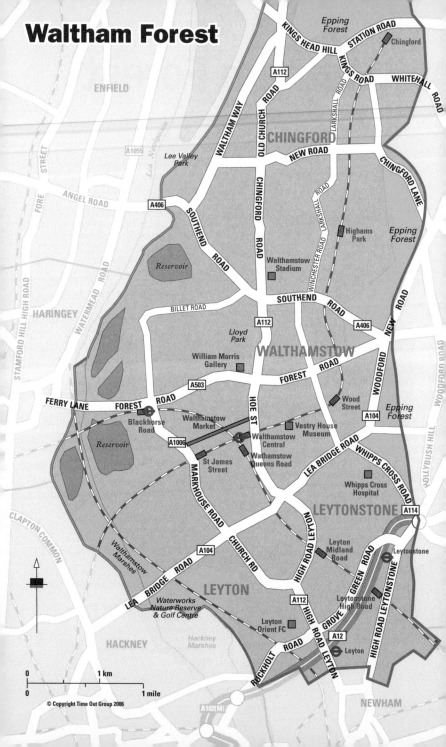

Waltham Forest

excellent transport links. The Central Line whisks commuters to the heart of the City, while the A12 runs east to Essex and the A102 speeds traffic south across the Thames. This area is set to go upmarket, as Olympic hysteria sweeps through north-east London. The much-publicised blocks of flats built on the four corners of Leyton Orient's football ground are the first evidence of the desire to attract greater youth and affluence to the neighbourhood.

For now, Leyton remains more inner city than suburban. There are some tranquil terraced rows and the restored Coronation Gardens are a joy, but there are almost as many industrial zones and concrete estates, filling in spaces created by wartime bombing. Cutting through it all is the drab High Road Leyton, which must be one of the longest high streets in Europe when combined with its northern extension in Walthamstow.

Along the High Road, you'll find a very limited selection of shops and supermarkets (a run-of-the-mill Tesco at one end and Asda at the other), a good public library, but a bizarre lack of cash machines or banks – a persistent local complaint. There are a couple of Pakistani canteens, and some culinary variation is offered by the growing Portuguese community who have opened a restaurant and café opposite the library. Overall, though, the prevalence of takeaways over quality eateries is a cause of disappointment for the middle classes. At the south end of the district is the vast Leyton Mills shopping mall, with plenty of central London brands yet little atmosphere.

An important new development in Leyton is the £10m Score sports centre on Oliver Road, behind the football ground. The facility offers a huge indoor sports hall, high-quality outdoor pitches, a nursery and a Primary Care Trust. Leyton Orient's award-winning community work has always extended way beyond the provision of mere football coaching and this centre enables work to continue on problem estates, with refugees and with the ethnically diverse population.

Lee Valley Park is a welcome green space that sprawls north and south along the River Lea (confusingly, both Lea and Lee are acceptable spellings for the waterway). In addition, there's a riding school, an ice-rink and marina (mainly used by narrow-

boats) and miles of meadows for walking in the Walthamstow Marshes. Also here is the Waterworks Nature Reserve & Golf Centre – a novel use for what used to be the Essex Filter Beds, which were built to purify London's drinking water in 1849.

Leytonstone

First impressions of Leytonstone are not very appealing. Emerge from the tube station and you'll find a handful of independent retailers scratching a living alongside bottom-end chainstores and empty premises. The loudest voices on the street will be South African, whose adopted home, Zulu's on the High Road, pulls in huge crowds at weekends but is the bane of many residents' lives. Indeed, 20,000 Saffies are reckoned to live in

---

STATISTICS

BOROUGH MAKE-UP
Population 220,180
Average weekly pay £479.70
Ethnic origins
  White 64.49%
  Mixed 3.55%
  Asian or Asian British 14.75%
  Black or Black British 15.42%
  Chinese or other 1.79%
Students 9.24%
Retirees 9.43%

HOUSING STOCK
Borough size 38.8km²
No. of households 93,714
Detached 3.4%
Semi-detached 16.3%
Terraced 41.5%
Flats (purpose-built) 24.7%
Flats (converted) 13.3%
Flats (both) 38%

CRIME PER 1,000 OF POPULATION
(English average in brackets)
Burglary 8 (6.4)
Robbery 8 (1.4)
Theft of vehicle 7 (4.5)
Theft from vehicle 14 (10)
Violence against the person 28 (16.5)
Sexual offences 1 (0.9)

MPs & COUNCIL
MPs *Leyton & Wanstead* Harry Cohen (Labour); *Walthamstow* Neil Gerrard (Labour)
CPA 1 star; subject to review

Lloyd Park, a local asset that's also home to the William Morris Gallery. *See p279.*

Leytonstone and Leyton, adding colour or aggravation, depending on whether your house is within earshot of the bar and you want a decent night's sleep.

New blocks of flats on the High Road confirm Leytonstone's reputation as a target for first-time buyers, with the 15-minute Central Line journey to Liverpool Street a strong lure. Once settled, these newcomers may find they don't want to leave: Leytonstone is scruffy but generally safe, with a strong sense of community that shows itself in an annual arts festival and car-free day. There's an increasingly bohemian edge provided by 491 Gallery on Grove Green Road, which calls itself a Sustainable Community Regeneration Art Project (SCRAP), and the tiny Vertigo cinema next door.

Most of Leytonstone's late-Victorian terraces are occupied by middle-class British and Asian families, who rub along pretty harmoniously. Upper Leytonstone has a Hindu temple, while Bushwood claims the mosque; right by the junction of Church Lane and the High Road is St John's, whose vicar is a popular figure for his work to bring together locals of all faiths and none.

You'll find every community out enjoying the greenery of Epping Forest and Wanstead Flats (across borough boundaries in Redbridge; *see p272*). There's a mooted return for the legendary Leytonstone cows, who until the early 1990s were free to roam and often caused havoc – and hilarity – at the busy Green Man roundabout.

Restaurants & cafés

A trio of fine Italian restaurants grace Walthamstow Village and its surrounding area: charming trattoria La Ruga, hearty Mondragone and family-friendly La Cafeteria. Otherwise, Walthamstow is largely served by takeaway kebabs, pizzas and Chinese outlets, of varying quality, but it has a genuine gem in pie and mash shop L Manze on Walthamstow High Street. Opened in 1929, it's a welcome authentic respite from the ubiquitous fast food.

Leytonstone's High Road has a broad mix of international eateries, but only a handful are worth checking out, notably Singburi (Thai), Chopsticks (Chinese) and the Elche (Spanish). Nearby Café Larosh (Indian) on Church Lane is also rated.

Café Larosh *7 Church Lane, E11 1HG (8518 7463).*
La Cafeteria *841 Forest Road, E17 4AT (8527 1926).*
Chopsticks *686 Leytonstone High Road, E11 3AA (8539 7802).*
Elche *567-569 Leytonstone High Road, E11 4PB (8558 0008/www.elcherestaurant. co.uk).*
L Manze *76 Walthamstowe High Street, E17 7LD (8520 2855).*
Mondragone *25-27 Orford Road, E17 9NL (8923 1113).*
La Ruga *59 Orford Road, E17 9NJ (8520 5008).*
Singburi *593 Leytonstone High Road, E11 4PA (8281 4801).*

TRANSPORT

Tube stations *Central* Leyton, Leytonstone; *Victoria* Blackhorse Road, Walthamstow Central
Rail stations *one* St James Street, Walthamstow Central, Wood Street, Highams Park, Chingford; *Silverlink* Blackhorse Road, Walthamstow Queens Road, Leyton Midland Road, Leytonstone High Road
Main bus routes *into central London* 48, 55, 56; *night buses* N55; *24-hour buses* 69

Bars & pubs

Leyton and Leytonstone hide a few havens for the pub connoisseur. Just minutes from Leyton tube station, the Birkbeck Tavern is a gem of a pub; the William IV would also be a credit to any neighbourhood. In Leytonstone, the North Star pub is a welcoming spot – as long as you're in the mood for a noisy crowd. The Sir Alfred Hitchcock Hotel (Hitch was born in Leytonstone) recalls a grander age, though the hotel bar's interior is a little scruffy. Raucous Zulu's is popular with local South Africans and is rammed at weekends.

Over in Walthamstow, the Flower Pot is a marvellously archaic den, with an interior apparently untouched since the war (possibly even the first one). The Nag's Head is a little more refined (as is Orford Road, where it's situated): it's popular with Pimms drinkers and jazz fans. The Village, on the same strip, is tattier, but has a great selection of beers.

Birkbeck Tavern *45 Langthorne Road, E11 4HL (8539 2584).*
Flower Pot *128 Wood Street, E17 3HX (8520 3600).*
Nag's Head *9 Orford Road, E17 9LP (8520 9709).*
North Star *24 Browning Road, E11 3AR (8989 5777).*
Sir Alfred Hitchcock Hotel *147 Whipps Cross Road, E11 1NP (8530 3724).*
Village *31 Orford Road, E17 9NL (8521 9982).*
William IV *816 Leyton High Road, E10 6AE (8556 2460).*
Zulu's *640 Leytonstone High Road, E11 3AA (8558 6846/www.zulus.co.uk).*

Shops

Waltham Forest is not what you would call a shopping destination – a relative dearth of large stores and attractive curios, coupled with the proximity of the North Circular Road, with its access to out-of-town superstores, means that residents are more likely to leave the borough and do their shopping in Stratford, Ilford or beyond.

Unless, of course, they're car-less: which is where Walthamstow's epic street market – the borough's beating heart – comes into its own. A teeming strip of some 450 stalls and 300 shops stretching the length of the High Street (linking Hoe Street to St James's Street), it's open every day except Sunday.

For conventional chain stores, the Selborne Walk shopping centre at the High Street's east end suffices, while Hoe Street has a continuous chain of shops and takeaways running south to High Road Leyton.

Apart from two large supermarkets (Asda and Tesco), which attract residents from Stratford and Walthamstow, Leyton and Leytonstone have very little to entice the curious shopper.

Arts & attractions

Galleries & museums

Vestry House Museum *Vestry Road, E17 9NH (8509 1917/www.lbwf.gov.uk).* Local history museum.
William Morris Gallery *Lloyd Park, Forest Road, E17 4PP (8527 3782/www.lbwf.gov.uk).*

Open spaces

Coronation Gardens *Oliver Road, E10.*
Epping Forest *Rangers Road, E4.* A wonderful space for walking, jogging, cycling, riding and picnicking; stop at the visitors' centre (8505 0028) for information and maps.
Langthorne Park *Birch Grove, E11*
Lee Valley Park *Waltham Abbey, E17.* Large green space that sprawls into the boroughs of Enfield and Haringey.
Lloyd Park *Forest Road, E17.* Peaceful spot, with excellent amenities: tennis courts, a skate park, café, duck ponds, an aviary and gardens.
Walthamstow Marshes *Lea Bridge Road, E17.* Ideal for walks by the River Lea, the marshes employ a pleasingly low-tech method of horticultural maintenance: a herd of cows is let loose in July to munch the grass until it's gone.

Waltham Forest

Sport & fitness

Waltham Forest's five public centres are managed by Greenwich Leisure – and it's doing a decent job. Score, a massive community sports project costing £10m, opened in summer 2005.

Gyms & leisure centres

Bannatyne's Health & Fitness Club Chingford 2 Morrison Avenue, E4 8SA (8503 2266/www.bannatyne.co.uk). Private.
Cathall Leisure Centre Cathall Road, E11 4LA (8539 8343/www.gll.org).
Greens Health & Fitness Larkswood Leisure Park, 175 New Road, E4 9EY (8523 7474/ www.greensonline.co.uk). Private.
Kelmscott Leisure Centre Markhouse Road, E17 8RN (8520 7464/www.gll.org).
Larkswood Leisure Centre Larkswood Leisure Park, New Road, E4 9EY (8496 1555/www.gll.org).
Leyton Leisure Lagoon 763 High Road, E10 5AB (8558 8858/www.gll.org).
Results Health & Leisure Studio 14A Hickman Avenue, E4 9JG (8523 5133/ www.resultshealthstudio.co.uk). Private.
Waltham Forest Pool & Track 170 Chingford Road, E17 5AA (8527 5431/www.gll.org).

Other facilities

Lee Valley Ice Centre Lea Bridge Road, E10 7QL (8533 3154/www.leevalleypark.org.uk).
Lea Valley Riding Centre Lea Bridge Road, E10 7QL (8556 2629/www.leevalleypark.org.uk).
Score 100 Oliver Road, Leyton E10 5JY (8556 5973).

Spectator sports

Walthamstow Stadium Chingford Road, E4 8SJ (8498 3300/www.wsgreyhound.co.uk). Greyhound racing.
Leyton Orient Football Club Matchroom Stadium, Brisbane Road, E10 5NE (8926 1111/ 1010/www.leytonorient.com).

Schools

WHAT THE PARENTS SAY:

‘We moved house three years ago to put us in the catchment area for the Yardley School, one of the top five Waltham Forest primaries, and Chingford Foundation School, one of the top five secondary schools. My previous address presented me with quite a dilemma regarding secondary schools as, apart from an all-girls school in the vicinity, they were all pretty poor.

We also looked at the local grammar schools, and my daughter has been seeing a private tutor to assist with entrance exams. The competition for the local grammars is fierce, with Woodford County High for Girls in Redbridge (see p278)

only taking 5% of the possible 120 places from Waltham Forest, and the other, Latymer School in Enfield (see p292), having 1,600 applicants for 160 places. All the other really good schools are either fee-paying or Catholic or faith schools.

Waltham Forest Council is currently working very hard to improve education in the borough, and recently had a great Ofsted inspection. The borough has also been lucky enough to be included in the first wave of the government BSF [Building Schools for the Future] initiative, so there are good prospects on the horizon.’
Amanda Shepherd, mother of two, Chingford

Primary

There are 50 state primary schools in Waltham Forest, nine of which are church schools. There are also six independent primaries, including two faith schools and one Montessori school. See www.eduaction.com and www.ofsted.gov.uk for more information.

Secondary

Aveling Park School Aveling Park Road, E17 4NR (8527 5794/www.avelingparkschool.ik.org).
Chingford Foundation School Nevin Drive, E4 7LT (8529 1853/www.chingford-school.co.uk).
Connaught School for Girls Connaught Road, E11 4AB (8539 3029). Girls only.
George Mitchell School Farmer Road, E10 5DN (8539 6198).
Heathcote School Normanton Park, E4 6ES (8498 5110).
Highams Park School Handsworth Avenue, E4 9PJ (8527 4051/www.highamspark. waltham.sch.uk).
Holy Family Technology College www.holyfamily.waltham.sch.uk; Walthamstow House site 1 Shernhall Street, E17 3EA (8520 0482); Wiseman House site Shernhall Street, E17 9RT (8520 3587).
Kelmscott School Markhouse Road, E17 8DN (8521 2115).
The Lammas School 150 Seymour Road, E10 6LX (8988 5860).
Leytonstone School Colworth Road, E11 1JD (8988 7420).
McEntee School Billet Road, E17 5DP (8527 3750).
Norlington Boys' School Norlington Road, E10 6PZ (8539 3055). Boys only.
Rush Croft School Rushcroft Road, E4 8SG (8531 9231/www.rushcroft.waltham.sch.uk).
Tom Hood School Terling Close, E11 3NT (8534 3425).
Walthamstow Girls' School Church Hill, E17 9RZ (8509 9446/www.walthamstow school.net). Girls only.
Warwick Boys' School www.warwick-waltham.co.uk; Lower School Brooke Road, E17 3ND; Upper School Barrett Road, E17 9HJ (8520 4173). Boys only.
Willowfield School Clifton Avenue, E17 6HL (8527 4065/www.willowfield.waltham.sch.uk).

**Walthamstow
street market.**
See p279.

Property

WHAT THE AGENTS SAY:

'Walthamstow is one of the few London areas left – especially around the Wood Street end – where a big three-bedroom house is still affordable. Plus you've got Epping Forest right behind you. It also has a thriving street market, and the Selbourne Walk shopping centre is pretty good. Transport is handy for London – good buses, overground trains and the tube. The conservation area has its own unique village atmosphere, with mock Tudor buildings and the Vestry House Museum. A lot of the development flow, though, is going outwards – to Leyton mostly, because it's near Stratford. Because of the Olympics, you know?'

Ali Khan, Village Estates, Walthamstow

Average property prices

Detached £286,899
Semi-detached £217,115
Terraced £170,104
Flat £114,908

Local estate agents

Alan Harvey *658 High Road, E11 3AA (8539 4000/www.alanharvey.co.uk).*
Allen Davies & Co *342 High Street, E10 5PW (8539 2121/www.allendavies.co.uk).*

COUNCIL TAX

A	up to £40,000	£869.75
B	£40,001-£52,000	£1,014.70
C	£52,001-£68,000	£1,159.66
D	£68,001-£88,000	£1,304.62
E	£88,001-£120,000	£1,594.54
F	£120,001-£160,000	£1,884.45
G	£160,001-£320,000	£2,174.37
H	over £320,000	£2,609.24

Central Estate Agents *179 Hoe Street, E17 3AP (8520 0033/www.central-estates. co.uk).*
Clarke Hillyer *www.clarkehillyer.co.uk; 2 offices in the borough (Chingford 8529 7100/Walthamstow 8521 6121).*
Kingsbridge Properties *Marlborough Business Centre, 96 George Lane, E18 1AD (8989 9811).*
Outlook *429-431 High Road, E10 5EL (8558 9900/www.outlookproperty.com).*
Village Estates *54-56 Hoe Street, E17 4PG (8223 0784/www.villageestates.org.uk).*

Other information

Council

Waltham Forest Council *Town Hall, Forest Road, E17 4JF (8496 3000/www.waltham forest.gov.uk).*

Hospitals

Thorpe Coombe Hospital *714 Forest Road, E17 3HR (8520 8971/www.nelmht.nhs.uk).*
Whipps Cross University Hospital *Whipps Cross Road, E11 1NR (8539 5522/ www.whippsx.nhs.uk).*

Legal services

Walthamstow CAB *167 Hoe Street, E17 3AL (0870 126 4026/www.walthamforestcab. org.uk).*

Local newspapers

www.guardian-series.co.uk.
The Guardian series of newspapers publishes various local papers for east London and west Essex, including the *Walthamstow Guardian, Chingford Guardian, Leyton & Leystonstone Guardian* and *Waltham Forest Independent.*

Allotments

Council Allotments *Environmental Services, Greenspace Group, Low Hall Depot, Argall Avenue, E10 7AS (8496 3000).*

Waltham Forest

Enfield

Welcome to the northern suburbs: land of IKEA, pitch and putt, and amateur dramatics. Despite odd attempts to jazz up the district, stability remains the norm. Yes, thrills might be in short supply, but you do get abundant parkland, plenty of family homes and the opulent tranquillity of Winchmore Hill.

Neighbourhoods

Edmonton

Edmonton doesn't have an awful lot to recommend it. It's a corner of Enfield where suburban life gently ebbs and flows but rarely changes. One hairdresser's closes down and is instantly replaced by another. Twin and triplet towers of council estates blot the landscape, seemingly designed to display a lack of charisma.

Edmonton Green is a likeable if rudimentary shopping area and transport terminal, which is currently undergoing a much-needed overhaul. Construction is due for completion by 2007 (did we imagine a collective cheer when the bulldozers took to the multistorey car park in June 2005?). Elsewhere, more renewal has been promised; the Lower Lea Valley area is set for development as part of the 2012 Olympic plans. The recently opened IKEA (scene of farcical, and near-fatal, madness when a mob tried to rush through its doors on opening night in February 2005) has perked up the environs of Upper Edmonton somewhat. Helping things along, many areas of nearby wasteland have been converted into not-unattractive housing estates in recent years.

Palmers Green and Southgate

As many late-night travellers through north London have discovered (when the well-used N29 night bus terminates here without warning), Palmers Green technically stretches past the bus station at the crossing of Green Lanes and the North Circular and towards Wood Green. To locals, however, Palmers Green 'proper' is the stretch of Green Lanes between the Triangle (a junction at the base of Aldermans Hill) and St John's Church on Bourne Hill, along with the many surrounding roads of Edwardian semis to the north and south. The roads laddered along Aldermans Hill ('the Lakes estate' in agent-speak as they're all named after British lakes) are popular with kiddied-up professional couples.

Over the past few years this part of Palmers Green has tried to gentrify and emulate the north London 'villages' of Highgate and Crouch End. Success has been limited. A reasonable attempt has been made in the immediate surrounds of Palmers Green station – a weekly farmers' market in the car park, a popular café-cum-jazz bar called the Waiting Rooms in the station itself – but, on the whole, Palmers Green belongs to unchanging suburbia.

The PG stretch of Green Lanes is full of the usual stores and supermarkets; despite middle-class resistance some years ago, the

Highs & Lows

▲ **Schools** Enfield has loads – and people compete from all over London to get into the Latymer School, one of the top mixed grammars in the country
Transport links It's well served by both rail and tube (there are four Zone 4 Piccadilly Line stations), so getting into the West End is as fast as from tubeless Hackney

Lack of decent bars Excluding the odd inoffensive pub, is there a single desirable nightspot in Enfield?
Chavs Although Eros nightclub – the Burberry Brigade's second home – is ▼ north near Enfield Town, lairy chavs spill out in packs all over the borough

Waiting Rooms café at **Palmers Green station**.

Big Three fast-food chains have all been able to entrench themselves in and around the Triangle. At night, the area isn't particularly friendly.

This district is home to a large Greek community; a memorable night came in 2004 when Greece's national football team won the European Cup, creating a swell of national pride in Palmers Green that manifested itself in street parties, fireworks, beeping car horns, and the occasional attempt to tip over passing buses.

Broadly encompassing the N14 postcode, Southgate is predominantly residential. Property ranges from the semi-detached Edwardian rows near Palmers Green to the high-priced stand-alones towards Winchmore Hill. The neighbourhood is very child-friendly, flanked as it is by two fairly large parks (Oakwood and Grovelands) offering a variety of activities such as pitch and putt and a boating lake. On the border with Barnet to the north-east is the Chicken Shed Theatre, which runs a drama club for both able-bodied and disabled children. Performances are often of a high standard (annual pantos are especially popular) and the waiting list to join is long.

Circling the Zone 4 tube station, Southgate Circus is the main hub of the area, with a clutch of half-decent eateries (long-standing Spanish joint La Paella is probably the best), sandwich delis, and a M&S food store round the corner towards Oakwood. Snaking away in the direction of Cockfosters, the south end of Chase Side is the area's main strip, though it offers little more exciting than a few chain restaurants and

pubs. The area's main landmark is Southgate station: a fine art deco specimen designed by Charles Holden in the 1930s.

Winchmore Hill

Bounded to the west by the junction of Green Lanes with Green Dragon Lane (by the former Green Dragon pub) and to the east by Grovelands Park, Winchmore Hill is the prettiest and most tranquil of Enfield's southern neighbourhoods. The Green, a cute grassy square, rests at the heart of the district. It's a throwback to Winchmore Hill's days as a quiet hamlet, and is duly speed-bumped to preserve the peace. The overland rail station is nearby.

Proximity to Grovelands Park is a boon for the many residents with young children; the parents themselves can expend energy at Winchmore Hill's excellent lawn tennis club or on the nearby Enfield Golf Course.

Property here tends to be more lavish than in neighbouring wards. Broadwalk – a long residential road linking Winchmore Hill to Palmers Green and Southgate – features some of the most expensive (and, some would say, tasteless) properties in the borough. No doubt many of its residents would prefer this road to be gated. Given the hotchpotch of ill-matching architectural styles along its length, aesthetes might agree.

Restaurants & cafés

Hardly known as an area of gastronomic excellence, Enfield does possess the odd delight. Family-run Café Anjou gallantly flies the Gallic flag in Palmers Green; down

Enfield

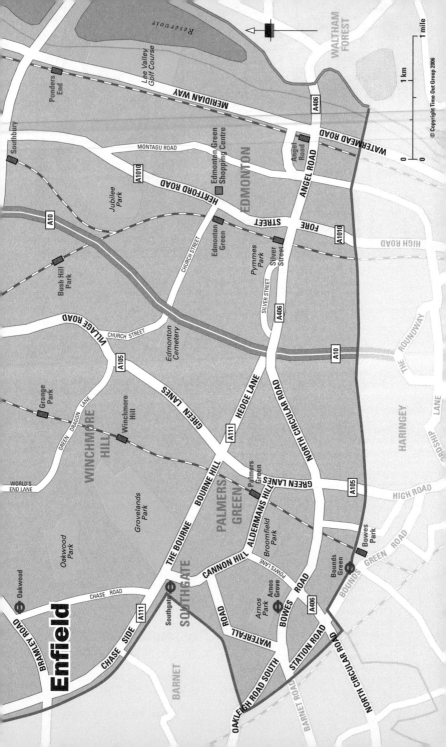

the road, Di Nero's sandwich deli (source of bizarrely delicious mayonnaise) continues the fight against the fast-food chains at lunch. The Waiting Rooms in Palmers Green station was once fantastic for salads, pastries and breakfasts, but a change in ownership has seen overall quality decline a jot. Up in Southgate, the likes of Spanish brasserie La Paella hold fast against chains such as Pizza Express on Chase Side. North is Dylan's, bringing a touch of contemporary elegance to deepest Cockfosters. Winchmore Hill has local faves fish restaurant Sargasso Sea and Italian Regatta, plus a well-used branch of Pizza Express. If Edmonton has a culinary speciality at all, it's uninviting chicken takeaways.

Café Anjou *394 Green Lanes, N13 5PD (8886 7267).*
Dylan's Restaurant *21 Station Parade, Cockfosters Road, EN4 0DW (8275 1551/ www.dylansrestaurant.com).*
Di Nero's *335 Green Lanes, N13 4TY (8886 1440).*
La Paella *9 Broadway, N14 6PH (8882 7868).*
Regatta *10-12 The Green, N21 1AY (8886 5471/www.regattarestaurant.co.uk).*
Sargasso Sea *10 Station Road, N21 3RB (8360 0990/www.sargassosea.co.uk).*
Waiting Rooms *Palmers Green Station, Aldermans Hill, N13 4PN (8886 7781).*

Bars & pubs

Palmers Green has a surplus of pubs; whether you'd want to drink in them is another matter. The Fox (an immense old boozer that's been tarted up) is something of a social hub, although the popular comedy nights are no more; many find it too young and brash, and are put off by particularly gruff bouncers. Elsewhere, the Inn on the Green in Palmers Green and the New Crown in Southgate, are fine for what they are – unimaginative chain pubs. Nicer is Ye Olde Cherry Tree, which draws a slightly older crowd. Down by the North Circular, the once-iconic Manhattan pub is now renamed and rebranded as a Sports Zone boozer. In Winchmore Hill, the Green Dragon pub was bought out by chain Jim Thompsons a few years ago – the old name is still used by most locals (it retains a pleasant beer garden, too). Better is the inviting Kings Head, in a grand Victorian building on Winchmore Hill Green that's recently had a makeover. In Edmonton,

the pubs that aren't chain joints tend to be intimidating backwater boozers – try the few on Church Street if you're desperate, though these are often peopled by the barely legal from local schools.

Of course, a round-up of Enfield's nightlife wouldn't be complete without a mention of the chav-tastic Enfield Town (don't try the George unless you're well-stocked with Burberry clothing) or the dreadful Eros superclub – home to the same crowd of alcopop-quaffing blondes and brawns every night (plus the odd minor Spurs player).

The Fox *413 Green Lanes, N13 4JD (8886 9674).*
Inn on the Green *295 Green Lanes, N13 4XS (8886 3760).*
Jim Thompson at the Green Dragon *889 Green Lanes, N21 2QP (8360 0005).*
Kings Head *1 The Green, N21 1BB (8886 1988/www.geronimo-inns.co.uk).*
New Crown *80-84 Chase Side, N14 5PH (8882 8758).*
Ye Olde Cherry Tree *22 The Green, N14 6EN (8447 8022).*

STATISTICS

BOROUGH MAKE-UP
Population 276,335
Average weekly pay £481.10
Ethnic origins
White 77.11%
Mixed 2.96%
Asian or Asian British 7.77%
Black or Black British 10.45%
Chinese or other 1.71%
Students 9.33%
Retirees 11.23%

HOUSING STOCK
Borough size 81.2km^2
No. of households 117,000
Further figures not available

CRIME PER 1,000 OF POPULATION
(English average in brackets)
Burglary 8 (6.4)
Robbery 4 (1.4)
Theft of vehicle 7 (4.5)
Theft from vehicle 10 (10)
Violence against the person 19 (16.5)
Sexual offences 1 (0.9)

MPs & COUNCIL
MPs *Edmonton* Andrew Love (Labour); *Enfield, Southgate* David Burrowes (Conservative)
CPA 3 stars; improving well

Shops

Palmers Green has a brace of good bookshops on Green Lanes: small-but-ample Palmers Green Bookshop, and the excellent British Red Cross shop next door, entirely dedicated to cut-price, second-hand literature. A surprising find on this stretch is the Only Place for Pictures, a boutiquey stop for prints, posters and frames. Palmers Green Antique Centre is also popular.

For clothing, Catwalk serves women and men – stocking brands like Miss Sixty and Elle for the former, Diesel and Replay for the latter. Similar labels are available elsewhere in the borough, at Zucchero in Southgate and X-It in Winchmore Hill. Slightly more upmarket are Angel Boutique (women's) and Twenty-One the Green (men's) on Winchmore Hill Green. Also on the Green you'll find various independent shops, such as garden centre King Easton and homeware outfit Dantel on the Green. Back in Southgate, look out for Kate Kuba's sale shop (up to 70 per cent off previous season's stock), AMT for sportswear and Italian deli Italcibo. Aside from an IKEA and other retail park usuals nearby, shopping options in Edmonton are pretty bleak – let's hope the regeneration of the shopping centre, due for completion in 2007, improves things.

AMT Sports *43 Chase Side, N14 6BP (8882 5741).*
Angel Boutique *7 Wades Hill, The Green, N21 1BD (8886 4500).*
British Red Cross Shop *383 Green Lanes, N13 4JG (8886 7467).*
Catwalk Clothing *321-323 Green Lanes, N13 4TY (8882 3880).*
Dantel on the Green *24 The Green, N21 1AY (8886 8456).*

IKEA *Glover Drive, N18 3HF (0845 355 2255/www.ikea.co.uk).*
Italcibo *25 Ashfield Parade, N14 5EH (8886 4074).*
Kate Kuba *49 Chase Side, N14 5BU (8886 1185/www.katekuba.co.uk).*
King Easton *The Green, off Station Road, N21 3NB (8886 8783).*
The Only Place for Pictures *358 Green Lanes, N13 5TJ (8886 8717).*
Palmers Green Antique Centre *472 Green Lanes, N13 5PA (8350 0878).*
Palmers Green Bookshop *379 Green Lanes, N13 4JG (8882 2088).*
Twenty-One the Green *21 The Green, N21 3NL (8882 4298).*
X-It *754 Green Lanes, N21 3RE (8364 1903).*
Zucchero *10 Ashfield Parade, N14 5AB (8886 5044).*

Arts & attractions

Cinemas & theatres

Chicken Shed Theatre *Chase Side, N14 4PE (8351 6161/www.chickenshed.org.uk).* Lively performances by all-inclusive theatre group.
Cineworld Enfield *Southbury Leisure Park, 208 Southbury Road, EN1 1YQ (0871 200 2000/www.cineworld.co.uk).*
Millfield Theatre *Silver Street, N18 1PJ (8807 6680/www.millfieldtheatre.co.uk).*
UCI Lee Valley *Lee Valley Leisure Complex, Picketts Lock Lane, N9 0AS (0871 224 4007/ www.uci.co.uk).*

Galleries & museums

Museum of Domestic Design & Architecture (MoDA) *Middlesex University, Cat Hill, EN4 8HT (8411 5244/www.moda. mdx.ac.uk).* Past exhibitions have included outrageous wallpaper designs and an investigation into suburbia.

Other attractions

Forty Hall Estate *Forty Hill, EN2 9HA (8363 8196).* Henry VIII's hunting lodge dates back to the 13th century; it has a museum and some suitably regal grounds.

Open spaces

Arnos Park *Waterfall Road, N14.*
Broomfield Park *Aldermans Hill, N13.*
Bush Hill Park *Lincoln Road, EN1.*
Grovelands Park *The Bourne, N21.* Arguably Enfield's most attractive park. Features the grand Grovelands Estate, now a private hospital.
Jubilee Park *Galliard Road, EN3.*
Oakwood Park *Oakwood Park Road, N14.*
Pymmes Park *Victoria Road, N18.*
Town Park *Essex Road, EN2.*
Trent Park *Cockfosters Road, EN4.* Enfield's largest open space: 900 acres of woodland and greenery, most of which is open to the public.

TRANSPORT
Tube stations *Piccadilly* Arnos Grove, Southgate, Oakwood, Cockfosters
Rail stations *one* Silver Street, Edmonton Green, Southbury, Turkey Street; *WAGN* Palmers Green, Winchmore Hill, Grange Park, Enfield Chase, Gordon Hill, Crews Hill; Bush Hill Park, Edmonton Green; Angel Road, Ponders End, Brimsdown, Enfield Lock
Main bus routes *into central London* 149, 259; *night buses* N29, N91, N279; *24-hour buses* 149

'I can literally walk into the countryside, yet it's only half an hour on the tube to get into central London. People are just starting to realise this – we used to have problems getting people to come out to our theatre in Enfield, but now our Christmas shows are all sold out.'

Joseph Morton, actor and programme director at the Chicken Shed Theatre Company

Sport & fitness

There's a decent spread of sports and leisure centres in Enfield, but the situation will improve further when the existing Edmonton Leisure Centre is replaced with a spanking new centre in 2007 (the existing centre will remain open until then). The borough also has the new and very successful Southbury Leisure Centre (the only significant indoor space since the Lee Valley Leisure Centre closed).

Gyms & leisure centres

Albany Leisure Centre *505 Hertford Road, EN3 5XH (8804 4255/www.enfieldleisure centres.co.uk).*
Arnos Pool *Bowes Road, N11 0BD (8361 9336/www.enfieldleisurecentres.co.uk).*
Brunswick Health & Fitness *311B Chase Road, N14 6JS (8886 9111).* Private.
David Lloyd *Caterhatch Lane, EN1 4LF (8364 5858/www.davidlloydleisure.co.uk).* Private.
Edmonton Leisure Centre *Plevna Road, N9 0BU (8379 2462/www.enfieldleisurecentres.co.uk).*
LA Fitness *www.lafitness.co.uk; 18 East Barnet Road, EN4 8RQ (8440 2796); Winchmore Hill Road, N14 6AA (8886 8883).* Private.
Park Health & Fitness Club *Southgate Hockey Centre, Trent Park, Snakes Lane, EN4 0PS (8441 5855).* Private.
Southbury Leisure Centre *192 Southbury Road, EN1 1YP (8245 3201).*
Southgate Leisure Centre *Winchmore Hill Road, N14 6AD (8882 7963/www.enfieldleisure centres.co.uk).*

Other facilities

Southgate Hockey Centre *Trent Park, Snakes Lane, EN4 0PS (8440 7574/www.southgatehc.org.uk).*
Trent Park Equestrian Centre *Trent Park Stables, Bramley Road, N14 4XS (8363 8630/www.trentpark.com).* One of the largest riding schools in London.
Trent Park Golf Club *Bramley Road, N14 4UW (8367 4653/www.trentparkgolf.com).*

Schools

WHAT THE PARENTS SAY:

‘Enfield is good for primary schools. Two that stand out for me are Walker and Hazelwood. My son goes to Walker, which is pretty middle-class and aesthetically nice, but also benefits from strong leadership. It does very well in the league tables.

There are some fairly good state options at secondary level, but there is no genuine choice over where your kids will end up going, and this makes the transition process a nightmare for parents. Ashmole School (in Barnet, *see p301*) is popular and I know a family who moved to get into it. Its admissions policy is extremely tight. I want my youngest to go to Highlands, which is very inclusive and has good pastoral care. Other secondary schools in Enfield include Broomfield, which struggles to shake off its poor reputation despite genuinely improving under a new head, and the Latymer School, which is good for arts and music but is very hard to get into – thousands sit the entrance exam each year.’
Tami Hedley, mother of two, Palmers Green

Primary

There are 71 state primary schools in Enfield, 16 of which are church schools. There are also six independent primary schools, including one faith school. See www.enfield.gov.uk and www.ofsted.gov.uk for more information.

Secondary

Albany School *Bell Lane, EN3 5PA (8804 1648).*
Aylward School *Windmill Road, N18 1NB (8803 1738).*
Bishop Stopford's School *Brick Lane, EN1 3PU (8804 1906/www.bishop-stopfords-school.co.uk).*
Broomfield School *Wilmer Way, N14 7HY (8368 4710).*
Chace Community School *Churchbury Lane, EN1 3HQ (8363 7321/www.chace.enfield.sch.uk).*
Edmonton County *Great Cambridge Road, EN1 1HQ (8360 3158).*

RECYCLING

No. of bring sites 57 (for nearest, visit www.recycleforlondon.com)
Household waste recycled 11%
Main recycling centre Barrowell Green Recycling Centre, Barrowell Green, Winchmore Hill, N21 3AU (8379 1000)
Other recycling services home composting; fridge, furniture and electrical item collection; washable nappies refund promotion; anti-junk mail promotion
Council contact Waste Reduction Service, London Borough of Enfield, Carterhatch Depot, 7 Melling Drive, Enfield EN1 4BS (8379 1000)

Enfield County School *Holly Walk, EN2 6QG (8363 3030/www.enfieldcs.enfield.sch.uk).* Girls only; mixed sixth form.
Enfield Grammar School *Market Place, EN2 6LN (8363 1095).* Boys only.
Highlands School *148 Worlds End Lane, N21 1QQ (8370 1100/www.highlands.enfield.sch.uk).*
Kingsmead School *Southbury Road, EN1 1YQ (8363 3037/www.kingsmead.org).*
The Latymer School *Haselbury Road, N9 9TN (8807 4037/www.latymer.co.uk).*
Lea Valley High School *Bullsmoor Lane, EN3 6TW (01992 763666/www.lvhs.org.uk).*
St Anne's Catholic High School for Girls *Oakthorpe Road, N13 5TY (8886 2165/ www.st-annes.enfield.sch.uk).* Girls only.
St Ignatius College *Turkey Street, EN1 4NP (0199 271 7835).* Boys only.
Salisbury School *Turin Road, N9 8DQ (8372 5678).*
Southgate School *Sussex Way, EN4 0BL (8449 9583/www.southgate.enfield.sch.uk).*
Winchmore School *Laburnum Grove, N21 3HS (8360 7773/www.winchmore.enfield.sch.uk).*

Property

WHAT THE AGENTS SAY:

❝It's never had a great reputation, Edmonton. But it seems to be over the worst now. It's quite close to the Olympics – we hear Picketts Lock stadium will be used for Olympic training – so now Edmonton's on the up. About 70 per cent of our sales were properties bought to let, but we're now getting a lot of first-time buyers. People are starting to invest in the area. There's no tube, no restaurants, and the shopping centre is no Brent Cross, but it's in Zone 4 and you can be in the City in 20 minutes on the overland train.❞
Nick Dean, Adam Kennedy, Edmonton

Average property prices
Detached £479,685
Semi-detached £239,713
Terraced £175,540
Flat £126,813

Local estate agents
Brien Firmin *www.brienfirmin.com; 2 offices in the borough (Green Lanes 8889 9944/ Winchmore HIll 8360 9696).*
Equity Estate Agents *9 Lancaster Road, EN2 0DW (8367 7999/www.equityestate agents.com).*
James Hayward *181 Chase Side, EN2 0PT (8367 4000/www.james-hayward.co.uk).*
Lanes *www.lanesproperty.co.uk; 4 offices in the borough (Enfield Town 8342 0101/Enfield Southbury Road 8362 7680/Enfield Highway 8804 2253/Palmers Green 8882 8068).*
Peter Barry *946 Green Lanes, N21 2AD (8360 4777/www.peterbarry.co.uk).*
Townends *913 Green Lanes, N21 2QP (8360 8111/www.townends.co.uk).*

Other information

Council
Enfield Council *Civic Centre, Silver Street, EN1 3XY (8379 1000/www.enfield.gov.uk).*

Hospitals
Chase Farm Hospital *The Ridgeway, EN2 8JL (0845 111 4000/www.london.nhs.uk).*
North Middlesex Hospital *Sterling Way, N18 1QU (8887 2000/www.northmid.nhs.uk).*

Legal services
Enfield CAB *10 Little Park Gardens, EN2 6PQ (0870 126 4664/www.adviceguide.org.uk).*
Palmers Green CAB *Southgate Town Hall, Green Lanes, N13 4XD (0870 126 4664/ www.adviceguide.org.uk).*

Local newspapers
Enfield Advertiser/Gazette *8364 4040/ www.icnorthlondononline.co.uk*

Allotments
Call the council's Parks Business Unit (8379 3722/www.enfield.gov.uk) for assistance with local allotment sites.

COUNCIL TAX

A	up to £40,000	**£819.25**
B	£40,001-£52,000	**£955.79**
C	£52,001-£68,000	**£1,092.33**
D	£68,001-£88,000	**£1,228.87**
E	£88,001-£120,000	**£1,501.95**
F	£120,001-£160,000	**£1,775.03**
G	£160,001-£320,000	**£2,048.12**
H	over £320,000	**£2,457.74**

Enfield

Barnet

Clinging to the outer reaches of the Northern Line, Barnet encompasses the Jewish district of Golders Green, the idealistic housing project of Hampstead Garden Suburb and the busy high streets of the Finchleys. Head further north, and you'll reach the land of footballers' mansions, highfalutin' golf clubs and the self-sufficient market town of High Barnet.

Neighbourhoods

Golders Green and Hendon

Golders Green's existence is linked to the building of the Northern Line in 1907. In the following decades, the area's green fields were covered in residential buildings. Today, the district is centred on a major junction where the Golders Green Road crosses the Finchley Road, close to the busy bus terminal and Golders Green tube.

Shops spread out in four directions from this junction. Golders Green Road (which heads north-west to the North Circular) has retained a number of small, individual shops as well as generic chainstores and a cosmopolitan selection of restaurants. The area has become synonymous with Jewish London, hence the presence of numerous kosher coffee bars, salt beef bars, butchers and, of course, Bloom's, the iconic Jewish restaurant. Many of the district's businesses close from sunset on Friday to sunset on Saturday to observe the Jewish Shabbat. The weekly reopening on Saturday night sees Golders Green buzzing with young people; local bakeries do a swift trade in salmon and cream cheese bagels. Sunday is a busy shopping day too.

Just up the hill towards Hampstead, Golders Hill Park is a much-loved local resource, attractively laid out and with a well-equipped playground. Families come here to feed the deer, admire the aviary and enjoy a snack and ice-cream in the friendly café. The recent opening of the London Jewish Cultural Centre in Ivy House (former home of ballerina Anna Pavlova) further up the hill made a welcome addition to the local cultural scene. However, the future of the Golders Green Hippodrome, long a home of the BBC Concert Orchestra, remains uncertain.

Brutally bisected by the traffic-choked Watford Way (A41) and adjacent to the start of the M1, Hendon struggles to have much of an identity. The proximity of the UK's first large enclosed shopping centre, Brent Cross (opened in 1976), has had a draining effect on local shops, with Brent Street, the area's supposed high street, a dingy affair. Despite its lack of character, the area functions well in practical terms, with an excellent library just by the imposing Town Hall, a pleasant green space in Hendon Park, and Barnet Copthall Leisure Centre. A cluster of tutorial and sixth-form colleges and Middlesex University add a youthful touch.

Hampstead Garden Suburb

Founded in 1907 by the heiress Dame Henrietta Barnett, Hampstead Garden Suburb was envisioned as a piece of idealistic social engineering aimed at providing housing for all social classes, from workers' cottages to grand residences for the toffs. Gardens and green spaces played a central part in Dame Barnet's vision, with an average density of eight dwellings to an acre, which allowed for ample gardens. Today, bordered by the arterial Falloden Way (the A1) and Finchley Road (A598), Hampstead Garden Suburb remains something of a well-kept secret, though it is growing in popularity. The attractive Arts and Crafts-style houses, with their noticeably well-tended gardens, are much sought-after and command premium prices.

Despite its appealing veneer, there is something distinctly stand-offish about the neighbourhood. The great Lutyens churches in the central square each bear stern notices forbidding ball games against their walls. There are no shops

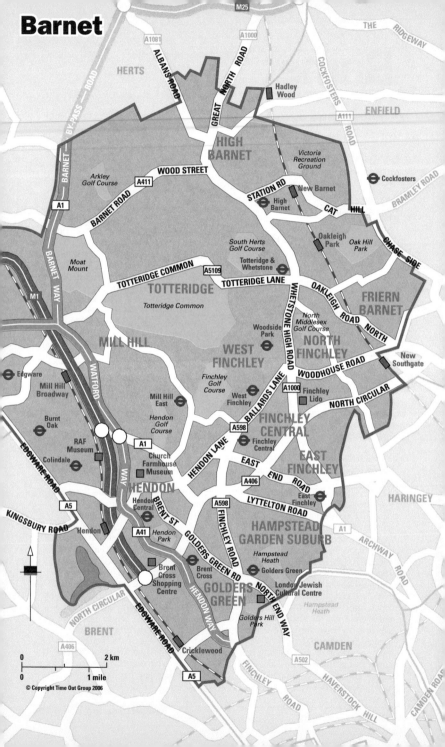

within Hampstead Garden Suburb (let alone pubs or cafés), but residents are well catered for by nearby Temple Fortune, where businesses range from veteran kosher fishmongers to branches of M&S and Waitrose.

East Finchley and Finchley Central

To those not in the know, the relationship between the various Finchleys – divided by the thundering North Circular (A406) – can be bewildering.

East Finchley has a more liberal feel than its namesakes: its proximity to Muswell Hill and Highgate, and a mixed housing stock (including desirable Victorian and Edwardian dwellings), attracts writers, journalists and musicians.The high street – officially the High Road/Great North Road and duly traffic-clogged – is narrow enough to allow for life on a human scale. It offers a homely range of shops and an increasing number of cafés and restaurants. The jewel in the local crown, however, is the Phoenix Cinema. Opened in 1910 and thought to be the UK's oldest continuously operating picture house, this art deco gem is one of the capital's few remaining independent cinemas and is loyally supported by locals, who fought successfully to save it from developers in the mid 1980s. Beside the tube line, Cherry Tree Wood and its playground is popular with yummy mummies, toddlers in tow. This is the site of a well-supported community festival every summer.

Heading up into Finchley Central is College Farm, formerly the main farm for Express Dairies and a reminder of the neighbourhood's rural past. The pastoral feel is long lost, with Finchley Central suffering from the high volume of traffic passing through its congested high street (Ballards Lane). Good transport links (both tube and buses) attract a mixed community, including a sizeable Jewish population, Japanese expats (catered for by the nearby Oriental City shopping complex at Colindale and shops like Atari-ya on the way to Golders Green), Asians and a recent influx of young Poles. Just off Ballards Lane, Victoria Recreation Ground offers residents a respite from the traffic and is popular with local families.

West Finchley and North Finchley

Although boasting its own tube station, West Finchley is primarily residential, lacking a real shopping centre and existing in Finchley Central's shadow. Plus points for 'burb lovers are its peaceful streets (away from the hustle and bustle of Finchley Central), its views over the Green Belt and its proximity to Finchley Golf Course.

Tally Ho Corner at North Finchley is marked by the towering Artsdepot, a controversial recent development that houses an arts centre, a bus depot and a block of luxury apartments. For recreation, locals can also head to the Finchley Lido; once a classic 1930s lido, now redeveloped, this still incorporates a swimming pool as well as a bowling alley, a Vue cinema and the obvious fast-food outlets. The high street at North Finchley is dominated by chainstores, with the desirable residences tucked away in the peaceful streets around Woodside Park (where you'll also find the nearest tube station).

Totteridge

How deceptive appearances can be. Drive up Whetstone High Road past B&Q, then past an impersonal tower block housing Barnet Council's offices, and there seems little to recommend this particular north London hill. Turn left into Totteridge Lane, however, and you enter a green and pleasant land of tree-lined lanes and large houses. Home to the seriously

Highs & Lows

▲ **Tranquility** Lots of greenery and a general lack of hubbub make for a peaceful life
Bagels Golders Green and Hendon have the best bagel bakeries of any London borough

Northern line Plagued by signal problems and industrial unrest; waiting for a train going up the right branch is also a chore
Staidness Some people like the changeless lethargy of the ▼ borough; many will find it a little lifeless and dull

Hendon Town Hall.
See p293.

wealthy (including notable footballers
and, of course, their wives), the mansions
here are discreetly set well back from the
road, relishing their view over London's
green belt. The prestigious South Herts
Golf Club, with its course designed by
golf legend Harry Vardon, is among
the area's hidden assets. In comparison,
the high street is pretty humdrum,
despite its inevitable Waitrose and M&S
outlets; a few decent restaurants, like the
boisterous Al Fresco, enjoy a good local
following nonetheless.

Friern Barnet

During the 19th century this part of
outer London became best known for
Colney Hatch, properly known as the
Middlesex County Pauper Lunatic Asylum.
Today, what was the asylum has been
reinvented as Princess Park Manor, a gated
development boasting luxurious properties
plus gyms, a bar and tennis courts – very
much in demand by young professionals.
Outside the gates, however, the immediate
area is pretty drab to say the least. There's
no tube either, so commuters must go via
New Southgate rail.

Head north towards Whetstone and the
picture is better; tree-lined roads by Friern
Barnet Lane boast large houses and the
North Middlesex Golf Course. Just south

of the course lies Friary Park, which has
landscaped grounds, a playground and
a cheap, child-friendly café. It's a popular
spot, attracting both locals and families
from neighbouring areas.

High Barnet

Positioned at the end of the Northern
Line, High Barnet relishes its out-of-
town location, with many residents
never going 'down London'. The plus
side to this parochialism is an old-
fashioned community feel, so events
like the Christmas street parade, church
fêtes and cricket on the green fill the
calendar. Barnet even has a professional
football team (nicknamed the Bees,
currently in Coca-Cola League Division
Two), which commands a loyal following.
A source of pride is Barnet market,
granted a charter by King John in 1199.
For centuries this plied a thriving cattle
trade; today cheerful chaps purvey fruit
and veg, particularly popular with Barnet's
many retirees. The easy access to green
spaces is much appreciated by residents,
who enjoy walking their dogs, cycling and
flying kites on the Common and Hadley
Green (where the Battle of Barnet was
fought in 1471, during the War of the Roses).

There are downers. The Bull Arts Centre,
once a venue for great stand-up acts and

STATISTICS

BOROUGH MAKE-UP
Population 318,471
Average weekly pay £541.10
Ethnic origins
White 74.03%
Mixed 3.02%
Asian or Asian British 12.33%
Black or Black British 6%
Chinese or other 4.62%
Students 10.23%
Retirees 10.10%

HOUSING STOCK
Borough size 86.6km²
No. of households 131,376
Detached 11.4%
Semi-detached 31.2%
Terraced 18.1%
Flats (purpose-built) 28.3%
Flats (converted) 10.2%
Flats (both) 38.5%

CRIME PER 1,000 OF POPULATION
(English average in brackets)
Burglary 8 (6.4)
Robbery 4 (1.4)
Theft of vehicle 6 (4.5)
Theft from vehicle 11 (10)
Violence against the person 22 (16.5)
Sexual offences 1 (0.9)

MPs & COUNCIL
MPs *Chipping Barnet* Theresa Villiers
(Conservative); *Finchley & Golders
Green* Rudi Vis (Labour); *Hendon*
Andrew Dismore (Labour)
CPA 2 stars; improving well

bands, was sacrificed for the newly built Artsdepot in North Finchley. As a result, local cultural stimulation is sorely lacking. On the High Street, the area's affluence is far from evident, and at night Barnet's yob element comes to the fore. Commuters working in London and using the tube can rely on getting a seat in the morning, but with the Northern Line's frequent signal problems, depending on the service can be distinctly problematic.

Barnet has seen a recent influx of families with young children from Muswell Hill and Crouch End, drawn by more affordable property prices, houses with large gardens and good schools. Nevertheless, this part of town remains resolutely untrendy.

Restaurants & cafés

Golders Green's long-established Jewish population make this a good place in which to sample Jewish cuisine, encompassing Ashkenazi (Russian and East European) and Sephardi (Middle Eastern) food, both on offer in Barnet. Eating at iconic Jewish restaurant Bloom's is a vintage experience, from the traditional *haimishe* (home-style) Ashkenazi fare to the elderly clientele. For a livelier atmosphere head to Dizengoff's, which serves generous portions of Israeli-style grilled meats and salads, as does Solly's Exclusive. Hendon also has its fair share of kosher restaurants, including modern Eighty-Six Bistro Bar, dairy specialist Isola Bella Café and Sephardi Mama's.

Of course, it's not only Jewish food on offer around here. Café Japan has a loyal fan base drawn by its top-notch sushi; Kimchee offers tasty Korean dishes while, in Temple Fortune, Beyoglu specialises in traditional Turkish cuisine. Other kosher options include La Fiesta (Argentinian) and Met Su Yan (Asian). Leon and Tony Manzi's fish restaurant, the Two Brothers, is a much-loved Finchley Central stalwart; another is sedate Indian restaurant Rani.

On the whole, Barnet noticeably lacks upmarket eateries; bar/restaurant outfits N20 and the Haven in Whetstone do their best. On the same road are bustling Italian Al Fresco, and the unreconstructed trattoria La Tavola. Up in High Barnet, curry houses and fast-food chains predominate. Dory's Café is a friendly example of that vanishing breed, the caff, and serves a great fry-up. Newcomers include Totally Thai and Ergens, a smart Turkish restaurant. Best of the bunch is Emchai, a funky, family-friendly noodle bar that would not be out of place in Soho.

Al Fresco *1327 High Road, N20 9HR (8445 8880).*
Beyoglu *1031 Finchley Road, NW11 7ES (8455 4884).*
Bloom's *130 Golders Green Road, NW11 8HB (8455 1338).*
Café Japan *626 Finchley Road, NW11 7RR (8455 6854).*
Dizengoff's *118 Golders Green Road, NW11 8HB (8458 7003).*
Dory's Café *3 St Albans Road, EN5 4LN (8440 1954).*

Barnet

Eighty-Six Bistro Bar 86 Brent Street, NW4 2ES (8202 5575).
Emchai 78 High Street, EN5 5SN (8364 9993).
Ergens 98-100 High Street, EN5 5XQ (3234 4066).
La Fiesta 239 Golders Green Road, NW11 9PN (8458 0444).
Haven Bistro & Bar 1363 High Road, N20 9LN (8445 7419/www.haven-bistro.co.uk).
Isola Bella Café 63 Brent Street, NW4 2EA (8203 2000).
Kimchee 887 Finchley Road, NW11 8RR (8455 1035).
Mama's Kosher Restaurant & Takeway 53 Brent Street, NW4 2EA (8202 5444).
Met Su Yan 134 Golders Green Road, NW11 8HP (8458 8088).
N20 1111 High Road, N20 0PT (8445 8080).
Rani 7 Long Lane, N3 2PR (8349 4386/ www.raniuk.com).
Solly's Exclusive 148A Golders Green Road, NW11 8HE (ground floor & takeaway 8455 2121/first floor 8455 0004).
La Tavola 1357 High Road, N20 9HR (8445 0525).
Totally Thai 192 High Street, EN5 5SZ (8441 1413).
Two Brothers Fish Restaurant 297-303 Regents Park Road, N3 1DP (8346 0469).

Black Bull 1446 High Road, N20 9BJ (8445 3578).
Catcher in the Rye 317 Regents Park Road, N3 1DP (8343 4369).
Claddagh Ring 10 Church Road, NW4 4EA (0871 223 6629).
Gallery 407-411 Hendon Way, NW4 3LH (8202 4000).
Greyhound Church End, NW4 4JT (8457 9730).
Orange Tree 7 Totteridge Lane, N20 8NX (8343 6961).
White Lion 50 St Albans Road, EN5 4LA (8449 4560).
Ye Old Mitre Inn 58 High Street, EN5 5SJ (8449 6582).
Ye Old Monken Holt 193 High Street, EN5 5SU (8449 4280).

Bars & pubs

Hendon's drinking scene ranges from traditional pub the Greyhound to the in-your-face Claddagh Ring, which pulls in a young crowd up for a serious drinking session and live music. An eye-catching addition is the refurbished Gallery, formerly a pub but now reincarnated as a nightclub, bar and restaurant, aimed at those wanting a West End-style night on the town. Over in Finchley Central, the revamped Catcher in the Rye, with its TV football screens, reasonably priced pub grub and quiz nights, is also popular.

One of Totteridge's best-known pubs is the Orange Tree, which gets top points for its picturesque location down leafy Totteridge Lane. The Black Bull on the high street offers a good range of beers and a peaceful atmosphere; cocktail drinkers should try bar-cum-restaurants N20 and the Haven (for both, *see p297*). Meanwhile, memories of High Barnet's past role as as a staging post linger on in a number of traditional pubs, among them Ye Old Mitre Inn, Ye Olde Monken Holt and the White Lion.

Shops

The borough's best-known retail attraction, Brent Cross Shopping Centre, opened in 1976 and was a herald of the mall shopping syndrome now prevalent across the UK. Positioned among a sprawl of flyovers by the North Circular and junction one of the M1, the centre is a busy bubble of consumerism, containing 110 shops and cafés. Respectable stalwarts such as John Lewis, M&S and Fenwick's mix with more modish chains, including Jigsaw, Hobbs and Karen Millen. Despite being near a tube station, the automobile is very much king at Brent Cross, with its ample car parks heaving with vehicles. Plans are afoot to modernise the centre, with an increased focus on pedestrian access and lifestyle shopping.

For shopping on a more human scale, Golders Green is well served: alongside the inevitable charity shops and chains are quirkier one-offs, such as Franks

TRANSPORT

Tube stations *Northern* Golders Green, Brent Cross, Hendon Central, Colindale, Burnt Oak, Edgware; East Finchley, Finchley Central, Mill Hill East, West Finchley, Woodside Park, Totteridge & Whetstone, High Barnet

Rail stations *Thameslink* Cricklewood, Hendon, Mill Hill Broadway; *WAGN Railway* New Southgate, Oakleigh Park, New Barnet, Hadley Wood

Main bus routes *into central London* 13, 16, 82, 113, 189; *night buses* N13, N16; *24-hour buses* 83, 134, 189, 266

(an old-fashioned clothing store) and Toyteck (for gizmo addicts). The local Jewish population is catered for by several kosher businesses and specialist bookshops. Just up the road, genteel, old-fashioned Temple Fortune boasts a number of small independents, including Brian's (kids' shoes), the Bookworm (kid's books), and Joseph's Book Store. High Barnet has the Spires, a pleasant, low-level shopping centre constructed around small open-air squares, which offers Monsoon, Ottakar's, WH Smith, Game and Tchibo. For more characterful shops, head down the Monken Hadley end of the high street to find Bargain Buys (a useful Aladdin's cave of household goods from doormats to padlocks), Wanders (elegant footware) and the Present (fancily wrapped gifts).

On the food front, the borough's most distinctive feature is the number of vintage Jewish food shops, including kosher wine specialist Amazing Grapes, classic Jewish deli Platters, fishmongers Stoller and JA Corney, and bustling bagel bakeries Carmelli, Daniel's and Hendon Bagel Bakery. Barnet's Japanese residents are catered for by branches of Atari-Ya, and Oriental City shopping centre/food court (just over the borough border in Brent), while Asian food shops include well-established Bina, Goodeats and Q Stores.

Supermarkets are a-plenty, of course, with upmarket Waitrose particularly well respected. High Barnet's food market (held on Wednesdays and Saturdays) dates back to the 12th century and today functions as a traditional fruit and veg outpost; Rita's fish stall is also a particular draw. There are plans to develop and cover the market, and add an underground car park.

Amazing Grapes *94 Brent Street, NW4 2ES (8202 2631).*
Atari-Ya Foods *595 High Road, N12 0DY (8446 6669); 15-16 Monkville Parade, Finchley Road, NW11 0AL (8458 7626).*
Bargain Buys *4 Hadley Parade, EN5 5SX (8440 7983).*
Bina *241 Golders Green Road, NW11 9PN (8458 2366).*
The Bookworm *1177 Finchley Road, NW11 0AA (88201 9811).*
Brent Cross Shopping Centre *NW4 3FP (8202 8095/www.brentcross.co.uk).*
Brian's Shoes *2 Halleswelle Parade, Finchley Road, NW11 0DL (8455 7001/www.brians shoes.com).*
Carmelli Bakery *126-128 Golders Green Road, NW11 8HB (8455 2074).*

Daniel's *12-13 Halleswelle Parade, Finchley Road, NW11 0DL (8455 5826).*
Franks *72-74 Golders Green Road, NW11 8LP (8455 2251).*
Goodeats *124 Ballards Lane, N3 2PA (7349 2373).*
Hendon Bagel Bakery *35-37 Church Road, NW4 4DU (8203 6969).*
JA Corney *16 Halleswelle Parade, Finchley Road, NW11 0DL (8455 9588).*
Joseph's Book Store *2 Ashbourne Parade, Finchley Road, NW11 0AD (8731 7575/ www.josephsbookstore.com).*
Oriental City *399 Edgware Road, NW9 0JJ (8200 0009/www.orientalcity.com).*
Platters *10 Halleswelle Parade, Finchley Road, NW11 0DL (8455 7345).*
The Present *220-222 High Street, Hadley Green, EN5 5SZ (8441 6400).*
Q Stores *19 Lodge Lane, N12 8JG (8446 2495).*
Sam Stoller & Son *28 Temple Fortune Parade, Finchley Road, NW11 0QS (8458 1429).*
Toyteck *61 Golders Green Road, NW11 8EL (8455 3899).*
Wanders *180 High Street, EN5 5SZ (8449 2520).*

Arts & attractions

Cinemas & theatres

Artsdepot *5 Nether Street, N12 0GA (8449 0048/www.artsdepot.co.uk).* Multidisciplinary arts venue, featuring comedy, dance and theatre productions, plus lots for kids.
Cineworld Staples Corner *Staples Corner Retail Park, Geron Way, NW2 6LW (0871 220 8000/www.cineworld.co.uk).*
Odeon Barnet *Great North Road, New Barnet, EN5 1AB (0871 224 4007/ www.odeon.co.uk).*
Phoenix Cinema *52 High Road, N2 9PJ (8444 6789/www.phoenixcinema.co.uk).*
Vue Finchley Lido *Great North Leisure Park, Chaplin Square, N12 0GL (0871 224 0240/ www.myvue.com).*

Galleries & museums

Artsdepot Gallery *5 Nether Street, N12 0GA (8369 5464/www.artsdepot.co.uk).*
Barnet Museum *31 Wood Street, EN5 4BE (8440 8066/www.barnetmuseum.co.uk).* Local history museum, holding everything from archaeological remains to a fine costume collection.
Church Farmhouse Museum *Greyhound Hill, NW4 4JR (8203 0130/www.churchfarmhouse museum.co.uk).* A 17th-century farmhouse with Victorian-period rooms.
Jewish Museum *80 East End Road, N3 2SY (8349 1143/www.jewishmuseum.org.uk).* Sister museum to the one in Camden (see p132).
Royal Air Force Museum *Grahame Park Way, NW9 5LL (8205 2266/www.rafmuseum. org.uk).* More than 100 aircraft (including a Spitfire and a Lancaster Bomber) are displayed on the site of the original London Aerodrome.

Other attractions

London Jewish Cultural Centre *Ivy House, 94-96 North End Road, NW11 7SX (8457 5000/www.ljcc.org.uk).* A Jewish hub, with a range of courses, exhibitions, films, music and lectures.

Open spaces

Cherry Tree Wood *Summerlee Avenue, N2.* A popular local park, with grass and woodland, plus a playground, two tennis courts and a multi-sports pitch.

College Farm *Fitzalan Road, N3 3PG (chairperson 8458 2214/www.collegefarm trust.co.uk).* Formerly an Express Dairies farm. A charity has now been established to save this site from developers.

Coppetts Wood & Glebelands Nature Reserve *Colney Hatch Lane, N11.* A mixture of woodlands scrub, grassland and ponds.

Darlands Lake Nature Reserve *off Totteridge Lane, N20.*

Friary Park *Friary Road, N12.* An Edwardian park forming the grounds of Friary House.

Golders Hill Park *West Heath Road, NW3.*

Hendon Park *Queens Road, Shirehall Lane, Park View Gardens, NW4.* Large formal park with a play area, eight tennis courts, two multi-sports courts and a basketball court.

Oak Hill Park & Woods *Church Hill Road, Herts EN4.* Meadows, streams and ancient woodland, plus a playground and golf area.

Scratchwood & Moat Mount *Mill Hill, NW7.* The largest area of woodland in Barnet, mostly made up of oak and hornbeam.

Victoria Recreation Ground *Lawton Road, Victoria Road, Park Road, EN4.* A Victorian park with grassy areas, a formal rose garden and various sports facilities.

RECYCLING

No. of bring sites 51 (for nearest, visit www.recycleforlondon.com)
Household waste recycled 13.5%
Main recycling centre Summers Lane Civic Amenity & Recycling Centre, Summers Lane, Finchley, N12 0PD (8362 0752)
Other recycling services green waste collection; home composting; 'block cleanse' service (free skip to take general waste and green garden waste, three times a year); white goods collection; hazardous waste collection
Council contact Nicola Buck, Environmental Services Manager – Waste Strategy, London Borough of Barnet, Building 4, North London Business Park, Oakleigh Road South, New Southgate, N11 1NP (8359 7400)

Sport & fitness

There's a decent mix of clubs and centres in Barnet. Greenwich Leisure: a new centre at Burnt Oak, buzzing Barnet Copthall (with its new gym), Compton Sports Centre and the lively Hendon Youth Sports Centre. The private chains are well represented in the borough too. Possibly the most attractive option, though, is the spectacular Laboratory Spa at Hendon's Fiveways Corner – assuming your purse strings can handle the strain. Golfers will be in their element; there are more golf courses in leafy Barnet than any other London borough, with plenty more nearby in Hertfordshire.

Gyms & leisure centres

Barnet Burnt Oak Leisure Centre
Watling Avenue, Middx HA8 0NJ (8201 0982/ www.gll.org).

Barnet Copthall Leisure Centre
Champions Way, off Great North Way, NW4 1PX (8457 9900/www.gll.org).

Church Farm Swimming Pool
Church Hill Road, EN4 8XE (8368 7070/ www.gll.org).

Compton Leisure Centre *Sunny Way, Summers Lane, N12 0QB (8361 8658/ www.gll.org).*

David Lloyd *Leisure Way, High Road, N12 0QZ (8492 2250/www.davidlloydleisure.co.uk).* Private.

Esporta *264 Royal Drive, Princess Park Manor, Friern Barnet Road, N11 3BG (8362 8444/www.esporta.com).* Private.

Finchley Lido Leisure Centre *Great North Leisure Park, High Road, N12 0AE (8343 9830/www.gll.org).*

Fitness First *Old Priory Road Shopping Centre, 706 High Road, N12 9QL (8492 2500/ www.fitnessfirst.com).* Private.

Hendon Leisure Centre *Marble Drive, NW2 1XQ (8455 0818/www.gll.org).*

Holmes Place *www.holmesplace.co.uk; 108-110 Cricklewood Lane, NW2 2DS (8453 7200; 260 Hendon Way, NW4 3NL (8203 9421).* Private.

Laboratory Spa & Health Club *1A Hall Lane, NW4 4TJ (8201 5500/spa 8201 5588/ www.labspa.co.uk).* Private.

LA Fitness *www.lafitness.co.uk; The Academy, East End Road, N3 2JA (8346 7253); 152-154 Golders Green Road, NW11 8HE (8731 7312).* Private.

Oakleigh Park School of Swimming
100 Oakleigh Road North, N20 9EZ (8445 1911/www.swimoakleighpark.co.uk).

Queen Elizabeth's Leisure Centre
Meadway, EN5 5RR (8441 2933/ www.gll.org).

Finchley Lido Leisure Centre.

Other facilities

Arkley Golf Club *Rowley Green Road, Arkley, EN5 3HL (8449 0394/www.club-noticeboard. co.uk/arkley).*

Finchley Golf Club *Nether Court, Frith Lane, NW7 1PU (8346 2436/www.finchleygolfclub. co.uk).*

Hendon Golf Club *Ashley Walk, Devonshire Road, NW7 1DG (8346 6023/www.hendongolf club.co.uk).*

Hollywood Bowl *Great North Leisure Park, High Road, N12 0QZ (8446 6667/www. hollywoodbowl.co.uk).*

Mill Hill Golf Club *100 Barnet Way, NW7 3AL (8959 2339/www.millhillgolf club.co.uk).*

North Middlesex Golf Course *Friern Barnet Lane, N20 0NL (8445 1604/ www.northmiddlesexgc.co.uk).*

Old Fold Manor Golf Club *Old Fold Lane, Hadley Green, EN5 4QN (8440 9185/ www.oldfoldmanor.co.uk).*

South Herts Golf Club *Links Drive, Totteridge, N20 8QU (8445 2035/ www.southherts.co.uk).*

Spectator sports

Barnet FC *Underhill Stadium, Barnet Lane, EN5 2DN (8441 6932/www.barnetfc. premiumtv.co.uk).*

Schools

WHAT THE PARENTS SAY:

'Barnet is well provided with primary schools. We chose the Martin Primary School in East Finchley, a community school with an inclusive and stimulating atmosphere. Other highly regarded Barnet primaries include Moss Hall and Brooklands. Brooklands is large and parents like it, but it doesn't suit working parents as the settling-in period for reception takes forever! Tetherdown, across the border in Haringey, is also highly regarded… but you practically have to live next door to get a place.

As for secondary schools, Barnet is quite well known for its high standards, and families relocate to the borough to take advantage of this. There are a number of selective state schools, the most well known being the Henrietta Barnett girls' school, and Latymer School (*see p292*) over in Enfield is close by. They are highly competitive and your child might have a one-in-ten chance of getting in – if, of course, he or she has a private tutor. Mill Hill County has scholarships for music, and also gives preference to borough employees. For comprehensives, a lot of people head for the border with Haringey, and many children go to Fortismere (*see p96*), which is particularly strong on the arts. The Compton School is also well thought of, and is very well equipped.'

Kate Fuscoe, mother of two, East Finchley

Primary

There are 75 state primaries in Barnet, including 24 church schools and six Jewish schools. There are also 25 independent primary schools, including seven faith schools, one international school and one theatre school. See www.barnet.gov.uk and www.ofsted.gov.uk for more information.

Secondary

Ashmole School *Cecil Road, N14 5RJ (8361 2703/www.ashmole.barnet.sch.uk).*

Bishop Douglass RC High School *Hamilton Road, N2 0SQ (8444 5211/www.bishopdouglass. barnet.sch.uk).*

Christ's College Finchley *East End Road, N2 0SE (8349 3581/www.christscollege finchley.com).* Boys only; mixed sixth form.

Compton School *Summers Lane, N12 0QG (8368 1783/www.compton.barnet.lgfl.net).*

Copthall School *Pursley Road, NW7 2EP (8959 1937/www.copthall.barnet.lgfl.net).* Girls only.

East Barnet School *Chestnut Grove, EN4 8PU (8440 4162/www.eastbarnet.barnet.sch.uk).*

Finchley Catholic High School *Woodside Lane, N12 8TA (8445 0105/www.finchley catholic.org.uk).* Boys only.

Friern Barnet School *Hemington Avenue, N11 3LS (8368 2777/www.friern.barnet.sch.uk).*

Barnet

Hasmonean High School Boys' site *Holders Hill Road, NW4 1NA (8203 1411/www.hasmonean. co.uk);* Girls' site *2 Page Street, NW7 2EU (8203 4294/www.hasmonean.co.uk).* Jewish.
Hendon Foundation School *Golders Rise, NW4 2HP (8202 9004).*
Henrietta Barnett School *Central Square, NW11 7BN (8458 8999/www.hbschool.org.uk).*
London Academy *Green Lane, Edgware, HA8 8BT (8958 5310/www.londonacademy.org.uk).*
Mill Hill County High School *Worcester Crescent, NW7 4LL (0844 477 2424/ www.mhchs.org.uk).*
Queen Elizabeth's Girls' School *High Street, EN5 5RR (8449 2984/www.qegschool.org.uk).*
Queen Elizabeth's Boys' School *Queen's Road, EN5 4DQ (8441 4646/www.qebarnet. co.uk).* Boys only.
Ravenscroft School *Barnet Lane, Totteridge, N20 8AZ (8445 9205/www.ravenscroft. barnet.sch.uk).*
St James' Catholic High School *Great Strand, NW9 5PE (8358 2800/www.st-james.barnet.sch.uk).*
St Mary's CE High School *Downage, NW4 1AB (8203 2827).*
St Michael's Catholic Grammar School *Nether Street, N12 7NJ (8446 2256/www.st-michaels.barnet.sch.uk).* Girls only.
Whitefield Community School *Claremont Road, NW2 1TR (8455 4114/www.whitefield. barnet.sch.uk).*

Property

WHAT THE AGENTS SAY:

❛It's not a trendy or fashionable borough, but you get a lot of house for your money if you don't mind the travel. It's reassuringly boring – there's more of a Horlicks feeling around here. A big drawback, though: the school catchment areas have narrowed so much that families are either moving away or having to pay privately.❜
David Bettis, Bennett & Hall, Finchley

Average property prices

Detached £619,520
Semi-detached £313,754
Terraced £232,065
Flat £174,635

COUNCIL TAX		
A	up to £40,000	**£830.60**
B	£40,001-£52,000	**£969.04**
C	£52,001-£68,000	**£1,107.47**
D	£68,001-£88,000	**£1,245.90**
E	£88,001-£120,000	**£1,522.76**
F	£120,001-£160,000	**£1,799.63**
G	£160,001-£320,000	**£2,076.50**
H	over £320,000	**£2,491.80**

Local estate agents

Bennett & Hall *2 Long Lane, N3 2PT (8346 2208/www.bennett-hall.co.uk).*
Douglas Martin *18 Central Circus, NW4 3AS (8202 6333/www.douglasmartin.co.uk).*
Ellis & Co *www.ellisandco.co.uk; 5 offices in the borough (Barnet 8441 7700/Finchley 8349 3131/Golders Green 8455 1014/Hampstead Garden Suburb 8458 8448/Mill Hill 8959 3281).*
Jeremy Leaf & Co *www.jeremyleaf.co.uk; 2 offices in the borough (East Finchley 0871 271 7516/North Finchley 0871 271 7515).*
Martyn Gerrard *www.martyngerrard.co.uk; 4 offices in the borough (East Finchley 8883 0077/Finchley Central 8346 0102/North Finchley 8445 2222/Whetstone 8446 2111).*
Richard James *52A The Broadway, NW7 3LH (8959 9191/www.richardjames.biz).*

Other information

Council

Barnet Council *Hendon Town Hall, The Burroughs, NW4 4BG (8359 2000/ www.barnet.gov.uk).*
Barnet Council First Contact Unit *8359 2277/first.contact@barnet.gov.uk.*

Hospitals

Barnet General Hospital *Wellhouse Lane, EN5 3DJ (0845 111 4000/www.bcf.nhs.uk).*
Edgware Community Hospital *Burnt Oak Broadway, Middx HA8 0AD (8952 2381/ www.barnet.nhs.uk).*
Finchley Memorial Hospital *Granville Road, N12 0JE (8349 6300/www.barnet.nhs.uk).*

Legal services

Finchley CAB *23-35 Hendon Lane, N3 1RT (0870 128 8080/www.barnetcab.org.uk).*
Hendon CAB *40-42 Church End, NW4 4JT (0870 128 8080/www.barnetcab.org.uk).*
New Barnet CAB *30 Station Road, New Barnet, EN5 1PL (0870 128 8080/www.barnetcab.org.uk).*

Local newspapers

The Archer *www.the-archer.co.uk.* Community newspaper for East Finchley run entirely by volunteers.
Barnet Times *www.barnettimes.co.uk.*
Edgware & Mill Hill Times *www.edgwaretimes.co.uk.*
Hendon & Finchley Times *www.hendontimes.co.uk.*

Allotments

London Borough of Barnet *Greenspaces Officer, Building 4, North London Business Park, Oakleigh Road South, N11 1NP (8359 7820/www.barnet.gov.uk).*
Barnet Federation of Allotments & Horticultural Societies *www.kitchengardens.dial.pipex.com.*

Barnet

Brent

A microcosm of the entire city, Brent encompasses the urban and suburban, the prosperous and the poorly off, the dynamic and the dull. Irish, Asian, Afro-Caribbean, Portuguese and East European communities have all settled in the borough. Local perks include cutting-edge theatre and a taste of Paradise (by way of Kensal Green).

Neighbourhoods

Kilburn and Brondesbury

The A5, across which Kilburn squats, has been a major thoroughfare since Roman times. In the 19th century the area became associated with Irish immigrants, many of whom came to build the railways. It still is (a parade takes place every St Patrick's Day), though changes are afoot.

Attracted by the Emerald Isle's boom economy, many of north-west London's Irish community have returned to their homeland. Consequently, several of the area's pubs have changed hands. You'll still find plenty of Irish bars, but a peppering of gastropubs has recently spiced up the High Road. Whether this marks the beginnings of Kilburn's march towards middle-class affluence remains to be seen.

The area's ethnic mix has also broadened, and is reflected in the shops, budget restaurants and takeaways along the High Road. Throw into the pot a small street market (on Kilburn Square), countless discount stores and low-price chains and you have some idea of the mishmash that makes up modern Kilburn. Three landmarks on the High Road show this diversity: the Tricycle Theatre is not only a top fringe venue, but now includes a cinema, bar and café; the former Gaumont State Cinema is an old-school bingo hall; and what was Biddy Mulligans (one of London's most famous Irish pubs) is now the Southern K, an Australian-themed bar.

The Victorian residential district of Brondesbury lies to the north of Kilburn and is served by a rail station on the Silverlink Metro line. The area has good transport links into the West End too, including Zone 2 tube stations at Kilburn and Kilburn Park, plus numerous buses. This accessibility, rather than any latent flowering of prosperity or funkiness, has kept house prices fairly high.

Kensal Rise and Kensal Green

Compared with the rough edges of Harlesden to the west, there's a relaxed feel to Kensal Green. Though the compact late-Victorian terraces are similar in style to many found in the neighbouring district, here they're more likely to be snapped up by young professionals. The constantly busy Harrow Road lies at the southern boundary of the borough; on the other side, in Kensington & Chelsea, is Kensal Green cemetery, final resting place of some of our most famous Victorian writers. Another literary connection is at the centre of Kensal Green's tentative moves upmarket: Paradise by Way of Kensal Green, named after a GK Chesterton poem, was one of London's first

Brent

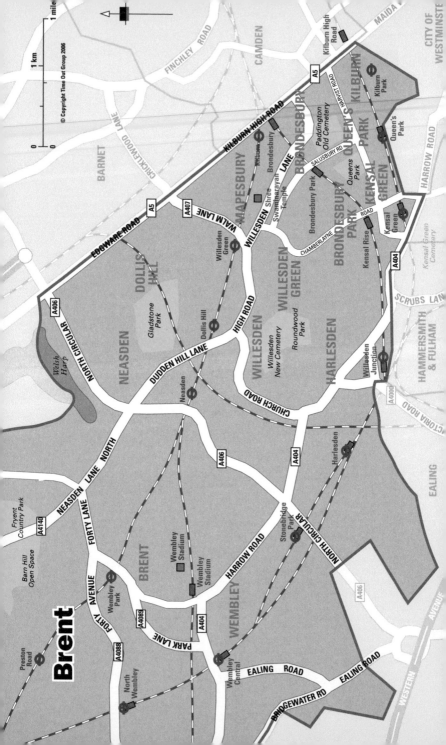

gastropubs in the early 1990s. In the residential area off Chamberlayne Road, Victorian terraces give way to wider, tree-lined streets as you head north into suburban Kensal Rise. Prim and proper 1930s semis flourish here, and stone cladding isn't unknown.

Harlesden

Harlesden gets a bad press – so much so that Brent Council has launched a 'Love Where You Live' campaign to improve the image of the borough's 'most challenging' neighbourhoods. Yet while the high crime rates around the Stonebridge Estate (to the north-west) are undeniable, and police minibuses often sport riot shields as they patrol the streets, this multicultural area throbs with vitality by day, with Afro-Caribbean and Asian businesses much in evidence on the High Street.

At the centre of Harlesden is the Jubilee Clock, an elaborate landmark erected in 1887. Most of the borough's housing was built during the late Victorian era following the establishment of a tramway service to central London. Today, the transport links are provided by the Bakerloo Line (a short walk down Acton Lane), the rail line at Willesden Junction, and a plentiful supply of buses. Though you'll find gritty urban deprivation in Harlesden if you look for it, and some of the flats look decidedly forebidding, you can also discover quiet, well-kept Victorian terraces (the area around St John's Avenue, for instance). House prices are relatively modest. To the north of the borough is Roundwood Park, a capacious green space containing a children's play area, an aviary and a bowling green, while to the north-east, acting as a green buffer between Harlesden and upmarket Brondesbury Park, is Willesden Sports Centre (due to reopen at the end of 2006).

Willesden and Willesden Green

Virtually free of chain stores – the exception is a Sainsbury's, tucked out of the way – Willesden High Road accommodates shops and services for a huge range of cultures. It's a pretty grimy thoroughfare, though, and you won't find anything in the way of boutiques or posh restaurants. Somehow the road maintains an old-fashioned feel, despite

STATISTICS
BOROUGH MAKE-UP
Population 270,391
Average weekly pay £459.70
Ethnic origins
White 45.27%
Mixed 3.27%
Asian or Asian British 27.73%
Black or Black British 19.86%
Chinese or other 3.41%
Students 11.92%
Retirees 9.56%

HOUSING STOCK
Borough size 44.2km^2
No. of households 102,625
Detached 6.5%
Semi-detached 27.7%
Terraced 18.9%
Flats (purpose-built) 26.9%
Flats (converted) 18.8%
Flats (both) 45.7%

CRIME PER 1,000 OF POPULATION
(English average in brackets)
Burglary 10 (6.4)
Robbery 8 (1.4)
Theft of vehicle 6 (4.5)
Theft from vehicle 10 (10)
Violence against the person 34 (16.5)
Sexual offences 1 (0.9)

MPs & COUNCIL
MPs *Brent East* Sarah Teather (Liberal Democrat); *Brent South* Dawn Butler (Labour)
CPA 3 stars; improving well

the constant slow-moving traffic and line of buses emerging from Willesden Garage. At the western end of the High Road (by White Hart Lane) is a small bi-weekly street market that is currently under threat.

As with Kilburn, Willesden has long been associated with Irish expats: there are plenty of Irish pubs, though several drinking holes are now primarily populated by Antipodean punters. A prime resource for locals is the Willesden Green Library Centre. It is housed in relatively new premises that also contain a bookshop, licensed café and cinema. Late Victorian terraces make up much of Willesden's housing stock (a high proportion of them converted into flats), though there are larger houses off Walm Lane near Willesden Green tube station. Here thirtysomething

Brent

professionals have gained a foothold, congregating in the Green, a modish bar-restaurant opposite the station.

Queen's Park, Brondesbury Park and Mapesbury

Like a stream of pinot grigio, prosperity is flowing northward from Notting Hill. It has found a promising channel along Harvist Road towards Queen's Park tube, then up Salusbury Road towards residential Brondesbury Park and Mapesbury. Harvist Road is lined with stately Victorian edifices overlooking the grassy serenity of Queen's Park. At a busy little junction, it meets the area's main shopping street, Salusbury Road. Here you'll discover swanky estate agents, posh cafés and a gastropub. Media types who dream of a Notting Hill apartment have started to populate the area, but Queen's Park is still economically mixed, so you'll also find workshops and the odd launderette nearby.

As Salusbury Road becomes Brondesbury Park, shops are replaced by substantial residential abodes. These become grander as you continue, including several gated mansions, though things change once again as you approach the scruffier environs of Willesden High Road. Parallel to Brondesbury Park is the busier, slightly less select Willesden Lane, linking Willesden and Kilburn. This rather grey road is enlivened by the bright new Shree Swaminarayan Hindu temple halfway along. To the north of here are the sedate streets of Mapesbury, home of the spacious 1930s semi, company cars parked neatly outside. This is a conservation area and house prices of £800,000 aren't unknown.

Dollis Hill and Neasden

Seemly Edwardian terraces line the streets of residential Dollis Hill. The Jubilee Line station appears to mark the divide between urban Willesden and outer London suburbia. The population is comfortably off, though not rich, with British Asian, English and Irish families well represented, plus an increasing number of Antipodeans. The area is only served by local shops (residents scoot off to Willesden, Neasden or the Brent Cross Shopping Centre for more provisions), but its main amenity is Gladstone Park. This large lawned space rises to a hilltop occupied by Dollis Hill House – once used as a retreat by Victorian prime minister William Gladstone, now awaiting restoration. One of the suburban roads leading off the park is Melrose Avenue, where, in the 1970s, mass murderer Dennis Nilson lived at No.195. The remains of 13 of Nilson's victims were found at the address after his arrest.

Neasden (meaning nose-shaped hill) has long been the butt of jokes, especially in *Private Eye*, though no one seems to know why. Perhaps it is the remarkable unremarkableness of this suburb, consisting, as it does, of a busy traffic island, a shopping street that's bisected by the North Circular Road, and row upon row of late Victorian, Edwardian and 1930s housing. Nevertheless, there's a diverting multicultural mix to the area; witness the variety of shops to be found along the 1930s parade of Neasden Lane. If you're after posh clothing, haute cuisine or nightlife, you'll need to take the Jubilee Line elsewhere.

TRANSPORT

Tube stations *Bakerloo* Kilburn Park, Queen's Park, Kensal Green, Willesden Junction, Harlesden, Stonebridge Park, Wembley Central, North Wembley, South Kenton, Kenton; *Jubilee* Kilburn, Willesden Green, Dollis Hill, Neasden, Wembley Park, Kingsbury, Queensbury; *Metropolitan* Wembley Park, Preston Road, Northwick Park; *Piccadilly* Alperton, Sudbury Town
Rail stations *Chiltern Railways* Wembley Stadium, Sudbury & Harrow Road; *Silverlink* Kilburn High Road, Queen's Park, Kensal Green, Brondesbury, Brondesbury Park, Kensal Rise, Willesden Junction, Harlesden, Stonebridge Park, Wembley Central, North Wembley, South Kenton, Kenton
Main bus routes *into central London* 6, 16, 18, 36, 52, 98, 189, 263; *night buses* N16, N18, N36, N52, N98, N266; *24-hour buses* 6, 43, 83, 189, 220, 260, 266

Restaurants & cafés

It has to be said, Brent isn't noted for gastronomy. But things are improving. Where bright young things have bought housing, restaurants are opening and pubs are developing a gastro bent. The process is in its early stages in Kilburn, but the area (which crosses into Camden borough) does contain worthwhile budget bistros such as Small & Beautiful and a branch of Little Bay. Also inexpensive is the cluster of South Indian restaurants along Willesden Lane: Vijay, Geeta and (the best) Kovalam. Otherwise, you'll find a civilised café at the Tricycle Theatre.

The endearingly weird Paradise by Way of Kensal Green has been overtaken in the gastro stakes by handsome pub conversion William IV. Over in Willesden, Sabras is well loved for Gujarati vegetarian cooking. Near the tube station is the delightfully authentic Japanese Sushi-Say; across the road is the smart new Pizza on the Wood; around the corner there's a branch of Turkish/oriental bar-restaurant Shish, and Little Star, part of the Little Bay group.

Harlesden's dining scene is barely in its infancy; the most welcoming spot is cosy Os Amigos, a Portuguese restaurant and bar with hearty food, though its compatriot Cantinho da Madeira Tapas Bar is also a possibility. Queen's Park is better served, with Penk's (French/global), Hugo's (modern bistro/brunch), a branch of Baker & Spice (posh café) and the Salusbury gastropub leading the way. Close to Dollis Hill, Saravanas serves commendable South Indian dishes, but Neasden has little choice; the best bet lies north of the North Circular, where New Kabana cooks authentic North Indian karahi food.

Baker & Spice 75 Salusbury Road, NW6 6NH (7604 3636).
Cantinho da Madeira Tapas Bar 208 High Street, Harlesden, NW10 4SY (8961 9239).
Geeta 57-59 Willesden Lane, NW6 7RL (7624 1713).
Hugo's 21-25 Lonsdale Road, NW6 6RA (7372 1232).
Kovalam 12 Willesden Lane, NW6 7SR (7625 4761/www.kovalamrestaurant.co.uk).
Little Bay 228 Belsize Road, NW6 4BT (7372 4699).
Little Star 26 Station Parade, NW2 4NH (8830 5221).
New Kabana 43 Blackbird Hill, NW9 8RS (8200 7094).
Os Amigos 25 Park Parade, NW10 4JG (8961 9161).
Paradise by Way of Kensal Green 19 Kilburn Lane, W10 4AE (8969 0098).
Penk's 79 Salusbury Road, NW6 6NH (7604 4484/www.penks.com).
Pizza on the Wood 76 Walm Lane, NW2 4RA (8459 3311).

Family-friendly **Kensal Rise**. See p303.

Sabras 263 High Road, NW10 2RX (8459 0340).
Salusbury 50-52 Salusbury Road, NW6 6NN (7328 3286).
Saravanas 77-81 Dudden Hill Lane, NW10 1BD (8459 4900/2400/www.saravanas.co.uk).
Shish 2-6 Station Parade, NW2 4NH (8208 9292).
Small & Beautiful 351 Kilburn High Road, NW6 2QJ (7328 2637).
Sushi-Say 33B Walm Lane, NW2 5SH (8459 2971).
Tricycle Theatre Café 269 Kilburn High Road, NW6 7JR (7372 6611/www.tricycle.co.uk).
Vijay 49 Willesden Lane, NW6 7RF (7328 1087).
William IV 786 Harrow Road, NW10 5LX (8969 5944).

Bars & pubs

Brent's changing demographics are most noticeable in its pubs, with several big old Irish boozers undergoing conversion. In Kilburn, this has produced a brace of good pubs – the moodily lit Black Lion and the North London Tavern (drink Pedigree, dine on risotto, listen to trip hop). There's also Australian theme pub the Southern K. The process started earlier in Kensal Green, where the district's young urbanites also have three nice pubs to lounge in: Paradise and William IV for food (*see p307*), and the Greyhound for a nice pint of Adnams.

Willesden Green's young homeowners concentrate themselves in the Green, a congenial bar-restaurant opposite the tube station, while Australians congregate at the Crown. The least intimidating of Willesden's Irish pubs is Flynn's Bar.

Apart from Young's pub the Grand Junction Arms (with a beer garden by the canal), most Harlesden boozers are of the hard-drinking, resolutely male variety; Queen's Park, in contrast, has convivial gastropub the Salusbury (*see p307*). Nearly all Neasden's hostelries are grouped around the shopping parade on Neasden Lane; Irish locals come to imbibe before a night at Dicey's (a raucous nightclub above a bar). At least the Wetherspoons pub, the Outside Inn, has cheap beer.

Black Lion *274 Kilburn High Road, NW6 2BY (7625 1635/www.blacklionguesthouse.com).*
Crown *335-339 High Road, NW10 2JT (8459 4771).*
Dicey's *The Galway Hooker, Neasden Shopping Centre, 289-295 Neasden Lane, NW10 1QR (8450 9922).*
Flynn's Bar *117 High Road, NW10 2SL (no phone).*
Grand Junction Arms *Canal Bridge, Acton Lane, NW10 7AD (8965 5670).*
Green *110 Walm Lane, NW2 4RS (8452 0909/www.thegreennw2.com).*
Greyhound *64-66 Chamberlayne Road, NW10 3JJ (8969 8080).*
North London Tavern *375 Kilburn High Road, NW6 7QB (7625 6634).*
Outside Inn *312-314 Neasden Lane, NW10 0AD (8452 3140).*
Southern K *205 Kilburn High Road, NW6 7HY (7624 2066).*

Shops

If not after delis and food shops (of which Brent has a decent selection), the choicest shopping in the borough is to be had in Kensal Rise. Chamberlayne Road, and the area just off it, is Brent's answer to Crouch End. High up the eponymous Rise is high-end interiors shop Maisonette, darling of *Elle Decoration* magazine. On the same road is Laars, with kidswear as well as designer goods. Kuddyco is crammed full of unusual gifts cherry-picked from around the globe, while Flirty Flowers specialises in country-style blooms. Get your sofa re-upholstered at Michael Blackstaffe – or buy a new one

at IKEA, off the North Circular Road. You might also try Willesden Market, for the usual odds and ends, or Willesden Green Architectural Salvage for large second-hand items like fireplaces. Music lovers should head to Hawkeye Record Store for reggae, or to Mandy's Irish Shop on the High Road for traditional (you guessed it) Irish folk.

Now for the food. Just away from Kensal Rise station is L'Angolo, a fine (if scruffy-looking) Italian deli; there are Spanish and Portuguese versions (such as Delicias de Portugal) on Harrow Road. In Kilburn, a beguiling mix of shops sell edible wares from Thailand, Italy, the Middle East and South Asia – as well as Ireland, of course. Try the small street market on Kilburn Square. In Willesden, Edward's Bakery has been providing traditional cakes since 1908, Colombo Trader caters for fans of Sri Lankan cuisine, and Blue Mountain Peak is ace for West African groceries. If you're still hungry, try Bab's Bakery for Ghanaian delights (any turkey tail fans out there?).

L'Angolo *120 College Road, NW10 5HD (8969 5757).*
Bab's Bakery *76 Craven Park Road, NW10 4AE (8965 2849).*
Blue Mountain Peak *4 Craven Park Road, NW10 4AB (8965 3859).*
Colombo Trader *316-318 High Road, NW10 2EN (8459 8589).*
Delicias de Portugal *1008 Harrow Road, NW10 5NS (8960 7933).*
Edward's Bakery *269 High Road, NW10 2RX (8459 3001).*
Flirty Flowers *98A Chamberlayne Road, NW10 3JN (8960 9191).*
Hawkeye Record Store *2 Craven Park Road, NW10 4AB (8961 0866).*
IKEA *Brent Park, 2 Drury Way, North Circular Road, NW10 0TH (0845 355 1141/ www.ikea.co.uk).*

Kilburn Square Market *Kilburn Square, W6.*
Kuddyco *117 Chamberlayne Road, NW10 3NS (8968 6617/www.kuddyco.com).*
Laars *60 Chamberlayne Road, NW10 3JH (8962 0011).*
Maisonette *79 Chamberlayne Road, NW10 3ND (8964 8444/www.maisonette.uk.com).*
Mandy's Irish Shop *161 High Road, NW10 2SG (8459 2842).*
Michael Blackstaffe *4 Station Terrace, NW10 5RS (8969 0932).*
Willesden Green Architectural Salvage *189 High Road, NW10 2SD (8459 2947).*
Willesden Market *White Hart High Road, NW10.*

Arts & attractions

Cinemas & theatres
Tricycle Theatre & Cinema *269 Kilburn High Road, NW6 7JR (7328 1000/www.tricycle. co.uk).* As well as the titular theatre and cinema, there's a rehearsal studio, visual arts studio, café-bar and art gallery.
Willesden Green Belle Vue Cinema *Willesden Green Library Centre, 95 High Road, NW10 2SU (0871 223 6049).*

Galleries & museums
Brent Museum *Willesden Green Library Centre, 95 High Road, NW10 2SU (8204 6870/ www.brent.gov.uk/grangemuseum).* Local history museum (formerly the Grange Museum of Community History), set to open in the Willesden Green Library Centre in spring 2006.

Other attractions
Willesden Green Library Centre *95 High Road, NW10 2SU (8937 3400).* Not just a library, it also has a cinema, museum and café.

Open spaces

Barnhill Open Space *Barn Hill Road, HA9.* Attached to Fryent Country Park.
Fryent Country Park *Fryent Way, NW9.*
Gladstone Park *Dollis Hill Lane, NW2.*
King Edward VII Park *Park Lane, HA9.*
Preston Park *College Road, HA9.*
Queen's Park *Chevening Road, NW6.*
Roundwood Park *Harlseden Road, NW10.*
Welsh Harp Reservoir *Birchen Grove, NW9.* Enormous expanse of open water, marshes, trees and grassland.
Woodcock Park *Shaftesbury Avenue, HA3.*

Sport & fitness

Considering the size of Brent, there's a smaller selection of health clubs than you might expect, particularly since the closure of Crystal Planet Fitness Centre.

Nevertheless, Brent's council-run facilities are very well equipped. The Willesden Sports Centre is closed for refurbishment until the end of 2006.

Gyms & leisure centres
Bridge Park Community Leisure Centre *Harrow Road, NW10 0RG (8937 3730).*
Cannons *Sidmouth Road, NW2 5JY (8451 7863/www.cannons.co.uk).* Private.
Charteris Road Sports Centre *24-30 Charteris Road, NW6 7ET (7625 6451/ www.leisureconnection.co.uk).*
Fitness First *www.fitnessfirst.co.uk; The Atlip Centre, 197 Ealing Road, HA0 4LW (8903 6464); 1st Floor, 632-640 Kingsbury Road, NW9 9HN (8204 5858); 105-109 Salusbury Road, NW6 6RG (7328 8333).* Private.
Genesis Gym *333 Athlon Road, HA0 1EF (8566 8687).* Private.
LivingWell *Hilton Hotel, Empire Way, HA9 8DS (8795 4118/www.livingwell.com).* Private.
The Manor Health & Leisure *307 Cricklewood Broadway, NW2 6PG (8450 6464/ www.themanorhealthandleisure.co.uk).* Private.
Vale Farm Sports Centre *Watford Road, HA0 3HG (8908 6545/www.leisureconnection. co.uk).*

Spectator sports
Wembley Arena & Conference Centre/ Wembley Stadium *Elvin House, Stadium Way, HA9 0DW (Arena 8902 8833/Stadium 8795 9000/box office 0800 600 0870/ www.wembleystadium.com).* International boxing bouts, snooker and basketball tournaments, and showjumping events take place infrequently at the refurbished Arena. The lavish new Wembley Stadium is due to be complete by spring 2006; at the time of press, many still have their doubts about this.

Schools

WHAT THE PARENTS SAY:
6Brent has a large number of Muslim, Jewish and Christian faith schools, including the well-known Islamia [set up by the man formerly known as Cat Stevens] and the Jewish Free School. My eldest children went to Salusbury Primary School, one of the largest primaries in Brent; it had a highly transient population when they were there, but is more desirable these days. Mora Primary School is smaller and favoured by Muslim parents. My youngest daughter is one of a minority of British pupils there, and part of an even smaller minority of white British pupils.

Of the secondary schools in the borough, I'm considering Kingsbury High and Preston Manor for my youngest.9
Sally Long, mother of three, Cricklewood

Brent

Primary

There are 60 state primary schools in Brent, 16 of which are church schools, one a Jewish school, and one an Islamic school. There are also ten independent primaries, including five faith schools, one Montessori school, and two Welsh schools. See www.brent.gov.uk and www.ofsted. gov.uk for more information.

Secondary

Alperton Community School *Ealing Road, HA0 4PW (8902 2293).*
Capital City Academy *Doyle Gardens, NW10 3ST (8838 8700/www.capitalcityacademy.org).*
Cardinal Hinsley High RC Boys' School *Harlesden Road, NW10 3RN (8965 3947/8497).* Boys only.
Claremont High School *Claremont Avenue, HA3 0UH (8204 4442/www.claremonthigh.co.uk).*
Convent of Jesus and Mary Language College *Crownhill Road, NW10 4EP (8965 2986/www.cjmhs.brent.sch.uk).* Girls only.
Copland School *Cecil Avenue, HA9 7DU (8902 6362).*
Jewish Free School (JFS) *The Mall, HA3 9TE (8206 3100/www.jfs.brent.sch.uk).*
John Kelly Technology College *Crest Road, NW2 7SN (boys 8452 8700/girls 8452 4842).* Boys and girls taught separately.
Kingsbury High School *Princes Avenue, NW9 9JR (8204 9814/www.kingsburyhigh.org.uk).*
Preston Manor High School *Carlton Avenue East, HA9 8NA (8385 4040/www.pmanor. brent.sch.uk).*
Queens Park Community School *Aylestone Avenue, NW6 7BQ (8438 1700/www.qpcs. brent.sch.uk).*
St Gregory's RC High School *Donnington Road, HA3 0NB (8907 8828/www.stgregorys. harrow.sch.uk).*
Wembley High Technology College *East Lane, HA0 3NT (8385 4800/www.whtc.co.uk).*

COUNCIL TAX

A	up to £40,000	£789.43
B	£40,001-£52,000	£921.00
C	£52,001-£68,000	£1,052.57
D	£68,001-£88,000	£1,184.14
E	£88,001-£120,000	£1,447.28
F	£120,001-£160,000	£1,710.42
G	£160,001-£320,000	£1,973.57
H	over £320,000	£2,368.28

Property

WHAT THE AGENTS SAY:

‘Willesden's in Zone 2 on the Jubilee Line and there are a lot of open spaces. The properties are largely Victorian and Edwardian and, in the last couple of years, the gentrification process has truly taken hold. Like any area in transition,

though, there are still problems with crime. You have to be aware of who's around you – but you can say that of most inner-city areas. The high street was killed by Brent Cross Shopping Centre. It's mainly estate agents and pubs now – no proper shopping. The other side to that is that Brent Cross is only five minutes away by car.’
Terry Miles, Camerons, Willesden Green

Average property prices

Detached £426,835
Semi-detached £261,743
Terraced £239,966
Flat £158,637

Local estate agents

Camerons *90 Walm Lane NW2 4QY (8459 0091/www.cameronslondon.com).*
Freshsteps *399 Kilburn High Road, NW6 7QE (7372 9000/www.freshsteps.co.uk).*
Hoopers *www.hoopersestateagents.co.uk; 2 offices in the borough (Kenton 8206 1484/ Neasden 8450 1633).*
Margo's *62 Chamberlayne Road, NW10 3JJ (8960 3030/www.margos.co.uk).*

Other information

Council

Brent Council *Town Hall, Forty Lane, HA9 9HD (switchboard 8937 1234/customer services 8937 1200/www.brent.gov.uk).*

Hospitals

Central Middlesex Hospital *Acton Lane, Park Royal, NW10 7NS (8965 5733/ www.nwlh.nhs.uk).*
Northwick Park *Hospital Watford Road, HA1 3UJ (8864 3232/www.nwlh.nhs.uk).*
St Mark's Hospital *Watford Road, HA1 3UJ (8864 3232/www.nwlh.nhs.uk).*
Willesden Hospital *Harlesden Road, NW10 3RY (8438 7000).*

Legal services

Brent CAB *270-272 High Road, NW10 2EY (0845 050 5250/www.brentcab.co.uk).*
Brent Community Law Centre *8451 1122/ www.lawcentres.org.uk.*

Local newspapers

Harrow Times *01923 216 343/ www.harrowtimes.co.uk.*
Harrow & Wembley Observer *8427 4404/ www.icharrow.co.uk.*
Willesden & Brent Times *8962 6868/ www.wbtimes.co.uk.*

Allotments

Council *Allotments Officer, Barham Park Offices, 660 Harrow Road, Wembley, Middx HA0 2HB (Phil Bruce-Green 8937 5633).*

Ealing

Belle of the 'burbs, Ealing is a generally prosperous spot surrounded by plentiful green space and exuding gentility. But the borough is far from homogeneous, and also includes the thriving multicultural district of Acton, diverse transport options and a wide variety of housing.

Neighbourhoods

Acton

For many, Acton is somewhere you just pass through on the way to Heathrow, so it's quite a surprise to leave the A40 and find such a thriving neighbourhood. Not all the area is prospering – North and West Acton have their share of neglected council blocks and industrial estates – but South Acton and East Acton are full of smart houses, parks, sports fields and upmarket private schools.

In Acton Town, the High Street has all the usual banks, fast-food franchises and supermarkets, plus the imposing Acton Library and Town Hall. Pubs like the Captain Cook and Redback Tavern cater to the large Australian population, while the mosques and halal tandoori joints provide for the Pakistani community.

The district is swamped by 1930s mock-Tudor housing, but you can still find some impressive Victorian detached residences and brick terraces, particularly around Creffield Road. Other upmarket areas include South Acton, Acton Green and Bedford Park, which all benefit from being near the shops and restaurants of Chiswick High Road (in the borough of Hounslow; see p320). Further north, the streets around Acton Park are jammed with Clerkenwell-style office conversions, while East Acton has long rows of posh semis, sports grounds and the Saudi-sponsored independent school, the King Fahad Academy.

The north and west of Acton are the least attractive places to live in the borough. West Acton is dominated by train tracks and industrial estates, and North Acton is an unappealing jumble of industrial developments and retail parks, cut off from the rest of the district by the traffic mayhem on the A40 (Western Avenue).

This is one of the most ethnically mixed areas in west London and also one of the best integrated. There is a panoply of churches and faith centres, all of which seem to pull in large congregations. The transport links are excellent too: numerous tube stops, overland train stations, and the A40 and M4 right on the doorstep.

Ealing and Hanger Hill

By turns elegant, bijou and brash, Ealing has come a long way since Ealing Studios produced its famous comedies on the edge of Walpole Park. Sure, the area has its share of tower blocks and housing estates – most notably around Argyle Road – but Ealing is overwhelmingly upper middle-class, and it shows. The district is ultra-suburban, with tree-lined avenues full of independent faith schools and stately detached homes with gravel drives.

From a resident's perspective, the main attractions (apart from the houses) are the schools and transport links. Ealing is packed with primary and secondary schools – mostly of the private, opted-out variety.

Highs & Lows

Community unity Acton is one of London's most ethnically mixed areas, and one of the most integrated
Villagey W5 The two- and three-bedroom cottages around Ealing's Meadvale Road are stunning

Price of life Ultra-moneyed, ultra-suburban, you have to have a lot of cash (and a Merc or two) before you can live in Ealing's bijou swathes
Acton ugliness Close to the money of Ealing, North and West Acton remain neglected and down at heel

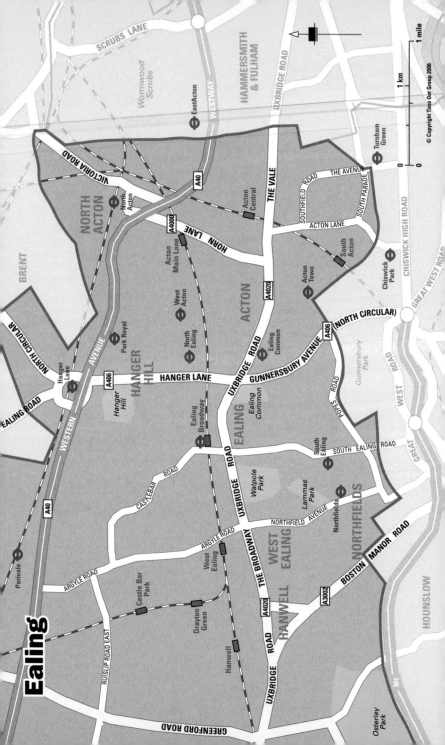

There are numerous parks and sporting clubs too, where kids can let off steam. As with Acton, commuters have a choice of half a dozen train and tube stations, while the A40 and M4 provide easy access to Heathrow and the South-west.

Lawyers, executives and wealthy ladies with lap dogs congregate on Ealing Green, which rivals Chiswick in terms of genteel affluence. Two Mercedes in the drive seems to be the minimum requirement to live around here, and this is reflected in property prices. The most extravagant properties are north of the Broadway towards Hanger Hill: there are some veritable palaces, with flamboyant Italian marble porticos, Grecian columns and more beds than the average Londoner has rooms.

The main civic centre is on Ealing Broadway; the streets around the tube station are packed with banks, cafés, restaurants, and chain pubs and shops. Things get more residential as you head south, but South Ealing is still a well-to-do area. Houses may be mock-Tudor, but they're huge, and there are plenty of shops and restaurants along Ealing South Road.

The grand housing extends to the streets around Ealing Common. The common itself is divided in two by train tracks, but from here it's only a short stroll south to huge Gunnersbury Park (just over the borough border in Hounslow), one of the few surviving manor house estates in west London. By contrast, Argyle Road in the north-west is dominated by retirement villages and uninspiring planned housing. It's a relatively downmarket area, but house prices are low and there are grand views towards the Brent Valley.

Hanwell, Northfields and West Ealing

Bound by Northfield Avenue and Boston Road, Hanwell is the poorer cousin of Ealing, but most residents can still afford two vehicles in the carport. The mood is sleepy and suburban. The streets are lined with identical rows of tidy terraced homes and pebble-dashed semis, plus the occasional church. Uxbridge Road cuts through the middle of town, providing the usual high-street amenities and, should you need it, a Rolls-Royce garage.

Hanwell and Northfields (the next district south) both score highly for green open

spaces; there are recreation grounds and sporting clubs every few hundred metres. Uxbridge Road passes between the vast Kensington and City of Westminster Cemeteries, final resting place for many of west London's wealthiest residents. For golfers, it's a short putt to the courses of Osterley Park and the Brent Valley.

The most appealing streets are east of Northfield Avenue in West Ealing. There are some huge detached houses here, particularly around Lammas Park, and the south end of Northfield Avenue holds an array of restaurants. For transport to central London, there are tube stops at Boston Manor and Northfields, overland train stations at Hanwell and West Ealing, and the congested M4.

Ealing

Restaurants & cafés

The highest concentration of restaurants is in Ealing, reflecting, no doubt, the division of disposable income in the borough. As well as chain options in the vicinity of the Broadway, such as Nando's, Carluccio's and Mamma Amalfi's, independent eateries covering a wide ethnic spread are thrown into the mix. Friendly Café Grove serves breakfast and Polish specialities, and, to the south, the Ealing Park Tavern is a huge, very popular gastropub with a great back garden. Heading towards Acton, Sushi-Hiro, near Ealing Common, may not look like much, but the sushi is swimmingly fresh. There are also a couple of accomplished Caribbean eateries, BB's and Tyme – the latter is particularly good.

Acton has a tiny but authentic Sichuan restaurant and a couple of pubs serving above-average fare on budding hotspot Churchfield Road, including Italian-accented gastropub the Rocket. There's also a rustic Russian, Rasputin, on the High Street.

BB's *3 Chignell Place, off Uxbridge Road, W13 0TJ (8840 8322/www.bbscrabback.co.uk).*
Café Grove *65 The Grove, W5 5LL (8810 0364).*
Ealing Park Tavern *222 South Ealing Road, W5 4RL (8758 1879).*
Rasputin *265 High Street, W3 9BY (8993 5802).*
Rocket *11-13 Churchfield Road, W3 6BD (8993 6123/www.therocketw3.co.uk).*
Sichuan Restaurant *116 Churchfield Road, W3 6BY (8992 9473).*
Sushi-Hiro *1 Station Parade, Uxbridge Road, W5 3LD (8896 3175).*
Tyme *133 Uxbridge Road, W13 9AU (8840 7222/www.tyme.co.uk).*

Bars & pubs

Ealing is not the best neighbourhood for a pub crawl, but there are a handful of good drinking holes. The area's oldest and most attractive pubs tend to be found in South Ealing – in the vicinity of St Mary's Road, where the original Ealing village developed. Take the cosy Red Lion, for example, which is a stone's throw from Ealing Film Studios and has been fuelling its incumbents with good ales and excellent bar food for years. A little further south is gastropub Ealing Park Tavern (*see p313*).

The Broadway, with its many chain shops, coffee stops and fast-food restaurants, boasts the usual names, All Bar One, Hog's Head and O'Neills included. Cocktail lovers will enjoy the sassy and good-humoured Baroque bar with its arty black and white photos, while, further north, past West Ealing station, is Drayton Court where punters can relax in the lounge area or landscaped garden, or get rowdy in the sports bar.

Acton's contribution to the west London pub scene is, at best, modest. The best pickings are to be found near the Uxbridge Road/High Street and adjoining Steyne Road, which offer a slew of chain bars and pubs, such as half-decent JD Wetherspoon outfit, the Red Lion & Pineapple. A couple of boozers on Churchfield Road have been done up, including the Rocket (*see above*). Further north, the Grand Junction Arms is an unexpected find in an unpromising industrial neighbourhood, with its seasonal ales and large beer garden overlooking the Grand Union Canal.

Baroque *94 Uxbridge Road, W13 8RA (8567 7346/www.baroque-ealing.co.uk).*
Drayton Court *2 The Avenue, W13 8PH (8997 1019).*
Grand Junction Arms *Acton Lane, NW10 7AD (8965 5670).*
Red Lion *13 St Mary's Road, W5 5RA (8567 2541).*
Red Lion & Pineapple *281 High Street, W3 9PJ (8896 2248).*

TRANSPORT

Tube stations *Central* East Acton, North Acton, West Acton, Hanger Lane, Perivale, Greenford, Northolt; *District* Turnham Green, Chiswick Park, Acton Town, Ealing Common, Ealing Broadway; *Piccadilly* Acton Town, Ealing Common, North Ealing, Park Royal, South Ealing, Northfields, Boston Manor
Rail stations *First Great Western Link* Acton Main Line, Ealing Broadway, West Ealing, Hanwell, Southall, Drayton Green, Castle Bar Park, South Greenford, Greenford; *Silverlink* Acton Central, South Acton
Main bus routes *into central London* 95, 207, 260, 607, E3, H91; *Night buses* N7, N11, N105, N207; *24-hour buses* 65, 83, 105, 140, 266
Development plans Proposed West London Tram running from Uxbridge to Shepherd's Bush

Ealing

Ealing Common

Shops

Although it's not an area you would travel to for an afternoon's browse, Ealing has sufficient retail resources for local needs. Ealing Broadway is the borough's undisputed shopping hub. Facing each other on this thoroughfare, the Ealing Broadway Centre and the smaller Arcadia Centre contain a wide array of chains (Sofa Workshop, HMV, Morrisons, M&S, Monsoon and TK Maxx, to name a few), interspersed with smaller units. Outside, there's a Polish deli, Parade, and, on the High Street, an organic food store, As Nature Intended, alongside various other independents – it's worth exploring the streets around the back and sides of the Broadway Centre. A bus ride east towards Hanwell is a well-established farmers' market (9am-1pm Sat).

Choice is rather more limited in Acton, with a basic, chain-dominated high street – although, above it, Churchfield Road is showing early signs of a more interesting scene. The Vintage Home Shop, whose owner also runs a clothing emporium in Portobello Road, is well worth a look, while contemporary florist Heart & Soul provides a splash of colour. To the south, the area's Antipodean expats flock to A Taste of Home, which stocks foodstuffs and beer imported from Australia, New Zealand and South Africa.

Arcadia Centre *1-8 The Broadway, W5 2NH (8567 0854).*
As Nature Intended *17-21 High Street, W5 5DB (8840 1404/www.asnatureintended.uk.com).*
Ealing Broadway Centre *The Broadway, W5 5JY (8567 3453/www.ealingbroadway shopping.co.uk).*\

Ealing Farmers' Market *Leeland Road, W13 (www.lfm.org.uk).*
Heart & Soul *73 Churchfield Road, W3 6AX (8896 3331/www.heart-n-soul.co.uk).*
Parade Delicatessen *8 Central Buildings, The Broadway, W5 2NT (8567 9066).*
A Taste of Home *81 Gunnersbury Lane, W3 8HQ (8992 7800).*
The Vintage Home Store *105 Churchfield Road, W3 6AH (8993 4162).*

Arts & attractions

Cinemas & theatres

Cineworld Ealing *59-61 New Broadway, Uxbridge Road, W5 5AH (0871 200 2000/ www.cineworld.co.uk).*
The Questors Theatre *12 Mattock Lane, W5 5BQ (8567 0011/www.questors.org.uk).* The largest local community theatre in Europe, and host to around 20 shows a year.
Vue Acton *Royale Leisure Park, Western Avenue, W3 0PA (0871 224 0240/www.myvue.co.uk).*

Galleries & museums

PM Gallery & House *Mattock Lane, W5 5EQ (8567 1227/www.ealing.gov.uk).* This grand manor house in Walpole Park, designed by John Soane in 1800, is west London's largest contemporary arts venue.

Open spaces

Acton Green Common *South Parade, W4.* Small common near Turnham Green tube station.
Acton Park *The Vale, W4.*
Blondin Park & Nature Area *Boston Manor & Windmill Road, W5.* Community orchard, wildflower meadow and pond.
Drayton Green *Drayton Bridge Road, W5.*
Ealing Common *Uxbridge Road, W5.* Accessible and popular open meadowland.
Fox Wood Nature Reserve *Fox Lane, W5.* This nature reserve is one of Ealing's last remaining woodland areas.

Ealing

Hanger Hill Park *Hillcrest Road, W5.* This park boasts beautifully managed flower beds, a playground and ancient oak trees.
Lammas Park *Culmington Road, W5.* Around 25 acres (10 hectares) of preened parkland with a playground, tennis courts and a nature area.
Montpelier Park *Montpelier Road, W5.* Recently developed nature area with a woodland glade and a wildlife pond.
Walpole Park *Mattock Lane, W5 5EQ.* A child-friendly park, with jazz and comedy festivals in summer.

Sport & fitness

There's a broad choice of public leisure centres, though none is outstanding (many are affiliated to local schools, so it's wise to check opening times before you visit). There are also plenty of private options, including three of the big-name chains (Holmes Place, Fitness First and David Lloyd). But if you really want to push the boat out, try the Park Club, a posh country club in the middle of Acton, with rows of 4WDs in its car park.

Gyms & leisure centres

Acton Swimming Baths *Salisbury Street, W3 8NW (8992 8877/www.leisureconnection. co.uk).*
David Lloyd *Greenford Road, Greenford, Middx UB6 0HX (8422 7777/www.davidlloyd leisure.co.uk).* Private.
Dormers Wells Leisure Centre *Dormers Wells Lane, Southall, Middx UB1 3HX (8571 7207/www.ealing.gov.uk).*
Dragons Health Club *Rowdell Road, Northolt, Middx UB5 6AG (8841 5611/ www.dragons.co.uk).* Private.
Elthorne Sports Centre *Westlea Road, off Boston Road, W7 2AD (8579 3226/ www.ealing.gov.uk).*
Featherstone Sports Centre *Montague Waye, Southall, Middx UB2 5HF (8813 9886/ www.ealing.gov.uk).*
Fitness First *The Oaks Shopping Centre, High Street, W3 6RD (8993 0364/www.fitness first.co.uk).* Private.
Gold's Gym *54-62 Uxbridge Road, W7 3SU (8840 0044/www.goldsgym.com).* Private.
Greenford Sports Centre *Ruislip Road, Greenford, Middx UB6 9RX (8575 9157/ www.ealing.gov.uk).*
Gurnell Leisure Centre *Ruislip Road East, W13 0AL (8998 3241/www.leisureconnection. co.uk).*
Holmes Place *5th floor, Ealing Broadway Centre, Town Square, W5 5JY (8579 9433/ www.holmesplace.com).* Private.

Northolt Swimarama *Eastcote Lane North, Northolt, Middx UB5 4AB (8422 1176/ www.leisureconnection.co.uk).*
The Park Club *East Acton Lane, W3 7HB (8743 4321/www.theparkclub.co.uk).* Private.
Twyford Sports Centre *Twyford Crescent, W3 9PP (8993 9095/www.ealing.gov.uk).*
West London YMCA *14 Bond Street, W5 5AA (8832 1600/www.westlondonymca.org).* Private.

Schools

WHAT THE PARENTS SAY:

‘The school situation in Ealing is as diverse as the community. There are faith schools, single-sex schools, both private and state, scattered throughout the borough. A few of the primary schools are oversubscribed and very popular, with families moving specially into the catchment area; likewise with one or two of the secondaries.

The headmaster of Drayton Manor High School, Sir Pritpal Singh, has recently been knighted for doing such a fantastic job turning the school around – needless to say, that's the one parents fight to get their children into. It's in the top 100 schools at the moment for both A-level and GCSE results. The juggling act required to provide every child with somewhere to go leaves some parents feeling dissatisfied, but on the whole things work reasonably well, with many local children being sent to the borough's range of private schools.’
Jane Boehm, mother of three, South Ealing

Primary

There are 66 state primary schools in Ealing, including 13 church schools. There are also 12 independent primaries, including a drama school, a Greek school, a Japanese school and four faith schools. See www.ealing.gov.uk and www.ofsted.gov.uk for more information.

Secondary

Acton High School *Gunnersbury Lane, W3 8EY (8752 0005).*
Brentside High School *Greenford Avenue, W7 1JJ (8575 9162/www.www.brentside high.ealing.sch.uk).*
Cardinal Wiseman RC School *Greenford Road, Middx UB6 9AW (8575 8222/ www.wiseman.ealing.sch.uk).*
Dormers Wells High School *Dormers Wells Lane, Southall, Middx UB1 3HZ (8813 8671).*
Drayton Manor High School *Drayton Bridge Road, W7 1EU (8357 1900).*

The Ellen Wilkinson School for Girls *Queen's Drive, W3 0HW (8752 1525/ www.ellen-wilkinson-school.co.uk).* Girls only.
Elthorne Park High School *Westlea Road, W7 2AD (8566 1166).*
Featherstone High School *11 Montague Waye, Southall, Middx UB2 5HF (8843 0984/www.featherstonehigh.ealing. sch.uk).*
Greenford High School *Ruislip Road, Greenford, Middx UB6 9RX (8578 9152/ www.greenford.ealing.sch.uk).*

LUDLOW ROAD

Ealing

BRENTHAM WAY

Des res W5 streets

Northolt High School *Eastcote Lane,*
Northolt, Middx UB5 4HP (8864 8544/
www.northolt-high.ealing.sch.uk).
Twyford CE High School *Twyford Crescent,*
W3 9PP (8752 0141/www.twyford.ealing.sch.uk).
Villiers High School *Boyd Avenue, Southall,*
Middx UB1 3BT (8813 8001/www.villiers.
ealing.sch.uk).
The West London Academy *Bengarth Road,*
Northolt, Middx UB5 5LQ (8841 4511/
www.westlondonacademy.co.uk).

Property

WHAT THE AGENTS SAY:

❛Property is cheap in Ealing compared to
Chiswick and Fulham. It's very leafy and nice
here; Ealing borough's symbol is a tree. Most
buyers are white and middle-class. We also have
a lot of Poles here; Ealing has the biggest Polish
community outside Warsaw. Because of World
War II, I suppose. They had to go somewhere.
They came here.❜
John Procinski, Haart, Ealing

❛Acton is good value for money. It's a safe
place to live, plenty of nightlife – we have a
very cosmopolitan cross-section of people. The
trendies who are renting in more expensive areas
– Bayswater, Kensington, places like that – can't
afford to buy there, so they're now buying here.
We also have lots of new leisure facilities and
exclusive gyms.

East Acton is very family-oriented. There
are about six primary schools, and quite a
few secondaries dotted around Acton and
Hammersmith. Acton Town could do with
a tube station nearer the High Street, but it's
got all the necessary amenities.❜
Billy Rowe, Churchill, East Acton

Average property prices
Detached £529,956
Semi-detached £290,587
Terraced £235,528
Flat £168,571

Local estate agents
Adams *www.adamsproperty.co.uk; 2 offices*
in the borough (Ealing 8566 3738/Hanwell
8579 8070).
Brendons *Royal Chambers, 104 Pitshanger*
Lane, W5 1QX (8998 6500/www.brendons.
co.uk).
Churchill *18 Old Oak Common Lane,*
W3 7EL (8749 9798/www.churchillestate
agents.co.uk).
Goodman Estate Agents *12 Market Place,*
W3 6QS (8993 0566/www.goodmanestates.
co.uk).

Robertson Smith & Kempson
www.rskhomes.co.uk; 4 offices in the borough
(Acton 8896 3996/Ealing Broadway 8840
7677/7885/Hanway 8566 2339/Northfields
8566 2340).
Sinton Andrews *www.sintonandrews.co.uk;*
3 offices in the borough (Ealing 8566 1990/
Hanwell 8567 3219/Northfields 8840 5151).

Other information

Council
Ealing Council *Perceval House, 14-16*
Uxbridge Road, W5 2HL (8825 5000/
www.ealing.gov.uk).

Hospitals
Clayponds Hospital *Sterling Place, W5 4RN*
(8560 4011)
The Ealing Hospital *Uxbridge Road, Southall,*
Middx UB1 3HW (8967 5000/www.ealing
hospital.org.uk).

Legal services
Community Advice Prgramme *Old Stable*
Block, Ealing Town Hall Annexe, W5 2UQ
(8579 3861).
Ealing Legal Centre *Church Avenue, UB2*
4DF (8574 2434).
Law for All *102-104 High Street, W3 6QX;*
The Meeting House, 17 Woodville Road, W5
2SE; Viking Community Centre, Radcliffe Way,
UB5 6HR; The Citadel, Leeland Road, W13
9HH (8758 0668).
Southall Rights *54 High Street, Southall,*
Middx UB1 3DB (8571 4920).

Local newspapers
Ealing Gazette/Ealing Informer *8579*
3131/www.icealing.co.uk.
Ealing Times *01494 755000/*
www.ealingtimes.co.uk.

Allotments
Council allotments For a list of allotment
sites in the borough, including contact details,
visit the Ealing Council website at www.ealing.
gov.uk.
Ealing & Hanwell Allotment Association
Nigel Sumner, Secretary, 66 Chatworth Gardens,
W3 9LW (www.allotments.org). Well-organised
society, with a great website.

Hounslow

Transport links – the rumbling A4, nearby Heathrow Airport – are both a boon and a blight to chic Chiswick. But the district also contains the unequivocal delights of historic houses, waterside pubs, and swish restaurants. Want more? Tell retail junkies about the shops here and you'll Turnham Green with envy.

Neighbourhoods

Chiswick

Lush and leafy Chiswick has long been a desirable part of London, swankier and better equipped with shops and restaurants than neighbouring Hammersmith, and much closer to the capital's heart than the nether reaches of Hounslow borough. Two main thoroughfares cut through it from east to west: Chiswick High Road (A315), the main shopping street and a continuation of Hammersmith's King Street; and the thundering, six-lane A4 (Great West Road) on its way to join the M4. The A4 is anchored by Chiswick Roundabout to the west and Hogarth Roundabout to the east, named after one-time resident, 18th-century artist and satirist William Hogarth, and the site of Fuller's vast Griffin Brewery (Chiswick is one of their ales).

Lined with shops and restaurants, Chiswick High Road is bustling by day and night, the abundance of SUVs and yummy-mummies pushing all-terrain buggies testament to the neighbourhood's popularity with wealthy, middle-class families. At the west end is Chiswick Business Park, a gleaming, high-tech office complex designed by Richard Rogers on the site of the old Gunnersbury bus depot. The triangular-shaped park nearby is, confusingly, called Turnham Green, while Chiswick Common sits next to Turnham Green tube station at the top end of prime shopping spot Turnham Green Terrace. North of here (and just over the borough border in Ealing) is 19th-century Bedford Park, London's first garden suburb and still an exclusive residential area.

But it's the southern half of Chiswick that is most sought after, with notable riverside stretches (prone to flooding) at Chiswick

Mall – whose spectacular Georgian residences have mini gardens across the road next to the Thames, facing Chiswick Eyot – and Strand-by-the-Green, whose waterside pubs are popular with walkers and cyclists heading along the Thames Path to Kew and beyond. Tiny Church Street is full of architectural gems, while Corney Reach, just to the south, is a more modern residential complex.

Also in great demand is the Grove Park area. Huge houses from all eras squat on a network of wide, hushed, tree-lined streets, with a smattering of shops around Chiswick rail station to break the residential norm. To the south lie Duke's Meadows – largely inaccessible to the public unless you keep an allotment, belong to the health club or can use the Civil Service sports fields – and beyond that Chiswick and Barnes Bridges.

Cultural pickings are surprisingly slim, with residents having to travel to Shepherd's Bush, Hammersmith or Brentford if they want to catch a movie, a play or a concert.

Highs & Lows

▲ **Riverside location** Though prone to flooding in parts, the riverside stretches of Chiswick are some of London's most desirable

Family-friendliness Bustling Chiswick High Road, leafy residential streets and the river mean an abundance of middle-class families

Lack of culture Chiswick residents must travel elsewhere for a film or a play

▼ **Tube frustration** Despite an adjacent Piccadilly Line, only the slower, less reliable District Line serves Chiswick

Hounslow

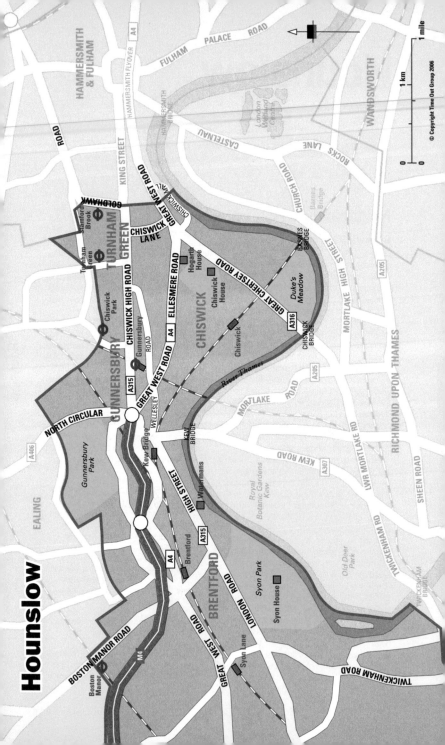

Still, there's an abundance of historic houses to enjoy, including Hogarth's House; Chiswick House, a supremely elegant, 18th-century Palladian villa surrounded by spacious, statue-filled grounds; and lion-topped Syon House, visible from Kew Gardens across the river. Chiswick is increasingly fashionable with celebs and media types (the offices of the BBC and Sky are within striking distance) – so much so that members' club Soho House is planning a new venture here, along with a brasserie and hotel, for summer 2006.

Transport in and out of London is good, though the proximity of Heathrow airport also means a constant stream of jets overhead. And although the Piccadilly Line runs adjacent to the slower and less reliable District Line, it's only the latter that serves tube stations within Chiswick boundaries.

Restaurants & cafés

Middle-class sensibilities (and incomes) mean Chiswick is packed with eating options, mostly located in the retail heartland of Chiswick High Road and its offshoots Devonshire Road and Turnham Green Terrace. There's a café on every corner, it seems, though Starbucks and Caffè Nero dominate; hurrah, then, for photo-gallery-cum-café Classic Image and a branch of upmarket pâtisserie Maison Blanc. There's no lack of family-friendly restaurant chains on the High Road (ASK, Pizza Express, Strada, Zizzi, Nando's, Tootsies, Giraffe…), plus brasserie Balans, posh burger joint Gourmet Burger Kitchen and Southwestern specialist the Coyote.

Newer arrivals include Italian bar and grill Frankie's (the brainchild of jockey Frankie Dettori and chef Marco Pierre White) and Sam's, a swish Modern European restaurant housed in a former paper factory (chef Rick Stein is an investor). There's also decent gastropub Devonshire House and a branch of the bright and breezy FishWorks mini chain (though, sadly, South African fish specialist FishHoek has closed). Non-European food is a rarity, though – with only Silks & Spice (Thai/Malaysian) and Woodlands (South Indian vegetarian) on offer; you'll have to head to nearby Hammersmith for more variety.

Last but by no means least, Chiswick is home to two fabulous French outposts: La Trompette (part of the mini empire of Nigel Platts-Martin and Bruce Poole, and one of the capital's best restaurants full stop) and classic bistro Le Vacherin.

Balans *214 Chiswick High Road, W4 1PD (8742 1435/www.balans.co.uk).*
Classic Image Café Gallery *15 Devonshire Road, W4 2EU (8995 9977).*
The Coyote *2 Fauconberg Road, W4 3JY (8742 8545/www.thecoyote.co.uk).*
Devonshire House *126 Devonshire Road, W4 2JJ (8987 2626/www.thedevonshirehouse.co.uk).*
FishWorks *6 Turnham Green Terrace, W4 1QP (8994 0086/www.fishworks.co.uk).*
Frankie's *68 Chiswick High Road, W4 1SY (8987 9988/www.frankiesitalianbarandgrill.com).*
Gourmet Burger Kitchen *131 Chiswick High Road, W4 2ED (8995 4548/www.gbkinfo.co.uk).*
Maison Blanc *26-28 Turnham Green Terrace, W4 1QP (8995 7220/www.maisonblanc.co.uk).*
Sam's Brasserie & Bar *11 Barley Mow Passage, W4 4PH (8987 0555/www.sams brasserie.co.uk).*

There are still some old-style retailing opportunities left in Chiswick.

Silks & Spice *95 Chiswick High Road, W4 2EF (0871 200 0999/www.silksandspice.com).*
La Trompette *5-7 Devonshire Road, W4 2EU (8747 1836/www.latrompette.co.uk).*
Le Vacherin *76-77 South Parade, W4 5LF (8742 2121/www.levacherin.co.uk).*
Woodlands *12-14 Chiswick High Road, W4 1TH (8994 9333/www.woodlandsrestaurant.co.uk).*

Bars & pubs

Lovers of traditional pubs will hail Chiswick with a hearty cheer. It really has some beauties, thanks to the proximity of Fuller's brewery and a gorgeous stretch of the Thames. The Bell & Crown and the City Barge are the best riverside pubs: both are child-friendly, with decent pub grub, waterside terraces and Fuller's ales. Nearer Turnham Green tube, Devonshire House is great for a meal (*see p321*), as is Gunnersbury's Pilot, with its stripped floorboards and Mediterranean menu. The

Old Pack Horse (open fires, leather sofas, Thai food) is among Chiswick High Road's finest, but for a pint of Fuller's within barrel-rolling distance of the brewery, head for the Mawson Arms.

Barflies have less to clink cocktail glasses over. The best Chiswick has to offer is a couple of chains on the High Road (All Bar One and Pitcher & Piano), though there are bars attached to both Frankie's and Sam's. The district also crosses the borough boundary into Ealing (*see p314*) and Richmond (*see p173*) where more fine hostelries can be found.

Bell & Crown *11-13 Thames Road, Strand-on-the-Green, W4 3PL (8994 4164).*
City Barge *27 Strand-on-the-Green, W4 3PH (8994 2148).*
Mawson Arms *110 Chiswick Lane South, W4 2QA (8994 2936).*
Old Pack Horse *434 Chiswick High Road, W4 5TF (8994 2872).*
Pilot *56 Wellesley Road, W4 4BZ (8994 0828).*

Tube stations *District* Stamford
Brook, Turnham Green, Chiswick
Park, Gunnersbury; *Piccadilly* , Boston
Manor, Osterley, Hounslow East,
Hounslow Central, Hounslow West
Rail stations *Silverlink* Gunnersbury;
South West Trains Barnes Bridge,
Chiswick, Kew Bridge, Brentford, Syon
Lane, Isleworth, Hounslow, Feltham
Main bus routes *into central London*
27, 94; *night buses* N9, N11;
24-hour buses 27, 65, 94, 266, 285
River leisure boat services to/from
central London and Kew Pier

Shops

Most of the retail action happens on or near Chiswick High Road, on the stretch between Chiswick Lane and the Sainsbury's superstore on Acton Lane. Devonshire Street and Turnham Green Terrace – facing each other on opposite sides of the High Road – also have notable clusters of shops. As befits the area's upmarket character, the options are all a lot smarter than Hammersmith with its pound shops and Primark.

Matters domestic hold sway, so there's an abundance of interiors and bathroom outlets among the usual mobile phone shops, banks and off-licences. Chains exist – including Woolies, WH Smith, a food-only M&S and Waterstone's, the sole bookshop – but Chiswick's strength lies in its abundance of independents. Foodies do well, with a brace of fish shops (Covent Garden Fishmongers and the wet fish counter at the front of FishWorks restaurant, *see p321*); lovely continental deli Mortimer & Bennett; Theobroma Cacao, one of London's best chocolatiers; and As Nature Intended, a large organic healthfood store selling everything from rice cakes to cleaning products.

Local tots are a well-dressed lot, thanks to branches of JoJo Maman Bébé, Neck & Neck, Petit Bateau and Gap, as well as one-offs Chiswick Shoes and the Little Trading Company, which deals in second-hand clothes, toys, books, even school uniforms. Women fare better than men when it comes to clothing, with branches of Noa Noa, East and Phase 8, though surfie dudes of both sexes will enjoy the large White Stuff store. Locals are lucky to have London's only

Jurlique day spa, which stocks the full range of organic Australian skincare, on their doorstep. There are also branches of the Body Shop and Space NK.

For furnishings with an oriental bent, try Baan Rama and Djinn; for gifts and jewellery, there's London Zu and an Oliver Bonas. The only area that's badly served is music, though things have improved with the recent arrival of a branch of Fopp. But throw into the mix some excellent charity shops, three floors of antiques at the Old Cinema, and long-standing Wheelers Garden Centre (next to Turnham Green tube station) and Chiswick has enough to satisfy the fussiest shopaholic.

As Nature Intended *201 Chiswick High Road, W4 2DR (8742 8838).*
Baan Rama *14 Devonshire Road, W4 2HD (8995 7732/www.baanrama.co.uk).*
Chiswick Shoes *1 Devonshire Road, W4 2EU (8987 0525).*
Covent Garden Fishmongers *37 Turnham Green Terrace, W4 1RG (8995 9273).*
Djinn *44 Devonshire Road, W4 2HD (8994 9200/www.djinninteriors.co.uk).*
Jurlique Day Spa & Sanctuary *300-302 Chiswick High Road, W4 1NP (8995 2293/ www.apotheke20-20.co.uk).*
Little Trading Company *7 Bedford Corner, The Avenue, W4 1LD (8742 3152).*
London Zu *6 Devonshire Road, W4 2HD (8747 4629/www.londonzu.com).*
Mortimer & Bennett *33 Turnham Green Terrace, W4 1RG (8995 4145/www.mortimer andbennett.com).*
The Old Cinema *160 Chiswick High Road, W4 1PR (8995 4166).*
Space NK *172 Chiswick High Road, W4 1PR (8994 3184/www.spacenk.com).*
Theobroma Cacao *43 Turnham Green Terrace, W4 1RG (8996 0431/www.theobroma-cacao.co.uk).*
Wheelers Garden Centre *Cato's Yard, Turnham Green Terrace, W4 1LS (8747 9505).*
White Stuff *34-38 Turnham Green Terrace, W4 1QP (8994 8028/www.whitestuff.com).*

Arts & attractions

Cinemas & theatres

Cineworld Feltham *Leisure West, TW13 7EX (0871 220 8000/www.cineworld.co.uk).*
Watermans *40 High Street, TW8 0DS (8232 1010/www.watermans.org.uk).* Multipurpose arts centre, offering theatre, films, exhibitions, workshops and more.

Galleries & museums

Gunnersbury Park Museum *Popes Lane, W3 8LQ (8992 1612).* Local history museum.

Hounslow

Kew Bridge Steam Museum *Green Dragon Lane, TW8 0EN (8568 4757/www.kbsm.org).* Lots of lovely steam engines, housed in a Victorian pumping station.

Other attractions

Chiswick House *Burlington Lane, W4 2RP (8995 0508/www.english-heritage.org.uk).* Palladian villa designed in 1725, with interiors by William Kent. Run by English Heritage.
Hogarth's House *Hogarth Lane, Great West Road, W4 2QN (8994 6757).* Country home of the great 18th-century painter, engraver and satirist William Hogarth.
Osterley House & Park *off Jersey Road, TW7 4RB (8232 5050/www.nationaltrust. org.uk/osterley).* Former Tudor house turned into a swish neo-classical villa by Robert Adam, now in the care of the National Trust. Fabulous park too.
Syon House & Park *London Road, TW8 (8560 0881/www.syonpark.co.uk).* Family seat of the Duke of Northumberland, with interiors by Robert Adam. The extensive grounds include the London Butterfly House, the Tropical Experience and a garden centre.

Open spaces

Boston Manor Park *Boston Manor Road, TW8.*
Chiswick Common *Chiswick Common Road, W4.*
Cranford Countryside Park *The Parkway, TW5.* Historic ruins in this 144-acre park include the medieval St Dunstan's Church and graveyard.
Gunnersbury Park Estate *Popes Lane, W3.* Large leafy park, with formal gardens, lawns, lakes, historic buildings and a museum.
Hounslow Heath *Staines Road TW4.*
Hounslow Urban Farm *Faggs Road, TW14 0LZ (8751 0850/www.hounslow.info/ urbanfarm).*
Pevensey Road Open Space & Nature Reserve *Pevensey Road, TW13.*
Turnham Green *Chiswick High Road, W4.*

Sport & fitness

CIP, which manages most of the public leisure centres in Hounslow, has had its work cut out bringing some very outdated facilities up to scratch. The organisation has made a commendable start with the installation of smart Life Centre gyms in Brentford Fountain, Feltham Airparcs, Isleworth Rec and New Chiswick. The Lampton Sports Centre opened in 2005.

Gyms & leisure centres

Brentford Fountain Leisure Centre *658 Chiswick High Road, TW8 0HJ (0845 456 2935).*
David Lloyd *Southall Lane, TW5 9PE (8573 9378/www.davidlloydleisure.co.uk).* Private.
Esporta *www.esporta.co.uk; Riverside Drive, Duke's Meadows, W4 2SX (8987 1800); Chiswick Business Park, 566 Chiswick High Road, W4 5YA (8987 5800).* Private.
Feltham Airparcs Leisure Centre *Uxbridge Road, TW13 5EG (8894 9156/www.hounslow. info).*
Heston Pool *New Heston Road, TW5 0LW (8570 4396/www.hounslow.info).*
Hogarth Health Club *1 Airedale Avenue, W4 2NW (8995 4600/www.thehogarth.co.uk).* Private.
Isleworth Recreation Centre *Twickenham Road, TW7 7EU (0845 456 2980/www. hounslow.info).*
Lampton Sports Centre *Lampton Avenue, TW3 4EP (8814 0342/www.hounslow.info).*
New Chiswick Pool *Edensor Road, W4 2RG (8742 7987/www.hounslow.info).*
West 4 *10A Sutton Lane North, W4 4LD (8747 1713/www.west4healthclub.co.uk).* Private.

Other facilities

Chiswick Tennis Club *Burlington Lane, W4 3EU (07946 096933/www.chiswicktennis club.co.uk).* Private.

Schools

WHAT THE PARENTS SAY:

'I was looking for a co-educational school for my three children; I chose Chiswick Community School because my children went to Belmont Primary School (one of the best primary schools in Chiswick) and therefore had many friends who also transferred there. My advice to parents is to become as involved as possible in your child's school life, especially at secondary level. At primary schools parents meet teachers and other parents regularly, but at secondary school it is very different.'
Sally Smith, mother of three and joint PTA chair, Chiswick Community School

Primary

There are 60 state primary schools in Hounslow, including seven church schools. There are also seven independent primaries, including one international school. See www.hounslow.gov.uk and www.ofsted.gov.uk for more information.

Secondary

Brentford School for Girls *5 Boston Manor Road, TW8 0PG (8847 4281).* Girls only.
Chiswick Community School *Burlington Lane, W4 3UN (8747 0031/www.chiswick. hounslow.sch.uk).*
Cranford Community College *High Street, Cranford, TW5 9PD (8897 2001/www.cranford. hounslow.sch.uk).*
Feltham Community College *Browells Lane, TW13 7EF (8831 3000/www.feltham. hounslow.sch.uk).*
The Green School for Girls *Busch Corner, TW7 5BB (8321 8080/www.green.hounslow. lgfl.net).* Girls only.
Gumley House RC Convent School for Girls *St John's Road, TW7 6XF (8568 8692).* Girls only; mixed sixth form.
Gunnersbury Catholic School *The Ride, Boston Manor Road, TW8 9LB (8568 7281/ www.gunnersbury.com).* Boys only; mixed sixth form.
The Heathland School *Wellington Road South, TW4 5JD (8572 4411/www.heathland. hounslow.sch.uk).*
Heston Community School *Heston Road, Heston, TW5 0QR (8572 1931).*
Hounslow Manor School *Prince Regent Road, TW3 1NE (8572 4461).*
Isleworth & Syon School for Boys *Ridgeway Road, TW7 5LJ (8568 5791).* Boys only; mixed sixth form.m
Lampton School *Lampton Avenue, TW3 4EP (8572 1936/www.lampton.hounslow. sch.uk).*
Longford Community School *Tachbrook Road, TW14 9PE (8890 0245).*
St Mark's Catholic School *106 Bath Road, TW3 3EJ (8577 3600/www.st-marks.hounslow. sch.uk).*

Property

WHAT THE AGENTS SAY:

'I'd be hard pushed to find anything bad to say about Chiswick – it's so nice here. Perhaps the odd bit of aircraft noise from Heathrow, but that's all. Chiswick is very green, with loads of parks and open spaces, but you can still get to central London quickly. The links out of London are very good too. There's a lot of wealth coming into Chiswick – a lot of celebs.'
Neil Laman, Foxtons, Chiswick

COUNCIL TAX

A	up to £40,000	£880.41
B	£40,001-£52,000	£1,027.15
C	£52,001-£68,000	£1,173.88
D	£68,001-£88,000	£1,320.62
E	£88,001-£120,000	£1,614.09
F	£120,001-£160,000	£1,907.56
G	£160,001-£320,000	£2,201.03
H	over £320,000	£2,641.24

Average property prices

Detached £422,326
Semi-detached £238,832
Terraced £225,558
Flat £177,845

Local estate agents

Featherstone-Leigh *Chardin House, Chardin Road, W4 1RJ (8994 6567/www.featherstone-leigh.co.uk).*
First Choice Residential *www.firstchoice residential.co.uk; 2 offices in the borough (Isleworth 8758 9100/Hounslow 8570 7000).*
Fletchers *58 Turnham Green Terrace, W4 1QP (8987 3000/www.fletcherestates.com).*
Quilliam Property Services *206 High Street, TW8 8AH (8847 4737/www.quilliam.co.uk).*

Other information

Council

London Borough of Hounslow *Civic Centre, Lampton Road, Hounslow, Middx TW3 4DN (8583 2000/www.hounslow.gov.uk).*
Out-of-hours emergency line *8583 2222.*

Hospitals

West Middlesex Hospital *Twickenham Road, TW7 6AF (8560 2121/www.west-middlesex-hospital.nhs.uk).*

Legal services

Brentford & Chiswick CAB *Old Town Hall, Heathfield Terrace, W4 4JN (8994 4846/www.citizensadvice.org.uk).*
Hounslow CAB *2nd Floor, 45 Treaty Centre, High Street, TW3 1ES (8570 2983).*
Hounslow Law Centre *51 Lampton Road, TW3 1LY (8570 9505/www.hounslowlaw centre.org.uk).*

Local newspapers

The Chiswick *www.thechiswick.com.*
Hounslow Guardian *www.hounslowguardian.co.uk.*

Allotments

For information on allotments in the borough, contact the Lettings Team, CIP, Treaty Centre, High Street, Hounslow, TW3 1ES (0845 456 2828/www.hounslow.info/allotments).

Hounslow

Travelcard Zones

Explanation of Zones

	Station outside the zones
D	Station in Zone D
C	Station in Zone C
B	Station in Zone B
A	Station in Zone A
	Station in Zone 6 and Zone A
6	Station in Zone 6
5	Station in Zone 5
4	Station in Zone 4
3	Station in Zone 3
	Station in both zones
2	Station in Zone 2
	Station in both zones
1	Station in Zone 1

7.04

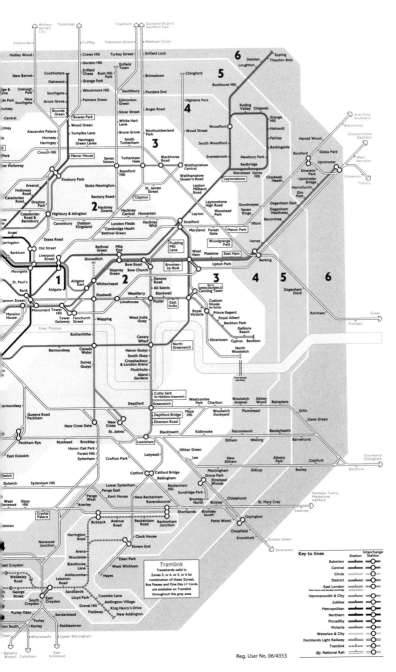

Tube & Rail Map

Reg. User No. 06/4353

Useful contacts

SERVICES & TRADESMEN

Directories 020 London
www.020.co.uk.
BT Directory
www.thephonebook.bt.com.
Tradesmens Directory *www.*
thetradesmensdirectory.co.uk.
Yellow Pages *www.yell.com.*
Builders Federation of
Master Builders *www.find*
abuilder.co.uk. Database of
registered practitioners.
Chimneys National
Association of Chimney
Sweeps *01785 811732/*
www.nacs.org.uk.
Electricians Electrical
Contractors' Association
7313 4800/www.eca.co.uk.
Electrical engineering and
building services.
National Inspection
Council for Electrical
Installation Contracting
(NICEIC) *0870 013 0431/*
www.niceic.org.uk. Where to
find an NICEIC-approved
electrician.
Glazing Glass & Glazing
Federation *www.ggf.org.uk.*
Database of registered glaziers.
Infestation British Pest
Control Association *0870*
6092687/www.bpca.org.uk.
For private pest control.
Alternatively, local councils
will address most common
problems.
Plumbers Association
of Plumbing & Heating
Contractors *024 7647 0626/*
www.aphc.co.uk.
Institute of Plumbing
& Heating Engineering
01708 472791/www.iphe.org.uk.
Find approved members.
Removals British
Association of Removers
01923 699480/www.bar.co.uk.

HOME EMERGENCIES

Power cuts EDF ENERGY
0800 028 0247.
Electrical enquiries
London Energy *0800 096*
9000. 24-hours.
Gas leaks National Grid
0800 111999/non-emergencies
0845 605 6677/www.national
grid.com.

Water leaks Thames Water
leakline *0800 714614/non-*
emergencies 0845 920 0800/
www.thames-water.com.
Locksmiths Master
Locksmiths Association
0800 783 1498/non-
emergencies 01372 262 255/
www.locksmiths.co.uk.

HEALTH & SUPPORT

Complementary medicine
British Homeopathic
Association *0870 444 3950/*
www.trusthomeopathy.org.
Where to find a homeopathic
doctor/chemist.
Institute for
Complementary Medicine
7237 5165/www.i-c-m.org.uk.
Dentists Find a Dentist
www.bda-findadentist.org.uk.
Hospitals For local hospitals,
see relevant borough chapter.
NHS services NHS Direct
0845 4647/www.nhsdirect.
nhs.uk. Health information.
Alternatively, find your nearest
NHS health service at
www.nhs.uk/england.
Helplines Alcoholics
Anonymous *0845 769 7555/*
www.alcoholics-anonymous.
org.uk.
ChildLine *0800 1111/*
www.childline.org.uk.
Contact-a-Family *0808 808*
3555/www.cafamily.org.uk.
Support for parents of children
with disabilities.
Greater London Action
on Disability *7346 5800/*
textphone *7326 4554/*
www.glad.org.uk.
London Lesbian & Gay
Switchboard *7837 7324/*
www.queery.org.uk.
Narcotics Anonymous
0845 373 3366/www.ukna.org.
National Missing Persons
Helpline *0500 700 700/*
www.missingpersons.org.
Samaritans *08457 909090/*
www.samaritans.org.uk.
Victim Support *0845 303*
0900/www.victimsupport.com.
Pregnancy & birth
British Pregnancy
Advisory Service *08457*
304030/www.bpas.org.

National Childbirth Trust
0870 770 3236/www.nct
pregnancyandbabycare.com.
Sexual health Brook *7284*
6040/helpline 0800 018 5023/
www.brook.org.uk. Advice for
young people.
Sexual Health Information
Line *0800 567123/*
www.playingsafely.co.uk.
Terrence Higgins
Trust/Lighthouse *helpline*
0845 122 1200/www.tht.org.uk.
Advice and counsel for those
with HIV/AIDS.

CHILDREN

Childminding Childminders
7935 3000/www.babysitter.co.uk.
Universal Aunts *7738 8937/*
www.universalaunts.co.uk.
Schools BBC Education
www.bbc.co.uk/education.
Ofsted *www.ofsted.gov.uk.*

LEGAL SERVICES

Legal advice Citizens'
Advice Bureau
www.citizensadvice.org.uk.
Community Legal Service
Direct *0845 345 4345/*
www.clsdirect.org.uk.
Legal Aid Legal Services
Commission *7759 0000/*
www.legalservices.gov.uk.
Solicitors Law Society
helpline 0870 606 6575/
www.solictors-online.com.
Find a solicitor in your area.

PUBLIC TRANSPORT

Information Transport
for London *7222 1234/*
www.tfl.gov.uk. Information,
maps and service updates for
tubes, trains, buses, DLR and
river services
Journey Planner
www.journeyplanner.org.
Route advice.
National Rail Enquiries
0845 748 4950/
www.nationalrail.co.uk.
Oyster Card *0870 849 9999/*
www.oystercard.com.
Rail services
Chiltern Railways
www.chilternrailways.co.uk.
c2c *www.c2c-online.co.uk.*
Eurostar *www.eurostar.com.*

ESTATE AGENTS

London-wide chains; locals are listed in each borough.

Adam Kennedy
www.adamkennedy.co.uk.
Bairstow Eves
www.bairstoweves.co.uk.
Barnard Marcus
www.sequencehome.co.uk.
Belvoir
www.belvoirlettings.com.
Dexters
www.dexters.co.uk.
Douglas & Gordon *www.douglasandgordon.com.*
Ellis & Co
www.ellisandco.co.uk
Felicity J Lord
www.fjlord.co.uk.
Foxtons
www.foxtons.co.uk.
Haart *www.haart.co.uk.*
Hampton's International
www.hamptons.co.uk.

Hotblack Desiato
www.hotblackdesiato.co.uk
John D Wood & Co
www.johndwood.co.uk.
Keatons
www.keatons.com
Kinleigh Folkard & Hayward *www.kfh.co.uk.*
Regents Estate Agents
www.regents.co.uk.
Wates Residential
www.watesresidential.co.uk.
Winkworth
www.winkworth.co.uk.
Your Move *www.your-move.co.uk.*

Property websites
www.findaproperty.co.uk;
www.hotproperty.co.uk;
www.primelocation.com

First Great Western
www.firstgreatwestern.co.uk.
one *www.onerailway.com.*
Silverlink
www.silverlink-trains.com.
Southern
www.southernrailway.com.
South Eastern Trains
www.setrains.co.uk.
South West Trains
www.southwesttrains.co.uk.
Thameslink
www.thameslink.co.uk.
WAGN *www.wagn.co.uk.*
Coaches Green Line Travel *0870 608 7261/*
www.greenline.co.uk.
National Express *0870 580 8080/www.nationalexpress.com*
Complaints Travel Watch
7505 9000/www.londontravel watch.org.uk.

DRIVING & CYCLING
Breakdown services
AA (Automobile Association) *information 0800 444999/breakdown 0800 887766/www.theaa.co.uk.*
ETA (Environmental Transport Association)
01932 828882/www.eta.co.uk.
Green motoring.
RAC (Royal Automobile Club) *breakdown 0800 828282/office & membership 08705 722722/www.rac.co.uk.*
Congestion Charge
0845 900 1234/
www.cclondon.com.

Cycling **London Cycle Network** *7974 2016/*
www.londoncyclenetwork.org.
London Cycling Campaign
7234 9310/www.lcc.org.uk.
OY Bike *www.oybike.com.* Hire.
Sustrans *www.sustrans.org.uk.*
Promoting cycling.
Disabled services **Dial a Ride** *7027 5823/5824/*
www.tfl.gov.uk.
Wheelchair Travel & Access Mini Buses *01483 233640/www.wheelchair-travel.co.uk.*
Parking NCP *0870 606 7050/*
www.ncp.co.uk.
Vehicle hire **Alamo** *0870 400 4508/www.alamo.com.*
Avis *08705 900500/*
www.avis.co.uk.
Easycar *www.easycar.com.*
Enterprise *0870 607 7757/*
www.enterprise.co.uk.
HGB Motorcycles *01895 676 451/www.hgbmotorcycles. co.uk.*
Taxis Transport for London's website (www.tfl.gov.uk) has a licensed minicab database. Alternatively, text HOME to 60835 for firms in your area, or call 8758 2000.
Lady Cabs *7272 3300.*
Women-only mini-cab drivers.
Radio Taxis *7272 0272.*
Book black cabs in advance.
Scooterman *0870 242 6999/*
www.scooterman.co.uk. Be driven home in your own car.

SPORT
London Active Partnership
7815 7828/www.londonactive partnership.org. Encouraging access to organised sport.
London Sports Forum for Disabled People *7354 8666/*
www.londonsportsforum.org.uk.
Sport England *08458 508 508/www.sportengland.org.*
Find your local sports centre.

USEFUL WEBSITES
Time Out London
www.timeout.com/london.
Premier source for information about happenings in the capital.
BBC London
www.bbc.co.uk/london. Online news, travel, weather, sport and entertainment.
Greater London Authority
www.london.gov.uk. See what the mayor and co are up to.
Gumtree *www.gumtree.com.*
Online community noticeboard.
House.co.uk
www.house.co.uk. Home management advice from British Gas.
IamMoving.com
www.iammoving.com. Notify people of your new address.
Loot *www.loot.com.* Buy and sell in London.
London Farmers' Markets
www.lfm.org.uk. Find your nearest market.
LondonTown
www.londontown.com. The official tourist board website.
Meteorological Office
www.met-office.gov.uk.
Weather forecasts.
Post Office
www.postoffice.co.uk. Find your nearest post office.
Recycle for London
www.recycleforlondon.com.
Find your nearest 'bring site' or recycling centre.
Streetmap
www.streetmap.co.uk.
Useful A-to-Z-like resource.
StreetSensation
www.streetsensation.co.uk.
Panoramic 'streetscapes' of over 3,000 London streets, showing you what's where.
This is London
www.thisislondon.co.uk.
The *Evening Standard* online.
UpMyStreet.com
www.upmystreet.com. Services and information, broken down by neighbourhood.

Useful contacts

Index

Index

Advertisers' Index

Index